SUBMARINES

WORLD WAR I TO THE PRESENT

SUBMARINES

WORLD WAR I TO THE PRESENT

CHRIS BISHOP & DAVID ROSS

CHARTWELL
BOOKS

Quarto is the authority on a wide range of topics.

Quarto educates, entertains and enriches the lives of our readers—enthusiasts and lovers of hands-on living.

www.quartoknows.com

This edition published in 2016 by

CHARTWELL BOOKS
an imprint of Book Sales
a division of Quarto Publishing Group USA Inc.
142 West 36th Street, 4th Floor
New York, New York 10018
USA

Editorial and design by
Amber Books Ltd
74–77 White Lion Street
London
N1 9PF
United Kingdom
www.amberbooks.co.uk
Appstore: itunes.com/apps/amberbooksltd
Facebook: www.facebook.com/amberbooks
Twitter: @amberbooks

ISBN 978-0-7858-3446-5

Printed in China

10 9 8 7 6 5 4 3 2 1

Picture Credits:
Art-Tech: 12, 46, 47, 71, 81, 93, 104/105, 106, 122, 125, 128, 138, 176, 213, 217, 254/255, 286, 352
Cody Images: 7, 10, 13, 22, 30, 33, 43, 44, 73, 78, 80, 83, 91, 92, 94, 95, 96, 107, 114, 150, 152, 162, 163, 164, 170, 178, 187, 198, 205, 225, 226, 233, 234, 243, 250, 268, 281, 289, 296
Getty Images: 85, 108, 136, 140, 343
Suddeutscher Verlag: 134
U.S. Department of Defense: 294, 297, 346, 350, 373
U.S. Navy: 315

All artworks © Amber Books and Art-Tech, except page 359 top © BAE Systems

Contents

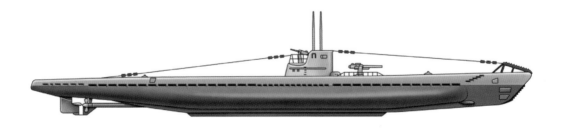

Introduction

The emergence of the submarine from August 1914 as a major strategic weapon was swift, and, to many, unexpected. Its early successes forced the warring navies into a drastic reconsideration of how war should be carried on at sea.

HARDLY MORE THAN A MONTH into World War I, the basis of naval warfare was changed for ever. On 5 September 1914, a British light cruiser, HMS *Pathfinder*, was sunk by the German submarine U-21, becoming the first victim of a free-fired torpedo. On the morning of 22 September, three Royal Navy armoured cruisers, *Aboukir*, *Cressy* and *Hogue*, of Cruiser Force C, based at Harwich, were sunk in just over an an hour by U-9, a petrol-engined boat launched in 1910.

These events exposed a huge and potentially fatal gap in Britain's defences. The British Admiralty had underestimated the threat of submarines. Now, suddenly and glaringly, the vulnerability of surface ships was exposed. After decades of experiment, and dismissal of its value by many senior officers, the age of the submarine had arrived.

The submarines of 1914–18 could not travel underwater for long, or go very deep. In effect they were surface ships capable of submersion for relatively brief periods. But their crucial feature was their ability to approach unseen and fire weapons from below the surface, striking the relatively unprotected undersides of far bigger ships. This invisibility and potential destructiveness created a submarine 'mystique' from the start. Many naval officers considered it a 'sneak' weapon, but whatever their attitude, they could not forgo the use of submarines as long as the other side had them.

The Submariners

Conditions on board these submarines were unpleasant in the extreme, especially during the periods of submergence. The boat was formed

▲ **K-class (Royal Navy)**

HMS K-12 was commissioned in August 1917. The K-class submarines were large, fast, steam-propelled vessels designed to operate as part of a surface battle fleet.

▲ **Russian Navy Project 971 Shchuka-B SSN**
This class is designated 'Akula' by NATO. These fast and quiet vessels marked a large step forward in Russian submarine design.

around an engine room, flotation tanks and torpedo tubes. Somewhere, accommodation and living space got fitted in for the men who made it all work. Tiny, cramped living space, damp, mould, bad air, dependence on temperamental machinery – together these made for a tough environment.

Submariners in all navies were something of a separate breed. Their world was a tiny one and in all operating conditions it was highly dependent on team spirit, co-operation and trust. The formality of the surface navy could not be replicated on board a submarine, yet discipline and determination were vital in order for the boat to be an effective fighting unit. Much depended on the leadership given by the captain. Submariners of all nations were more at risk than surface sailors. In Germany's World War II *Kriegsmarine*, out of 40,000 men who served in U-boats, more than 32,000 perished.

The Nuclear Era
Up to the mid-1950s, conditions on board submarines changed little. The advent of the nuclear vessel brought changes, for two reasons: firstly it had more available space; and secondly its capacity for remaining underwater and for extended cruises meant that more attention had to be given to crew amenities. But submarines remained a tight and risky environment. Submariners were no less dependent on technology

to sustain their lives than astronauts. Soviet Russia, in its haste to catch up with the American lead in nuclear propulsion, either underestimated or ignored the dangers associated with nuclear reactors. Its first generations of crews paid a heavy price in radiation burns and sickness. In the United States, Admiral Rickover, the 'father' of the nuclear submarine, was as obsessive about safety as he was about everything else, and the radiation safety record of US nuclear submarines is unmatched.

The Submarine's New Role
With the introduction of nuclear propulsion in the 1950s, the role of the submarine began to change. Huge sums were being invested in the development of long-range missiles at this time. These took two forms, the first being intercontinental ballistic missile (ICBM) which is fired at a steep angle to rise above the atmosphere and follow a predetermined trajectory to a target. Having reached maximum altitude it continues without power, governed by gravity and its own aerodynamic qualities. When submarine-launched, the ICBM is referred to as a SLBM (submarine-launched ballistic missile).

The cruise or guided missile has a shorter range, travels within the Earth's atmosphere under powered flight, and its course can be altered in the course of flight from a control point, and also (in more recent types) by sensors and navigational equipment installed on the missile itself.

While land-based missile sites could be identified and themselves become targets, the nuclear submarine's ability to remain submerged for lengthy periods offered the possibility of a new strategic development. In the lengthy Cold-War stand-off (1946–90) between the North Atlantic Treaty Organisation (NATO) powers and the Warsaw Pact countries led by Soviet Russia, submarines assumed an increasingly important role as missile platforms, and consequently also as hunters of missile-carrying boats. From this came the designations of SSBN (ballistic missile nuclear submarine), SSGN (guided missile nuclear submarine) and SSN (nuclear submarine, fitted with torpedoes or other missiles designed for anti-submarine and anti-ship attack: known first as 'hunter-killer' and later as 'fast attack' boats). Between 1945 and 1991, the Soviet Union produced 727 submarines – 492 with diesel-electric or closed-cycle propulsion and 235 with nuclear propulsion. The United States in the same period built 212 submarines – 43 with diesel-electric propulsion and 169 nuclear-powered. Deterrence of attack by the other side was the avowed intention. By 1970 the capacity for mutual destruction was so great that both sides agreed strategic arms limitation treaties in 1974 and 1979 (SALT I and II), which had some effect in slowing the arms race.

Post-Cold War: the Submarine's Role Changes Again

The collapse of the Soviet Union in 1989–90 and the emergence of the Russian Federation marked the end of the Cold War period, and a long pause in Russian submarine construction. The Strategic Arms Reduction Treaties known as START I and II in 1991 and 2010 have resulted in a large decrease in the deployed nuclear arsenals of the two major powers.

In 2015 an authoritative American report put the USA's current SLBM strength under START II at 14 SSBNs each with 20 launchers. Out of 1550 deployed warheads in the USA's nuclear arsenal, 1090 were carried on submarines. The comparative figures for Russia were eight SSBNs, with a total of 128 launchers and 640 nuclear warheads deployed on submarines, out of a total of 1335.

Mutual deterrence continues to be a basic plank in defence strategy. For six countries (Britain, China, France, Russia, and the United States, recently joined by India), the nuclear submarine forms one arm of the normative triadic defence/attack structure, comprising aircraft-borne weapons, land-launched missiles, and submarine missiles.

▲ **Scorpène**

Two Scorpène-type submarines, *O'Higgins* and *Carrera*, were acquired by the Chilean Navy in 2006. One is seen here cruising off the Chilean coast.

Chapter 1

World War I: 1914–18

Most of the submarines in action in 1914 were of a primitive type, but from the earliest days of the war their capacity for surprise attack and destruction became clear. Yet, although operations in the North Sea, the Atlantic and the Baltic, by both British and German boats, revealed the submarine's huge strategic value, the naval authorities on both sides remained preoccupied by surface warfare and battleship engagements.

The German U-boat offensive came close to cutting off Great Britain's main supply lines. But the submarine remained essentially a surface vessel with the capacity to submerge for relatively brief periods. Its gun was seen to be as essential as its torpedoes. And its very success focused attention on the means of detecting and destroying it.

◀ **Deck gun**
British submariners drill with a 12-pounder deck gun aboard a British E-class submarine.

Developments before 1914

By 1914, the submarine or submersible boat had quite a long history, going all the way back to the eighteenth century.

THE ANTECEDENTS of the World War I submarine really start with the inclusion of the torpedo as part of its armament in 1879, and, around the same time, the development of electric accumulators and motors of sufficient power to propel a boat underwater. Even at this stage there were two views of what a navy needed: one was a boat that could operate wholly and continuously submerged; the other was for a boat that was primarily a surface craft, but which could submerge and travel underwater for relatively brief periods.

This second view prevailed, partly because it was technically more feasible and partly because it was easier for the naval strategists of the time to understand. It was this approach that led to the adoption of the long, narrow torpedo-boat hull rather than the more bulbous, fish-shaped hull of many early submersibles. This hull design would prevail right into the 1950s.

Another influence was the improvement of naval guns, especially the development of the quick-firing gun, which made surface torpedo-boats vulnerable. France produced the first effective naval submarine, the electric-powered *Gustave Zédé* (1893), named for its designer.

The US Navy led during the 1890s in promoting experiments with gasoline and electric engines, and John Holland's *Holland* (1900), with gasoline and electric motors, was a major step forward. In 1900, six navies possessed a total of 10 submarines, with 11 under construction. The British Royal and German Imperial navies were not among them. France had 14 built or on the stocks, the United States had two, Turkey had two (of 1880s vintage), and Italy, Spain and Portugal had one each.

New Century

During the 1900s, some important developments took place. Great Britain decided it had to have submarines and its first five were built to Holland's design. Home-designed B- C- and D-classes followed, each one larger than its predecessor. The German

▲ **British D- and E-class**
Royal Navy submarines, including E1 and D2, sit in a dockyard somewhere on the English coast. E1 served mainly in the Baltic and was scuttled to avoid capture by advancing German forces near Helsinki, Finland. D2 served in the North Sea before being sunk with all hands in November 1914.

▲ **USS** *Seal*

One of four G-class boats, commissioned on 28 October 1912, USS *Seal* was allocated the unusual hull number of 19 from June 1916 until 1920. During World War I it was used almost exclusively as a training boat.

Navy, though sceptical, began to build submarines from 1906 and took a lead in using heavy oil rather than vaporous and flammable gasoline, or cumbrous steam machinery, for surface travel. From 1907, the Germans and the British were both building 'overseas' submarines intended primarily for operations in the North Sea, and between 1908 and 1914 the Germans ordered 42 of these, of which 29 were available for service in August 1914. Boats of this type displaced around 508 tonnes (500 tons) and with the D-class (1906) the British too began to use paired diesel engines and twin propellers.

Up to the start of the war, the biggest submarine fleet was the French. The French Navy saw its submarines as compensating for its lack of large capital ships, and naval exercises from the days of *Gustave Zédé* onwards convinced them that the submarine had a role as a potential destroyer of surface warships. By 1906, submarine flotillas were established at Dunkirk, Cherbourg, Rochefort and Toulon – all important naval ports – with the purpose of operating defensively against any approaching hostile fleet. The French were also the first to send submarines to remote colonial bases, for the same purpose. This French perception of the submarine's role was influential and in other navies it was also seen essentially as a defensive craft. Britain followed the French example by establishing flotilla bases at Devonport, Portsmouth, Harwich and Dundee, to maintain a watch in the western approaches, the English Channel and the North Sea.

United States Left Behind

These European developments, part of the 'arms race' of the 1900s, left the United States somewhat behind after its early start. US submarines remained small and were used only for patrols close to the coast. But the European nations were preparing for a war, while the United States was not. Nobody, however, appears to have appreciated the possibilities of the submarine as a wide-ranging commerce raider and certainly none of the pre-1914 boats were designed with this role in mind.

Naval exercises had shown convincingly by 1910 that a submarine could approach a battleship undetected and fire torpedoes at it, and this aspect of a submarine's offensive power was appreciated by the more perceptive naval strategists; but they still had much to learn about its potential.

Submarine forces
1914

By the eve of World War I, 16 navies included submarines in their fleets, with a total of around 400, but these craft were relatively small and generally intended for short sea operations, not for venturing out into the oceans.

ALMOST EVERY EUROPEAN power maintained a submarine fleet, although as yet submarines had not been tested in a full-scale war. But they would prove to have a decisive influence in naval combat.

Denmark and Sweden
Submarine construction was a specialized activity and the Fiat-San Giorgio yard at La Spezia, Italy, built boats for several navies. Typical was the petrol-engined *Dykkeren*, bought by the Danish Navy in 1909 and used for inshore patrols. In World War I Denmark was neutral, and coastal patrol was essential to ensure belligerent vessels did not enter territorial waters. Sunk in a collision with a Norwegian steamer in 1916, *Dykkeren* was salvaged, but broken up in 1918. Pre-war submarines had been armed with self-propelled torpedoes for attacking enemy ships, but *Dykkeren* had no deck gun, as this was not a feature of pre-war submarines.

During the war the belligerent powers fitted their boats with deck guns. This permitted them to approach enemy merchant ships on the surface and signal them to stop for searching (an early war policy), and later to sink small or unarmed ships that did not warrant expenditure of torpedoes. Up to 1914 most submarines carried no more than two to four torpedoes. Most war-built submarines had one and sometimes two guns of 75mm or 100mm (3- or 4in) calibre; however, the tendency was for deck guns to become bigger, and several later German submarines carried 150mm (5.9in) guns.

Sweden was to remain neutral in both world wars, but always maintained a strong defensive fleet. Its submarine tradition began in 1902 with *Hajen*, rebuilt and extended in 1916, but still a relatively primitive boat with a paraffin engine for surface work and a single 457mm (18in) torpedo tube.

France
The French had been pioneers in submarine design and began the war with a fleet of over 60 submarines in a range of types, including the 16-strong Brumaire

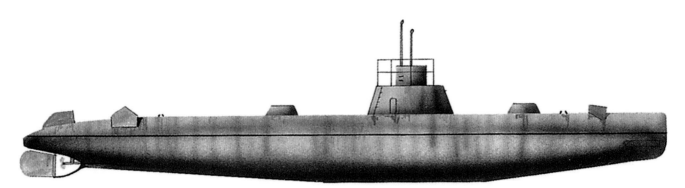

▲ Dykkeren

Danish Navy, coastal submarine, 1909

Dykkeren proved to have many mechanical and structural problems, and the Danish Navy did not look to Fiat-San Giorgio for further boats, instead building other Italian designs, from Whitehead, under licence in Denmark, as the Havmanden and Aegir classes. These had diesel engines rather than *Dykkeren's* kerosene motors.

Specifications	
Crew: 35	Displacement: Surfaced: 107 tonnes (105 tons);
Powerplant: Twin screw petrol engine;	Submerged: 134 tonnes (132 tons)
one electric motor	Dimensions (length/beam/draught): 34.7m x
Max Speed: Surfaced: 12 knots;	3.3m x 2m (113ft 10in x 10ft 10in x 6ft 6in)
Submerged: 7.5 knots	Commissioned: June 1909
Surface Range: 185km (100nm) at 12 knots	Armament: Two 457mm (18in) torpedo tubes

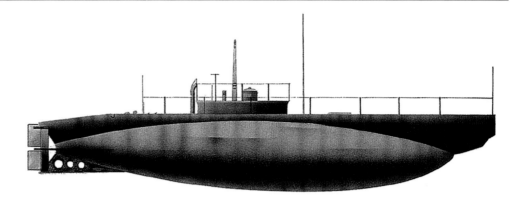

▲ Hajen

Swedish Navy, coastal submarine, 1900s

Hajen was in essence a Holland boat whose designer, Carl Richson, had studied submarine building in the United States. Two reload torpedoes could be carried, and two similar boats were built in 1909. In 1916, *Hajen* was given diesel engines, and a deck platform to raise the minimal bridge structure. Decommissioned in 1922, it is kept as a museum boat.

Specifications

Crew: 15

Powerplant: Single screw paraffin engine; electric motor

Max Speed: Surfaced: 9.5 knots; Submerged: 7 knots

Surface Range: Not known

Displacement: Surfaced: 108 tonnes (107 tons); Submerged: 130 tonnes (127 tons)

Dimensions (length/beam/draught): 19.8m x 3.6m x 3m (65ft x 11ft 10in x 9ft 10in)

Commissioned: July 1904

Armament: One 457mm (18in) torpedo tube

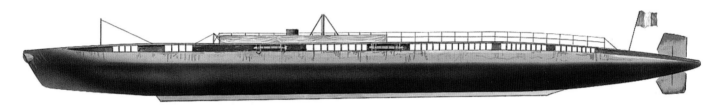

▲ Frimaire

French Navy, patrol submarine, World War I

Possession of a shallow keel prevented the Brumaire-class submarines from excessive rolling, but they were difficult to operate in anything other than a calm sea. They had limited success in warfare, though *Bernouilli* penetrated the naval base at Cattaro and torpedoed an Austrian destroyer. Three were lost in 1914–18.

Specifications

Crew: 29

Powerplant: Two-shaft diesel engines; electric motors

Max Speed: Surfaced: 13 knots; Submerged: 8 knots

Surface Range: 3150km (1700nm) at 10 knots

Displacement: Surfaced: 403 tonnes (397 tons); Submerged: 560 tonnes (551 tons)

Dimensions (length/beam/draught): 52.1m x 5.14m x 3.1m (170ft 11in x 17ft 9in x 10ft 2in)

Commissioned: August 1911

Armament: Six 450mm (17.7in) torpedo tubes

▲ Gustave Zédé

French Navy, patrol submarine, 1914

With eight torpedo tubes, *Gustave Zédé* was well armed for a 1914 submarine. The deck gun was a wartime addition. The two reciprocating steam engines developed 1640hp (1223kW). They were oil-fired, enabling rapid shutdown on diving. Steam could be retained in the two boilers for a surface restart.

Specifications

Crew: 32

Powerplant: Twin screw reciprocating engines; electric motors

Max Speed: Surfaced: 9.2 knots; Submerged: 6.5 knots

Surface Range: 2660km (1433nm) at 10 knots

Displacement: Surfaced: 862 tonnes (849 tons); Submerged: 1115 tonnes (1098 tons)

Dimensions (length/beam/draught): 74m x 6m x 3.7m (242ft 9in x 19ft 8in x 12ft 2in)

Commissioned: May 1913

Armament: Eight 450mm (17.7in) torpedo tubes

class, of which *Frimaire*, launched in 1911, was one of the first. Active in the Mediterranean throughout the war, it was stricken in 1923. The most unusual feature of the class was its lack of a conning-tower, which gave it a minimal surface profile but also made it very 'wet' and restricted the range of vision. Essentially it was a torpedo-boat hull with capacity for brief submergence.

Although by 1914 diesel fuel, far less flammable than petrol, was becoming standard, experimentation with steam turbines continued, partly through the quest for speed and partly because early diesel engines

lacked power and reliability. The second *Gustave Zédé*, completed in 1914, could make 10 knots on the surface, but its reciprocating steam turbines were exchanged in 1921–22 for German diesels cannibalized from U-165. It followed what was to be the standard submarine design, with a conning tower, and a 75mm (3in) gun on the foredeck.

Germany and Austria-Hungary

The Imperial German Navy had 30 U-boats in service at the start of the war. The first U-boat came into service in 1906, and U-1 had the double hull

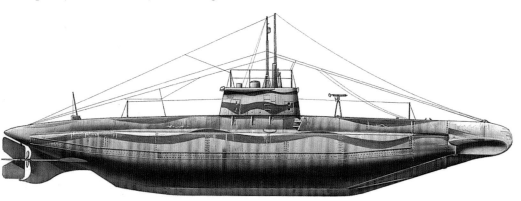

▲ UB-4

Imperial German Navy, coastal submarine, North and Adriatic Seas, 1914

Built and then disassembled in sections, these compact vessels were transported by rail to their base-ports, reassembled and put on active service. Most worked in the North Sea from German-held Antwerp, or from Pola on the Adriatic. Four of the eight UB-4 class were lost in the war.

Specifications

Crew: 14	Submerged: 144 tonnes (142 tons)
Powerplant: Single screw; diesel/electric motors	Dimensions (length/beam/draught): 28m x 2.9m
Max Speed: Surfaced: 6.5 knots; Submerged:	x 3m (92ft 3in x 9ft 9in x 10ft)
5.5 knots	Commissioned: April 1915
Surface Range: 2778km (1599nm) at 5 knots	Armament: Two 457mm (18in) torpedo tubes
Displacement: Surfaced: 129 tonnes (127 tons);	

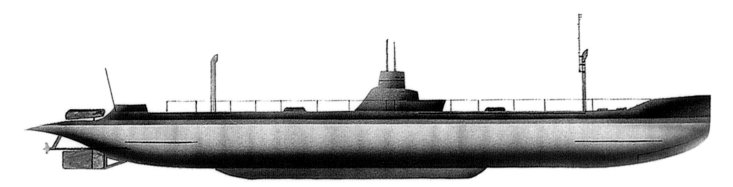

▲ U-1

Imperial German Navy, coastal submarine, North Sea, 1915

Designed by Krupps, U-1 was an improved version of their Karp- and Forelle-type submarines sold to Russia in 1904. Trim tanks were fitted, as well as the Körting kerosene engines (which had the disadvantage of not being reversible). The profile clearly shows the torpedo-boat ancestry of submarines of this period.

Specifications

Crew: 22	Displacement: Surfaced: 241 tonnes (238 tons);
Powerplant: Twin screws; heavy oil (kerosene)/	Submerged: 287 tonnes (283 tons)
electric motors	Dimensions (length/beam/draught): 42.4m x
Max Speed: Surfaced: 10.8 knots; Submerged:	3.8m x 3.2m (139ft x 12ft 6in x 10ft 6in)
8.7 knots	Commissioned: August 1906
Surface Range: 2850km (1536nm) at 10 knots	Armament: One 450mm (17.7in) torpedo tube

and twin screws that would be typical of twentieth-century German submarines. It had only a single torpedo tube. U-1 served throughout the war, but as a training and test boat only. Some German boats ran on petrol or kerosene at first, but diesel engines were introduced from 1908.

Like other navies, the German *Marinamt* initially saw submarines as short-range craft, with the North Sea as the prime theatre of operation. None of the early U-boat classes numbered more than four, and the U-31 class, introduced in 1913, was the first to number more than 10. By this time, intensive future planning was going on, but the work was going into the UB-class, developed from 1914 and intended for coastal and short-range operations – it would be deployed in the North Sea, the Mediterranean-Adriatic and the Black Sea – and the UC-class, intended for minelaying.

The war-plan for Germany's U-boats was that they should be distributed in flotillas of 12, with each responsible for a 96.6km (60-mile) wide front. Kiel was the prime base. One flotilla at sea would patrol the Heligoland Bight, while a second would act as relief. Another flotilla would guard the approaches to Kiel, and a fourth, based at Emden, would undertake longer-range patrols using 'overseas boats'. A fifth flotilla would be held at Kiel as a reserve force. But the numbers available in August 1914 fell far short of what the plan required.

The Austro-Hungarian Empire had six submarines in 1914, numbered German-style as U-1 to U-6. All were built in 1909–11 and were based at Adriatic ports, with Pola serving as the prime base; all would see action in the Adriatic. Austria also had the world's first torpedo factory, the Whitehead works at Fiume, but long before 1914, Whitehead (a British engineer) had established works in both Britain and France.

Great Britain

By the start of World War I, the Royal Navy had 87 submarines in service, the largest fleet of all. The pioneer class were the A-boats of 1902, and the 11-strong B-class followed in 1904. They were fitted with two 457mm (18in) torpedo tubes. The C-class of 19 boats followed in 1906–10. Britain did not wholly dispense with petrol engines until 1913, and it was reported that all RN petrol submarines carried a cage of white mice, whose squeaks would give warning against escaping fumes.

The form of things to come was established by the eight D-class boats built between 1908 and 1912, with diesel engines and a range of 4630km (2880 miles). Radio was a standard fitment for the first time on a British submarine, using a retractable aerial attached to the conning tower mast.

In 1913, the E-class, which was perhaps the Royal Navy's most successful World War I submarine, was introduced. Diesel-powered, and based on the

▲ **B-1**

Royal Navy, coastal submarine, Baltic and Dardanelles, 1914–15

The B-class were first intended to be stationed at Dover for Channel defence, though draft war plans also envisaged operations in the Baltic. By 1914 they were really obsolete, but saw active war service as far afield as the Dardanelles. Note the small hydroplanes fitted to the conning tower sides.

Specifications

Crew: 16

Powerplant: Single screw petrol engine, one electric motor

Max Speed: Surfaced: 13 knots; Submerged: 7 knots

Surface Range: 2779km (1500nm) at 8 knots

Displacement: Surfaced: 284 tonnes (280 tons); Submerged: 319 tonnes (314 tons)

Dimensions (length/beam/draught): 41m x 4.1m x 3m (135ft x 13ft 6in x 9ft 10in)

Commissioned: October 1904

Armament: Two 475mm (18in) torpedo tubes

D-class, this was a substantially larger and more formidable craft than its predecessors, displacing 677 tonnes (667 tons) on the surface and 820 tonnes (807 tons) submerged, and with five 457mm (18in) torpedo tubes and a 12-pounder deck gun. (The first eight, *E-1* to *E-7* plus two built for the Royal Australian Navy, AE-1 and AE-2, had only four tubes and no deck gun.) A total of 55 were built, at 12 different yards, including six adapted as minelayers. Various modifications were introduced up to the completion of E-56 in June 1916, including more powerful electric motors, giving a marginally increased submerged speed of 10 knots compared to 9.5.

In 1914, British submarines were deployed in eight flotillas of unequal numbers: Flotilla No. 1 at Devonport had two boats; No. 2 at Portsmouth had

▲ **C-25**

Royal Navy, patrol submarine, North Sea, 1918

The C was the first large British class, with 37 boats in service by 1910. They were mostly deployed in the North Sea and English Channel, in the hope of intercepting U-boats in transit to the Atlantic, or engaged in minelaying. C3 was packed with explosive and blown up as part of the operation to block the German base at Zeebrugge on 23 April 1918.

Specifications

Crew: 16

Powerplant: Single screw petrol engine; one electric motor

Max Speed: Surfaced: 12 knots; Submerged: 7.5 knots

Surface Range: 2414km (1431nm) at 8 knots

Displacement: Surfaced: 295 tonnes (290 tons); Submerged: 325 tonnes (320 tons)

Dimensions (length/beam/draught): 43m x 4m x 3.5m (141ft x 13ft 1in x 11ft 4in)

Commissioned: 1909

Armament: Two 457mm (18in) torpedo tubes

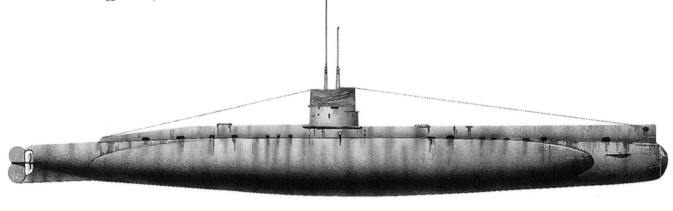

Specifications

Crew: 25

Powerplant: Twin screw diesel engines; electric motors

Max Speed: Surfaced: 14 knots; Submerged: 9 knots

Surface Range: 2038km (1100nm) at 10 knots

Displacement: Surfaced: 490 tonnes (483 tons);

Submerged: 604 tonnes (595 tons)

Dimensions (length/beam/draught): 50m x 6m x 3m (163ft x 20ft 6in x 10ft 5in)

Commissioned: August 1908

Armament: Three 457mm (18in) torpedo tubes, one 12-pounder gun

▲ **D-1**

Royal Navy, patrol submarine, North Sea, 1916

D-class boats could transmit by radio as well as receive. External ballast tanks gave improved buoyancy, and battery capacity enabled them to remain submerged through the daylight hours. D-1 'torpedoed' two cruisers during a 1910 naval exercise, helping to convince the Royal Navy of the offensive power of submarines.

four; Nos. 3 and 4, both at Dover, had six and eight respectively; No. 5, at The Nore, had six; No. 6 on the Humber had six; No. 7 had three boats on the Tyne and three at Leith; No. 8, at Harwich, had 19, including all the newest and largest.

A further five flotillas and numerous additional bases would be added in the course of the war, but this disposition clearly shows the great majority of Royal Navy submarines placed to counter any venture by the German Navy across the North Sea towards British shores. As with France, some boats were deployed to colonial stations. Six of the B-class

boats were sent to Gibraltar and Malta in 1906, and in 1910 six of the C-class were towed to Hong Kong. In August 1914, three of these were still with the China Squadron.

Italy

The Italian Navy had only one submarine in 1900, but, spurred on by developments in France, submarine construction started from around 1904, using Italian-originated designs and concentrating on the small boats that would be most useful around the Italian coast and in the inlets of the Adriatic.

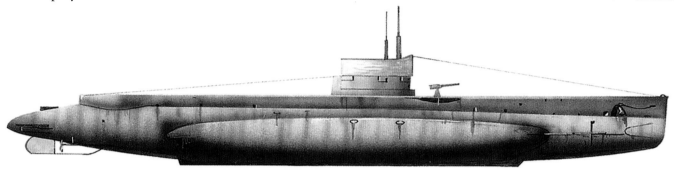

▲ E-11

Royal Navy, patrol submarine, Baltic Sea, Dardanelles, 1915

In October 1914, E-11 failed to gain entry to the Kattegat, but in August 1915, during a 29-day patrol in the Dardanelles and the Sea of Marmara, it sank the Turkish battleship *Barbarousse Haireddine*, a gunboat, seven transports and 23 sailing craft. The smaller vessels were sunk using the newly fitted deck gun.

Specifications

Crew: 30

Powerplant: Two twin-shaft diesel engines; two electric motors

Max Speed: Surfaced: 14 knots; Submerged: 9 knots

Surface Range: 6035km (3579nm)

Displacement: Surfaced: 677 tonnes (667 tons); Submerged: 820 tonnes (807 tons)

Dimensions (length/beam/draught): 55.17m x 6.91m x 3.81m (181ft x 22ft 8in x 12ft 6in)

Commissioned: 1913

Armament: Five 457mm (18in) torpedo tubes; one 12-pounder gun

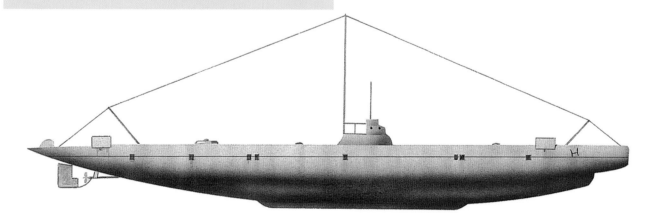

▲ Fisalia

Italian Navy, patrol submarine, Adriatic, World War I

Fisalia was one of the first of a class of eight boats that were among the first Italian submarines to have diesel engines. They were good sea boats with excellent manoeuvrability. *Fisalia* served in the Adriatic during World War I.

Specifications

Crew: 40

Powerplant: Twin screw diesel engines; electric motors

Max Speed: Surfaced: 12 knots; Submerged: 8 knots

Surface Range: Not known

Displacement: Surfaced: 256 tonnes (252 tons); Submerged: 310 tonnes (305 tons)

Dimensions (length/beam/draught): 45m x 4.2m x 3m (148ft 2in x 13ft 9in x 9ft 10in)

Commissioned: February 1912

Armament: Two 450mm (17.7in) torpedo tubes

BRITISH SUBMARINE CLASSES 1914–18, PRE-WAR BUILD			
Class	Number	Launched	Note
A	10	1903–05	
B	10	1904–06	
C	41	1906–10	
D	8	1908–11	First GB diesel-engined
E	11	1911–14	
V	1	1914	

BRITISH SUBMARINE CLASSES 1914–18, WARTIME BUILD			
Class	Number	Launched	Note
E	40	1914–18	
S	3	1914–15	Trans to Italy Oct 1915
V	2	1915	
W	4	1914–15	Trans to Italy Aug 1916
F	3	1915–16	
G	14	1916–17	
J	7	1915–17	Trans to Australia; 1 sank
K	17	1916–17	
M	3	1917–18	
H	43	1915–19	
L	32	1917–18	
R	10	1918	First 'hunter-killer' sub

The first Italian class was named after the lead boat *Glauco* in 1905 and five were built between 1905 and 1909. Italy began to build diesel/electric powered submarines with the eight boats of the Medusa class, including *Fisalia*, in 1910–12.

By 1914, there were 20 boats in Italy's submarine squadron, including the pioneer *Delfino* of 1892. Also there were two experimental midget submarines of the Alfa class, built in 1913. They did not last beyond 1916, but the Italian Navy retained an interest in midget craft and built more from 1915. In the course of the war its prime adversary was the Austro-Hungarian fleet in the Adriatic. Intended for inshore and shallow-sea service, Italy's World War I submarines, though effective, were quite small. The most effective boats in 1914 were *Nereide* and *Nautilus*; *Nereide* was sunk in the Adriatic on 5 August 1915 by the Austrian U-5.

Japan and Russia

Japan and Russia had fought a naval war in 1904–05 and although submarines did not play a significant part, the war stimulated the interest of both navies in submarines as anti-warship and coastal defence units. Imperial Japan's first submarine squadron consisted of six small submarines of the American Holland type and a Japanese variant. Intended for coastal work, they played no part in oceanic operations. In

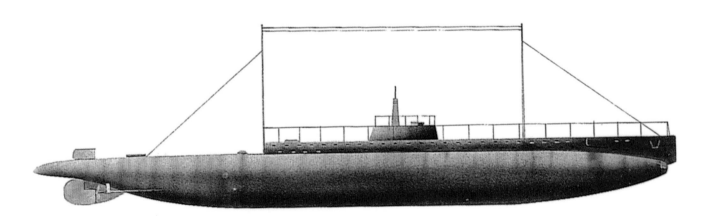

▲ Nereide

Italian Navy, patrol submarine, Adriatic, 1915

Nereide was designed by Curio Bernardis, whose influence on Italian submarine design was to be very strong. A deck-mounted third torpedo tube, though part of the design, was not installed. Despite a reputation for efficiency, *Nereide*'s war record appears to have been uneventful until its fatal duel with *U-5*.

Specifications

Crew: 35

Powerplant: Twin screws; diesel/electric motors

Max Speed: Surfaced: 13.2 knots; Submerged: 8 knots

Surface Range: 7412km (4000nm) at 10 knots

Displacement: Surfaced: 228 tonnes (225 tons);

Submerged: 325 tonnes (320 tons)

Dimensions (length/beam/draught): 40m x 4.3m x 2.8m (134ft 2in x 14ft 1in x 9ft 2in)

Commissioned: July 1913

Armament: Two 450mm (17in) torpedo tubes

1914, the Japanese had 12 submarines, of which the largest were five C1–C2 Vickers class boats, built in 1909–11, displacing from 295 to 325 tonnes (290 to 320 tons) on the surface, with two 457mm (18in) torpedo tubes. The others were considerably smaller. Japan's submarine base was the Kure naval yard on the Inland Sea.

In the later nineteenth century, Russia's Tsarist government had taken a keen interest in submarines, with a view to the protection of naval harbours. In 1914, Imperial Russia had between 30 and 40 small submarines on active duty, with a maximum range of around 241km (150 miles), based at Baltic and Black Sea ports. Most had been purchased from the United States, Britain, France and Germany, although some were built in Russian yards.

In the Baltic Sea, Russia had 11 submarines in 1914, organized in three divisions: two active, with four boats each; and one for training. Of these, only one, the one-off *Akula* of 1908, was really capable of longer-range missions.

United States

In the early twentieth century, the designer John Holland had given the United States a world lead in submarine design, but by 1917 several European fleets could boast submarines of greater performance and endurance than the United States possessed. In April 1917, when it entered the war against Germany, the United States had 12 classes of submarine and a total of 42 boats. *Grayling*, one of three D-class boats built in 1909–10, was petrol-engined, with four 457mm (18in) torpedo tubes.

America's first diesel-powered submarine was E-1, commissioned at Groton in February 1912. The US Navy was to make relatively little use of its submarines in the war; their operational range was limited and the Navy, mistakenly, did not anticipate hostile action close to the American coast. Grayling was in service until 1922.

The E- and F-classes of 1911–12 were diesel-engined with four torpedo tubes; all were re-engineered in 1915. F-4 sank in March 1915 off Pearl Harbor, but the wreck was successfully salvaged from 91m (299ft) in a pioneering deep-water retrieval operation.

Limitations

The submarines of 1914 had many shortcomings. Perhaps the most serious was their lack of punch. The 457mm (18in) torpedo would not penetrate the armour plating of a Dreadnought-type battleship, though it could and did sink armoured cruisers and pre-Dreadnoughts. The torpedo stock was limited, and with only one or two forward-facing tubes, a destructive salvo could not be fired. Their speed was slow on the surface and even slower under water. This prevented them from keeping up with surface ships, whether friendly or hostile. Their low silhouettes, while making them hard to detect on

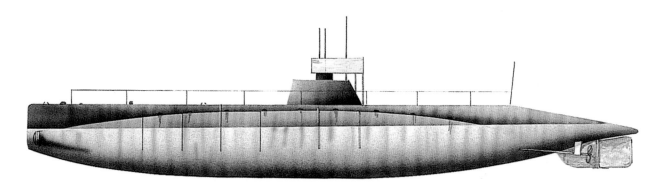

▲ **USS Grayling**

US Navy, patrol submarine, Atlantic, 1917–18

Grayling was flagboat of Submarine Division 3 of the Atlantic Fleet in 1910. It and the other D-class boats were used in offshore patrols on the east coast, but had no success in intercepting the long-range U-boats that appeared late in the war. On 14 September 1917, it sank at the dock, but was lifted and remained in commission until 1922.

Specifications

Crew: 15

Powerplant: Two twin screw petrol engines; two electric motors

Max Speed: Surfaced: 12 knots; Submerged: 9.5 knots

Surface Range: 2356km (1270nm) at 10 knots

Displacement: Surfaced: 292 tonnes (288 tons); Submerged: 342 tonnes (337 tons)

Dimensions (length/beam/draught): 41m x 4.2m x 3.6m (135ft x 13ft 9in x 12ft)

Commissioned: June 1909

Armament: Four 457mm (18in) torpedo tubes

the surface, had the disadvantages of making them hard to steer and navigate in anything other than calm conditions, and of making them susceptible to accidental ramming by ships that had simply failed to notice them. Many had only the most rudimentary kind of bridge structure. Their small size and limited space restricted the amount of stores that could be carried. Their capacity for underwater navigation and manoeuvre was very limited. Nevertheless, they had the huge advantage of stealth. In 1914, there was no way of detecting a submerged submarine. It was a completely new piece on the chessboard of naval war, and it did not conform to the old rules.

At international conferences between 1899 and 1907, certain rules of naval warfare had been agreed by the European powers. A warship encountering an enemy merchant vessel was expected to seize it as a 'prize' and sink it only as a last resort. Its crew should be taken prisoner. A neutral vessel suspected of carrying war goods to the enemy should be stopped, searched and seized in the same way if its cargo was suspect. This protocol, going back to the days of sail, took no account of the way in which a submarine was organized and managed.

The capacity to attack from a submerged position was the whole point. To surface and investigate was

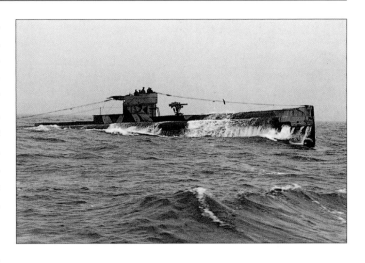

▲ **Royal Navy E-class**

Submarines travelled on the surface whenever possible and consequently, for many years, surface performance was given priority in design.

to invite retaliation from an armed merchantman; or, quite possibly faster than the submarine, it could just zig-zag away. Also, a submarine had no space whatsoever for holding prisoners. These were some of the reasons why admirals decided to discount or ignore the potential of the submarine as a commerce raider, and to see it as part of the defensive line against hostile warships.

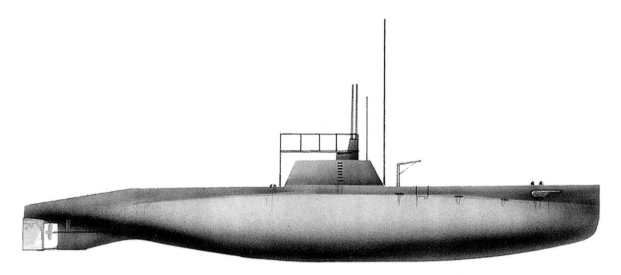

▲ **F-4**

US Navy, F-class coastal submarine, Pacific Fleet, 1914

F-4, originally to be named *Skate*, was launched in January 1912. From August 1914 it was attached to the First Submarine Group, Pacific Torpedo Flotilla. The cause of its disastrous dive was tentatively suggested as seepage of seawater into the battery compartment, causing power failure and loss of control.

Specifications

Crew: 35

Powerplant: Twin screw diesels; electric motors

Max Speed: Surfaced: 13.5 knots; Submerged: 5 knots

Surface Range: 4260km (2300nm) at 11 knots

Displacement: Surfaced: 335 tonnes (330 tons); Submerged: 406 tonnes (400 tons)

Dimensions (length/beam/draught): 43.5m x 4.7m x 3.7m (142ft 9in x 15ft 5in x 12ft 2in)

Commissioned: January 1912

Armament: Four torpedo tubes

Operations in European seas
1914–18

Much submarine action went on in the seas around the European continent, in particular the Baltic Sea, North Sea and Mediterranean.

IN THE BALTIC SEA, submarines played a key strategic role for a time, and in the Dardanelles they participated effectively in the first big combined military operation.

Baltic Sea

Danzig (now Gdansk) was a German city in 1913 when the four boats of the U-19 class were completed there. U-21 of this class was the first submarine to sink a ship with a self-propelling torpedo, when it hit the cruiser HMS *Pathfinder* on 5 September 1914. A new armament variation was to adapt a submarine to lay mines off an enemy harbour or across a shipping route.

The German Navy constructed several specialized submarines with vertical mine-launching tubes through their hulls: UC-74, launched in October 1917, was one of six. In 1918 it was transferred to the Austrian Navy for Adriatic operations against Italy, but kept its German crew; the others in the class served in the North Sea and the Baltic; only two

GERMAN SUBMARINE CLASSES 1914–18, PRE-WAR BUILD			
Class	Number	Launched	Note
U1	1	1906	Petrol engine
U2	1	1908	Petrol engine
U3	2	1909	Petrol engine
U5	4	1910	Petrol engine
U9	4	1910–11	Petrol engine
U13	3	1910–11	Petrol engine
U16	1	1911	Petrol engine
U17	2	1912	Petrol engine
U19	4	1912–13	Diesel; ocean-going
U23	4	1913	Diesel; ocean-going
U27	4	1913	Diesel; ocean-going
U31	11	1913	Diesel; ocean-going

survived the war. Eighteen mines were carried, and the class also had three 508mm (20in) torpedo tubes and a 86mm (3.4in) deck gun.

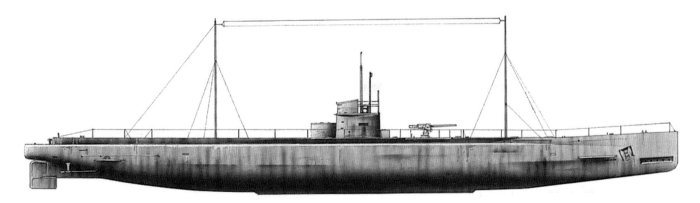

▲ U-21

Imperial German Navy, patrol submarine, Mediterranean, 1916

One of the most successful World War I U-boats, U-21 was unusual in having a single captain, Otto Hersing, throughout the war. It returned from its Mediterranean exploits to rejoin the High Seas Fleet at Kiel in March 1917. It foundered in the North Sea on 22 February 1919 while being towed to Britain to be handed over.

Specifications

Crew: 35

Powerplant: Two shafts; diesel/electric motors

Max Speed: Surfaced: 15.4 knots; Submerged: 9.5 knots

Surface Range: 9265km (5500nm) at 10 knots

Displacement: Surfaced: 660 tonnes (650 tons);

Submerged: 850 tonnes (837 tons)

Dimensions (length/beam/draught): 64.2m x 6.1m x 3.5m (210ft 6in x 20ft x 11ft 9in)

Commissioned: February 1913

Armament: Four 508mm (20in) torpedo tubes; one 86mm (3.4in) gun

In the course of the war, the majority of new British submarines were built for open-sea work, but a small class of coastal submarines was built in 1913–15 as the F-class, and used extensively on coastal patrols. A second batch was cancelled in 1914, in favour of the longer-range E-class boats. F-1 had a short service life, being broken up in 1920.

In October 1914, three British E-boats were dispatched to the Baltic and two got through, to support the Russians against the German Baltic Fleet. In August to September, four more were sent (one lost on the way), and four C-class boats were towed to Archangel and delivered to the Baltic via canal barges. Originally intended to hinder German landing operations, they also were used to prevent shipments of iron ore from neutral Sweden to Germany.

The E-boats were armed with five 457mm (18in) torpedo tubes plus a 5.4kg (12-pounder) deck gun. They had good surface speed, but their wireless sets had limited range and their captains had to rely on carrier pigeons while on remote patrols. The E-boats were also much less reliable than their German equivalents.

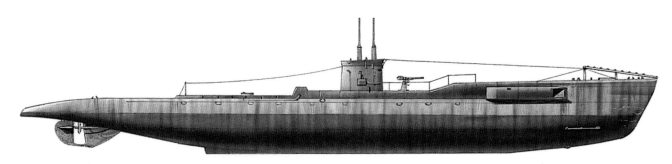

Specifications

Crew: 26

Powerplant: Two-shafts; diesel/electric motors

Max Speed: Surfaced: 11.8 knots; Submerged: 7.3 knots

Surface Range: 18,520km (10,000nm) at 10 knots

Displacement: Surfaced: 416 tonnes (410 tons); Submerged: 500 tonnes (492 tons)

Dimensions (length/beam/draught): 50.6m x 5.1m x 3.6m ((166ft x 17ft x 12ft)

Commissioned: October 1916

Armament: Three 508mm (20in) torpedo tubes; one 86mm (3.4in) gun; 18 mines

▲ UC-74

Imperial German Navy, minelayer, Adriatic, World War I

The mine-tubes were set in the forward part of the hull, below the raised fairing. The boat's Austrian service was arranged to assist the Austrian fleet even though Germany and Italy were not in a state of war at the time. At the end of the war, UC-74 was ceded to France and was scrapped in 1921.

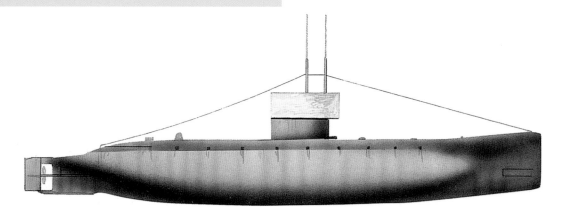

▲ F-1

Royal Navy, F-class coastal submarine, 1915

The three F-class were double-hulled. Diving depth was 30m (99ft). It does not seem that any was fitted with a deck gun, probably because of their small size and limited crew number. With limited endurance and offensive power, they were used only for inshore patrols, and no major encounters are recorded. All were broken up by 1922.

Specifications

Crew: 20

Powerplant: Twin screw diesel engines; electric motors

Max Speed: Surfaced: 14 knots; Submerged: 8.7 knots

Surface Range: 5556km (3000nm) at 9 knots

Displacement: Surfaced: 368 tonnes (363 tons); Submerged: 533 tonnes (525 tons)

Dimensions (length/beam/draught): 46m x 4.9m x 3.2m (151ft x 16ft x 10ft 6in)

Commissioned: March 1915

Armament: Three 457mm (18in) torpedo tubes

The British flotilla was based at Reval (now Tallinn) and its presence in the Baltic intimidated the Germans, who quickly organized convoys to protect merchantmen. German propaganda blasted 'British pirate submarines' in the Baltic, just as British newspapers did about the U-boats in the North Sea. However, until well into 1915, all the sinkings of German vessels in the Baltic were due to mines.

The E-boats began to show more results in the summer of 1915. On 19 August, E-1 fired a torpedo into the cruiser *Moltke*, and although it failed to sink it, the Germans abandoned their planned occupation of Riga. By September, there were five E-boats in Baltic waters.

In October, E-8 sank the German cruiser *Prinz Adelbert*, already damaged in July by E-9, and in the next month E-19 sank the light cruiser *Undine*. Tight defence of the Kattegat eventually kept the E-boats at bay, except for those already in the Baltic. When Russia signed a peace treaty with Germany in 1918, four British E-class and three C-class submarines were scuttled by their crews off Helsinki.

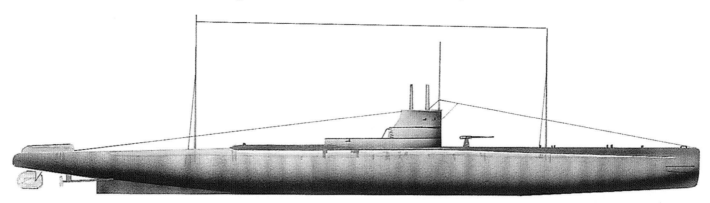

▲ **G-1**

Royal Navy, patrol submarine, North Sea, 1915–18

In autumn 1915, a new flotilla of G- and E-class boats was formed at Blyth, Northumberland, to operate with units of the Grand Fleet, but their slow speed made this an impossible project. *G-7* was the last British submarine lost in World War I, failing to return from a North Sea patrol on 1 November 1918.

Specifications

Crew: 31

Powerplant: Twin screw diesel; electric motors

Max Speed: Surfaced: 14.25 knots; Submerged: 9 knots

Surface Range: 4445km (2400nm) at 12.5 knots

Displacement: Surfaced: 704 tonnes (693 tons); Submerged: 850 tonnes (836 tons)

Dimensions (length/beam/draught): 57m x 6.9m x 4.1m (187ft x 22ft x 13ft 6in)

Commissioned: August 1915

Armament: Four 457mm (18in) torpedo tubes; one 533mm (21in) torpedo tube; one 76mm (3in) gun

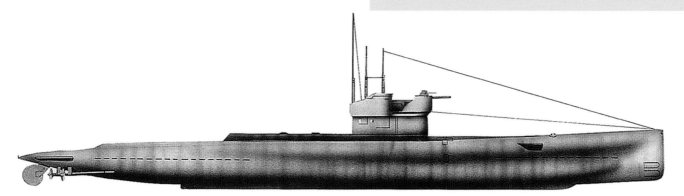

Specifications

Crew: 44

Powerplant: Triple screw diesel; electric motors

Max Speed: Surfaced: 17 knots; Submerged: 9.5 knots

Surface Range: 9500km (5120nm) at 12.5 knots

Displacement: Surfaced: 1223 tonnes (1204 tons); Submerged: 1849 tonnes (1820 tons)

Dimensions (length/beam/draught): 84m x 7m x 4.3m (275ft 7in x 23ft x 14ft)

Commissioned: November 1915

Armament: Six 457mm (18in) torpedo tubes; one 76mm (3in) gun

▲ **J-1**

Royal Navy, fast submarine, 1918

With three 12-cylinder diesel engines, producing 3600hp (2685kW), this was the Royal Navy's most powerful submarine yet, although its speed was not enough to keep up with the British Grand Fleet. The J-class also had better sea endurance than previous British classes. After the war, the six surviving boats were passed on to the Royal Australian Navy.

The Dardanelles, May 1915 to January 1916

The Gallipoli campaign, centred on the Dardanelles Straits, was the first major naval campaign in which submarines played an active supporting role. French and British, and one Australian, contended with U-boats and surface vessels. The first British boats despatched were five B-class, too small and underpowered to be really effective in the powerful currents, though B-11 sank the Turkish battleship *Messoudieh* in December 1915; they were followed by five E-class boats plus the Australian Navy's AE-2. Four French submarines also took part. The disastrous Allied campaign ended in January 1916, when the British withdrew their forces.

The activities of Allied submarines were a bright spot in the dismal story, though all four French and four British submarines were lost in the effort. However, they had sunk seven Turkish warships, 16 transports and supply ships, plus 230 steamers and small vessels.

On the other side, U-21 sank HMS *Triumph* off Anzac Bay on 25 May 1915, and another battleship, HMS *Majestic*, two days later. U-21's feat in voyaging from Kiel to Pola without refuelling was remarkable. U-21 joined the German U-boat flotilla based at Cattaro (now Kotor) on the Adriatic, in July 1915. On 8 February 1916 it sank a French armoured cruiser off the Syrian coast.

U-21 survived the war, having sunk some 40 Allied ships. UB-14, notionally transferred to the Austrian Navy but with an all-German crew, was, like other UB- and UC-boats, transported overland in sections to Pola, and in a highly successful career sank numerous merchant ships. It took HMS E-20 by surprise on 6 November 1915, surfacing and sinking the British submarine with a single torpedo fired from 500m (547yds), in one of the few sub-versus-sub engagements to occur in the first years of the war.

North Sea

Perhaps one of the most famous and effective actions by a U-boat occurred in the North Sea in the first few months of the war. The British Admiralty sought to keep the German High Seas Fleet bottled up in its ports, which required an aggressive deployment of cruisers and light warships in the North Sea. Cruiser Force C, consisting of HMS *Aboukir*, HMS *Hogue* and HMS *Cressy*, were sent out on patrol, as part of this strategy. All the cruisers were at least 10 years old and obsolete, even by the standards of 1914.

On 22 September 1914, the fleet was spotted by U-9, one of the fastest and most advanced submarine types of its time. The slow-moving cruisers presented an easy target and each was sunk in turn by torpedo within the space of just an hour. The action proved the effectiveness of the new U-boats against slow-moving cruisers.

Despite their early successes, the North Sea became increasingly difficult for U-boats to traverse. The British E-9 sank the German light cruiser *Hela* and the German destroyer S-116 in the North Sea in mid-September 1914. Though the German High

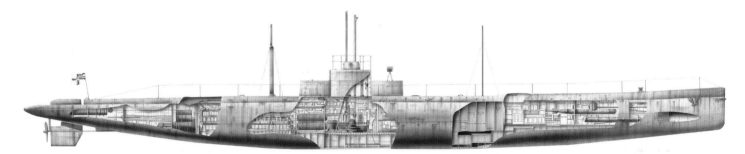

▲ **U-9**

Imperial German Navy, patrol submarine, 1914

U-9 had four Körting kerosene engines, which tended to make smoke and required a dismountable funnel. This was the first submarine on which the torpedo tubes were successfully reloaded while the boat was submerged. Its despatch of the British cruisers on 22 September 1914 with its six torpedoes demonstrated early in the war the power of the type.

Specifications

Crew: 29	601 tons
Powerplant: Four kerosene engines; electric motors	Dimensions (length/beam/draught): 57.3m
Max Speed: Surfaced: 26.3 km/h (14.2 knots);	(188ft) x 6m (19.7ft) x 3.5m (11.5ft)
Submerged: 14.8km/h (8.0kn)	Commissioned: April 1910
Surface Range: 6216km (3356nm) at	Armament: four 45cm (17.7in) torpedo tubes
15.9km/h (8.6 knots)	(two bow, two stern); six torpedoes; 1 x 37mm
Displacement: Surface: 425 tons; Submerged:	(1.46in) deck gun

Seas Fleet made plans for drawing the British Grand Fleet within range of its submarine squadrons, the only major naval battle of the war, in the North Sea off Jutland in May 1916, did not involve submarines on either side.

In the last year of the war there were fierce struggles between German destroyers and British submarines in the North Sea, with merchant convoys between Britain and Scandinavia as the target or protectee. L-class submarines played a large part. L-10 sank the German destroyer S-33 on 3 October 1918 just before being sunk by other German vessels.

Mediterranean

By a pre-war agreement with the British, the French fleet operated largely in the Mediterranean, where French submarines had relatively few opportunities to show their prowess. Small numbers of kills were scored in the Adriatic by the Italian submarines against the Austrians, though Austrian and German U-boats scored kills of their own in return.

Balilla, built in Italy for the German Navy and intended as U-42, was taken over by the Italians in 1915, but sunk in the Adriatic on 14 July 1916 after attack by Austrian torpedo boats. It was in the

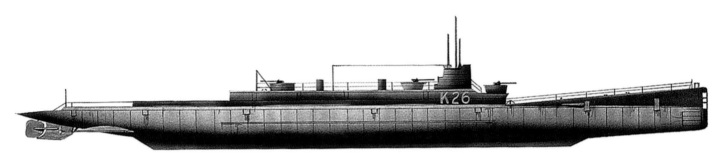

▲ K-Class
Royal Navy, fleet submarine, 1919

The product of the British Admiralty's desire to have a submarine that could keep up with battlecruisers, the K-class was undoubtedly fast but had few other positive features. They were deployed in two fleet flotillas from 1917, intended to get between an enemy fleet and its base, but they were never engaged in combat.

Specifications

Crew: 40	Displacement: Surfaced: 2174 tonnes (2140 tons); Submerged: 2814 tonnes (2770 tons)
Powerplant: Twin screw; steam turbines; electric motors	Dimensions (length/beam/draught): 100.6m x 8.1m x 5.2m (330ft x 26ft 7in x 17ft)
Max Speed: Surfaced: 23 knots; Submerged: 9 knots	Commissioned: 1916
Surface Range: 5556km (3000nm) at 13.5 knots	Armament: 10 533mm (21in) torpedo tubes; three 102mm (4in) guns

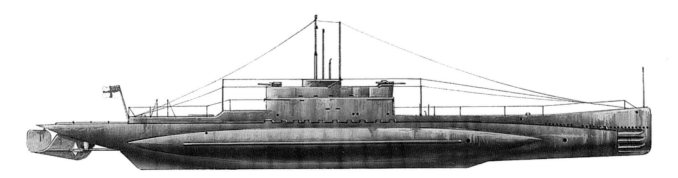

Specifications

Crew: 36	Submerged: 1097 tonnes (1080 tons)
Powerplant: Twin screw diesel; electric motors	Dimensions (length/beam/draught): 72.7m x 7.2m x 3.4m (238ft 6in x 23ft 8in x 11ft 2in)
Max Speed: Surfaced: 17.5 knots; Submerged: 10.5 knots	Commissioned: 1918
Surface Range: 7038km (3800nm) at 10 knots	Armament: Four 533mm (21in) torpedo tubes; one 102mm (4in) gun
Displacement: Surfaced: 904 tonnes (890 tons);	

▲ L-Class
Royal Navy, patrol submarine, 1918

The first L-class boats had 457mm (18in) torpedo tubes but later ones had 533mm (21in) tubes. These were the Royal Navy's largest patrol submarines, though still of relatively modest size. Introduced late in the war, most served on through the 1920s, and three survived as training boats to 1946.

Austrian-Italian submarine war that aerial spotting of submerged boats first became a regular practice. One of the most effective Italian submarine classes of the war was the F-class of 1916, which was well equipped, with two periscopes and with Fessenden signalling apparatus (like some British submarines, including the K-class), which was capable of sending Morse code messages from under the surface. The F-class was a small submarine with two 450mm (17.7in) torpedo tubes and a 76mm (3in) deck gun, and some actually remained in service into the 1930s.

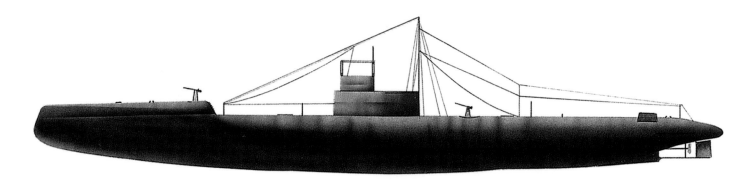

▲ Balilla

Italian Navy, patrol submarine, Adriatic, World War I

The influence of the designer Cesare Laurenti was notable on *Balilla*. Its prominent raised bow casing was unique in its three-strong class; the two sister boats had a flush deck and an additional bow tube. The design was sold to Japan and became the basis of the Japanese Navy's F1- and F2-classes in 1919–21.

Specifications

Crew: 38	Submerged: 890 tonnes (876 tons)
Powerplant: Two-shafts; diesel/electric motors	Dimensions (length/beam/draught): 65m x 6m
Max Speed: Surfaced: 14 knots; Submerged:	x 4m (213ft 3in x 19ft 8in x 13ft 1in)
9 knots	Commissioned: August 1913
Surface Range: 7041km (3800nm) at 10 knots	Armament: Four 450mm (17.7in) torpedo tubes;
Displacement: Surfaced: 740 tonnes (728 tons);	two 76mm (3in) guns

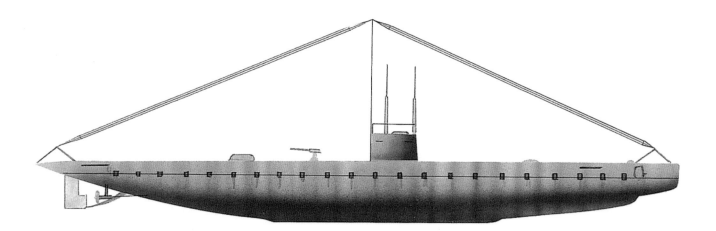

Specifications

Crew: 54	Submerged: 324 tonnes (319 tons)
Powerplant: Twin screw diesel engines; electric	Dimensions (length/beam/draught): 45.6m x
motors	4.2m x 3m (149ft 7in x 13ft 9in x 10ft)
Max Speed: Surfaced: 12.5 knots; Submerged:	Commissioned: April 1916
8.2 knots	Armament: Two 450mm (17.7in) torpedo tubes;
Surface Range: 2963km (1600nm) at 8.5 knots	one 76mm (3in) gun
Displacement: Surfaced: 226 tonnes (262 tons);	

▲ F-1

Italian Navy, patrol submarine, coastal service, World War I

Improved versions of the preceding Medusa class, the 21 F-class boats were built by Fiat-San Giorgio at La Spezia, to a design of Cesare Laurenti, whose consortium with Fiat built submarines for several nations. The 76mm (3in) gun is mounted in an unusual stern-facing position. The F-class served all round the Italian coast.

Operations in the Atlantic
1915–17

By far the most crucial of World War I submarine activities was the long campaign in the Atlantic Ocean by German U-boats against British and Allied merchant ships.

ALTHOUGH HARDLY ANTICIPATED by the German High Command in 1914, the Atlantic campaign was seen by 1917 as a means of achieving victory. The long-range U-boats of 1914 and 1915 were few in number, with only five likely to be on station at any given time. Slow on the surface, with low-calibre guns, they were not well suited to the task of commerce raids on the high seas. Their prime asset was the surprise attack with torpedoes, which was forbidden by international convention.

In February 1915, the German Navy announced a policy of partially unrestricted submarine warfare, claiming it as retaliation for the British blockade of German ports. Rescinded later in the year, the policy was renewed in the spring of 1916 and finally became an unrestricted campaign from 1 February 1917 until the end of the war, involving all shipping in the 'war zone' surrounding the British Isles.

By February 1917, over 110 U-boats could be deployed, 46 of them in the Atlantic, and between then and April 1917, U-boats sank 1,889,847 tonnes (1,860,000 tons) of merchant shipping, for the loss of nine of their own number. British wheat supplies were down to six weeks' worth, and in May and June a further 1,320,860 tonnes (1,300,000 tons) of shipping were sunk. The huge scale of this relentless attrition forced the British to try all sorts of countermeasures, with relatively little success, until the convoy system was adopted from May 1917.

By the autumn of 1917, Germany was losing between six and 10 U-boats a month. In that year, 6,235,878 tons (6,335,944 tonnes) of British, Allied and neutral shipping were sunk by U-boats, almost half the total for the whole war. But in April, the United States had declared war on Germany, and though the U-boats sank another 2,709,738 tonnes (2,666,942 tons) in 1918, the chance of starving Britain into submission had passed by May 1917.

Long-Range Subs

The success of the U-boats in the Atlantic encouraged the German Navy to build large, long-range submarines with powerful guns as well as torpedoes. To avoid British supremacy on the surface, the German Deutschland class of merchant U-boats was also introduced, each 96m (315ft) long with two large

▲ **Deutschland (U-155)**

Imperial German Navy, cargo submarine, Atlantic 1916

The profile shows the boat in its original unarmed mercantile form. Three were built like this and four were converted to combat boats while under construction. An addition of two 148mm (5.9in) deck guns changed the appearance. As U-155, this submarine sank 43 ships, with a gross register tonnage of 120,434.

Specifications

Crew: 56

Powerplant: Twin screw diesel engines; electric motors

Max Speed: Surfaced: 12.4 knots; Submerged: 5.2 knots

Surface Range: 20,909km (11,284nm)

Displacement: Surfaced: 1536 tonnes (1512 tons); Submerged: 1905 tonnes (1875 tons)

Dimensions (length/beam/draught): 65m x 8.9m x 5.3m (213ft 3in x 29ft 2in x 17ft 5in)

Commissioned: March 1916

Armament: None

GERMAN SUBMARINE CLASSES 1914–18, WARTIME BUILD			
Class	Number	Launched	Note
U43	8	1914–15	Diesel; ocean-going
UB I	17	1915	Coastal patrol
UC I	15	1915	Coastal minelayer
UB II	30	1915–16	Coastal patrol
U51	6	1915–16	Diesel; ocean-going
UC II	64	1915–17	Coastal minelayer
U57	12	1916	Diesel; ocean-going
U63	3	1916	Diesel; ocean-going
U135	4	1916–18	Diesel; ocean-going
U81	6	1916	Diesel; ocean-going
UE I	10	1916	Ocean minelayer
U87	6	1916–17	Diesel; ocean-going
U151	7	1916–17	'Merchant cruiser'
U139	3	1916–18	'Merchant cruiser'
U93	22	1916–18	Diesel; ocean-going
UC III	16	1916–18	Coastal minelayer
UE II	9	1916–18	Ocean minelayer
UB III	96	1916–19	Coastal patrol
U142	1	1918	'Merchant cruiser'

cargo compartments. These submarines could carry 700 tonnes (690 tons) of cargo at 12- to 13-knot speeds on the surface and at 7 knots submerged. In June 1916, *Deutschland* made a voyage to the still-neutral United States to load with nickel, tin and rubber.

Deutschland itself became U-155 when fitted with torpedo tubes and deck guns, and, with seven similar submarines, it served in a combat role during the latter stages of the war. A few made long voyages south to the Azores and the African coast, where they operated generally unmolested against shipping operating in the area, though U-154 was torpedoed by the British submarine E-35 off the coast of Portugal in May 1918.

Late in the war, the German High Command decided to take the war to US shores. This required submarines with very long range, which was feasible for the Deutschland class. A purpose-built, long-range naval 'cruiser' design was developed as well,

▼ **Deutschland (U-155)**

Deutschland's conning tower was quite small and low-set compared with the great bulk of its hull, giving it a low profile on the surface. This was important in its task of evading the British blockade of Germany.

armed with six torpedo tubes and 22 torpedoes, and at least two 150mm (5.9in) deck guns.

One of the most remarkable voyages by a cruiser U-boat began on 14 April 1918, when U-151 left Kiel to attack shipping along the American Atlantic coast and lay mines off major coastal outlets. The Americans were not expecting trouble off their own shores and had taken no precautions. U-151 carried on without interference, seizing and sinking three schooners and laying its remaining mines across Delaware Bay.

It spent three days trawling the sea bottom off New York with a cable-cutter, severing two telegraph lines. On 2 June, U-151 sank the liner *Carolina*, on its way from Puerto Rico to New York. By this time, there was a degree of panic along the US Eastern Seaboard, but U-151 safely returned to Kiel on 20 July 1918, after having covered 17,570km (10,915

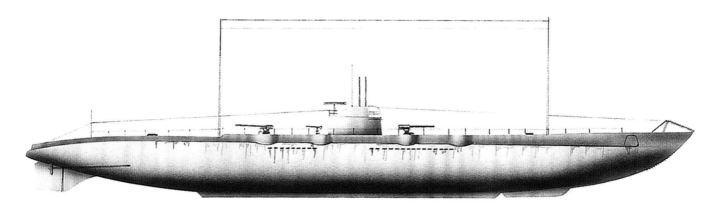

▲ U-139

Imperial German Navy, commerce raider, Atlantic, 1917

Purpose-built as a cruiser-killer, U-139 had six torpedo tubes compared to U-155's two, and carried 18 reloads. The deck guns were on barbette-type mountings extending from a central fairing. The command centre in the conning tower was armour-plated, reflecting the expectation of surface gunfights with armed merchantmen.

Specifications

Crew: 62

Powerplant: Twin shafts; diesel/electric motors

Max Speed: Surfaced: 15.8 knots; Submerged: 7.6 knots

Surface Range: 23,390km (12,630nm) at 8 knots

Displacement: Surfaced: 1961 tonnes (1930 tons); Submerged: 2523 tonnes (2483 tons)

Dimensions (length/beam/draught):94.8m x 9m x 5.2m (311ft x 29ft 9in x 17ft 3in)

Commissioned: December 1917

Armament: Six 508mm (20in) torpedo tubes; two 150mm (5.9in) guns

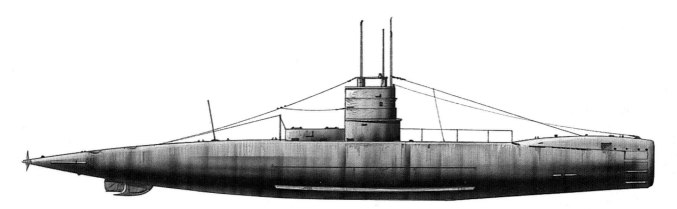

Specifications

Crew: 36

Powerplant: Single screw, diesel/electric 1200 hp motors

Max Speed: Surfaced: 15 knots; Submerged: 9.5 knots

Surface Range: 3800km (2048nm) at 8 knots

Displacement: Surfaced: 416 tonnes (410 tons); Submerged: 511 tonnes (503 tons)

Dimensions (length/beam/draught): 49.9m x 4.6m x 3.5m (163ft 9in x 15ft x 11ft 6in)

Commissioned: April 1918

Armament: Six 457mm (18in) torpedo tubes

▲ R-Class

Royal Navy, patrol submarine, North Sea and Western Approaches, 1918

The bulbous bow section contained the most up-to-date hydrophone instruments. Two electric motors each delivered 1200hp (895kW) for high submerged speed while the 8-cylinder diesel was rated at only 210hp (157kW). In November 1918, two R-class were based at Blyth and four at Killybegs on the northwest coast of Ireland.

miles) and sent 27 ships to the bottom, including four that were sunk by mines.

Encouraged by this success, U-140, U-156 and U-117 were sent over as well, but the Americans were now on the alert and there were fewer easy pickings. U-156 was lost with all hands on the return voyage when it struck a mine off Bergen, Norway,

on 25 September 1918. Another trio of long-range submarines, U-155, U-152 and U-139, were on their way across the Atlantic when the war ended.

Naval historians have generally discounted the value of their role, with the view that if the German Navy had built more of the medium-sized 'Mittel U-boot' typified by the U-81 and U-87 classes, armed with 16 torpedoes and with a range of 18,000km (11,220 miles), of which 46 were built between 1915 and 1918, the impact on Allied shipping would have been much greater. The cruisers sank less than 2 per cent of total tonnage sent to the bottom by U-boats.

Countermeasures

One result of the U-boat onslaught was to force the British into intensive work on countermeasures. Explosive sweeps towed by trawlers were not very effective. The first effective depth-charge was produced in January 1916, and the first submarine lost to a depth-charge was U-68 on 22 March. On 6 July, UC-7 was detected by hydrophones and sunk by depth charges. A submerged submarine was no longer beyond attack.

The Q-ships, or disguised merchantmen, sank nine U-boats. Also noteworthy was the development, during the war, of the concept of an anti-submarine submarine. British submarines sank 18 German U-boats during the conflict, 13 in 1917–18. These were very largely surface encounters, dependent on

US SUBMARINE CLASSES 1914–18			
Class	Number	Launched	Note
A	7	1901–03	Stationed in Philippines
B	3	1906–07	Stationed in Philippines
C	5	1906–09	
D	3	1909–10	
E	2	1911	
F	4	1911–12	
G	4	1911–13	
H	9	1913–16	H4–7 and 8–9 originally for Russia
K	8	1913–14	
L	11	1915–17	7 based Ireland as Class AL, 1918
M	1	1915	
N	7	1916–17	
O	16	1917–18	
R	27	1917–19	6 launched by Nov 1918

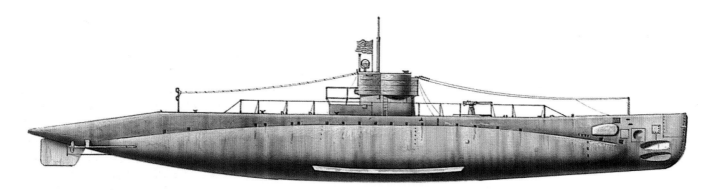

▲ O-Class

US Navy, patrol submarine, 1918

The quickly built O-class's 457mm (18in) torpedo tubes, limited range and diving depth of 61m (200ft) would have hampered their value as combat boats. US submarine design had some catching-up to do in 1918. *O-12*, renamed *Nautilus*, was used in an unsuccessful attempt to reach the North Pole in 1930.

Specifications

Crew: 29

Powerplant: Two shafts; diesel/electric motors

Max Speed: Surfaced: 14 knots; Submerged: 10.5 knots

Surface Range: 10,191km (5500nm) at 11.5 knots

Displacement: Surfaced: 529 tonnes (521 tons); Submerged: 639 tonnes (629 tons)

Dimensions (length/beam/draught): 52.5m x 5.5m x 4.4m (172ft 3in x 18ft 1in x 14ft 5in)

Commissioned: July 1918

Armament: Four 457mm (18in) torpedo tubes; one 76mm (3in) gun

▲ HMS R7

The 10 R-class were the first submarines designed to hunt down and attack other submarines. Five hydrophones with bearing instruments were mounted in the bow.

keen look-out work, and might develop into duels in which, on two occasions, the British boat was sunk.

This led to British development of the R-class submarine, which was intended specifically for the hunting role. They were relatively small craft, 49.7m (163ft) long and displacing 416.5 tonnes (410 tons) on the surface, with only one propeller (most contemporary submarines had two). Diesel engines could drive them at 9 knots on the surface but, once submerged, large batteries permitted their electric motors to drive them underwater at the high speed of 15 knots for two hours (8–10 knots was the common speed for submerged submarines until after World War II).

These prototypes of the later 'hunter-killer' were also equipped with hydrophones as underwater listening equipment. Six forward torpedo tubes made them potent weapons, but the R-class submarines appeared too late to have any actual effect on the war. Britain's long-delayed introduction of the convoy system in mid-1917 was the single most effective check on submarine attacks.

United States

At the outbreak of the war the United States was lagging behind the great powers of Europe in submarine development. During the war years, the US Navy built the H-, K-, L-, N-, O- and finally R-class submarines, but failed to keep pace with European improvements.

Nevertheless, when the United States declared war on Germany in April 1917, the US Navy wanted to get its submarines involved. K-class boats were really not meant for blue-water operations, but the Navy decided to tow the eight K-1 to K-8 boats to the Mediterranean. This proved to be a disaster, with K-3, K-4, K-6 and K-7 lost in a storm, while the survivors were kept in the Azores for the rest of the war. The Navy also tried to tow a number of L-class boats across the Atlantic. Caught in a storm, they were cast off, and remarkably all made it to Ireland, from where they conducted uneventful coastal patrols. A further eight boats of the new O-class were on their way across the Atlantic when the war ended. Only one O-class boat was used on active patrol, from July 1918; the other 16 were completed after the Armistice of 11 November, though seven remained on the Navy list through World War II, and were used for training.

▲ **Walrus (K-4)**

US Navy, patrol submarine, Azores, 1917

K-4 never carried the proposed name *Walrus*. The K-class class of eight boats were of relatively small size compared to post-war American submarines. The hull form is still reminiscent of earlier American types. Their 950hp (708kW) Nelseco diesel engines gave a lot of trouble. K-4 was based first at Hawaii, then at Key West, Florida.

Specifications

Crew: 31

Powerplant: Twin screw diesel; electric motors

Max Speed: Surfaced: 14 knots; Submerged: 10.5 knots

Surface Range: 8334km (4500nm) at 10 knots

Displacement: Surfaced: 398 tonnes (392 tons);

Submerged: 530 tonnes (521 tons)

Dimensions (length/beam/draught): 47m x 5m x 4m (153ft 10in x 16ft 9in x 13ft 2in)

Commissioned: October 1914

Armament: Four 457mm (18in) torpedo tubes

Forces at the end of the war
1917–18

More submarines were lost in the course of the war through accidents, grounding, scuttling by their own crews and capture than by outright sinking in combat. This also reflects the relatively late development of effective anti-submarine weapons.

IN THE YEARS BETWEEN 1914 and 1918, Germany built over 300 submarines, far more than any other country, and amounting to almost half of the world's stock. Out of a total of 373 it had lost 178, but they had sunk 5708 ships, around 15 vessels for each submarine, or 32 ships for each U-boat lost. Although the U-boats failed to win the war, it has been pointed out that they were more thwarted than actually defeated, and were never driven from the seas despite the intensive efforts made by the Royal Navy in 1917–18 to pen them in at their home bases.

In terms of manpower the whole U-boat force numbered less than a single army division, and while the pace and volume of U-boat construction cost the German economy dearly, it was clear that the submarine was unchallenged for economy of force. It was also plain that the whole basis of naval planning and strategy must be changed.

Quite apart from maintaining an effective submarine force, it became clear that any viable

SUBMARINE FLEETS, 1914 AND 1918 COMPARED			
Country	1914	1918	War Losses
Austria-Hungary	6	19	8
France	55	60	14
Germany	24	134	173
Great Britain	74	168	56
Italy	22	78	8
Japan	12	15	0
Sweden	9	12	0
Russia	29	44	17
United States	27	79	1

navy would have to vastly increase its stock of anti-submarine craft and weapons to combat enemy submarines in a future war. Every country, therefore, had to look at its resources and decide on future policy, even while reducing its submarine numbers from wartime levels.

France

France ended the war with a varied collection of submarines. Fourteen had been lost, including the Brumaire-class boat *Foucault*, the first submarine to be sunk by air attack (by two seaplanes, on 15 September 1916), and around 19 had been put into commission, making the fleet five stronger than it had been in 1914.

The steam-powered *Dupuy de Lôme*, launched in September 1915, was refitted with cannibalized German diesels after the war. Other wartime classes were the Amphitrite class (eight boats, built 1914–16), of which one was lost; Bellone class (three boats, 1914–17); Diane class (two boats, 1915–17), of which one was lost; Armide class (three boats, 1915–16); Joessel-Fulton class (two boats, 1917–19); and the Lagrange class (four boats, 1917–24), of which only two saw war service.

After a succession of medium-sized submarine classes, these were bigger, at 920–1320 tonnes (905–1299 tons) surfaced and submerged; and more heavily armed, with eight 457mm (18in) torpedo tubes and two 7.5cm (3in) deck guns. Not the least important addition, however, was *Roland Morillot*, the captured UB-18, commissioned into the French Navy in 1917; this boat, with others acquired as war reparations, would influence French post-war designs. One class that did not long survive the war was the 16-strong one that included *Euler* (launched 1912), with only a single integral torpedo tube, plus four carried in drop collars and two in external cradles, and no gun.

Specifications

Crew: 54	Displacement: Surfaced: 846 tonnes (833 tons);
Powerplant: Twin screw, three cylinder	Submerged: 1307 tonnes (1287 tons)
reciprocating steam engine; electric motors	Dimensions (length/beam/draught): 75m x 6.4m
Max Speed: Surfaced: 15 knots; Submerged:	x 3.6m (246ft x 21ft x 11ft 10in)
8.5 knots	Commissioned: September 1915
Surface Range: 10,469km (5650nm) at 10 knots	Armament: Eight 450mm (17.7in) torpedo tubes

▲ **Dupuy de Lôme**

French Navy, patrol submarine, Mediterranean, World War I

Provided with a minimal tower, and a closable steam funnel, *Dupuy* was commissioned in July 1916 and attached to the Morocco flotilla from 1917 to the the end of the war. It was used to bombard the scene of a local uprising in 1917, and was mistakenly attacked by a British vessel in the same year. It was scrapped in 1935.

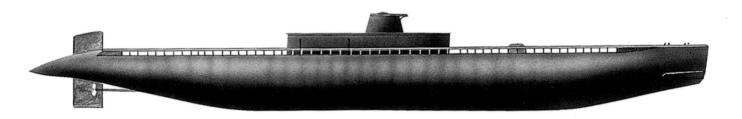

▲ **Euler**

French Navy, patrol submarine, Mediterranean/Adriatic, World War I

One of the Brumaire class, powered by two German MAN diesels of 840hp (626kW) built under licence, *Euler* had a 75mm (3in) deck gun added in 1916. Four of the same design were built in England as the Royal Navy's W-class, but sold to Italy in 1915. All saw service in the Mediterranean and Adriatic seas.

Specifications

Crew: 35	Submerged: 560 tonnes (551 tons)
Powerplant: Twin screw diesel engines; electric	Dimensions (length/beam/draught): 52m x 5.4m
motors	x 3m (171ft x 17ft 9in x 10ft 3in)
Max Speed: Surfaced: 14 knots; Submerged:	Commissioned: October 1912
7 knots	Armament: One 450mm (17.7in) torpedo tube;
Surface Range: 3230km (1741nm) at 10 knots	four drop collars; two external cradles
Displacement: Surfaced: 403 tonnes (397 tons);	

Germany

In November 1918, all remaining German U-boats were surrendered or scuttled. By the end of the war, 134 were in service out of 373 commissioned, and a total of 176, including boats under repair or not yet in commission, were handed over. Among them was U-60, launched on 5 July 1916, which sank over 40 Allied ships in the course of its wartime career, and was grounded on 21 November 1918 and later broken up.

In the final months of the war a new class of fast submarines was under construction at Kiel. Class leader was U-160, and eight out of 13 were completed. With six 509mm (20in) torpedo tubes and two 104mm (4.1in) guns, and a surface speed of 16.2 knots, they would have been a powerful commerce raiding force, but came too late to have any influence on events.

Under the terms of the Treaty of Versailles, Germany was banned from possessing submarines. All the U-boats that had passed into the possession of the Allies were eventually scrapped or sunk in target practice. But no treaty clause could nullify the fact that among German technicians there was at least as great a degree of expertise in submarine design and construction as in any other country.

Great Britain

Losses in the Royal Navy were high, with 56 submarines lost by the end of the war through a variety of causes including 'friendly fire' or 'friendly ramming'. Among the wartime classes of British submarines were the M-class of 1917–18, with diesel and electric propulsion, mounting a massive 305mm (12in) battleship gun in front of the conning tower. This weapon was in principle capable of giving the M-class ships the firepower and hitting range that torpedoes of the time lacked. The gun could be fired underwater from periscope depth, but had to be loaded on the surface. Only three were built; the first two were completed near the end of the war and never used in action. Although it now appears cumbersome and impracticable, a 30.5cm (12in) M-class shell struck the battlecruiser HMS *Hood* during a naval exercise in 1922, and this ship was declared disabled.

The British G-class of 14 boats was built primarily to counter the threat of ocean-going U-boats. To reach the Atlantic, German vessels had to pass through the English Channel or make a long detour round the Shetland Islands, and the G-class were intended as interceptors for both submarines and surface craft. Four torpedo tubes of 457mm (18 in) were fitted, with a fifth of 533mm (21in), whose torpedoes were intended for armour piercing.

The G-class submarines were quite fast on the surface, for their time, able to make 14.25 knots, but reports that new German U-boats could reach 22 knots led to the building of seven J-class submarines in 1915, capable of maintaining 17 knots. J-1 inflicted severe damage on the German battleships *Grosser Kürfurst* and *Kronprinz* on 5 November 1916.

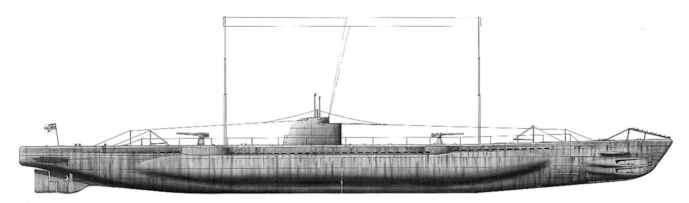

▲ U-160

Imperial German Navy, commerce raider, World war I

Good seagoing boats and well armed, the U-160 boats were intended to carry out attacks on the surface whenever possible. Based on the design of U-93, these were among the 46 submarines known as 'Mittel-U' – a middle size between the smaller U-boats and the large cruisers.

Specifications

Crew: 39	Submerged: 1016 tonnes (1000 tons)
Powerplant: Two shafts; diesel; electric motors	Dimensions (length/beam/draught): 71.8m x
Max Speed: Surfaced: 16.2 knots; Submerged:	6.2m x 4.1m (235ft 6in x 20ft 6in x 13ft 6in)
8.2 knots	Commissioned: February 1918
Surface Range: 15,372km (8300nm) at 8 knots	Armament: Six 509mm (20in) torpedo tubes; two
Displacement: Surfaced: 834 tonnes (821 tons);	104mm (4.1in) guns

Although many petrol-engined submarines were still in use in 1914, World War I submarines were generally driven by diesels on the surface and by electric motors when submerged. But the British Admiralty's preoccupation with surface speed led to the building of the K-class in 1915–19. These large submarines, intended to operate with battle fleets as scouts for surface warships, were powered by steam turbines, which had to be shut down on diving, with movable lids to cover the two funnels. The K-boats steamed at 23.5 knots on the surface, while electric motors gave them a 10-knot submerged speed, and 10 533mm (21in) torpedo tubes plus three 102mm (4in) guns made them formidable on paper, but five were lost in accidents. Seventeen boats of this class, unsuccessful and deeply disliked (by their crews), were built. Most of the big ships they were intended to engage were now sufficiently armoured to absorb hits from torpedoes and survive, and were also protected at anchor by torpedo nets. All but one of the K-class boats were scrapped in 1926. The most effective British submarines built during the war years were the E-, H- and L-classes.

By the end of the war, the number of submarines in the British Royal Navy had risen to 137 in service, with a further 78 under construction. A programme of scrapping and cancellation was rapidly introduced to bring the numbers down to a peacetime level that would nevertheless ensure the Royal Navy's continued superiority.

Italy

Italy's submarine fleet in 1918 included several boats passed on from the British Royal Navy, including

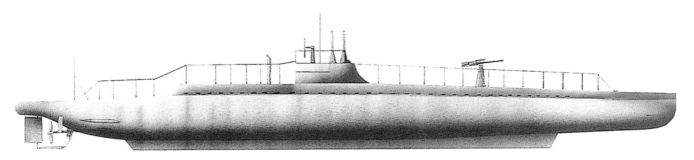

▲ **W-2**

Royal Navy, then Italian, coastal submarine, Adriatic, 1915–18

Ordered after an official visit to the Schneider yard at Toulon, this small British-built class used the design of the French Brumaire boats, with external torpedoes mounted in six Drzewiecki drop collars. Unsuitable for British conditions, the W-class was sold on to the Italian Navy in 1915, and saw service in the Adriatic Sea.

Specifications

Crew: 19

Powerplant: Twin screw diesel; electric motors

Max Speed: Surfaced: 13 knots; Submerged: 8.5 knots

Surface Range: 4630km (2500nm) at 9 knots

Displacement: Surfaced: 336 tonnes (331 tons); Submerged: 507 tonnes (499 tons)

Dimensions (length/beam/draught): 52.4m x 4.7m x 2.7m (172ft x 15ft 5in x 8ft 10in)

Commissioned: February 1915

Armament: Two 457mm (18in) torpedo tubes

Specifications

Crew: 60

Powerplant: Twin screw diesel; electric motors

Max Speed: Surfaced: 15 knots; Submerged: 9 knots

Surface Range: 7112km (3840nm) at 10 knots

Displacement: Surfaced: 1619 tonnes (1594 tons); Submerged: 1977 tonnes (1946 tons)

Dimensions (length/beam/draught): 90m x 7.5m x 4.9m (295ft 7in x 24ft 7in x 16ft)

Commissioned: September 1917

Armament: Four 533mm (21in) torpedo tubes; one 305mm (12in) gun

▲ **M-1**

Royal Navy, submarine gunboat, 1917

The M-class submarines were adapted from the hulls of four K-class boats then under construction. The big guns were designed for the Formidable-class battleship, and 50 shells could be carried. M-1 and M-2 had 457mm (18in) torpedo tubes; M-3 had 533mm (21in) tubes. M-1 sank in November 1925 after colliding with a Swedish cargo steamer.

four of Class W2, built to Italian–French design with two integral 457mm (18in) torpedo tubes and two externally mounted drop-collar torpedoes. They were transferred in 1916 and broken up in 1919. Also transferred in the previous year were three Class S1 boats, also of Italian design, and perhaps considered more suitable for Mediterranean service. Eight British H-class boats were transferred in 1916–17.

But Italy had been actively building on its own account. Wartime classes were the two Pacinotti boats (1916), of which one was sunk in 1917; the F-class – most numerous Italian class with 21 boats – of small submarines, 262 tonnes (258 tons) surfaced, 319 tonnes (314 tons) submerged, with two 457mm (18in) torpedo tubes. Designed and built by Fiat-San Giorgio at La Spezia, it had begun in 1913 as

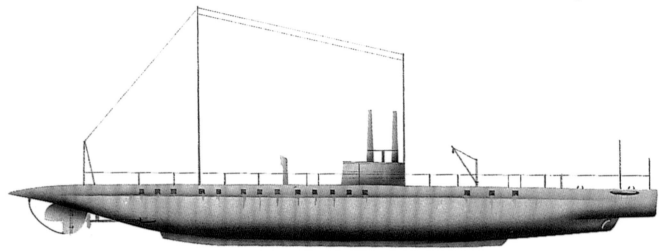

Specifications

Crew: 31	Submerged: 330 tonnes (324 tons)
Powerplant: Twin screw diesel; electric motors	Dimensions (length/beam/draught): 45m x 4.4m
Max Speed: Surfaced: 13 knots; Submerged:	x 3.2m (148ft x 14ft 5in x 10ft 6in)
8.5 knots	Commissioned: 1914
Surface Range: 2963km (1600nm) at 8.5 knots	Armament: Two 457mm (18in) torpedo tubes,
Displacement: Surfaced: 270 tonnes (265 tons);	one 12-pounder gun

▲ S-1

Royal Navy, then Italian, coastal submarine, Adriatic, 1915–18

Like the W-class, the S-class was a British borrowing of a European design, in this case an Italian Laurenti boat, with a partial double hull, and 10 watertight compartments – a more ambitious design than British boats of the period. Only three were built, and after a short time based at Yarmouth, they were transferred to the Italian Navy in 1915.

Specifications

Crew: 35	Submerged: 938 tonnes (923 tons)
Powerplant: Twin shafts; diesel/electric motors	Dimensions (length/beam/draught): 67m x 6m x
Max Speed: Surfaced: 16 knots; Submerged:	3.8m (220ft x 19ft 8in x 12ft 6in)
9.8 knots	Commissioned: November 1917
Surface Range: 3218km (1734nm) at 11 knots	Armament: Six 450mm (17.7in) torpedo tubes;
Displacement: Surfaced: 774 tonnes (762 tons);	two 76mm (3in) guns

▲ Agostino Barbarigo

Italian Navy, coastal submarine, 1918

This was one of the Provana-class boats, completed too late for combat work. Novel features included separation of the batteries in four watertight compartments, as a safety measure. Fore and aft 76mm (3in) guns were mounted. Even for a coastal boat, the diving depth of 50ms (155ft) was a limiting factor on operations.

an export class, with three supplied to each of Brazil, Portugal and Spain. The N-class of six boats followed in 1917–18, then the X2 coastal minelayer, a class of two boats in 1917; the Pietro Micca class of six boats built 1917–19 (three after the end of hostilities); and four boats of the Provana class in 1917–19.

In addition, Italy built six A-class midget submarines in 1915–16. At the end of the war, Italy emerged with an enhanced submarine fleet while its foremost rival, the defeated Austria-Hungary, could boast none.

Neutral Nations

Among some of the non-belligerent nations, submarine-building did not stop during the war years. Rather, extension of submarine capability was seen as necessary to maintain the integrity of territorial waters against intrusion from the vessels of warring powers.

Spain preserved neutrality during World War I, and in 1918 had a modest submarine fleet, the American-built Holland-type boat *Isaac Peral*, launched in July 1916, and three A-class boats completed in 1917.

Specifications

Crew: 35

Powerplant: Twin screw diesel; electric motors

Max Speed: Surfaced: 15 knots; Submerged: 8 knots

Surface Range: 5386km (2903nm) at 11 knots

Displacement: Surfaced: 499 tonnes (491 tons);

Submerged: 762 tonnes (750 tons)

Dimensions (length/beam/draught): 60m x 5.8m x 3.4m (196ft 10in x 19ft x 11ft 2in)

Commissioned: July 1916

Armament: Four 457mm (18in) torpedo tubes; one 76mm (3in) gun

▲ Isaac Peral

Spanish Navy, patrol submarine, 1916

Built by the Fore River Co., this was Spain's first and, for several years, its only substantial submarine. The 76mm (3in) gun was fixed to a collapsible mount. Based at Cartagena, the boat was hulked in the 1930s and played no part in the Civil War combat.

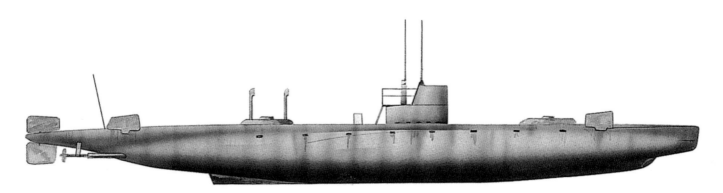

Specifications

Crew: 30

Powerplant: Single screw petrol engines; electric motors

Max Speed: Surfaced: 14.8 knots; Submerged: 6.3 knots

Surface Range: 8338km (4500nm) at 10 knots

Displacement: Surfaced: 189 tonnes (186 tons);

Submerged: 233 tonnes (230 tons)

Dimensions (length/beam/draught): 42.4m x 4.3m x 2.1m (139ft x 14ft x 6ft 11in)

Commissioned: 1909

Armament: Two 457mm (18in) torpedo tubes

▲ Hvalen

Swedish Navy, test boat, Baltic Sea, 1915

Hvalen was a small boat, with a single screw and two torpedo tubes, apparently bought so that Swedish naval architects could study an up-to-date submarine from a major builder. On patrol in late 1915, *Hvalen* was shelled by a German gunboat, *Meteor*, in Swedish territorial waters, causing a diplomatic incident.

Sweden in 1918 had 13 submarines, of which 12 had been completed during the war years. All were home built, except for *Hvalen*, bought in 1909 from Fiat-San Giorgio, and which made one of the earliest long voyages (on the surface) by a submarine, from La Spezia to Sweden. It was stricken in 1919 and sunk as a target in 1924.

Japan

Japan's contribution to the Allied victory had been comparatively small, and its submarine force had played no part. During the war Japan built only three submarines. Japanese naval planners, however, followed the events of the war at sea with great attention, and, with a vast ocean at their east side, perceived the advantages of the long-range submarine. At the end of the war, Japan was handed nine U-boats as part of German war reparations, and these would be subjected to intensive study.

Russia

In the war years the Russian Empire had built 32 submarines, of which the Bars class accounted for 24. Built between 1914 and 1917, these were an enlarged version of the pre-war Morzh class: a single-hulled boat with four 457mm (18in) torpedo tubes, but also mounting a further eight in drop-collar release mechanisms. Most carried a 37mm (1.5in) AA gun. A serious defect was their lack of interior bulkheads;

RUSSIAN SUBMARINE CLASSES 1914–18, PRE-WAR BUILD			
Class	Number	Launched	Note
Delfin	1	1903	Sunk 1904; salvaged
Kasatka	6	1904–05	Baltic and Black Sea
Som	7	1904–07	Baltic and Black Sea
Karp	3	1907	Black Sea
Akula	1	1908	Diesel motor; Baltic
Minoga	1	1908	Diesel, Black and Caspian Seas
Kaiman	4	1910–11	Baltic
Morzh/Nerpa	3	1911–13	Black Sea
Narval	3	1914	Black Sea

RUSSIAN SUBMARINE CLASSES 1914–18, WARTIME BUILD			
Class	Number	Launched	Note
Bars	24	1915–17	Baltic
Krab	1	1915	Minelayer; Black Sea
Sviatoi Georgi	1	1916	Italian built
AG 'Holland'	6	1916–17	7 built after 1918; US reclaimed 6

another was their short range, only 740km (460 miles). They were active both with the Baltic and Black Sea fleets, six of them with the former. Fifteen survived the war, nine having been sunk in action or scuttled. Russia, between 1918 and 1921, was caught

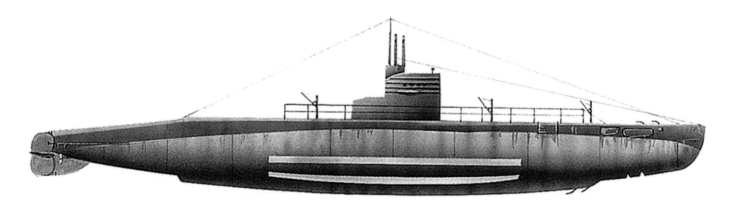

▲ **H-4**

Imperial Russian Navy, coastal submarine, 1917

The Russian Holland boats (Class AG, 'American Golland') were ordered in three batches. Two were delivered between June 1916 and early 1917, but only the first five were commissioned. The second batch remained unassembled when the Revolution came. Batch three was not despatched, and was eventually bought by the US Navy (H-4 to H-9).

Specifications

Crew: 27

Powerplant: Twin screw; diesel/electric motors

Max Speed: Surfaced: 12.5 knots; Submerged: 8.5 knots

Surface Range: 1750nm (3240km; 2010 miles) at 7 knots

Displacement: Surfaced: 370 tonnes (365 tons); Submerged: 481 tonnes (474 tons)

Dimensions (length/beam/draught): 45.8m x 4.6m x 3.7m (150ft 3in x 15ft 4in x 12ft 5in)

Commissioned: October 1916

Armament: Four 450mm (17in) torpedo tubes

up in revolution and civil warfare. While only seven submarines are known to have been lost in action, many more were scuttled to prevent them falling into the hands of the Germans or the Bolsheviks.

This was the fate of the Karp class, two boats scuttled at Sebastopol on 26 April 1919; also of the Narval class (Holland 31A) of three boats, a superior design to the Bars, with watertight bulkheads and a crash-diving tank; and of the one-off *Krab*, the first submarine designed specifically as a minelayer, ordered in 1908, but commissioned only in 1915, later than the first German UC-boats. Unlike these, its mines were laid in horizontal stern-discharging galleries.

In 1915, 17 H-class (Holland-602 type) submarines had been ordered from the Electric Boat Co. in America and, in 1917, 11 were assembled in British Columbia, shipped to Vladivostok in kit form and brought over the Trans-Siberian Railway for assembly. H-4, however, was cancelled as a Russian order and bought by the US Navy in 1918, renumbered in 1920 as SS-147, and served until 1930.

The Holland-602 was built for several navies: the United States and British Navies already had 'H' boats of essentially the same design. It was considered an effective class within the limitations of its size, 398 tonnes (392 tons) surfaced, 529 tonnes (521 tons) submerged, and range, 3800km (2361 miles). The Baltic boats were scuttled in 1918; the Black Sea boats passed to the Ukrainian, then the Soviet, Navy.

United States

In 1918, the US Navy had a total of 79 submarines. None had been lost to enemy action; F-4 had foundered and H-1 had been wrecked in the Gulf of Mexico. The L-class boats based at Berehaven in Ireland returned home, as did the K-class from the Azores. Two further divisions of four L- and four O-class arrived on the European coast too late to join in hostilities. For war service the L-boats had been classed AL to distinguish them from the British L-class. They were the first American submarines to be fitted with a deck gun, which was partially retractable into the deckhouse.

The N-class was a smaller, lower-powered version of the L-class; it was without a deck gun but with the same number of torpedo tubes, four 457mm (18in). Unlike the L-class, however, it was used exclusively on coastal defence patrols. At the end of 1918, R-15 to R-20 were deployed to Hawaii to form the first squadron at the new submarine base of Pearl Harbor.

Although the United States' boats had made no 'kills' in the war, their crews had learned a great deal about the tactics of submarine warfare – and its hazards. All Berehaven boats were attacked at least twice by Allied ships or planes. As the war ended, 59 submarines were being built in the United States, but most of the older boats were plainly obsolete or in a worn-out condition.

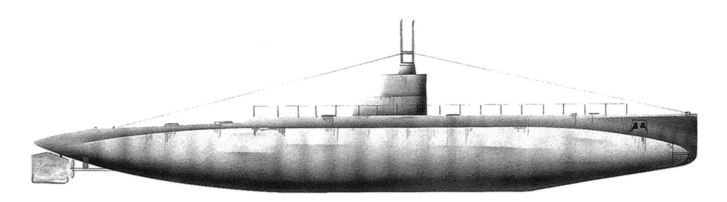

▲ **N-1**

US Navy, patrol submarine, World War I

Seven boats formed the N-class, the first US submarines to have metal rather than canvas-protected bridges. The lower-powered diesels, 300hp (224kW), were much more reliable and the same policy was used on subsequent types. *N-2* was used to try out an air-independent propulsion system, but it was not developed further.

Specifications

Crew: 35	Submerged: 420 tonnes (414 tons)
Powerplant: Twin screw; diesel/electric motors	Dimensions (length/beam/draught): 45m x 4.8m
Max Speed: Surfaced: 13 knots; Submerged:	x 3.8m (147ft 4in x 15ft 9in x 12ft 6in)
11 knots	Commissioned: December 1916
Surface Range: 6485km (3500nm) at 5 knots	Armament: Four 457mm (18in) torpedo tubes
Displacement: Surfaced: 353 tonnes (348 tons);	

Specifications

Crew: 35	Submerged: 556 tonnes (548 tons)
Powerplant: Twin screw diesel; electric motors	Dimensions (length/beam/draught): 51m x 5.3m
Max Speed: Surfaced: 14 knots; Submerged:	x 4m (167ft 4in x 17ft 4in x 13ft 1in)
8 knots	Commissioned: February 1915
Surface Range: 6270km (3380nm) at 11 knots	Armament: Four 457mm (18in) torpedo tubes;
Displacement: Surfaced: 457 tonnes (450 tons);	one 76mm (3in) gun

▲ **L-3**

US Navy, patrol submarine, Atlantic 1917–18

Eleven boats formed the L-class. Although the United States' first 'ocean-going' submarines, they were really intended for coastal defence. To the crews they were 'pig-boats', partly because of their shape, partly because of their typical submarine living conditions. In action they made 21 U-boat sightings and four attacks, but without success.

The Submarines of 1918

The submarines of 1918, apart from those most recently delivered, had seen hard service and were often in poor condition. Even the newest were largely based on pre-1914 designs, and though more up-to-date equipment and instruments had been fitted, their packed and narrow hulls were not easily adaptable for the installation of new equipment. They were slow, often also slow to dive, and in order to communicate required the rigging of tall radio masts. There had been little progress in engine development during the war. Also, they were vulnerable to the anti-submarine warfare (ASW) techniques that, though still crude, had been brought to a high pitch of intensity, especially by the British Royal Navy. Now that the war was over, few would survive in the major navies for more than a couple of years.

But though its importance in naval warfare was beyond doubt, the future of the submarine was ringed by question marks. The basic question was not 'Do we need submarines?', but 'What more can submarines do?' The notion of the submarine as essentially a coastal defence and anti-warship vessel had been discredited. The role of submarines in long-front coastal defence had not been particularly distinguished, though more effective at 'choke points' like the entrances to the English Channel and the Straits of Otranto. What they excelled at was exactly what made the high naval authorities most nervous – commerce raids, stealth and surprise attacks.

Technical Issues

A raft of technical questions demanded answers. Submarines could be single-hulled or double-hulled, or single-hulled with external saddle-tanks. But which was best? Also, surfaced, submerged and in-between (diving/surfacing) characteristics had to be balanced. Wartime experience had shown that rapid diving was extremely desirable, but so too was surface speed, and a submarine designed for the first was not likely to be so good at the second. A central issue was reserve buoyancy, the volume and placing of the tanks, which were flooded for the boat to submerge, or emptied for the boat to operate on the surface; this had a direct impact on the boat's surface performance.

The single-hull submarine had to have all its tanks inside the pressure hull, reducing the space available for everything else. But it was cheaper and faster to build, and offered less resistance than a double hull in submerged performance because of its smaller area. The double hull, with its greater area, also had a higher freeboard when surfaced and was capable of higher surface speeds because more of the surface was in contact with the water. The space between the hulls could be used not only for flooding/voiding tankage, but for fuel storage and even for weapon stowage, in pressure-proof containers. More space was made available inside the pressure hull. But a double-hull boat took longer to dive.

The British Royal Navy attempted to square the circle with the saddle tank, fixing external tanks around a single hull (beginning with the D-class in 1906) and despite experiments with double hulls, remained faithful to this solution. The Imperial German Navy favoured the double hull, partly in the interest of good sea-keeping on the surface, though it too had single-hulled boats, normally smaller types like the UB-coastal and UC-minelayer classes. The United States' Navy opted for the double hull with its World War I designs and did not abandon it until the nuclear era.

It was generally accepted, and would be for another 25 years, that externally mounted guns were an essential part of the combat submarine's armoury. Here again questions arose. In the war, the gun had been a supplement to the limited stock of torpedoes, used for attack rather than for defence. But the development of ASW tactics, using escort ships and aircraft, made defence, especially anti-aircraft defence, important. What kind of gun or guns should a submarine have? To this and many other issues, there was no simple answer. Periscope location was also debated.

At this time, though the control room was located within the hull, submarines had a bridge, or command and navigating post, mounted on the conning tower, reflecting the fact that most of its time would be spent on the surface. A periscope with eyepiece mounted in the conning tower could be extended further beyond the boat than one that descended to the control room inside the pressure hull. In the engine-room there was no practical alternative to dual power, but there was clearly room for improvement in the diesel engines. The form of drive was also a matter of choice, with the diesels either driving electrical generators or turning the drive shafts directly, in which case they had to be de-clutched from the drive shafts when it was necessary to recharge the batteries. All in all, the technical challenges were enormous.

▲ **U-boats surrender**
Crews line up on the decks as three U-boats prepare to surrender at an unidentified British base, November 1918. Most were scrapped or sunk in target practice over the next few years.

Chapter 2

The Interwar Years: 1919–38

Submarine development followed some
strange courses, as strategists and designers struggled
to define the role of the submarine and to build boats to
fulfil it. Important technical challenges were also being
tackled, notably in engine efficiency and in underwater
detection. By 1930, the lines of development were becoming
clear, and substantial numbers of submarines were built
in the following decade. The majority were intended for
relatively short-range work, but the concept of the
long-distance cruising submarine was also elaborated,
especially by Japan. All nations agreed not to engage
in commerce-raiding. By the late 1930s, Germany was
emerging once again as a formidable naval power,
and at the end of the decade, with war looming,
submarine construction began to accelerate.

◀ O-class
HMS *Oberon* and three other O-class submarines moored alongside the depot ship HMS *Maidstone*,
probably at Malta, in the late 1920s.

New potential

The 1920s were a decade of experiment for designers and builders, as, in conjunction with the various navies, they explored the operational potential of the submarine.

TECHNIQUES CONTINUED to move forward with greater use of welding. A welded hull was much more resistant to vibration and less prone to tiny leaks than a riveted one, and stronger steels were also introduced, to facilitate deeper diving. Bow diving planes were introduced and crews were trained to operate a more sophisticated arrangement of tanks to allow for working in a variety of conditions, with greater or less salinity or temperatures.

The MAN works in Germany, Vickers in England, and Nelson Engine Co. in the Unites States had all provided engines for the combat submarines and in the 1920s and 1930s international competition intensified to develop a compact and lightweight diesel engine that could produce enough power for a meaningful increase in speed. New names began to appear in the United States, with Winton and Fairbanks-Morse producing submarine diesels. Various drive systems were used. Some engines were reversible and could be used for manoeuvring. Others were not and the commander had to change over to the battery-driven electric motors. Drive by diesels through generator sets emerged as the best compromise, providing maximum flexibility for directing power for any combination of battery charging, propulsion and manoeuvring operations.

Alongside these developments, important improvements were under way in underwater detection and communication. The primitive hydrophone listening devices of World War I were elaborated into steadily more complex and bulky detection equipment. Simple hydrophones were a passive mode of detection, but from late in the war, active systems were made possible by the French development of the transducer, based on the piezoelectric effect of passing an alternating current through a quartz crystal, causing it to vibrate and send out 'waves' whose impact on a solid object could

▲ **Cruiser submarine**
Carrying four 132mm (5.2in) deck guns, the one-off British X-1 was an attempt by the Royal Navy to combine the stealth of a submersible with the surface fighting ability of a cruiser.

▲ **Krupp workshops**

German Type II and Type VII U-boats undergo service checks in the docks at Krupp's Germania shipyard in Kiel, 1939. Krupp were Nazi Germany's largest steelmaker, and were consequently involved in the production of many of the *Kriegsmarine*'s U-boats.

be traced. From the late 1920s, most new French and British submarines carried early forms of this sonar array. But submariners found that active sonar was better at finding submarines from surface ships than vice versa. Submarine-to-shore communication by radio was assisted by the development of a worldwide network of transmitting/receiving stations, though a boat could use high-frequency radio only when surfaced, and masts were needed. But development of VLF radio, which could reach a submerged submarine if it was within range of a transmitter, meant that British submarines, for example, could keep in touch while in the Mediterranean or the North Atlantic: this was a considerable boost to their value as scouts.

New Fleets

By the 1930s, most navies had come to the view that the submarine's prime importance and value in warfare lay in its ability to operate on its own, or

with a tactical group, in patrol and reconnaissance. Improved communication and undersea detection systems played a considerable part in this. Although the economic depression of the early 1930s caused cancellation and cut-backs of building orders, technical development continued.

Italy and France followed a dynamic policy of submarine design and construction, with a variety of types, though no class was built in large numbers. Soviet Russia also began the construction of a substantial submarine fleet. At opposite sides of the Pacific Ocean, the Japanese Empire and the United States were drawing up plans for a future war. Surreptitiously at first, then openly under Hitler's Reich, the German Navy re-entered the submarine domain with a new generation of U-boats and a powerful vision of how to use them. In the late 1930s, Italian and German submarine crews went on active service in support of the Nationalist side in the Spanish Civil War.

The war legacy
1919–29

After 1918, the navies of the world faced vital issues: among them were the reduction of submarine fleets, the post-war role of the submarine and even whether it should be abolished.

WHEN THE FIRST International Conference on Limitation of Naval Armaments began in Washington in October 1921, the British tried to ban submarines altogether. The reason was simple: although Britain had a large fleet of submarines itself, it also still had the world's largest merchant fleet. The Washington Treaty that resulted from the 1921 conference did manage to impose restrictions on the numbers of major surface warships, but not on submarines. Like it or not, submarines were here to stay.

Despite the horrendous loss of Allied shipping to a relatively small number of U-boats, navies in the 1920s seemed to shy away from full acceptance of the submarine. Germany itself was forbidden to build them, though very soon the embargo was being bypassed. In Britain and France the submarine was still seen mainly as an adjunct to the surface fleet, and design focused on building larger submarines that could travel fast on the surface.

One lesson well learned from the war years was that submarines had more effective uses than coastal defence work, and this was one reason for the increase in size. France received 10 U-boats in 1919, and after inspection of these, nine boats of the Requin class were built in 1923–26, of 990 tonnes (974 tons) surfaced and 1464 tonnes (1441 tons) submerged, with 10 550mm (21.7in) torpedo tubes and a 76mm (3in) deck gun. Part of their role was protection of outlying colonial territories and islands. Modernized in 1935–37, they served in World War II. *Requin* is seen with full radio gear fixed to dismountable masts; *Espadon*, of the same class, is in submersible configuration. A medium-size and range boat, *Galathée*, was one of three completed between 1923 and 1927; they too had the larger-size 533mm (21in) torpedo tubes (seven). From 1925, 31 submarines of the Redoutable class were built up to 1930, in three sets, of increasing power and speed. Displacing 1595 tonnes (1570 tons) surfaced

FRENCH SUBMARINE CLASSES 1920–38			
Class	Number	Launched	Note
O'Byrne	3	1919–20	Stricken by 1935
Joessel	2	1920	Stricken 1935
Maurice Callot	1	1921	Stricken 1936
Pierre Chailley	1	1921	Stricken 1936
Requin	9	1924–27	Last survivor scrapped 1946
Sirène	4	1925–26	Last survivor sunk 1944
Ariane	4	1925–27	Last survivor sunk 1942
Circe	4	1925–27	Last survivor sunk 1943
Redoutable	31	1928–37	Last 4 broken up 1952
Saphir	6	1928–35	Last one stricken 1949
Argonaute	4	1929–32	All broken up 1946
Diane	9	1930–32	Last 3 broken up 1946
Orion	2	1931	Broken up 1943
Surcouf	1	1934	Sunk 1942
Minerve	6	1934–38	Last one broken up 1954

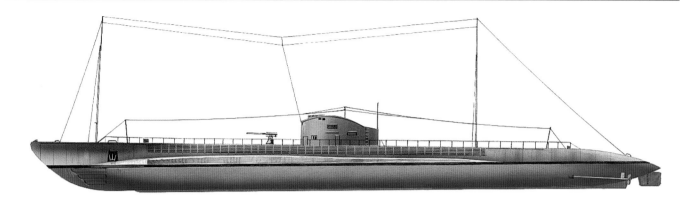

▲ Requin

French Navy, patrol submarine, Mediterranean, 1942

Requin was seized by the Germans at Bizerta in December 1942 and passed to the Italians as *FR113*. It was scuttled on 9 September 1943. Another, *Souffleur*, was sunk by the British submarine *Parthian* on 29 June 1941. *Marsouin* and *Narval* evaded German capture at Toulon, but *Narval* was sunk by a mine en route for Malta in December 1940.

Specifications

Crew: 54

Powerplant: Twin screw diesel; electric motors

Max Speed: Surfaced: 15 knots; Submerged: 9 knots

Surface Range: 10,469km (5650nm) at 10 knots

Displacement: Surfaced: 974 tonnes (990 tons); Submerged: 1464 tonnes (1441 tons)

Dimensions (length/beam/draught): 78.25m x 6.84m x 5.10m (256ft 7in x 22ft 6in x 16ft 9in)

Commissioned: July 1924

Armament: 10 550mm (21.7in) torpedo tubes

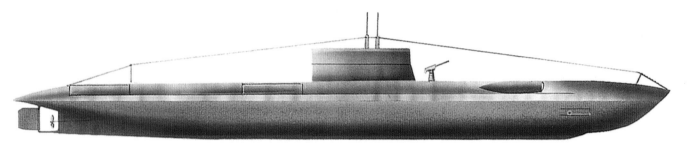

▲ Galathée

French Navy, patrol submarine, 1940

Galathée formed part of the Vichy French fleet at Toulon from June 1940, but these boats saw little or no action. When the Germans occupied Toulon on 27 November 1942, it was scuttled. Refloated in 1945, it was not recommissioned and was eventually sold as a derelict hulk in 1955.

Specifications

Crew: 41

Powerplant: Twin screw diesel; electric motors

Max Speed: Surfaced: 13.5 knots; Submerged: 7.5 knots

Surface Range: 6485km (3500nm) at 7.5 knots

Displacement: Surfaced: 619 tonnes (609 tons);

Submerged: 769 tonnes (757 tons)

Dimensions (length/beam/draught): 64m x 5.2m x 4.3m (210ft x 17ft x 14ft)

Commissioned: December 1925

Armament: Seven 551mm (21.7in) torpedo tubes; one 76mm (3in) gun

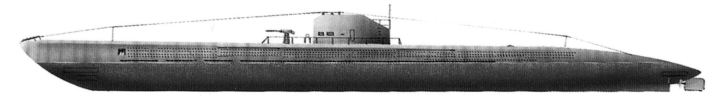

▲ Espadon

French Navy, then Italian transport submarine, Mediterranean, 1943

Captured at Bizerta with *Requin* and *Phoque* of the same class, and commissioned into the *Regia Marina* as FR114, *Espadon* was undergoing conversion to a transport boat at Castellamare di Stabia, but with the fall of Italy in September 1943, it was scuttled. Though raised by the Germans, it was not recommissioned.

Specifications

Crew: 54

Powerplant: Twin screw diesel engines; electric motors

Max Speed: Surfaced: 15 knots; Submerged: 9 knots

Surface Range: 10,469km (5650nm) at 10 knots

Displacement: Surfaced: 1168 tonnes (1150

tons); Submerged: 1464 tonnes (1441 tons)

Dimensions (length/beam/draught):78.2m x 6.8m x 5m (256ft 9in x 22ft 5in x 16ft 9in)

Commissioned: May 1926

Armament: 10 533mm (21in) torpedo tubes; one 100mm (3.9in) gun

and 2117 tonnes (2084 tons) submerged, the original armament was nine 21.7in (551mm) and two 15.7in (399mm) torpedo tubes, one 100mm (3.9in) deck gun and two 13.2mm (0.5in) AA machine guns.

Prohibitions

Germany was prohibited from building submarines, but a hint of what might have been is the design of U-112, projected in the last months of the war as a large, heavily armed submarine with eight 533mm (21in) torpedo tubes, four 127mm (5in) guns and two 20mm (0.8in) AA guns. Though a keel was never laid, this concept of the submarine cruiser, which was also intended to carry a spotter aircraft, was highly influential, not least on the Imperial Japanese Navy. Meanwhile, by 1922, the Germans were

circumventing the ban on submarine-building by using a front-company as a submarine design office in the Netherlands. This was at first not so much a political as an industrial move: several large German companies had acquired great expertise in submarine construction and were determined to capitalize on it. But soon the German Navy was discreetly involved. Confidential negotiations with several governments, including Estonia, Finland and Turkey, would ultimately lead to construction orders. From mid-decade, Germany and Russia co-operated in clandestine development of new submarine types.

British Developments

After the war, Great Britain scrapped 90 submarines and cancelled orders for 31 under construction,

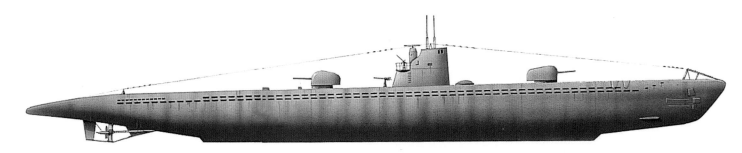

▲ U-boat Cruiser

Imperial German Navy, projected cruiser design

A German submarine that might have been. Drawings showed a boat with twin gun turrets and heavy AA armament. With a projected surface speed of 23 knots, they were intended to sink other ships while surfaced, reserving torpedoes for large targets. Many elements of the design went into the Type XI U-boats of World War II.

Specifications

Crew: 110	tons); Submerged: 3688 tonnes (3630 tons)
Powerplant: Two shafts, diesel; electric motors	Dimensions (length/beam/draught): 115m x
Max Speed: Surfaced: 23 knots; Submerged:	9.5m x 6m (377ft x 31ft x 20ft)
7 knots	Commissioned: N/A
Surface Range: 25,266km (13,635nm) at	Armament: Eight 533mm (21in) torpedo tubes;
12 knots	four 127mm (5in) guns; two 30mm (1.18in)
Displacement: Surfaced: 3190 tonnes (3140	and two 20mm (0.8in) AA guns

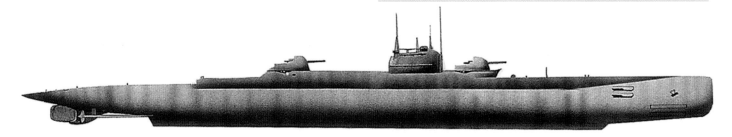

Specifications

Crew: 75	Dimensions (length/beam/draught): 110.8m x
Powerplant: Twin screw diesel; electric motors	9m x 4.8m (363ft 6in x 29ft 10in x 15ft 9in)
Max Speed: Surfaced: 19.5 knots	Commissioned: December 1925
Surface Range: 23,000km (12,400 nm)	Armament: Six 533mm (21in) torpedo tubes; four
Displacement: Surfaced: 3098 tonnes (3050	132mm (5.2in) guns
tons); Submerged: 3657 tonnes (3600 tons)	

▲ X-1

Royal Navy, experimental submarine

Britain's final attempt to produce a ship that combined the qualities of a submersible and a surface-combat vessel. Double-hulled, *X-1* carried ASDIC and range-finding instruments. The fire-control platform could be raised 0.6m (2ft) in action. Though it handled well and its mechanical problems might have been resolved, it remained a one-off.

though a further 24 were completed. The British 'submarine monitor' M-1 was lost with all hands in a collision with a surface vessel in 1925, and the Admiralty used the remaining two of the class for experiments. M-2 was fitted with a watertight seaplane hangar in place of the big gun, as well as a catapult ramp for launching the seaplane. It sank off Portland, England, in 1932, and was found on the bottom with the hangar doors and the hatch to the hangar flooded. M-3 was converted to a minelayer, and survived to be sold off in 1932.

The Royal Navy launched the one-off X-1 type in 1925, with four 5.2in (132mm) guns in twin turrets set fore and aft of the tower and six 21in (533mm) torpedo tubes. Powered by two Admiralty diesels with two ex-U-boat MAN diesels

for battery-charging, and two electric motors, it had a theoretical power output of 8000hp (6000kW) and was intended for long-range cruising to and between foreign stations, but although it had good handling qualities, a potential surface speed of 20 knots, and could travel halfway around the world without refuelling, its engines were chronically unreliable, and it was scrapped in 1936.

Italian Navy

In 1927, the Italian Navy received its first large submarines, the four Balilla class boats of which *Domenico Millelire* was one, built by Ansaldo-San Giorgio. An emergency auxiliary motor was provided in addition to two diesels and two electric motors. All made long ocean cruises in the 1930s to boost the

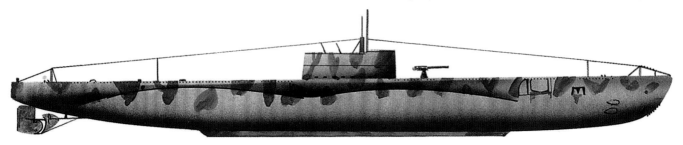

Specifications

Crew: 76	Submerged: 2275 tonnes (2240 tons)
Powerplant: Twin screw diesels; one auxiliary motor; two electric motors	Dimensions (length/beam/draught): 97m x 8.5m x 4m (319ft 3in x 27ft 9in x 13ft 1in)
Max Speed: Surfaced: 17.5 knots; Submerged: 8.9 knots	Commissioned: September 1927
Surface Range: 7401km (3800nm) at 10 knots	Armament: Six 533mm (21in) torpedo tubes; one 102mm (4in) gun
Displacement: Surfaced: 1585 tonnes (1560 tons);	

▲ Domenico Millelire

Italian Navy, Balilla-class submarine, 1941

In order to get under anti-submarine nets and avoid entanglement, submarines involved in inshore attacks, or having to pass through narrow protected straits, had a pair of heavy wires rigged from bow to tower and stern. These were intended to lift the base of the net without the hull being touched.

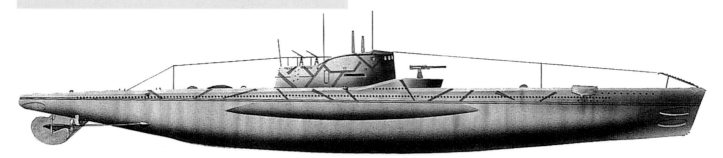

▲ Giovanni Bausan

Italian Navy, Pisani-class patrol submarine

The Pisani class suffered from instability problems, which were partly rectified by fitting bulges to the bows, but this, and their obsolescent design, meant that little use was made of them as combat boats in World War II. *Des Genys* was used as a battery-charging hulk and *Marcantonio Colonna* was broken up in 1943. Only *Vettor Pisani* survived the war.

Specifications

Crew: 48	Submerged: 1075 tonnes (1058 tons)
Powerplant: Twin screw diesel; electric motors	Dimensions (length/beam/draught): 68.2m x 6m x 4.9m (223ft 9in x 20ft 16ft 2in)
Max Speed: Surfaced: 15 knots; Submerged: 8.2 knots	Commissioned: March 1928
Surface Range: 9260km (5000nm) at 8 knots	Armament: Six 533mm (21in) torpedo tubes; one 120mm (4in) gun
Displacement: Surfaced: 894 tonnes (880 tons);	

prestige of Mussolini's Fascist state, and were involved on the Nationalist side in the Spanish Civil War. Also among the considerable range of Italian submarines of the 1920s were the Pisano class, medium-to-large boats of 894 tonnes (880 tons) surfaced and 1075 tonnes (1058 tons) submerged, but with a relatively short range of 9260km (5754 miles) at 8 knots.

Giovanni Bausan, one of the four, launched March 1928, was used as a training ship in 1940–42, when it was converted to an oil hulk. In April 1929, *Ettore Fieramosca* was launched, a one-off design which incorporated a seaplane hangar as an extension of the conning tower, though a plane was never installed.

The unwieldy craft was laid up in June 1941. A more serviceable design was that of the Fratelli Bandiera class, also of 1929; four boats that survived through World War II (engaged on training and transport duties) to be discarded in 1948.

Japan

In accordance with a new naval strategy, Japan's ocean-going boats began to appear from 1919, with I-21 as the first. It was based on Italian drawings of the Fiat-Laurenti F1-type. In 1924, its number was altered to RO-2 and a new I-21 was built, based on the design of the German UB-125, which Japan had

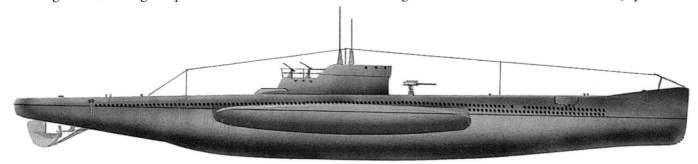

Specifications

Crew: 52	Displacement: Surfaced: 880 tonnes (866 tons);
Powerplant: two diesel engines; two electric	Submerged: 1114 tonnes (1096 tons)
motors	Dimensions (length/beam/draught): 69.8m x
Max Speed: Surfaced: 15.1 knots; Submerged:	7.2m x 5.2m (229ft x 23ft 8in x 17ft)
8.2 knots	Commissioned: August 1929
Surface Range: 8797km (4750nm) at 8.5 knots	Armament: Eight 533mm (21in) torpedo tubes

▲ **Fratelli Bandiera**

Italian Navy, patrol, then transport submarine

Like the Pisani class, the four Bandiera boats had to be modified to obviate stability problems in heavy seas, which slowed them down. They were used for training and transport in World War II; one, *Santorre Santarosa*, was torpedoed and scuttled in January 1943; the others were stricken in 1948.

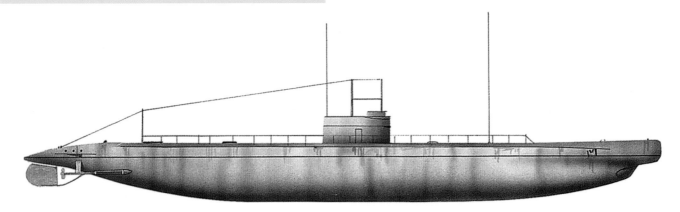

▲ **I-21**

Imperial Japanese Navy, patrol submarine, 1930

Marking the start of the Japanese Navy's interest in ocean-going submarines, built at the Kawasaki Yard in Kobe, *I-21* was a large boat for 1920, but was later reclassified as a second-class RO type. Its career was relatively brief, being stricken in 1930, by which time Japanese submarine design had made considerable strides.

Specifications

Crew: 45	Displacement: Surfaced: 728 tonnes (717 tons);
Powerplant: Twin screw diesel; electric motors	Submerged: 1063 tonnes (1047 tons)
Max Speed: Surfaced: 13 knots; Submerged:	Dimensions (length/beam/draught): 65.6m x 6m
8 knots	x 4.2m (215ft 3in x 19ft 8in x 13ft 9in)
Surface Range: 19,456km (10,500nm) at	Commissioned: November 1919
8 knots	Armament: Five 457mm (18in) torpedo tubes

acquired at the end of the war. The original I-21 was stricken in 1930. By then, Japanese submarine technology was well embarked on its own unique course. Designers were instructed to work on boats with a high surface speed, able to keep up with a battle-fleet or a fast cruiser squadron, and the concept of the 'submarine cruiser' was pursued with maximum enthusiasm at the new Submarine School that had been set up at Kure in 1920.

Japan also played host to several hundred German technicians and ex-naval officers. The KD-1 submarine, completed in 1924, was said to be partly based on the British L-class, but had a double hull, displacing 1525 tonnes (1500 tons) surfaced and 2469 tonnes (2430 tons) submerged. Its range was a remarkable 37,000km (23,000 miles) but its engines were inadequate. More successful was KD-2, completed in 1925 and based on U-139. Its range was half that of KD-1. It was armed with eight 533mm (21in) torpedo tubes, 16 torpedoes and a 120mm (4.8in) deck gun. From 1924, the Imperial Japanese Navy reclassified its submarines under the rubrics I (first-class submarine), RO (medium or coastal submarine), and HA (small or midget type).

US Navy

The US Navy obtained six U-boats as war prizes in 1919, including U-140, and US Navy officers quickly found the German vessels superior to US submarines in almost every respect. This discovery came too late to change the S-class currently under construction, of which no fewer than 51 were launched between 1919 and 1925. Following a basic order for an 813-tonne (800-ton) patrol boat, three prototypes were built, of which S1, from the Electric Boat Co., and S3, designed by the USN Bureau of Construction and Repair and built at the Portsmouth Navy Yard, were accepted. S1 was a single-hull design and 25 were built on this models. The others, based on S3, were double-hulled, with the conning tower set distinctly behind the mid-point.

S1 was one of the first submarines to have retractable bow planes. All the S-class had four forward 533mm (21in) torpedo tubes, and some had a stern tube. Various deck guns were fitted at different times. In 1923, S1 was experimentally fitted with a cylindrical hangar to hold a partially dismantled Martin MS-1 floatplane. Despite their shortcomings, even more apparent by 1941, 42 of the S-boats were

JAPANESE SUBMARINE CLASSES, 1920–38			
Class	Number	Launched	Note
L4	10	1922–26	Patrol/training. Based on GB 'L-class'
KD1	1	1924	Fleet boat
KD2	1	1925	Training boat
J1	4	1926–29	Long-range cruiser
KR5	4	1927–28	Minelayer
KD3	9	1927–30	Training boats
KD4	3	1929–30	Patrol boats
KD5	3	1932	Patrol boats
KD6	8	1934–38	Patrol boats
J1 (modified)	1	1932	Seaplane carrier
J2	1	1935	Seaplane carrier
J3	2	1937–38	Seaplane carrier/command boat

still in service in December 1941, in both the Atlantic and Pacific fleets. Six were transferred to Britain's Royal Navy as the P-class in 1942 (one later passed on to the Polish navy and lost through friendly fire) and seven were lost through wreck or enemy action. S-class boats sank 14 Japanese ships in the Pacific, but by mid-1943 they were relegated to the training role. Wartime alterations included modification of the tower to allow for installation of AA guns, and new shear structure to accommodate periscope and masts.

Cruiser submarines form only part of a pattern of design and construction that by the mid-1920s also embraced the more modest objective of improving the small-to-medium size patrol submarine, primarily for work in coastal waters, but also as an ocean-going attack boat. Design work was going ahead in several countries, including the Netherlands and the recently formed Soviet Russia. A secret German–Soviet co-operation agreement was made in 1926, and the drawings for four types, U-105, UB-48, U-122 (minelayer) and U-139 (cruiser) were passed on. A six-year programme for 12 submarines was initiated. By 1928, this had been enlarged to 18 large and five small submarines, and Soviet Russia's first two classes, Dekabrist and Leninets, resulted from this. In 1930, the sunken and salvaged British L-55 was recommissioned and became an additional test-bed for Soviet engineers, who also had their own submarine tradition to draw on.

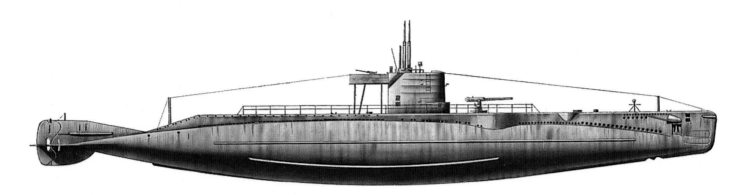

Specifications

Crew: 42

Powerplant: Twin shaft diesels

Max Speed: Surfaced: 14.5 knots; Submerged:
11 knots

Surface Range: 6333km (3420nm) at 6.5 knots

Displacement: Surfaced: 864 tonnes (850 tons);

Submerged: 1107 tonnes (1090 tons)

Dimensions (length/beam/draught): 64.3m x
6.25m x 4.6m (211ft x 20ft 6in x 15ft 3in)

Commissioned: September 1922

Armament: Four 533mm (21in) torpedo tubes;
one 102mm (4in) gun

▲ **S-28**

US Navy, patrol submarine

The S-class formed the backbone of America's inter-war submarine fleet, and marked a real advance on the wartime classes. They were the first USN boats to have 533mm (21in) tubes. These proved unsuitable for the Mark 14 torpedo developed prior to World War II and they fired the older (and more reliable) Mark 10.

Technical developments
1920s–1930s

From modest beginnings with simple externally mounted hydrophones, the quest was on to enable submarines to track their targets and communicate with land while submerged.

THE USE OF PULSED SOUND waves to detect the distance and course of an underwater vessel had been experimented with since at least 1914, and the principle of the hydrophone was well known. Originally, this was simply a microphone extended into the water that could pick up sound waves, such as those of a turning propeller, though soon it was elaborated into a pair of directional microphones fixed on a revolvable mount.

But it was 1920 before the ASDIC system was given sea trials by the Royal Navy, and the JP submarine hydrophone by the US Navy. ASDIC combined hydrophones with a sound emitter whose pulses would reflect off any solid body they met. Range could be calculated by the length of time the echo took to return. The first submarine with an operational ASDIC system was H-32 (commissioned April 1919) in 1922, followed by some of the L-class boats.

The sets were placed on the deck of the hull. But only seven were installed on submarines by 1926. As an 'Anti-Submarine Detection' device it was relatively primitive, confined to low speeds and short range, and was hard to interpret. Effective depth finding would not be achieved until the summer of 1944.

Although British naval planners would place great reliance on ASDIC, it was far from dependable. The Italian submarine *Iride* fired a torpedo at the British destroyer HMS *Havock*, on anti-belligerent patrol off Spain, on 31 August 1937; the destroyer had picked up *Iride*'s ASDIC signal, but failed to hold it (the torpedo missed).

In 1938, the Type 129 ASDIC set was designed, as an attack set, and would be the standard British system in World War II. It was the first to be located inside a streamlined keel dome set at the fore-end of the ballast-keel, and could be used for echo-detection ranging, hydrophone-listening and underwater communication.

As with radar, there is a myth that only the British possessed underwater detection systems, but this is not the case. In the 1930s, the Germans too were working on underwater listening devices, of several kinds. One was the TAG (*Torpedoalarmgerät* or torpedo alarm), which listened for approaching torpedoes; another was the NHG (L), which was intended to tell an ASW vessel which side a submarine was approaching from; and then there was the multiple-receiver GHG (*Gruppehörgerät*), using a minimum of 24 microphones distributed along the sides of a Type II U-boat to 48 on a Type VIIC. The US Navy, too, was experimenting with echo-ranging gear, though in a rather lethargic manner. By 1933, only five boats had been fitted.

One of the submarine designers' prime tasks was to come up with a diesel engine that was compact, reliable and sufficiently powerful to drive the boat at a speed better than 10 knots, which was as much as most pre-1920s submarines could achieve. There were other demands, including the improvement of communications systems and diving mechanisms, and improving manoeuvrability when submerged.

The new larger submarines were often slow to dive, a potentially fatal shortcoming now that aerial detection was a regular feature of life for submariners. Amidst the various concerns for improvement of the vessel, most countries, with the exception of Japan, paid little attention to its armament, and the technology of torpedoes remained at a World War I stage.

▲ Argonaute

French Navy, coastal submarine for Mediterranean service

This Schneider-Laubeuf design for a 'second-class' (i.e. smaller, not ocean-going) boat was a successful and effective one, with good handling qualities and a fast diving time. They served in the Mediterranean, for which they were designed. Completed in 1932, *Argonaute* also provided better crew accommodation than its predecessors.

Specifications

Crew: 89

Powerplant: Twin shaft diesels; electric motors

Max Speed: Surfaced: 15 knots; Submerged: 8 knots

Surface Range: 10,747km (5800nm) at 10 knots

Displacement: Surfaced: 2753 tonnes (2710 tons); Submerged: 4145 tonnes (4080 tons)

Dimensions (length/beam/draught): 116m x 10.4m x 4.6m (381ft x 34ft x 15ft 6in)

Commissioned: November 1927

Armament: Four 533mm (21in) torpedo tubes; two 152mm (6in) guns; 60 mines

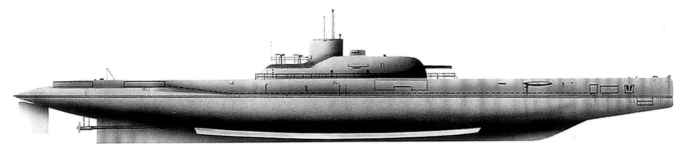

▲ Surcouf

French Navy, submarine gunboat, Atlantic 1942

Described as a 'corsair-submarine', *Surcouf* was intended as a commerce raider, equipped with a Besson MB411 floatplane and a 4.5m (15ft) motorboat, and with room to hold around 40 prisoners. Its cruising endurance was a maximum 90 days. Its designers did not anticipate attacks from the air, as it took two minutes to dive.

Specifications

Crew: 118

Powerplant: Twin screw diesel; electric motors

Max Speed: Surfaced: 18 knots; Submerged: 8.5 knots

Surface Range: 18,530km (10,000nm) at 10 knots

Displacement: Surfaced: 3302 tonnes (3250 tons); Submerged: 4373 tonnes (4304 tons)

Dimensions (length/beam/draught): 110m x 9.1m x 9.07m (360ft 10in x 29ft 9in x 29ft 9in)

Commissioned: October 1929

Armament: Two 203mm (8in) guns; eight 551mm (21.7in) and four 400mm (15.75in) torpedo tubes

BRITISH SUBMARINE CLASSES, 1920-38			
Class	Number	Launched	Note
X1	1	1925	'Commerce raider'; 4 13cm (5.2in) guns
O	9	1926-29	First with ASDIC; 3 built for Chile, 1929
P	6	1929	Far East service; scrapped 1946
R	4	1930	Far East service; scrapped 1946
S	12	1930-37	
River	3	1932-35	Final effort at a 'fleet' submarine
Porpoise	6	1932-38	Minelayers; scrapped 1946
T	15	1935-38	More built 1940-42
U	3	1938	More built 1939-40

British ships *Achates* and *Westcott* in 1942 when trying to oppose Operation Torch, along with a sister boat, *Actéon*. They serve as a reminder that practical, medium-size boats were also being built at this time, though the headlines were grabbed by the end-product of the drive for size, the huge *Surcouf*. Launched on 18 October 1929, this was the largest submarine in the world until the introduction of the Japanese 400 class, displacing 3302 tonnes (3250 tons) surfaced, and 4373 tonnes (4304 tons) submerged. *Surcouf* carried two 203mm (8in) guns and a seaplane hangar as well as 12 torpedo tubes, eight of 550mm (21.7in) and four of 400mm (15.75in). It proved to be a clumsy vessel with an embarrassing history of mishaps, but in June 1940 it escaped from Brest and was taken over by the Royal Navy at Plymouth. Later crewed by Free French sailors, it was lost in collision with a freighter in the Gulf of Mexico, on 18 February 1942.

French Developments

In France, the submarine *Fulton* had been laid down as early as 1913, intended to be driven by 4000hp (2983kW) turbines, but these were displaced by diesel motors. The original machinery was responsible for the rearwards elongation of the conning tower. Between 1929 and 1932, five boats of the Argonaute class were completed for service in the Mediterranean, armed with six 550mm (21.7in) torpedo tubes and a 75mm (3in) gun. *Argonaute*, manned by a Vichy French crew, was sunk by the

Royal Navy

In 1926, Britain launched HMS *Oberon*, first of the nine O-class submarines. With a surface displacement of 1513 tonnes (1490 tons) and 1922 tonnes (1892 tons) submerged, eight 533mm (21in) torpedo tubes, and a 102mm (4in) gun, they were intended for long-distance patrol, with a range of up to 15,550km (9660 miles). Britain still maintained fleets across the globe, and the O-class were intended to serve anywhere from Portsmouth to Hong Kong (*Otway* and *Oxley*, at first sent to the Royal Australian Navy, were returned

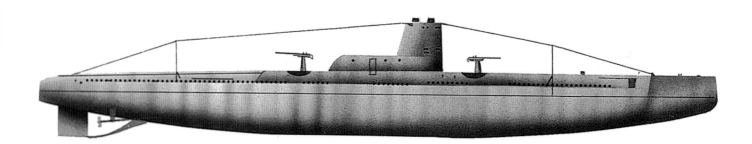

▲ Fulton

French Navy, fast submarine

With its sister-boat *Joessel*, *Fulton* was meant to make 20 knots with steam turbines, but the diesels actually fitted gave 16.5 knots, still above average. Two integral bow tubes were fitted, with four hull-mounted tubes and two external cradles. The conning towers were rebuilt in the 1920s. Both boats were stricken in 1935.

Specifications

Crew: 45

Powerplant: Twin screw diesel engines; electric motors

Max Speed: 16.5 knots surfaced

Surface Range: 7964km (4300nm) at 10 knots

Displacement: Surfaced: 884 tonnes (870 tons);

Submerged: 1267 tonnes (1247 tons)

Dimensions (length/beam/draught): 74m x 6.4m x 3.6m (242ft 9in x 21ft x 11ft 10in)

Commissioned: April 1919

Armament: Eight 450mm (17.7in) torpedo tubes; two 75mm (3in) guns to Britain in 1931). These were boats of traditional configuration and size, in line from World War I classes, though they incorporated many improvements, such as a longer periscope to allow them to cruise at periscope depth without danger of being rammed. Maximum diving depth was 152m (500ft).

The Oberons were easily identifiable with their long tower and high-mounted gun. These were the first British boats equipped with VLF radio, operable at periscope depth, also with Type 116 ASDIC. This system was installed in a large vertical

tube that passed through the pressure hull; it was soon replaced by Type 118/9, which was fitted close to the hull. The slightly larger Parthian class were completed in 1930–31 and stationed at first with the China Squadron. In World War II they were adapted to lay 18 M2 mines from the torpedo tubes, and sent to the Mediterranean. *Parthian* was lost in the Adriatic on 11 August 1943; only one of the class survived the war.

Of similar size to the O-class, but with six 533mm (21in) torpedo tubes and one 102mm (4in) gun,

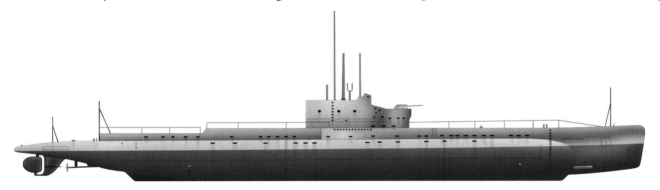

▲ HMS Oberon

Royal Navy, patrol submarine, China Squadron

Completed in 1927, *Oberon* was of an advanced design for the period, and with up-to-date instrumentation. One defect was the riveted saddle tanks, which contained additional fuel, but tended to leave a trail of leakage. Placed in reserve between 1937 and 1939, it was used in World War II primarily for training, and decommissioned in July 1944.

Specifications

Crew: 54	Displacement: Surfaced: 1513 tonnes (1490
Powerplant: Twin screw diesel; electric motors	tons); Submerged: 1922 tonnes (1892 tons)
Max Speed: Surfaced: 13.7 knots; Submerged:	Dimensions (length/beam/draught): 83.4m x
7.5 knots	8.3m x 4.6m (273ft 8in x 27ft 3in x 15ft)
Surface Range: 9500km (5633nm) at 10 knots	Commissioned: 1927
	Armament: Eight 533mm (21in) torpedo tubes

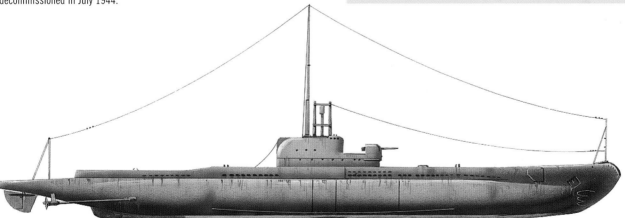

Specifications

Crew: 53	tons); Submerged: 2072 tonnes (2040 tons)
Powerplant: Twin shaft diesel; electric motors	Dimensions (length/beam/draught): 88.14m x
Max Speed: Surfaced: 17.5 knots; Submerged:	9.12m x 4.85m (289ft 2in x 29ft 11in x 16ft)
8.6 knots	Commissioned: June 1929
Surface Range: 9500km (5633nm) at 10 knots	Armament: Eight 533mm (21in) torpedo tubes;
Displacement: Surfaced: 1788 tonnes (1760	one 102mm (4in) gun

▲ HMS Parthian

Royal Navy, patrol submarine/minelayer, Mediterranean, 1940–41

New higher-capacity batteries gave the Parthian class greater underwater endurance. If not carrying mines, they took 14 torpedoes of the standard British Mark VIII type. *Parthian* sank the Italian submarine *Diamante* on 20 June 1940 and the Vichy French *Souffleur* on 25 June 1941, as well as numerous Axis merchant vessels.

SURCOUF

The French Navy's *Surcouf* was the largest of the submarine cruisers built by several navies during the 1920s. None was a success, and by the 1930s only Japan maintained an interest in long-range submarines capable of carrying aircraft.

Armament

The 203mm (8in) guns and gun-laying equipment were not new, as many guns in good condition were available from decommissioned surface ships. The twin turret weighed 185 tonnes (182 tons) and could be ready to fire within three minutes of surfacing, sending a 120kg (264lb) shell a distance of 27,500m (90,223ft).

Holding cell

Although the design provided for a 5m (16ft) motorboat, it was unusable and *Surcouf* never carried one on active service. The submarine was also said to have prison space for 40 men, but this was also usable as a cargo space.

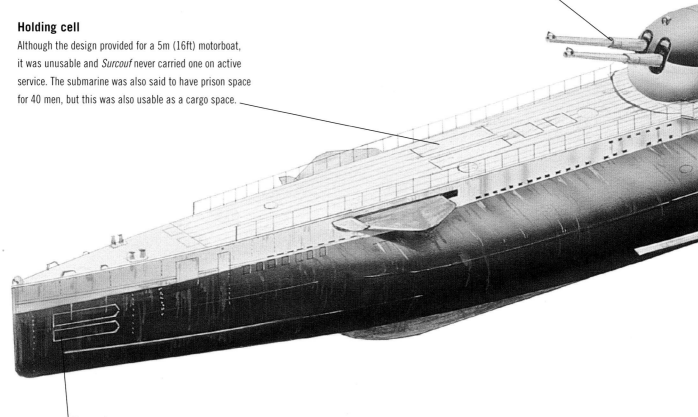

Torpedoes

Six forward torpedo tubes were installed, four of 550mm (21.4in), two of 400mm (15.6in), and two externally-mounted triple sets, formed of one 550mm tube and two of 400mm.

Floatplane

A Besson MB-41-0 floatplane with a 400km (248 mile) range was originally carried in a hangar behind the tower. After a crash-landing in July 1933 it was replaced by an MB-41-1 model. Both were wood-framed. In 1938 a Breguet gyroplane was tested as a possible replacement.

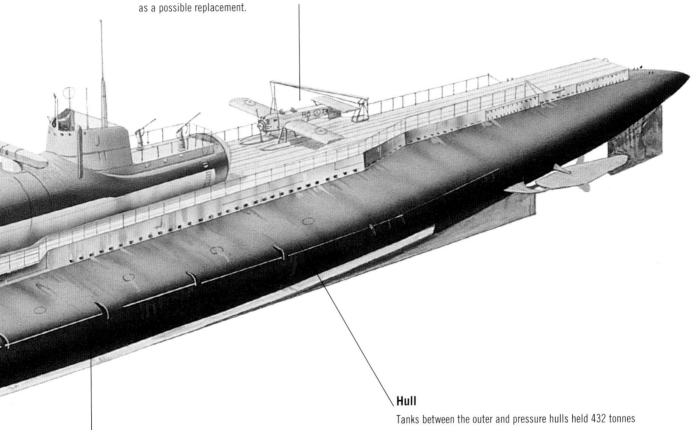

Hull

Tanks between the outer and pressure hulls held 432 tonnes (425 tons) of diesel oil, and four torpedoes were carried in the superstructure. These tanks increased buoyancy and allowed the pressure hull to be made of steel almost 2.54cm (1in) thick, giving the vessel diving capability to over 150m (492ft).

Colour scheme

Originally painted in French naval grey, *Surcouf* was repainted in 'dark Prussian blue' from 1934 until 1940. From then it was painted in two-tone grey.

the six-strong Porpoise class entered service between 1932 and 1938. Sometimes known as the Grampus class, it was the only British submarine designed specifically for minelaying, though six each of the E- and L-classes had been converted for the purpose during the war.

Drawing on experience with the converted M-3 in 1927, the class carried 50 mines stored on racks between the pressure hull and the floodable deck casing. Mines were laid while running on the surface. *Porpoise*'s range of 16,400km (10,190 miles) was slightly greater than that of *Oberon* or *Parthian*.

Italian Types

Italy in the 1930s continued to expand an impressive range of submarine types. Minelaying was seen as a key aspect of submarine work, and many boats were converted for this purpose. *Filippo Corridoni*, launched 1930, was designed as a minelayer, capable of carrying up to 24 mines, and also armed with four 533mm (21in) torpedo tubes and a 102mm (4in) gun. Surprisingly, its speeds were undistinguished: 11.5 knots on the surface, 7 knots submerged.

With its sister boat *Bragadin* it survived until the dispersal of the Italian fleet in 1948. In 1933, the *Sirena* class was introduced, classed as a coastal submarine, capable of diving to 100m (330ft). Two 13mm (0.5in) AA guns were added to the 100mm (3.9in) deck gun during World War II. *Galatea* was the sole member of the class to survive the war.

Long-range cruising was the purpose of the *Calvi* class, one of which was *Enrico Tazzoli*, launched in October 1935. Like many Italian submarines, it was semi-secretly involved in the Spanish Civil war. Refitted as a transport boat in 1942, it was sunk by aircraft in the Bay of Biscay in May 1943 while on a voyage to Japan, along with the transport submarine *Barbarigo*.

Yet another large Italian type was *Pietro Micca*, launched at Taranto as a prototype in March 1935, and though no others followed, it was a reliable and useful boat, storing 20 mines in vertical trunks and also fitted with six 533mm (21in) torpedo tubes and two 120mm (4.7in) guns. In late 1940 it was converted for transporting ammunition and fuel, but its career was terminated by the British submarine HMS *Trooper* in the Otranto Straits on 29 July 1943.

Japanese Subs

More rigorously and successfully than any other navy, the Japanese worked on the concept of the large cruising, aircraft-carrying, fleet-escorting submarine. This was not a random decision but a carefully worked-out policy, anticipating trans-Pacific war with the United States and how it should be waged. The boats I-7 and I-8, launched in July 1935, had a range of 26,600km (16,530 miles) at a speed of 16 knots. The diesel motors could produce a maximum speed of 23 knots. Diving depth was

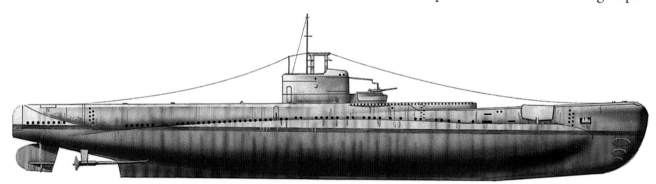

Specifications

Crew: 61	tons); Submerged: 2086 tonnes (2053 tons)
Powerplant: Twin screw diesels; electric motors	Dimensions (length/beam/draught): 81.5m x 9m
Max Speed: Surfaced: 15 knots; Submerged:	x 3.75m (267ft x 29ft 9in x 13ft 9in)
8.75 knots	Commissioned: August 1932
Surface Range: 10,191km (5500nm) at 10 knots	Armament: Six 533mm (21in) torpedo tubes; one
Displacement: Surfaced: 1524 tonnes (1500	102mm (4in) gun

▲ HMS Porpoise

Royal Navy, Grampus-class minelayer, Malacca Straits, January 1945

Porpoise was recognizable from the others in its class by the external fuel tanks terminating about 18m (60ft) short of the bow structure. They served at various times in the West Indies, the Mediterranean and the China Station. Five were lost in World War II, including *Porpoise* itself, sunk by Japanese aircraft in the Malacca Straits on 19 January 1945.

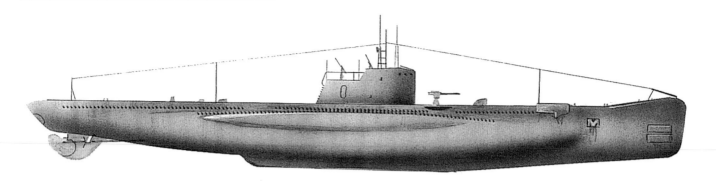

Specifications

Crew: 55

Powerplant: Twin screw diesels; electric motors

Max Speed: Surfaced: 11.5 knots; Submerged:

7 knots

Surface Range: 16,668km (9000nm) at 8 knots

Displacement: Surfaced: 996 tonnes (981 tons);

Submerged: 1185 tonnes (1167 tons)

Dimensions (length/beam/draught): 71.5m x 6m

x 4.8m (234ft 7in x 20ft 2in x 15ft 9in)

Commissioned: March 1950

Armament: Four 533mm (21in) torpedo tubes;

one 102mm (4in) gun; up to 24 mines

▲ Filippo Corridoni

Italian Navy, minelayer, Mediterranean, 1942

Mines were carried in two tubes. Seventeen different mine types were used by Italy, plus German versions. Some 54,457 were laid, mostly of moored types, accounting for 32 vessels, including 11 submarines. *Corridoni* was also used as a transport boat between Italy and North Africa. It was stricken in 1948.

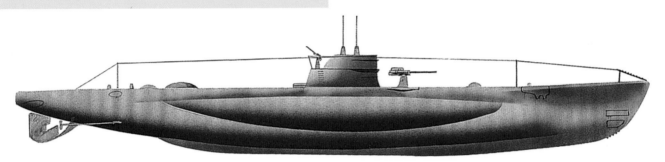

▲ Galatea

Italian Navy, coastal submarine, Mediterranean, 1941

International agreements limited the size of coastal submarines to 610 tonnes (600 tons) and the Italians and French both had several '600' designs, though size tended to creep up with successive variants. Most of the Sirena class saw intensive action in the Mediterranean in 1940–43, and all except *Galatea* were lost. It was stricken in 1948.

Specifications

Crew: 45

Powerplant: Twin screw diesel; electric motors

Max Speed: Surfaced: 14 knots; Submerged:

7.7 knots

Surface Range: 9260km (5000nm) at 8 knots

Displacement: Surfaced: 690 tonnes (679 tons);

Submerged: 775 tonnes (701 tons)

Dimensions (length/beam/draught): 60.2m x

6.5m x 4.6m (197ft 5in x 21ft 2in x 15ft)

Commissioned: October 1933

Armament: Six 533mm (21in) torpedo tubes;

one 100mm (3.9in) gun

Specifications

Crew: 76

Powerplant: Twin screw diesels; electric motors

Max Speed: Surfaced: 17.5 knots; Submerged:

9 knots

Surface Range: 7041km (3800nm) at 10 knots

Displacement: Surfaced: 1473 tonnes (1450

tons); Submerged: 1934 tonnes (1904 tons)

Dimensions (length/beam/draught): 87.7m x

7.8m x 4.7m (288ft x 25ft 7in x 15ft 5in)

Commissioned: April 1928

Armament: Six 533mm (21in) torpedo tubes;

one 120mm (4.7in) gun

▲ Enrico Tazzoli

Italian Navy, attack submarine then transport, 1943

Like the Balilla class, which it resembled, the Calvi class was designed by the civilian Ansaldo team. With a full double hull, and improved crew facilities, it was meant for long-range work. Prior to conversion as a transport, *Tazzoli* had sunk 96,553 gross registered tonnage (GRT) of Allied shipping in the Atlantic and Mediterranean.

99m (325ft) and they could cruise independently for up to 60 days.

When war came, I-7 and I-8 sank seven merchant ships before I-7 was sunk by the USS *Monaghan* on 22 June 1943. I-8's seaplane was removed and the hangar adapted to carry four Kaiten 'human torpedoes' or suicide submarines. It was sunk on 30 March 1945 in the Okinawa landings. In 1939, the I-15 or B-1 type was introduced, a slightly larger, more streamlined version of the aircraft-fitted scouting submarine, of which 20 were completed. One of these, I-19, sank the US carrier *Wasp* on 15 September 1942. Two were modified, like *I-8*, to carry Kaiten manned torpedoes.

Not all Japan's first-class submarines were giants. The legacy of U-139 lived on in the 33 successive Kaidai or KD-class boats, culminating in KD7, designed in 1939. Displacing 1656 tonnes (1630 tons) surfaced and 2644 tonnes (2602 tons) submerged, with a range of 15,000km (9320 miles), they carried six 533mm (21in) torpedo tubes and a stock of 12 Type 95 torpedoes.

I-176 is the only Japanese submarine of this class to have sunk a US one, USS *Corvina*, in November 1943. It also severely damaged the cruiser USS *Chester* in October 1942. Later converted to a transport role, I-176 was blown up in May 1944 by depth charges from US destroyers.

US Navy V-boats

The US Navy also felt the lure of the big cruising submarine. The ability of the U-151 and similar classes to strike at the American coast had made a deep impression. Drawing on the U-boat designs, nine boats, known as the V-boats, were built between 1919 and 1934. In fact, they formed five separate types. Originally designated only by the V and a number, they received names in 1931. The basic aim was to find an acceptable 'fleet boat' design, on the lines of the German cruisers. V-1 to V-3, later named *Barracuda*, *Bass* and *Bonita*, were not considered successes, partly because of unreliable and underpowered motors, and because they failed to make the required surface and submerged speeds of 21 knots and 9 knots.

ITALIAN SUBMARINE CLASSES, 1920–38			
Class	Number	Launched	Note
Mameli	4	1926–28	Ocean-going; last one stricken 1948
Pisani	4	1927–28	Ocean-going; last one stricken 1947
Balilla	4	1927–28	Ocean-going; all out of action 1943
Bandiera	4	1929	Ocean-going; last one stricken 1948
Ettore Fieramosco	1	1930	Intended as seaplane carrier
Bragadin	2	1929–30	Minelayers; stricken 1948
Settembrini	2	1930–31	Ocean-going; last one stricken 1947
Squalo	4	1930	Ocean-going; last one stricken 1948
Argonauta	7	1931–32	Coastal; last one stricken 1948
Sirena	12	1933	Coastal; last one stricken 1948
Archimede	4	1933–34	Two transferred to Spain, 1937
Glauco	2	1935	Originally for Portugal; stricken 1948
Calvi	3	1935	None survived WWII
Micca	1	1935	Minelayer; sunk 1943
Argo	2	1936	Originally for Portugal; lost WWII
Perla	10	1936	Coastal; two passed to Spain, 1937
Adua	17	1936–38	Another 2 sold to Brazil, 1937
Brin	5	1938–39	Ocean-going; last one stricken 1948
Marcello	11	1937–39	Two converted for cargo work, 1943
Foca	3	1937–38	Minelayers; last 2 stricken 1948

Decommissioned in 1937, they were re-entered and overhauled in 1942–43, converted to cargo carrying, but never used in this role. *Bass* was scuttled as a sonar target in 1945. V-4, commissioned in April 1928 and later named *Argonaut*, was the United States' only purpose-built minelaying submarine. It was also the largest US submarine until the nuclear generation; at 116m (382ft) it was longer than its own diving depth of 91m (300ft). In a sense it was a mirror-image of Japan's long-range boats, fulfilling the US side of the same war-plan scenario. Sixty Mark XI moored mines were carried. Despite its size,

lack of engine-space meant it was under-powered, its diesels producing only 15 knots. In World War II *Argonaut* was re-engined and converted to a troop carrier. It was lost off the Solomon Islands on 10 January 1943.

V-5 and V-6, *Narwhal* and *Nautilus*, were commissioned in 1930. Displacing 2770 tonnes (2730 tons) surfaced and 3962 tonnes (3900 tons) submerged, they carried two 150mm (6in) guns, as did *Argonaut*. Plans for accommodating a seaplane were dropped and the boats never undertook the scouting missions, but both served usefully.

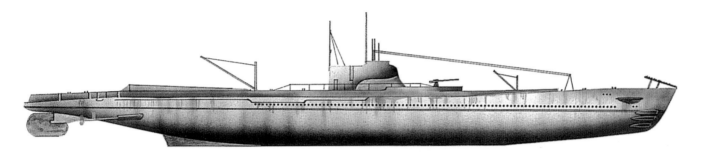

▲ I-7

Imperial Japanese Navy, Type Junsen 3 large patrol submarine, 1942

This was an expanded version of the KD-6 patrol submarine design. The intended scouting role of I-7 and I-8 was heavily curtailed by American use of carrier-borne attack planes, though both were refitted with extra AA guns in 1942. They were not well adapted to attack mode despite being fast on the surface. Destroyers were faster.

Specifications

Crew: 100

Powerplant: Twin screw diesel; electric motors

Max Speed: Surfaced: 23 knots; Submerged: 8 knots

Surface Range: 26,600km (14,337nm) at 16 knots

Displacement: Surfaced: 2565 tonnes (2525 tons); Submerged: 3640 tonnes (3583 tons)

Dimensions (length/beam/draught): 109.3m x 9m x 5.2m (358ft 7in x 29ft 6in x 17ft)

Commissioned: July 1935

Armament: Six 533mm (21in) torpedo tubes; one 140mm (5.5in) gun

▲ USS Bass

US Navy, V-boat, Atlantic, 1942

Originally V-2, *Bass* was twice the size of the S-boats, with only two more torpedo tubes. It served with Submarine Division 20 in the Caribbean and Pacific. Put on reserve in 1937, recommissioned in 1940, it was part of Submarine Squadron 3, Submarine Division 31, Atlantic Fleet. A fire on 17 August 1942 killed 25 crewmen.

Specifications

Crew: 85

Powerplant: Twin shaft diesel engines; electric motors

Max Speed: Surfaced: 18 knots; Submerged: 11 knots

Surface Range: 11,118km (6000nm) at 11 knots

Displacement: Surfaced: 2032 tonnes (2000 tons); Submerged: 2662 tonnes (2620 tons)

Dimensions (length/beam/draught): 99.4m x 8.3m x 4.5m (326ft x 27ft 3in x 14ft 9in)

Commissioned: December 1924

Armament: Six 533mm (21in) torpedo tubes; one 76mm (3in) gun

Nautilus was adapted as a seaplane refueller and in World War II both were used as troop carriers on secret missions of both invasion and troop retrieval. They were withdrawn and broken up in 1945. V-7, *Dolphin*, commissioned in 1932, was only half the size of the previous two and was not considered a success though its dimensions are close to those of the wartime Gato and Balao classes.

V-8 and V-9, *Cachalot* and *Cuttlefish*, were the smallest of the V-boats and though they incorporated numerous innovations, from air conditioning (*Cuttlefish*) to partially welded hulls and sophisticated fire-control, they were not effective in wartime conditions and were relegated to training activities from late 1942. The air conditioning was an immediate success, though other navies were slow to follow the Americans in this. Given the environment they operated in, damp and humidity had always been features of submarine life, but a drier atmosphere was now needed as more sophisticated electrical equipment came into use. Crew comfort was a secondary consideration.

The V-boats have come in for some criticism, with the skipper of one heard to say: 'They were too large for easy handling, too slow in submerging, and too easily seen as targets.' They were, however, perhaps necessary milestones in the search for the 'fleet boat' that the US Navy needed.

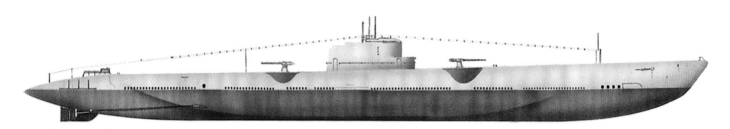

▲ USS Argonaut

US Navy, V-boat, Pacific 1942

On 1 December 1941, *Argonaut* was stationed off Midway on a reconnaissance patrol. Soon after Pearl Harbor it was converted to a transport and special operations role. In June 1942, along with USS *Nautilus*, it landed 211 US Marines to raid Makin Island, by far the biggest submarine landing yet attempted.

Specifications

Crew: 89	tons); Submerged: 4145 tonnes (4080 tons)
Powerplant: Twin shaft diesels; electric motors	Dimensions (length/beam/draught): 116m x 10.4m x 4.6m (381ft x 34ft x 15ft 6in)
Max Speed: Surfaced: 15 knots; Submerged: 8 knots	Commissioned: November 1927
Surface Range: 10,747km (5800nm) at 10 knots	Armament: Four 533mm (21in) torpedo tubes; two 152mm (6in) guns, 60 mines
Displacement: Surfaced: 2753 tonnes (2710	

Specifications

Crew: 60	tons); Submerged: 2275 tonnes (2240 tons)
Powerplant: Twin screw diesel engines; electric motors	Dimensions (length/beam/draught): 97m x 8.5m x 4m (319ft 3in x 27ft 9in x 13ft 3in)
Max Speed: Surfaced: 17 knots; Submerged: 8 knots	Commissioned: March 1932
Surface Range: 11,112km (6000nm) at 10 knots	Armament: Six 533mm (21in) torpedo tubes; one 102mm (4in) gun
Displacement: Surfaced: 1585 tonnes (1560	

▲ USS Dolphin

US Navy, V-boat

Originally V-7, it was smaller than the previous V-boats, and represented an attempt to pack their features and technology into a structure that offered more destructive power per ton of displacement. This problem was resolved more effectively by later designs. *Dolphin* was used through World War II as a training boat, and was broken up in 1946.

Submarine deployment
1930s

The building of very large submarines was given up by most countries, but the numbers of operative boats were growing steadily, despite international conferences aimed at limiting them.

AT THE TALKS preceding the London Naval Treaty in 1930–31, Great Britain again sought the abolition of submarines as combat craft. At that time, the Royal Navy had just over 50, all capable of firing 533mm (21in) torpedoes, and 27 of them had six front tubes for firing salvoes.

Of the other powers, the United States had the largest fleet, 81 boats, though the majority were of the not very satisfactory S-class. France had 66 submarines, Japan had 72 and Italy had 46, but the two latter countries also had substantial building programmes. The Treaty itself limited the size of new submarines to 2032 tonnes (2000 tons) and gun calibre to 130mm (5.1in).

This was no great restriction, since most navies, except Japan's, had abandoned the concept of the very large submarine and wanted to build more medium-sized boats, which were cheaper to build and easier to deploy in a variety of situations.

Great Britain, the United States and Japan agreed not to exceed a total submarine tonnage of 53,545 tonnes (52,700 tons), which was the current British total; France and Italy refused to be bound by this. Neither the Soviet Union nor Germany were represented at these talks.

France

French submarine policy continued to be dictated by the French Navy's relative lack of major surface ships. Of its 66 boats, more than two-thirds were capable of long-range sea-going. Organized in flotillas, squadrons and divisions, submarines were based at Dunkirk and Cherbourg on the Channel coast, Brest and Lorient on the Atlantic, and Toulon on the Mediterranean. On the North African coast there were squadrons or divisions based at Casablanca and Oran, with a flotilla HQ at Bizerta. Divisions were also based at Beirut (Libya), Djibouti on the Red Sea and Saigon in French Indo-China (Vietnam).

Henri Poincaré, launched at Lorient in April 1929, was one of the first series of Redoutable-class boats, double-hulled and classified as first class or ocean-going, and commissioned in December 1931. Thirty-one of the class were built, in three groups, with 19 in 1924–28, six in 1929–30, and six in 1930–31. Up to 11 torpedo tubes were carried, including six or seven externally mounted. Diving depth was 80m (262ft). Group I's diesel engines produced 6000hp (4474kW); later series were higher powered. They were effective boats whose main defect was a relatively slow dive-time (45–50 seconds), which in World War

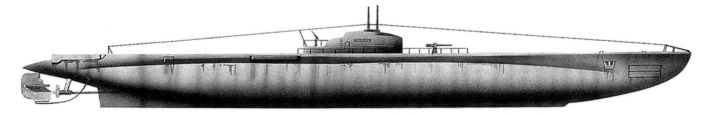

▲ Henri Poincaré
French Navy, surface raider

The double-hulled Redoutable class was designed as an advance on the Requin boats and were heavily armed with torpedoes. Their function was that of surface raiders and defenders of the maritime supply line between France and its colonies. In World War II they did very little of either before most were scuttled.

Specifications

Crew: 61

Powerplant: Twin screw diesel; electric motors

Max Speed: Surfaced: 17–20 knots; Submerged: 10 knots

Surface Range: 18,530km (10,000nm) at 10 knots

Displacement: Surfaced: 1595 tonnes (1570 tons); Submerged: 2117 tonnes (2084 tons)

Dimensions (length/beam/draught): 92.3m x 8.2m x 4.7m (302ft 10in x 27ft x 15ft 5in)

Commissioned: April 1929

Armament: Nine 550mm (21.7in) and two 400mm (15.7in) torpedo tubes; one 82mm (3.2in) gun

II conditions was potentially fatal. *Henri Poincaré* was scuttled with six others of the class at Toulon on 27 November 1942; it was salvaged by the Italians and recommissioned, but was sunk in September 1943.

British Subs

In Great Britain, 17 further L-class submarines were commissioned after the end of World War I. With their high-mounted 102mm (4in) gun and raised bridge on a long conning tower, they had a distinctive appearance. By the 1930s they were obsolescent and most were scrapped during the decade. Two remained in service in World War II, L-23 and L-27, both as training boats. Stricken in 1946, L-23 foundered off Nova Scotia while on tow to a breaker's yard. The successor to the L-class was the O-class, intended to to have greater sea endurance, for service in the Far East.

HMS *Odin*, built at Chatham Naval Dockyard, was lead ship of a second batch of six, launched in 1928–29. Compared to *Oberon* it was slightly longer and wider, with a differently shaped 'ram' bow and retractable bow hydroplanes mounted quite high

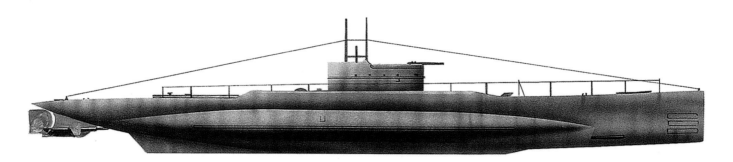

▲ L-23

Royal Navy, patrol submarine, North Sea, 1940

Laid down at Vickers, Barrow in Furness, and completed at Chatham Royal Navy Dockyard, L-23 was commissioned on 5 August 1924. By 1929, 30 boats of the class remained, of which 10 were in reserve. By 1939, only a handful remained. In February 1940, L-23 had a narrow escape from a depth-charge attack from German destroyers.

Specifications

Crew: 36

Powerplant: Twin screw diesel; electric motors

Max Speed: Surfaced: 17.5 knots; Submerged: 10.5 knots

Surface Range: 8338km (4500nm)

Displacement: Surfaced: 904 tonnes (890 tons);

Submerged: 1097 tonnes (1080 tons)

Dimensions (length/beam/draught): 72.7m x 7.2m x 3.4m (238ft 6in x 23ft 8in x 11ft 2in)

Commissioned: July 1919

Armament: Four 533mm (21in) torpedo tubes; one 102mm (4in) gun

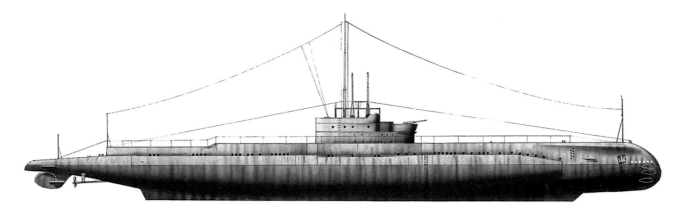

Specifications

Crew: 54

Powerplant: Twin screw diesel; electric motors

Max Speed: Surfaced: 17.5 knots; Submerged: 8 knots

Surface Range: 9500km (5633nm) at 10 knots

Displacement: Surfaced: 1513 tonnes (1490 tons); Submerged: 1922 tonnes (1892 tons)

Dimensions (length/beam/draught): 83.4m x 8.3m x 4.6m (273ft 8in x 27ft 3in x 15ft)

Commissioned: May 1928

Armament: Eight 533mm (21in) torpedo tubes

▲ HMS Odin

Royal Navy, O-class long-range patrol submarine, Mediterranean, 1940

The O-class is more properly named after HMS *Odin* than *Oberon*, which is shorter, lighter and less powerful than the subsequent boats. Apart from *Odin*, *Orpheus* and *Oswald* were also sunk by Italian destroyers, and *Olympus* struck a mine off Malta. *Osiris* and *Otus* were scrapped at Durban, South Africa, in September 1946.

on the pressure hull. Like the L-class, the gun was mounted on the forepart of the tower, but the bridge was stepped up in order to provide a wider view. *Odin* had a surface speed of 17.5 knots as against *Oberon*'s 15.5, but in most respects there were no significant differences. *Odin* was sunk on 14 June 1940, off Taranto, by the Italian destroyer *Strale*. Only one of the six survived World War II. Three boats of the O-class were built for Chile in 1929, to form the Capitan O'Brien class. They long outlived the British boats, being decommissioned in 1957–58.

Italian Torpedoes

Italian submarines of the 1930s have been criticized for a low ratio of destructive power to weight, and for being too big and bulky to escape detection in clear Mediterranean waters. But they also had positive aspects in combat, among which were very effective torpedoes, produced by the Whitehead plant at Fiume and the naval ordnance factory at Naples. Fiume produced a torpedo that could travel up to 4000m (4400yds) at 50 knots, or 12,000m (13,100 yds) at 30 knots, with a 250kg (551lb) warhead. Italy also produced the magnetically activated torpedo, which exploded underneath a ship's keel, usually breaking its back. (The inventor, Carlo Calosi, was taken to the United States in 1944 after Italy's surrender and passed on details of how to disrupt the torpedo's magnetic field and render it harmless.)

The Squalo class of medium submarines numbered four, completed at Monfalcone in 1930–31, the single-hull design being based on Curio Bernardis'

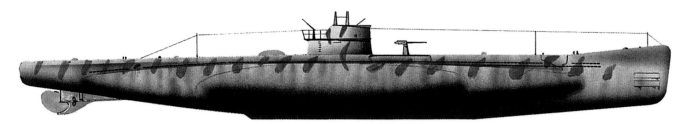

▲ Delfino

Italian Navy patrol submarine/transport, Mediterranean, 1942

In an active career *Delfino* was first with the 2nd Submarine Squadron at La Spezia. Then, after a Black Sea cruise, it was based at Naples, before deploying to the Red Sea. In 1940 it was attached to the 51st Squadron, 5th Submarine Division, on the island of Leros. From 1942 it operated as a transport boat from Taranto.

Specifications

Crew: 52

Powerplant: Two diesel engines, two electric motors

Max Speed: Surfaced: 15 knots; Submerged: 8 knots

Surface Range: 7412km (4000nm) at 10 knots

Displacement: Surfaced: 948 tonnes (933 tons); Submerged: 1160 tonnes (1142 tons)

Dimensions (length/beam/draught): 70m x 7m x 7m (229ft x 23ft x 23ft)

Commissioned: April 1930

Armament: Eight 533mm (21in) torpedo tubes, one 102mm (4in) gun

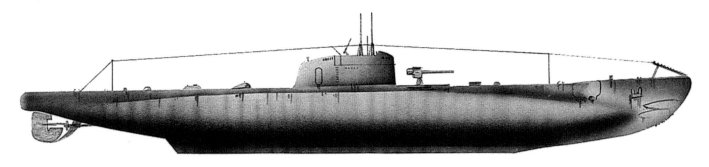

Specifications

Crew: 46

Powerplant: Twin screws, diesel/electric motors

Max Speed: Surfaced: 14 knots; Submerged: 8 knots

Surface Range: 9260km (5000nm) at 8 knots

Displacement: Surfaced: 807 tonnes (794 tons);

Submerged: 1034 tonnes (1018 tons)

Dimensions (length/beam/draught): 63m x 6.9m x 4.5m (207ft x 22ft 9in x 14ft 8in)

Commissioned: December 1936

Armament: Six 533mm (21in) torpedo tubes; one 100mm (3.9in) gun

▲ Velella

Italian Navy, surface raider, Atlantic 1940–41

A good sea-boat, *Velella* also saw much action. Though classed as coastal, it was among the submarines sent to Bordeaux for Atlantic service, making four patrols between November 1940 and August 1941. Its sinking in September 1943, while opposing Allied landings at Salerno, was on the day before the Armistice (already signed) was announced.

SOVIET SUBMARINE CLASSES, 1920–38			
Class	Number	Launched	Note
AG	6	1920–21	Two reclaimed by United States; last one sunk 1943
Series I 'Dekabrist'	6	1928–29	Last one stricken c.1958
Series II 'Leninets'	6	1931	Last one broken up 1959
Series III 'Shchuka'	4	1930–31	Last one broken up 1958
Series IV 'Pravda'	3	1934	Last one broken up 1956
Series V 'Losos'	19	1933–35	Last one broken up 1958
Series Vb 'Strelad'	12	1934	Stricken 1950
Series Vbii 'Sayda'	9	1935	Last one broken up 1958
Series VI 'M1'	30	1933–34	Small boats; last ones broken up 1950s
Series VIb 'M53'	20	1934–35	Small boats; last ones broken up 1950s
Series XI 'Voroshilovets'	6	1935–36	Stricken 1950
Series IX 'Nalim'	3	1935–36	All lost in WWII
Series X 'Shch126'	33	1935–37	Last ones broken up 1958
Series XII 'M87'	4	1936–37	Last ones broken up in 1950s
Series IXb 'S4'	4	1936–38	More built from 1939
Series XIII 'L13'	7	1937–38	Stricken 1950
Series XIV 'K1'	5	1937–38	Minelayer; more built from 1939
Series XV 'Mest'	4	1937	More built from 1939

for Fratelli Bandiera. Stability problems when diving and surfacing were resolved by an enlarged bow design. Operational diving depth was 90m (297ft). The Squalo boats were assigned first to the 2nd Squadron at La Spezia, then to the 4th Squadron at Naples; in 1936, they were involved in Spanish Civil War operations. In 1937, all four were transferred to the Red Sea. Back in the Mediterranean during World War II, *Delfino* sank the Greek cruiser *Helli* in harbour on 15 August 1940, although Italy and Greece were not yet at war. On 1 August 1941, it shot down an attacking Sunderland flying boat. After 29 missions and 67 training sorties, it sank on 23 March 1942 after colliding with a pilot boat off Taranto.

The economic slump of the 1930s caused Portugal to cancel a 1931 order for two submarines from Italy. The boats, *Argo* and *Velella*, were finally completed for Italy's *Regia Marina* in August 1937. Portugal's Atlantic-facing coast is very different to Italy's, but the boats were of relatively standard type. *Velella* was first attached to the 42nd squadron of the 4th Submarine Group at Taranto, then saw service in the Red Sea with the Submarine Flotilla of Italian East Africa before returning to the Mediterranean. From

US SUBMARINE CLASSES, 1918–39			
Class	Number	Launched	Note
O	7	1918	
R	18	1918–19	1 lost 1942
S	51	1920–25	7 lost
V1-3	3	1925–27	*Barracuda, Bass* and *Bonita* from 1931
V4 *Argonaut*	1	1928	Minelayer; lost 1943
V5-6 *Narwhal*	2	1930	Intended seaplane carriers; 66mm (2.6in) guns
V7 *Dolphin*	1	1932	Carried a motor boat
V8-9 *Cachalot*	2	1933–34	Submarine cruisers
Porpoise	10	1935–37	4 lost
Salmon	6	1937–38	
Sargo	10	1939	4 lost

December 1940 it was part of the Italian squadron at Bordeaux for a few months, making four Atlantic patrols. Once again in the Mediterranean, it was sunk in the Gulf of Salerno by the British submarine HMS *Shakespeare* on 7 September 1943.

The Soviet Union

Soviet Russia's submarine fleet was greatly expanded in the 1930s to become numerically the world's largest, though most of the boats were small. The most numerous class, the M- ('Baby') boats, from 1933, totalled 111, with a surfaced displacement ranging from 160 tonnes (158 tons) to 285 tonnes (281 tons). Submarines had to be distributed among the four sea fleets. The S- or Shch-class (from *Shchuka*, 'Pike'), intended to be 200-strong, numbered 88 submarines, all designated as coastal. With a range of 11,100km (6900 miles), they operated with the Baltic, Black Sea, Northern and Pacific fleets. *Shch 303*, *Ersh*, was part of the Baltic fleet. Thirty-two of the class were lost in World War II, but *Shch 303* was one of the survivors, and was not finally broken up until 1958.

United States

USS V-6 was launched on 15 March 1930 and commissioned on 1 July that year, as one of the few large American submarines of the period. The name *Nautilus* was given in February 1931. At Pearl Harbor it was flagship of Submarine Division 12, then relocated to San Diego as flagship of Submarine Division 13 from 1935 to 1938 before returning to Pearl Harbor. The rest of its career was spent in the Pacific, where it saw much action during World War II, in 14 patrols that encompassed sea battles, troop landings and reconnaissance missions. *Nautilus* was

▲ Shch 303

Soviet Navy, patrol submarine, Baltic Sea, 1941

The Baltic was a difficult sea from every point of view. For most of World War II it was a German pond (with Finnish help), with the Soviet fleet hemmed in at Kronstadt and Leningrad, where Submarine Brigades 1 and 2 were based. Only submarines could slip by, and 26 were lost in 1941 alone. It was very late in the war before the Soviet Union gained control.

Specifications

Crew: 45

Powerplant: Twin screw diesel engines; electric motors

Max Speed: Surfaced: 12.5 knots; Submerged: 8.5 knots

Surface Range: 11,112km (6000nm) at 8 knots

Displacement: Surfaced: 595 tonnes (586 tons); Submerged: 713 tonnes (702 tons)

Dimensions (length/beam/draught): 58.5m x 6.2m x 4.2m (192ft x 20ft 4in x 13ft 9in)

Commissioned: November 1931

Armament: Six 533mm (21in) torpedo tubes, two 45mm (1.8in) guns

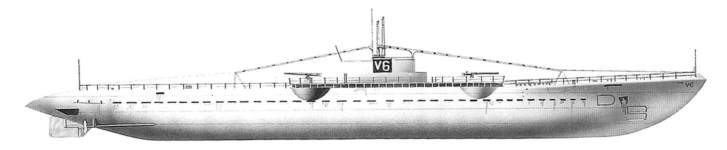

Specifications

Crew: 90

Powerplant: Twin screw diesel engines; electric motors

Max Speed: Surfaced: 17 knots; Submerged: 8 knots

Surface Range: 33,336km (18,000nm) at 10 knots

Displacement: Surfaced: 2773 tonnes (2730 tons); Submerged: 3962 tonnes (3900 tons)

Dimensions (length/beam/draught): 113m x 10m x 4.8m (370ft x 33ft 3in x 15ft 9in)

Commissioned: March 1930

Armament: Six 533mm torpedo tubes; two 152mm (6in) guns

▲ USS Nautilus (V-6)

US Navy, V-boat, later transport, Pacific, World War II

Commissioned as V-6, *Nautilus* was to be a heavily armed ocean-going boat with trans-Pacific range. However, the US Navy made the strategic decision to opt for more compact fleet boats. In 1940, *Nautilus* was modified to carry 19,320 gallons (73,134 litres) of aviation fuel, but retained its tubes and sank three freighters in the course of the war. It was scrapped in 1945.

decommissioned at Philadelphia on 30 June 1945 and scrapped in 1946.

Yugoslavia

The Kingdom of Yugoslavia had four submarines to patrol its Adriatic coast, two of British L-type (intended as L-67 and L-68, but cancelled in 1919), completed for Yugoslavia by Vickers-Armstrong in 1927–28; and two built in France, all based at Kotor. When the Italians captured Kotor, three were seized and one escaped to link up with the British Navy to make it to Britain. *Osvetnik*, built at Nantes, France in 1929, became the Italian *Francesco Rismondo* and, after the Italian surrender, sailed for Corsica, but was seized and scuttled by the Germans on 18 September 1943. *Osvetnik* was a medium-size boat, of 630 tonnes (620 tons) surfaced and 809 tonnes (796 tons) submerged, and with an operational depth of 80m (262ft). Another of the Yugoslav boats, *Nebojsa*, escaped to Alexandria and was later used by the British. It was last heard of at Malta in August 1945.

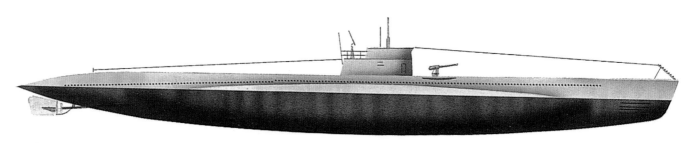

Specifications

Crew: 45

Powerplant: Two diesel engines; two electric
  motors

Max Speed: Surfaced: 14.5 knots; Submerged:
  9.2 knots

Surface Range: 5003km (2700nm) at 10 knots

Displacement: Surfaced: 676 tonnes (665 tons);

Submerged: 835 tonnes (822 tons)

Dimensions (length/beam/draught): 66.5m x
  5.4m x 3.8m (218ft 2in x17ft 9in x 12ft 4in)

Commissioned: 929

Armament: Six 551mm (21.7in) torpedo tubes;
  one 100mm (3.9in) gun

▲ **Ostvetnik (N1)**

Yugoslav Navy, patrol submarine, Adriatic

Built at the Ateliers de le Loire, Nantes, *Osvetnik* and its sister boat *Smeli* were designed by the French architect Simonot on the lines of French '600' type boats and had many French features, including the 551mm (21.7in) torpedo tubes. The diesel engines were by MAN, and the electric motors from CGE, Nancy. After capture, modifications were made to the conning tower structure.

Return of the U-boats
1935–39

Renewal of Germany's U-boat programme began from 1935. But the British response was surprisingly mild, and U-boat chief Karl Dönitz did not succeed in getting the number of submarines that he needed.

ADOLF HITLER came to power in Germany in 1933. In March 1935, he repudiated the Versailles Treaty. In the same year, Germany signed a naval arms limitation treaty with Great Britain, the terms allowing Germany to have 45 per cent of the naval strength of the British, and a 100 per cent match in submarines. Considering British memories of 1914–18, this was a remarkable concession, usually explained by excessive confidence in the London Submarine Agreement, signed by Germany in 1936, that submarines in war would respect international law and rescue the crews of sunken ships; and also in the detection capabilities of ASDIC.

The building of new German submarines began immediately; the plans already existed and Command of the *Reich*'s First Submarine Flotilla was given to *Kapitän-sur-See* Karl Dönitz, a submarine veteran of World War I. From 1935, he began to develop ideas that had long been discussed among ex-U-boat officers, on how to make the submarine a really

▲ **U-32**

This grainy photograph shows U-32 moving through friendly waters, probably off northern Germany. The stripes painted on the conning tower are the distinguishing marks used by warships of the 'Non-Interventionist Committee', patrolling shipping lanes off the Spanish coast during 1938–39.

effective weapon. Allied convoys from 1917 had proved able to fend off lurking U-boats. However, if a group of U-boats, a 'wolfpack', concentrated their attacks on a convoy, they might be able to overwhelm the escorts and inflict major damage. Dönitz had many other ideas, including scepticism about the effectiveness of ASDIC. Looking ahead, he felt he needed 300 ocean-going submarines if the task should be to cut British supply lines in the event of war. This would take several years to achieve, and Dönitz found that submarines were not the top priority of the Nazi High Command.

U-Boat Menace

Karl Dönitz had learned his craft in U-boats during World War I. The Imperial German Navy was the first to make extensive use of submarines in attacking an enemy's supply lines, and in spite of the primitive nature of the boats of the period, achieved considerable success.

U-boats wreaked havoc on British shipping in the Mediterranean, and the unrestricted submarine warfare of 1917 and 1918 came within a whisker of bringing Britain to its knees. It was a major reason why after the war Germany was denied a submarine force under the terms of the Treaty of Versailles. In spite of the ban, Germany set up clandestine U-boat design offices in Holland in 1922 and in Berlin in 1927. In 1932, months before Hitler's rise to power, the Weimar government approved a naval building plan which included 16 U-boats.

Rearmament

The rise of the Nazis accelerated the navy's plans. In 1935, Hermann Göring announced Germany's intent to rearm, repudiating the Treaty of Versailles. Hitler managed to push through an Anglo-German naval agreement that allowed German warship construction up to a ceiling of 45 per cent of the Royal Navy. Curiously, since the British had painful experience of what submarines could do, the agreement also allowed Germany to match the Royal Navy's submarine force, ton for ton.

Dönitz was given command of Germany's first post-war submarine flotilla in 1935 and set about training a new U-boat fleet that could succeed where his generation had, by a narrow margin, failed. Once in charge of the German submarine force, he was able to define the types of boat best suited to near and distant operations, as well as the number required to beat a fully-organized convoy system.

U-Boat Construction

Design of Type 1A (U-25 and U-26) went back to the pre-Hitler period, and construction began in in 1934. It was not an effective craft: handling was tricky, it was difficult to keep level at periscope depth, and it rolled violently. Type IIA, comprising U-1 to U-9, were completed in 1935. The design was newly tested and proved by a submarine launched at Turku, Finland, as a supposedly commercial venture backed by the German front-company in The Hague. This boat, known first as CV-707, was launched in May 1933 and later sold to the Finnish Government as *Vesikko*.

U-2, like most other early U-boats, was used for training. Its small size limited it to coastal patrols and forays into the the North and Baltic Seas. *U-2* was lost in a collision in the Baltic Sea in April 1944 while on a training run as part of the 22nd (training) flotilla. The first active group was Dönitz's *U-Flotille Weddigen*, formed of U-7 to U-9.

U-3 made five combat patrols and sank two ships of neutral nations, one Danish and one Swedish, and with the other training boats was part of the fleet supporting the German invasion of Norway in April 1940. It was then transferred to a training flotilla, the 21st. Captured by the British in May 1945, it was scrapped that year.

Training boats were essential to produce a new generation of U-boat crews, but there was a sense of urgency about producing submarines that would fulfil the ocean-going, commerce-raiding role. These would have to be substantially bigger than

the Type II, and the need was filled by the Type VII design, tested in the Finnish Vetehinen class (launched 1930) under the same auspices as the CV-707, though the Type VII, intended for the Atlantic, was larger.

U-32 was an early Type VIIA, launched in 1937, and one of the few ready for ocean combat in 1939. Although the Type VII would go through several stages of improvement, it could already dive in under 30 seconds and reach a depth of 100m (330ft) and go even deeper to 200m (660ft) in an emergency. It could travel submerged at 7.6 knots for two hours, or at 2 knots for 130 hours. Perhaps its main defect was its limited range: 10,000km (6200 miles).

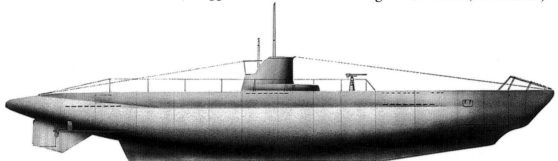

▲ U-2

German Navy, Type IIA coastal submarine

Though not a large boat, U-2 was built in a very short time: laid down in February 1935 and commissioned on 25 July of the same year, at the Deutsche Werke, Kiel. Its entire career was spent as a training boat, under 10 successive commanders. It sank on 8 April 1944 after colliding with a trawler. Though raised the next day, it was stricken from the active list.

Specifications

Crew: 25	Dimensions (length/beam/draught): 40.9 x 4.1 x
Powerplant: Diesel engine; electric motor	3.8m (1134.2 x 13.5 x 12.5ft)
Max Speed: Surfaced: 17.8 knots; Submerged:	Commissioned: 6 August 1935
8.3 knots	Armament: Six torpedoes (three bow tubes);
Surface Range: 1945km (1050nm)	1 x 2cm (0.8in) gun
Displacement: 258/308t (254/303 tons) s/d	

Specifications

Crew: 44	Dimensions (length/beam/draught): 64.5 x 5.8 x
Powerplant: Diesel engine; electric motors	4.4m (211.6 x 19 x 14.4ft)
Max Speed: Surfaced: 16 knots; Submerged:	Commissioned: 8 October 1936
8 knots	Armament: 11 torpedoes (4 bow/1 stern tubes);
Surface Range: 7964km (4300nm)	one 8.8cm (3.5in) and one 2cm (0.8in) gun
Displacement: 636/757t (626/745 tons) s/d	

▲ U-32

German Navy, Type VIIA patrol submarine

U-32 was one of the first Type VIIA boats, laid down at Germaniawerft, Kiel, in March 1936 and commissioned on 15 April 1937. Ten VIIA were built, and the class was immediately popular with crews, who realized that they had a submarine superior to any other. Payload was 11 torpedoes, or 22 TMA/33 TMB mines. U-32 made nine combat patrols and sank a total tonnage of 116,836GRT.

Great Britain

The official British view in the late 1930s, expressed even by Winston Churchill, was that 'the sub had been mastered'. Confidence in the combination of ASDIC detectors with depth charge throwers fitted on destroyers and sloops meant that they thought that a submarine threat could be readily dealt with, and the role of submarines in the Royal Navy was not seen as a priority.

Contemporary with the German developments, a new class of ocean-going submarine, the Triton or T-class was developed from 1935, and 15 had been built by September 1939. The smaller Undine or U-class was under construction at the same time, with 15 completed by the outbreak of war. Both classes would be extended, with 53 of the T-class ultimately built, and 49 of the Undines. The first three U-class were seen as training vessels, but their operational value was soon perceived.

Most served in the North Sea and Mediterranean, in the latter with the 10th Submarine Flotilla based at Malta. The first three had two external bow torpedo tubes in addition to the four integral tubes, but these were not applied to the rest of the class. *Undine* itself had a short career, being scuttled off Heligoland when immobilized by anti-submarine warfare surface craft in January 1940.

Italy

Commissioned just before World War II were three Italian minelayers of the Foca class, built by Tosi at Taranto. The 100mm (6in) gun was originally installed in the after part of the conning tower, but was later placed more conventionally on the deck facing forward. Mines were carried in both vertical and horizontal tubes, a total of 28.

The class had an operational depth of 100m (330ft). *Zoea* was seized by the Allies after the fall of Italy and used in late 1943 to run supplies to the garrisons on the islands of Samos and Leros. It was discarded in 1947.

Another class completed by CRDA, *Monfalcone*, just before hostilities began, was the 11-strong *Marcello*, built 1938–39, large and well-armed ocean-going boats, considered by some experts to be the best of the large Italian submarines, whose number included *Barbarigo* and *Dandolo*. In 1939–40 they were stationed in the Mediterranean, but 10 were transferred to Bordeaux in August 1940.

▲ **Torpedo loading**
A U-boat crew bring a torpedo on board. Initial problems with reliability were soon overcome and as German torpedoes improved, so the U-bootwaffe quickly became a deadly fighting force.

The Type VII carried between 11 and 14 torpedoes. Early boats also had a deck gun, but as the war progressed, this was often replaced with heavy anti-aircraft armament.

The Type IX class was designed for ocean warfare. Loosely based on the far smaller Type II, it differed fundamentally in having a double hull. This increased useable internal volume by enabling fuel and ballast tanks to be sited externally. In turn, the extra hull improved survivability by cushioning the inner (pressure) hull from explosive shock and gave the boats greatly improved handling on the surface.

Early Type IXs had enough range to operate in the southern hemisphere, mounting long patrols into the South Atlantic. Later versions with increased range could reach the Indian Ocean and even the Pacific without refuelling.

As Atlantic raiders, they never achieved the success rate of the U-boats, and four were sunk. In early 1941, *Dandolo* returned to the Mediterranean, where it torpedoed the cruiser HMS *Cleopatra* in July 1943. Ultimately, the only member of the class to survive the war, *Dandolo*, was scrapped in 1947. Two of the class were converted to cargo-carrying; one of them, *Comandante Cappellini*, was commissioned (at Singapore) in the *Reichsmarine* as UIT-24, and later in the Japanese Navy as I-503, one of only two boats to serve in all three Axis navies.

Poland

The German invasion of Poland in September 1939 was the action that finally triggered World War II. Poland, with a short Baltic coast, had five submarines in 1939, three French-built minelayers of the Wilk class (1931), and *Orzel* and *Sep*, built in the Netherlands and commissioned in 1939. On 14 September 1939, all were ordered to head for British ports, but only *Orzel* and *Wilk* succeeded. *Orzel* sank two German troop transports on 8 April 1940 while opposing the invasion of Norway, but was sunk by a mine on 8 June.

Specifications

Crew: 31	Submerged: 752 tonnes (740 tons)
Powerplant: Twin screw diesel; electric motors	Dimensions (length/beam/draught): 54.9m x
Max Speed: Surfaced: 11.2 knots; Submerged:	4.8m x 3.8m (180ft x 16ft x 12ft 9in)
10 knots	Commissioned: October 1937
Surface Range: 7041km (3800nm) at 10 knots	Armament: Four 533mm (21in) torpedo tubes;
Displacement: Surfaced: 554 tonnes (545 tons);	one 76mm (3in) gun

▲ HMS Undine

Royal Navy, U-class patrol submarine, Mediterranean, World War II

Unlike most submarines, the U-class did not have a separate hatch for the gun crew. HMS *Unity* was the first British submarine to have a propeller for optimum submerged performance: on this class the electric motors developed more power than the diesels. Most were attached to the 10th flotilla at Malta, and 16 were lost in the Mediterranean.

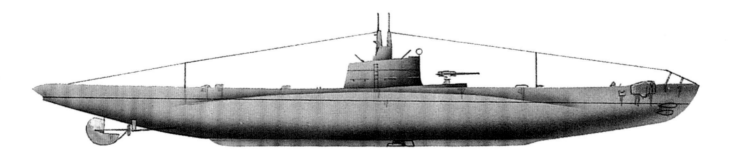

▲ Zoea

Italian Navy, coastal minelayer

Described as coastal boats despite their size, the class was also heavily armed for minelayers. One photo of *Atropo* shows the gun mounted on the conning tower, perhaps a temporary arrangement. *Foca* was lost off Palestine in October 1940; *Atropo* was used by the Allies in the same way as *Zoea*.

Specifications

Crew: 60	Displacement: Surfaced: 1354 tonnes (1333
Powerplant: Twin screw diesel engines; electric	tons); Submerged: 1685 tonnes (1659 tons)
motors	Dimensions (length/beam/draught): 82.8m x
Max Speed: Surfaced: 15.2 knots; Submerged:	7.2m x 5.3m (271ft 8in x 23ft 6in x 17ft 5in)
7.4 knots	Commissioned: February 1936
Surface Range: 15,742km (8500nm) at 8 knots	Armament: Six 533mm (21in) torpedo tubes; one
	100mm (3.9in) gun

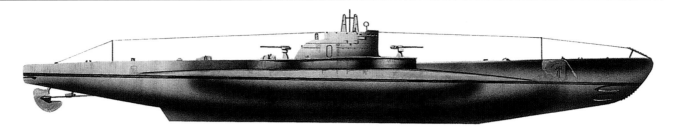

Specifications

Crew: 57

Powerplant: Twin screw diesel engines; electric
    motors

Max Speed: Surfaced: 17.4 knots; Submerged:
    8 knots

Surface Range: 4750km (2560nm) at 17 knots

Displacement: Surfaced: 1080 tonnes (1063

tons); Submerged: 1338 tonnes (1317 tons)

Dimensions (length/beam/draught): 73m x 7.2m
    x 5m (239ft 6in x 23ft 8in x 16ft 5in)

Commissioned: November 1937

Armament: Eight 533mm (21in) torpedo tubes;
    two 100mm (3.9in) guns

▲ Dandolo

Italian Navy, patrol submarine

As with numerous other Italian classes, 'stability bulges' were added to the single hull to improve performance on diving and surfacing, but the Marcello class handled well both on the surface and submerged. All were built by CRDA at Monfalcone.

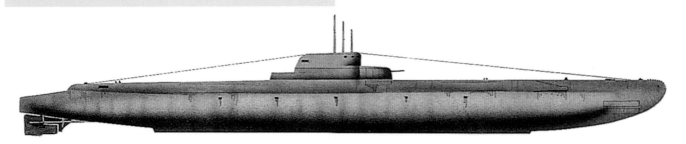

Specifications

Crew: 56

Powerplant: Twin screw diesel; electric motors

Max Speed: Surfaced: 15 knots; Submerged:
    8 knots

Surface Range: 13,300km (7169nm) at 10 knots

Displacement: Surfaced: 1117 tonnes (1100

tons); Submerged: 1496 tonnes (1473 tons)

Dimensions (length/beam/draught): 84m x 6.7m
    x 4m (275ft 7in x 22ft 13ft 1in)

Commissioned: 1938

Armament: 12 550mm (21.7in) torpedo tubes;
    one 105mm (4in) gun

▲ Orzel

Polish Navy, patrol submarine

Poland had a five-strong submarine squadron in 1939, three Wilk class minelayers and two patrol boats. *Orzel*'s sister boat *Sep* escaped to Sweden and was interned. Similar to the Dutch O19 class, they were excellent boats, of welded construction with double hulls and powered by two Sulzer 6QD42 six-cylinder diesels and two Brown-Boveri electric motors.

Spanish Civil War
1936–39

The conflict in Spain between Nationalist and Republican forces provided Italy and Germany with opportunities to test their new submarines in action.

WHEN CIVIL WAR BEGAN in July 1936, the Spanish Navy had 12 submarines, 6 B-class dating from from 1921–23 and six more modern C-class, commissioned in 1936. All were in the Republic's hands, though little effective use was made of them. Help was sought by the Nationalists from the sympathetic governments of Italy and Germany. German aid came in late 1936 with Operation Ursula. Two new submarines, U-33 and U-34, were sent to Spain. On 12 December, U-34 sank the Spanish C-3, but soon afterwards both U-boats were recalled. Four Italian submarines, *Iride* and *Onice* of the *Perla* class (temporarily given Spanish names, *Gonsales Lopes* and *Aquilar Tablada*), and *Galileo Galilei* and *Galileo Ferraris* of the Archimede class, were hired out to the Nationalists. In addition, two other Archimede class boats, *Archimede* and *Evangelista Torricelli*, were sold to the Nationalists and renamed *General Sanjurjo* and *General Mola*.

Evangelista Torricelli was commissioned in 1934 and secretly sold to the Nationalist forces in Spain in 1937. While still under Italian colours, *Torricelli* disabled the Spanish cruiser *Miguel de Cervantes* in 1937; as *General Mola* it sank the merchant ship *Ciudad de Barcelona* in May 1937 and the British *Endymion* in January 1938. Spanish neutrality in World War II helped extend their longevity and *General Mola* was not decommissioned until 1958.

Many other Italian submarines served on short deployments. Among them was *Enrico Toti* of the

Balilla class, launched in 1928, a sister-ship of *Domenico Millelire*. *Toti* and the others were too large to be effective in off-shore patrolling, being designed for long-range transit to Italy's colonies in northeast Africa. During World War II it sank a British submarine in a surface gun battle, on 15 October 1940, now thought to be HMS *Triad*, though often said to be HMS *Rainbow*, which was more probably lost through collision at the same time. Laid up in April 1943, *Toti* saw no further service.

Also involved off Spain were all four boats of the Mameli class, including *Giovanni da Procida*. Medium-sized, they were better suited to the task, although their

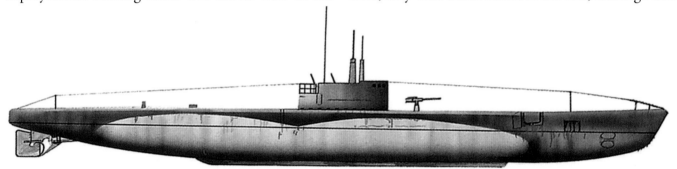

▲ **Enrico Toti**

Italian Navy, patrol submarine, Mediterranean, 1940

The only Italian submarine to sink a Royal Navy submarine in World War II, *Toti* was already quite elderly on 15 October 1940. It was attached to the 40th Squadron of the 4th Submarine Group at Taranto, making patrols into the Ionian Sea. After its exploit, it was used as a training boat.

Specifications

Crew: 76	tons); Submerged: 1934 tonnes (1904 tons)
Powerplant: Twin screw diesels; electric motors	Dimensions (length/beam/draught): 87.7m x
Max Speed: Surfaced: 17.5 knots; Submerged:	7.8m x 4.7m (288ft x 25ft 7in x 15ft 5in)
9 knots	Commissioned: April 1928
Surface Range: 7041km (3800nm) at 10 knots	Armament: Six 533mm (21in) torpedo tubes;
Displacement: Surfaced: 1473 tonnes (1450	one 120mm (4.7in) gun

SUBMARINES OF THE SPANISH CIVIL WAR: NATIONALIST FORCES

Class	Name	Note
Archimede (Italian)	*General Mola* (ex *Archimede*)	Purchased 1937
	General Sanjurjo (ex *Evangelista Torricelli*)	Purchased 1937
	General Mola II (ex *Galileo Galilei*)	Hired 1937–38
	General Sanjurjo II (ex *Galileo Torricelli*)	Hired 1937–38
Perla (Italian)	*Gonsalez Lopez* (ex-*Iride*)	Hired 1937–38
	Aguilar Tablada (ex-*Onice*)	Hired 1937–38
Type VII (German)	U-33	Operation Ursula, 1936
	U-34	Operation Ursula, 1936

SUBMARINES OF THE SPANISH CIVIL WAR: REPUBLICAN FORCES

Class	Built	Name	Note
B	1921–23	1	Scuttled April 1939
		2	Survived war
		3	Scuttled April 1939
		4	Scuttled April 1939
		5	Sunk 12 October 1936
		6	Sunk 19 September 1936
C	1927–29	1	Sunk 9 November 1936
		2	Not involved in war
		3	Sunk 21 December 1936
		4	Not involved in war
		5	Lost December 1936
		6	Scuttled November 1937

design, based on World War I U-boats, was showing its age. After its Spanish deployment, *Giovanni da Procida* next saw active service in June 1940, in the unsuccessful effort to stop the transfer of French war materiel and personnel to North Africa in June 1940, after the French surrender. It was deployed in the eastern Mediterranean from August 1940 and, after the armistice with Italy, it was eventually brought into in a US anti-submarine warfare training programme in 1943–44 along with eight other Italian submarines.

The Italian submarines sank a number of ships of other nations as well as Spanish vessels, causing an international outcry. Other naval powers, especially Britain and France, instituted coastal surface patrols, and there were a number of close encounters between surface ships and submerged submarines. Germany joined in this, sending U-boats again, though with 'peacekeeping' intention. Around 15 U-boats made 47 patrols.

By the end of the war on 1 April 1939, the Republican submarine fleet was reduced to eight, through combat or scuttling. Only one B-class remained, and three C-class.

The Spanish Civil War was yet another demonstration of the power of submarines as commerce raiders. It also showed up the limitations of ASDIC in the failure of British patrol vessels to locate, identify or stop the activities of the Italian submarines. But this was a very small-scale rehearsal for things soon to come.

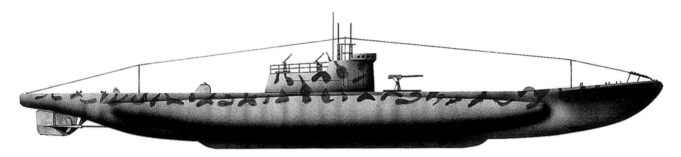

▲ Giovanni da Procida

Italian Navy, patrol submarine

The Mameli class, based partly on World War I U-boats, was designed by the Cavallini Bureau, with a cylindrical hull that could reach greater depths than previous Italian types. Its saddle-tank design was a model for the Archimede and Brin classes, though there was much experimentation with bow and stern shapes.

Specifications

Crew: 49	Submerged: 1026 tonnes (1010 tons)
Powerplant: Twin shaft diesel engines; electric motors	Dimensions (length/beam/draught): 64.6m x 6.5m x 4.3m (212ft x 21ft 4in x 14ft)
Max Speed: Surfaced: 17 knots ; Submerged: 7 knots	Commissioned: April 1928
Surface Range: 5930km (3200nm) at 10 knots	Armament: Six 533mm (21in) torpedo tubes; one 102mm (4in) gun
Displacement: Surfaced: 843 tonnes (830 tons);	

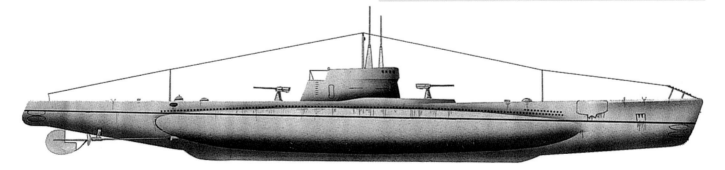

Specifications

Crew: 55	Submerged: 1026 tonnes (1010 tons)
Powerplant: Twin shaft diesel engines; electric motors	Dimensions (length/beam/draught): 64.6m x 6.5m x 4.3m (212ft x 21ft 4in x 14ft)
Max Speed: Surfaced: 17 knots; Submerged: 7 knots	Commissioned: April 1934
Surface Range: 5930km (3200nm) at 10 knots	Armament: Six 533mm (21in) torpedo tubes; one 102mm (4in) gun
Displacement: Surfaced: 843 tonnes (830 tons);	

▲ General Mola

Spanish Navy (ex-Italian), patrol submarine

General Mola and *General Sanjurjo* outlasted all their Italian sister boats, which, if they survived World War II, were stricken with other Italian naval units in 1948. The two ex-Archimede class boats made patrols in Spanish waters during World War II, with large neutrality symbols on the conning towers. They remained on the active list until September 1959, when both were decommissioned.

Chapter 3

World War II: 1939–45

The submarines of 1939 were not very different in the essentials to their predecessors of 20 years before. Indeed, many of them were still of World War I design. All that was to change swiftly, however, as a deadly struggle was waged in and below the world's seas. Would Hitler's wolfpacks succeed where the Kaiser's raiders had failed? In Germany, construction of submarines reached unprecedented levels, but could not match the ever-increasing losses. Yet even as the Battle of the Atlantic was won by the Allies, Germany was developing new submarines far superior to any yet built, and another submarine war was being fought in the vastness of the Pacific, as the Japanese were gradually forced back from their early conquests.

◀ U-47

The close-up shot of U-47's conning tower shows many details, including the port-side navigation light, the hardwood deck planking, the free-flooding holes, and the casing of the airtrunk feeding air to the diesel engines.

Preparations for war

Twenty-six navies possessed a total of 777 submarines in September 1939. Those with more than 10 were Denmark (11), France (77), Germany (65), Great Britain (69), Italy (107), the Netherlands (29), Sweden (24), the Soviet Union (about 150), United States (100), Japan (65).

THE OTHER SUBMARINE-OWNING nations were Argentina (3), Brazil (4), Estonia (2), Finland (5), Greece (6), Latvia (2), Norway (9), Peru (5), Poland (5), Portugal (4), Romania (1), Siam (Thailand) (4), Spain (9), Turkey (9), Yugoslavia (4). Some of these countries would preserve neutrality, but the great majority of existing submarines, plus many yet unbuilt, would be caught up in the global battles to come.

In the larger navies, the submarine arm was established as a separately run command under a flag officer. Submarine strength was grouped in flotillas, each with its own senior officer. Flotilla size was usually from eight to 10 boats. Submarines required a range of facilities and were normally based only at large naval depots. Even before World War I, the submarine tender or depot ship had been introduced,

at first a converted merchant vessel, which could carry submarine stores and supplies and provide accommodation and messing-space for crews – it was impossible for a submarine crew to inhabit their boat in dock, as there were not enough bunks when the watch system was not in use.

The British HMS *Maidstone*, commissioned in May 1938, was a typical purpose-built depot ship with workshops, auxiliary engines, laundries, medical facilities and salvage equipment, as well as ammunition (100 torpedoes). It could service nine submarines and was intended to accompany a flotilla to remote locations. In World War II, *Maidstone* served in the Mediterranean, the Far East and South Africa. Britain, Japan and the United States all used tenders to support submarine operations.

▲ **HMS *United* (P44)**

The Royal Navy produced 51 boats of the U-class. Effective combat boats, the U-class suffered heavy losses. Direction-finding and radar antennas are noticeable. Also in the picture are a minesweeper and barrage balloon.

▲ **Battle sub**
Surcouf after its hand-over to the Free French, in the Firth of Clyde, near Faslane, Scotland, late 1940.

By 1939, submarines were in many ways vastly more capable of effective combat than they had been in 1918. After the experiments of the 1920s, it was generally accepted that the medium-sized patrol-attack boat was the most versatile and useful type, and it formed the backbone of the European submarine fleets. They could fire torpedo salvoes with large warheads that could sink any battleship. Radio communication enabled close direction of operations. Mechanical reliability of diesel engines, whether two- or four-stroke, had greatly improved. Stronger construction and design improvements had made crash diving remarkably fast, and new submarines could now operate to depths of around 100m (330ft).

Some form of underwater detection apparatus was in use by all large navies, though this was, of course, a threat as well as an asset to submarine operation.

The least progress had been made with surface endurance, and speeds both surfaced and submerged remained slow. Manoeuvring and maintaining trim while submerged was still a difficult business, and underwater endurance time, though improved, was still limited.

Though the 533mm (21in) torpedo was now standard, the quality of torpedoes varied greatly between the different navies. The United States in particular suffered badly from defective torpedoes in the the first year of the Pacific War. The most effective were those of the Japanese and the Italians. In 1939, all torpedoes were still straight-running, which meant the submarine had to be lined up to fire. The sophistication and lethal power of torpedoes was greatly increased in the course of the war. Mine-design also was worked on to enable detonation at greater depths.

Submarine deployment
1939-40

Events began to move quickly in the course of 1940. Germany established a strong strategic position by overcoming Norway and France, opening the Atlantic to U-boat raids.

GERMANY'S FAST VICTORIES along the Atlantic seaboard quickly neutralized France's naval forces and immediately threatened Britain's supply lines with North America.

France

Twenty-three new submarines were ordered or under construction in France in September 1939. When the German *Blitzkrieg* was launched in June 1940, submarines were based at Cherbourg (2nd, 12th and part of the 16th Submarine Divisions); Brest (6th, 8th, 13th, 16th and 18th Divisions, also the unique *Surcouf*); and Toulon (1st, 15th, 17th, 19th and 21st). The strength of a division varied between two and six boats. In North Africa, *Oran* had the 14th and 18th; at Bizerta were boats from the 1st, also the 3rd, 4th, 7th, 9th and 20th. The 11th was at Sousse, Tunisia; some of the 3rd and all of the 10th were at Beirut. There were also two 1st Submarine Division boats at Dakar in Senegal.

When German forces entered Toulon, France's main submarine base, in November 1942, 12 submarines were undergoing refit. Eleven were scuttled, but *Casabianca* slipped out and joined the Free French forces in North Africa, and had an adventurous wartime career in seven secret missions, bringing agents, weapons and supplies to Corsica and the southern French coast until 1944. *Casabianca* was one of the third series of Redoutable-class submarines, launched at Nantes in February 1935, with a diesel power rating of 8600hp (6413kW) and a surface speed of 20 knots. The only third-series boat to survive the war, it was sent to the United States for a refit in 1944 after being hit in a blue-on-blue air attack, and was finally stricken in 1952.

Germany

By the summer of 1939, the German Navy had 57 U-boats, of which 46 were operational, with the majority being Type II coastal boats, allocated to seven flotillas. An unprecedented building programme was about to begin that sent the numbers rising steadily, but not until between August 1942 and August 1943 would there be 100 U-boats at sea at any one time.

As in 1914, the U-boats announced their presence in an emphatic way. On the first day of the war, U-30, one of the first Type VII boats, sank the liner

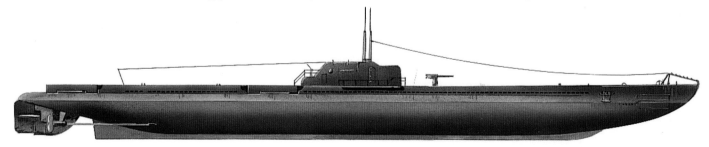

▲ **Casabianca**

French Navy, patrol submarine, Mediterranean 1942

First based at Brest with the 2nd Division, *Casabianca* made two wartime patrols off Norway in 1940, then was deployed to Dakar in Senegal until October 1941. After escaping Toulon, it reached Algiers on 30 November 1942, and operated with the 8th Royal Navy Flotilla from Oran, sinking an Axis ASW patrol vessel.

Specifications

Crew: 61

Powerplant: Two twin-shaft diesel engines; two electric motors

Max Speed: Surfaced: 17–20 knots; Submerged: 10 knots

Surface Range: 18,530km (10,000nm) at 10 knots

Displacement: Surfaced: 1595 tonnes (1570 tons);

Submerged: 2117 tonnes (2084 tons)

Dimensions (length/beam/draught): 92.3m x 8.2m x 4.7m (210ft x 18ft 7in x 10ft 9in)

Commissioned: February 1935

Armament: Nine 550mm (21.7in) and two 400mm (15.7in) torpedo tubes; one 100mm (3.9in) gun

▲ Torpedo loading

RN submariners loading a torpedo at the Malta naval base. The Mark VIII was by far the most frequently used torpedo type by the British in World War II.

Athenia without warning. Another Type VIIA, U-29, sank the British aircraft carrier HMS *Courageous* off Ireland on 17 September 1939, and a Type VIIB, U-47, made a daring entry into the Scapa Flow anchorage and sank the battleship HMS *Royal Oak*, on 14 October. From mid-1940, the main operational bases were mostly outside Germany, though Kiel was always the prime base. At the end of 1940, U-boats were operating from major bases at Lorient, St Nazaire, Brest and La Pallice in France, and Bergen, Trondheim and Kristiansand in Norway.

The 16-strong Type IID, introduced from June 1940, was the most advanced version of Type II, with supplementary saddle tanks giving it a range almost double that of the original IIA, enabling it to patrol beyond the British Isles. Like all Type IIs, it was hampered by limited torpedo capacity, carrying

only six. As the size of the U-boat fleet grew, the Type IIs were generally used as training boats. The *Reichsmarine*'s urgent need for more and bigger submarines was met by the Type VII. By 1937, it was already being modified, and Type VIIB had twin rudders, greatly helping manoeuvrability, and with the stern tube placed between them inside the pressure hull, allowing for submerged reloading.

The surrender of France in June 1940 made it possible for Germany to base U-boats on the French Atlantic coast, with no need to pass repeatedly through the heavily guarded English Channel or the North Sea. At Brest, Lorient, St Nazaire and La Pallice, massive concrete 'pens' were built to house the three main U-boat combat flotillas.

This inaugurated the 'Happy Time' – June 1940 to February 1941 – when with little interference, the U-boats raided freely into the Atlantic. From June to October they sank 270 Allied ships. The spoils were shared by Type IX boats, which were bigger and with a greater range, introduced in August 1938 when U-37 was commissioned.

U-505, commissioned in August 1941, was one of 54 Type IXC boats, with larger fuel tanks giving a range of 12,660 miles (20,370km). Powered by two supercharged nine-cylinder diesels, it made 18.3 knots on the surface. Having sunk eight ships on previous patrols, U-505 was captured intact on 4 June 1944 in the South Atlantic by destroyers from an American task force using HF/DF (high frequency direction-finding) and supported by air reconnaissance; an indication of how intense the U-boat hunt had become. Its secret cipher code books were retrieved and delivered to the Decryption Establishment at Bletchley Park, England. In all, 191 IX-class boats were built, in six sub-classes, of which IXC and IXC40 combined made up 141. IXC40 was virtually identical to IXC, but slightly larger and with an extra 740km (460-mile) range.

Great Britain

The Royal Navy had six operational submarine squadrons in September 1939. The 1st, with nine boats, was at Malta; the 2nd with 10 boats, at Dundee; the 4th, with 16 boats, was with the China fleet at Hong Kong; the 5th, with 11 boats, was at Portsmouth; the 6th, with six boats, at Blyth; and the 7th with two boats was at Freetown, Sierra Leone. Sixteen boats were in the North Sea, while the western side of the country had none. This distribution of forces would soon change.

The British T-class was intended to supersede the O-, P- and R-class submarines, and was built strictly within the London Treaty limits. The T-boats were built to operate in all major theatres of action, and eventually did so. Considering their overall size, it was remarkable that they should have incorporated 10 forward-facing torpedo-tubes, six internal and four externally mounted. This enabled them to fire a massive salvo, intended to destroy a large warship. Seventeen torpedoes were carried. Later T-class submarines had the midship tubes reversed to fire astern but, by this time, it was clear that commerce raiding and destruction of small escort vessels was a more regular task than trying to sink battleships.

Fifty-three were built between October 1937 and March 1942, in three groups: 15 in 1935–38, seven in 1939, and 31 in 1940–42. *Thistle* was one of the first group, launched in October 1937, with a riveted hull, divided into six watertight compartments. Like some previous British classes, the 100mm (4in) gun was set on a raised mounting.

Many of the class served in the Mediterranean, where their size was a disadvantage, making them too visible from the air. Sixteen were lost in the war years, and 13 Axis submarines were sunk by T-class boats. The 31 'Group 3' boats, with all-welded hulls, were retained after the war and modernized. Four went to the Royal Netherlands Navy and three to Israel (one, *Totem*, was lost in transit). The last T-class boats, much modernized and lengthened, were withdrawn in 1977 and 1978.

The Norway Campaign

Thistle was sunk off Norway by U-4 on 10 April 1940, during the failed effort to prevent German occupation. This was the first major submarine confrontation, with all available U-boats, including training craft, mobilized to support the invasion fleet, and 20 British submarines among the opposing forces. Though the Polish submarine *Orzel* sank a German transport ship on 8 April, and HMS *Sterlet* sank the gunnery training ship *Brummer* on 14 April, the British submarines achieved few successes in this campaign and were gradually forced away from the Norwegian coast by anti-submarine warfare (ASW) planes and trawlers.

Only one Norwegian submarine escaped to join up with the British forces. Nine U British submarines were lost off Norway between April and August 1940, only one to a U-boat, and four U-boats were sunk by air and surface ship attacks.

The Dutch Contribution

Until the commissioning of O-19 and O-20 in 1939, submarines of the Royal Netherlands Navy were designated as O, for service in home waters, and K, for service in the Dutch West and East Indies. When German forces overran the Netherlands in June 1940, 12 O-class and five K-class submarines joined the Royal Navy in Portsmouth and Singapore and were immediately deployed in British flotillas. The Dutch were the largest group of 'free' boats from defeated nations, which also included Greek, Norwegian, Free French and Polish vessels. O-19 and O-20 are of particular interest as the first submarines to be equipped with any form of the snorkel apparatus that

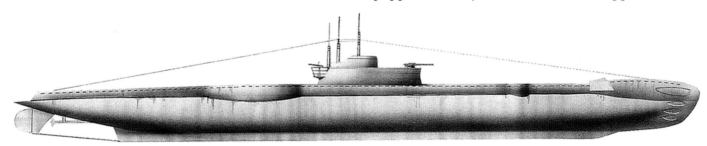

▲ Thistle

Royal Navy, T-class patrol submarine, North Sea, 1940

Commissioned on 4 July 1939, *Thistle* was patrolling off Stavanger when it fired torpedoes at the Type IIA *U-4*, but without success, and itself fell victim to *U-4*. Many modifications were made to the T-class, providing it with Type 267 and 291 radar for sea and air detection, in addition to the integral Type 129 ASDIC.

Specifications

Crew: 59	tons); Submerged: 1600 tonnes (1575 tons)
Powerplant: Twin screw diesel; electric motors	Dimensions (length/beam/draught): 80.8m x 8m
Max Speed: Surfaced: 15.25 knots; Submerged:	x 4.5m (265ft x 26ft 6in x 14ft 9in)
9 knots	Commissioned: October 1938
Surface Range: 7041km (3800nm) at 10 knots	Armament: 10 533mm (21in) torpedo tubes; one
Displacement: Surfaced: 1107 tonnes (1090	100mm (4in) gun

▲ **Marconi class**
Lead boat of Italy's Marconi class, *Guglielmo Marconi* was launched at Monfalcone on 27 July 1939. It disappeared in the Atlantic at the end of October 1941.

enabled the boat to run on its diesel engines while submerged. O-20, working from Singapore, was sunk in the South China Sea in December 1941 but O-19 survived until July 1945, when it grounded on a Pacific reef and had to be destroyed.

Italy

Italian submarine deployment had two main aspects: protection of the long domestic coastline and the islands; and maintaining connection with Italian colonial possessions in North and East Africa. With its existing fleet plus an ongoing building programme, it did not lack boats to fulfil these roles. Around 30 of its submarines were of a size and endurance for oceanic work, and 28 were despatched to the Atlantic from June 1940, to make Atlantic patrols in the latitudes south of Lisbon, from the base of Bordeaux. Eight other boats were in the Red Sea flotilla at Massawa. The remainder of the fleet was spread across Mediterranean bases, La Spezia, Naples, Messina, Taranto, Fiume, Tobruk and Leros.

Convoy attack and commerce raiding was the purpose of the four Ammiraglio Cagni-class submarines, laid down in September to October

1939. They mounted 14 torpedo tubes, though of 450mm (17.7in) calibre, considered adequate to deal with merchant vessels. Each boat carried 36 torpedoes, more than twice the capacity of most other submarines. The original high conning tower was designed for Indian Ocean conditions, but for Atlantic operations it was reduced to a lower German-style form.

Cagni, part of the Italian flotilla at Bordeaux in late 1942, sank a tanker and a Greek sloop. These were the *Regia Marina*'s largest attack submarines, but were not hugely successful. *Cagni* accounted for less than 10,000 gross registered tonnage (GRT) of Allied shipping in two long patrols and, like other large boats, it was converted in 1943 to a transport role. It surrendered at Durban in September 1943. Two Cagni class boats were sunk by British U-class submarines and a third was scuttled. *Cagni* was the only member of the class to survive the war, and was broken up in 1948.

Japan

Still pursuing their decade-long objective of building up a force of long-range scouting submarines and fleet supports, the Japanese introduced the B1 Type or I-15 class in 1939. These 20 large boats were of streamlined design, with a rounded seaplane hangar set forward of the conning tower, carrying a Yokosuka E14Y 'Glen' floatplane. Twin diesels produced 12,400hp (9200kW), giving a best surface speed of 23.5 knots, and operating range was 26,000km (16,155 miles). This enabled them to undertake trans-Pacific operations. I-17 and I-25 shelled land installations at Santa Barbara, California and Fort Stevens, Oregon, respectively. In August 1942, I-25's floatplane dropped two bombs on the Oregon mainland, starting a forest fire.

As the progress of the war increasingly showed the faulty nature of the Japanese submarine strategy,

some members had the hangar removed and replaced by a second 140mm (5.5in) gun to operate as attack submarines; and I-36 and I-37 were modified to carry Kaiten manned torpedoes. Only one of the I-15-class survived the war; I-15 itself was sunk on 14 December 1942. For all its size and firepower, it had failed to sink any Allied vessel.

The Soviet Union

By 1939, the Soviet Union had more submarines than any other country, though more than half were of the small M-class, only useful for inshore work and harbour protection: something the Soviets took seriously. The Soviet Navy had to dispose its forces among the Baltic, Black Sea, Northern and Pacific

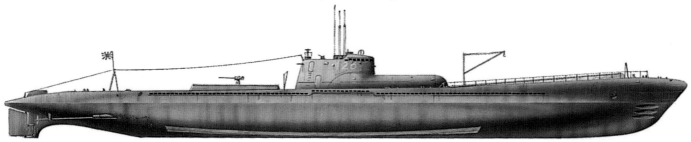

▲ I-15

Imperial Japanese Navy, Type B-1 patrol submarine, Pacific, 1942

In the Guadalcanal battles of August 1942, the Japanese deployed the big submarines in a screen in advance of the fleet, with the senior officer in a command boat. Co-ordination was difficult, but either I-15 or I-19 hit the battleship *North Carolina* with a torpedo and I-15 narrowly missed USS *Washington*.

Specifications

Crew: 100	Submerged: 3713 tonnes (3654 tons)
Powerplant: Twin shaft diesel; electric motors	Dimensions (length/beam/draught): 102.5m x
Max Speed: Surfaced: 23.5 knots; Submerged:	9.3m x 5.1m (336ft x 30ft 6in x 16ft 9in)
8 knots	Commissioned: March 1939
Surface Range: 45,189km (24,400nm) at 10 knots	Armament: Six 533mm (21in) torpedo tubes; one
Displacement: Surfaced: 2625 tonnes (2584 tons);	140mm (5.5in) and two 25mm (0.96in) AA guns

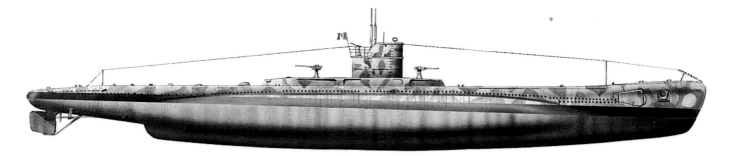

Specifications

Crew: 85	Submerged: 1707 tonnes (1680 tons)
Powerplant: Two diesel engines, two electric	Dimensions (length/beam/draught): 87.9m x
motors	7.76m x 5.72m (200ft 5in x 17ft 7in x 13ft)
Max Speed: Surfaced: 17 knots; Submerged:	Commissioned: July 1940
9 knots	Armament: 14 450mm (17.7in) torpedo tubes; two
Surface Range: 22,236km (12,000nm) at 11 knots	100mm (3.9in) guns
Displacement: Surfaced: 1528 tonnes (1504 tons);	

▲ Ammiraglio Cagni

Italian Navy, long-range patrol submarine, South Atlantic, 1943

Built at Monfalcone to a Bernardis design, this boat made some of the longest patrols of any World War II submarine, operating into the South Atlantic for up to 135 days. After surrendering at Durban, it returned to Italy in January 1944 and was used as a training boat by the Allied forces at Palermo.

fleets. These formed a set of very different undersea environments for submarines, in terms of temperature range, salinity, currents and depths, but the planners appear to have allocated vessels to bases and switched them without great regard for these aspects.

The Soviet plans of the later 1920s began to bear fruit with the construction of a substantial fleet, beginning with the Dekabrist class or Series I, of which six were built from 1927. The second design was the L- or Leninets class of minelaying submarine, inaugurated with six boats in 1931–32, followed by six in 1935–36, seven in 1937–38 and five in 1939–40. The first group were shared between the Black Sea and Baltic fleets, the second was all with the Pacific fleet, and the others were distributed between the Baltic, Black Sea, and Northern fleets. Some historians have suggested that some features were copied from the British L-55, sunk in the Baltic in 1919, salvaged and reinstated two years later, and certainly the Soviet class, though double-hulled, also had a British-style saddle ballast-tank, unlike the preceding double-hulled *Dekabrist*.

They were among the larger Soviet submarines, and the first group were distinctly underpowered, with German diesels of 2200hp (1600kW), replaced from Group 2 on with engines of 4200hp (3100kW). Groups 3 and 4 also had two stern-mounted torpedo tubes fitted. They carried 20 mines in stern galleries, modelled on the pioneer Krab design of the 1900s. Four L-class boats were lost during World War II; and the survivors were decommissioned between 1956 and 1963.

BRITISH SUBMARINE CLASSES, 1939–45			
Class	Number	Launched	Note
S	50	1939–45	Pre-war class, North Sea/coastal
T	38	1940–45	Ocean-going; pre-war design
U	46	1939–	North Sea, Mediterranean
P611	4	1940	Turkish order transferred to RN
V	22	1941–44	Improved U-class
X-craft	20	1942	Midget type
XE	12		Midget type
Amphion	16	1943–45	Only 2 completed by May 1945

Wilhelm Gustloff and Goya

As the Red Army advanced towards the Baltic coast, refugees both civilian and military left German-held ports on commandeered transport ships. One of these, the former cruise-liner *Wilhelm Gustloff*, was sunk on 30 January 1945 by the Shchuka class submarine S-13, with a loss of life estimated to exceed 9000.

Another packed vessel, the 5314-tonne (5230-ton) *Goya*, was sunk in the Baltic by torpedoes from L-3 on 16 April. Estimates of the number on board range from 6100 to 7000: only 183 survived. These sinkings rank as the greatest single events of human destruction yet caused by submarines.

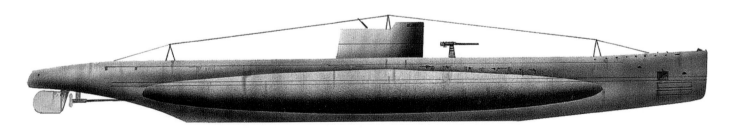

Specifications

Crew: 50

Powerplant: Twin screw diesel; electric motors

Max Speed: Surfaced: 15 knots; Submerged: 9 knots

Surface Range: 11,112km (6000nm) at 9 knots

Displacement: Surfaced: 1219 tonnes (1200 tons); Submerged: 1574 tonnes (1550 tons)

Dimensions (length/beam/draught): 81m x 7.5m x 4.8m (265ft 9in x 24ft 7in x 15ft 9in)

Commissioned: July 1931

Armament: Six 533mm (21in) torpedo tubes; one 100mm (3.9in) gun

▲ **L-3**

Soviet Navy, patrol submarine/minelayer, Baltic Sea 1944–45

Submarine war in the Baltic Sea was dominated by extensive minefields and massive nets, often many miles long, set by the Germans and Finns, which the Soviet boats had to skirt. Meanwhile, until the end of 1944, the surface was dominated by German ships. L-3's conning tower has been preserved as a memorial.

The Mediterranean and Black Seas
1940–45

The Mediterranean, lined on its south coast by French and Italian colonies and with the British protectorate of Egypt at the east end, was a strategic sea, made even more so as it was the passage to the Suez Canal and the short route to India and Africa.

AXIS POSSESSION OF SUEZ would be a major blow to the Allied war effort. When hostilities with Italy began in June 1940, the Royal Navy was in effective control of the eastern and western Mediterranean, with the Italians in control of the central area. With aircraft able to overfly any part, the role of submarines was all the more important, although they were dangerously visible at low depths.

Early Deployment

Italy had 49 submarines in three main groups, a western one operating between Gibraltar and Siciliy, a second centred in the Gulf of Genoa, and the third between Greece and Alexandria. The Royal Navy moved 10 submarines to Alexandria in 1940 and further deployments followed, though between surface ships and mines, nine were sunk by the end of 1940. Five Greek boats joined the British squadron, and a flotilla of 10 U-class boats were based at Malta from early 1941, and these smaller craft turned out to be very effective performers in the Mediterranean. In June 1941, 25 British and

ITALIAN SUBMARINE CLASSES, 1939–45			
Class	Number	Launched	Note
CA1-2	2	1938–39	Midget sub
Liuzzi	4	1939–40	Larger version of pre-war Brin class
Marconi	6	1939–40	Ocean-going
Cagni	4	1940	Ocean-going; largest Italian WWII sub
Acciaio	13	1941–42	Last survivor discarded 1966
CB	21	1941–43	Midget sub; 9 completed after Sep 1943
CA3-4	2	1942	Modified CA1; scuttled 1943
Flutto Type 1	9	1942–43	12 originally ordered
Flutto Type 2	3	1944	15 originally ordered
Romolo	2	1943	Transport sub; 12 originally ordered
S1	11	1943	Ex-U-boats repossessed by Germany 1943

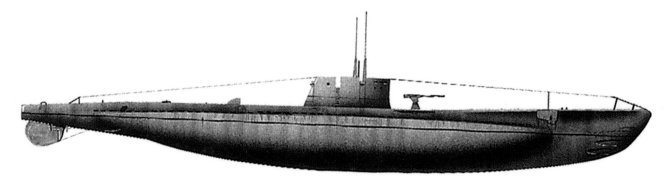

Specifications

Crew: 45

Powerplant: Twin screw diesel engines; electric motors

Max Speed: Surfaced: 14 knots; Submerged: 8 knots

Surface Range: 4076km (2200nm) at 10 knots

Displacement: Surfaced: 690 tonnes (680 tons);

Submerged: 861 tonnes (848 tons)

Dimensions (length/beam/draught): 60m x 6.5m x 4m (197ft 6in x 21ft x 13ft)

Commissioned: November 1936

Armament: Six 533mm (21in) torpedo tubes; one 100mm (3.9in) gun

▲ **Dagabur**

Italian Navy, patrol submarine, Mediterranean/Red Sea, 1941

Built at the Tosi yard, Taranto, *Dagabur* was completed in April 1937. Several of the Adua class had their conning towers reduced in size during the war, and two, *Gondar* and *Sciré*, were fitted with cylindrical containers for three SLC manned torpedoes. Only one of the class, *Alagi*, survived the war, though three were sold to Brazil in 1937.

Allied boats were on service, but failed to do more than slightly hinder the transfer of the *Afrika Korps* to North Africa. Sixty-nine Axis ships were sunk by submarines, with a GRT of 305,000 during 1941. By the end of 1941, despite losses, there were 28 Allied submarines in the Mediterranean.

For most of the year only 10 Italian submarines had been operational, but from September 10 U-boats entered this theatre, and by the end of the year they had put Britain's eastern Mediterranean battle squadron out of action, with the loss of the carrier *Ark Royal* and the sinking or disabling (with Italian help) of three battleships and a cruiser. In April 1943, the British flotilla moved from Malta to Alexandria, but continuing losses held the Allied number down to 12 in April 1942, compared to 16 U-boats plus the Italians. By summer, reinforcements had brought the numbers up to 23 British boats. Further temporary reinforcements arrived to support the Allied landings in North Africa in October 1942.

The constant crossings of the Mediterranean by Axis supply convoys offered many attack opportunities but they were normally heavily escorted, and Allied forces never succeeded in more than partial disruption, though in some cases three quarters of a convoy's strength was sunk. In September 1943, the Italian war effort collapsed and an armistice was sought, but U-boats remained highly active.

Submarine Actions

Dagabur, completed in 1937, was one of 17 Adua-class boats, very similar to the Perla class, but of more restricted range, and able to go slightly deeper, to 80m (262ft). *Dagabur* attacked the cruiser HMS *Bonaventure* on 30 March 1941, but the Perla-class *Ambra* successfully sank it. As the Malta-bound convoy of Operation Pedestal ploughed its way eastwards in August 1942, *Dagabur* was among the forces sent to prevent it. On 12 August, the destroyer HMS *Wolverine*, having located it on the surface through Type 271 radar, charged at a full 27 knots and rammed *Dagabur*, sinking it instantly.

A much larger boat was *Remo*, one of only two completed submarines of its class, intended to form 12 cargo-carrying long-range boats between Europe and Japan. Cargo capacity was 610 tonnes (600 tons). Its limited armament was intended for self-defence. *Remo* never got very far, being sunk in

the Gulf of Taranto by the U-class HMS *United* on 15 July 1943.

Flutto was the lead boat of eight medium-range submarines (four others were cancelled or uncompleted) intended to form part of a large wartime building programme, though two others, *Tritone* and *Gorgo*, were completed before it. By now, Italian conning towers had a lower profile. During the Allied landings on Sicily, *Flutto* was operating in the Straits of Messina, when it was sunk on 11 July 1943 by three British motor torpedo boats, one of six Italian submarines sunk in the same week. One of the Flutto class, *Marea*, was involved in secret intelligence missions on the Italian coast in November to December 1943, on behalf of the Allies.

Midget Submarines

Midget submarines had always been a specialism of the Italian Navy, and semi-submersible 'human torpedoes' manned by frogmen, deployed from the specially modified Adua class submarine *Scirè*, made several attempts on shipping at Gibraltar, and seriously damaged the British battleships *Valiant* and *Queen Elizabeth* in Alexandria harbour in December 1941. Between June 1940 and September 1943, Italian underwater craft and explosive motor torpedo boats sank seven merchant vessels and five warships.

During the war, the CB midget class, intended as an anti-submarine weapon, was designed. Of 72 planned, only 22 were laid down, with six built in January to May 1941 and transferred to the Black Sea in early 1942, based at Yalta. CB2 has been credited with the torpedoing of a Soviet submarine, *Shch-208*, on 18 June 1942, though Soviet records ascribe the loss to a mine in August. With the Italian surrender the CBs passed into Romanian hands and were scuttled in 1944. A further 16 were wholly or partially completed in 1943; five were surrendered to Great Britain, the others were taken over by the German Navy. None of these saw active service, as far as is known, though CB20 passed to the post-war Yugoslav Navy and remained in service until 1959.

U-boats in the Med

Germany's 23rd U-boat Flotilla was formed at Salamis, Greece, on 11 September 1941, with nine boats, three Type VIIB and six VIIC, moved from

Lorient. U-331 sank the British battleship *Barham* on 25 November, but the U-boat deployment was not a general success. The 23rd Flotilla was merged into the larger 29th, based first at La Spezia, Italy, then Toulon, France.

In all, 68 U-boats were sent to the Mediterranean, against the wishes of Dönitz; none survived the war. A small contingent of Type II coastal U-boats, six in all, were transported to the Black Sea as the 30th Flotilla, based at Constanta, Romania, and disturbing the Soviet hegemony of that water; one was sunk by aircraft and the rest were scuttled,

in August to September 1944. U-73 (Type VIIB), commissioned on 30 September 1940, was stationed with the 7th Flotilla at St Nazaire before transferring to the Mediterranean in January 1942 to join the 29th Flotilla at Salamis. Five other Type VIIBs, known as the Goeben group, were deployed there around this time. The aim was to assist the Afrika Korps by cutting off the British supply line between Alexandria and Tobruk. On 11 August 1942, U-73 made a major contribution by sinking the carrier HMS *Eagle*, with four torpedoes. It was sunk by American destroyers on 16 December 1943.

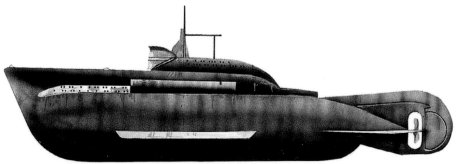

Specifications

Crew: 4

Powerplant: Single screw diesel; one electric motor

Max Speed: Surfaced: 7.5 knots; Submerged: 6.6 knots

Surface Range: 2660km (1434nm) at 5 knots

Displacement: Surfaced: 25 tonnes (24.9 tons); Submerged: 36 tonnes (35.9 tons)

Dimensions (length/beam/draught): 15m x 3m x 2m (49ft 3in x 9ft 10in x 6ft 9in)

Commissioned: August 1943

Armament: Two 450mm (17.7in) torpedoes in external canisters

▲ CB12

Italian Navy, midget submarines, Black Sea, 1942

These were built far inland, in Milan by Caproni Toliedo, but could be moved on special rail trucks. The torpedoes were mounted in external collars. Maximum diving depth was 55m (180ft), and they were equipped to carry 10 man-days of provisions. They were of very similar dimensions to the British X-boats, and, though still slow-speed, were slightly faster.

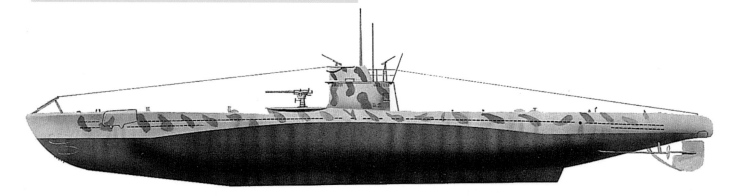

▲ Flutto

Italian Navy, patrol submarine, 1942

Completed in March 1943, *Flutto* was one of only three of its class to be engaged in action; all were lost. Two were fitted with cylinders for manned torpedoes, set alongside the tower and not replacing the gun as happened with the Adua class. After the war, *Nautilo* was passed to the Yugoslav Navy, and *Marea* to the Soviets.

Specifications

Crew: 50

Powerplant: Twin screw diesel engines; electric motors

Max Speed: Surfaced: 16 knots; Submerged: 7 knots

Surface Range: 10,000km (5400nm) at 8 knots

Displacement: Surfaced: 973 tonnes (958 tons); Submerged: 1189 tonnes (1170 tons)

Dimensions (length/beam/draught): 63.2m x 7m x 4.9m (207ft x 23ft x 16ft)

Commissioned: November 1942

Armament: Six 533mm (21in) torpedo tubes; one 100mm (3.9in) gun

▲ **10th Submarine Flotilla**

In June 1941, the British submarines stationed at Lazzaretto Creek, Malta, were grouped as the 10th Submarine Flotilla, and the Lazzaretto itself was named HMS *Talbot*. The nearest submarine is HMS *Upholder*.

Black Sea Patrols

U-19 (Type IIB), commissioned on 16 January 1936, had had a distinguished record with the 1st Flotilla at Brest, sinking 14 merchant ships and one warship in the course of 20 patrols. In October 1942, it was assigned to the newly formed 30th Flotilla based at Constanza, Romania. The six boats, all Type IIB, had to be dismantled in order to be transferred to the Black Sea. The sections were transported by barge up the Elbe to Dresden, then overland to Linz on the Danube, where they were reassembled and made their own way down the Danube to Constanza.

Between 21 January 1943 and 10 September 1944, U-19 carried out 11 patrols. The U-boats had only limited success, though Soviet supremacy in the Black Sea was challenged. In August 1944,

Romania surrendered and the Constanza base was no longer tenable. U-19 was scuttled off the Turkish coast on 10 September. Apart from U-9, which was sunk by Soviet aircraft on 20 August, the other boats of the flotilla were also scuttled in August to September.

Numbers and Losses

Over a hundred British submarines, with 10 French, eight Greek, four Dutch and two Polish boats, were involved in Mediterranean operations, and usually between 20 and 30 at a time. Their contribution in hindering supplies to Axis armies in North Africa was a vital one, with more than a million tons of shipping sunk. Forty-five British submarines were lost in the Mediterranean, of which 22 probably

▲ HMS *Unbroken*

The crew of HMS *Unbroken* line the deck at Malta in the summer of 1942. Commissioned in January 1942, *Unbroken* was on loan to the Soviet Navy from 1944 to 1949.

succumbed to mines. Nineteen were sunk by surface ships, three by aircraft and only one by a submarine. Sixteen Italian and five German submarines were sunk by Allied submarines. Altogether, 136 Italian submarines were involved, but many had been converted to a transport role to help in getting supplies across. Sixty-six were lost in total, against 41 new boats completed during the time Italy was at war.

Sixty-two U-boats were deployed in the Mediterranean, though there were never more than 25 in action at any one time. Between them, they sank 95 ships, totalling some 500,000 GRT, and forced Allied ships to move in convoy. By sinking the British depot ship *Medway*, they seriously affected the Royal Navy's submarine operations. By the end of the war, all U-boats operating in the Mediterranean had been destroyed.

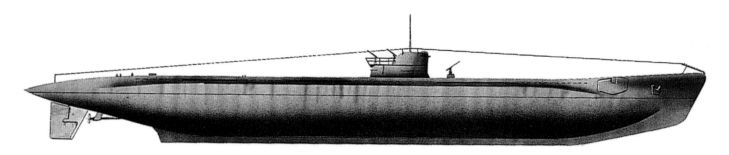

▲ Remo

Italian Navy, transport submarine, 1943

The large hull extended over four watertight holds. Two 450mm (17.7in) torpedo tubes were mounted in the bow. *Remo* was torpedoed while on the surface; *Romolo* was also sunk three days later. None of the other boats in the class were completed, though two, R-11 and R-12, were scuttled, refloated and used as oil storage hulks after the war.

Specifications

Crew: 63	tons); Submerged: 2648 tonnes (2606 tons)
Powerplant: Twin screws, diesel/electric motors	Dimensions (length/beam/draught): 70.7m x
Max Speed: Surfaced: 13 knots; Submerged:	7.8m x 5.3m (232ft x 25ft 9in x 17ft 6in)
6 knots	Commissioned: March 1943
Surface Range: 22,236km (12,000nm) at 9 knots	Armament: Two 450mm (17.7in) torpedo tubes;
Displacement: Surfaced: 2245 tonnes (2210	three 20mm (0.8in) guns

The Battle of the Atlantic
1940–43

A titanic struggle was fought out between Axis submarines and Allied convoy-protection craft. If the U-boats could prevent Allied ships from reaching Britain, the war would be as good as won.

A MASSIVE BUILDING PROGRAMME was launched by Germany from the end of 1939, concentrating primarily on the Type VII and Type IX, but for the first two years of the war the U-boat command remained chronically short of long-range boats. Only from three to five were out at any one time, and though their rate of success was high, it was mid-1940 before new commissionings exceeded losses.

The British began to use convoys immediately, but escorting forces were small. U-boat captains developed the tactic of surface night-attacks in order to avoid ASDIC detection, and for a time this, combined with radio contact and direction, and the wolfpack system, brought excellent results, even with only 10 or 12 U-boats active at any one

time. Realizing that they had been overconfident about the effectiveness of ASDIC, the British began to develop further countermeasures from the spring of 1941, by which time 13 new U-boats were being commissioned each month.

The British were able to gauge the qualities of a Type VIIC when U-570 was captured with its crew on its first patrol, south of Iceland, on 27 August 1941. It was incorporated into the Royal Navy as HMS *Graph*. Germany's declaration of war against the United States (11 December 1941) made it possible for the U-boats to operate in the former Pan-American Security Zone, and the first half of 1942 was known as a second 'Happy Time' for U-boats in the western Atlantic. By February

▲ **Under attack**
A Type IXB boat, probably U-106, as seen from one of two attacking Short Sunderland flying boats just before sinking in the Bay of Biscay, on 2 August 1943.

▲ Resupply mission

View from the tower: crewmen on deck wear security ropes as Type XIV U-459 resupplies U-boats at sea.

1942, they were active off the eastern coastline of Canada and the United States. Type IXC boats could strike as far away as Trinidad. Type VII, with shorter range, were refuelled and resupplied by the 10 submarines of Type XIV, capable of holding 439 tonnes (432 tons) of fuel. A Type XIV could enable 12 Type VII boats to stay operational for four weeks, or five Type IX boats for five weeks. Type XB minelayers were also used as supply boats.

Between January and July 1942, 681 ships, a GRT of around 3.5 million, were sunk for the loss of 11 U-boats. But convoys along the US coast, and ever-more intensive countermeasures, began turning the tide from mid-1942. In August 1942, 140 U-boats were operational, with 50 on patrol and 20 on passage at any time. Even though their numbers were still increasing, the attrition rate climbed faster, until by mid-1943 the destruction rate of U-boats exceeded the number being commissioned.

Until 1942, the depth charge was the only anti-submarine weapon, essentially a drum of high explosive with a hydrostatically set switch, which had been improved since World War I, with a weighted Mark IV version from the end of 1940 to speed up its descent. It could break a pressure hull at 6m (20ft) and force a submarine to surface from a detonation 12m (40ft) away. Later, improved depth charges and other devices were introduced. The 'Hedgehog', which threw a set of charges ahead of the pursuing vessel, was not very effective, as they exploded only on contact. By 1944, the 'Squid', a three-barrelled mortar, with an ASDIC link to explode at the correct depth, was much feared by submariners and contributed to the short service life of the later U-boats.

Its exploits from August 1939 to April 1941 made the Type VIIB U-48 the single most successful submarine of World War II. In 12 patrols, between September 1939 and June 1941, it sank a total of 51 Allied ships, with a GRT of 306,875, plus a Royal Navy sloop. From June 1941, it was used as a training boat with the 26th Flotilla, but after heavy wear and tear was decommissioned in October 1943, and finally scuttled on 3 May 1945. Others of the 24 VIIBs had shorter lives. U-100, commissioned on 30 May 1940, was a very successful boat, which sank 25 ships on six patrols, with a total GRT of 135,614, plus others damaged. On 17 March 1941, it was sunk after being rammed by the British destroyer HMS *Vanoc*. U-100 had surfaced in foggy conditions but was caught by *Vanoc*'s Type 286 radar, the first U-boat to fall victim to this technology. On the same day *Vanoc* and HMS *Walker* depth-charged its sister VIIB boat U-99, forcing it to the surface, where the crew scuttled it. On the previous day it had sunk six

Allied merchant ships, making a total of 38 sunk, a GRT of 244,658.

'Stay hard' – the Laconia Incident

On 12 September 1942, U-156 sank the British liner *Laconia* in the South Atlantic. It proved to be transporting 1800 Italian prisoners of war. Three U-boats and the Italian submarine *Cappelini* picked up survivors, but they and the lifeboats were attacked by a US Liberator aircraft. This resulted in Dönitz's order to U-boats not to pick up survivors, unless for interrogation. 'Stay hard,' it said. 'Remember, the enemy does not care about women and children when he bombs Germany's towns and cities.' U-156 was a member of the four-strong *Eisbär* wolfpack, based at Lorient but operating in the South Atlantic, where they sank 24 ships off the South African coast in October to November 1942.

At the end of 1942, two wolfpack groups, *Falke* and *Habicht*, were operating west of Ireland, with

▲ U-47 victorious

The crew of U-47 taking the salute from the crew of the German battleship *Scharnhorst* on its return from the successful attack at Scapa Flow in October 1939.

a total of 29 boats. But by this time, however, the work of the Ultra codebreakers, and the use of high-frequency direction-finding equipment, helped the Allies to identify U-boat locations and re-route convoys accordingly. The wolfpacks enjoyed less success, though appalling weather conditions also played a part. Convoy TM 1, of nine oil tankers sailing from the Caribbean to North Africa, was intercepted in the Atlantic west of Gibraltar on 3–5 January 1943 by the 10 U-boats of the *Delfin* wolfpack, plus four others. Only two of the nine tankers reached Gibraltar.

U-106 was a typical Type IXB boat. Laid down on 26 November 1939 at AG Weser, Bremen, it was launched on 17 June 1940 and commissioned on 24 September. The speed of construction meant that the U-boats had few refinements. US submariners in particular would be struck by the austerity of their operating conditions. U-106 sank 22 ships during its career, with a total GRT of 138,581, and survived three depth-charge attacks before being sunk off Spain by British and Australian Sunderlands on 2 August 1943.

Type XB, designed as minelayers, were the largest of the World War II U-boats. Eight were commissioned, capable of carrying 66 mines of SMA (Schachtmine A) moored type, with 18 placed in vertical shafts set forward and independent of the pressure hull. A further 48 were in side-shafts set into the saddle tanks. U-118, commissioned on 6 December 1941, made four operational patrols, but only one sortie as a minelayer, in January to February 1943, sinking four merchant vessels.

Before and and after that, it was used as a supply boat for attack submarines operating in the West Atlantic. On 12 June 1943, it was sunk to the southwest of the Canary Islands by air-dropped depth depth charges from Avengers flying from the US escort carrier *Bogue*. The XB boats had a slow diving time compared to the smaller German submarines and this made them particularly vulnerable to air attack. Only two survived the war.

At the start of 1943, over two hundred U-boats were available for operations. In the war's largest convoy action, in March, 40 U-boats attacked convoys HX229 and SC122, sinking 22 ships for the loss of one U-boat. It seemed that the concerted onslaught of submarines in large numbers might defeat the convoy system. But this was the last great

▲ **Preparing for sea**
Lowering a torpedo into HMS *Unbroken*, 1942. Torpedoes were prepared at the depot before loading.

success of the wolfpacks. The turn of fortune was due to several factors, including the Allied deployment of long-range reconnaissance aircraft, the improvement of radar systems, the use of escort carriers to despatch attack planes, the use of larger convoys, and more effective deployment of surface ASW forces in fast-moving support groups. Improved efficiency of British and US radar meant that the favoured night surface attacks by U-boats were no longer safe. Above and below the surface, they were detectable at all times. In May 1943, 26 convoy ships were sunk, but 27 U-boats were lost in the process. Overall, U-boat casualties outnumbered the new commissions, and Allied air patrols turned the Bay of Biscay into the 'valley of death'. Six U-boats were destroyed there by aircraft in May 1943. The U-boats were withdrawn from the North Atlantic. In late 1943, the combination of intercepted intelligence and increasing ASW skills by both aircraft and surface ships made any part of the Atlantic area an increasingly risky place for U-boats. In one attack on the combined convoys ON 202 and ONS 18, on 20 September 1943, the 14 boats of the *Leuthen* wolfpack concentrated their initial attack on the escort vessels, sinking three but losing two of their number in the process.

Mainstay of the Fleet

Throughout the war, the Type VII, in its various sub-classes, remained the *Reichsmarine*'s main attack submarine. A total of 709 were built. For the purposes of the German Navy as understood in 1935, its size, range, seaworthiness, speed, armament, manoeuvrability, construction cost and crewing requirement were all adequate and added up to an effective war machine that was further improved in its later variants, of which the most numerous was the VIIC, with 507 commissioned.

U-210, which was commissioned in February 1942, a typical Type VIIC in design, exemplified the increasing hazards faced by the German submarine fleet. It would have joined the 9th Flotilla at Brest, but its first and only patrol lasted from 18 July to 6 August 1942. Having set off from Kiel, it was ordered to join the Atlantic *Pirat* wolfpack, which had a patrol line across the standard convoy route; then the *Steinbrinck* pack in the North Atlantic, about 645km (400 miles) northeast of Newfoundland. Eastbound Convoy SC 94 was spotted on 5 August, but on the 6th, as U-210 closed in, it was detected by the Canadian destroyer *Assiniboine*. Forced by depth charges to surface, the submarine engaged the destroyer in a gun battle that ended when *Assiniboine*, its bridge on fire, rammed and sank the U-boat. Nevertheless, the *Steinbrinck* pack sank 11 out of 36 ships in the convoy.

U-511 (Type IXC) was commissioned at DeutscheWerft, Hamburg, on 8 December 1941. Initially, it was used as a test platform for experimental rockets at the Peenemünde base. A rack for six 30cm (11.8in) Wurfkörper 42 Spreng artillery rockets was fitted to the deck. These were successfully fired from a depth of 12m (39ft), and might with further development have become a major weapon. However, the problem of accurate aiming was not resolved and U-511 was assigned from August 1942 to the 10th Flotilla at Lorient, making four patrols as far as the Caribbean Sea, and sinking three merchant ships. Its final mission for the *Reichsmarine* was to carry passengers and cargo to Penang, Malaya, between May and August 1943, sinking two ships en route. Passed on to a Japanese crew, it was sold to Japan on 16 September, becoming RO-500. It was scuttled by the Americans on 30 April 1946.

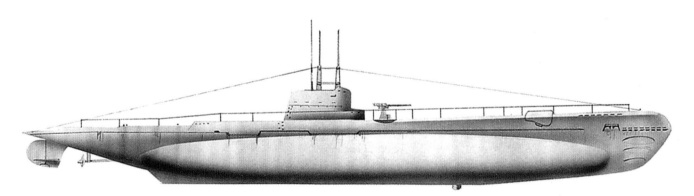

▲ **Seraph**

Royal Navy, S-class patrol submarine, Mediterranean, 1943

Seraph played a key role in the secret preparations for the Allied landings in North Africa, including the depositing of the body of 'the man who never was' on the Spanish coast in Operation Mincemeat in early 1943. In 1944, it was converted as a fast target boat for ASW exercises and was stricken in 1963.

Specifications

Crew: 44	Submerged: 1005 tonnes (990 tons)
Powerplant: Twin screw diesel; electric motors	Dimensions (length/beam/draught): 66.1m x
Max Speed: Surfaced: 14.7 knots; Submerged:	7.2m x 3.4m (216ft 10in x 23ft 8in x 11ft 2in)
9 knots	Commissioned: October 1941
Surface Range: 11,400km (6144nm) at 10 knots	Armament: Six 533mm (21in) torpedo tubes; one
Displacement: Surfaced: 886 tonnes (872 tons);	76mm (3in) gun

Supply Boats

U-459 (Type XIV) was the first purpose-built refuelling and supply boat, of which 10 were commissioned between November 1941 and March 1943. It had no torpedo tubes, but carried two 3.7cm (1.5in) and one 200mm (0.8in) AA guns. Its supply tanks held 439 tonnes (432 tons) of fuel oil. From the bases at St Nazaire, and then Bordeaux, U-459 made six Atlantic patrols, with 63 refuelling meetings, between 29 March 1942 and 24 July 1943; on one occasion running so short itself that another 'milch cow', U-462, had to refuel it.

Attacked off Cape Ortegal, Spain by RAF Wellingtons on 24 July 1943, U-459 was severely damaged and scuttled. By the end of 1943, the Type XIV boats had been virtually eliminated and, in May 1944, work on a planned further 14 was cancelled, together with plans for a larger version to be known as Type XX.

U-530 (Type IXC/40) was commissioned in October 1942 and spent its career in the Atlantic with the 10th and 33rd Flotillas. The 10th was based at Lorient, the 33rd notionally at Flensburg, though many of its boats were still on service in the Atlantic.

U-530 did not have a particularly distinguished record as an attack boat, and was used on at least one patrol as a fuel tanker, but on 23 June 1944 it made an important mid-ocean rendezvous with the Japanese I-52, to transfer a Naxos radar detector, two operators, and a navigator to guide the huge Japanese submarine, with a cargo of gold and strategic materials, to Germany. I-52 was soon afterwards sunk by depth charges and homing torpedoes from USS *Bogue*'s Avengers. U-530 proceeded to make the last U-boat patrol into the Caribbean. At the end of the war the boat surrendered in Mar del Plata, Argentina. Transferred to the United States, it was sunk, after tests, as a target on 28 November 1947.

By early 1943, air attacks were taking such a toll of U-boats in the Atlantic that some submarines were converted as 'flak-boats' to provide anti-aircraft protection, especially for the 'milch-cow' supply boats. A Type VIIC, U-441, commissioned in February 1942, attached to the 1st Flotilla at Brest, and part of the big *Haudegen* wolfpack of January 1943, was the first of four boats to complete conversion. The bridge was extended fore and aft in an enlarged 'wintergarden' to allow for two fast-firing quadruple 2cm (0.8in) Flakvierling guns and a 3.7cm (1.5in) Flak gun, as well as additional MG42 machine guns. Around 20 additional crew were needed, bringing the total to 67. On its first flak patrol as Uflak-1, it shot down an RAF Sunderland, but was badly damaged by three Beaufighters on its second patrol. A flak boat could not cope with concerted attack by several aircraft, and U-441, like the others involved, was re-converted from October 1943 and resumed basic combat duties. Ironically, an aircraft was its downfall: sunk on 8 June 1944 in the English Channel by depth charges from a Liberator of No. 224 Squadron RAF.

British Production

Germany's drive to build more and more U-boats gave it the world's largest submarine fleet, despite the ever-increasing rate of destruction. The British rate of increase was far more modest, but there were very few German merchantmen for the Royal Navy to attack, and the task of the British submarines was to attack German and Italian naval craft, including, of course, submarines. British submarines played virtually no part in the wider Battle of the Atlantic, though actively engaged on patrols in the approaches to the British Isles. The S-class was chosen for an accelerated construction programme in 1941, with 50 being built between 1941 and 1945, in three groups with slightly varying specifications. Though bigger than the original S-boats, they were still only medium-large compared to many of their adversaries. Powered on the surface by two Admiralty-pattern diesel engines, many made by Paxman (who provided engines for over half the British wartime submarine fleet), the two electric motors were rated at 1300hp (969kW). These could be used as generators when the diesels were engaged in direct drive, either to recharge the batteries or to provide auxiliary power.

The third group, including HMS *Seraph*, had an additional torpedo tube, stern-facing and externally mounted, and some later boats mounted a 100mm (4in) gun. The S-class was an effective design, serving mainly around the British coasts and in the Mediterranean, though some were fitted with external fuel tanks and operated in the Far East. Fast to dive, they had an operational depth of 76m (249ft). Seventeen were lost to enemy action and one, HMS *Seal*, was captured by the Germans. From

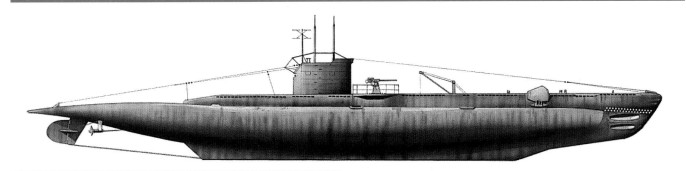

Specifications

Crew: 37	Submerged: 752 tonnes (740 tons)
Powerplant: Twin screw diesel; electric motors	Dimensions (length/beam/draught): 61m x 4.8m
Max Speed: Surfaced: 11.25 knots; Submerged:	x 3.8m (200ft x 16ft x 12ft 9in)
9 knots	Commissioned: September 1944
Surface Range: 7041km (3800nm) at 8 knots	Armament: Four 533mm (21in) torpedo tubes;
Displacement: Surfaced: 554 tonnes (545 tons);	one 76mm (3in) gun

▲ **HMS Vagabond**

Royal Navy, V-class patrol submarine

Commissioned on 19 September 1944, *Vagabond* was powered by two 6-cylinder Davey-Paxman engines generating 400hp (298kW) compared to the original U-class's 307hp (229kW) Admiralty diesels. Diving depth was 91m (300ft). V-boats carried the DF loop at the rear of the tower casing, not on top as in the U-class.

1943 to 1945, one of the class, HMS *Sturgeon*, was manned by a Dutch crew as *Zeehond*.

The British V-class, of which 42 were ordered but only 22 completed, was a development of the slightly smaller U-class. Official designation was 'U-class long-hull'; they were 62.33m (204ft 6in) long compared with the the U-class length of 58m (191ft). To create further confusion, seven V-class had U-names and four U-class had V-names. The V-class had thicker steel plates, 19.05mm (.75in) rather than 12.7mm (.5in), and a greater degree of welding in construction, enabling them to dive faster and deeper. The U- and V-classes were the first British submarines to have diesel-electric drive, with the diesels feeding two Paxman diesel generators. British submarines had been most active in the Mediterranean Sea, and the reduction of combat operations following the collapse of Italy deprived the V-class of much possible action. Two V-class went to the Free French Navy, and one each to the Norwegian and Greek free forces.

Between August 1941 and May 1945, 78 convoys sailed to North Russian ports, tagged as 'PQ outward bound' and 'QP or RA homewards'. Convoy PQ 17, of 35 ships, lost 24 of them between 1 and 13 July 1942 to a sustained attack by 10 U-boats and a large force of *Luftwaffe* dive-bombers and torpedo planes. Believing mistakenly that German capital ships were on the way, the British Admiralty ordered the convoy to scatter, leaving the merchant ships open to U-boat attack. It was the biggest convoy disaster of the war.

Norwegian harbours at Narvik and Hammerfest were added to Trondheim as forward bases, both for convoy attack and for weather reporting and intelligence-gathering. The 13th Flotilla, based at Trondheim, formed of 55 Type VIIC and VIIC/41 boats, was operational right up to the final surrender in May 1945. Formed into two wolfpacks, *Keil* and *Donner*, in April 1944 they made repeated attacks on the returning convoy RA 59, sinking one freighter, but losing U-277, U-959 and U-674, all Type VIIC boats. The scale of the German effort was prodigious. From September 1939 until May 1943, almost 600 U-boats were built and put into action (not all in the Atlantic campaigns) and 250 had been lost. They still had over 400 in service, far more than any other navy. But in their prime purpose, in this war, they had been defeated.

The U-Boats wrought massive destruction on Allied shipping, sinking 14,732,680 tonnes (14,500,000) tons over all the oceans of the world. Out of this total, some 12,095,992 tonnes (11,904,954 tons) was sunk in the North Atlantic alone. Although the U-Boats were eventually fitted with Dutch-invented 'Schnorchel' tubes, allowing them to charge their batteries while operating below the surface, thus making them harder to find, between June and December 1944, 140 did not return to their bases.

The U-Boat Command paid a huge price in the loss of their personnel: of 40,900 officers and men involved, 25,870 were killed (63 per cent) and another 5338 taken prisoner of war.

U-boat operations – Atlantic Theatre

The Battle of the Atlantic was one of the key campaigns of World War II. Lasting from the first day of the conflict to the last, it was a war of weapons and tactics, with the early German advantage giving way to an Allied victory as new technology proved decisive.

The successful prosecution of Britain's war in Europe depended upon a steady flow of shipping reaching the United Kingdom from across the Atlantic and from the Empire beyond. The primary weapon employed by Germany in its attempts to strangle this flow was the U-boat, though at the outbreak of war elements within the *Kriegsmarine*'s high command expected great things from surface raiders. However, although these achieved some successes, many were hunted down by the much larger Royal Navy. U-boats, on the other hand, were much harder to find, and presented a serious threat to Britain's Atlantic lifeline.

The capture of France and Norway in 1940 meant that Germany's U-boats no longer had to make the long and dangerous transit up the North Sea and around the northern coasts of the British Isles to reach the main shipping lanes. Based in French Atlantic ports, the few boats available to the *Kriegsmarine* were able to wreak havoc in Britain's

western approaches as well as in convoy attacks in mid-Atlantic and on British shipping off West Africa.

America's entry into the war in December 1941 saw the *Kriegsmarine* extend its U-boat operations to the North American coast. The US Navy was slow to institute convoys, and the U-boats had an easy time finding targets at night, silhouetted as they were by the bright lights of American cities. A general blackout would have cut losses, but was delayed by six months primarily due to opposition from the tourist trade! In the meantime, the U-boats were wreaking havoc on America's coastal trade; so much so in fact that the German crews called this their second 'Happy Time', the first being June–November 1940.

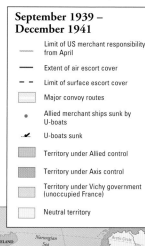

**September 1939 –
December 1941**

— Limit of US merchant responsibility from April

— Extent of air escort cover

-- Limit of surface escort cover

☐ Major convoy routes

• Allied merchant ships sunk by U-boats

↙ U-boats sunk

▨ Territory under Allied control

▨ Territory under Axis control

▨ Territory under Vichy government (unoccupied France)

☐ Neutral territory

▶ **September 1939 – May 1940**

In 1939, Admiral Karl Dönitz had only 56 U-boats in service, of which only 22 were ocean-going types. Initially, pickings for the U-boat commanders were rich, as their boats sank merchantmen returning individually to Britain. Even when convoys were established, they could only be escorted through 15 degrees of longitude at either end of the transatlantic route due to a lack of suitable escorts. Even so, the U-boats were little more than a nuisance – until the fall of France.

▶ June 1940 – March 1941

The lessons of 1917, when unrestricted U-boat warfare had almost brought Britain to its knees, had been largely forgotten by the Royal Navy between the wars, though the British were quick to re-establish convoys in the face of the U-boat threat. Even so, losses were heavy once the U-boats began operating from French ports, reaching 1.6 million tonnes (1.57 million tons) between June and November 1940. The British were particularly unprepared for the German tactic of night-time surface attacks. So successful were the U-boats that their commanders and crews were to remember this period as the 'Happy Time'.

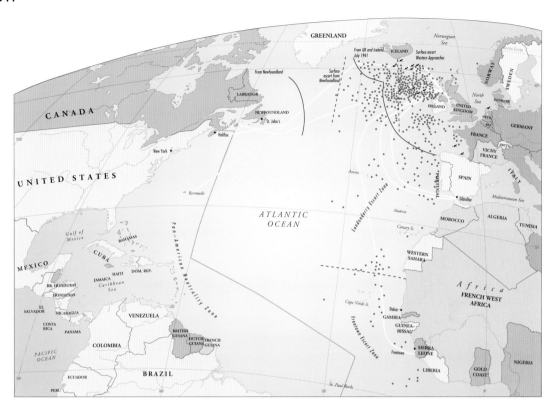

▶ April – December 1941

In 1941, the *Kriegsmarine* still had too few U-boats to control the convoy routes. Improvements in British convoy tactics and the advent of a new type of escort, the corvette, made the U-boat mission harder. Increasing Canadian strength and the decision by the United States to escort convoys out of their ports further strengthened the British position. The American decision involved the US Navy in a 'secret' shooting war, in which US escorts attacked if first attacked by U-boats. However, the introduction of 'Wolfpack' tactics – the use of multiple boats making coordinated attacks on a single convoy – negated the effects of improved British convoy tactics.

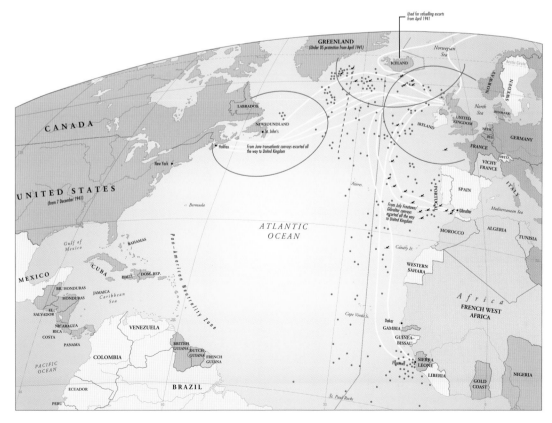

▶ **January 1942 – February 1943**

In July 1942 the Americans finally instituted a convoy system, so the U-boats moved south to the Caribbean where they could strike at the vital oil supplies coming out of Maracaibo. As the US convoy system expanded to include these areas, the U-boats prepared to move back to the shipping lanes of the North Atlantic. By now, the *Kriegsmarine* had more than 300 U-boats in service, and by November 1942 Allied shipping was being sunk at a rate of more than 700,000 tonnes (689,000 tons) every month.

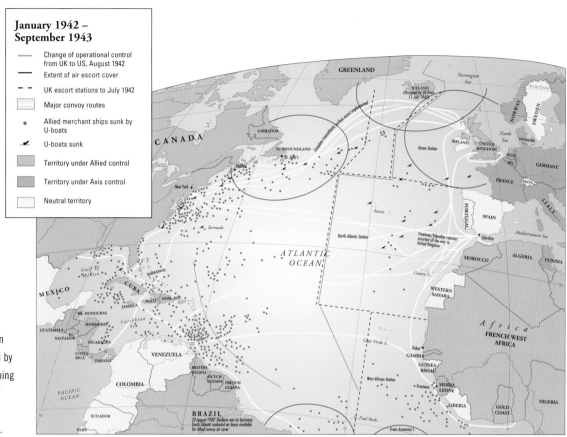

January 1942 –
September 1943

—— Change of operational control from UK to US, August 1942
—— Extent of air escort cover
- - - UK escort stations to July 1942
☐ Major convoy routes
• Allied merchant ships sunk by U-boats
⚓ U-boats sunk
☐ Territory under Allied control
☐ Territory under Axis control
☐ Neutral territory

▶ **March – September 1943**

Between May and August 1943, 98 new U-boats were commissioned – but 123 were lost in action. Each of those losses represented a trained crew perished or taken prisoner. By the end of 1943, the *Kriegsmarine* knew that the average U-boat was unlikely to survive for more than three or four patrols, many being sunk by Allied aircraft as they transited the Bay of Biscay. In 1943, the U-boats sank 463 ships of 2.6 million tonnes (2.55 million tons): in 1944, though more than 400 boats were in commission, they sank only 132 ships totalling 770,000 tonnes (758,000 tons).

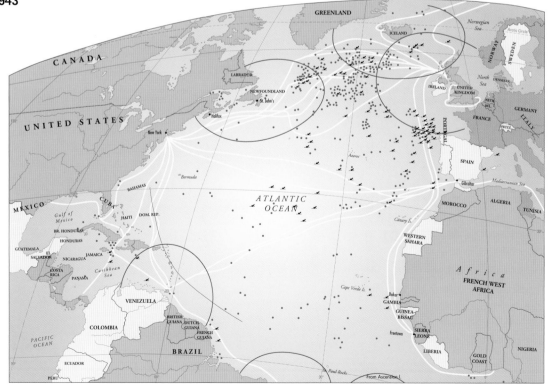

Tonnage definitions

The success of a U-boat or a commander was sometimes calculated by the number of ships destroyed or damaged, but was more often measured in the tonnage of shipping sunk. However, there is more than one type of tonnage measure, depending on the type of vessel.

THERE ARE FOUR CATEGORIES by which tonnage of a vessel is calculated: gross registered, net registered, deadweight and displacement tonnage.

• Gross Registered Tonnage, sometimes known simply as Registered Tonnage and generally abbreviated as GRT, is a measure of volume where 100 cubic feet is considered the equivalent of a ton. This is the total internal capacity of a vessel.

• Net Registered Tonnage is a commercial measure, describing only that part of the Registered Tonnage that is used to carry commercial freight. All spaces that are not revenue producing – the engine compartment, ship's stores, crew spaces and the like – are deducted from the registered tonnage.

• Deadweight Tonnage is the carrying capacity of a vessel in terms of weight rather than volume, and is measured in tons or tonnes.

• Displacement Tonnage is the actual weight of the ship and is equal to the weight of water displaced by the vessel. It is measured in imperial tons (2240 pounds per ton) or in metric tonnes (1000 kilograms).

Most U-boat records were measured in GRT or Displacement Tonnage. GRT was applied to merchant vessels as well as to auxiliary warships such as Armed Merchant Cruisers or AMCs, Merchant Aircraft Carriers (MAC ships), and small vessels like trawlers pressed into patrol or anti-submarine duties. Displacement Tonnage refers solely to vessels built as warships.

Kriegsmarine officer ranks

There were minor differences between the *Kriegsmarine* and the Allies, the latter having no equivalent for *Fregattenkapitän,* which could be described as a junior Captain's rank.

KRIEGSMARINE RANK	BRITISH EQUIVALENT	US EQUIVALENT
Fähnrich zur See	Midshipman, cadet	Midshipman, cadet
Oberfähnrich zur See	No equivalent	Ensign
Leutnant zur See	Sub-Lieutenant	Lieutenant – Junior Grade
Oberleutnant zur See	Lieutenant	Lieutenant
Kapitänleutnant	Lieutenant-Commander	Lieutenant-Commander
Korvettenkapitän	Commander	Commander
Fregattenkapitän	No equivalent	No equivalent
Kapitän zur See	Captain	Captain

U-Boat Combat Flotillas

Once a U-boat and its crew had completed their training, they were assigned to a combat, or 'Front', *flottille* (flotilla). The six prewar combat flotillas bore the brunt of operations for the first two years of the war. Originally based at Kiel and Wilhelmshaven, the Front flotillas were transferred to bases in Norway and France after those countries were conquered in the campaigns of 1940. The new bases enabled the boats to reach their main patrol areas more quickly, without having to make the perilous voyage around the British Isles. By the end of the war, 16 active flotillas had been established and had seen combat in war zones as far afield as the Caribbean, the Indian Ocean and the East Indies. However, the bulk of operational U-boats and their crews fought and died in the key battlegrounds of the Atlantic.

1 Unterseebootsflottille

Plans for German rearmament, circumventing the provisions of the Treaty of Versailles, had been under way since the days of the Weimar Republic in the 1920s. That rearmament came into the open in 1935, two years after Hitler came to power.

Nazi Germany's first U-boat unit, *U-Flottille* Weddigen, was officially founded on 27 September 1935 under the command of Fregkpt. Karl Dönitz, later to become commander of the U-boat arm, commander-in-chief of the Navy, and last Führer of the Reich after Hitler's suicide in 1945. The flotilla was named after Kptlt. Otto Weddigen, who as commander of U-9 sank the armoured cruisers HMS *Aboukir*, HMS *Cressy* and HMS *Hogue* in September 1914.

In 1939 the flotilla, based at Kiel, was renamed 1. *Unterseebootsflottille* (1st Flotilla). Its first boats had been dispatched into the North Sea before the

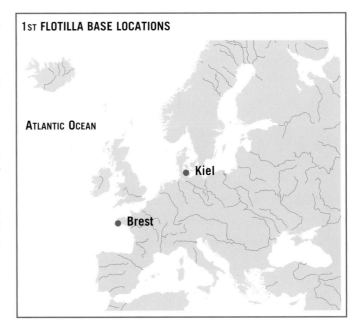

1ST FLOTILLA BASE LOCATIONS

ATLANTIC OCEAN

Kiel

Brest

▼ **Under attack**

1st Flotilla boats served throughout the war, seeing early triumph change to defeat. Here, U-625 is about to be sunk by a Canadian Sunderland in 1944.

▲ U-563

The crew of U-563 pose beneath the conning tower of their Type VIIC in the summer of 1942. The U-boat was sunk with all hands on 31 May 1943, southwest of Brest, by depth charges from British and Australian Handley Page Halifax and Sunderland aircraft.

Commanders

Kpt. z. S. Karl Dönitz *(Sep 1935 – Dec 1935)*	Korvkpt. Hans Eckermann *(Sep 1939 – Oct 1940)*
Kpt. z. S. Loycke *(Jan 1936 – Sep 1937)*	Korvkpt. Hans Cohausz *(Nov 1940 – Feb 1942)*
Kptlt. Hans-Günther Looff	Kptlt. Heinz Buchholz *(Feb 1942 – Jul 1942)*
(Oct 1937 – Sep 1939)	Korvkpt. Werner Winter *(Jul 1942 – Sep 1944)*

1ST FLOTILLA INSIGNIA

Many U-boats had insignia (*Bootswappen*) painted on their conning towers. The first examples were individual, but later boats often carried a flotilla insignia as well. This is the 1st Flotilla's emblem.

1ST FLOTILLA	
Type	**Boats on strength**
Type IIB	14
Type IIC	8
Type IID	13
Type VIIB (after 1941)	3
Type VIIC (after 1941)	81
Type VIIC/41 (after 1941)	2
Type XB (after 1941)	2

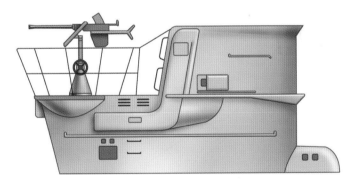

▲ Type VIIB conning tower

Early Type VII boats had simple conning towers, with little or no provision for anti-aircraft armament. By 1940, however, boats were being fitted with a widened bridge to allow the carriage of a single C/30 2cm (0.8in) cannon. The gun was known to have reliability problems, so the conversion was considered to be an interim measure until an improved twin mounting was available. Early war towers were also fitted with wave deflectors halfway up and around the bridge.

outbreak of war, and achieved some successes against Britain's coastal convoys. However, it was clear that the small Type II boats were only marginally effective in a long-distance war, and they began to be replaced by the larger Type VII boats.

Atlantic bases

The *Wehrmacht*'s victory in the Battle of France in 1940 allowed the *Kriegsmarine* to base its U-boats on the French Atlantic coast, doing away with the need for the long and risky passage around the British Isles. In January 1941 construction of massive concrete pens began in the French ports, and from June 1941 the 1st Flotilla was based at Brest in Brittany.

The flotilla was the basic command unit of the *Kriegsmarine* for organizational purposes, but boats were often moved from flotilla to flotilla. Control of boats on operations was held by the various *Führer der Unterseeboote*, or FdU, or even by the commander-in-chief himself. Once they left port on patrol, the 1st Flotilla's boats were directed by FdU *West* from a base at Paris, which was later moved to Angers. Many of the *Kriegsmarine*'s top aces served at one time or another with the 1st Flotilla, including Otto Kretschmer, Erich Topp, Adalbert Schnee, Reinhard Suhren and Wolfgang Lüth.

Star commanders
1935–45

The 1st Flotilla served throughout the most active phases of World War II, and numbered among its commanders many U-boat aces.

Grossadmiral Karl Dönitz

In September 1935 Karl Dönitz took command of the *U-Flottille* Weddigen with the Type II boats U-7, U-8 and U-9. On 1 January 1936 he became the *Führer der Unterseeboote* (FdU), a position that was renamed *Befehlshaber der Unterseeboote* (BdU) after the outbreak of war. He had been a successful U-boat captain in World War I and remained in the trade between the wars, developing the wolfpack tactics that concentrated U-boats on a convoy to attack it in strength.

Korvettenkapitän Adalbert Schnee

Schnee was born on 31 December 1913 in Berlin. He joined the *Kriegsmarine* as part of Crew 34. In May 1937 he joined the U-boat arm, serving under *Oberleutnant* Otto Kretschmer aboard U-23. His first command was U-6, followed by U-60, U-121, U-201 and U-2511, the first Type XXI boat to make an operational patrol in the last days of the war. He made 12 patrols, sinking 21 ships totalling 90,847 GRT and two auxiliary warships of 5700 GRT as well as damaging three ships with a total tonnage of 28,820 GRT. He was awarded the Oak Leaves to the Knight's Cross after his seventh patrol in U-201, during which he sank over 41,000 GRT of shipping.

Kapitänleutnant Rolf Mützelburg

Born on 23 June 1913 at Kiel, Mützelburg joined the *Reichsmarine* as part of Crew 32. After two years on minesweepers, he joined the U-boat arm in October 1939. He received his first combat experience on Schepke's U-100. He commanded U-10 in 1940 before taking command of U-203. In seven patrols, his boat sank 19 ships for a total of 81,987 GRT and damaged three more totalling 17,052 GRT. Awarded the Knight's Cross in November 1941, he received the Oak Leaves in July 1942. Mützelburg died accidentally while swimming on his last patrol on 11 September 1942. Diving from the conning tower, he struck the deck with his head and shoulder when

STAR COMMANDERS		
Commander	Patrols	Ships Sunk
Grossadmiral Karl Dönitz	None	None
Korvettenkapitän Adalbert Schnee	12	21
Kapitänleutnant Rolf Mützelburg	7	19
Kptlt. Friedrich Guggenberger	10	14

▲ **Admiral Dönitz**
Admiral Karl Dönitz (right) shown with propaganda minister Albert Speer, following the surrender of Nazi Germany, May 1945.

the boat lurched suddenly in the swell. He was buried at sea on 12 September 1942.

Kapitänleutnant Friedrich Guggenberger

Born in Munich in 1915, Guggenberger joined the *Reichsmarine* as part of Crew 32. His first U-boat was U-28, commanded by Günther Kuhnke. During the autumn of 1940 Guggenberger took over U-28, and later he commanded U-81, U-847 and U-513. He made 10 patrols, sinking 14 ships of 41,025 GRT plus one auxiliary warship of 1150 GRT. His greatest triumph was the sinking of the 22,963-tonne (22,600-ton) British carrier HMS *Ark Royal* in the Mediterranean in November 1941. Guggenberger died on 13 May 1988 at Erlenbach am Main.

Early U-boat organization
1935–39

To the outside world, the *Kriegsmarine*'s U-boat arm seemed to spring into existence in an astonishingly short time in 1935, but in fact it was the product of years of secret planning.

UNDER THE TERMS of the Treaty of Versailles, the German *Reichsmarine* had specifically been barred from designing or building submarines, but the clandestine work of the 1920s and 1930s meant that Germany was already well into the process of U-boat development when Hitler came to power. When Hermann Göring announced that the Third Reich was casting aside the shackles of Versailles, most of the preliminary work on the first boats for the German Navy had already been done.

The first U-boat officers and crewmen had been trained at the *U-Abwehrschule* at Kiel, established on 1 October 1933. Nominally intended to teach anti-submarine tactics, it was actually used to provide theoretical instruction for future U-boat officers and crews. U-boat building did not get under way until 1935, but all of the preparatory work was done in the preceding two years.

U-boats in service
The first Type IIA boats were completed in 1935, with U-1 to U-6 being reserved as training boats while U-7, U-8 and U-9 were assigned to the *U-Flottille* Weddigen, under the command of Karl

CREW 36 EMBLEM

Germany hosted the Olympic Games in 1936, and many officers who joined the *Kriegsmarine* in Crew 36 adopted the Olympic rings for their commands, including the 1st Flotilla boats U-20, U-23 and U-59.

Dönitz. The U-boat school, initially at Kiel, was moved to Neustadt north of Lübeck. A second flotilla, the *Flottille* Salzwedel, was established on the North Sea at Wilhelmshaven in September 1936, followed by *Flottille* Lohs, *Flottille* Emsmann and *Flottille* Wegener at Kiel and *Flottille* Hundius at Wilhelmshaven.

U-boat headquarters was established aboard the depot ship *Hai* at Kiel, where Dönitz, now promoted to *Kapitän zur See* and *Kommodore*, set up his staff. Although numbers of U-boats in service were still relatively small, Dönitz's aim was to create a large administration network that would be able to control the large number of submarines which he hoped and believed would be entering service in the near future.

Specifications

Crew: 44	Dimensions (length/beam/draught): 64.5 x 5.8 x 4.4m (211.6 x 19 x 14.4ft)
Powerplant: Diesel/electric	Commissioned: Jul 1936 – April 1937
Max Speed: 29.6/14.8km/hr (16/8kt) surf/sub	Armament: 11 torpedoes (4 bow/1 stern tubes); 1 x 8.8cm (3.5in) and 1 x 2cm (0.8in) guns
Surface Range: 7964km (4300nm)	
Displacement: 636/757 tonnes (626/745 tons) surf/sub	

▲ **U-27 – U-36**

Type VIIA

The first Type VII boats were commissioned in 1936, in time to serve alongside British and French vessels on neutrality patrol during the Spanish Civil War. A total of 10 were built before construction was switched to the improved Type VIIB.

U-9

TYPE IIB

Built by Germania-Werft at Kiel, U-9 was laid down on 8 April 1935 and was launched on 30 July of the same year. The boat was commissioned into 1st Flotilla on 21 August.

U-9 WAS ONE OF THE BOATS sent out on patrol before the outbreak of war. After that she had a successful combat career in the first year of the war, during which she sank eight ships totalling more than 24,000 GRT, as well as the French submarine *Doris*.

The war in the North Sea was very much what the small Type II boats had been designed for, the short distances involved meaning that their low endurance was no real handicap. However, all that was about to change. Although successful, the Type II boats were too small for the Atlantic campaign, and U-9 was transferred to 24 Flotilla at Danzig, where she was used as a torpedo instruction boat. She was then moved to 21 Flotilla at Pillau, where she was used as a school boat to train new recruits.

U-9 Commanders

Korvkpt. Hans-Günther Looff *(Aug 1935)*	Wolfgang Kaufmann *(Jun 1940 – Oct 1940)*
Oblt. Werner von Schmidt	Kptlt. Joachim Deecke *(Oct 1940 – Jun 1941)*
(Sep 1935 – Oct 1937)	Kptlt. Hans-Joachim Schmidt-Weichert
Kptlt. Ludwig Mathes *(Oct 1937 – Sep 1939)*	*(Jul 1941 – Apr 1942; Oct 1942 – Sep 1943)*
Oblt. Max-Martin Schulte	Oblt. Heinrich Klapdor *(Sep 1943 – Aug 1944)*
(Sep 1939 – Dec 1939)	Oblt. Martin Landt-Hayen *(Apr 1944)*
Oblt. Wolfgang Lüth *(Dec 1939 – Jun 1940)*	Kptlt. Klaus Petersen *(Apr 1944 – Jun 1944)*

After two years spent as a training boat, U-9 was dismantled and shipped overland to the Black Sea, where she mounted a further 12 patrols. U-9 was sunk on 20 August 1944 while in harbour at Konstanza on the Black Sea by bombs during a raid by Soviet aircraft.

Specifications

Crew: 25

Powerplant: Diesel/electric

Max Speed: 33/15.4km/hr (17.8/8.3kt) surf/sub

Surface Range: 3334km (1800nm)

Displacement: 283/334 tonnes (279/329 tons) surf/sub

Dimensions (length/beam/draught): 42.7 x 4.1 x 3.8m (140.1 x 13.5 x 12.5ft)

Commissioned: 21 Aug 1935

Armament: 6 torpedoes (3 bow tubes); 1 x 2cm (0.8in) gun

IRON CROSS EMBLEM

U-9 was the first boat to carry an individual insignia, a metal Iron Cross being mounted on the conning tower of the boat during the pre-war period. This was to commemorate the famous U-9 of World War I.

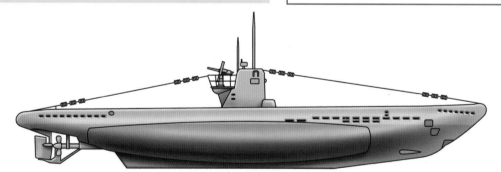

U-9 TIMETABLE		
Patrol Dates	**Operational Area**	**Ships Sunk**
25 Aug 1939 – 15 Sep 1939	Reconnaissance of English coast	0
16 Jan 1940 – 22 Jan 1940	North Sea	2
5 Feb 1940 – 17 Feb 1940	North Sea	2
14 Mar 1940 – 20 Mar 1940	North Sea submarine hunting	0
4 Apr 1940 – 24 Apr 1940	Norwegian invasion	0
5 May 1940 – 30 May 1940	Low Countries	4

▲ U-9

Type IIB

Known as 'canoes' to their crews, the Type II coastal boats carried too few torpedoes to be really effective in combat, and most became training vessels.

U-201

TYPE VIIC

Laid down on 20 January 1940, U-201 was a Type VIIC boat, a member of the largest class of submarines ever built and the mainstay of the *U-Bootwaffe* throughout the war.

A HIGHLY SUCCESSFUL BOAT, commanded by U-boat ace Adalbert Schnee for much of its existence, U-201 carried out nine patrols in the Atlantic between April 1941 and February 1943. In that time the boat accounted for more than 100,000 GRT of Allied merchant shipping as well as sinking a fighter/catapult ship and an anti-submarine warfare (ASW) trawler.

U-201 took part in Operation *Paukenschlag*, the U-boat offensive on the east coast of the United States. Schnee was succeeded by Günther Rosenberg in 1942, and it was under his command that U-201 was sunk with all hands on 17 February 1943 in the North Atlantic by depth charges from the British destroyer HMS *Viscount*. The boat was previously thought to have been sunk east of Newfoundland by the destroyer HMS *Fame*. This attack actually sank U-69.

U-201 Commanders
Kptlt. Adalbert Schnee (Jan 1941 – Aug 1942)
Kptlt. Günther Rosenberg (Aug 1942 – Feb 1943)

U-201 TIMETABLE		
Patrol Dates	Operational Area	Ships Sunk
22 Apr 1941 – 18 May 1941	Transit from Kiel to Brest	2
18 May 1941 – 19 Jul 1941	Central N Atlantic	0
14 Aug 1941 – 25 Aug 1941	W of Ireland/W of Portugal	3
14 Sep 1941 – 30 Sep 1941	W/SW of Ireland	5
29 Oct 1941 – 9 Dec 1941	W of Ireland	0
24 Mar 1942 – 21 May 1942	US East Coast	3
27 June 1942 – 8 Aug 1942	Central Atlantic SE of the Azores	6
6 Sep 1942 – 26 Oct 1942	Central Atlantic/Caribbean	3
27 Dec 1942 – 29 Dec 1942	Returned after developing fault	0
3 Jan 1943 – 17 Feb 1943	N Atlantic	0

U-441

TYPE VIIC FLAK CONVERSION

U-boats in transit across the Bay of Biscay were becoming increasingly vulnerable to aggressive Allied aircraft attacks, and it was decided to give the U-boats the chance to fight back.

IN APRIL–MAY 1943, U-441 was rebuilt as U-Flak 1, the first of three U-Flak boats. Designed to lure aircraft into battle, she was equipped with an enlarged bridge on which were mounted two Flakvierling 2cm (0.8in) quad mounts and a 3.7cm (1.5in) Flak gun, along with extra MG 42 machine guns. The crew was increased from around 46 to 67.

On her first patrol, U-441 shot down a Sunderland aircraft, but was still vulnerable. With the boats unable to fight off Allied air attacks, Admiral Dönitz

U-441 Commanders	
Kptlt. Klaus Hartmann *(Feb 1942 – May 1943)*	Kptlt. Klaus Hartmann *(Aug 1943 – Jun 1944)*
Kptlt. Götz von Hartmann *(May 1943 – Aug 1943)*	

decided that the U-Flak experiment had failed. In late 1943, U-Flak 1 was converted back to a more conventional configuration.

U-441 was sunk with all hands on 8 June 1944 in the English Channel by depth charges from a Liberator of No. 224 Sqn RAF.

Specifications

Crew: 67

Powerplant: Diesel/electric

Max Speed: 31.5/14.1km/hr (17/7.6kt) surf/sub

Surface Range: 12,040km (6500nm)

Displacement: 773/879 tonnes

(761/865 tons) surf/sub

Dimensions (length/beam/draught): 67.1 x

6.2 x 4.8m (220.1 x 20.34 x 15.75ft)

Commissioned: 21 Feb 1942

Armament: 14 torpedoes; 1 x 3.7cm (1.5in)

and 2 x quad 2cm (0.8in) guns

▲ **U-441**

Type VIIC Flak conversion

In spite of her impressive anti-aircraft armament, U-441 was severely damaged on each of the patrols she mounted as a Flak boat, and she was converted back to normal Type VIIC configuration.

U-441 TIMETABLE		
Patrol Dates	**Operational Area**	**Ships Sunk**
17 Sep 1942 – 27 Sep 1942	Transit from Kiel to Trondheim	0
1 Oct 1942 – 7 Nov 1942	Transit to Brest, patrol N of Ireland	0
7 Dec 1942 – 11 Dec 1942	Returned after developing fault	0
13 Dec 1942 – 22 Jan 1943	Central Atlantic	1
27 Feb 1943 – 11 Apr 1943	Central N Atlantic	0
22 May 1943 – 25 May 1943	Bay of Biscay	1
8 July 1943 – 13 Jul 1943	Bay of Biscay	0
17 Oct 1943 – 8 Nov 1943	NW coast of Spain	0
18 Jan 1944 – 14 Mar 1944	W and NW of the British Isles	0
1 May 1944 – 3 May 1944	Returned after developing fault	0
20 May 1944 – 28 May 1944	Western English Channel	0
6 June 1944 – 8 June 1944	Normandy Invasion Front	0

U-556

Type VIIC

On 27 May 1941, U-556 was ordered to collect the War Diary of the battleship *Bismarck*, then being chased down by the Royal Navy.

U-556 HAD ALREADY had a successful patrol when she was ordered to close with the *Bismarck*. Force H (aircraft carrier *Ark Royal* and battlecruiser *Renown*) came within the boat's sights, but U-556 was at the end of

U-556 TIMETABLE		
Patrol Dates	**Operational Area**	**Ships Sunk**
1 May 1941 – 30 May 1941	Transit from Kiel to Lorient	5
19 June 1941 – 27 June 1941	N Atlantic	0

a patrol and had no more torpedoes. The boat had not reached the battleship by the time the

Bismarck was pounded into ruin and sank. The U-boat herself did not last much longer. She was sunk on 27 June on her next patrol, southwest of Iceland, by depth charges from the corvettes HMS *Nasturtium*, HMS *Celandine* and HMS *Gladiolus*. Five of her crew were killed and 41 survived.

U-556 Commander

Kptlt. Herbert Wohlfarth *(Feb 1941 – Jun 1941)*

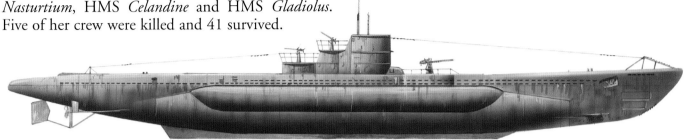

▲ U-556

Type VIIC

U-556 was one of a number of boats ordered to attack Convoy HX 113 in June 1941. Located by the convoy escorts on 27 June, U-556 was depth-charged and forced to the surface, where she was destroyed.

Specifications

Crew: 44	Dimensions (length/beam/draught): 67.1 x 6.2
Powerplant: Diesel/electric	x 4.8m (220.1 x 20.34 x 15.75ft)
Max Speed: 31.5/14.1km/hr (17/7.6kt) surf/sub	Commissioned: 6 Feb 1941
Surface Range: 12,040km (6500nm)	Armament: 14 torpedoes (4 bow/1 stern tubes);
Displacement: 773/879 tonnes (761/865 tons)	1 x 3.7cm (1.5in) and 2 x twin 2cm (0.8in) guns

Convoy HG 76

DECEMBER 1941

HG 76 was an important convoy comprising 32 ships sailing from Gibraltar in December 1941. Powerfully escorted, it was targeted by equally strong U-boat forces.

U-BOATS INVOLVED IN THE BATTLE included Wolfpack *Seeräuber*, comprising U-67 (Type IXC), U-107 (Type IXB), U-108 (Type IXB), U-131 (Type IXC), U-434 (Type VIIC). The group was reinforced by U-125 (Type IXC), U-71, U-567, U-574 and U-751 (all Type VIIC). They faced the Royal Navy's 36th Escort Group under Commander F. J. Walker, including two sloops, *Deptford* and

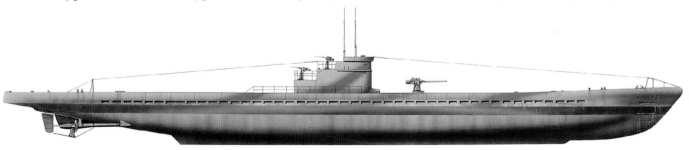

▲ U-107

Type IXB

Although a part of 2. Flottille, U-107 took part in the attack on convoy HG 76. While unsuccessful in this operation, U-107 did sink 37 ships over the course of 14 patrols, making her one of the most successful U-boats of the war.

Specifications

Crew: 48–55	Dimensions (length/beam/draught): 76.5 x 6.8 x
Powerplant: Diesel/electric	4.7m (251 x 22.31 x 15.42ft)
Max Speed: 33.7/13.5km/hr (18.2/7.3kt) surf/sub	Commissioned: Jul 1936 – Apr 1937
Surface Range: 16,110km (8700nm)	Armament: 22 torpedoes (4 bow/2 stern tubes);
Displacement: 1068/1197 tonnes	1 x 8.8cm (3.5in), 1 x 3.7cm (1.5in) and 1 x 2cm
(1051/1178 tons) surf/sub	(0.8in) guns

Convolvulus, *Penstemon*, *Gardenia*, *Samphire* and *Vetch*. The group was supported by the prototype escort carrier *Audacity* and the escort destroyers *Blankney*, *Exmoor* and *Stanley*.

The battle around the convoy was to be one of the most important of the war. At this time, U-boats seemed to be sinking merchantmen at will, but the strength of the escort of HG 76, as well as the presence of the escort carrier, promised to be more of a challenge.

The loss of four boats in this battle came as a severe shock to the U-boat arm. The strong escort allied to the aggressive tactics developed by Commander Walker had defeated a wolfpack for the first time, but until these could be applied to every convoy, losses would continue to mount. The battle around HG 76 was a portent of things to come.

▲ **Depth charges**

Depth charges were the convoy escort's primary weapon in the struggle against the U-boat – at least when the boat was submerged.

CONVOY HG 76 BATTLE TIMETABLE	
Date	Event
16 Dec	Contact is established. U-67, U-108 and U-131 are driven off by the escorts
17 Dec	U-131 is repeatedly attacked and damaged by aircraft from the *Audacity*. Unable to dive, the crew scuttle the boat
17/18 Dec	U-434 keeps contact during the night, but in the morning is detected by the escort and sunk. Two Fw 200 Condors are shot down by Martlets (Grumman Wildcats) from the *Audacity*. U-107 and U-67 are driven off by the convoy escort
19 Dec	U-574 sinks HMS *Stanley*. Lit up by 'snowflake' illuminating rounds, the boat is forced to dive. Damaged by depth charges from the *Stork*, U-574 is forced to the surface, where it is rammed and sunk. While the escort is occupied, U-108 sinks one ship
20/21 Dec	U-107 maintains contact, but the wolfpack is unable to penetrate the escort
21 Dec	Reinforced by U-71, U-567 and U-751 the wolfpack presses home its attack. U-567, under ace commander Endrass, sinks one ship, but is herself sunk by the *Deptford*. U-751 finds the *Audacity*, and sinks the escort carrier
22 Dec	The convoy escort is reinforced by two destroyers. U-71 and U-125 are driven off
23 Dec	U-751 loses contact

Wolfpack groups *Star, Specht & Fink*
APRIL 1943

The spring of 1943 saw the Battle of the Atlantic coming to a climax. U-boats were in service in large numbers, but Allied escort forces were also getting stronger.

THE *STAR* WOLFPACK was formed in April 1943, incorporating the *Meise* Group, which had been operating southeast of Greenland, together with a number of new boats. The group was instructed to form a patrol line south of Iceland, with the aim of intercepting a westbound convoy. Convoy ONS 5 passed the northern end of the patrol line, but bad weather meant that only five boats made contact, and only one ship was sunk. On 1 May, the *Star* boats were directed to an eastbound convoy, SC 128, which had been sighted and lost by another wolfpack, the 18-strong *Specht* Group. Now numbering 30 boats, the combined wolfpacks were renamed Group *Fink*.

After searching for SC 128, the *Fink* boats again encountered ONS 5, which had been delayed by a storm. ONS 5 was a slow outward-bound convoy of 42 ships that had sailed for North America on 22 April. It was given the crack B7 Escort Group led by Commander Peter Gretton, which was reinforced later by the 1st and 3rd Support Groups.

Early in May, Ultra intelligence and high-frequency direction-finding intercepts warned the British of an imminent attack by the powerful wolfpack. On the night of 3 May the boats attacked the escort, with the operation being directed by

Admiral Dönitz himself from his headquarters. Scenting a major success, the admiral urged his U-boat commanders to press home their attacks. However, the escorts proved so effective at keeping the U-boats at bay by night that they switched to submerged attacks by day.

On 5 May the convoy lost 12 ships. However, this was the last occasion when the U-boats would make such a killing, and it came at a very high cost. The convoy escort attacked more than 15 boats in the fog that had descended, and six were destroyed, with another seven sustaining serious damage.

Following these severe losses, over the next few weeks the U-boats were unable to successfully attack any other convoy.

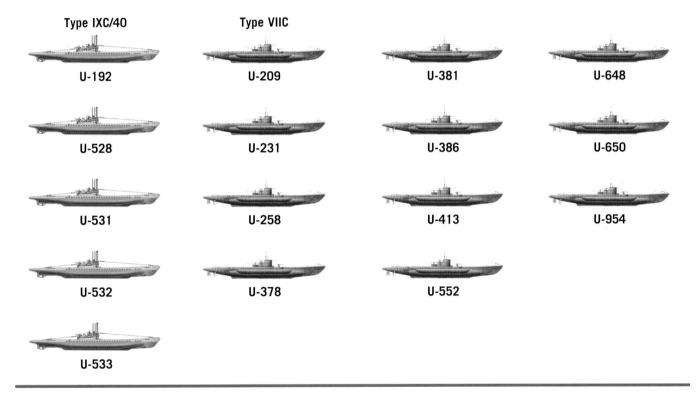

Type IXC/40 — U-192, U-528, U-531, U-532, U-533

Type VIIC — U-209, U-231, U-258, U-378; U-381, U-386, U-413, U-552; U-648, U-650, U-954

BOATS THAT SERVED WITH 1ST FLOTILLA (111 BOATS)					
U-Boat	Type	Commissioned	Flotilla(s)	Patrols	Fate
U-8	IIB	5-Aug-35	13 Apr 1940 – 30 Jun 1940 from U-Bootschulflottille	1 patrol	to 24. Flottille
U-9	IIB	21-Aug-35	1 Sep 1935 – 30 Jun 1940	19 patrols. 7 ships sunk: total 16,669 GRT; 1 warship sunk: total 561 t/552 tons; 1 warship damaged: total 419 t/412 tons	to 24. Flottille
U-10	IIB	9-Sep-35	27 Sep 1935 – 3 Oct 1937 from U-Bootschulflottille	5 patrols. 2 ships sunk: total 6356 GRT	to 3. Flottille
U-11	IIB	21-Sep-35	1 Jul 1940 – 30 Nov 1940 (school boat) from U-Bootschulflottille	None	to 21. Flottille
U-13	IIB	30-Nov-35	1 Sep 1935 – 31 May 1940	9 patrols. 9 ships sunk: total 28,056 GRT	Sunk 31 May 1940, southeast of Lowestoft, by depth charges from the sloop *HMS Weston*. 26 survivors (no casualties)
U-15	IIB	7-Mar-36	1 Mar 1936 – 30 Jan 1940	5 patrols. 3 ships sunk: total 4532 GRT	Sunk with all hands 30 Jan 1940 in the North Sea; accidentally rammed by the German torpedo boat *Iltis*. 25 dead

BOATS THAT SERVED WITH 1ST FLOTILLA (111 BOATS)

U-Boat	Type	Commissioned	Flotilla(s)	Patrols	Fate
U-17	IIB	3-Dec-35	1 Dec 1935 – 31 Oct 1939	4 patrols. 3 ships sunk: total 1825 GRT	to U-Ausbildungsflottille
U-18	IIB	4-Jan-36	4 Jan 1936 – 1 Aug 1939	14 patrols. 3 ships sunk: total 1985 GRT; 1 ship damaged: total 7745 GRT; 1 warship damaged: total 57t/56 tons	to 3. Flottille
U-19	IIB	16-Jan-36	1 Jan 1936 – 30 Apr 1940	20 patrols. 14 ships sunk: total 35,430 GRT; 1 warship sunk: total 448t/441 tons	to 1. U-Ausbildungsflottille
U-20	IIB	1-Feb-36	1 Jan 1940 – 30 Apr 1940 from 3. Flottille	17 patrols. 14 ships sunk: total 37,669 GRT; 1 ship damaged beyond repair: total 844 GRT; 1 ship damaged: total 1846 GRT	to 1. U-Ausbildungsflottille
U-21	IIB	3-Aug-36	1 Aug 1936 – 30 Jun 1940	7 patrols. 5 ships sunk: total 10,706 GRT; 1 aux warship sunk: total 605 GRT; 1 cruiser damaged: total 11,685t/11,500 tons	to 21. Flottille
U-22	IIB	20-Aug-36	1 Jan 1940 – 27 Mar 1940 from 3. Flottille	7 patrols. 6 ships sunk: total 7344 GRT; 2 auxiliary warships sunk: total 3633 GRT; 1 warship sunk: total 1499t/1475 tons	Missing with all hands 27 March 1940 in the North Sea/ Skagerrak, possibly lost to a mine. 27 dead
U-23	IIB	24-Sep-36	1 Sep 1936 – 30 Jun 1940	16 patrols. 7 ships sunk: total 11,094 GRT; 2 warships sunk: total 1433t/1410 tons; 3 ships damaged beyond repair: total 18,199 GRT; 1 ship damaged: total 1005 GRT; 1 warship damaged: total 57t/56 tons	to 21. Flottille
U-24	IIB	10-Oct-36	18 Oct 1939 – 30 Apr 1940 from 3. Flottille	20 patrols. 1 ship sunk: total 961 GRT; 5 warships sunk: total 580t/571 tons; 1 ship a total loss: total 7886 GRT; 1 ship damaged: total 7661 GRT	to 1. U-Ausbildungsflottille
U-56	IIC	26-Nov-38	1 Jan 1940 – 31 Oct 1940 from 5. Flottille	12 patrols. 3 ships sunk: total 8860 GRT; 1 auxiliary warship sunk: total 16,923 GRT; 1 ship damaged: total 3829 GRT	to 24. Flottille
U-57	IIC	29-Dec-38	1 Jan 1940 – 3 Sep 1940 from 5. Flottille	11 patrols. 11 ships sunk: total 48,053 GRT; 1 auxiliary warship sunk: total 8240 GRT; 1 ship damaged beyond repair: total 10,191 GRT; 2 ships damaged: total 10,403 GRT	to 22. Flottille
U-58	IIC	4-Feb-39	1 Jan 1940 – 31 Dec 1940 from 5. Flottille	12 patrols. 6 ships sunk: total 16,148 GRT; 1 auxiliary warship sunk: total 8401 GRT	to 22. Flottille
U-59	IIC	4-Mar-39	1 Jan 1940 – 31 Dec 1940 from 5. Flottille	13 patrols. 16 ships sunk: total 29,514 GRT; 2 auxiliary warships sunk: total 864 GRT; 1 ship damaged beyond repair: total 4943 GRT; 1 ship damaged: total 8009 GRT	to 22. Flottille
U-60	IIC	22-Jul-39	1 Jan 1940 – 18 Nov 1940 from 5. Flottille	9 patrols. 3 ships sunk: total 7561 GRT; 1 ship damaged: total 15,434 GRT	to 21. Flottille
U-61	IIC	12-Aug-39	1 Jan 1940 – 14 Nov 1940 from 5. Flottille	10 patrols. 5 ships sunk: total 19,668 GRT; 1 ship damaged: total 4434 GRT	to 21. Flottille
U-62	IIC	21-Dec-39	1 Jan 1940 – 30 Sep 1940 from 5. Flottille	5 patrols. 1 ship sunk: total 4581 GRT; 1 warship sunk: total 1372t/1350 tons	to 21. Flottille
U-63	IIC	18-Jan-40	18 Jan 1940 – 25 Feb 1940	1 patrol. 1 ship sunk: total 3840 GRT	Sunk 25 Feb 1940 in the North Sea south of the Shetlands by depth charges and torpedoes from the destroyers HMS Escort, HMS Inglefield, HMS Imogen and the submarine HMS Narwhal. 1 dead and 24 survivors
U-79	VIIC	13-Mar-41	13 Mar 1941 – 30 Sep 1941	6 patrols. 2 ships sunk: total 2983 GRT; 1 warship damaged b/r: total 635t/625 tons;1 ship damaged: total 10,356 GRT	to 23. Flottille
U-80	VIIC	8-Apr-41	8 Apr 1941 – 30 Apr 1941 (training)	None	to 26. Flottille
U-81	VIIC	26-Apr-41	26 Apr 1941 – 30 Nov 1941	17 patrols. 23 ships sunk: total 39,711 GRT; 1 auxiliary warship sunk: total 1150 GRT; 1 aircraft carrier (HMS Ark Royal) sunk: total 22,960t/22,600 tons; 1 ship damaged beyond repair: total 5917 GRT; 2 ships damaged: total 14,143 GRT	to 29. Flottille
U-83	VIIB	8-Feb-41	8 Feb 1941 – 31 Dec 1941	12 patrols. 5 ships sunk: total 8425 GRT; 1 auxiliary warship sunk: total 91 GRT; 1 ship damaged: total 2590 GRT; 1 auxiliary warship damaged: total 6746 GRT	to 23. Flottille
U-84	VIIB	29-Apr-41	29 Apr 1941 – 7 Aug 1943	8 patrols. 6 ships sunk: total 29,905 GRT; 1 ship damaged: total 7176 GRT	May have been sunk with all hands returning from the Caribbean on 7 Aug 1943 by a Mk 24 homing torpedo from a US Navy Liberator of VB-105. 46 dead. For many years the boat was erroneously thought to have been sunk southwest of the Azores on 24 Aug 1943 by torpedoes from an Avenger of the escort carrier USS Core
U-86	VIIB	8-Jul-41	1 Sep 1941 – 14 Dec 1943	7 patrols. 3 ships sunk: total 9614 GRT; 1 ship damaged: total 8627 GRT	Listed as missing with all hands 14 Dec 1943 in the North Atlantic after failing to answer radio calls. 50 dead. Previously believed to have been sunk 29 Nov 1943 east of the Azores by depth charges from aircraft of the escort carrier USS Bogue. That attack was actually against U-764, which escaped undamaged
U-116	XB		1 Feb 1942 – 6 Oct 1942 from 2 Flottille	4 patrols. 1 ship sunk by mines: total 4284 GRT; 1 damaged by mines: total 7093 GRT	Declared missing with all hands in Oct 1942 in the North Atlantic, details and position not known. The last radio message was sent on 6 Oct 1942. 56 dead
U-117	XB	25-Oct-41	1 Feb 1942 – 14 Oct 1942 from 2 Flottille	5 patrols. 2 ships damaged by mines: total 14,269 GRT	to 11. Flottille
U-137	IID	15-Jun-40	15 Jun 1940 – 19 Dec 1940	4 patrols. 6 ships sunk: total 24,136 GRT; 1 ship damaged: total 4917 GRT; 1 auxiliary warship damaged: total 10,552 GRT	to 22. Flottille
U-138	IID	27-Jun-40	27 Jun 1940 – 31 Dec 1940	5 patrols. 6 ships sunk: total 48,564 GRT; 1 ship damaged: total 6993 GRT	to 22. Flottille
U-139	IID	24-Jul-40	24 Jul 1940 – 3 Oct 1940 (training)	2 patrols	to 21. Flottille
U-140	IID	7-Aug-40	7 Aug 1940 – 31 Dec 1940	3 patrols. 3 ships sunk: total 12,410 GRT; 1 warship sunk: total 209t/206 tons	to 22. Flottille
U-141	IID	21-Aug-40	21 Aug 1940 – 23 Oct 1940 (training)	4 patrols. 4 ships sunk: total 6801 GRT; 1 ship damaged: total 5133 GRT	to 3. Flottille
U-142	IID	4-Sep-40	4 Sep 1940 – 16 Oct 1940 (training)	4 patrols	to 24. Flottille
U-143	IID	18-Sep-40	18 Sep 1940 – 2 Nov 1940 (training)	4 patrols. 1 ship sunk: total 1409 GRT	to 24. Flottille

U-Boat	Type	Commissioned	Flotilla(s)	Patrols	Fate
BOATS THAT SERVED WITH 1ST FLOTILLA (111 BOATS)					
U-144	IID	2-Oct-40	2 Oct 1940 – 19 Dec 1940 (training)	3 patrols. 1 warship sunk: total 209t/206 tons	to 22. Flottille
U-145	IID	16-Oct-40	16 Oct 1940 – 18 Dec 1940 (training)	3 patrols	to 22. Flottille
U-146	IID	30-Oct-40	30 Oct 1940 – 31 Dec 1940 (training)	2 patrols. 1 ship sunk: total 3496 GRT	to 22. Flottille
U-147	IID	11-Dec-40	Dec 1940 (training)	3 patrols. 3 ships sunk: total 8636 GRT	to 22. Flottille
U-149	IID	13-Nov-40	13 Nov 1940 – 31 Dec 1940 (training)	1 patrol. 1 warship sunk: total 209t/206 tons	to 22. Flottille
U-150	IID	27-Nov-40	27 Nov 1940 – 31 Dec 1940 (training)	None	to 22. Flottille
U-201	VIIC	25-Jan-41	25 Jan 1941 – 17 Feb 1943	9 patrols. 22 ships sunk: total 103,355 GRT; 2 aux warships sunk: total 5700 GRT; 2 ships damaged: total 13,386 GRT	Sunk with all hands 17 Feb 1943 in North Atlantic by depth charges from the British destroyer HMS Viscount. 49 dead. Previously thought to have been sunk east of Newfoundland by depth charges from the destroyer HMS Fame. This attack actually sank U-69
U-202	VIIC	22-Mar-41	22 Mar 1941 – 2 Jun 1943	9 patrols. 9 ships sunk: total 34,615 GRT; 5 ships damaged: total 42,618 GRT. One special operations mission, landing 4 saboteurs on Long Island, New York, on 12 Jun 1942	Sunk 2 Jun 1943 southeast of Cape Farewell, Greenland, by depth charges and gunfire from the sloop HMS Starling. 18 dead and 30 survivors
U-203	VIIC	18-Feb-41	18 Feb 1941 – 25 Apr 1943	11 patrols. 21 ships sunk: total 94,296 GRT; 3 ships damaged: total 17,052 GRT	Sunk 25 April 1943 south of Cape Farewell, Greenland, by depth charges from Swordfish aircraft of No. 811 Sqn off the escort carrier HMS Biter and by the destroyer HMS Pathfinder. 10 dead and 38 survivors
U-204	VIIC	8-Mar-41	8 Mar 1941 – 19 Oct 1941	3 patrols. 4 ships sunk: total 17,360 GRT; 1 warship sunk: total 1077t/1060 tons	Sunk with all hands 19 Oct 1941 near Tangier by depth charges from the corvette HMS Mallow and the sloop HMS Rochester. 46 dead
U-208	VIIC	5-Jul-41	1 Sep 1941 – 7 Dec 1941 from 5. Flottille (training)	2 patrols. 1 ship sunk: total 3872 GRT	Sunk with all hands 7 Dec 1941 in the Atlantic west of Gibraltar by depth charges from the destroyers HMS Harvester and HMS Hesperus. 45 dead. Previously thought to have been destroyed by the corvette HMS Bluebell, but this attack was probably against U-67 and caused only minor damage
U-209	VIIC	11-Oct-41	1 Mar 1943 – 7 May 1943 from 11. Flottille	7 patrols. 4 ships sunk: total 1356 GRT	Missing with all hands on 7 May 1943 in the North Atlantic in approximate position 52N, 38W. Possibly lost in a diving accident after being damaged on 4 May by a Canadian Catalina. 46 dead. Originally thought to have been sunk by the frigate HMS Jed and the sloop HMS Sennen on 19 May 1943; in fact U-954 was sunk.
U-213	VIID	30-Aug-41	1 Jan 1942 – 30 Apr 1942 from 5. Flottille (training)	3 patrols	to 9. Flottille
U-225	VIIC	11-Jul-42	1 Jan 1943 – 15 Feb 1943 from 5. Flottille (training)	2 patrols. 1 ship sunk: total 5273 GRT; 4 ships damaged: total 24,672 GRT	Sunk with all hands 15 Feb 1943 in the North Atlantic by depth charges from a Liberator aircraft of No. 120 Sqn RAF. 46 dead. Sinking previously credited to US Coast Guard cutter John C. Spencer on 21 Feb 1943 in the North Atlantic – actually against U-604, which escaped damage.
U-238	VIIC	20-Feb-43	1 Aug 1943 – 9 Feb 1944 from 5. Flottille (training)	3 patrols. 4 ships sunk: total 23,048 GRT; 1 ship damaged: total 7176 GRT	Sunk with all hands 9 Feb 1944 southwest of Ireland by depth charges from the sloops HMS Kite, HMS Magpie and HMS Starling. 50 dead
U-243	VIIC	2-Oct-43	1 Jun 1944 – 8 Jul 1944	1 patrol	Sunk 8 Jul 1944 in the Bay of Biscay west of Nantes by depth charges from a Sunderland of No. 10 Sqn RAAF. 11 dead and 38 survivors
U-247	VIIC	23-Oct-43	1 Jun 1944 – 1 Sep 1944 from 5. Flottille (training)	2 patrols. 1 ship sunk: total 207 GRT	Sunk with all hands 1 Sep 1944 near Land's End by depth charges from the Canadian frigates HMCS St. John and HMCS Swansea. 52 dead
U-263	VIIC	6-May-42	1 Nov 1942 – 20 Jan 1944	2 patrols. 2 ships sunk: total 12,376 GRT	Sunk with all hands 20 Jan 1944 in the Bay of Biscay near La Rochelle during deep dive trials. 51 dead
U-268	VIIC	29-Jul-42	1 Feb 1943 – 19 Feb 1943 from 8. Flottille (training)	1 patrol. 1 ship sunk: total 14,547 GRT	Sunk with all hands 19 Feb 1943 in the Bay of Biscay west of Nantes by depth charges from a Vickers Wellington of No. 172 Sqn RAF. 45 dead
U-271	VIIC	23-Sep-42	1 Jun 1943 – 28 Jan 1944 from 8. Flottille	3 patrols. No ships sunk or damaged. Served as a Flak boat September–November 1943	Sunk with all hands 28 Jan 1944 west of Limerick by depth charges from a US Navy PB4Y Liberator of VB-103. 51 dead
U-276	VIIC	9-Dec-42	1 Mar 1944 – 1 Jul 1944 from 8. Flottille	3 patrols	to 31. Flottille
U-292	VIIC/41	25-Aug-43	1 May 1944 – 27 May 1944 from 8. Flottille	1 patrol	Sunk with all hands 27 May 1944 west of Trondheim by depth charges from a Liberator of No. 59 Sqn RAF. 51 dead.
U-301	VIIC	21-Jan-43	1 Oct 1942 – 31 Dec 1942 from 5. Flottille	3 patrols	to 29. Flottille
U-304	VIIC	5-Aug-42	1 Apr 1943 – 28 May 1943 from 8. Flottille	1 patrol	Sunk with all hands 28 May 1943 southeast of Cape Farewell, Greenland, by depth charges from a Liberator of No. 120 Sqn RAF. 46 dead.
U-305	VIIC	17-Sep-42	1 Mar 1943 – 17 Jan 1944 from 8. Flottille	4 patrols. 2 ships sunk: total 13,045 GRT; 2 warships sunk: total 2601t/2560 tons	Lost with all hands in the North Atlantic 16 Jan 1944, possibly to one of its own torpedoes. 51 dead. Previously credited to the destroyer HMS Wanderer and the frigate HMS Glenarm on 17 Jan 1944. That attack probably sank U-377.

BOATS THAT SERVED WITH 1ST FLOTILLA (111 BOATS)

U-Boat	Type	Commissioned	Flotilla(s)	Patrols	Fate
U-306	VIIC	21-Oct-42	1 Mar 1943 – 31 Oct 1943 from 8. Flottille	5 patrols. 1 ship sunk: total 10,218 GRT; 2 ships damaged: total 11,195 GRT	Sunk with all hands 31 Oct 1943 in the Atlantic northeast of the Azores by depth charges from the destroyer HMS Whitehall and the corvette HMS Geranium. 51 dead
U-311	VIIC	23-Mar-43	1 Dec 1943 – 22 Apr 1944 from 8. Flottille	2 patrols. 1 ship sunk: total 10,342 GRT	Sunk with all hands on 22 Apr 1944 southwest of Iceland by depth charges from the frigates HMCS Matane and HMCS Swansea. 51 dead
U-331	VIIC	31-Mar-41	31 Mar 1941 – 14 Oct 1941	10 patrols. 1 auxiliary warship sunk: total 9135 GRT; 1 battleship sunk (HMS Barham): total 31,599t/31,100 tons; 1 warship damaged: total 378t/372 tons	to 23. Flottille
U-336	VIIC	14-Feb-42	1 Dec 1942 – 5 Oct 1943 from 5. Flottille	5 patrols. 1 ship sunk: total 4919 GRT	Sunk with all hands 5 Oct 1943 southwest of Iceland by rockets from a Hudson of No. 269 Sqn RAF. 50 dead. Previously credited to a US Navy Ventura of VB-128 on 4 Oct 1943, which actually sank U-279
U-353	VIIC	31-Mar-42	1 Oct 1942 – 16 Oct 1942 from 5. Flottille	1 patrol	Sunk 16 Oct 1942 in the North Atlantic by depth charges from the destroyer HMS Fame. 6 dead and 39 survivors
U-354	VIIC	22-Apr-42	1 Oct 1942 – 14 Oct 1942 from 5. Flottille	20 patrols. 1 ship sunk: total 7179 GRT; 1 warship sunk: total 1320t/1300 tons; 1 warship damaged beyond repair: total 11,603t/11,420 tons; 1 ship damaged: total 3771 GRT	to 11. Flottille
U-371	VIIC	15-Mar-41	15 Mar 1941 – 31 Oct 1941	19 patrols. 8 ships sunk: total 51,401 GRT; 1 aux warship sunk: total 545 GRT; 2 warships sunk: total 2323t/2286 tons; 2 ships damaged beyond repair: total 13,341 GRT; 4 ships damaged: total 28,072 GRT; 2 warships damaged: total 2540t/2500 tons	to 23. Flottille
U-372	VIIC	19-Apr-41	19 Apr 1941 – 13 Dec 1941	8 patrols. 3 ships sunk: total 11,751 GRT; 1 auxiliary warship sunk: total 14,650 GRT	to 29. Flottille
U-374	VIIC	21-Jun-41	1 Sep 1941 – 13 Dec 1941 from 5. Flottille	3 patrols. 1 ship sunk: total 3349 GRT; 2 auxiliary warships sunk: total 992 GRT	to 29. Flottille
U-379	VIIC	29-Nov-41	1 Jul 1942 – 8 Aug 1942 from 8. Flottille	1 patrol. 2 ships sunk: total 8904 GRT	Sunk 8 Aug 1942 in the North Atlantic southeast of Cape Farewell, Greenland, by ramming and depth charges from the corvette HMS Dianthus. 40 dead and 5 survivors
U-392	VIIC	29-May-43	1 Dec 1943 – 16 Mar 1944 from 5. Flottille	2 patrols	Sunk with all hands 16 Mar 1944 in the Straits of Gibraltar by depth charges from the frigate HMS Affleck, the destroyer HMS Vanoc and from 3 US Navy PBY Catalinas of VP-63. 52 dead
U-394	VIIC	7-Aug-43	1 Apr 1944 – 31 May 1944 from 5. Flottille	2 patrols	to 11. Flottille
U-396	VIIC	16-Oct-43	1 Jun 1944 – 30 Sep 1944 from 5. Flottille	5 patrols	to 11. Flottille
U-401	VIIC	10-Apr-41	10 Apr 1941 – 3 Aug 1941	1 patrol	Sunk with all hands 3 Aug 1941 southwest of Ireland by depth charges from the destroyer HMS Wanderer, the Norwegian destroyer St. Albans and the corvette HMS Hydrangea. 45 dead
U-405	VIIC	17-Sep-41	1 Mar 1942 – 30 Jun 1942 from 8. Flottille	11 patrols. 2 ships sunk: total 11,841 GRT	to 11. Flottille
U-413	VIIC	3-Jun-42	1 Nov 1942 – 20 Aug 1944 from 8. Flottille	8 patrols. 5 ships sunk: total 36,885 GRT; 1 warship sunk: total 1118t/1100 tons	Sunk on 20 Aug 1944 in the Channel south of Brighton by depth charges from the escort destroyer HMS Wensleydale and the destroyers HMS Forester and HMS Vidette. 45 dead and 1 survivor
U-415	VIIC	5-Aug-42	1 Mar 1943 – 14 Jul 1944 from 8. Flottille	7 patrols. 1 ship sunk: total 4917 GRT; 1 warship sunk: total 1362t/1340 tons; 1 ship damaged: total 5486 GRT	Sunk by a mine on 14 Jul 1944 west of the torpedo-net barrier at Brest. 2 crewmen killed
U-418	VIIC	21-Oct-42	1 May 1943 – 1 Jun 1943 from 8. Flottille	1 patrol	Sunk with all hands 1 Jun 1943 northwest of Cape Ortegal by rockets from a Bristol Beaufighter of No. 236 Sqn RAF. 48 dead
U-422	VIIC	10-Feb-43	1 Aug 1943 – 4 Oct 1943 from 8. Flottille	1 patrol	Sunk with all hands on 4 Oct 1943 north of the Azores by Avenger and Wildcat aircraft from the escort carrier USS Card. 49 dead. U-422 was being resupplied by 'milch cow' U-460, which was also sunk. A third boat, U-264, escaped with serious damage
U-424	VIIC	7-Apr-43	1 Oct 1943 – 11 Feb 1944 from 8. Flottille	2 patrols	Sunk with all hands 11 Feb 1944 southwest of Ireland by depth charges from the sloops HMS Wild Goose and HMS Woodpecker. 50 dead
U-426	VIIC	12-May-43	1 Nov 1943 – 8 Jan 1944 from 1. Flottille	2 patrols. 1 ship sunk: total 6625 GRT	Sunk with all hands 8 Jan 1944 west of Nantes by depth charges from an Australian Sunderland of No. 10 Sqn RAAF. 51 dead
U-435	VIIC	30-Aug-41	1 Jan 1942 – 30 Jun 1942 from 5. Flottille	8 patrols. 9 ships sunk: total 53,712 GRT; 1 auxiliary warship sunk: total 2456 GRT; 3 warships sunk: total 869t/855 tons	to 11. Flottille. Sunk with all hands 9 Jul 1943 west of Figueira, Portugal, by 4 depth charges from a Wellington of No. 179 Sqn RAF. 48 dead
U-439	VIIC	20-Dec-41	1 Nov 1942 – 4 May 1943 from 5. Flottille	4 patrols	Sunk on 4 May 1943 west of Cape Ortegal, Spain, in a collision with U-659. 40 dead and 9 survivors
U-440	VIIC	24-Jan-42	1 Sep 1942 – 31 May 1943 from 5. Flottille	5 patrols	Sunk with all hands 31 May 1943 northwest of Cape Ortegal, Spain, by depth charges from a Short Sunderland of No. 201 Sqn RAF. 46 dead
U-441	VIIC	21-Feb-42	1 Oct 1942 – 8 Jun 1944 (as U-Flak 1 from 1 May 1943 – 1 Nov 1943) from 5. Flottille	11 patrols. 1 ship sunk: total 7051 GRT	Converted as the first Flak boat with anti-aircraft armament in April/May 1943. Shot down a Sunderland on its first patrol, but was badly damaged by Beaufighters on its second. Returned to a normal configuration in Oct 1943. Sunk with all hands on 8 Jun 1944 in the English Channel by depth charges from a Liberator of No. 224 Sqn RAF. 51 dead

BOATS THAT SERVED WITH 1ST FLOTILLA (111 BOATS)

U-Boat	Type	Commissioned	Flotilla(s)	Patrols	Fate
U-456	VIIC	18-Sep-41	1 Dec 1942 – 12 May 1943 from 11. Flottille	11 patrols. 6 ships sunk: total 31,528 GRT; 1 auxiliary warship sunk: total 251 GRT; 1 warship (*HMS Edinburgh*) damaged: total 11,685t/11,500 tons	Almost certainly sunk with all hands in a diving accident on 12 May 1943 while avoiding the destroyer HMS *Opportune* in the North Atlantic. The boat was crash-diving after being badly damaged by a Fido homing torpedo from a Liberator of No. 86 Sqn RAF. 49 dead. Sinking was previously credited to the corvette *HMCS Drumheller*, the frigate HMS *Lagan* and a Canadian Sunderland of No. 423 Sqn
U-471	VIIC	5-May-43	1 Nov 1943 – 30 Apr 1944 from 5. Flottille	3 patrols	to 29. Flottille
U-556	VIIC	6-Feb-41	6 Feb 1941 – 27 Jun 1941	2 patrols. 6 ships sunk: total 29,552 GRT; 1 ship damaged: total 4986 GRT	Sunk 27 Jun 1941 southwest of Iceland by depth charges from the corvettes HMS *Nasturtium*, HMS *Celandine* and HMS *Gladiolus*. 5 dead and 41 survivors
U-557	VIIC	13-Feb-41	13 Feb 1941 – 4 Dec 1941	4 patrols. 6 ships sunk: total 31,729 GRT	to 29. Flottille
U-558	VIIC	20-Feb-41	20 Feb 1941 – 20 Jul 1943	10 patrols. 17 ships sunk: total 93,186 GRT; 1 auxiliary warship sunk: total 913 GRT; 1 warship sunk: total 940t/925 tons; 1 ship damaged beyond repair: total 6672 GRT; 2 ships damaged: total 15,070 GRT	Sunk 20 Jul 1943 in the Bay of Biscay northwest of Cape Ortegal by depth charges from a British Halifax and a US B-24 Liberator of No. 58 Sqn RAF and the 19th A/S Sqn. 45 dead and 5 survivors
U-559	VIIC	27-Feb-41	27 Feb 1941 – 31 Oct 1941	10 patrols. 4 ships sunk: total 11,811 GRT; 1 warship sunk: total 1077t/1060 tons	to 23. Flottille
U-561	VIIC	13-Mar-41	13 Mar 1941 – 31 Jan 1942	15 patrols. 5 ships sunk: total 17,146 GRT; 1 ship damaged beyond repair: total 5062 GRT; 1 ship damaged: total 4043 GRT	to 23. Flottille
U-562	VIIC	20-Mar-41	20 Mar 1941 – 31 Dec 1941	9 patrols. 6 ships sunk: total 37,287 GRT; 1 ship damaged: total 3359 GRT	to 29. Flottille
U-563	VIIC	27-Mar-41	27 Mar 1941 – 31 May 1943	6 patrols. 3 ships sunk: total 14,689 GRT; 1 warship sunk: total 1900t/1870 tons; 2 ships damaged: total 16,266 GRT	Sunk with all hands 31 May 1943 southwest of Brest by depth charges from British and Australian Handley Page Halifax and Sunderland aircraft. 49 dead
U-564	VIIC	3-Apr-41	3 Apr 1941 – 14 Jun 1943	9 patrols. 18 ships sunk: total 95,544 GRT; 1 warship sunk: total 914t/900 tons; 4 ships damaged: total 28,907 GRT	Sunk 14 Jun 1943 northwest of Cape Ortegal by depth charges from an Armstrong Whitworth Whitley of No. 10 OTU RAF. 28 dead and 18 survivors
U-565	VIIC	10-Apr-41	10 Apr 1941 – 31 Dec 1941	21 patrols. 3 ships sunk: total 11,347 GRT; 3 warships (including cruiser *HMS Naiad* and HM Submarine *Simoom*) sunk: total 7829t/7705 tons; 3 ships damaged: total 33,862 GRT	to 29. Flottille
U-566	VIIC	17-Apr-41	17 Apr 1941 – 24 Oct 1943	11 patrols. 6 ships sunk: total 38,092 GRT; 1 warship sunk: total 2301t/2265 tons	Scuttled 24 Oct 1943 in the North Atlantic west of Leixoes after being seriously damaged by depth charges from a Vickers Wellington of No. 179 Sqn RAF. 49 survivors and no casualties
U-574	VIIC	12-Jun-41	12 Jun 1941 – 19 Dec 1941	1 patrol. 1 warship sunk: total 1209t/1190 tons	Sunk 19 Dec 1941 in the North Atlantic east of the Azores by ramming and depth charges from the sloop HMS *Stork*. 28 dead and 16 survivors
U-582	VIIC	7-Aug-41	1 Jan 1942 – 5 Oct 1942 from 5. Flottille	4 patrols. 6 ships sunk: total 38,826 GRT	Sunk with all hands 5 Oct 1942 southwest of Iceland by depth charges from a US Navy Catalina of VP-73. 46 dead. Previously credited to a Hudson on the same day, which sank U-619
U-584	VIIC	21-Aug-41	1 Dec 1941 – 31 Oct 1943 from 5. Flottille	10 patrols. 3 ships sunk: total 18,478 GRT; 1 warship sunk: total 209t/206 tons. Landed 4 saboteurs south of Jacksonville, Florida, on 18 Jun 1942	Sunk with all hands 31 Oct 1943 in the North Atlantic by a Fido homing torpedo from Avenger aircraft of the escort carrier USS *Card*. 53 dead (including one man lost overboard on 10 Oct)
U-597	VIIC	20-Nov-41	1 Jul 1942 – 12 Oct 1942 from 8. Flottille	4 patrols. 2 ships sunk: total 9295 GRT; 1 ship damaged: total 6197 GRT	Sunk with all hands 12 Oct 1942 southwest of Iceland by depth charges from a Liberator of No. 120 Sqn RAF. 49 dead
U-599	VIIC	4-Dec-41	1 Sep 1942 – 24 Oct 1942 from 8. Flottille	1 patrol	Sunk with all hands 24 Oct 1942 northeast of the Azores by depth charges from a Liberator of No. 224 Sqn RAF. 44 dead
U-603	VIIC	2-Jan-42	1 Dec 1942 – 1 Mar 1944 from 5. Flottille	5 patrols. 4 ships sunk: total 22,406 GRT	Sunk with all hands 1 Mar 1944 in the North Atlantic by depth charges from the destroyer escort USS *Bronstein*. 51 dead
U-625	VIIC	4-Jun-42	1 Nov 1943 – 10 Mar 1944 from 13. Flottille	9 patrols. 3 ships sunk: total 18,751 GRT; 2 auxiliary warships sunk: total 939 GRT	Sunk with all hands 10 Mar 1944 west of Ireland by depth charges from a Sunderland of No. 422 Sqn RCAF. 53 dead
U-628	VIIC	25-Jun-42	1 Dec 1942 – 3 Jul 1943 from 5. Flottille	4 patrols. 4 ships sunk: total 21,765 GRT; 3 ships damaged: total 20,450 GRT	Sunk with all hands 3 Jul 1943 west of Cape Ortegal, Spain, by depth charges from a B-24 Liberator of No. 224 Sqn RAF. 49 dead
U-629	VIIC	2-Jul-42	1 Nov 1943 – 7 Jun 1944 from 11. Flottille	11 patrols	Sunk with all hands 7 Jun 1944 west of Brest by depth charges from a B-24 Liberator of No. 53 Sqn RAF. 51 dead. Previously credited to a 224 Sqn Liberator on 8 June, but that probably sank U-441.
U-632	VIIC	23-Jul-42	1 Jan 1943 – 6 Apr 1943 from 5. Flottille	2 patrols. 2 ships sunk: total 15,255 GRT	Sunk with all hands 6 Apr 1943 southwest of Iceland by depth charges from a B-24 Liberator of No. 86 Sqn RAF. 48 dead
U-637	VIIC	27-Aug-42	1 Jun 1944 – 5 Jul 1944 from 5. Flottille	3 patrols. 1 warship sunk: total 57t/56 tons	to 8. Flottille
U-643	VIIC	8-Oct-42	1 Jul 1943 – 8 Oct 1943 from 5. Flottille	1 patrol	Sunk 8 Oct 1943 in the North Atlantic by depth charges from Liberators of Nos. 86 and 120 Sqns. 30 dead and 18 survivors
U-651	VIIC	12-Feb-41	12 Feb 1941 – 29 Jun 1941	1 patrol. 2 ships sunk: total 11,639 GRT	Sunk 29 Jun 1941 south of Iceland by depth charges from destroyers HMS *Malcolm* and HMS *Scimitar*, corvettes HMS *Arabis* and HMS *Violet* and minesweeper HMS *Speedwell*. All 45 crew survived

BOATS THAT SERVED WITH 1ST FLOTILLA (111 BOATS)

U-Boat	Type	Commissioned	Flotilla(s)	Patrols	Fate
U-653	VIIC	25-May-41	25 May 1941 – 15 Mar 1944	8 patrols. 3 ships sunk: total 14,983 GRT; 1 warship sunk: total 853t/840 tons; 1 ship damaged: total 9382 GRT	Sunk with all hands 15 Mar 1944 in the North Atlantic by depth charges from a Swordfish of escort carrier HMS *Vindex*, and from sloops HMS *Starling* and HMS *Wild Goose*. 51 dead
U-654	VIIC	5-Jul-41	1 Nov 1941 – 22 Aug 1942 from 5. Flottille	4 patrols. 3 ships sunk: total 17,755 GRT; 1 warship sunk: total 914t/900 tons	Sunk with all hands 22 Aug 1942 in the Caribbean north of Colon by depth charges from a Douglas B-18 of US Army 45 BS. 44 dead
U-656	VIIC	17-Sep-41	1 Jan 1942 – 1 Mar 1942 from 5. Flottille	2 patrols	Sunk with all hands 1 Mar 1942 in the North Atlantic south of Cape Race by depth charges from a US Navy PBO-1 Hudson of patrol squadron VP-82. 45 dead. This was the first U-boat sunk by the US Navy
U-665	VIIC	22-Jul-42	1 Feb 1943 – 22 Mar 1943 from 5. Flottille	1 patrol. 1 ship sunk: total 7134 GRT	Sunk with all hands 22 Mar 1943 west of Ireland by depth charges from a Whitley of No. 10 Operational Training Unit RAF. 46 dead. Previously credited to a No. 172 Sqn Wellington in Biscay, which actually attacked U-448, causing no damage
U-669	VIIC	16-Dec-42	1 Jun 1943 – 7 Sep 1943 from 5. Flottille	2 patrols	Missing with all hands in the Bay of Biscay on or after 8 Sep 1943. 52 dead. Previously credited to a Canadian aircraft northwest of Cape Ortegal on 7 Sep, but that attack was actually against U-584 and caused no damage
U-722	VIIC	15-Dec-43	1 Aug 1944 – 30 Sep 1944 from 31. Flottille	3 patrols. 1 ship sunk: total 2190 GRT	to 11. Flottille
U-731	VIIC	3-Oct-42	1 May 1943 – 15 May 1944 from 8. Flottille	4 patrols	Sunk with all hands 15 May 1944 near Tangier by depth charges from HMS *Kilmarnock*, trawler HMS *Blackfly* and 2 US Navy PBY Catalinas from VP-63. 54 dead
U-732	VIIC	24-Oct-42	1 May 1943 – 31 Oct 1943 from 8. Flottille	3 patrols	Sunk 31 Oct 1943 near Tangier by depth charges from trawler HMS *Imperialist* and destroyer HMS *Douglas*. 31 dead and 18 survivors
U-736	VIIC	16-Jan-43	1 Apr 1944 – 6 Aug 1944 from 8. Flottille	2 patrols	Sunk 6 Aug 1944 west of St Nazaire by depth charges from frigate HMS *Loch Killin*. 28 dead and 19 survivors
U-740	VIIC	27-Mar-43	1 Apr 1944 – 6 Jun 1944 from 8. Flottille	2 patrols	Missing with all hands in the Channel after 6 Jun 1944. The boat may have been sunk on 7 Jun by a Liberator of No. 53 Sqn or on 8 Jun by a Liberator of No. 224 Sqn. 51 dead
U-741	VIIC	10-Apr-43	1 Nov 1943 – 15 Aug 1944 from 8. Flottille	5 patrols. 1 warship damaged: total 1651t/1625 tons	Sunk 15 Aug 1944 northwest of Le Havre by depth charges from corvette HMS *Orchis*. 48 dead and 1 survivor
U-743	VIIC	15-May-43	1 Jul 1944 – 21 Aug 1944 from 8. Flottille	1 patrol	Missing with all hands in the Atlantic or Arctic after 21 Aug 1944. 50 dead. Previously credited to corvette HMS *Porchester Castle* and frigate HMS *Helmsdale* on 9 Sep 1944, but the boat destroyed in that attack was U-484. A wreck discovered off the coast of Northern Ireland may be U-743, in which case she was probably lost to unknown causes in mid-September
U-754	VIIC	28-Aug-41	1 Dec 1941 – 31 Jul 1942 from 5. Flottille	3 patrols. 13 ships sunk: total 55,659 GRT; 1 ship damaged: total 490 GRT	Sunk with all hands 31 Jul 1942 north of Boston by a Lockheed Hudson of No. 113 Sqn RCAF. 43 dead
U-767	VIIC	11-Sep-43	1 May 1944 – 18 Jun 1944 from 8. Flottille	1 patrol. 1 warship sunk: total 1392t/1370 tons	Sunk 18 Jun 1944 southwest of Guernsey by depth charges from the destroyers HMS *Fame*, HMS *Inconstant* and HMS *Havelock*. 49 dead and 1 survivor
U-773	VIIC	20-Jan-44	1 Aug 1944 – 30 Sep 1944 from 31. Flottille	3 patrols	to 11. Flottille
U-821	VIIC	11-Oct-43	1 Mar 1944 – 10 Jun 1944 from 4. Flottille	2 patrols	Sunk on 10 Jun 1944 in the Bay of Biscay by attacks from 4 Mosquitoes of No. 248 Sqn and by depth charges from a Liberator of No. 206 Sqn RAF. 50 dead – 1 survivor
U-925	VIIC	30-Dec-43	1 Aug 1944 – 24 Aug? 1944 from 4. Flottille	1 patrol	Missing with all hands in the North Atlantic or Arctic on or after 24 August 1944. 51 dead
U-956	VIIC	6-Jan-43	1 Jul 1943 – 31 Dec 1943 from 5. Flottille	13 patrols. 1 warship sunk: total 1209t/1190 tons; 1 ship damaged beyond repair: total 7176 GRT	to 11. Flottille
U-963	VIIC	17-Feb-43	1 Aug 1943 – 31 Oct 1944 from 5. Flottille	10 patrols	to 11. Flottille
U-987	VIIC	8-Jul-43	1 Mar 1944 – 31 May 1944 from 5. Flottille	1 patrol	to 11. Flottille
U-1007	VIIC/41	18-Jan-44	1 Jun 1944 – 31 Jul 1944 from 31. Flottille	1 patrol	to 24. Flottille
U-1199	VIIC	23-Dec-43	1 Aug 1944 – 9 Nov 1944 from 8. Flottille	2 patrols. 1 ship damaged beyond repair: total 7176 GRT	to 11. Flottille
UB	British S class	30-Nov-40	30 Nov 1940 – May 1941	None; used for trials	Launched at Admiralty Dockyard Chatham on 27 Sep 1938. Commissioned into Royal Navy as HMS *Seal* 28 Jan 1939. Captured after being damaged while minelaying 29 Apr 1940. Transferred to 3. Flottille in May 1941
UD-1	British H class	21-Nov-40	Nov 1940 – Apr 1941	Trials boat	Originally commissioned as the US-built British submarine H 6 at Quebec in Canada on 10 Jun 1915. Interned after running aground at Schiermonnikoog in the Netherlands on 16 Jan 1916. Purchased by the Dutch Government and commissoned as O 8. Taken over by the German Navy on 14 May 1940 at Den Helder, Netherlands. Transferred to 3. Flottille
UD-4	Dutch O 21 class	28-Jan-41	Jan 1941 – Apr 1941	School boat	Laid down in 1938 as the Dutch submarine O 26. Captured while being built at the Rotterdam yard on 14 May 1940. Launched 23 May 1940 and commissioned on 28 Jan 1941. Transferred to 3. Flottille

2 Unterseebootsflottille

Founded a year after the 1st Flotilla, the 2nd U-Boat Flotilla was established on Germany's North Sea coast at Kiel in September 1936, but moved to Wilhelmshaven within weeks. It was known as the *U-Flottille Saltzwedel*, and its first commander was *Fregattenkapitän* Werner Scheer.

THE FLOTILLA WAS NAMED after World War I U-boat ace *Oberleutnant zur See* Reinhold Saltzwedel, who commanded UB-10, UC-10, UC-11, UC-21, UC-71 and UB-81 in the Great War. In the course of 22 patrols, he sank 111 ships for a total of 172,262 tonnes (170,526 tons). He was killed on 2 December 1917, when UB-81 was sunk by a mine in the English Channel. On 1 February 1935 Hitler unveiled the existence of a new U-boat force and on 16 March repudiated the terms of the Versailles Treaty. It was also at this time that the *Kriegsmarine* (Combat Navy) and *Unterseebootwaffe* (U-boat arm) were officially formed. Unknown to other nations at that time, Germany had already begun construction on 12 new U-boats as early as 1934 – by January 1935, the parts were awaiting assembly in Kiel and building began to be undertaken openly.

U-boat expansion

The Anglo-German Naval Agreement of 1935 allowed the *Kriegsmarine* to legally construct up to 35 per cent of the tonnage of the Royal Navy. Submarine tonnage allowed was up to 45 per cent and could be raised to 100 per cent with due notification. As part of that expansion, the Saltzwedel Flotilla was created.

2ND FLOTILLA BASE LOCATIONS

ATLANTIC OCEAN

Wilhelmshaven • • Kiel

• Lorient

2ND FLOTILLA INSIGNIA

The 2nd Flotilla insignia consisted of a U-boat transfixed by a shaft of lightning, otherwise known as the *Siegesrune*. This symbol was a runic depiction of the letter 'S', standing for *Sieg*, or victory.

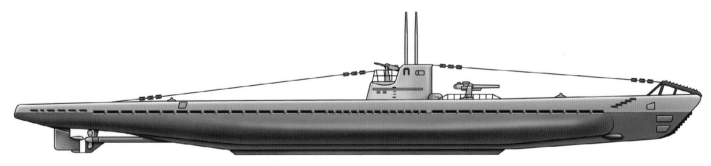

Specifications

Crew: 43	Dimensions (length/beam/draught): 72.4 x 6.2
Powerplant: Diesel/electric	x 4.3m (237.5 x 20.34 x 14.11ft)
Max Speed: 33/15.4km/hr (17.8/8.3kt) surf/sub	Commissioned: 6 April 1936
Surface Range: 12,410km (6700nm)	Armament: 14 torpedoes (4 bow/2 stern
Displacement: 876/999t (862/983 tons)	tubes); 1 x 10.5cm (4.1in) and 1 x 2cm
surf/sub	(0.8in) guns

▲ **U-25**

Type IA

The Type I was the precursor to the Type IX long-range boat, and its design began under the Weimar Republic. It was difficult to handle; the two completed examples had difficulty maintaining periscope depth and rolled heavily in any kind of sea.

▲ **Kiel harbour**

This 1939 photograph shows in the foreground the 2nd Flotilla boats U-27, U-33 and U-34 (all Type VIIAs) as well as two Type IIAs (background, left). Kiel was one of the chief bases and production areas for U-boats throughout the war.

2ND FLOTILLA	
Type	Boats on strength
Type IA	2
Type VIIA	10
Type VIIC	2
Type IX	5
Type IXB	14
Type IXC	27
Type IXC/40	28
Type XB	2
UA (originally built for Turkey)	1
Dutch Type O 21	1

The Saltzwedel Flotilla was intended for longer-range operations than the Weddigen Flotilla, and in addition to the two large Type IA boats, it contained the first examples of the new medium Type VII boats.

U-33 and U-34 were sent to the Mediterranean to support Nationalist Spain. U-34 encountered the Republican submarine C-3 and sank it – the first success for the *Kriegsmarine*'s fledgling U-boat arm. Three years later, Fritz-Julius Lemp's sinking of the

Montreal-bound liner *Athenia* in another Saltzwedel boat marked the beginning of Germany's U-boat war against England.

Leading the attack on the Americas, India, Africa and the oil-rich Caribbean merchant traffic, ace commanders like Werner Hartenstein and Reinhard Hardegen wreaked havoc among Allied trade shipping in distant waters.

However, while the 2nd U-boat Flotilla mounted some of the most shattering submarine offensives of

Commanders	
Fregkpt. Werner Scheer *(Sep 1936 – Jul 1937)*	Korvkpt. Heinz Fischer *(May 1940 – Jul 1941)*
Korvkpt. Hans Ibbeken *(Oct 1937 – Sep 1939)*	Korvkpt. Victor Schütze *(Aug 1941 – Jan 1943)*
Korvkpt. Werner Hartmann	Fregkpt. Ernst Kals *(Jan 1943 – Oct 1944)*
(Jan 1940 – May 1940)	

World War II, it was the intact capture of two of its boats, complete with their Enigma code machines, that would contribute greatly to the Allied defeat of Germany's U-boat arm.

Star commanders
1939–44

In the first years of the war, the 2nd Flotilla included the *U-Bootwaffe*'s long-range boats in its operational strength, and some of its Type IX commanders were particularly successful.

Korvettenkapitän Reinhard Hardegen

Born on 8 March 1913 in Bremen, Hardegen joined the Navy as part of Crew 33 soon after the Nazi seizure of power. In 1935 he began training as a naval aviator, but after being seriously injured in a crash he transferred to the U-boat arm in 1939. His first boat was the Type IXB U-124, in which he served under Kptlt. Wilhelm Schulz.

On 11 December 1940, Hardegen took command of the small Type IID boat U-147, which on its single patrol with Hardegen in command sank a Norwegian freighter of nearly 5000 GRT. On 16 May 1941, he succeeded Kptlt. Karl-Heinz Möhle in the successful Type IXB boat U-123. Even though he had been declared unfit for U-boat duty thanks to the injuries suffered in his pre-war plane crash, Hardegen sank five ships totalling more than 21,000 GRT on his first patrol off West Africa. U-123 was one of five boats sent by Dönitz on Operation *Paukenschlag*, or *Drumbeat*, the opening act of the U-boat offensive on the east coast of the United States. In this second 'Happy Time', U-123 sank nine ships for a total of 53,173 GRT. During his second *Drumbeat* patrol in March 1942, Hardegen sank a further 10 ships for a total of 57,170 tons. He was awarded the Oak Leaves to his Knight's Cross while still at sea.

Hardegen left U-123 at the end of July and spent the remainder of the war as an instructor. After the war he spent a year as a POW, returning

EDELWEISS EMBLEM

The crew of U-124 had served aboard U-64, lost off Norway in April 1940. German mountain troops rescued them and in gratitude they adopted the *Gebirgsjäger* emblem, the edelweiss.

to Bremen in 1946. Subsequently he became a successful businessman and a member of parliament.

Kapitänleutnant Fritz-Julius Lemp

Born on 19 February 1913 in Tsingtao, China, Lemp joined the *Reichsmarine* as part of Crew 31. His first command was U-28, on which he served briefly before taking command of U-30.

Lemp was operating west of the British Isles on the first day of the war when he sank a large vessel thought to be an armed merchant cruiser. In fact, it was the liner *Athenia*, and 112 of its passengers died in the incident. From a controversial start, Lemp went on to considerable success, sinking 17 ships and damaging one.

Promoted to command the Type IXB U-110, on 9 May 1941 Lemp was forced to the surface by the destroyers *Bulldog* and *Broadway* on his second patrol. His boat was captured by the British, a priceless intelligence coup, and Lemp was mysteriously killed, or possibly committed suicide.

STAR COMMANDERS		
Commander	Patrols	Ships Sunk
Korvettenkapitän Reinhard Hardegen	5	21
Kapitänleutnant Fritz-Julius Lemp	10	19
Kapitän zur See Wolfgang Lüth	15	46

Kapitän zur See Wolfgang Lüth

Born on 15 October 1913 in Riga, Latvia, Wolfgang Lüth joined the Navy as part of Crew 33. He transferred to U-boats in February 1937 and served aboard U-27 on neutrality patrol during the Spanish Civil War. His first combat command was the Type IIB boat U-9, in which he made six patrols. Transferring to the Type IID U-138, he sank four ships on his first patrol. He transferred to the large Type IX U-43, and in five patrols sank 12 ships

totalling 69,169 tonnes (68,077 tons). In May 1942 Lüth commissioned the new long-range Type IXD2 boat U-181. On his first patrol off South Africa and in the Indian Ocean, Lüth's boat sank 12 ships for a total of more than 55,000 GRT, for which he was awarded Oak Leaves to the Knight's Cross. His next patrol, at 205 days the second longest of the war, saw U-181 sink a further 10 ships of more than 45,000 GRT. In January 1944, after more than five years of uninterrupted duty on U-boats, *Korvettenkapitän* Wolfgang Lüth became the commanding officer of the 22nd Flotilla, the unit responsible for training future U-boat commanders. Lüth then became the youngest commander of the *Marineschule*, the German Naval Academy, at Flensburg-Mürwik. He died on 13 May 1945 at the *Marineschule*, shot in error by one of his own sentries.

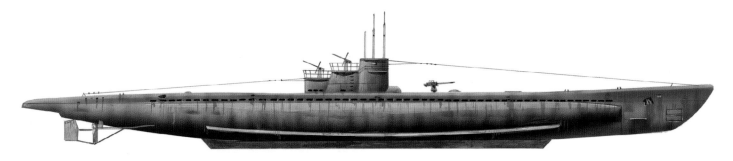

Specifications

Crew: 48–50

Powerplant: Diesel/electric

Max Speed: 33.7/13.5km/hr (18.2/7.3kt) surf/sub

Surface Range: 16,110km (8700nm)

Displacement: 1068/1197t (1051/1178 tons)

Dimensions (length/beam/draught): 76.5 x 6.8 x 4.7m (251 x 22.31 x 15.42ft)

Commissioned: 30 April 1940

Armament: 22 torpedoes (4 bow/2 stern tubes); 1 x 10.5cm (4.1in), 1 x 3.7cm (1.5in) and 1 x 2cm (0.8in) guns

▲ **U-123**

Type IXB

One of the most successful U-boats of the war, U-123 under her three Knight's Cross-winning commanders sank 42 merchant ships totalling 219,924 GRT, one auxiliary warship of 3209 GRT and the British submarine P615.

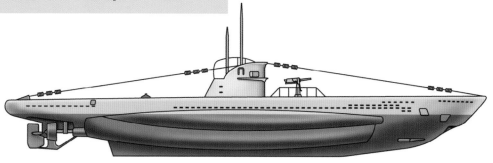

Specifications

Crew: 25

Powerplant: Diesel/electric

Max Speed: 23.5/13.7km/hr (12.7/7.4kt) surf/sub

Surface Range: 6389km (3450nm)

Displacement: 319/370t (314/364 tons)

Dimensions (length/beam/draught): 44 x 4.9 x 3.9m (144.4 x 16.8 x 12.8ft)

Commissioned: Jun 1940 – Jan 1941

Armament: 6 torpedoes (3 bow tubes); 1 x 2cm (0.8in) gun

▲ **U-137 – U-152**

Type IID

Many of the most successful U-boat captains got their first command experience aboard the small Type II coastal boats. The Type IID was the last variant to be built, and had a longer range than earlier boats.

U-30
TYPE VIIA

Launched in August 1936, U-30 was one of the first Type VII boats to enter service with the _Kriegsmarine_ and would serve until the end of World War II.

ON 3 SEPTEMBER 1939, U-30 became notorious when she was responsible for the first U-boat sinking of the war. On patrol south of Rockall at the outbreak of war, U-30 torpedoed the 13,799-tonne (13,581-ton) passenger liner _Athenia_ by mistake. Hitler had announced that passenger liners were not to be attacked. U-30's commander, Fritz-Julius Lemp, almost had his career wrecked by the scandal, but he persuaded Dönitz and the high command that he had made a genuine error: because the target was darkened and was zig-zagging, he took it to be

an Armed Merchant Cruiser, or AMC, which would have made the vessel a valid target. U-30 went on to make six combat patrols, sinking 15 merchant ships

U-30 Commanders

Kptlt. Hans Cohausz _(Oct 1936 – Oct 1938)_	Oblt. Kurt Baberg _(Apr 1941 – Mar 1942)_
Kptlt. Hans Pauckstadt _(Feb 1938 – Aug 1938)_	Oblt. Hermann Bauer _(Mar 1942 – Oct 1942)_
Kptlt. Fritz-Julius Lemp _(Nov 1938 – Sep 1940)_	Kptlt. Franz Saar _(Oct 1942 – Dec 1942)_
Kptlt. Robert Prützmann _(Sep 1940 – Mar 1941)_	Oblt. Ernst Fischer _(May 1943 – Dec 1943)_
Kptlt. Paul-Karl Loeser _(Apr 1941 – Apr 1941)_	Oblt. Ludwig Fabricius _(Dec 1943 – Dec 1944)_
Kptlt. Hubertus Purkhold _(Apr 1941 – Apr 1941)_	Oblt. Günther Schimmel _(Jan 1945 – Jan 1945)_

▶ **U-30 before the war**

U-30 is seen here along with other _Flottille Salzwedel_ boats at Hamburg in December 1937, en route to their new base at Wilhelmshaven.

Specifications

Crew: 44	Dimensions (length/beam/draught): 64.5 x 5.8 x 4.4m (211.6 x 19 x 14.4ft)
Powerplant: Diesel/electric	
Max Speed: 29.6/14.8km/hr (16/8kt) surf/sub	Commissioned: 8 Oct 1936
Surface Range: 7964km (4300 nm)	Armament: 11 torpedoes (4 bow/1 stern tubes);
Displacement: 636/757t (626/745 tons) surf/sub	1 x 8.8cm (3.5in) and 1 x 2cm (0.8in) guns

▲ **U-30**

Type VIIA

Much more capable than the tiny Type II boats known to their crews as 'canoes', the Type VII was to bear the brunt of the _U-Bootwaffe_'s war. U-30 was one of the earliest Type VIIs to enter service, commissioning in October 1936.

totalling over 82,300 tonnes (81,000 tons). She was the first U-boat to make use of the newly captured French bases, entering Lorient on 7 July 1940 after her fifth patrol. After one more patrol U-30 was transferred to the 24th Flotilla in the Baltic where she was used for torpedo training. Used in the last months of the war as a range boat and as a school boat for training new U-boat crewmen, U-30 was scuttled on 4 May 1945 in Kupfermühlen Bay. The wreck was broken up for scrap in 1948.

U-30 TIMETABLE

Patrol Dates	Operational Area	Ships Sunk
22 Aug 1939 – 27 Sep 1939	Southwestern approaches	3
9 Dec 1939 – 14 Dec 1939	W of British Isles	0
23 Dec 1939 – 17 Jan 1940	Mining in Irish Sea off Liverpool	5
11 Mar 1940 – 30 Mar 1940	Norway/Orkneys/Shetland	0
3 Apr 1940 – 4 May 1940	Norway	0
8 Jun 1940 – 24 Jul 1940	Wolfpack operations SW of Ireland	7
5 Aug 1940 – 27 Aug 1940	WNW of Rockall	2

U-106

TYPE IXB

One of the more successful U-boats of the war, U-106 was a Type IXB boat laid down at AG Weser in Bremen in November 1939 and commissioned in September 1940.

IN 10 PATROLS, U-106 sank 21 Allied merchantmen totalling 132,540 GRT. However, on 23 October 1941, two days into the boat's fourth patrol, U-106 graphically illustrated the perils of North Atlantic operations. When the replacement watch opened the conning tower hatch, they found that all four members of the previous watch had been washed overboard in stormy seas.

In July 1942 U-106 suffered a further loss. Two days out of Lorient, it came under attack from a Czech-crewed Vickers Wellington of No. 311 Sqn RAF. The boat was damaged, the commander was wounded and the first officer was killed.

U-106 was sunk on 2 August 1943, northwest of Cape Ortegal, Spain. Damaged by a Canadian Wellington of No. 407 Sqn RCAF, the boat tried to rendezvous with some E-boats that would escort her back to base, but was spotted by an RAF Sunderland of No. 228 Sqn, which was driven off by its gunners. However, an Australian Sunderland of No. 461 Sqn joined the fight and U-106 was sunk. Twenty-two of the crew died; 36 survivors were picked up by German torpedo boats.

U-106 Commanders

Kptlt. Jürgen Oesten *(Sep 1940 — Oct 1941)*   *(Jun 1943 – Aug 1943)*

Kptlt. Hermann Rasch *(Oct 1941 – Apr 1943)*

Oblt. Wolf-Dietrich Damerow

U-106 TIMETABLE

Patrol Dates	Operational Area	Ships Sunk
4 Jan 1941 – 10 Feb 1941	NW of Rockall	2
26 Feb 1941 – 17 Jun 1941	Central Atlantic	8
11 Aug 1941 – 11 Sep 1941	SW of Ireland	0
21 Oct 1941 – 22 Nov 1941	North Atlantic	1
3 Jan 1942 – 22 Feb 1942	US Coast	5
15 Apr 1942 – 29 Jun 1942	Gulf of Mexico	5
25 Jul 1942 – 28 Jul 1942	Damaged by aircraft in Bay of Biscay	0
22 Sep 1942 – 26 Dec 1942	Gulf of St Lawrence/Central Atlantic	1
17 Feb 1943 – 2 Aug 1943	Azores/Canaries	0
19 Mar 1941 – 5 Apr 1941	Sunk off northern Spain	0

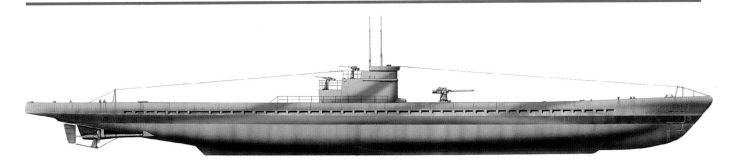

Specifications

Crew: 48–50

Powerplant: Diesel/electric

Max Speed: 33.7/13.5km/hr (18.2/7.3kt) surf/sub

Surface Range: 16,110km (8700nm)

Displacement: 1068/1197t (1051/1178 tons) surf/sub

Dimensions (length/beam/draught): 76.5 x 6.8 x 4.7m (251 x 22.31 x 15.42ft)

Commissioned: 30 April 1940

Armament: 22 torpedoes (4 bow/2 stern tubes); 1 x 10.5cm (4.1in), 1 x 3.7cm (1.5in) and 1 x 2cm (0.8in) guns

▲ **U-106**

Type IXB

Unlike the Type VII boats, many of the Type IXs, like U-106, retained their 8.8cm (3.5in) deck guns until late in the war. U-106 actually used her gun to sink the American tanker SS *Rochester* off the mouth of the Chesapeake in January 1942.

U-505

TYPE IXC

Laid down at Deutsche Werft, Hamburg, in June 1940, U-505 was commissioned on 28 August 1941 and served with the 2nd Flotilla from January 1942 until her capture on 4 June 1944.

U-505 MADE 12 PATROLS from 1 February 1942, sinking eight ships totalling 44,962 GRT. On 2 November 1942, the boat was attacked by a Lockheed Hudson of No. 53 Sqn RAF. The aircraft was shot down, but the boat was damaged and the second officer and a lookout were seriously wounded. The commander of U-505, Kptlt. Peter

Zschech, committed suicide while under a heavy depth charge attack on 24 October 1943. The first officer, *Oberleutnant* Paul Meyer, saved the boat and brought her back to port.

U-505 was captured at sea west of Africa on 4 June 1944, the first vessel taken as a prize on the high seas by the US Navy in the 20th century.

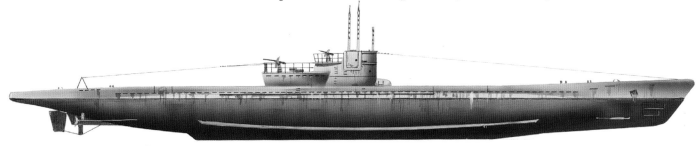

Specifications

Crew: 48–50

Powerplant: Diesel/electric

Max Speed: 33.9/13.5km/hr (18.3/7.3kt) surf/sub

Surface Range: 20,370km (11,000nm)

Displacement: 1138/1232t (1120/1232 tons) surf/sub

Dimensions (length/beam/draught): 76.8 x 6.8 x 4.7m (252 x 22.31 x 15.42ft)

Commissioned: 26 Aug 1941

Armament: 22 torpedoes (4 bow/2 stern tubes); 1 x 10.5cm (4.1in), 1 x 3.7cm (1.5in) and 1 x 2cm (0.8in) guns

▲ **U-505**

Type IXC

U-505 sailed three times on patrol in August 1943, returning each time after strange sounds were heard on diving. A number of French dockyard workers were arrested – suspected of sabotage – and shot by the Gestapo.

The capture was made by ships and aircraft of the US Navy Task Group 22.3, comprising the escort carrier USS *Guadalcanal* and the destroyer escorts USS *Pillsbury*, USS *Chatelain*, USS *Flaherty*, USS *Jenks* and USS *Pope*. Towed to the United States, U-505 is still in existence and is currently on display at the Chicago Museum of Science and Industry.

▶ **U-boat captured**

U-505 was one of the few German U-boats to be captured on the high seas. Taken off West Africa two days before D-Day, it was towed first to Bermuda.

U-505 Commanders

Korvkpt. Axel-Olaf Loewe *(Aug 1941 – Sep 1942)*	Oblt. Paul Meyer *(Oct 1943 – Nov 1943)*
Kptlt. Peter Zschech *(Sep 1942 – Oct 1943)*	Oblt. Harald Lange *(Nov 1943 – 4 Jun 1944)*

U-505 TIMETABLE		
Patrol Dates	**Operational Area**	**Ships Sunk**
19 Jan 1942 – 3 Feb 1942	Transit around Britain from Kiel to Lorient	0
11 Feb 1942 – 7 May 1942	Central Atlantic off Freetown	4
7 Jun 1942 – 25 Aug 1942	Central Atlantic/Caribbean	3
4 Oct 1942 – 12 Dec 1942	Central Atlantic/Caribbean	1
1 Jul 1943 – 13 Jul 1943	Mechanical damage forced early return	0
1 Aug 1943 – 2 Aug 1943	Unidentifiable faults forced early return	0
14 Aug 1943 – 15 Aug 1943	Unidentifiable faults forced early return	0
21 Aug 1943 – 22 Aug 1943	Unidentifiable faults forced early return	0
18 Sep 1943 – 30 Sep 1943	Mechanical damage forced early return	0
9 Oct 1943 – 7 Nov 1943	Captain's suicide forced early return	0
25 Dec 1943 – 2 Jan 1944	Biscay, rescuing German warship survivors	0
16 Mar 1944 – 4 Jun 1944	Central Atlantic off Freetown	0

U-843
Type IXC/40

Laid down at AG Weser, Bremen, in April 1942, U-843 was commissioned in March 1943 and made her first operational patrol in October 1943.

BY THE TIME U-843 had completed her training and entered operational service, the Battle of the Atlantic had swung decisively in favour of the Allies. In place of the multiple sinkings made by earlier Type IX boats, U-843 managed to destroy only one Allied merchant vessel, west-southwest of Ascension Island on her way to join the *Monsun* boats operating in the Far East. After transferring to the 33rd Flotilla, U-843 returned from Batavia in the Dutch East Indies, carrying a cargo of zinc. The boat never delivered her cargo. Reaching Bergen safely, U-843 headed for Kiel but was sunk on 9 April 1945 in the Kattegat, west of Gothenburg, by rockets from Mosquito fighter-bombers of Nos. 143, 235 and 248 Sqns RAF. Forty-four crewmen were killed and 12 survived.

U-843 Commanders

Kptlt. Oskar Herwartz *(Mar 1943 – Apr 1945)*

U-843 TIMETABLE		
Patrol Dates	Operational Area	Ships Sunk
7 Oct 1943 – 12 Oct 1943	Transit from Kiel to Trondheim	0
15 Oct 1943 – 15 Dec 1943	S of Greenland/SW of Ireland	0
19 Feb 1944 – 11 Jun 1944	Indian Ocean	1
Oct 1944	Transferred to 33. Flotille at Batavia	0
10 Dec 1944 – 3 Apr 1945	Transit from Far East to Bergen	0
6 Apr 1945 – 9 Apr 1945	Sunk in transit from Bergen to Germany	0

The *Laconia* incident

SEPTEMBER 1942

Far from being the bestial Nazis depicted by Hollywood, most U-boat commanders were scrupulous in their observance of the rules of war.

ON 12 SEPTEMBER 1942, U-156 under the command of Kptlt. Werner Hartenstein torpedoed a large target in the South Atlantic in position 05.05S, 11.38W. The vessel was the British liner *Laconia* (20,011 tonnes/19,695 tons), which sank at 23:23. The liner was carrying a 136-man crew, around 80 civilians – and 1800 Italian prisoners of war with 160 Polish guards.

Shortly after the sinking, the crew of U-156 heard Italian voices coming from those struggling in the water. Hartenstein immediately began rescue operations and radioed for assistance, both in code to nearby U-boats and in clear to be picked up by any other vessel. The U-boat commander promised not to attack any vessel coming to the rescue. By dawn,

U-156 had picked up nearly 200 survivors and over the next hours had another 200 on tow in lifeboats.

Into attack

U-506 (Kptlt. Erich Würdemann) arrived on 15 September and continued rescue operations. The two boats were joined by U-507 under Korvkpt. Harro Schacht and the Italian submarine *Cappellini*. The boats headed for shore, filled like sardine cans with survivors and towing lifeboats.

On the morning of 16 September, the surfaced – and hence vulnerable – boats were attacked by an American B-24 Liberator bomber operating out of Ascension Island. On seeing the Red Cross flags, the pilot radioed his base asking for instructions. He was

▲ **U-156**

Type IXC

U-156 was on its way to form part of the *Eisbar* wolfpack off the South African coast when it torpedoed the liner *Laconia*, carrying Italian prisoners of war. The boat's commander, Kptlt. Hartenstein, immediately began a rescue operation.

Specifications

Crew: 48–50

Powerplant: Diesel/electric

Max Speed: 33.9/13.5km/hr (18.3/7.3kt) surf/sub

Surface Range: 20,370km (11,000nm)

Displacement: 1138/1252t (1120/1232 tons) surf/sub

Dimensions (length/beam/draught): 76.8 x 6.8 x 4.7m (252 x 22.31 x 15.42ft)

Commissioned: 26 Aug 1941

Armament: 22 torpedoes (4 bow/2 stern tubes); 1 x 10.5cm (4.1in), 1 x 3.7cm (1.5in) and 1 x 2cm (0.8in) guns

told to attack, and at 12:32 the U-boats were forced to cut loose the lifeboats and submerge. However, neutral Vichy French warships from Dakar arrived at that point, and most of those in the water were rescued. Once the U-boats were able to surface and unload their survivors, it was found that around 1500 of those travelling aboard the liner had been saved.

The *Laconia* incident became a scandalous rather than heroic incident because it prompted one of the most controversial orders Dönitz ever issued. Up until that time, U-boats had often helped the survivors of their victims with supplies, water – even directions to the nearest land. In what became known as the *Laconia* Order, Dönitz made it clear that from

henceforth, U-boats were not to take part in any rescue operations; survivors were to be left in the sea to fend for themselves. The only exceptions were senior merchant officers, who might be interrogated for convoy information. Dönitz ended the order with the admonition to:

'Stay hard. Remember, the enemy does not care about women and children when he bombs Germany's towns and cities.'

This order was one of the key pieces of evidence used against Dönitz at Nuremberg in 1946, and some observers felt that he was simply being punished for being too efficient at his job. Dönitz eventually served over 11 years in prison.

Wolfpack *Eisbär*
AUGUST 1942

Against Admiral Dönitz's wishes, the *Kriegsmarine* high command ordered that a U-boat force be sent away from the main battlefield of the Atlantic to take the war to the Allies in distant waters.

UNLIKE MANY OTHER wolfpacks, which tended to be ad hoc organizations of whichever boats happened to be in an operational area at the time, the *Eisbär* (Polar Bear) Group was a unit from the start. Four Type IXC boats – U-68, U-156, U-172 and U-504, all from the 2nd Flotilla at Lorient – sailed in company in August 1942, heading for South African waters. En route they attacked convoy SL 119 off the Spanish coast, sinking one vessel. The boats then operated independently on their way south, arranging to rendezvous in the South Atlantic.

U-156 sank the liner *Laconia* north of Ascension Island, setting in motion what was to become known as the *Laconia* Incident, but the boat was damaged by a subsequent air attack. U-159, already operating in the central Atlantic, was ordered to join up with the

Eisbär boats as a replacement. After refuelling from the 'milch cow' U-459 at a pre-arranged rendezvous well to the south of St Helena, the four boats reached their operational area off the Cape of Good Hope at the beginning of October.

Far from the main theatre of operations, merchant ships were still sailing independently. Over the next six weeks the *Eisbär* boats patrolled the South African coast from the Cape into the Indian Ocean as far north as Durban and between them sank 24 ships.

By mid-November most of the boats had used up their torpedoes and were ordered to return to Lorient. U-504 returned on 11 December, followed by U-68 on 12 December, U-172 on 27 December and U-159 on 5 January 1943. U-156 had returned with combat damage on 16 November.

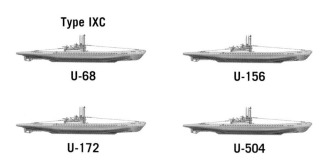

Type IXC

U-68

U-156

U-172

U-504

U-159

BOATS THAT SERVED WITH 2ND FLOTILLA (91 BOATS)

U-Boat	Type	Commissioned	Flotilla(s)	Patrols	Fate
U-25	IA	6-Apr-36	1 Apr 1936 – 1 Aug 1940	5 patrols. 7 ships sunk: total 33,209 GRT; 1 auxiliary warship sunk: total 17,046 GRT; 1 ship damaged: total 7638 GRT	Lost with all hands around 1 Aug 1940 in the North Sea north of Terchelling, probably in the minefield laid on 3 Mar by the destroyers HMS *Express*, HMS *Esk*, HMS *Icarus* and HMS *Impulsive*. 49 dead
U-26	IA	6-May-36	1 May 1936 – 1 Jul 1940	6 patrols. 11 ships sunk: total 48,645 GRT; 1 ship damaged: total 4871 GRT; 1 warship damaged: total 539t/530 tons	Scuttled 1 Jul 1940 southwest of Ireland after being heavily damaged by depth charges from the corvette HMS *Gladiolus* and bombs from an Australian Sunderland flying boat. 48 survivors – no casualties
U-27	VIIA	12-Aug-36	12 Aug 1936 – 20 Sep 1939	1 patrol. 2 ships sunk: total 624 GRT	Sunk 20 Sept 1939 west of Scotland by depth charges from the destroyers HMS *Fortune* and HMS *Forester*. 38 survivors – no casualties
U-28	VIIA	12-Sep-36	12 Sep 1936 – 9 Nov 1940	6 patrols. 11 ships sunk: total 42,252 GRT; 1 auxiliary warship sunk: total 4443 GRT; 1 ship a total loss: total 9577 GRT; 2 ships damaged: total 10,067 GRT	to 24. Flottille
U-29	VIIA	16-Nov-36	16 Nov 1936 – 1 Jan 1941	7 patrols. 11 ships sunk: total 62,765 GRT; 1 aircraft carrier (HMS *Courageous*) sunk: total 22,861t/22,500 tons	to 24. Flottille
U-30	VIIA	8-Oct-36	8 Oct 1936 – 30 Nov 1940	6 patrols. 15 ships sunk (including liner *Athenia*, first sinking of the war): total 86,165 GRT; 1 auxiliary warship sunk: total 325 GRT; 1 ship damaged: total 5642 GRT; 1 battleship (HMS *Barham*) damaged: total 31,599t/31,100 tons	to 24. Flottille
U-31	VIIA	28-Dec-36	28 Dec 1936 – 2 Nov 1940	7 patrols. 11 ships sunk: total 27,751 GRT; 2 auxiliary warships sunk: total 160 GRT; 1 battleship (HMS *Nelson*) damaged by a U-31-laid mine: total 34,495t/33,950 tons	Sunk with all hands 11 Mar 1940 in Jadebusen by RAF Blenheim bomber. 58 dead. Raised in Mar 1940, repaired and returned to service. Sunk again on 2 Nov 1940 NW of Ireland by depth charges from the destroyer HMS *Antelope*. 2 dead and 44 survivors
U-32	VIIA	15-Apr-37	15 Apr 1937 – 30 Oct 1940	9 patrols. 20 ships sunk (including largest ship sunk by U-boats, the 43,030t/42,350-ton liner *Empress of Britain*): total 116,836 GRT; 4 ships damaged: total 32,274 GRT; 1 warship damaged: total 8128t/8000 tons	Sunk 30 Oct 1940 northwest of Ireland by depth charges from the destroyers HMS *Harvester* and HMS *Highlander*. 9 dead and 33 survivors
U-33	VIIA	25-Jul-36	25 Jul 1936 – 12 Feb 1940	3 patrols. 10 ships sunk: total 19,261 GRT; 1 ship damaged beyond repair: total 3670 GRT	Sunk 12 Feb 1940 in the Firth of Clyde by depth charges from the minesweeper HMS *Gleaner*. 17 survivors, 25 dead
U-34	VIIA	12-Sep-36	12 Sep 1936 – 30 Sep 1940	7 patrols. 19 ships sunk: total 91,989 GRT; 3 warships sunk: total 2403t/2365 tons; 2 ships damaged: total 4957 GRT. Sank the Spanish submarine C-3 on 12 Dec 1936 while on neutrality patrol during the Spanish Civil War	to 21. Flottille
U-35	VIIA	3-Nov-36	3 Nov 1936 – 29 Nov 1939	3 patrols. 4 ships sunk: total 7850 GRT; 1 ship damaged: total 6014 GRT	Sunk 29 Nov 1939 in North Sea by depth charges from destroyers HMS *Kingston*, HMS *Icarus* and HMS *Kashmir*. 43 survivors – no casualties
U-36	VIIA	16-Dec-36	1 Sept 1939 – 4 Dec 1939 from U-Bootschulflottille	2 patrols. 2 ships sunk: total 2813 GRT; 1 ship damaged: total 1617 GRT	Sunk with all hands southwest of Kristiansand, torpedoed by the British submarine HMS *Salmon*. 40 dead
U-37	IX	4-Aug-38	1 Jan 1940 – 30 Apr 1941 from 6. Flottille	11 patrols. 53 ships sunk: total 200,125 GRT; 2 warships sunk: total 2443t/2404 tons; 1 ship damaged: total 9494 GRT. Second highest scoring U-boat in terms of numbers of vessels sunk	to 26. Flottille
U-38	IX	24-Oct-38	1 Jan 1940 – 30 Nov 1941 from 6. Flottille	11 patrols. 35 ships sunk: total 188,967 GRT; 1 ship damaged: total 3670 GRT	to 24. Flottille
U-41	IX	22-Apr-39	1 Jan 1940 – 5 Feb 1940 from 6. Flottille	3 patrols. 7 ships sunk: total 24,888 GRT; 1 ship damaged: total 8096 GRT	Sunk with all hands 5 Feb 1940 south of Ireland by depth charges from the destroyer HMS *Antelope*. 49 dead
U-43	IX	26-Aug-39	1 Jan 1940 – 30 Jul 1943 from 6. Flottille	14 patrols. 21 ships sunk: total 117,036 GRT; 1 ship a total loss: total 9131 GRT; 1 ship damaged: total 10,350 GRT	Sunk with all hands 30 Jul 1943 southwest of the Azores by a Fido homing torpedo from an Avenger of the escort carrier USS *Santee*. 55 dead
U-44	IX	4-Nov-39	1 Jan 1940 – 13 Mar 1940 from 6. Flottille	2 patrols. 8 ships sunk: total 30,885 GRT	Destroyed with all hands on or around 13 Mar 1940 by a mine laid by the destroyers HMS *Express*, HMS *Esk*, HMS *Icarus* and HMS *Impulsive*. 47 dead. Originally credited to depth charges from the destroyer HMS *Fortune*
U-64	IXB	16-Dec-39	16 Dec 1939 – 13 Apr 1940	1 patrol	Sunk 13 Apr 1940 near Narvik, Norway, by a bomb and machine-gun fire from a Swordfish floatplane of HMS *Warspite*. 8 dead and 38 survivors
U-65	IXB	15-Feb-40	15 Feb 1940 – 28 Apr 1941	6 patrols. 12 ships sunk: total 66,174 GRT; 3 ships damaged: total 22,490 GRT	Sunk with all hands 28 Apr 1941 in the North Atlantic southeast of Iceland by depth charges from the destroyer HMS *Douglas*. 50 dead. Originally credited to depth charges from the corvette HMS *Gladiolus*. That attack was actually on U-96 and inflicted no damage
U-66	IXC	2-Jan-41	2 Jan 1941 – 6 May 1944	9 patrols. 33 ships sunk: total 200,021 GRT; 2 ships damaged: total 22,674 GRT; 2 MTBs damaged: total 65t/64 tons	Sunk 6 May 1944 west of the Cape Verde Islands by depth charges and gunfire from Avengers and Wildcats of the escort carrier USS *Block Island*, and ramming by the destroyer escort USS *Buckley*. 24 dead and 36 survivors
U-67	IXC	22-Jan-41	22 Jan 1941 – 16 Jul 1943	7 patrols. 13 ships sunk: total 72,138 GRT; 5 ships damaged: total 29,726 GRT	Sunk 16 Jul 1943 in the Sargasso Sea by depth charges from an Avenger of VC-13 from the escort carrier USS *Core*. 48 dead and 3 survivors
U-68	IXC	11-Feb-41	11 Feb 1941 – 10 Apr 1944	10 patrols. 32 ships sunk: total 197,453 GRT; 1 auxiliary warship sunk: total 545 GRT	Sunk 10 Apr 1944 northwest of Madeira by depth charges and rockets from Avengers and Wildcats of the escort carrier USS *Guadalcanal*. 56 dead and 1 survivor
U-103	IXB	5-Jul-40	5 Jul 1940 – 1 Jan 1944	11 patrols. 45 ships sunk: total 237,596 GRT; 3 ships damaged: total 28,158 GRT	to 24. Flottille
U-104	IXB	19-Aug-40	19 Aug 1940 – 28 Nov 1940	1 patrol. 1 ship sunk: total 8240 GRT; 1 ship damaged: total 10,516 GRT	Missing with all hands on or after 28 Nov 1940 northwest of Ireland. May have struck a mine northwest of Tory Island. 49 dead. Previously credited to depth charges from the corvette HMS *Rhododendron* on 11 Nov 1940. That attack was actually against U-103 and inflicted no damage

U-Boat	Type	Commissioned	Flotilla(s)	Patrols	Fate
			BOATS THAT SERVED WITH 2ND FLOTILLA (91 BOATS)		
U-105	IXB	10-Sep-40	10 Sep 1940 – 2 Jun 1943	9 patrols. 22 ships sunk: total 123,924 GRT; 1 warship sunk: total 1571t/1546 tons	Sunk with all hands 2 Jun 1943 near Dakar by depth charges from a French Potez-CAMS 141 flying boat of *Flottille d'exploration 4E*, French Naval Air Force. 53 dead
U-106	IXB	24-Sep-40	24 Sep 1940 – 2 Aug 1943	10 patrols. 22 ships sunk: total 138,581 GRT; 2 ships damaged: total 12,634 GRT; 1 auxiliary warship damaged: total 8246 GRT; 1 battleship (HMS *Malaya*) damaged: total 31,599t/31,100 tons	Sunk 2 Aug 1943 northwest of Cape Ortegal, Spain, by depth charges from British and Australian Sunderland flying boats from Nos. 228 and 461 Sqns. 22 dead and 36 survivors
U-107	IXB	8-Oct-40	8 Oct 1940 – 18 Aug 1944	14 patrols. 37 ships sunk: total 207,375 GRT; 2 auxiliary warships sunk: total 10,411 GRT; 3 damaged: total 17,392 GRT; 1 auxiliary warship damaged: total 8246 GRT	Sunk with all hands 18 Aug 1944 in the Bay of Biscay west of La Rochelle by depth charges from a Sunderland of 201 Sqn. 58 dead. U-107 under Kptlt. Günther Hessler had previously completed the most successful patrol of the war, sinking 14 ships of 88,090 GRT around the Canaries and off Freetown
U-108	IXB	22-Oct-40	22 Oct 1940 – 31 Aug 1943	11 patrols. 25 ships sunk: total 118,722 GRT; 1 auxiliary warship sunk: total 16,644 GRT	to 8. Flottille
U-109	IXB	5-Dec-40	5 Dec 1940 – 4 May 1943	9 patrols. 12 ships sunk: total 79,969 GRT; 1 ship damaged: total 6548 GRT	Sunk with all hands 4 May 1943 south of Ireland by 4 depth charges from a Liberator of No. 86 Sqn RAF. 52 dead
U-110	IXB	21-Nov-40	21 Nov 1940 – 9 May 1941	2 patrols. 3 ships sunk: total 10,149 GRT; 2 ships damaged: total 8675 GRT	Captured on 9 May 1941 south of Iceland by the destroyers HMS *Bulldog*, HMS *Broadway* and the corvette HMS *Aubretia*. The boat was allowed to sink on 10 May to preserve the secret of her capture and the capture of an intact Enigma coding machine. 15 dead and 32 survivors
U-111	IXB	19-Dec-40	19 Dec 1940 – 4 Oct 1941	2 patrols. 4 ships sunk: total 24,176 GRT; 1 ship damaged: total 13,037 GRT	Sunk 4 Oct 1941 southwest of Tenerife by depth charges from the anti-submarine trawler HMS *Lady Shirley*. 8 dead and 44 survivors
U-116	XB	26-Jul-41	26 Jul 1941 – 31 Jan 1942	4 patrols. 1 ship sunk by mines: total 4284 GRT; 1 ship damaged by mines: total 7093 GRT	to 1. Flottille
U-117	XB	25-Oct-41	25 Oct 1941 – 31 Jan 1942	5 patrols. 2 ships damaged by mines: total 14,269 GRT	to 1. Flottille
U-122	IXB	30-Mar-40	30 Mar 1940 – 22 Jun 1940	2 patrols. 1 ship sunk: total 5911 GRT	Missing with all hands around 22 Jun 1940 in North Sea or the Bay of Biscay. Boat may have been lost in an underwater collision with the vessel *San Filipe* on 22 June, or by depth charges from the corvette HMS *Arabis* on 23 Jun. 49 dead
U-123	IXB	30-May-40	30 May 1940 – 1 Aug 1944	12 patrols. 42 ships sunk: total 219,924 GRT; 1 auxiliary warship sunk: total 3209 GRT; 1 warship sunk: total 694t/683 tons; 5 ships damaged: total 39,584 GRT; 1 auxiliary warship damaged: total 13,984 GRT	Taken out of service at Lorient, France, 17 Jun 1944. Scuttled 19 Aug 1944. Surrendered to France in 1945 and became the French submarine *Blaison*. Stricken 18 Aug 1959 as Q165
U-124	IXB	11-Jun-40	11 Jun 1940 – 2 Apr 1943	11 patrols. 46 ships sunk: total 219,178 GRT; 2 warships sunk: total 5868t/5775 tons; 4 ships damaged: total 30,067 GRT	Sunk with all hands 2 Apr 1943 west of Oporto by depth charges from the corvette HMS *Stonecrop* and the sloop HMS *Black Swan*. 53 dead
U-125	IXC	3-Mar-41	3 Mar 1941 – 6 May 1943	7 patrols. 17 ships sunk: total 82,873 GRT	Sunk with all hands 6 May 1943 east of Newfoundland: rammed by the destroyer HMS *Oribi* and finished off by gunfire from the corvette HMS *Snowflake*. 54 dead
U-126	IXC	22-Mar-41	22 Mar 1941 – 3 Jul 1943	6 patrols. 24 ships sunk: total 111,564 GRT; 2 ships damaged beyond repair: total 14,173 GRT; 5 ships damaged: total 37,501 GRT	Sunk with all hands 3 Jul 1943 northwest of Cape Ortegal, Spain, by depth charges from a British Wellington of No. 172 Sqn RAF. 55 dead
U-127	IXC	24-Apr-41	24 Apr 1941 – 15 Dec 1941	1 patrol	Sunk with all hands 15 Dec 1941 west of Gibraltar by depth charges from the Australian destroyer HMAS *Nestor*. 51 dead
U-128	IXC	12-May-41	12 May 1941 – 17 May 1943	6 patrols. 12 ships sunk: total 83,639 GRT	Sunk 17 May 1943 in the South Atlantic south of Pernambuco by gunfire from the US destroyers USS *Moffett*, USS *Jouett* and depth charges from two US Navy Mariner aircraft of Patrol Sqn VP-74. 7 dead and 47 survivors
U-129	IXC	21-May-41	1 Jul 1941 – 1 Jul 1944 from 4 Flottille	10 patrols. 29 ships sunk: total 143,748 GRT	Taken out of service at Lorient 4 Jul 1944. Scuttled 18 Jul 1944
U-130	IXC	11-Jun-41	1 Sep 1941 – 12 Mar 1943 from 4 Flottille	6 patrols. 21 ships sunk: total 127,608 GRT; 3 auxiliary warships sunk: total 34,407 GRT; 1 ship damaged: total 6986 GRT	Sunk with all hands 12 Mar 1943 west of the Azores by depth charges from the destroyer USS *Champlin*. 53 dead
U-131	VIIC	1-Jul-41	1 Nov 1941 – 17 Dec 1941 from 4 Flottille	1 patrol. 1 ship sunk: total 4016 GRT	Sunk 17 Dec 1941 northeast of Madeira by depth charges and gunfire from the escort destroyers HMS *Exmoor*, HMS *Blankney*, destroyer HMS *Stanley*, corvette *HMS Penstemon* and sloop HMS *Stork*, and by depth charges from a Martlet aircraft of the escort carrier HMS *Audacity*. 47 survivors
U-153	IXC	19-Jul-41	1 Jun 1942 – 13 Jul 1942 from 4. Flottille	2 patrols. 3 ships sunk: total 16,186 GRT	Sunk with all hands 13 Jul 1942 near Panama by depth charges from the destroyer USS *Lansdowne*. 52 dead
U-154	IXC	2-Aug-41	1 Feb 1942 – 3 Jul 1944 from 4. Flottille	8 patrols. 10 ships sunk: total 49,288 GRT; 1 ship damaged beyond repair: total 8166 GRT; 2 ships damaged: total 15,771 GRT. One of its commanders, Oblt. Oskar Kusch, was executed on 12 May 1944 after being denounced by his former first officer for *Wehrkraftzersetzung* (sedition and defeatism)	Sunk with all hands 3 Jul 1944 west of Madeira by depth charges from the destroyer escorts USS *Inch* and USS *Frost*. 57 dead
U-156	IXC	4-Sep-41	1 Jan 1942 – 8 Mar 1943 from 4. Flottille	5 patrols. 20 ships sunk: total 97,205 GRT; 3 ships damaged: total 18,811 GRT; 1 warship damaged: total 1209t/1190 tons. On 12 Sep 1942 U-156 sank the liner *Laconia* west of Africa in what has become known as the *Laconia* Incident	Sunk with all hands at 13:15 on 8 Mar 1943 east of Barbados by depth charges from a US Navy Catalina of VP-53. 53 dead
U-157	IXC	15-Sep-41	1 Jun 1942 – 13 Jun 1942 from 4. Flottille	2 patrols. 1 ship sunk: total 6401 GRT	Sunk with all hands 13 Jun 1942 northeast of Havana by depth charges from the Coast Guard cutter USCG *Thetis*. 52 dead

BOATS THAT SERVED WITH 2ND FLOTILLA (91 BOATS)					
U-Boat	Type	Commissioned	Flotilla(s)	Patrols	Fate
U-161	IXC	8-Jul-41	1 Jan, 1942 – 27 Sep 1943 from 4. Flottille	6 patrols. 13 ships sunk: total 60,407 GRT; 1 warship sunk: total 1148t/1130 tons; 1 ship damaged beyond repair: total 3305 GRT; 5 ships damaged: total 35,672 GRT; 1 warship damaged: total 5537t/5450 tons	Sunk with all hands 27 Sept 1943 in the South Atlantic near Bahia by depth charges from a US Navy Mariner aircraft of VP-74. 53 dead
U-162	IXC	9-Sep-41	1 Feb 1942 – 3 Sep 1942 from 4. Flottille	3 patrols. 14 ships sunk: total 82,027 GRT	Sunk 3 Sept 1942 near Trinidad by depth charges from the destroyers HMS *Vimy*, HMS *Pathfinder* and HMS *Quentin*. 2 dead and 49 survivors
U-168	IXC/40	10-Sep-42	1 Mar 1943 – 30 Sep 1944 from 4. Flottille	4 patrols. 2 ships sunk: total 6568 GRT; 1 auxiliary warship sunk: total 1440 GRT; 1 ship damaged: total 9804 GRT	to 33. Flottille
U-173	IXC	15-Nov-41	1 Jul 1942 – 16 Nov 1942	2 patrols. 1 auxiliary warship sunk: total 9359 GRT; 2 auxiliary warships damaged: total 18,713 GRT; 1 warship damaged: total 1656t/1630 tons	Sunk with all hands 16 Nov 1942 off Casablanca by depth charges from the destroyers USS *Woolsey*, USS *Swanson* and USS *Quick*. 57 dead
U-183	IXC/40	1-Apr-42	1 Oct 1942 – 30 Sep 1944 from 4. Flottille	6 patrols. 4 ships sunk: total 19,260 GRT; 1 ship damaged beyond repair: total 6993 GRT	to 33. Flottille
U-184	IXC/40	29-May-42	1 Nov 1942 – 21 Nov 1942 from 4. Flottille	1 patrol. 1 ship sunk: total 3192 GRT	Listed as missing with all hands 21 Nov 1942 in the North Atlantic east of Newfoundland. 50 dead. Loss previously attributed to a mid-Atlantic depth charge attack on 20 Nov 1942 by the Norwegian corvette *Potentilla*. That attack was probably against U-264 and inflicted no damage.
U-189	IXC/40	15-Aug-42	1 Apr 1943 – 23 Apr 1943 from 4. Flottille	1 patrol	Sunk with all hands 23 April 1943 east of Cape Farewell, Greenland, by depth charges from a Liberator aircraft of No. 120 Sqn RAF. 54 dead
U-190	IXC/40	24-Sep-42	1 Mar 1943 – 30 Sep 1944 from 4. Flottille	6 patrols. 1 ship sunk: total 7015 GRT; 1 warship sunk: total 599t/590 tons	to 33. Flottille
U-191	IXC/40	20-Oct-42	1 Apr 1943 – 23 Apr 1943 from 4. Flottille	1 patrol. 1 ship sunk: total 3025 GRT	Sunk with all hands 23 Apr 1943 southeast of Cape Farewell, Greenland, by depth charges from the destroyer HMS *Hesperus*. 55 dead
U-193	IXC/40	10-Dec-42	1 May 1943 – 31 Mar, 1944 from 4. Flottille	3 patrols. 1 ship sunk: total 10,172 GRT	to 10. Flottille
U-501	IXC	30-Apr-41	30 Apr 1941 – 10 Sep 1941	1 patrol. 1 ship sunk: total 2000 GRT	Sunk 10 Sep 1941 in the Straits of Denmark south of Angmagsalik, Greenland, by depth charges and ramming from the Canadian corvettes HMCS *Chambly* and HMCS *Moosejaw*. 11 dead and 37 survivors
U-502	IXC	31-May-41	31 May 1941 – 5 Jul 1942	4 patrols. 14 ships sunk: total 78,843 GRT; 2 ships damaged: total 23,797 GRT	Sunk with all hands 5 Jul 1942 in the Bay of Biscay west of La Rochelle by depth charges from a Wellington of No. 172 Sqn. 52 dead. This was the first successful use of Leigh Light equipment
U-503	IXC	10-Jul-41	10 Jul 1941 – 15 Mar 1942	1 patrol	Sunk with all hands 15 Mar 1942 southeast of Newfoundland by depth charges from a US Navy Lockheed PBO-1 Hudson of VP-82. 51 dead. This was the second U-boat sunk by the US Navy
U-504	IXC	30-Jul-41	1 Jan 1942 – 30 Jul 1943 from 4. Flottille	7 patrols. 15 ships sunk: total 74,959 GRT; 1 ship damaged beyond repair: total 7176 GRT	Sunk with all hands 30 Jul 1943 northwest of Cape Ortegal, Spain, by depth charges from the sloops HMS *Kite*, HMS *Woodpecker*, HMS *Wren* and HMS *Wild Goose*. 53 dead
U-505	IXC	26-Aug-41	1 Feb 1942 – 4 Jun 1944 from 4. Flottille	12 patrols. 8 ships sunk: total 44,962 GRT. Kptlt. Zschech committed suicide while under depth charge attack on 24 Oct 1943; the I WO, Meyer, brought the boat back to port	Captured at sea west of Africa on 4 Jun 1944 by US Navy Task Group 22.3 – escort carrier USS *Guadalcanal*, destroyer escorts USS *Pillsbury*, USS *Chatelain*, USS *Flaherty*, USS *Jenks* and USS *Pope*. 1 dead and 59 survivors. The boat survives and is currently on display at the Chicago Museum of Science and Industry
U-507	IXC	8-Oct-41	1 Mar 1942 – 13 Jan 1943	4 patrols. 19 ships sunk: total 77,144 GRT; 1 ship damaged: total 6561 GRT. Involved in the rescue of 1500 survivors of the *Laconia* in Sep 1942	Sunk with all hands 13 Jan 1943 in the South Atlantic northwest of Natal by depth charges from a US Navy PBY Catalina of VP-83. 55 dead (including one survivor from the merchant ship *Baron Dechmont*, sunk 3 Jan)
U-518	IXC	25-Apr-42	1 Oct 1942 – 31 Oct 1944 from 4. Flottille	7 patrols. 9 ships sunk: total 55,747 GRT; 3 ships damaged: total 22,616 GRT	to 33. Flottille
U-519	IXC	7-May-42	1 Nov 1942 – 31 Jan 1943 from 4. Flottille	2 patrols	Missing with all hands in the Bay of Biscay on or after 31 Jan 1943. 50 dead. May have been sunk by a Wellington of No. 172 Sqn RAF, which was shot down as it attacked an unidentified U-boat on 4 Feb 1943. Previously credited to a USAAF B-24 on 10 Feb, but that attack was actually against U-752
U-520	IXC	19-May-42	1 Oct 1942 – 30 Oct 1942 from 4. Flottille	1 patrol	Sunk with all hands 30 Oct 1942 east of Newfoundland by depth charges from a Canadian Douglas B-18 Digby aircraft of No. 10 Sqn RCAF. 53 dead
U-521	IXC	3-Jun-42	1 Oct 1942 – 2 Jun 1943 from 4. Flottille	3 patrols. 3 ships sunk: total 19,551 GRT; 1 auxiliary warship sunk: total 750 GRT	Sunk 2 Jun 1943 in the North Atlantic southeast of Baltimore by depth charges from the US patrol craft PC-565. 51 dead and 1 survivor
U-522	IXC	11-Jun-42	1 Oct 1942 – 23 Feb 1943	2 patrols. 7 ships sunk: total 45,826 GRT; 2 ships damaged: total 12,479 GRT	Sunk with all hands 23 Feb 1943 southwest of Madeira by depth charges from the sloop HMS *Totland*. 51 dead
U-531	IXC/40	28-Oct-42	1 Apr 1943 – 6 May 1943 from 4. Flottille	1 patrol	Sunk with all hands 6 May 1943 northeast of Newfoundland by depth charges from the destroyer HMS *Vedette*. 54 dead. Previously credited to destroyer HMS *Oribi* and corvette HMS *Snowflake*, but they probably sank U-125
U-532	IXC/40	11-Nov-42	1 Apr 1943 – 30 Sep 1944 from 4. Flottille	4 patrols. 8 ships sunk: total 46,895 GRT; 2 ships damaged: total 13,128 GRT	to 33. Flottille

BOATS THAT SERVED WITH 2ND FLOTILLA (91 BOATS)					
U-Boat	Type	Commissioned	Flotilla(s)	Patrols	Fate
U-534	IXC/40	23-Dec-42	1 Jun 1943 – 31 Oct 1944 from 4. Flottille	3 patrols	to 33. Flottille
U-536	IXC/40	13-Jan-43	1 Jun 1943 – 20 Nov 1943 from 4. Flottille	2 patrols. U-536 was involved in the attempt to pick up some of the top U-boat commanders held at Camp Bowmanville in Canada, but their escape attempt failed	Sunk 20 Nov 1943 northeast of the Azores by depth charges from the frigate HMS *Nene* and the corvettes HMCS *Snowberry* and HMCS *Calgary*. 38 dead and 17 survivors
U-538	IXC/40	10-Feb-43	1 Nov 1943 – 21 Nov 1943 from 4. Flottille	1 patrol	Sunk with all hands 21 Nov 1943 southwest of Ireland by depth charges from the frigate HMS *Foley*. 55 dead
U-545	IXC/40	19-May-43	1 Dec 1943 – 10 Feb 1944 from 4. Flottille	1 patrol. 1 ship damaged: total 7359 GRT	Scuttled with heavy damage west of the Hebrides on 10 Feb 1944, after a depth charge attack by a Canadian Wellington of No. 407 Sqn (which was shot down by the boat) and another Wellington of No. 612 Sqn RAF. 56 survivors were rescued by U-714; 1 crewman was killed
U-547	IXC/40	16-Jun-43	1 Jan 1944 – 30 Sep 1944 from 4. Flottille	3 patrols. 2 ships sunk: total 8371 GRT; 1 auxiliary warship sunk: total 750 GRT	to 33. Flottille
U-548	IXC/40	30-Jun-43	1 Apr 1944 – 30 Sep 1944 from 4. Flottille	4 patrols. 1 warship sunk: total 1468t/1445 tons	to 33. Flottille
U-801	IXC/40	24-Mar-43	1 Nov 1943 – 17 Mar 1944 from 4. Flottille	2 patrols	Sunk 17 Mar 1944 near the Cape Verde Islands by Fido homing torpedo from Avengers of escort carrier USS *Block Island*, and by depth charges and gunfire from destroyer USS *Corry* and destroyer escort USS *Bronstein*. 10 dead and 47 survivors
U-802	IXC/40	12-Jun-43	1 Feb 1944 – 30 Nov 1944 from 4. Flottille	4 patrols. 1 ship sunk: total 1621 GRT	to 33. Flottille
U-821	VIIC	11-Oct-43	1 Nov 1943 – 31 Dec 1943 from 4. Flottille	Torpedo/underwater detection training	to 24. Flottille
U-841	IXC/40	6-Feb-43	1 Jul 1943 – 17 Oct 1943 from 4. Flottille	1 patrol	Sunk 17 Oct 1943 east of Cape Farewell, Greenland, by depth charges from the frigate HMS *Byard*. 27 dead and 27 survivors
U-842	IXC/40	1-Mar-43	1 Aug 1943 – 6 Nov 1943 from 4. Flottille	1 patrol	Sunk with all hands 6 Nov 1943 in the western North Atlantic by depth charges from the sloops HMS *Starling* and HMS *Wild Goose*. 56 dead
U-843	IXC/40	24-Mar-43	1 Nov 1943 – 30 Sep 1944 from 4. Flottille	4 patrols. 1 ship sunk: total 8261 GRT	to 33. Flottille
U-856	IXC/40	19-Aug-43	1 Mar 1944 – 7 Apr 1944 from 4. Flottille	1 patrol	Sunk 7 Apr 1944 east of New York by depth charges from destroyer USS *Champlin* and destroyer escort USS *Huse*. 27 dead and 28 survivors
U-858	IXC/40	30-Sep-43	1 May 1944 – 30 Sep 1944 from 4. Flottille	2 patrols	to 33. Flottille
U-868	IXC/40	23-Dec-43	1 Aug 1944 – 30 Sep 1944 from 4. Flottille	2 patrols. 1 warship sunk: total 683t/672 tons	to 33. Flottille
U-1223	IXC/40	6-Oct-43	1 Aug 1944 – 29 Dec 1944 from 4. Flottille	1 patrol. 1 warship damaged beyond repair: total 1392t/1370 tons; 1 ship damaged: total 7134 GRT	to 33. Flottille
U-1225	IXC/40	10-Nov-43	1 Jun 1944 – 24 Jun 1944 from 31. Flottille	1 patrol	Sunk with all hands 24 Jun 1944 northwest of Bergen by depth charges from a Consolidated Catalina of No. 162 Sqn RCAF
U-1226	IXC/40	24-Nov-43	1 Aug 1944 – 30 Sep 1944 from 31. Flottille	1 patrol	to 33. Flottille
U-1227	IXC/40	8-Dec-43	1 Aug 1944 – 31 Dec 1944 from 31. Flottille	1 patrol. 1 warship damaged beyond repair: total 1392t/1370 tons	to 33. Flottille
U-1228	IXC/40	22-Dec-43	1 Aug 1944 – 31 Oct 1944 from 31. Flottille	2 patrols. 1 warship sunk: total 914t/900 tons	to 33. Flottille
UA	Turkish	20-Sep-39	Apr 1941 – Dec 1941 from 7. Flottille	9 patrols. 7 ships sunk: total 40,706 GRT; 1 damaged: total 7524 tons	back to to 7. Flottille
UD-3	Dutch O 21 class	8-Jun-41	Aug 1941 – Sep 1942 from 5. Flottille	3 patrols. 1 ship sunk: total 5041 GRT	to 10. Flottille

▶ **U-boat pens**

This photograph shows the inside of one of the U-boat pens on the French Atlantic coast. The thick concrete roofs of the pens allowed the U-boats to survive numerous air attacks by the RAF. The Type VIIA submarine on the left is probably U-30, identifiable from the dog emblem on the conning tower. The emblem represented the crew mascot 'Schnurzel', a dog who remained at the base while U-30 was on patrol.

3 Unterseebootsflottille

The 3rd U-boat Flotilla was founded on 4 October 1937 under the command of *Kapitänleutnant* Hans Eckermann and in its first incarnation existed until December 1939. It was refounded in March 1941, as the U-boat force fighting the Battle of the Atlantic expanded.

As with all of the early flotillas, the 3rd Flotilla was originally named after a notable U-boat commander of the Great War. Known as *U-Flottille* Lohs, it commemorated *Oberleutnant zur See* Johannes Lohs, who during World War I made 15 patrols in command of UC-75 and UB-57. He sank 76 ships for a total of 151,063 tonnes (148,677 tons), and he also destroyed the 1219-tonne (1200-ton) sloop HMS *Lavender*. Lohs was killed on 14 August 1918, when UB-57 was sunk by a mine.

The *Flottille* Lohs joined the 1st Flotilla at Kiel, followed by three more flotillas. The *Flottille* Wegener was to become the 7th Flotilla, the *Flottille* Hundius would be redesignated as the 6th Flotilla and the *Flottille* Emsmann became the 5th Flotilla.

Until the outbreak of war, the eight Type IIB boats of the *Flottille* Lohs were mainly used for training: indeed, a number were in the process of being transferred to the *U-Ausbildungsflottille* (U-boat training school flotilla) at Danzig, but became operational on the outbreak of hostilities. However, both the boats and the flotilla itself were too small to be operationally effective, and the *Flottille* Lohs was disbanded in December 1939.

Flotilla reborn

In January 1940, the organization of the German U-boat force underwent a radical restructuring. There were three main combat flotillas, the 1st and the 7th based at Kiel and the 2nd at Wilhelmshaven. The capture of the French Atlantic ports in the *Blitzkrieg* campaign of 1940 meant that the *Kriegsmarine*'s U-boat arm could now be based much closer to the main theatre of operations – the Atlantic Ocean to the west of the British Isles.

In 1940 and 1941, the three main combat flotillas were moved to new bases in France. However, the expansion of the U-boat war meant that three flotillas were not enough to control such an expanding force effectively. In March 1941, the 3rd U-boat Flotilla was recreated as an operational unit, and in September 1941 it was moved to La Pallice, France.

3RD FLOTILLA BASE LOCATIONS

ATLANTIC OCEAN

Kiel

La Pallice/La Rochelle

Chain of command

The restructuring of the U-boat arm in 1940 saw Karl Dönitz promoted to the rank of *Konteradmiral* and appointed *Befehlshaber der Unterseeboote Ops,* or Commander of U-boat Operations. Hans-Georg von Friedeburg was made BdU Org, or Commander of U-boat Organization. Beneath them, four Flag Officers for U-boats (*Führer des U-boote,* or FdU) were appointed, each responsible for a different

Commanders

Kptlt. Hans Eckermann *(Oct 1937 – Dec 1939)*

Korvkpt. Hans Rösing *(Mar 1941 – Jul 1941)*

Kptlt. Herbert Schultze *(Jul 1941 – Mar 1942)*

Kptlt. Heinz v. Reiche *(Mar 1942 – June 1942)*

Korvkpt. Richard Zapp *(June 1942 – Oct 1944)*

3RD FLOTILLA (1937–39, 1941–44)	
Type	**Boats ordered**
Type IIB (to 1940)	8
Type IID	5
Type VIIB	1
Type VIIC	90
Captured/foreign	4

U-570 was the first U-boat to be captured in the war, after she surrendered to an RAF Hudson of 269 Squadron on 27 August 1941.

construction of bomb-proof fortified bunkers. The first two pens were finished in October 1941, and the first boat to arrive from Atlantic operations was U-82, which made port on 19 November 1941. The initial commander of the flotilla was Hans Rösing, an experienced U-boat man and one of a handful of *Reichsmarine* officers who had secretly served as crewmembers on foreign-built submarines between the wars.

Over 100 boats under 3 Flotilla command passed through La Pallice and the nearby base at La Rochelle over the next two and a half years. They mounted 161 combat patrols. Since the flotilla was formed after the first 'Happy Time' and with boats too short-ranged to operate off the US coast in the second 'Happy Time', few of its commanders were able to run up massive scores.

In August 1944, the last U-boats left La Pallice and La Rochelle for Norway as American troops drove southwards from Normandy, and the flotilla was disbanded in October 1944.

operational area. The new 3rd Flotilla came under FdU *West*, based in Paris and later at Angers. By this time, the mainstay of the *U-bootwaffe* was the medium Type VII U-boat, and the first operational boats assigned to the new 3rd Flotilla were mostly Type VIICs, although four Type IIDs (longer-range Type IIs) served briefly in 1941.

French base

The base at La Pallice had originally been used as an alternative home port by the Italian boats located at Bordeaux from 1940. In April 1941 the *Kriegsmarine* decision to locate boats there saw the

3RD FLOTILLA INSIGNIA

Fewer 3rd Flotilla boats carried the unit badge – the turtle – than was common in other units, which may be why it is not as well known as the Bull of the 7th Flotilla or the Laughing Swordfish of the 9th Flotilla.

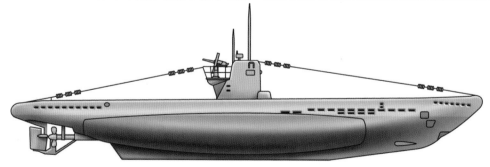

Specifications	
Crew: 25	Dimensions (length/beam/draught): 42.7 x 4.1
Powerplant: Diesel/electric	x 3.8m (140.1 x 13.5 x 12.5ft)
Max Speed: 33/15.4km/hr (17.8/8.3kt) surf/sub	Commissioned: 21 Aug 1935
Surface Range: 3334km (1800nm)	Armament: 6 torpedoes (3 bow tubes);
Displacement: 283/334t (279/329 tons) surf/sub	1 x 2cm (0.8in) gun

▲ U-10

Type IIB

In its first incarnation, the 3rd Flotilla operated a handful of small coastal boats like U-10. This boat had previously served with the 1st Flotilla, and was being used as a training boat until the outbreak of war, when it became operational.

Star commanders
1939–45

Although boasting fewer of the top U-boat aces among its number than other, more well-known formations, the 3rd Flotilla did have several successful captains.

Korvettenkapitän Peter-Erich Cremer

Peter-Erich Cremer was born on 25 March 1911 in Metz, Lorraine. After studying law, he joined the *Reichsmarine* as part of Crew 32. He served with coastal artillery units and aboard destroyers before transferring to U-boats in August 1940.

In January 1941 Cremer commissioned the Type IID boat U-152 before moving on to command the Type VIIC boat U-333. In eight patrols he sank six ships for a total of 26,873 GRT. On his third patrol, he was seriously wounded and spent several months in hospital. Early in 1943 he served on Dönitz's staff before returning to U-333. In 1944, Cremer commissioned the Type XXI 'Electro Boat' U-2519, but made no patrols. In the last days of the war he commanded a tank-destroyer battalion in the fight for Hamburg.

After the war, Cremer made a successful career in business, and wrote a memoir of his time with U-333. He died on 5 July 1992 in Hamburg.

Kapitänleutnant Heinz-Otto Schultze

Heinz-Otto Schultze was born on 13 September 1915 in Kiel, the son of World War I U-boat ace Otto Schultze. He joined the Navy with Crew 34. After training with surface ships, he entered the U-boat arm in May 1937 and served for two years aboard U-31. After some command experience aboard the Type II school boats U-9 and U-141, Schultze was given command of the new Type VIIC boat U-432, which was commissioned in April 1941. He left the boat in February 1942 and in March he joined the 12th Flotilla, where he took command of the new long-range Type IXD2 boat U-849.

In the course of seven patrols with U-432, Schultze sank 19 ships totalling 64,769 GRT, for which he was awarded the Knight's Cross. He died on 25 November 1943 when U-849, en route for the Indian Ocean on her first patrol, was attacked and sunk with all hands in the South Atlantic by a US Navy Liberator flying out of Ascension Island.

STAR COMMANDERS		
Commander	Patrols	Ships Sunk
Korvettenkapitän Peter-Erich Cremer	8	6
Kapitänleutnant Heinz-Otto Schultze	8	19
Korvettenkapitän Helmut Möhlmann	8	5

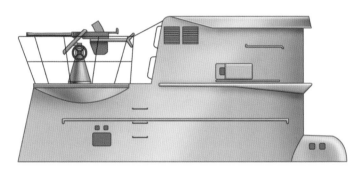

▲ **Type VIIB conning tower**

One of the problems with early Type VII boats was the rather cramped conditions on the bridge. There was little room for a full four-man bridge watch, and the 2cm (0.8in) gun mount had to be widened to make room for its crew. One of the modifications introduced with the Type VIIC boat was the enlargement of the tower by 6cm (2.4in) in width and 30cm (12in) in length.

Korvettenkapitän Helmut Möhlmann

Born on 25 June 1913 in Kiel, Helmut Möhlmann joined the Germany Navy with Crew 33. He served on the light cruiser *Nürnberg* and aboard the torpedo boat (light escort destroyer) *Luchs*. In April 1940 he transferred to the U-boat force. His first command was the school boat U-143, but he moved on to the Type VIIC boat U-571 in May 1941.

Möhlmann made eight patrols in the North Atlantic and the Arctic, sinking five ships totalling 33,511 GRT and damaging three more. He left the boat in May 1943 for a course at the Naval Academy at Berlin, going on to serve on the staff of BdU. From December 1944, he was the commander of the 14th Flotilla at Narvik, Norway. After the surrender, he spent more than four months in captivity. He died on 12 April 1977 at Prien am Chiemsee.

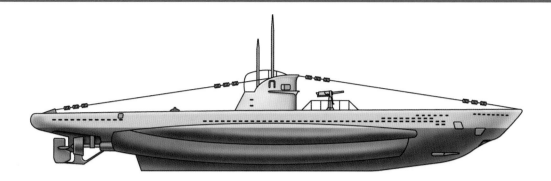

Specifications

Crew: 25

Powerplant: Diesel/electric

Max Speed: 23.5/13.7km/hr (12.7/7.4kt) surf/sub

Surface Range: 6389km (3450nm)

Displacement: 319/370t (314/364 tons)

Dimensions (length/beam/draught): 44 x 4.9 x 3.9m (144.4 x 16.8 x 12.8ft)

Commissioned: Jun 1940 – Jan 1941

Armament: 6 torpedoes (3 bow tubes); 1 x 2cm (0.8in) gun

▲ **U-141**

Type IID

U-141 was a training boat, whose first commander was Heinz-Otto Schultze. It briefly served as a combat boat with 3 Flotilla, mounting four patrols in 1941, during which it sank three ships and damaged another.

◀ **Krupp workshops**

Type II and Type VII U-boats undergo service checks in the docks at Krupp's Germania shipyard in Kiel, 1939. Krupp were Nazi Germany's largest steelmaker, and were consequently involved in the production of many of the *Kriegsmarine*'s U-boats.

U-333
TYPE VIIC

U-333 had a varied career after it was commissioned out of the Nordseewerke yard at Emden in August 1941, making 11 patrols before being destroyed in the English Channel in 1944.

ON ITS FIRST PATROL, U-333 sank three ships before encountering the German blockade runner *Spreewald*. The *Spreewald* was disguised as a Norwegian freighter, and was waiting to rendezvous with U-575 to be escorted into a Biscay port. However, the blockade runner was in the wrong position and was sunk in error by U-333. On its fourth patrol, U-333 fought an epic battle with the British corvette HMS *Crocus* on 6 October 1942. Rammed twice, the U-boat lost three men dead (including the first officer) and several men wounded, including its commander, Cremer. The boat was heavily damaged and limped back to base with help of a replacement first officer, Kptlt. Lorenz Kasch, from the U-107. The boat was directed to meet with the milchcow U-459, which had a doctor

U-333 Commanders

Kptlt. Peter-Erich Cremer *(Aug 1941 – Oct 1942)*

Kptlt. Helmut Kandzior *(Oct 1942 – Oct 1942)*

Kptlt. Lorenz Kasch *(Oct 1942 – Nov 1942)*

Oblt. Werner Schwaff *(Nov 1942 – May 1943)*

Korvkpt. Peter-Erich Cremer

(May 1943 – Jul 1944)

Kptlt. Hans Fiedler *(Jul 1944 – Jul 1944)*

THREE LITTLE FISHES EMBLEM

The emblem of U-333 was chosen by its first commander, Peter-Erich Cremer. The 'Three Little Fishes' were suitably nautical, and the number was selected to reflect that of the U-boat.

aboard to treat the wounded. On the way back to La Pallice U-333 was attacked by HMS *Graph*, the former U-570 which had been captured by the British, but the German boat managed to evade all four torpedoes fired in the encounter. Cremer then spent three months in hospital.

On its sixth patrol, U-333 shot down a Leigh-Light Wellington, but not before the British bomber dropped four depth charges, which damaged the boat. On its eighth patrol, U-333 narrowly avoided being sunk by a destroyer, and snapped its periscope while surfacing under the British ship. On its tenth patrol, U-333 was stuck on the bottom while avoiding depth charges.

U-333 was sunk with all hands on 31 July 1944 to the west of the Scilly Isles by depth charges from Royal Navy warships – the sloop HMS *Starling* and the frigate HMS *Loch Killin*.

▲ U-333

Type VIIC

U-333 was one of a number of boats newly equipped with a *Schnorchel*, which were sent to try to interrupt the flow of supplies across the Channel after the Normandy invasion. It was the first boat to be sunk by the Squid ahead-throwing mortar.

Specifications

Crew: 44

Powerplant: Diesel/electric

Max Speed: 31.5/14.1km/hr (17/7.6kt) surf/sub

Surface Range: 12,040km (6500nm)

Displacement: 773/879t (761/865 tons) surf/sub

Dimensions (length/beam/draught): 67.1 x 6.2 x 4.8m (220.1 x 20.34 x 15.75ft)

Commissioned: 6 Feb 1941

Armament: 14 torpedoes (4 bow/1 stern tubes); 1 x 3.7cm (1.5in) and 2 x twin 2cm (0.8in) guns

U-333 TIMETABLE

Patrol Dates	Operational Area	Ships Sunk
27 Dec 1941 – 9 Feb 1942	Transit from Kiel to La Pallice via N Atlantic	3
30 Mar 1942 – 26 May 1942	US coast off Florida	3
11 Aug 1942 – 24 Aug 1942	Central Atlantic – returned after damage	0
1 Sep 1942 – 23 Oct 1942	Central Atlantic – returned damaged	0
20 Dec 1942 – 2 Feb 1943	North Atlantic	0
5 Feb 1943 – 13 Apr 1943	North Atlantic	1
2 June 1943 – 31 Aug 1943	Central Atlantic	0
21 Oct 1943 – 1 Dec 1943	Off Spanish coast – returned damaged	0
10 Feb 1944 – 12 Feb 1944	North Atlantic, but returned with mechanical fault	0
14 Feb 1944 – 20 Apr 1944	North Atlantic	0
6 June 1944 – 13 June 1944	Channel invasion front	1
23 Jul 1944 – 31 Jul 1944	English Channel	0

U-570

TYPE VIIC

Laid down at the Blohm und Voss yard in Hamburg on 21 May 1940, U-570 was commissioned into the 3rd Flotilla in May of 1941. The boat set off on its only patrol on 23 August 1941.

THE BOAT BECAME FAMOUS because it was captured by the Royal Navy on 27 August 1941, south of Iceland. There were no casualties – all 44 members of the crew survived to be taken prisoner.

Captured on its first patrol

After leaving Trondheim, U-570 was ordered to patrol to the south of Iceland. The green crew were badly affected by the rough weather, and morale was low. While attempting to locate eastbound convoy HX 145, U-570 was spotted on the surface by an RAF Hudson of No. 269 Sqn, which dropped four depth charges before the boat could dive.

The inexperienced crew ran out on deck, waving white flags. The Hudson continued to circle until relieved by a Catalina of No. 209 Sqn. Before nightfall, an anti-submarine trawler arrived, which was reinforced by two destroyers and three more trawlers overnight.

The boat was taken in tow and with difficulty was beached on Iceland at Thorlakshafn. U-570 was repaired and taken into service as HM Submarine *Graph* on 19 September 1941, becoming operational in September 1942. It was stricken on 20 March 1944 after running aground near Islay.

U-570 Commander

Kptlt. Hans-Joachim Rahmlow *(May 1941 – Aug 1941)*

Once in captivity, *Kapitänleutnant* Rahmlow and his first officer, Lt. Berndt, were considered to have displayed cowardice by their fellow prisoners. Berndt was killed in an escape attempt, while Rahmlow was ostracized by his fellows for the rest of the war.

▼ **U-570 surface gun**

Royal Navy personnel board U-570 after its capture. Type VIICs carried an 8.8cm (3.5in) gun. This was effective in dealing with smaller vessels not considered worth a torpedo, but it was of little use in attacking escorted convoys.

▲ **U-570**

Type VIIC

The Type VIIC boats entered production from 1940. They were marginally longer than the preceding Type VIIB, the extra length being used to incorporate a larger control room to enable new sound-detection equipment to be fitted. This artwork shows U-570 in Royal Navy colours, after it became HM Submarine Graph.

Specifications

Crew: 44	Dimensions (length/beam/draught): 67.1 x 6.2 x 4.8m (220.1 x 20.34 x 15.75ft)
Powerplant: Diesel/electric	
Max Speed: 31.5/14.1km/hr (17/7.6kt) surf/sub	Commissioned: 6 Feb 1941
Surface Range: 12,040km (6500nm)	Armament: 14 torpedoes (4 bow/1 stern tubes);
Displacement: 773/879t (761/865 tons) surf/sub	1 x 8.8cm (3.5in) and 1x 2cm (0.8in) guns

U-571

TYPE VIIC

U-571 was laid down at the Blohm und Voss yard in Hamburg on 3 June 1940. The boat was commissioned under the command of Helmut Möhlmann on 22 May 1941.

The boat was assigned to 3rd Flotilla at Kiel, where it underwent working up training and from where it mounted its first patrol in Arctic waters. In October 1941, U-571 transferred from Kiel to 3rd Flotilla's French operating base at La Pallice. Under the command of *Kapitänleutnant* Helmut Möhlmann, U-571 went on seven patrols in the North Atlantic, off Gibraltar and in North American waters. Möhlmann transferred out of the boat in May 1943, going on to serve in staff positions. He was replaced by *Oberleutnant* Gustav Lüssow, who took the boat on her last two patrols into the Atlantic.

U-571 Commanders

Kptlt. Helmut Möhlmann

(May 1941 – May 1943)

Oblt. Gustav Lüssow

(May 1943 – 28 Jan 1944)

Fate

U-571 went on her last patrol in January 1944, when she joined the *Rügen* wolfpack that was dispersed widely in waters to the west of the British Isles. After unsuccesfully attacking a destroyer near Fastnet, U-571 was sunk with all hands on 28 January 1944 west of Ireland, by depth charges from an Australian Sunderland of No.461 Sqn.

U-571 TIMETABLE		
Patrol Dates	**Operational Area**	**Ships Sunk**
18 Aug 1941 – 27 Aug 1941	Arctic waters off the Kola Peninsula	1
22 Oct 1941 – 26 Nov 1941	Transit to La Pallice via Newfoundland and the Azores	0
21 Dec 1941 – 27 Jan 1942	Off Gibraltar	0
10 Mar 1942 – 7 May 1942	Newfoundland/US Coast/Bermuda	3
11 Jun 1942 – 7 Aug 1942	W of Portugal/Carolina coast/Florida coast/Gulf of Mexico	2
3 Oct 1942 – 14 Nov 1942	Central Atlantic	0
22 Dec 1942 – 19 Feb 1943	Central Atlantic/SW of the Azores/W of Portugal	0
25 Mar 1943 – 1 May 1943	W of Biscay/S of Greenland/Newfoundland waters	0
8 Jun 1943 – 1 Sep 1943	Central Atlantic off W Africa	0
8 Jan 1944 – 28 Jan 1944	W of Ireland	0

Specifications

Crew: 44

Powerplant: Diesel/electric

Max Speed: 31.5/14.1km/hr (17/7.6kt) surf/sub

Surface Range: 12,040km (6500nm)

Displacement: 773/879t (761/865 tons) surf/sub

Dimensions (length/beam/draught): 67.1 x 6.2 x 4.8m (220.1 x 20.34 x 15.75ft)

Commissioned: 6 Feb 1941

Armament: 14 torpedoes (4 bow/1 stern tubes); 1 x 3.7cm (1.5in) and 2 x twin 2cm (0.8in) guns

▲ **U-571**

Type VIIC

Early in the war Type VII boats could only operate out to the centre of the Atlantic, but in 1942 commanders realized that by careful engine management they could mount patrols as far as the US coast and even the Caribbean. On U-571's fifth patrol it was refuelled by U-459 and reached as far as the Gulf of Mexico.

U-960
TYPE VIIC

U-960 saw extremes of service in less than a year of combat. From patrols to the edge of the Arctic ice, it was transferred to the warm waters of the Mediterranean.

LAUNCHED AT BLOHM UND VOSS, Hamburg, in December 1942, U-960 was commissioned on 28 January 1943. It mounted two minelaying patrols in Soviet waters before moving to Atlantic operations for three months. On 27 April 1944, U-960 set off for the Mediterranean, probably passing through the Straits of Gibraltar on the night of 14/15 May.

Fate

On 17 May, U-960 attacked the destroyer USS *Ellyson* off Oran. The destroyer had survivors on board from U-616, which had been destroyed only five hours before to the east of Cartagena. U-960's attack missed, and Allied anti-submarine forces immediately started a Swamp operation. This involved every available unit being vectored onto the possible position of the U-boat. Four American destroyers formed a line across the U-boat's predicted path, and once an aircraft made radar contact early on the 19th the nearest destroyers raced in to attack.

Forced to the surface, U-960 exchanged fire with first two and then four destroyers, until attacked by a Wellington and a Ventura. The boat dived, but depth charges from the USS *Niblack* again forced the boat to the surface, where the surviving crew abandoned U-960 as it sank.

U-960 Commander

Oblt. Günther Heinrich *(Jan 1943 – May 1944)*

U-960 TIMETABLE		
Patrol Dates	Operational Area	Ships Sunk
3 Aug 1943 – 15 Aug 1943	Transit from Kiel to Narvik via Bergen	0
18 Aug 1943 – 1 Sep 1943	Minelaying patrol in Matochkin Strait	0
14 Sep 1943 – 10 Oct 1943	Minelaying/attack patrol in Soviet waters	2
14 Oct 1943 – 16 Oct 1943	Transit to Trondheim	0
4 Dec 1943 – 3 Feb 1944	Transit to La Pallice via N Atlantic	1
16 Feb 1944 – 18 Feb 1944	Returned with mechanical fault	0
19 Mar 1944 – 27 Mar 1944	Atlantic, but damaged by Mosquito attack	0
27 Apr 1944 – 19 May 1944	Transit to Mediterranean	0

Convoy TM 1
3 JANUARY 1943

Convoy TM 1 was a strategically important mission to supply fuel to the North African battle front. Escorted by four warships, the convoy was attacked by a wolfpack of 14 U-boats.

OPERATION *TORCH* had taken place in November 1942. The Allied landings in Northwest Africa were intended to eliminate the Axis armies in Africa and to provide a jumping-off point for the planned invasion of Sicily. Fuel was a vital necessity, so it was decided that instead of loaded tankers sailing from the Caribbean up to Nova Scotia, then travelling in convoy to Britain before sailing on to Gibraltar, convoys would be formed at Trinidad and go directly to Gibraltar and thence to North Africa. TM 1

CONVOY TM 1 BATTLE TIMETABLE	
Date	Event
29 Dec 1942	U-124 sights a part of the convoy heading for an assembly point
3 Jan 1943	U-514 locates the convoy and leaves one tanker abandoned and adrift. The hulk is sunk by U-105 three weeks later. Dönitz, realizing that such a large tanker convoy is likely to be heading direct for North Africa to support the victorious Allied offensives, orders his boats to ignore Convoy GUS 2, which a wolfpack had been preparing to attack, and to move instead against TM 1
4 Jan	Dönitz establishes Group *Delphin*, which with some other boats sets up a patrol line in the central Atlantic
8 Jan	U-381 sights the convoy. U-436, U-571 and U-575 head towards it. U-436 attacks in the evening, sinking a tanker and damaging another, before being damaged and driven off by the escort. U-571 and U-575 are unable to penetrate the screen
9 Jan	U-575 damages two tankers and newly arrived U-442 hits another. U-181 and U-134 are driven off, the latter damaged by depth charges. U-620 has also arrived, and shadows the convoy. At nightfall U-522 finishes off two damaged tankers, while U-442 and U-436 sink another. Meanwhile, U-511 sinks an independent ship not belonging to the convoy
10 Jan	U-522 damages a tanker, which is given the *coup de grâce* by U-620
11 Jan	U-571 attacks but fails to sink the two surviving tankers
12 Jan	U-511 is driven off by the escort
13 Jan	The escort is reinforced by the destroyer HMS *Quentin* and the corvettes HMS *Penstemon* and *Samphire*. Air cover also arrives
14 Jan	The two surviving tankers arrive at Gibraltar

was to be the first of these direct fuel convoys. The Germans were fully aware of the importance of fuel convoys. U-124 spotted a small part of TM 1 headed eastwards, and when U-514 came across nine tankers Admiral Dönitz realized that a large fuel convoy was heading direct from the Caribbean oilfields to the battle theatre of North Africa.

The vital importance of the convoy was clear. Dönitz ordered a number of boats assembled to attack convoy GUS 2 to ignore that target and attempt to intercept the tankers. The U-boat C-in-C ordered the *Delphin* pack together with some independent boats, into a patrol line on the convoy's predicted route.

The convoy commander received a warning of U-boat activity based on direction-finding bearings on U-boat radio transmissions, but curiously ignored an instruction from the Submarine Tracking Room to re-route. As a result, the nine tankers ran straight into the patrol line, being sighted by U-381 on 8 January.

The opponents

The wolfpack *Delphin* consisted of 10 boats, including U-134 (Kptlt. Schendel), U-181 (Korvkpt. Lüth), U-381 (Kptlt. von Puckler und Limburg), U-436 (KptlLt. Seibicke), U-442 (Korvkpt. Hesse), U-511 (Kptlt. Schneewind), U-522 (Kptlt.

Schneider), U-571 (Kptlt. Möhlmann), U-575 (Kptlt. Heydemann), and U-620 (Kptlt. Stein). They were reinforced by U-105 (Oblt. Nissen), U-124 (Korvkpt. Mohr), U-125 (Kptlt. Folkers) and U-514 (Kptlt. Auffermann). The convoy was escorted by Royal Navy Escort Group B5, which included the destroyer HMS *Havelock* and the corvettes HMS *Pimpernel*, HMS *Saxifrage* and HMS *Godetia*.

High toll

In two days of attacks, the U-boats succeeded in sinking seven out of nine tankers. However, the final attacks failed since by 12 January the escort had finally been reinforced by the destroyer HMS *Quentin* and the corvettes HMS *Penstemon* and HMS *Samphire*. The arrival of air cover ensured that the two remaining tankers finally arrived in Gibraltar on 14 January.

TM 1 suffered the highest percentage loss of any Atlantic convoy. Only two of the tankers eventually reached Gibraltar, the *Cliona* and the *Vanja*. On receiving the news of the convoy battle, the commander of *Panzerarmee Afrika*, General von Arnim, sent congratulations to Dönitz, thanking him for the substantial contribution the U-boats had made to the Axis battle for survival in the North African theatre.

Wolfpack group *Ritter*
FEBRUARY 1943

Ritter was one of three wolfpacks, along with the *Knappen* and *Neptun* groups, which were directed against convoy ON 166.

Wolfpacks *Ritter*, *Knappen* and *Neptun* were sent to attack convoy ON 166. Located in the central Atlantic by the independently operating U-604 on 20 February 1943, ON 166's escorts drove off the shadowing boat before the wolfpacks could concentrate.

However, by the next day the U-boats were in position. Over the next five days, in a battle covering 1600km (1000 miles) right up to Newfoundland waters, ON 166 lost 14 ships totalling more than 88,000 GRT. At least three U-boats from the combined wolfpacks were sunk.

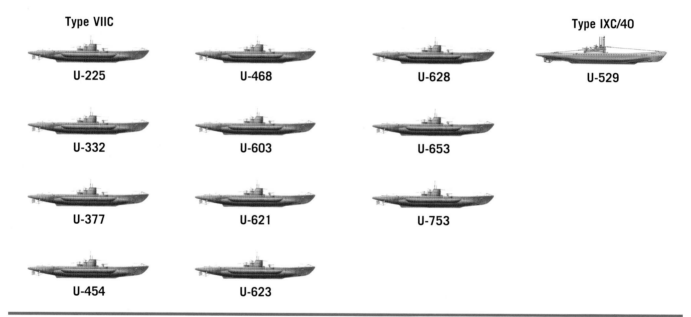

Type VIIC

U-225   U-468   U-628

Type IXC/40

U-529

U-332   U-603   U-653

U-377   U-621   U-753

U-454   U-623

BOATS THAT SERVED WITH 3RD FLOTILLA (108 BOATS)					
U-Boat	Type	Commissioned	Flotilla(s)	Patrols	Fate
U-10	IIB	9-Sep-35	4 Oct 1937 – 14 Apr 1939 from 1. Flottille	5 patrols. 2 ships sunk: total 6356 GRT	to U-Bootschulflottille
U-12	IIB	1-Sep-35	1 Sep 1935 – 8 Oct 1939	1 patrol	Sunk with all hands 8 Oct 1939 near Dover by a mine. 27 dead
U-14	IIB	18-Jan-36	18 Jan 1936 – 31 Oct 1939	6 patrols. 9 ships sunk: total 12,344 GRT	to U-Ausbildungsflottille
U-16	IIB	16-May-36	16 May 1936 – 25 Oct 1939	3 patrols. 1 ship sunk: total 3378 GRT; 1 auxiliary warship sunk: total 57 GRT	Sunk with all hands 25 Oct 1939 near Dover by depth charges from the ASW trawler HMS *Cayton Wyke* and the patrol vessel HMS *Puffin*. 28 dead
U-18	IIB	4-Jan-36	1 Sep 1939 – 1 Mar 1940 from 1. Flottille	14 patrols. 3 ships sunk: total 1985 GRT; 1 ship damaged: total 7745 GRT; 1 warship damaged: total 57t/56 tons	to U-Ausbildungsflottille
U-20	IIB	1-Feb-36	1 Feb 1936 – 31 Dec 1939	17 patrols. 14 ships sunk: total 37,669 GRT; 1 ship damaged beyond repair: total 844 GRT; 1 ship damaged: total 1846 GRT	to 1. Flottille
U-22	IIB	20-Aug-36	20 Aug 1936 – 31 Dec 1939	7 patrols. 6 ships sunk: total 7344 GRT; 2 auxiliary warships sunk: total 3633 GRT; 1 warship sunk: total 1497 GRT	to 1. Flottille
U-24	IIB	10-Oct-36	10 Oct 1936 – 17 Oct 1939	20 patrols. 1 ship sunk: total 961 GRT; 5 MTBs sunk: total 580 GRT; 1 ship a total loss: total 7886 GRT; 1 ship damaged: total 7661 GRT	to 1. Flottille
U-82	VIIC	14-May-41	14 May 1941 – 6 Feb 1942	3 patrols. 8 ships sunk: total 51,859 GRT; 1 warship sunk: total 1209t/1190 tons; 1 ship damaged: total 1999 GRT	Sunk with all hands 6 Feb 1942 north of the Azores by depth charges from the sloop HMS *Rochester* and the corvette HMS *Tamarisk*. The boat was attacking convoy OS 18 while returning from Operation *Drumbeat* off the US east coast. 45 dead

BOATS THAT SERVED WITH 3RD FLOTILLA (108 BOATS)

U-Boat	Type	Commissioned	Flotilla(s)	Patrols	Fate
U-85	VIIB	7-Jun-41	7 Jun 1941 – 14 Apr 1942	4 patrols. 3 ships sunk: total 15,060 GRT	Sunk with all hands 14 Apr 1942 off the US coast near Cape Hatteras by gunfire from the destroyer USS *Roper*. 46 dead. U-85 was the first of the Operation *Drumbeat (Paukenschlag)* U-boats to be sunk off the North American coast, three months after the campaign against American shipping started
U-132	VIIC	29-May-41	29 May 1941 – 4 Nov 1942	4 patrols. 8 ships sunk: total 32,964 GRT; 1 warship sunk: total 2252t/2216 tons; 1 ship damaged beyond repair: total 4367 GRT; 1 ship damaged: total 6690 GRT	U-132 and its crew probably died with its final victim on 4 Nov 1942; the ammunition ship *Hatimura* detonated in a massive explosion and U-132 was probably within the lethal radius. 47 dead. The sinking was originally attributed to RAF aircraft from No. 120 Sqn on 5 Nov 1942 southeast of Cape Farewell, Greenland. That attack was most likely against U-89, which was severely damaged
U-134	VIIC	26-Jul-41	1 Nov 1941 – 24 Aug 1943 from 5. Flottille	7 patrols. 3 ships sunk: total 12,147 GRT	Sunk with all hands 24 Aug 1943 in the North Atlantic near Vigo, Spain, by 6 depth charges from a Wellington of No. 179 Sqn RAF. 48 dead
U-138	IID	27-Jun-40	1 May 1941 – 18 Jun 1941 from 22. Flottille	5 patrols. 6 ships sunk: total 48,564 GRT; 1 ship damaged: total 6993 GRT	Sunk 18 Jun 1941 west of Cadiz by depth charges from destroyers HMS *Faulknor*, HMS *Fearless*, HMS *Forester*, HMS *Foresight* and HMS *Foxhound*. All 27 crew survived
U-141	IID	21-Aug-40	1 May 1941 – 30 Sept 1941 from 1. Flottille	4 patrols. 3 ships sunk: total 6801 GRT; 1 ship damaged: total 5133 GRT	to 21. Flottille
U-143	IID	18-Sep-40	1 Apr 1941 – 12 Sept 1941 from 22. Flottille	4 patrols. 1 ship sunk: total 1409 GRT	to 22. Flottille
U-146	IID	30-Oct-40	22 Sept 1941 – 31 Aug 1941 from 22. Flottille	2 patrols. 1 ship sunk: total 3496 GRT	to 22. Flottille
U-147	IID	11-Dec-40	Feb 1941 – 2 Jun 1941 from 22. Flottille	3 patrols. 3 ships sunk: total 8636 GRT	Sunk with all hands off Malin Head on 2 Jun 1941 by depth charges from destroyer HMS *Windermere* and corvette HMS *Periwinkle*. 26 dead
U-205	VIIC	3-May-41	3 May 1941 – 1 Nov 1941	11 patrols. 1 ship sunk: total 2623 GRT; 1 warship sunk: total 5537t/5450 tons	to 29. Flottille
U-206	VIIC	17-May-41	17 May 1941 – 30 Nov 1941	3 patrols. 2 ships sunk: total 3283 GRT; 1 warship sunk: total 940t/925 tons	Missing with all hands in the Bay of Biscay, west of St Nazaire, on about 30 Nov 1941. Possibly sunk in the minefield 'Beech' laid by RAF aircraft the previous year. 46 dead. Loss previously attributed to depth charges from a British Whitley aircraft of No. 502 Sqn; that attack is thought now to have been against U-71, which escaped without damage
U-212	VIIC	25-Apr-42	1 Nov 1943 – 21 Jul 1944 from 13. Flottille	15 patrols. 1 ship sunk: total 80 GRT	Sunk with all hands 21 Jul 1944 in the English Channel south of Brighton by depth charges from the frigates HMS *Curzon* and HMS *Ekins*. 49 dead
U-231	VIIC	14-Nov-42	1 May 1943 – 13 Jan 1944 from 5. Flottille (training)	3 patrols	Sunk 13 Jan 1944 northeast of the Azores by depth charges from a Vickers Wellington of No. 172 Sqn RAF. 7 dead and 43 survivors
U-241	VIIC	24-Jul-43	1 Apr 1944 – 18 May 1944 from 5. Flottille (training)	1 patrol	Sunk with all hands 18 May 1944 northeast of the Faroes by depth charges from a Catalina of No. 210 Sqn RAF. 51 dead
U-242	VIIC	14-Aug-43	1 Jun 1944 – 5 Jul 1944 from 5. Flottille (training)	7 patrols. 3 ships sunk: total 2595 GRT	to 5. Flottille
U-245	VIIC	18-Dec-43	1 Aug 1944 – 1 Oct 1944 from 5. Flottille (training)	3 patrols. 3 ships sunk: total 17,087 GRT	to 33. Flottille
U-246	VIIC	11-Jan-44	1 Aug 1944 – 30 Sep 1944 from 5. Flottille (training)	2 patrols	to 11. Flottille
U-257	VIIC	14-Jan-42	1 Oct 1942 – 24 Feb 1944 from 5. Flottille	6 patrols	Sunk 24 Feb 1944 in the North Atlantic by depth charges from the Canadian frigate HMCS *Waskesiu* and the British frigate HMS *Nene*. 30 dead and 19 survivors
U-258	VIIC	4-Feb-42	1 Sep 1942 – 20 May 1943 from 5. Flottille (training)	4 patrols. 1 ship sunk: total 6198 GRT	Sunk with all hands 20 May 1943 in the North Atlantic by depth charges from a Liberator of No. 120 Sqn RAF. 49 dead
U-259	VIIC	18-Feb-42	1 Sep 1942 – 15 Nov 1942 from 5. Flottille (training)	2 patrols	Sunk with all hands 15 Nov 1942 in the Mediterranean north of Algiers by depth charges from a Lockheed Hudson of No. 500 Sqn RAF. 48 dead
U-262	VIIC	15-Apr-42	1 Oct 1942 – 9 Nov 1944 from 5. Flottille (training)	10 patrols. 3 ships sunk: total 13,010 GRT; 1 warship sunk: total 940t/925 tons	to 33. Flottille
U-275	VIIC	25-Nov-42	1 Jun 1943 – 30 Sep 1944 from 8. Flottille	9 patrols. 1 ship sunk: total 4934 GRT; 1 warship sunk: total 1107t/1090 tons	to 11. Flottille
U-280	VIIC	13-Feb-43	1 Aug 1943 – 16 Nov 1943	1 patrol	Sunk with all hands 16 Nov 1943 southwest of Iceland by depth charges from a Liberator of No. 86 Sqn RAF. 49 dead
U-289	VIIC	10-Jul-43	1 Apr 1944 – 1 May 1944 from 8. Flottille	2 patrols. On 25 Apr 1944 U-289 landed 2 agents on Iceland	to 13. Flottille
U-332	VIIC	7-Jun-41	7 Jun 1941 – 29 Apr 1943	7 patrols. 8 ships sunk: total 46,729 GRT; 1 ship damaged: total 5964 GRT	Sunk with all hands 29 Apr 1943 north of Cape Finisterre, Spain, by depth charges from a Liberator of No. 224 Sqn RAF. 45 dead. Previously the sinking was credited to an Australian Sunderland on 2 May 1943, but that probably sank U-465.
U-333	VIIC	25-Aug-41	1 Jan 1942 – 31 Jul 1944 from 5. Flottille	12 patrols. 7 ships sunk: total 32,107 GRT; 1 ship damaged: total 8327 GRT; 1 warship damaged: total 940t/925 tons	Sunk with all hands 31 Jul 1944 west of the Scilly Isles by depth charges from the sloop HMS *Starling* and the frigate HMS *Loch Killin*. 45 dead
U-334	VIIC	9-Oct-41	1 Mar 1942 – 30 Jun 1942 from 8. Flottille	8 patrols. 2 ships sunk: total 14,372 GRT	to 11. Flottille

U-Boat	Type	Commissioned	Flotilla(s)	Patrols	Fate
			BOATS THAT SERVED WITH 3RD FLOTILLA (108 BOATS)		
U-341	VIIC	28-Nov-42	1 Jun 1943 – 19 Sep 1943 from 8. Flottille	2 patrols	Sunk with all hands 19 Sep 1943 southwest of Iceland by depth charges from a Liberator of No. 10 Sqn RCAF. 50 dead
U-343	VIIC	26-Mar-43	1 Apr 1944 – 31 May 1944 from 8. Flottille	5 patrols. 1 warship sunk: total 1372t/1350 tons	to 11. Flottille
U-352	VIIC	28-Aug-41	28 Aug 1941 – 9 May 1942	3 patrols	Sunk 9 May 1942 southwest of Cape Hatteras by depth charges from the US Coast Guard cutter *Icarus*. 15 dead and 33 survivors
U-373	VIIC	22-May-41	22 May 1941 – 8 Jun 1944	15 patrols. 3 ships sunk: total 10,263 GRT	Sunk 8 Jun 1944 in the Bay of Biscay west of Brest by depth charges from a Liberator of No. 224 Sqn RAF. 4 dead and 47 survivors. The same aircraft also sank U-441 20 minutes later
U-375	VIIC	19-Jul-41	1 Nov 1941 – 31 Dec 1941 from 5. Flottille	11 patrols. 9 ships sunk: total 16,847 GRT; 1 ship damaged b/r: total 6288 GRT; 1 warship damaged: total 2693t/2650 tons	to 29. Flottille
U-376	VIIC	21-Aug-41	1 Mar 1943 – 13 Apr 1943 from 11. Flottille	8 patrols. 2 ships sunk: total 10,146 GRT	Missing with all hands in the Bay of Biscay on or after 13 Apr 1943. 47 dead. Previously credited to a Wellington of No. 172 Sqn RAF on 10 Apr 1943 west of Nantes. The aircraft actually severely damaged U-465 in that attack
U-378	VIIC	30-Oct-41	1 Mar 1942 – 30 Jun 1942 from 8. Flottille	11 patrols. 1 warship sunk: total 1951t/1920 tons	to 11. Flottille
U-378	VIIC	30-Oct-41	1 May 1943 – 20 Oct 1943 from 11. Flottille	11 patrols. 1 warship sunk: total 1951t/1920 tons	Sunk with all hands 20 Oct 1943 in the North Atlantic by depth charges and gunfire from US Navy Avengers and Wildcats of the escort carrier USS *Core*. 48 dead
U-384	VIIC	18-Jul-42	1 Jan 1943 – 19 Mar 1943 from 5. Flottille	2 patrols. 2 ships sunk: total 13,407 GRT	Sunk with all hands 19 Mar 1943 southwest of Iceland by depth charges from a B-17 Fortress of No. 206 Sqn RAF. 47 dead. Previously credited to a Sunderland the next day, but that attack was actually against U-631 and caused no damage
U-391	VIIC	24-Apr-43	1 Oct 1943 – 13 Dec 1943 from 5. Flottille	1 patrol	Sunk with all hands 13 Dec 1943 in the Bay of Biscay northwest of Cape Ortegal by depth charges from a Liberator of No. 53 Sqn. 51 dead
U-398	VIIC	18-Dec-43	1 Aug 1944 – 31 Oct 1944 from 5. Flottille	2 patrols	to 33. Flottille
U-402	VIIC	21-May-41	21 May 1941 – 13 Oct 1943	8 patrols. 14 ships sunk: total 70,434 GRT; 1 auxiliary warship sunk: total 602 GRT; 3 ships damaged: total 28,682 GRT	Sunk with all hands 13 Oct 1943 in the central North Atlantic by a Fido acoustic torpedo dropped by a US Navy Avenger of the escort carrier USS *Card*. 50 dead
U-431	VIIC	5-Apr-41	5 Apr 1941 – 31 Dec 1941	16 patrols. 7 ships sunk: total 9752 GRT; 1 auxiliary warship sunk: total 313 GRT; 2 warships sunk: total 3605t/3548 tons; 1 ship damaged beyond repair: total 6415 GRT; 1 ship damaged: total 3560 GRT; 1 warship damaged: total 457t/450 tons	to 29. Flottille
U-432	VIIC	26-Apr-41	26 Apr 1941 – 11 Mar 1943	8 patrols. 19 ships sunk: total 64,769 GRT; 1 warship sunk: total 1362t/1340 tons; 2 ships damaged: total 15,666 GRT	Sunk 11 Mar 1943 in the North Atlantic by depth charges and gunfire from the Free French corvette *Aconit*. 26 dead and 20 survivors
U-433	VIIC	24-May-41	24 May 1941 – 16 Nov 1941	2 patrols. 1 ship damaged: total 2215 GRT	Foundered on 16 Nov 1941 in the Mediterranean south of Malaga, Spain, after being damaged by depth charges and gunfire east of Gibraltar by the corvette HMS *Marigold*. 6 dead and 38 survivors
U-444	VIIC	9-May-42	1 Jan 1943 – 11 Mar 1943 from 8. Flottille	2 patrols	Sunk 11 Mar 1943 in the North Atlantic by ramming and depth charges from the destroyer HMS *Harvester* and the Free French corvette *Aconit*. 41 dead and 4 survivors
U-451	VIIC	3-May-41	3 May 1941 – 21 Dec 1941	4 patrols. 1 warship sunk: total 448t/441 tons	Sunk 21 Dec 1941 near Tangier by depth charges from a Royal Navy Swordfish of No. 812 Sqn. 44 dead and 1 survivor
U-452	VIIC	29-May-41	29 May 1941 – 25 Aug 1941	1 patrol	Sunk with all hands 25 Aug 1941 southeast of Iceland by depth charges from the anti-submarine trawler HMS *Vascama* and from a Catalina of No. 209 Sqn RAF. 42 dead
U-458	VIIC	12-Dec-41	1 Jul 1942 – 31 Oct 1942 from 8. Flottille	7 patrols. 2 ships sunk: total 7584 GRT	to 29. Flottille
U-466	VIIC	17-Jun-42	1 Jan 1943 – 31 Mar 1944 from 5. Flottille	5 patrols	to 29. Flottille
U-468	VIIC	12-Aug-42	1 Feb 1943 – 11 Aug 1943 from 5. Flottille	3 patrols. 1 ship sunk: total 6537 GRT	Sunk 11 Aug 1943 near Bathurst by depth charges from a Liberator of No. 200 Sqn RAF, which was shot down. 44 dead and 7 survivors. The pilot of the Liberator, Flying Officer Lloyd Trigg RNZAF, was awarded a posthumous Victoria Cross based on the testimony of the surviving officers of the U-boat
U-469	VIIC	7-Oct-42	1 Mar 1943 – 25 Mar 1943 from 5. Flottille	1 patrol	Sunk with all hands 25 Mar 1943 south of Iceland by depth charges from a Flying Fortress of No. 206 Sqn RAF. 47 dead
U-476	VIIC	28-Jul-43	1 Apr 1944 – 25 May 1944	1 patrol	Badly damaged northwest of Trondheim 24 May 1944 by depth charges from a Catalina of No. 210 Sqn RAF which killed 34. Scuttled the next day by torpedoes from U-990. U-990 rescued 21 of the crew, but was itself sunk by a Liberator a few hours later. 19 of the rescued crewmen survived and two died
U-478	VIIC	8-Sep-43	1 Jun 1944 – 30 Jun 1944 from 5. Flottille	1 patrol	Sunk with all hands 30 Jun 1944 northeast of the Faroes by depth charges from a Canso (Canadian-built PBY Catalina) of No. 162 Sqn RCAF and a Liberator of No. 86 Sqn RAF. 52 dead

U-Boat	Type	Commissioned	Flotilla(s)	Patrols	Fate
BOATS THAT SERVED WITH 3RD FLOTILLA (108 BOATS)					
U-483	VIIC	22-Dec-43	1 Aug 1944 – 4 Sep 1944 from 5. Flottille	2 patrols. 1 warship damaged beyond repair: total 1321t/1300 tons	to 11. Flottille
U-484	VIIC	19-Jan-44	1 Aug 1944 – 9 Sep 1944 from 5. Flottille	1 patrol	Sunk with all hands 9 Sept 1944 northwest of Ireland by depth charges from the corvette HMS *Porchester Castle* and the frigate HMS *Helmsdale*. 52 dead
U-553	VIIC	23-Dec-40	1 Dec 1942 – 20 Jan 1943 from 7. Flottille	10 patrols. 13 ships sunk: total 64,612 GRT; 2 ships damaged: total 15,273 GRT	Missing with all hands in the central North Atlantic in Jan 1943. The boat sent its last message on 20 Jan 1943, reporting: 'Sehrohr unklar' (Periscope unclear). 47 dead
U-567	VIIC	24-Apr-41	24 Apr 1941 – 31 Oct 1941	3 patrols. 2 ships sunk: total 6809 GRT	to 7. Flottille
U-568	VIIC	1-May-41	1 May 1941 – 31 Dec 1941	5 patrols. 1 ship sunk: total 6023 GRT; 2 warships sunk: total 1880t/1850 tons; 1 warship damaged: total 1656t/1630 tons	to 29. Flottille
U-569	VIIC	8-May-41	8 May 1941 – 22 May 1943	9 patrols. 1 ship sunk: total 984 GRT; 1 ship damaged: total 4458 GRT	Scuttled 22 May 1943 in the North Atlantic after being badly damaged by depth charges from a pair of Grumman Avengers of the escort carrier USS *Bogue*. 21 dead and 25 survivors
U-570	VIIC	15-May-41	15 May 1941 – 27 Aug 1941	1 patrol	Captured by the Royal Navy on 27 Aug 1941 south of Iceland, after being damaged by a Lockheed Hudson of No. 269 Sqn RAF. 44 survivors – no casualties. Repaired and taken into service as HM Submarine *Graph* on 19 Sep 1941, becoming operational in Sep 1942. Taken out of service in Feb 1944. Stricken on 20 Mar 1944 after running aground near Islay. Broken up
U-571	VIIC	22-May-41	22 May 1941 – 28 Jan 1944	11 patrols. 5 ships sunk: total 33,511 GRT; 2 ships damaged beyond repair: total 13,658 GRT; 1 ship damaged: total 11,394 GRT	Sunk with all hands 28 Jan 1944 west of Ireland by depth charges from an Australian Sunderland of No. 461 Sqn. 52 dead
U-572	VIIC	29-May-41	29 May 1941 – 3 Aug 1943	9 patrols. 6 ships sunk: total 19,323 GRT; 1 ship damaged: total 6207 GRT	Sunk with all hands 3 Aug 1943 in the Caribbean northeast of Trinidad by depth charges from a Martin Mariner of US Navy Patrol Squadron VP-205. 47 dead. Former commander Kptlt. Heinz Hirsacker was the only U-boat captain to be found guilty of cowardice in the face of the enemy. He committed suicide on 24 Apr 1943, shortly before his scheduled execution
U-573	VIIC	5-Jun-41	5 Jun 1941 – 31 Dec 1941	4 patrols. 1 ship sunk: total 5289 GRT	to 29. Flottille
U-596	VIIC	13-Nov-41	1 Jul 1942 – 18 Nov 1942 from 8. Flottille	12 patrols. 12 ships sunk: total 41,411 GRT; 1 warship sunk: total 250t/246 tons; 2 ships damaged: total 14,180 GRT	to 29. Flottille
U-600	VIIC	11-Dec-41	1 Aug 1942 – 25 Nov 1943 from 5. Flottille	6 patrols. 5 ships sunk: total 28,600 GRT; 3 ships damaged: total 19,230 GRT	Sunk with all hands 25 Nov 1943 north of Punta Delgada by depth charges from the frigates HMS *Bazely* and HMS *Blackwood*. 54 dead
U-611	VIIC	26-Feb-42	1 Oct 1942 – 8 Dec 1942 from 5. Flottille	1 patrol	Sunk with all hands 8 Dec 1942 southeast of Cape Farewell by depth charges from a Liberator of No. 120 Sqn RAF. 45 dead. Previously credited to a US Navy PBY Catalina on 10 Dec, but that attack was probably against U-609, which was undamaged
U-613	VIIC	12-Mar-42	1 Nov 1942 – 23 Jul 1943 from 8. Flottille	4 patrols. 2 ships sunk: total 8087 GRT	Sunk with all hands 23 Jul 1943 south of the Azores by depth charges from the destroyer USS *George E. Badger*. 48 dead
U-615	VIIC	26-Mar-42	1 Sep 1942 – 7 Aug 1943 from 8. Flottille	4 patrols. 4 ships sunk: total 27,231 GRT	Scuttled after being damaged in one of the longest battles between a U-boat and aircraft. From the night of 5/6 Aug to 7 Aug, U-615 was attacked by 6 US Navy Mariners and 1 Ventura. U-615's battle let many other U-boats in the Caribbean come to the surface and escape to the east. 4 dead and 43 survivors
U-619	VIIC	23-Apr-42	1 Oct 1942 – 5 Oct 1942 from 5. Flottille	1 patrol. 2 ships sunk: total 8723 GRT	Sunk with all hands 5 Oct 1942 southwest of Iceland, by 4 depth charges from a Hudson of No. 269 Sqn RAF. 44 dead. Previously credited to destroyer HMS *Viscount* on 15 Oct 1942, but that attack almost certainly sank U-661
U-620	VIIC	30-Apr-42	1 Oct 1942 – 13 Feb 1943 from 8. Flottille	2 patrols. 1 ship sunk: total 6983 GRT	Sunk with all hands 13 Feb 1943 northwest of Lisbon by depth charges from a Catalina of No. 202 Sqn RAF. 47 dead. Another Catalina was credited with sinking U-620 the next day, but it probably targeted U-381 and caused no damage
U-625	VIIC	4-Jun-42	1 Oct 1942 – 31 Oct 1942 from 8. Flottille	9 patrols. 3 ships sunk: total 18,751 GRT; 2 auxiliary warships sunk: total 939 GRT	to 11. Flottille
U-630	VIIC	9-Jul-42	1 Apr 1943 – 6 May 1943 from 5. Flottille	1 patrol. 2 ships sunk: total 14,894 GRT	Sunk with all hands 6 May 1943 northeast of Newfoundland by depth charges from the destroyer HMS *Vidette*. 47 dead. Previously credited to a Catalina of No. 5 Sqn RCAF on 4 May 1943 south of Greenland, which actually damaged U-209
U-635	VIIC	13-Aug-42	1 Apr 1943 – 5 Apr 1943 from 5. Flottille	1 patrol. 1 ship sunk: total 9365 GRT; 1 ship damaged: total 5529 GRT	Sunk with all hands 5 Apr 1943 southwest of Iceland by depth charges from a Liberator of No. 210 Sqn RAF. 47 dead. Previously credited to depth charges from the frigate HMS *Tay*, which attacked U-306 the same day and inflicted no damage
U-645	VIIC	22-Oct-42	1 May 1943 – 24 Dec 1943 from 5. Flottille	3 patrols. 2 ships sunk: total 12,788 GRT	Sunk with all hands 24 Dec 1943 northeast of the Azores by depth charges from the destroyer USS *Schenck*. 55 dead

BOATS THAT SERVED WITH 3RD FLOTILLA (108 BOATS)					
U-Boat	Type	Commissioned	Flotilla(s)	Patrols	Fate
	VIIC	3-Apr-41	3 Apr 1941 – 31 Dec 1941	8 patrols. 2 ships sunk: total 8152 GRT; 1 auxiliary warship	to 29. Flottille. U-652 fought an inconclusive duel with
U-652				sunk: total 558 GRT; 2 warships sunk: total 2784t/2740 tons; 2 ships damaged: total 9918 GRT; 1 auxiliary warship damaged: total 10,917 GRT	the destroyer USS *Greer* on 4 Sep 1941 – three months before the US declaration of war
	VIIC	8-Oct-41	1 Mar 1942 – 30 Jun 1942 from 8. Flottille	7 patrols. 1 ship sunk: total 5196 GRT	to 8. Flottille
U-657	VIIC	12-Feb-42	1 Oct 1942 – 15 Oct 1942 from 5. Flottille	1 patrol. 1 ship sunk: total 3672 GRT	Sunk with all hands 15 Oct 1942 in the North Atlantic, rammed by destroyer HMS *Viscount*. 44 dead. Credited to a 120 Sqn Liberator, but the bomber probably depth-charged U-615 causing no damage
U-661	VIIC	3-Mar-43	1 May 1944 – 5 Aug 1944 from 5. Flottille	2 patrols	Sunk 5 Aug 1944 south of Brighton by depth charges from the frigate HMS *Stayner* and the escort destroyer HMS *Wensleydale*. 47 dead and 5 survivors
U-671	VIIC	20-Sep-43	1 Jun 1944 – 1 Jul 1944 from 5. Flottille	1 patrol	to 23. Flottille
U-677	VIIC	16-Jul-41	16 Jul 1941 – 7 Jul 1942	3 patrols. 5 ships sunk: total 25,390 GRT; 3 aux warships sunk: total 1429 GRT; 1 warship sunk: total 864 GRT; 4 ships damaged: total 37,093 GRT; 1 warship damaged: total 1209t/1190 tons	Sunk 7 Jul 1942 in American waters near Cape Hatteras by depth charges from a Lockheed Hudson of the 396th US Army Bomb Sqn. 39 dead and 7 survivors
U-701	VIIC	16-Mar-42	1 Oct 1942 – 3 Aug 1943 from 3. Flottille	5 patrols. 3 ships sunk: total 18,650 GRT	Damaged 3 Aug 1943 northwest of Cape Ortegal, Spain, by depth charges from a Handley-Page Hampden of No. 415 Sqn RCAF. Finished off by a B-24 of the USAAF's 4th A/S Sqn. 42 dead and 4 survivors
U-706	VIIC	5-Nov-42	1 Nov 1943 – 31 Dec 1943 from 8. Flottille	No patrols	to 21. Flottille
U-712	VIIC	27-Jul-43	1 May 1944 – 26 Jun 1944 from 5. Flottille	1 patrol	Sunk with all hands 26 Jun 1944 northwest of Ireland by depth charges from the destroyer HMS *Bulldog*. 52 dead
U-719	VIIC	5-Dec-42	1 Aug 1943 – 9 Feb 1944	2 patrols	Sunk with all hands 9 Feb 1944 southwest of Ireland by depth charges from the sloops HMS *Wild Goose* and HMS *Starling*. 49 dead
U-734	VIIC	24-May-41	24 May 1941 – 23 May 1943	7 patrols. 6 ships sunk: total 32,358 GRT; 2 auxiliary warships sunk: total 1134 GRT; 1 ship damaged: total 4799 GRT	Sunk 23 May 1943 in the North Atlantic by rockets from a Fairey Swordfish of the escort carrier HMS *Archer*. 29 dead and 17 survivors
U-752	VIIC	18-Jun-41	18 Jun 1941 – 13 May 1943	7 patrols. 3 ships sunk: total 23,117 GRT; 2 ships damaged: total 6908 GRT	Sunk with all hands 13 May 1943 in the North Atlantic by depth charges from corvette HMCS *Drumheller*, frigate HMS *Lagan* and from a Sunderland of No. 423 Sqn RCAF. 47 dead
U-753	VIIC	15-Oct-42	1 May 1943 – 8 Sep 1943 from 8. Flottille	2 patrols	Attacked and damaged off Cape Finisterre by a Wellington of No. 179 Sqn RAF. Retreated to Vigo in Spain where, unable to make repairs in the 24 hours allowed by international law, the boat was interned. Handed over to the British 23 Jul 1945 and sunk in Operation *Deadlight* on 13 Dec 1945
U-760	VIIC	13-Mar-43	1 Nov 1943 – 30 Sep 1944 from 8. Flottille	4 patrols. 1 ship sunk: total 1499 GRT	to 33. Flottille
U-763	VIIC	10-Dec-42	1 May 1943 – 31 Jan 1944 from 5. Flottille	5 patrols. 2 ships sunk: total 13,374 GRT; 1 warship sunk: total 940t/925 tons; 1 ship damaged: total 7176 GRT	to 29. Flottille
U-952	VIIC	17-Dec-42	1 Jun 1943 – 14 Oct 1944 from 5. Flottille	10 patrols. 1 ship sunk: total 1927 GRT	to 33. Flottille
U-953	VIIC	7-Jan-43	1 Aug 1943 – 31 Dec 1943 from 5. Flottille	6 patrols. 2 ships sunk: total 7353 GRT; 2 warships sunk: total 614/604 tons	to 11. Flottille
U-957	VIIC	28-Jan-43	1 Aug 1943 – 19 May 1944 from 5. Flottille	5 patrols. 2 ships sunk: total 9656 GRT; 1 auxiliary warship sunk: total 611 GRT	Sunk 19 May 1944 northwest of Algiers by destroyers USS *Niblack* and USS *Ludlow* and by Wellingtons and Venturas of Nos. 36 and 500 Sqns RAF. 31 dead and 20 survivors
U-960	VIIC	25-Mar-43	1 Mar 1944 – 7 Jun 1944 from 5. Flottille	2 patrols	Sunk 7 Jun 1944 west of Bordeaux by depth charges from a Sunderland of No. 228 Sqn RAF. 38 dead and 14 survivors
U-970	VIIC	1-Apr-43	1 Jun 1944 – 24 Jun 1944	1 patrol	Sunk 24 Jun 1944 in the Channel north of Brest by depth charges from destroyers HMS *Eskimo* and HMCS *Haida* and by depth charges from a Czech Liberator of No. 311 Sqn RAF. 1 dead and 51 survivors
U-971	VIIC	29-Apr-43	1 Jan 1944 – 1 Jul 1944 from 5. Flottille	1 patrol	to 23. Flottille
U-975	VIIC	12-May-43	1 Aug 1944 – 4 Sep 1944 from 5. Flottille	2 patrols. 1 ship damaged beyond repair: total 7176 GRT	to 11. Flottille
U-978	VIIC	2-Aug-43	1 Mar 1944 – 31 May 1944 from 5. Flottille	8 patrols. 1 warship damaged beyond repair: total 1077t/1060 tons	to 11. Flottille
U-992	VIIC	19-Aug-43	1 Mar 1944 – 4 Oct 1944 from 5. Flottille	3 patrols	Destroyed at Bergen on 4 Oct 1944 during an RAF air raid. 2 crew killed
U-993	British	30-Nov-40	May 1941 – 31 Jul 1941 from 5. Flottille	No patrols; used as trials boat	Used as a trials boat. Decommissioned 31 Jul 1941. Scuttled at Kiel 3 May 1945
UB	S class British	21-Nov-40	1. Flottille May 1941 – Aug 1941 from 5. Flottille	Trials boat	to 5. Flottille
UD-1	H class Dutch	8-Jun-41	1. Flottille Jun 1941 – Jul 1941	Trials boat	Launched 1 May 1940 as the O 25 at Wilton Feyenoord shipyard in Schiedam. Taken over by the German Navy on 14 May 1940. Completed and commissioned 8 Jun 1941. Transferred to 5. Flottille
UD-3	O 21 class Dutch	28-Jan-41	May 1941 – Jul 1941 from 5. Flottille	Trials boat	to 5. Flottille
UD-4	O 21 class		1. Flottille		

5 Unterseebootsflottille

The 5th U-boat Flotilla, *U-Flottille* Emsmann, was founded on 1 December 1938 under the command of one of the few experienced U-boat officers serving with the *Kriegsmarine*, *Kapitän zur See* Hans Rudolf Rösing.

THE FLOTILLA WAS NAMED in honour of a U-boat ace of World War I, *Oberleutnant* Hans Joachim Emsmann. Emsmann commanded the boats UB-5, UB-10, UB-40 and UB-116. On 10 patrols, he sank 27 ships totalling 9369 tonnes (9221 tons). He was killed on 28 October 1918, when UB-116 struck a mine while attempting to break into the Royal Navy fleet anchorage at Scapa Flow, a feat achieved more successfully 21 years later by *Kaptänleutnant* Prien.

The *U-Flottille* Emsmann was part of the expansion of the *U-bootwaffe*'s organization which took place in the late 1930s, in accordance with the Anglo-German Naval Treaty of 1935. Since by treaty the tonnage of submarines allowed to be built was limited, the 5th Flotilla was never more than six boats strong, and the boats on strength were the smaller and less capable Type IIC coastal submarines.

Most of the boats were still in training at the outbreak of war, but they were rushed into operational service, making numerous short patrols in the North Sea and off the British coast. However, the flotilla was disbanded at the end of 1939, most of its boats being assigned to the 1st Flotilla. The 5th Flotilla was resurrected as a training unit in 1941.

Kapitän zur See Hans Rudolf Rösing

Hans Rudolf Rösing was born on 28 September 1905 in Wilhelmshaven, and joined the interwar *Reichsmarine* in Crew 24. He commanded U-11, U-35, U-10 and U-48, sinking 12 ships totalling 60,702 GRT in just two patrols in the last-mentioned boat, for which he was awarded the Knight's Cross.

Rösing was one of a handful of German officers who secretly served aboard foreign-built submarines

Commander

Kpt. z. S. Hans Rudolf Rösing

(Dec 1938 – Dec 1939)

5TH FLOTILLA BASE LOCATION

ATLANTIC OCEAN

● Kiel

between the wars. This was the only way that the *Reichsmarine*, hampered by the terms of the Treaty of Versailles, could gain any submarine experience. He commissioned the Type IIB boat U-11 in September 1935. Although it was primarily a training boat, Rösing commanded a patrol to the Azores in 1937.

In 1938, he became the first and only commander of the *Flottille* Emsmann, later redesignated as the 5th Flotilla. On its disbandment he took command of the highly successful 7th Flotilla in January 1940, making two patrols in U-48.

From September 1940 to February 1941, he served as liaison officer with the Italian submarine force in Bordeaux. From March to August 1941, Rösing was commander of the 3rd Flotilla. In July 1942, he became the FdU *West*, where he was responsible for all U-boats stationed in France. After the surrender, Rösing spent more than a year as a POW. In 1956, Hans Rudolf Rösing joined the *Bundesmarine*, retiring in 1965 as *Konteradmiral*.

5TH FLOTILLA INSIGNIA

U-boat insignia varied from the overtly military through humorous to personal emblems of the commander. Many had an underwater theme, the rarely seen 5th Flotilla's insignia being a seahorse.

In 1966, he was decorated for his postwar achievements with the *Bundesverdienstkreuz* (Federal Merit Cross). Rösing died on 16 December 2004 at Kiel, aged 99.

U-59

U-59 was a Type IIC boat and was laid down on 5 October 1937 at Deutsche Werke, Kiel. It was commissioned on 4 March 1939 under the command of *Oberleutnant* Harald Jürst, who was promoted to *Kapitänleutnant* soon after. The boat was assigned to the 5th Flotilla, where it underwent combat training until the outbreak of war. The boat then became operational, mounting four patrols before being transferred to 1 Flotilla on 1 January 1940.

U-59 Commanders	
Kptlt. Harald Jürst *(Mar 1939 – Jul 1940)*	Oblt. Günter Poser *(Dec 1941 — Jul 1942)*
Joachim Matz *(Jul 1940 – Nov 1940)*	Oblt. Karl-Heinz Sammler *(Jul 1942 – Jun 1943)*
Kptlt. Baron Siegfried von Forstner *(Nov 1940 – Apr 1941)*	Oblt. Hans-Jürgen Schley *(Jun 1943 – Jun 1944)*
Oblt. Günter Gretschel *(Apr 1941 – Dec 1941)*	Ltn. Herbert Walther *(Jul 1944 – Apr 1945)*

▲ **Type IIC conning tower**
The hatch is open on this Type IIC conning tower. The periscope housing can be seen immediately behind the open hatch. The commander would have stood at the front-right of the tower, next to the voice tube.

At the outbreak of war, U-59 was part of a patrol line southwest of Norway. On its second patrol, the boat sank two fishing boats and an anti-submarine trawler off the Orkney Islands. The third patrol saw U-59 laying mines in shallow waters off Great Yarmouth, Norfolk. The mines sank a minesweeper and a small coastal vessel. On her last patrol with 5th Flotilla, in December 1939, U-59 sank three vessels totalling more than 4000 GRT. The boat returned to Kiel, where she bacame part of the 1st Flotilla, the 5th Flotilla having been disbanded.

U-59 continued to serve as a combat boat to the end of 1940. Under the command of Joachim Matz and Baron Siegfried von Forstner, the boat made a further nine patrols, the combined totals of its successes with the 5th and 1st Flotillas reaching 16 ships sunk for a total of 29,514 GRT, along with two auxiliary warships sunk, and two ships totalling nearly 13,000 GRT damaged.

School boat

In January 1941, as most of the Type II boats were withdrawn from general combat roles, U-59 was transferred to the 22nd Flotilla at Gotenhafen in the Baltic, becoming a school boat where new U-boat crewmen received initial training. It was transferred to the 19th Flotilla in July 1944. U-59 was finally scuttled in the Kiel Arsenal on 3 May 1945.

BOATS THAT SERVED WITH 5TH FLOTILLA (7 BOATS)					
U-Boat	Type	Commissioned	Flotilla(s)	Patrols	Fate
U-56	IIC	26-Nov-38	26 Nov 1938 – 31 Dec 1939 (training and combat)	12 patrols. 3 ships sunk: total 8860 GRT; 1 auxiliary warship sunk: total 16,923 GRT; 1 ship damaged: total 3829 GRT	to 1. Flottille
U-57	IIC	29-Dec-38	29 Dec 1938 – 31 Dec 1939 (training and combat)	11 patrols. 11 ships sunk: total 48,053 GRT; 1 auxiliary warship sunk: total 8240 GRT; 1 ship damaged beyond repair: total 10,191 GRT; 2 ships damaged: total 10,403 GRT	to 1. Flottille
U-58	IIC	4-Feb-39	4 Feb – 31 Dec 1939 (training and combat)	12 patrols. 6 ships sunk: total 16,148 GRT; 1 auxiliary warship sunk: total 8401 GRT	to 1. Flottille
U-59	IIC	4-Mar-39	4 Mar – 31 Dec 1939 (training and combat)	13 patrols. 16 ships sunk: total 29,514 GRT; 2 auxiliary warships sunk: total 864 GRT; 1 ship damaged beyond repair: total 4943 GRT; 1 ship damaged: total 8009 GRT	to 1. Flottille
U-60	IIC	22-Jul-39	22 Jul – 31 Dec 1939 (training)	9 patrols. 3 ships sunk: total 7561 GRT; 1 ship damaged: total 15,434 GRT	to 1. Flottille
U-61	IIC	12-Aug-39	12 Aug – 31 Dec 1939 (training)	10 patrols. 5 ships sunk: total 19,668 GRT; 1 ship damaged: total 4434 GRT	to 1. Flottille
U-62	IIC	21-Dec-39	21 – 31 Dec 1939 (training)	5 patrols. 1 ship sunk: total 4581 GRT; 1 warship sunk: total 1372t/1350 tons	to 1. Flottille

6 Unterseebootsflottille

The 6th U-boat Flotilla, *U-Flottille* Hundius, was founded at Kiel on 1 October 1938 under the command of Korvkpt. Werner Hartmann. The first dedicated long-range flotilla, it was equipped with early examples of the new, large Type IX boats then entering service.

THE NEW FLOTILLA WAS named in commemoration of *Kapitänleutnant* Paul Hundius, who in World War I commanded UB-16, UC-47 and UB-103. On 20 patrols, he sank 67 ships totalling 96,809 tonnes (95,280 tons). He was killed on 16 September 1918, when his boat was sunk by depth charges.

German pre-war planning called for a balanced force of U-boats, comprising small Type IIs, medium Type VIIs and large Type IX boats. The Type IXs began to commission in 1938 and 1939, and were assigned to the newly formed *U-Flottille* Hundius.

At around 1016 tonnes (1000 tons), the Type IX had been built as a result of a *Kriegsmarine* study of potential operations against the two major potential enemies, Britain and France. The Type IX design was developed to enable German interdiction of sea lines of communication in the Mediterranean, along the Atlantic coast and as far south as West Africa.

Operations

The Type IX boats of the *U-Flottille* Hundius quickly completed their training and moved to Wilhelmshaven for operations on the outbreak of war. Three of the eight boats were lost before the flotilla was disbanded in December 1939. U-39 was depth-charged and sunk on 14 September, northwest

6TH FLOTILLA BASE LOCATIONS

ATLANTIC OCEAN

Kiel • • Danzig

• St Nazaire

Commanders

Korvkpt. Werner Hartmann *(Oct 1938 – Dec 1939)* Korvkpt. Carl Emmermann
Korvkpt. Wilhelm Schulz *(Aug 1941 – Jan 1942)* *(Nov 1943 – Aug 1944)*

of Ireland. All 44 crew survived the first U-boat loss of the war. U-40 was sunk by mines on 13 October, with only three of the 48 crew being picked up. U-42 was sunk on the same day, southwest of Ireland, by depth charges from the destroyers HMS *Imogen* and HMS *Ilex*. Twenty of the 46 crew survived.

Rebirth of the flotilla

The flotilla was refounded as the 6th Flotilla in July 1941 at Danzig. During the first months of its existence, its crews were under training in the Baltic, but in February 1942 the flotilla was moved as a combat-capable unit to St Nazaire in France. Since it was primarily tasked with Atlantic operations, it was largely equipped with Type VIIC boats.

The approach of Allied armies after the invasion of Normandy meant that the Atlantic bases had to be abandoned. Surviving 6th Flotilla boats were transferred to Norway in August 1944 and the unit was disbanded.

6TH FLOTILLA INSIGNIA

Originally carried by Otto von Bülow's U-404, the 6th Flotilla emblem was a U-boat silhouette over a stylized Viking ship prow. It may have also been used by the 23rd Flotilla under von Bülow's command.

6TH FLOTILLA (1939 AND 1941–44)	
Type	Boats assigned
Type IXA	8
Type VIIB	1
Type VIIC	81
Type VIIC/41	1

Star commanders
1941–45

The first incarnation of the 6th Flotilla did not last long enough for any ace commanders to emerge, but from 1941 the reformed flotilla was in action in the hotbed of the North Atlantic.

Korvettenkapitän Carl Emmermann

Carl Emmermann was born on 6 March 1915 in Hamburg. He joined the Navy with Crew 34. For some years he was training officer at the *Marineschule* Mürwik, but with the outbreak of war he transferred to the U-boat arm. In November 1940, he served aboard U-A, a large boat being built for Turkey but taken over by the *Kriegsmarine* in 1939.

In November 1941, Emmermann's first command was the Type IXC boat U-172. He completed five patrols – in the Caribbean, with the wolfpack *Eisbär* in South African waters, and in the North and South Atlantic. He sank 26 ships totalling 152,778 GRT. On his fifth and last patrol, he rescued half the crew of U-604, which had been scuttled after air attacks. He became commander of the 6th Flotilla in November 1943, before going on to head the test unit for the new Type XXIII boat. He ended the war in command of a naval infantry battalion in Hamburg. Emmermann survived the war and died in March 1990.

Korvettenkapitän Otto von Bülow

Otto von Bülow was born on 16 October 1911 in Wilhelmshaven. He joined the *Reichsmarine* with Crew 30. After initial service aboard a pre-dreadnought and a pocket battleship, he transferred to U-boats in April 1940. After gaining command experience with the training boat U-9, he commissioned U-404 in August 1941.

In five patrols Bülow sank 14 ships of 71,450 GRT as well as the Royal Navy destroyer HMS *Veteran*. He attacked the escort carrier HMS *Biter*, thinking it was

STAR COMMANDERS		
Commander	Patrols	Ships Sunk
Korvettenkapitän Carl Emmermann	5	26
Korvettenkapitän Otto von Bülow	5	15

the USS *Ranger*, and claimed it sunk after hearing four explosions. In the event all four were premature detonations. Even so, he was awarded the Knight's Cross with Oak Leaves. Bülow then commanded a training flotilla and one of the new Type XXI boats.

After the war, he joined the *Bundesmarine*, eventually commanding a destroyer squadron. Otto von Bülow died on 5 January 2006, aged 94.

ARMOURED GAUNTLET EMBLEM

This armoured gauntlet emblem probably refers to the 15th-century knight Götz von Berlichingen, who lost his hand in combat and had an iron fist attached in its place. U-586 and U-2527 used the insignia.

▲ **Keeping watch**

Crew at their stations monitor instumentation. Conditions in the U-boats were cramped and uncomfortable, ranging from stuffy tropical humidity to freezing Arctic temperatures, depending on the location of the boat.

U-37
TYPE IX

U-37's long career saw the boat become the second highest scoring U-boat of the war in terms of numbers of vessels sunk.

THE BOAT WAS BUILT at Germania Werft in Kiel. It was laid down in March 1937 and entered service in August 1938, the first Type IX to be commissioned. It served with the *U-Flottille* Hundius for the first months of the war, before the long-range boats were transferred to the 2nd Flotilla and the Hundius Flotilla was disbanded.

One of the most successful submarines in history, U-37 made 11 patrols under four commanders in two years, sinking 53 merchant ships totalling

200,000 GRT. On its second patrol, U-37 carried the tactical commander in the first attempt to mount a controlled, co-ordinated wolfpack operation. On its third patrol, U-37 landed two agents on the Irish coast in Donegal.

U-37 was removed from active service in May 1941, becoming a training boat in the Baltic for the rest of the war. It was scuttled on 8 May 1945 in Sonderburg Bay.

U-37 Commanders

Kptlt. Heinrich Schuch *(Aug 1938 – Sep 1939)*

Korvkpt. Werner Hartmann *(Sep 1939 – May 1940)*

Kptlt. Victor Oehrn *(May 1940 – Oct 1940)*

Kptlt. Asmus Nicolai Clausen *(Oct 1940 – May 1941)*

Kptlt. Ulrich Folkers *(May 1941 – Nov 1941)*

Kptlt. Gustav Janssen *(Nov 1941 – Jun 1942)*

Kptlt. Albert Lauzemis *(Jul 1942 – Jan 1943)*

Kptlt. Hinrich Kelling *(Jan 1943 – Nov 1943)*

Oblt. Peter Gerlach *(Nov 1943 – Jan 1944)*

Oblt. Wolfgang Seiler *(Jan 1944 – Dec 1944)*

Kptlt. Eberhard von Wenden *(Dec 1944 – May 1945)*

Specifications

Crew: 48–55

Powerplant: Diesel/electric

Max Speed: 33.7/14.3km/hr (18.2/7.7kt) surf/sub

Surface Range: 15,000km (8100nm)

Displacement: 1049/1172t (1032/1153 tons) surf/sub

Dimensions (length/beam/draught): 76.5 x 6.5 x 4.7m (251 x 21.33 x 15.42ft)

Commissioned: 4 Aug 1938

Armament: 22 torpedoes (4 bow/2 stern tubes); 1 x 10.5cm (4.1in), 1 x 3.7cm (1.5in) and 1 x 2cm (0.8in) guns

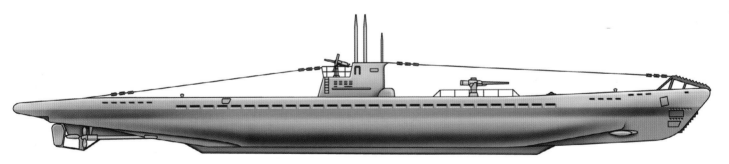

U-37 TIMETABLE		
Patrol Dates	**Operational Area**	**Ships Sunk**
19 Aug 1939 – 15 Sep 1939	W of the Iberian Peninsula	0
5 Oct 1939 – 8 Nov 1939	Central Atlantic	8
28 Jan 1940 – 27 Feb 1940	SW of Ireland	8
30 Mar 1940 – 18 Apr 1940	Escorting raider Faroes/Shetlands	3
15 May 1940 – 9 Jun 1940	NW of Cape Finisterre	10
1 Aug 1940 – 12 Aug 1940	Transit from Wilhemshaven to Lorient	1
17 Aug 1940 – 30 Aug 1940	W of the British Isles	6
24 Sep 1940 – 22 Oct 1940	W of the British Isles	6
28 Nov 1940 – 7 Jan 1941	W of Spain/W of Africa	6
30 Jan 1941 – 18 Feb 1941	Central Atlantic off Freetown	3
27 Feb 1941 – 22 Mar 1941	North Atlantic	2

▲ **U-37**

Type IX

Although the Type IX was designed as a long-range boat, early examples like U-37 did not have the reach of later variants. Even so, the boat was highly successful in the Atlantic. On her fifth patrol, under the command of Kptlt. Victor Oehrn, U-37 sank 10 ships totalling more than 40,000 tonnes (39,368 tons), eight of them in the space of just seven days.

U-87

TYPE VIIB

Built by Flenderwerft at Lübeck, U-87 was commissioned into the 6th Flotilla in August 1941, and after a period of training with the flotilla went on her first patrol in December of that year.

U-87's FIVE patrols accounted for five ships totalling 38,014 GRT. Early in 1942, Hitler feared an Allied landing in Norway, and ordered Dönitz to divert boats from the Atlantic. U-87 was one of the boats used to set up a patrol line west of the Faroes. She was sunk with all hands on 4 March 1943, west of Oporto, by depth charges from HMCS *Shediac* and HMCS *St. Croix*.

U-87 TIMETABLE		
Patrol Dates	Operational Area	Ships Sunk
24 Dec 1941 – 30 Jan 1942	Transit from Kiel to La Pallice	2
22 Feb 1942 – 27 Mar 1942	Norwegian Sea	0
19 May 1942 – 8 Jul 1942	Minelaying and patrol off Boston	2
31 Aug 1942 – 20 Nov 1942	N of Cape Verde Islands	1
9 Jan 1943 – 4 Mar 1943	Azores/Canaries	0

U-87 Commander

Kptlt. Joachim Berger *(Aug 1941 – Mar 1943)*

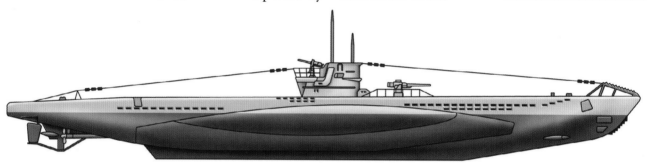

Specifications

Crew: 44

Powerplant: Diesel/electric

Max Speed: 31.9/14.8km/hr (17.2/8kt) surf/sub

Surface Range: 12,040km (6500nm)

Displacement: 765/871t (753/857 tons) surf/sub

Dimensions (length/beam/draught): 66.5 x 6.2 x 4.7m (218.1 x 20.34 x 15.4ft)

Commissioned: 19 Aug 1941

Armament: 14 torpedoes (4 bow/1 stern tubes); 1 x 8.8cm (3.5in) and 1 x 2cm (0.8in) guns

▲ **U-87**

Type VIIB

U-87 entered service with the kind of armament typical of Type VII boats before the rise of Allied air power forced a change. The main gun was an 8.8cm (3.5in) artillery piece, with a 2cm (0.8in) AA gun mounted on the conning tower.

U-404

TYPE VIIC

Commanded by Otto von Bülow, U-404 was commissioned in August 1941 and became operational in December, in time to take part in U-boat operations against the United States.

U-404's FIRST PATROL was as part of the *Schlei* wolfpack operating west of Rockall, but the boats were ordered home early to prepare for operations off the US east coast.

On its second patrol, the boat initially operated off the Canadian coast before moving south to operate off New Jersey. The inexperienced crew did well, sinking four ships, although one was actually a

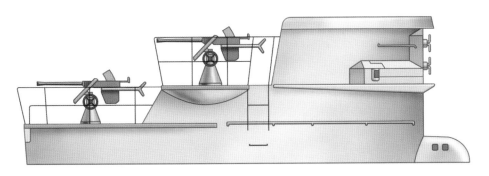

◀ **Type VIIC 'winter garden' conning tower**

Adding extra anti-aircraft guns meant increasing the size of the turret of the Type VIIC. Bridge Conversion II saw the addition of a 'winter garden' platform abaft the conning tower. The unreliable 2cm (0.8in) C/30 guns were replaced by improved C/38 weapons, based on an Army Flak gun.

U-404 TIMETABLE		
Patrol Dates	**Operational Area**	**Ships Sunk**
17 Jan 1942 – 1 Feb 1942	Transit from Kiel to St Nazaire	0
14 Feb 1942 – 4 Apr 1942	Central Atlantic/US coast	4
6 May 1942 – 14 Jul 1942	US Atlantic coast/Bermuda	6 + 1 destroyer
23 Aug 1942 – 13 Oct 1942	W of Ireland/off Newfoundland	1
21 Dec 1942 – 6 Feb 1943	N Atlantic	0
21 Mar 1943 – 3 May 1943	S of Greenland	3
24 Jul 1943 – 28 Jul 1943	Transit through Biscay	0

U-404 Commander

Korvkpt. Otto von Bülow *(Aug 1941 – Jul 1943)*

Oblt. Adolf Schönberg *(Jul 1943 – Jul 1943)*

Chilean neutral and should not have been attacked. The next patrol, off New York, initially offered no targets, but when the boat moved south to Bermuda she sank seven vessels.

On 25 April 1943, on her sixth patrol, U-404 fired four torpedoes at a carrier identified as the USS *Ranger*. Hearing four explosions, Korvpt. Otto von Bülow claimed to have sunk the ship.

However, the target was actually the escort carrier HMS *Biter*. The explosions were a consequence of premature detonations and caused no damage.

Nevertheless, the Supreme Command of the Armed Forces announced the sinking, and von Bülow was awarded Oak Leaves to the Knight's Cross. The *Führer der Unterseeboote* was not as certain, and later disallowed the claim.

Fate

U-404 was sunk with all hands on 28 July 1943 in the Bay of Biscay northwest of Cape Ortegal by depth charges from two USAAF B-24s of the 4th A/S Sqn and from a Liberator of No. 224 Sqn RAF. All 51 crew were killed in the attack.

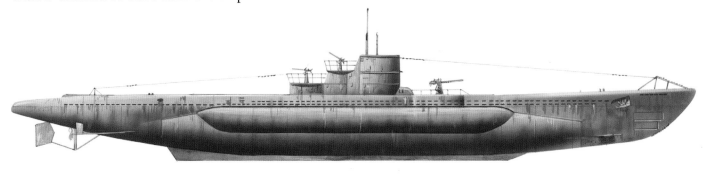

▲ **U-404**

Type VIIC

By 1942, the threat posed by Allied convoy escorts and aircraft meant that U-boats rarely had a chance to use their main gun, and heavier AA protection was necessary. Soon the big gun would be removed in favour of more AA guns.

Specifications

Crew: 44

Powerplant: Diesel/electric

Max Speed: 31.5/14.1km/hr (17/7.6kt) surf/sub

Surface Range: 12,040km (6500nm)

Displacement: 773/879t (761/865 tons) surf/sub

Dimensions (length/beam/draught): 67.1 x 6.2 x 4.8m (220.1 x 20.34 x 15.75ft)

Commissioned: 6 Feb 1941

Armament: 14 torpedoes (4 bow/1 stern tubes); 1 x 2cm (0.8in) quad and 2 x 2cm (0.8in) guns

U-757
TYPE VIIC

Laid down at the *Kriegsmarine-Werft* in Wilhelmshaven, U-757 was commissioned in February 1942 and after operational training with the 6th Flotilla was ready for combat in September.

LIKE MOST BOATS that entered service in the later stages of the war, U-757 had little chance of running up the huge scores typical of earlier years. In five patrols, she sank only two ships. On her third patrol, U-757 was damaged when the ammunition ship she had just torpedoed, exploded. On her fourth patrol, an explosion aboard the boat forced her early return. On 8 January 1944, in the North Atlantic

U-757 Commander
Korvkpt. Friedrich Deetz *(Feb 1942 – Jan 1944)*

southwest of Ireland, on her fifth patrol, U-757 was sunk with all hands by depth charges from the frigate HMS *Bayntun* and the corvette HMCS *Camrose*. All 49 crew were killed.

▲ **U-757**

Type VIIC

U-757 spent most of its operational career in the central Atlantic, mounting patrols from the waters west of Ireland to as far south as the Azores. Late in 1943, the boat had to abandon four patrols because of mechanical faults.

Specifications

Crew: 44	Dimensions (length/beam/draught): 67.1 x 6.2
Powerplant: Diesel/electric	x 4.8m (220.1 x 20.34 x 15.75ft)
Max Speed: 31.5/14.1km/hr (17/7.6kt) surf/sub	Commissioned: 6 Feb 1941
Surface Range: 12,040km (6500nm)	Armament: 14 torpedoes (4 bow/1 stern tubes);
Displacement: 773/879t (761/865 tons) surf/sub	1 x 8.8cm (3.5in) quad and 2 x 2cm (0.8in) guns

Convoy ON 127
9 SEPTEMBER 1942

ON 127 was a westbound convoy travelling across the North Atlantic from Britain to Canada. It consisted of 32 merchant ships, protected by an inexperienced Canadian escort group.

ON 127 WAS ESCORTED by the Canadian Escort Group C4, which comprised the destroyers HMCS *St. Croix* and HMCS *Ottawa* and the corvettes HMCS *Amherst*, HMCS *Arvida*, HMCS *Sherbrooke* and the British corvette HMS *Celandine*.

The attack on ON 127 achieved considerable success at very little cost to the U-boat force. Unusually, every

boat involved in the operation actually used their weapons in the battle – all too often, many of the boats deployed in such an attack never made contact with a target. The Germans were helped by the poor tactics used by the Canadian escorts. Lacking radar and the latest direction-finding equipment, the escorts made extensive use of 'Snowflake' illuminating rockets. However, instead of lighting up the U-boats on the surface, all the pyrotechnics achieved was to ruin the night vision of the Allied lookouts while at the same time letting every U-boat within miles know the exact location of their targets. Attacked by the *Vorwarts* wolfpack, the convoy lost seven ships plus the destroyer HMCS *Ottawa,* and several merchantmen were damaged.

CONVOY ON 127 BATTLE TIMETABLE	
Date	Event
9 Sep	Convoy is sighted by U-584. U-Boat command orders wolfpack *Vorwarts* to concentrate and attack. Group *Vorwarts* was made up of 12 boats – U-91, U-92, U-96, U-211, U-218, U-380, U-404, U-407, U-411, U-584, U-594 and U-608
10 Sep	U-584 loses contact during the night, but it is regained at about noon when U-96 sights the merchantmen and their escorts. U-96 makes a submerged daylight attack, sinking 2 ships and damaging a tanker. As the other *Vorwarts* group boats arrive through the night, they mount a series of attacks. U-659 damages a tanker. U-608, attacking about the same time, does not score any hits
11 Sep	U-404 and U-218 each damage a tanker, while U-92 and U-594 mount unsuccessful attacks. U-584 finishes off the tanker previously hit by U-659. During the day, U-96 uses its gun to sink a Portuguese trawler that had lost contact with the convoy
12 Sep	The wolfpack continues to press home its attacks through the night of 11/12 September. U-380 makes an unsuccessful attack while U-404 damages a tanker. U-92 takes a shot at the escorting destroyer *Ottawa,* but misses. U-584 sinks a ship, while U-211 damages 2 more. Both are finished off by U-608. The escorts have little success against the wolfpack, only U-659 sustaining any damage, which is not serious enough to stop the boat returning to its French base
13 Sep	As the night of 12/13 September closes in, the U-boats again press home their attacks, but only U-407 and U-594 make contact with the main body of the convoy and both fail to hit any targets. U-594 sinks a straggler as daylight breaks, and U-91 sinks the destroyer *Ottawa.* U-411 launches a torpedo at one of the corvettes but misses, and U-92 loses contact with the convoy. The U-boats now break off the attack: during the night the escort has been reinforced by the British destroyer HMS *Witch* and the American destroyer USS *Annapolis,* and the convoy has now come within range of aircraft based in Newfoundland

Wolfpacks *Falke, Habicht* & *Haudegen*

JANUARY 1943

There is a perception that the *Kriegsmarine*'s U-boat wolfpacks were fearsome hunters of the deep, homing in on every merchantman crossing the Atlantic in convoy and sinking Allied vessels at will.

This was far from the case, as the boats in the large *Falke* and *Habicht* groups discovered in the winter of 1942/43, when the Battle of the Atlantic approached its climax.

The *Falke* and *Habicht* groups were formed to the west of Ireland at the end of 1942. With 29 boats available, the two groups could have wreaked considerable destruction on even the most heavily defended convoy.

However, Ultra codebreakers and high-frequency direction-finding equipment meant that the Allies knew almost as much about U-boat deployments as did their commanders in France, and convoys were routed around known U-boat concentrations.

Missed contact

Nothing having crossed the U-boat patrol line, both groups were ordered westwards in an attempt to intercept eastbound ON convoys. The boats were combined into a new group, known as *Haudegen,* which covered almost 480km (300 miles) of sea southeast of Cape Farewell, Greenland. Several convoys were sighted by independent boats, and small groups of *Haudegen* boats were detached to try

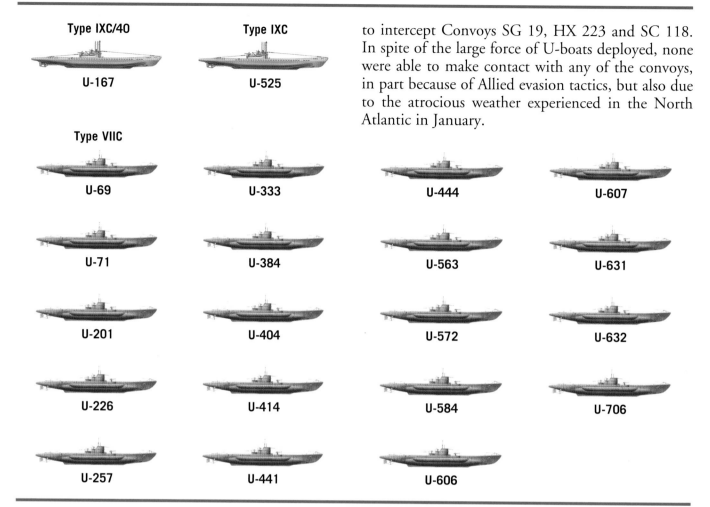

Type IXC/40 — U-167
Type IXC — U-525

Type VIIC

U-69   U-333   U-444   U-607

U-71   U-384   U-563   U-631

U-201   U-404   U-572   U-632

U-226   U-414   U-584   U-706

U-257   U-441   U-606

to intercept Convoys SG 19, HX 223 and SC 118. In spite of the large force of U-boats deployed, none were able to make contact with any of the convoys, in part because of Allied evasion tactics, but also due to the atrocious weather experienced in the North Atlantic in January.

BOATS THAT SERVED WITH 6TH FLOTILLA (91 BOATS)					
U-Boat	Type	Commissioned	Flotilla(s)	Patrols	Fate
U-37	IX	4-Aug-38	1 Apr 1938 – 31 Dec 1939	11 patrols. 53 ships sunk: total 200,125 GRT; 2 warships sunk: total 2443t/2404 tons; 1 ship damaged: total 9494 GRT. Second highest scoring U-boat in terms of numbers of vessels sunk	to 2. Flottille
U-38	IX	24-Oct-38	24 Oct 1938 – 31 Dec 1939	11 patrols. 35 ships sunk: total 188,967 GRT; 1 ship damaged: total 3670 GRT	to 2. Flottille
U-39	IX	10-Dec-38	10 Dec 1938 – 14 Sep 1939	1 patrol	Depth-charged and sunk 14 Sept 1939 northwest of Ireland by the destroyers HMS *Faulknor*, HMS *Foxhound* and HMS *Firedrake*. No casualties – 44 survivors. First U-boat sunk in the war
U-40	IX	11-Feb-39	11 Feb 1939 – 13 Oct 1939	2 patrols	Sunk by mines 13 Oct 1939 in the English Channel. 45 dead and 3 survivors
U-41	IX	22-Apr-39	22 Apr 1939 – 31 Dec 1939	3 patrols. 7 ships sunk: total 24,888 GRT; 1 ship damaged: total 8096 GRT	to 2. Flottille
U-42	IX	15-Jul-39	15 Jul 1939 – 13 Oct 1939	1 patrol. 1 ship damaged: total 4803 GRT	Sunk 13 Oct 1939 southwest of Ireland by depth charges from the destroyers HMS *Imogen* and HMS *Ilex*. 26 dead and 20 survivors
U-43	IX	26-Aug-39	26 Aug 1939 – 31 Dec 1939	14 patrols. 21 ships sunk: total 117,036 GRT; 1 ship a total loss: total 9131 GRT; 1 ship damaged: total 10,350 GRT	to 2. Flottille
U-44	IX	4-Nov-39	4 Nov 1939 – 31 Dec 1939	2 patrols. 8 ships sunk: total 30,885 GRT	to 2. Flottille
U-87	VIIB	19-Aug-41	19 Aug 1941 – 4 Mar 1943	5 patrols. 5 ships sunk: total 38,014 GRT	Sunk with all hands 4 Mar 1943 west of Oporto by depth charges from the Canadian warships HMCS *Shediac* and HMCS *St. Croix*. 49 dead
U-136	VIIC	30-Aug-41	30 Aug 1941 – 11 Jul 1942	3 patrols. 5 ships sunk: total 23,649 GRT; 2 warships sunk: total 1880t/1850 tons; 1 ship damaged: total 8955 GRT	Sunk with all hands 11 Jul 1942 in Atlantic west of Madeira by the Free French destroyer *Léopard*, the frigate HMS *Spey* and the sloop HMS *Pelican*. 45 dead
U-209	VIIC	11-Oct-41	11 Oct 1941 – 30 Jun 1942	7 patrols. 4 ships sunk: total 1356 GRT	to 11. Flottille
U-223	VIIC	6-Jun-42	1 Feb 1943 – 31 Oct 1943 from 8. Flottille (training)	6 patrols. 2 ships sunk: total 12,556 GRT; 1 warship sunk: total 1966t/1935 tons; 1 ship damaged beyond repair: total 4970 GRT; 1 warship damaged beyond repair: total 1321t/1300 tons	to 29. Flottille

U-Boat	Type	Commissioned	Flotilla(s)	Patrols	Fate
**BOATS THAT SERVED WITH 6TH FLOTILLA (91 BOATS)**					
U-226	VIIC	1-Aug-42	1 Jan 1943 – 6 Nov 1943 from 5. Flottille (training)	3 patrols. 1 ship sunk: total 7134 GRT	Sunk with all hands 6 Nov 1943 in the North Atlantic east of Newfoundland by depth charges from the British sloops HMS *Starling*, HMS *Woodcock* and HMS *Kite*. 51 dead
U-228	VIIC	12-Sep-42	1 Mar 1943 – 5 Oct 1944 from 5. Flottille (training)	6 patrols	Stricken at Bergen, Norway, 5 Oct 1944 and broken up
U-229	VIIC	3-Oct-42	1 Mar 1943 – 22 Sep 1943 from 5. Flottille (training)	3 patrols. 2 ships sunk: total 8352 GRT; 1 ship damaged: total 3670 GRT	Sunk with all hands 22 Sep 1943 in the North Atlantic southeast of Cape Farewell, Greenland, by the destroyer HMS *Keppel*. 50 dead
U-251	VIIC	20-Sep-41	20 Sep 1941 – 30 Jun 1942	9 patrols. 2 ships sunk: total 11,408 GRT	to 11. Flottille
U-252	VIIC	4-Oct-41	4 Oct 1941 – 14 Apr 1942	1 patrol. 1 ship sunk: total 1355 GRT. A spy was landed on Iceland on this boat's only patrol	Sunk with all hands 14 Apr 1942 southwest of Ireland by depth charges from the sloop HMS *Stork* and the corvette HMS *Vetch*. 44 dead
U-253	VIIC	21-Oct-41	1 Sep 1942 – 25 Sep 1942 from 8. Flottille	1 patrol	Sunk with all hands 25 Sep 1942 northwest of Iceland, probably by a British mine. 45 dead. Previously credited to a British Catalina, but that was probably an ineffective attack against U-255
U-260	VIIC	14-Mar-42	1 Oct 1942 – 31 Oct 1944 from 8. Flottille (training)	9 patrols. 1 ship sunk: total 4893 GRT	to 33. Flottille
U-261	VIIC	28-Mar-42	1 Sep 1942 – 15 Sep 1942	1 patrol	Sunk with all hands 15 Sep 1942 west of the Shetlands by depth charges from an Armstrong-Whitworth Whitley of No. 58 Sqn RAF. 43 dead
U-264	VIIC	22-May-42	1 Nov 1942 – 19 Feb 1944	5 patrols. 3 ships sunk: total 16,843 GRT	Sunk 19 Feb 1944 in the North Atlantic by depth charges from the sloops HMS *Woodpecker* and HMS *Starling*. No casualties – 52 survivors
U-269	VIIC	19-Aug-42	1 Nov 1943 – 25 Jun 1944 from 11. Flottille	5 patrols	Sunk 25 Jun 1944 in the Channel southeast of Torquay by depth charges from the frigate HMS *Bickerton*. 13 dead and 39 survivors
U-270	VIIC	5-Sep-42	1 Apr 1943 – 13 Aug 1944	6 patrols. 1 warship damaged beyond repair: total 1392t/1370 tons	Stricken 1 Jul 1944 after extensive damage from British Wellington and Fortress aircraft. Recommissioned early Aug. Sunk on 13 Aug 1944 in the Bay of Biscay west of La Rochelle by depth charges from an Australian Sunderland of No. 461 Sqn RAAF. No casualties – 71 survivors
U-277	VIIC	21-Dec-42	1 Jun 1943 – 31 Oct 1943 from 8. Flottille	5 patrols	to 13. Flottille
U-290	VIIC	24-Jul-43	1 May 1944 – 31 Jul 1944 from 8. Flottille	3 patrols	to 11. Flottille
U-308	VIIC	23-Dec-42	1 Jun 1943 – 4 Jun 1943 from 8. Flottille	1 patrol	Sunk with all hands 4 Jun 1943 northeast of the Faroes, torpedoed by the submarine HMS *Truculent*. 44 dead
U-312	VIIC	21-Apr-43	1 Dec 1943 – 31 Dec 1943 from 8. Flottille	12 patrols	to 11. Flottille
U-335	VIIC	17-Dec-41	1 Aug 1942 – 3 Aug 1942 from 8. Flottille	1 patrol	Sunk 3 Aug 1942 northeast of the Faroes, torpedoed by the submarine HMS *Saracen*. 43 dead and 1 survivor
U-337	VIIC	6-May-42	1 Jan 1943 – 3 Jan 1943 from 5. Flottille	1 patrol	Missing with all hands in the North Atlantic on or after 3 Jan 1943. 47 dead. Previously listed as sunk 15 Jan 1943 by depth charges from a Flying Fortress of No. 206 Sqn RAF. That attack was against U-632, which escaped without damage
U-340	VIIC	16-Oct-42	1 May 1943 – 2 Nov 1943 from 8. Flottille	3 patrols	Sunk 2 Nov 1943 near Tangier by depth charges from the sloop HMS *Fleetwood*, the destroyers HMS *Active* and HMS *Witherington* and a Wellington of No. 179 Sqn RAF. 1 dead and 48 survivors
U-356	VIIC	20-Dec-41	20 Dec 1941 – 27 Dec 1942	2 patrols. 3 ships sunk: total 13,649 GRT; 1 ship damaged: total 7051 GRT	Sunk with all hands 27 Dec 1942 north of the Azores by depth charges from the destroyer *HMCS St. Laurent* and corvettes HMCS *Chilliwack*, HMCS *Battleford* and HMCS *Napanee*. 46 dead
U-357	VIIC	18-Jun-42	1 Dec 1942 – 26 Dec 1942 from 8. Flottille	1 patrol	Sunk 26 Dec 1942 northwest of Ireland by depth charges from the destroyers HMS *Hesperus* and HMS *Vanessa*. 36 dead and 6 survivors
U-376	VIIC	21-Aug-41	21 Aug 1941 – 30 Jun 1942	8 patrols. 2 ships sunk: total 10,146 GRT	to 11. Flottille
U-377	VIIC	2-Oct-41	2 Oct 1941 – 30 Jun 1942	12 patrols	to 11. Flottille
U-380	VIIC	22-Dec-41	1 Sep 1942 – 30 Nov 1942 from 5. Flottille	12 patrols. 2 ships sunk: total 14,063 GRT; 1 ship damaged beyond repair: total 7178 GRT; 1 ship damaged: total 7191 GRT	to 29. Flottille
U-385	VIIC	29-Aug-42	1 Mar 1944 – 11 Aug 1944 from 5. Flottille	3 patrols	Sunk 11 Aug 1944 in the Bay of Biscay west of La Rochelle by depth charges from the sloop HMS *Starling* and from an Australian Sunderland of No. 461 Sqn. 1 dead and 42 survivors
U-386	VIIC	10-Oct-42	1 May 1943 – 19 Feb 1944	4 patrols. 1 ship sunk: total 1997 GRT	Sunk 19 Feb 1944 in the North Atlantic by depth charges from the frigate HMS *Spey*. 33 dead and 16 survivors
U-404	VIIC	6-Aug-41	6 Aug 1941 – 28 Jul 1943	7 patrols. 14 ships sunk: total 71,450 GRT; 1 warship sunk: total 1138t/1120 tons; 2 ships damaged: total 16,689 GRT	Sunk with all hands 28 Jul 1943 in Biscay northwest of Cape Ortegal by depth charges from 2 USAAF B-24s of the 4th A/S Sqn and from a Liberator of No. 224 Sqn RAF. 51 dead
U-405	VIIC	17-Sep-41	1 Mar 1943 – 1 Nov 1943 from 11. Flottille	11 patrols. 2 ships sunk: total 11,841 GRT	Sunk with all hands 1 Nov 1943 in the North Atlantic by ramming, small-arms fire and depth charges from the destroyer USS *Borie*. 49 dead

BOATS THAT SERVED WITH 6TH FLOTILLA (91 BOATS)

U-Boat	Type	Commissioned	Flotilla(s)	Patrols	Fate
U-411	VIIC	18-Mar-42	1 Sep 1942 – 13 Nov 1942 from 8. Flottille	2 patrols	Sunk with all hands 13 Nov 1942 west of Gibraltar by depth charges from a Hudson of No. 500 Sqn RAF. 46 dead. The destroyer HMS *Wrestler* had been credited with sinking this boat on 15 Nov 1942, but she actually sank U-98
U-414	VIIC	1-Jul-42	1 Jan 1943 – 30 Apr 1943 from 8. Flottille	3 patrols. 1 ship sunk: total 5979 GRT; 1 ship damaged: total 7134 GRT	to 29. Flottille
U-417	VIIC	26-Sep-42	1 Jun 1943 – 11 Jun 1943 from 8. Flottille	1 patrol	Sunk with all hands 11 Jun 1943 southeast of Iceland by depth charges from a Boeing Fortress of No. 206 Sqn RAF. 46 dead
U-436	VIIC	27-Sep-41	1 Sep 1942 – 26 May 1943 from 11. Flottille	8 patrols. 6 ships sunk: total 36,208 GRT; 2 ships damaged: total 15,575 GRT	Sunk with all hands 26 May 1943 west of Cape Ortegal by depth charges from the frigate HMS *Test* and the corvette HMS *Hyderabad*. 47 dead
U-437	VIIC	25-Oct-41	25 Oct 1941 – 5 Oct 1944	13 patrols	Damaged by British bombs at Bergen, Norway, 4 Oct 1944 and stricken 5 Oct 1944. Broken up in 1946
U-445	VIIC	30-May-42	1 Nov 1942 – 24 Aug 1944 from 8. Flottille	9 patrols	Sunk with all hands 24 Aug 1944 in the Bay of Biscay west of St Nazaire by depth charges from the frigate HMS *Louis*. 52 dead
U-456	VIIC	18-Sep-41	18 Sep 1941 – 30 Jun 1942	11 patrols. 6 ships sunk: total 31,528 GRT; 1 auxiliary warship sunk: total 251 GRT; 1 warship (HMS *Edinburgh*) damaged: total 11,685t/11,500 tons	to 11. Flottille
U-457	VIIC	5-Nov-41	5 Nov 1941 – 30 Jun 1942	Training	to 11. Flottille
U-465	VIIC	20-May-42	1 Oct 1942 – 2 May 1943 from 8. Flottille	4 patrols	Sunk with all hands 2 May 1943 north of Cape Finisterre by depth charges from an Australian Sunderland of No. 461 Sqn. 48 dead. Originally credited to another Australian Sunderland five days later, but that attack caused major damage to U-663
U-477	VIIC	18-Aug-43	1 Jun 1944 – 3 Jun 1944 from 5. Flottille	1 patrol	Sunk with all hands 3 Jun 1944 west of Trondheim, Norway, by depth charges from a Catalina of No. 162 Sqn RCAF. 51 dead
U-585	VIIC	28-Aug-41	28 Aug 1941 – 30 Mar 1942	3 patrols	Sunk with all hands 30 Mar 1942 north of Murmansk by a loose mine from a German minefield. 44 dead. Originally thought to have been sunk 29 Mar 1942 by the destroyer HMS *Fury*, which in fact attacked U-378 and caused no damage
U-586	VIIC	4-Sep-41	4 Sep 1941 – 30 Jun 1942	12 patrols. 2 ships sunk: total 12,716 GRT; 1 ship damaged: total 9057 GRT	to 29. Flottille
U-586	VIIC	4-Sep-41	1 Oct 1943 – 29 Feb 1944 from 13. Flottille	12 patrols. 2 ships sunk: total 12,716 GRT; 1 ship damaged: total 9057 GRT	to 11. Flottille
U-587	VIIC	11-Sep-41	11 Sep 1941 – 27 Mar 1942	2 patrols. 4 ships sunk: total 22,734 GRT, 1 auxiliary warship sunk: total 655 GRT	Sunk with all hands 27 Mar 1942 in the North Atlantic by depth charges from the escort destroyers HMS *Grove* and HMS *Aldenham* and the destroyers HMS *Volunteer* and HMS *Leamington*. 42 dead
U-588	VIIC	18-Sep-41	18 Sep 1941 – 31 Jul 1942	4 patrols. 7 ships sunk: total 31,492 GRT; 1 ship damaged: total 7460 GRT	Sunk with all hands 31 Jul 1942 in the North Atlantic by depth charges from the corvette HMCS *Wetaskiwin* and destroyer HMCS *Skeena*. 46 dead
U-589	VIIC	25-Sep-41	25 Sep 1941 – 30 Jun 1942	8 patrols. 1 ship sunk: total 2847 GRT; 1 auxiliary warship sunk: total 417 GRT	to 11. Flottille
U-590	VIIC	2-Oct-41	2 Oct 1941 – 9 Jul 1943	5 patrols. 1 ship sunk: total 5228 GRT; 1 ship damaged: total 5464 GRT	Sunk with all hands 9 Jul 1943 off the mouth of the Amazon by depth charges from a US Navy PBY Catalina aircraft of VP-94. 45 dead
U-591	VIIC	9-Oct-41	9 Oct 1941 – 30 Jun 1942	8 patrols. 4 ships sunk: total 19,932 GRT; 1 ship damaged: total 5701 GRT	to 11. Flottille
U-592	VIIC	16-Oct-41	16 Oct 1941 – 30 Jun 1942	10 patrols. 1 ship sunk: total 3770 GRT	to 11. Flottille
U-592	VIIC	16-Oct-41	1 Mar 1943 – 31 Jan 1944 from 11. Flottille	10 patrols. 1 ship sunk: total 3770 GRT	Sunk with all hands 31 Jan 1944 southwest of Ireland by depth charges from the sloops HMS *Starling*, HMS *Wild Goose* and HMS *Magpie*. 49 dead
U-598	VIIC	27-Nov-41	1 Jul 1942 – 23 Jul 1943 from 8. Flottille	4 patrols. 2 ships sunk: total 9295 GRT; 1 ship damaged: total 6197 GRT	Sunk 23 Jul 1943 in the South Atlantic near Natal by depth charges from two US Navy Liberators of VB-107. 43 dead and 2 survivors
U-608	VIIC	5-Feb-42	1 Sep 1942 – 10 Aug 1944 from 5. Flottille	10 patrols. 4 ships sunk: total 35,539 GRT	Sunk 10 Aug 1944 off La Rochelle by depth charges from the sloop HMS Wren and a Liberator of No. 53 Sqn RAF. No casualties – 52 survivors
U-609	VIIC	12-Feb-42	1 Aug 1942 – 7 Feb 1943	4 patrols. 2 ships sunk: total 10,288 GRT	Sunk with all hands 7 Feb 1943 in the North Atlantic by depth charges from the Free French corvette *Lobelia*. 47 dead
U-610	VIIC	19-Feb-42	1 Oct 1942 – 8 Oct 1943 from 5. Flottille	5 patrols. 4 ships sunk: total 21,273 GRT; 1 ship damaged: total 9551 GRT	Sunk with all hands 8 Oct 1943 in the North Atlantic by depth charges from a Sunderland of No. 423 Sqn RCAF. 51 dead
U-614	VIIC	19-Mar-42	1 Feb 1943 – 29 Jul 1943 from 8. Flottille	3 patrols. 1 ship sunk: total 5730 GRT	Sunk with all hands 29 Jul 1943 northwest of Cape Finisterre by depth charges from a Wellington of No. 172 Sqn RAF. 49 dead
U-616	VIIC	2-Apr-42	1 Jan 1943 – 31 May 1943 from 8. Flottille	9 patrols. 2 warships sunk: total 2216t/2181 tons; 2 ships damaged: total 17,754 GRT	to 29. Flottille
U-623	VIIC	21-May-42	1 Dec 1942 – 21 Feb 1943 from 8. Flottille	2 patrols	Sunk with all hands 21 Feb 1943 in the Atlantic by depth charges from a Liberator of No. 120 Sqn RAF. 46 dead

U-Boat	Type	Commissioned	Flotilla(s)	Patrols	Fate
BOATS THAT SERVED WITH 6TH FLOTILLA (91 BOATS)

BOATS THAT SERVED WITH 6TH FLOTILLA (91 BOATS)

U-Boat	Type	Commissioned	Flotilla(s)	Patrols	Fate
U-626	VIIC	11-Jun-42	1 Nov 1942 – 15 Dec 1942 from 5. Flottille	1 patrol	Missing with all hands on or after 14 Dec 1942. May have been sunk 15 Dec 1942 in the North Atlantic by depth charges from the US Coast Guard cutter *Ingham*. 47 dead
U-627	VIIC	18-Jun-42	1 Oct 1942 – 27 Oct 1942 from 5. Flottille	1 patrol	Sunk with all hands 27 Oct 1942 south of Iceland by depth charges from a Boeing B-17 Flying Fortress of No. 206 Sqn RAF. 44 dead
U-640	VIIC	17-Sep-42	1 May 1943 – 14 May 1943 from 5. Flottille	1 patrol	Sunk with all hands 14 May 1943 east of Cape Farewell by depth charges from a US Navy PBY Catalina of Patrol Squadron VP-84. 49 dead. Loss previously credited to depth charges from the frigate HMS *Swale* on 17 May 1943, which actually sank U-657
U-642	VIIC	1-Oct-42	1 Mar 1943 – 30 Nov 1943 from 5. Flottille	4 patrols. 1 ship sunk: total 2125 GRT	to 29. Flottille
U-648	VIIC	12-Nov-42	1 May 1943 – 23 Nov 1943 from 5. Flottille	4 patrols	Sunk with all hands 23 Nov 1943 northeast of the Azores by the frigates HMS *Bazely*, HMS *Blackwood* and HMS *Drury*. 50 dead. Other attacks thought to have been against U-648 actually targetted U-424, U-714 and U-843. None caused any damage
U-655	VIIC	11-Aug-41	11 Aug 1941 – 24 Mar 1942	1 patrol	Sunk with all hands 24 Mar 1942 in the Barents Sea, rammed by minesweeper HMS *Sharpshooter*. 45 dead
U-658	VIIC	5-Nov-41	1 Aug 1942 – 30 Oct 1942 from 8. Flottille	2 patrols. 3 ships sunk: total 12,146 GRT; 1 ship damaged: total 6466 GRT	Sunk with all hands 30 Oct 1942 east of Newfoundland by depth charges from a Lockheed Hudson of No. 145 Sqn RCAF. 48 dead
U-666	VIIC	26-Aug-42	1 Mar 1943 – 10 Feb 1944 from 5. Flottille	4 patrols. 1 warship sunk: total 1392t/1370 tons; 1 ship damaged: total 5234 GRT	Missing with all hands in the North Atlantic on or after 10 Feb 1944. 51 dead. Previously credited to aircraft from the escort carrier HMS *Fencer*, now thought to have been attacking a false target
U-668	VIIC	16-Nov-42	1 Apr 1944 – 31 May 1944 from 5. Flottille	6 patrols	to 13. Flottille
U-672	VIIC	6-Apr-43	1 Oct 1943 – 18 Jul 1944 from 5. Flottille	4 patrols	Sunk 18 Jul 1944 north of Guernsey by depth charges from frigate HMS *Balfour*. No casualties – 52 survivors
U-673	VIIC	8-May-43	1 Jun 1944 – 20 Jun 1944 from 5. Flottille	5 patrols	to 13. Flottille
U-673	VIIC	8-May-43	1 Aug 1944 – 24 Oct 1944 from 13. Flottille	5 patrols	Collided with U-382, ran aground and wrecked 24 Oct 1944 north of Stavanger. Raised 9 Nov 1944. Surrendered to Norway in 1945 and broken up
U-675	VIIC	14-Jul-43	1 May 1944 – 24 May 1944 from 5. Flottille	1 patrol	Sunk with all hands 24 May 1944 west of Alesund, Norway, by depth charges from a Short Sunderland of No. 4 Sqn RAF. 51 dead
U-680	VIIC	23-Dec-43	1 Aug 1944 – 30 Sep 1944 from 31. Flottille	4 patrols	to 11. Flottille
U-703	VIIC	16-Oct-41	16 Oct 1941 – 30 Jun 1942	13 patrols. 5 ships sunk: total 29,523 GRT; 1 auxiliary warship sunk: total 559 GRT; 1 warship sunk: total 1900t/1870 tons	to 11. Flottille
U-705	VIIC	30-Dec-41	1 Aug 1942 – 3 Sep 1942	1 patrol. 1 ship sunk: total 3279 GRT	Sunk with all hands 3 Sep 1942 west of Brest by depth charges from an Armstrong Whitworth Whitley of No. 77 Sqn RAF. 45 dead
U-742	VIIC	1-May-43	1 Apr 1944 – 31 May 1944 from 8. Flottille	2 patrols	to 13. Flottille
U-756	VIIC	30-Dec-41	30 Dec 1941 – 1 Sep 1942	1 patrol	Sunk with all hands 1 Sep 1942 in the North Atlantic by the corvette HMCS *Morden*. 43 dead. Previously credited to a US Navy Catalina the same day, which actually damaged U-91
U-757	VIIC	28-Feb-42	28 Feb 1942 – 8 Jan 1944	5 patrols. 2 ships sunk: total 11,313 GRT	Sunk with all hands 8 Jan 1944 southwest of Ireland by depth charges from the frigate HMS *Bayntun* and corvette HMCS *Camrose*. 49 dead
U-758	VIIC	5-May-42	5 May 1942 – 14 Oct 1944	7 patrols. 2 ships sunk: total 13,989 GRT	to 33. Flottille
U-766	VIIC	30-Jul-43	1 Mar 1944 – 21 Aug 1944 from 8. Flottille	5 patrols	Unable to put to sea 21 Aug 1944 at La Pallice. Surrendered to France and was commissioned into French service as the *Laubie* in 1947. Renamed Q335 and stricken 11 Mar 1963
U-964	VIIC	18-Feb-43	1 Oct 1943 – 16 Oct 1943 from 5. Flottille	1 patrol	Sunk 16 Oct 1943 southwest of Iceland by depth charges from a Liberator of No. 86 Sqn RAF. 47 dead and 3 survivors
U-967	VIIC	11-Mar-43	1 Oct 1943 – 29 Feb 1944 from 5. Flottille	3 patrols. 1 warship sunk: total 1321t/1300 tons	to 29. Flottille
U-972	VIIC	8-Apr-43	1 Dec 1943 – 1 Jan 1944 from 5. Flottille	1 patrol	Missing with all hands Jan 1944. 49 dead. May have been sunk by one of its own acoustic homing torpedoes
U-981	VIIC	3-Jun-43	1 Dec 1943 – 12 Aug 1944 from 5. Flottille	3 patrols	Sunk 12 Aug 1944 at La Rochelle by an air-laid mine and by depth charges from a Handley Page Halifax of No. 502 Sqn RAF. 12 dead and 40 survivors
U-982	VIIC	10-Jun-43	1 Feb 1944 – 1 Jul 1944 from 5. Flottille	1 patrol	to 24. Flottille
U-986	VIIC	1-Jul-43	1 Mar 1944 – 17 Apr 1944 from 5. Flottille	1 patrol	Usually recorded as sunk with all hands 17 Apr 1944 southwest of Ireland by depth charges from the destroyer HMS *Swift* and Canadian sub-chaser HMCS *PC-619*. 50 dead. However, that is far north of the return route to Lorient, and there is doubt about its fate
U-999	VIIC/41	21-Oct-43	1 Jun 1944 – 30 Jun 1944 from 5. Flottille	1 patrol	to 24. Flottille

7 Unterseebootsflottille

Last of the prewar U-boat flotillas to be formed, the 7th Flotilla was established as the *U-bootflottille* Wegener on 25 June 1938 at Kiel. After offically becoming the 7th Flotilla, the unit was transferred to St Nazaire over the autumn of 1940 and into 1941.

THE FLOTILLA WAS NAMED after Kptlt. Bernd Wegener, who commanded U-27 during World War I. On 10 patrols he sank 29 ships, becoming famous after his death on 19 August 1915. U-27 was sunk by the Q-ship *Barolong*, and the crew of the British vessel caused an international incident when they killed 10 of the survivors of U-27 in what became known as the *Barolong* Incident.

French success

Once established in France, the 7th Flotilla amassed a combat record second to none. It was home to many of the most successful aces. The first boat of

▼ **U-47 crew**

Gunther Prien and the crew of U-47 pose on deck after their triumphant return from sinking the battleship *Royal Oak* at Scapa Flow in the Orkneys.

7TH FLOTILLA BASE LOCATIONS

ATLANTIC OCEAN

Kiel

St Nazaire

The 'Snorting Bull' was originally the emblem of U-47, after Gunther Prien's nickname of 'the Bull'. Designed by Engelbert Endrass, it was later selected as the 7th Flotilla's insignia.

Commanders

Korvkpt. Ernst Sobe *(Jun 1939 – Dec 1939)*	Kptlt. Herbert Sohler *(May 1940 – Sep 1940)*
Korvkpt. Hans Rudolf Rösing	Korvkpt. Herbert Sohler *(Sep 1940 – Feb 1944)*
(Jan 1940 – May 1940)	Korvkpt. Adolf Piening *(Mar 1944 – May 1945)*

7TH FLOTILLA

Type	Boats assigned
Type VIIB	19
Type VIIC	89
Type VIIC/41	1
Type U-A	1

the flotilla to reach St Nazaire, on 29 September 1940, was U-46, commanded by future U-boat ace Engelbert Endrass. St Nazaire boats of the 6th and 7th Flotillas mounted 388 operational patrols between the end of 1940 and the summer of 1944.

Allied advances after the invasion of Normandy meant that most boats left for Norway in August and September 1944. The 7th Flotilla was disbanded in August 1944. Many of the unit's shore-based personnel were unable to escape, however, and they were used as ground troops defending the *Festung* Saint-Nazaire, which remained in German hands until the end of the war.

Only one boat remained at the base. Engineering problems meant that U-255 had been unable to sail for Norway. However, it was repaired by base personnel and went on a last minelaying patrol near Les Sables d'Olonne in April 1945 under the flotilla's last commander, Korvkpt. Piening. U-255 finally left St Nazaire on 7 May 1945 and surrendered five days later at sea.

▶ **Radio operator**
The strict control maintained by the high command over operational U-boats meant that the *Funkers*, or radio operators, were vital members of any boat's crew.

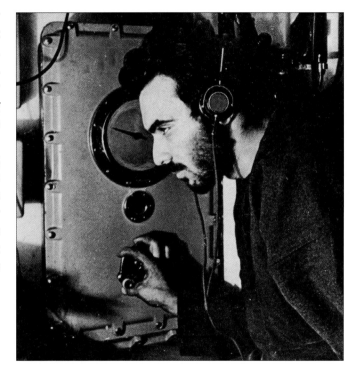

Star commanders
1939–45

The 7th Flotilla was the most successful U-boat formation of the war, numbering many of the highest-scoring commanders and boats in history in its ranks.

Fregattenkapitän Otto Kretschmer

The son of a teacher, Otto Kretschmer was the top submarine ace of World War II. Born at Heidau in Silesia, he spent eight months in England before joining the German Navy in 1930. In 1936, he transferred to the U-boat arm, commanding his first boat in 1937. As a wartime U-boat captain in U-23 and U-99, he sank 44 ships totalling 266,629 GRT. His motto on operations was 'One torpedo … one ship'. He was awarded the Knight's Cross with Oak Leaves on 4 November 1940, adding the Swords while in captivity on 26¾December 1941. On 17

March 1941, in a running battle with the destroyer HMS *Walker*, U-99 was forced to the surface by depth charges. Kretschmer was captured and with him 39 out of ¾ his crew of 43. After the war, Kretschmer entered the West German *Bundesmarine*, where he served with distinction, retiring with the rank of *Flotillenadmiral* in September 1970. He died in an accident on 5 August 1998 in Bavaria.

Korvettenkapitän Gunther Prien

Prien was the U-boat ace who became one of the Third Reich's earliest war heroes. On the night of 13/14 October 1939, Prien took the Type VII U-boat U-47 into the heavily defended Royal Navy base at Scapa Flow in the Orkneys. Penetrating the minefields and anti-submarine nets, he launched two torpedo attacks on HMS *Royal Oak*. The battleship sank in 15 minutes, and 24 officers and 800 men were killed. Prien made a skilful surface escape. He was awarded the Knight's Cross – the first to any U-boat commander – and each member of his crew received the Iron Cross (Second Class).

Born in Thuringia, Prien was a merchant seaman before joining the German Navy in 1934. He transferred to U-boats in 1935, and by the outbreak of war was in command of U-47. Described by William L. Shirer as 'clean-cut, cocky, a fanatical Nazi and obviously capable', he was one of the most successful of all U-boat commanders, sinking over 180,000 tonnes (177,158 tons) of British shipping in 18 months. He was awarded Oak Leaves in October

▲ **U-boat ace**

He was not the highest-scoring ace, but Prien's feat at Scapa Flow early in the war meant that he became the most famous of all U-boat commanders.

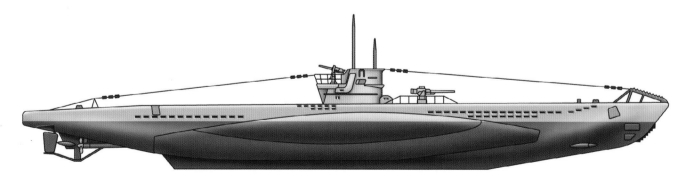

▲ **U-47**

Type VIIB

Launched on 29 October 1938, U-47 was commanded for its entire existence by Gunther Prien. The boat was always assigned to the *Wegener* Flotilla, which later became the 7th U-boat Flotilla.

Specifications	
Crew: 44	Dimensions (length/beam/draught): 66.5 x 6.2
Powerplant: Diesel/electric	x 4.7m (218.1 x 20.34 x 15.4ft)
Max Speed: 31.9/14.8km/hr (17.2/8kt) surf/sub	Commissioned: 17 Dec 1938
Surface Range: 12,040km (6500nm)	Armament: 14 torpedoes (4 bow/1 stern tubes);
Displacement: 765/871t (753/857 tons) surf/sub	1 x 8.8cm (3.5in) and 1 x 2cm (0.8in) guns

1940. Prien was killed in action on the night of 7/8 March 1941, when U-47 was thought to have been sunk by the British destroyer HMS *Wolverine*. However, recent research indicates that the destroyer actually attacked U-A and that U-47 was lost to unknown causes.

Fregattenkapitän Erich Topp

The third-highest scoring commander after Kretschmer and Lüth, Erich Topp sank 35 ships (200,629 tonnes/197,460 tons) in 12 patrols in U-57 and U-552. Topp began his naval career with Crew 34 and joined the U-boat force in October 1937. After four patrols commanding U-57, he transferred to U-552, known as the 'Red Devil' boat after Topp's

STAR COMMANDERS		
Commander	Patrols	Ships Sunk
Fregattenkapitän Otto Kretschmer	16	44
Kapitänleutnant Joachim Schepke	14	36
Fregattenkapitän Erich Topp	12	35
Korvettenkapitän Gunther Prien	10	31

personal emblem. Topp scored most of his successes in the North Atlantic against convoys and off the North American coast. After commanding the 27th Tactical Training Flotilla, Topp commissioned the 'Electro' boats U-3010 and U-2513. After the war, Topp served in the *Bundesmarine*, retiring in 1969 as a *Konteradmiral*. He died on 26 December 2005.

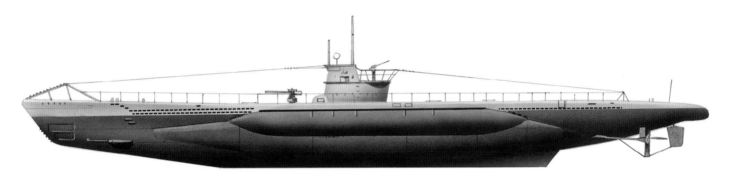

▲ U-99

Type VIIB

U-99 was the third boat commanded by Otto Kretschmer. In it, the top-scoring ace of the war sank 36 out of the 44 vessels he destroyed between September 1939 and his capture in March 1941.

Specifications

Crew: 44

Powerplant: Diesel/electric

Max Speed: 31.9/14.8km/hr (17.2/8kt) surf/sub

Surface Range: 12,040km (6500nm)

Displacement: 765/871t (753/857 tons) surf/sub

Dimensions (length/beam/draught): 66.5 x 6.2 x 4.7m (218.1 x 20.34 x 15.4ft)

Commissioned: 18 Apr 1940

Armament: 14 torpedoes (4 bow/1 stern tubes); 1 x 8.8cm (3.5in) and 1 x 2cm (0.8in) guns (1941)

▲ U-552

Type VIIC

Erich Topp commissioned U-552 in December 1940. The boat served with the 7th Flotilla until 1944, with Topp in command until August 1942. Under Topp and his successor Klaus Popp, U-552 sank 29 merchant ships of some 163,529 GRT.

Specifications

Crew: 44

Powerplant: Diesel/electric

Max Speed: 31.5/14.1km/hr (17/7.6kt) surf/sub

Surface Range: 12,040km (6500nm)

Displacement: 773/879t (761/865 tons) surf/sub

Dimensions (length/beam/draught): 67.1 x 6.2 x 4.8m (220.1 x 20.34 x 15.75ft)

Commissioned: 4 Dec 1940

Armament: 14 torpedoes (4 bow/1 stern tubes); 1 x 8.8cm (3.5in) and 1 x 2cm (0.8in) guns

U-48

TYPE VIIB

The most successful U-boat of World War II, U-48 was launched on 5 March 1939 and commissioned into the *Flottille* Wegener, later the 7th Flotilla, on 22 April.

UNDER THE SUCCESSIVE COMMANDS of Knight's Cross winners Herbert Schultze, Hans Rudolf Rösing and Heinrich Bleichrodt, U-48 sank more ships of a greater tonnage than any other submarine in World War II. On 12 patrols, the boat accounted for 51 merchant ships totalling 306,875 GRT, as well as sinking a Royal Navy sloop and damaging three ships for a total of 20,480 GRT. On its last mission in support of the *Bismarck*, U-48 joined in the search for survivors when the battleship was sunk, spending four days looking but with no success.

From June 1941 to 1945, U-48 was with the 26th and 21st Flotillas as a training boat. Decommissioned

in October 1943, U-48 was used as a non-operational instructional platform by the 3. *Unterseebootslehrdivision* (a training school known until 1940 as an *Unterseebootsschule*) at Neustadt. At the end of the war, the boat was still at Neustadt, where it was scuttled on 3 May 1945.

U-48 Commanders	
Kptlt. Herbert Schultze (Apr 1939 – May 1940)	Oblt. Diether Todenhagen
Korvkpt. Hans Rudolf Rösing	(Sep 1940 – Oct 1940)
(May 1940 – Sep 1940)	Kptlt. Herbert Schultze (Dec 1940 – Jul 1941)
Kptlt. Heinrich Bleichrodt	Oblt. Siegfried Atzinger
(Sep 1940 – Dec 1940)	(Aug 1941 – Sep 1942)

▼ U-48

Type VIIB

A standard Type VIIB boat, U-48 used her 8.8cm (3.5in) gun to sink a number of her victims, especially on early patrols.

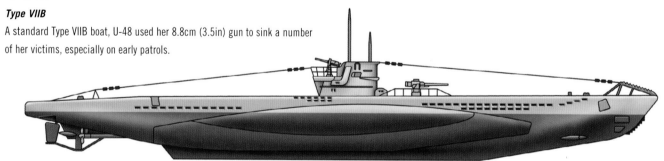

U-48 TIMETABLE		
Patrol Dates	**Operational Area**	**Ships Sunk**
19 Aug 1939 – 17 Sep 1939	W of Biscay	3
4 Oct 1939 – 25 Oct 1939	W of Finsterre	5
20 Nov 1939 – 20 Dec 1939	Orkneys/Channel approaches	4
24 Jan 1940 – 26 Feb 1940	Channel approaches	4
3 Apr 1940 – 20 Apr 1940	Norway	0
26 May 1940 – 29 June 1940	WNW of Finisterre	7
7 Aug 1940 – 28 Aug 1940	WSW of Rockall	5
8 Sep 1940 – 25 Sep 1940	W of British Isles	8
5 Oct 1940 – 27 Oct 1940	NW of Rockall	7
20 Jan 1941 – 27 Feb 1941	S of Iceland	2
17 Mar 1941 – 8 Apr 1941	S of Iceland	5
22 May 1941 – 21 June 1941	W of St Nazaire (supporting *Bismarck*)/N of the Azores/central Atlantic	0
June 1941 – 1945	Served wth 26 and 21 Flotillas as a training boat	
Oct 1943	Decommissioned: used by 3 ULD	
3 May 1945	Scuttled at Neustadt	

U-76
TYPE VIIB

Although a small number of boats under ace commanders were running up large scores in 1940 and 1941, most boats, like U-76, had less spectacular careers.

COMMISSIONED IN DECEMBER 1940 after being built by Bremer Vulkan, Vegesack, U-76 under the command of *Oberleutnant* Friederich von Hippel spent a shorter time than average in working up to combat standards. Normally, this could take up to six months, but U-76 went on its first patrol on 19 March 1941. After sinking a merchantman, the boat closed with Convoy SC 26. The boat was abandoned and sank after being forced to surface by depth charge attacks from the destroyer HMS *Wolverine* and the sloop HMS *Scarborough*. One crewman was killed; 42 were captured.

U-76 Commander

Oblt. Friederich von Hippel *(Dec 1940 – Apr 1941)*

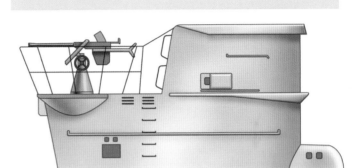

▲ **Type VIIB AA conversion**

In an attempt to increase the anti-aircraft defences of the Type VIIB boats without being forced to completely rebuild the conning tower, U-84 was fitted with a raised AA platform for an extra 2cm (0.8in) C/38 gun behind the bridge. This was not as effective as the 'winter garden' conversion, and the experiment proceeded no further.

U-76 TIMETABLE		
Patrol Dates	**Operational Area**	**Ships Sunk**
19 Mar 1941 – 5 Apr 1941	Central N Atlantic	1
5 Apr 1941	Boat was abandoned and sank after being forced to the surface by depth-charge attacks from destroyer HMS *Wolverine* and sloop HMS *Scarborough*. 1 crewman killed; 42 captured	

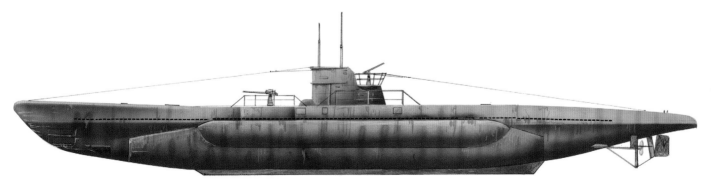

Specifications

Crew: 44

Powerplant: Diesel/electric

Max Speed: 31.9/14.8km/hr (17.2/8kt) surf/sub

Surface Range: 12,040km (6500nm)

Displacement: 765/871t (753/857 tons) surf/sub

Dimensions (length/beam/draught): 66.5 x 6.2 x 4.7m (218.1 x 20.34 x 15.4ft)

Commissioned: 3 Dec 1940

Armament: 14 torpedoes (4 bow/1 stern tubes); 1 x 8.8cm (3.5in) and 1 x 2cm (0.8in) guns

▲ **U-76**

Type VIIB

Although U-boats were not as fast as front-line warships, they could easily outpace merchant convoys. U-76 spent three days of her only patrol shadowing Convoy SC 26, although she was unable to mount any successful attacks.

U-553

TYPE VIIC

Laid down at Blohm und Voss, Hamburg, in November 1939, U-553 was launched on 7 November 1940 and commissioned into the 7th Flotilla in December of that year.

AFTER FOUR MONTHS working up at Kiel, U-553 set off for the flotilla's operational base in France. The boat went on to amass a respectable score. Commanded by *Korvettenkapitän* Karl Thurmann, U-553 sank 13 ships for a total of 64,612 GRT in its 10 sorties, and damaged two more vessels totalling 15,273 GRT.

In two years with the 7th Flotilla, the boat operated in the North Atlantic, off Canada and down the US east coast. It was at about this time that Type VII

U-553 Commander

Korvkpt. Karl Thurmann *(Dec 1940 – Jan 1943)*

commanders discovered that by careful regulation of engine speed they could stretch endurance more than had originally been expected, and the boat made one patrol as far south as the Caribbean.

The boat went missing in January 1943, after sending a last message saying 'Periscope unclear'.

U-553 TIMETABLE		
Patrol Dates	**Operational Area**	**Ships Sunk**
13 Apr 1941 – 2 May 1941	Transit from Kiel to St Nazaire	0
7 June 1941 – 19 Jul 1941	Azores/Newfoundland Bank	2
7 Aug 1941 – 16 Sep 1941	SW of Iceland	0
7 Oct 1941 – 22 Oct 1941	N Atlantic SE of Cape Farewell	3
1 Jan 1942 – 3 Feb 1942	Canadian waters	2
19 Apr 1942 – 24 June 1942	Canadian waters. Attacked several times, sustained damage	3
19 Jul 1942 – 17 Sep 1942	N Atlantic/Caribbean	4
November 1942	Transferred to 3rd Flotilla	
23 Nov 1942 – 18 Dec 1942	N Atlantic	1
16 Jan 1943 – 22 Jan 1943	W of Ireland	0
20 Jan 1943	Last communication from U-553	
22 Jan 1943	Declared lost with all hands to unknown causes. 47 dead	

Specifications

Crew: 44

Powerplant: Diesel/electric

Max Speed: 31.5/14.1km/hr (17/7.6kt) surf/sub

Surface Range: 12,040km (6500nm)

Displacement: 773/879t (761/865 tons) surf/sub

Dimensions (length/beam/draught): 67.1 x 6.2 x 4.8m (220.1 x 20.34 x 15.75ft)

Commissioned: 23 Dec 1940

Armament: 14 torpedoes (4 bow/1 stern tubes); 1 x 2cm (0.8in) quad and 2 x twin 2cm (0.8in) guns

▲ **U-553**

Type VIIC

By 1943 the anti-aircraft armament of U-boats was increasing dramatically to meet an equally increased threat. Firepower was greatly enhanced by the fitting of the Flakvierling quadruple 2cm (0.8in) anti-aircraft mounting.

Attack on convoy SC 7

OCTOBER 1940

SC 7 was one of the first convoys to suffer heavily from an effective wolfpack attack, and its terrible stuggle for life showed that the U-boat was a real threat to Britain's survival.

ON THE NIGHT of 21 September 1940, HX 72, a fast convoy consisting of 41 merchantmen, was attacked and 11 vessels were sunk. The commodore of the convoy was sure at least two U-boats had taken part in the attack. The senior officer of the escorts agreed. There was a suggestion that U-boats were beginning to co-ordinate their attacks. Slow convoy SC 7 was to put the matter beyond doubt.

The Canadian port of Sydney saw the gathering of a motley collection of ships, and convoy SC 7 got under way in the first week of October 1940. SC 7 was not expected to make more than 15km/hr (8kt) – in fact, some of the ships were so old and decrepit that they struggled to make 9km/hr (5kt).

Slaughter begins

In the early hours of 16 October, one of the stragglers was attacked. The convoy's single escort, the sloop HMS *Scarborough*, could do nothing. Late that night, the watch on the bridge of U-48 spotted the moonlit silhouette of a ship. As the boat closed, it became clear it was part of a convoy, a large one, weakly protected. U-48 sent a message to Lorient giving the convoy's course and speed. Five boats were ordered to close with the convoy and attack. U-48 went in first,

CONVOY SC 7 BATTLE TIMETABLE	
Date	Event
4/5 Oct	Departs Sydney, Cape Breton Island – 35 ships
16 Oct	One straggler sunk
17 Oct	One straggler sunk. Convoy spotted by U-48 – 2 ships sunk. U-46, U-99, U-100, U-123 vectored to intercept
18 Oct	7 ships sunk, 4 damaged
19 Oct	9 ships sunk
20 Oct	15 surviving ships of convoy reach Liverpool

sinking the 9650-tonne (9500 ton) tanker *Languedoc*. Two minutes later, the freighter *Scoresby* was hit.

The escort, now reinforced by sloops HMS *Leith*, HMS *Fowey* and corvettes HMS *Bluebell* and HMS *Heartsease*, spent a good deal of the 17th rounding up ships. The convoy was spread over 30km (18 miles) of ocean, and some ships did not even know there had been an attack.

But it was to be a brief respite. U-48 was shadowing SC 7 when it was forced to dive by a Sunderland flying boat, but it had passed enough information to ensure the convoy would be intercepted by U-38,

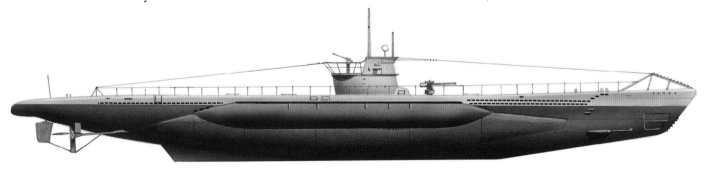

▲ **U-100**

Type VIIB

Joachim Schepke rivalled Gunther Prien in his popularity with Germany's Propaganda Ministry. His piratical appearance masked a capable commander who with U-3, U-19 and U-100 sank 36 ships in just 18 months..

Specifications

Crew: 44

Powerplant: Diesel/electric

Max Speed: 31.9/14.8km/hr (17.2/8kt) surf/sub

Surface Range: 12,040km (6500nm)

Displacement: 765/871t (753/857 tons) surf/sub

Dimensions (length/beam/draught): 66.5 x 6.2 x 4.7m (218.1 x 20.34 x 15.4ft)

Commissioned: 30 May 1940

Armament: 14 torpedoes (4 bow/1 stern tubes); 1 x 8.8cm (3.5in) and 1 x 2cm (0.8in) guns (1941)

U-46, U-100 and U-99, the last three commanded by ace commanders Endrass, Schepke and Kretschmer. SC 7 was just the second convoy to be attacked by a wolfpack.

On 18 October, seven ships were torpedoed and sunk, including the iron ore ship SS *Creekirk*, bound for Cardiff, Wales. With her heavy cargo, she sank like a stone, taking all 36 crew members with her. October 19 1940 was the blackest day of all, with the wolfpack sinking nine ships, including the SS *Empire Brigand*

with her cargo of trucks. She went down with six of her crew. Other casualties were the commodore's ship, SS *Assyrian*, and the SS *Fiscus* with its cargo of steel ingots. The convoy lost 20 ships out of 35, of which seven fell to Kretschmer's U-99. The total tonnage lost was 80,869 tonnes (79,592 tons).

The arrival in the vicinity of Convoy HX 79 diverted the wolfpack and they went on to sink 14 more ships from that convoy, making a total of 34 ships destroyed in 48 hours. No U-boats were lost.

Wolfpack group *West*
JUNE 1941

Formed in June 1941 from Type VII boats, mostly from 7th Flotilla and 1st Flotilla, together with a number of larger Type IX boats from 2nd Flotilla, the *West* group gathered southeast of the Newfoundland Bank. However, even in summer it was hard to find targets in the North Atlantic.

ON 20 JUNE, the group spread out northeastwards, forming a widely spaced line in the centre of the North Atlantic. No convoys were encountered, but a number of independently sailing merchantmen were sunk. On 24 June, U-203 (not part of the *West* group) sighted the westbound convoy OB 336 to the south of Greenland. OB convoys were outward bound to North America, and OB 336, consisting of

24 ships, had sailed from Liverpool. Taking a chance when offered, U-203 made an attack and sank two vessels. U-77, U-101, U-108, U-553 and U-558 of Group *West* were ordered to intercept and closed to

▼ **Scanning the horizon**
Well protected against the ocean spray, the crew of a U-boat search for potential prey in the North Atlantic, summer 1941.

shadow the convoy. However, the submarines lost the merchant vessels in fog – always a possibility in these waters, whatever the season – before any more could be sunk.

Late in June, Group *West*, together with some independent boats, was ordered eastwards after a Focke-Wulf Fw 200 Condor aircraft sighted Convoy OG 66 about 500km (290nm) west of Ireland. The OG convoys were routed from Britain to Gibraltar and West Africa, and the 55 ships of OG 66 had left Liverpool on 24 June. Further aircraft sightings were made on 30 June and 1 July, but the wolfpack was unable to close because of poor visibility caused by fog and bad weather.

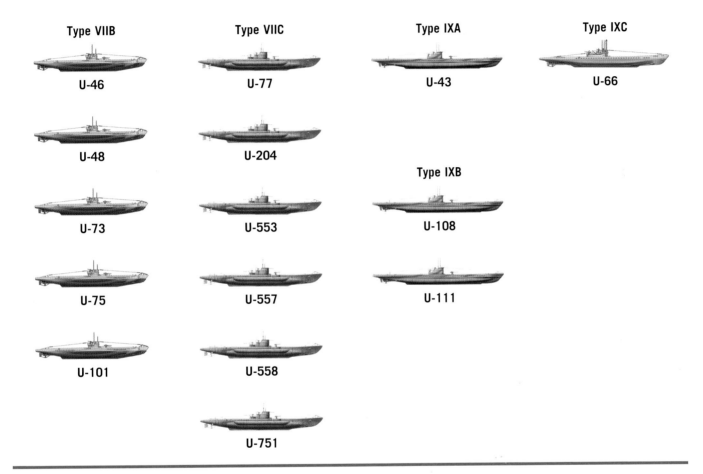

Type VIIB	Type VIIC	Type IXA	Type IXC
U-46	U-77	U-43	U-66
U-48	U-204		
U-73	U-553	Type IXB	
		U-108	
U-75	U-557	U-111	
U-101	U-558		
	U-751		

BOATS THAT SERVED WITH 7TH FLOTILLA (110 BOATS)					
U-Boat	Type	Commissioned	Flotilla(s)	Patrols	Fate
U-45	VIIB	25-Jun-38	25 Jun 1938 – 14 Oct 1939	2 patrols. 2 ships sunk: total 19,313 GRT	Sunk with all hands 14 Oct 1939 southwest of Ireland by depth charges from the destroyers HMS *Inglefield*, HMS *Ivanhoe* and HMS *Intrepid*. 38 dead
U-46	VIIB	2-Nov-38	2 Nov 1938 – 1 Sep 1941	13 patrols. 21 ships sunk: total 90,408 GRT; 2 auxiliary warships sunk: total 35,284 GRT; 1 ship a total loss: total 2080 GRT; 4 ships damaged: total 25,491 GRT	to 26. Flottille
U-47	VIIB	17-Dec-38	17 Dec 1938 – 7 Mar, 1941	10 patrols. 30 ships sunk: total 162,768 GRT; 1 battleship (HMS *Royal Oak*) sunk: total 29,618t/29,150 tons; 8 ships damaged: total 62,751 GRT	Missing with all hands 7 Mar 1941 in North Atlantic near the Rockall Banks. 45 dead. Previously recorded fate is probably an error: destroyer HMS *Wolverine* claimed to have sunk U-47 on 8 Mar 1941 after depth-charge attacks, but the *Wolverine* actually attacked Eckermann's U-A. U-47 may have hit a mine, or possibly fallen to an attack by corvettes HMS *Camellia* and HMS *Arbutus*
U-48	VIIB	22-Apr-39	22 Apr 1939 – 30 Jun 1941	12 patrols. 51 ships sunk: total 306,875 GRT; 1 warship sunk: total 1077t/1060 tons; 3 ships damaged: total 20,480 GRT. Most successful submarine of World War II both in terms of tonnage and numbers of ships sunk	to 26. Flottille
U-49	VIIB	12-Aug-39	12 Aug 1939 – 15 Apr 1940	4 patrols. 1 ship sunk: total 4258 GRT	Sunk 15 Apr 1940 near Narvik, Norway, by depth charges from the British destroyers HMS *Fearless* and HMS *Brazen*. 1 dead and 41 survivors

BOATS THAT SERVED WITH 7TH FLOTILLA (110 BOATS)

U-Boat	Type	Commissioned	Flotilla(s)	Patrols	Fate
U-50	VIIB	12-Dec-39	12 Dec 1939 – 6 Apr 1940	2 patrols. 4 ships sunk: total 16,089 GRT	Destroyed with all hands 6 April 1940 by mines laid by destroyers HMS *Express*, HMS *Esk*, HMS *Icarus* and HMS *Impulsive* 3 March 1940. 44 dead. Previously the loss was attributed to an attack by the destroyer HMS *Hero* 10 April 1940; but this was most probably against a false target
U-51	VIIB	6-Aug-38	6 Aug 1938 – 20 Aug 1940	4 patrols. 5 ships sunk: total 26,296 GRT; 1 auxiliary warship sunk: total 4724 GRT	Sunk with all hands 20 Aug 1940 in the Bay of Biscay west of Nantes, France, by a torpedo from the submarine HMS *Cachalot*. 43 dead
U-52	VIIB	4-Feb-39	4 Feb 1939 – 31 May 1941	8 patrols. 13 ships sunk: total 56,333 GRT	to 26. Flottille
U-53	VIIB	24-Jun-39	24 Jun 1939 – 23 Feb 1940	3 patrols. 7 ships sunk: total 27,316 GRT; 1 ship damaged: total 8022 GRT	Sunk with all hands 23 Feb 1940 in the North Sea, Orkney waters, by depth charges from the destroyer HMS *Gurkha*. 42 dead
U-54	VIIB	23-Sep-39	23 Sept 1939 – 20 Feb 1940	1 patrol	Missing with all hands 20 Feb 1940 in the North Sea, position unknown. 41 dead. The boat was possibly lost to mines laid by the destroyers HMS *Ivanhoe* and HMS *Intrepid* early in Jan 1940
U-55	VIIB	21-Nov-39	21 Nov 1939 – 30 Jan 1940	1 patrol. 6 ships sunk: total 15,853 GRT	Sunk 30 Jan 1940 in the English Channel southwest of the Scilly Isles by depth charges from the destroyer HMS *Whitshed*, the sloop HMS *Fowey*, the French destroyers *Valmy* and *Guépard*, and by depth charges from a British Sunderland aircraft of No. 228 Sqn. 1 dead and 41 survivors
U-69	VIIC	2-Nov-40	2 Nov 1940 – 17 Feb 1943 (front boat)	11 patrols. 16 ships sunk: total 67,500 GRT; 1 ship damaged beyond repair: total 5445 GRT; 1 ship damaged: total 4887 GRT	Sunk with all hands 17 Feb 1943 in the North Atlantic east of Newfoundland by depth charges from the British destroyer HMS *Fame*. 46 dead. Originally thought to have been sunk by destroyer HMS *Viscount*. That attack actually sank U-201
U-70	VIIC	23-Nov-40	23 Nov 1940 – 7 Mar 1941	1 patrol. 1 ship sunk: total 820 GRT; 3 ships damaged: total 20,484 GRT	Sunk 7 Mar 1941 southeast of Iceland, in position 60.15N, 14.00W, by British corvettes HMS *Camellia* and HMS *Arbutus*. 20 dead and 25 survivors
U-71	VIIC	14-Dec-40	14 Dec 1940 – 31 May 1943	10 patrols. 5 ships sunk: total 38,894 GRT	to 24. Flottille
U-73	VIIB	31-Oct-40	31 Oct 1940 – 30 Nov 1941	8 patrols. 4 ships sunk: total 24,694 GRT; 1 warship sunk: total 940t/925 tons; 1 ship damaged: total 97 GRT; 1 auxiliary warship damaged: total 11,402 GRT	to 29. Flottille
U-75	VIIB	19-Dec-40	19 Dec 1940 – 1 Oct 1941	5 patrols. 7 ships sunk: total 37,884 GRT; 2 warships sunk: total 756t/744 tons	to 23. Flottille
U-76	VIIB	3-Dec-40	3 Dec 1940 – 5 Apr 1941	1 patrol. 2 ships sunk: total 7290 GRT	Sunk 5 Apr 1941 south of Iceland by depth charges from the destroyer HMS *Wolverine* and the sloop HMS *Scarborough*. 1 dead and 42 survivors
U-77	VIIC	18-Jan-41	18 Jan 1941 – 31 Dec 1941	12 patrols. 14 ships sunk: total 31,186 GRT; 1 warship sunk: total 1067t/1050 tons; 1 ship damaged beyond repair: total 5222 GRT; 2 ships damaged: total 5384 GRT; 2 warships damaged: total 2926t/2880 tons	to 23. Flottille
U-88	VIIC	15-Oct-41	1 May 1942 – 30 Jun 1942 from 8. Flottille	3 patrols. 2 ships sunk: total 12,304 GRT	to 11. Flottille
U-93	VIIC	30-Jul-40	30 Jul 1940 – 15 Jan 1942	7 patrols. 8 ships sunk: total 43,392 GRT	Sunk 15 Jan 1942 in North Atlantic by the destroyer HMS *Hesperus*. 6 dead and 40 survivors
U-94	VIIC	10-Aug-40	10 Aug 1940 – 28 Aug 1942	10 patrols. 26 ships sunk: total 141,853 GRT; 1 ship damaged: total 8022 GRT	Sunk in the Caribbean Sea on 28 Aug 1942 by depth charges from a US Navy Catalina from patrol squadron VP-92, followed by ramming by the Canadian corvette HMCS *Oakville*. 19 dead and 26 survivors
U-95	VIIC	31-Aug-40	31 Aug 1940 – 28 Nov 1941	7 patrols. 8 ships sunk: total 28,415 GRT; 4 ships damaged: total 27,916 GRT	Sunk 28 Nov 1941 off the Spanish coast southwest of Almeria by the Dutch submarine HrMs *O 21*. 35 dead and 12 survivors
U-96	VIIC	14-Sep-40	14 Sep 1940 – 31 Mar 1943	11 patrols. 27 ships sunk: total 181,206 GRT; 1 ship damaged beyond repair: total 8888 GRT; 4 ships damaged: total 33,043 GRT	To 24. Flottille. Lothar-Günther Buchheim joined U-96 for one patrol as a war correspondent, which provided material for the best-selling novel, TV series and film *Das Boot (The Boat)*
U-97	VIIC	28-Sep-40	28 Sep 1940 – 31 Oct 1941	13 patrols. 15 ships sunk: total 64,404 GRT; 1 auxiliary warship sunk: total 6833 GRT; 1 ship damaged: total 9718 GRT	to 23. Flottille
U-98	VIIC	12-Oct-40	12 Oct 1940 – 15 Nov 1942	9 patrols. 10 ships sunk: total 48,878 GRT; 1 auxiliary warship sunk: total 10,549 GRT; 1 warship damaged: total 188t/185 tons	Sunk with all hands 15 Nov 1942 in North Atlantic west of Gibraltar, in position 36.09N, 07.42W, by depth charges from the British destroyer HMS *Wrestler*. 46 dead
U-99	VIIB	18-Apr-40	18 Apr 1940 – 17 Mar 1941	8 patrols. 35 ships sunk: total 198,218 GRT; 3 auxiliary warships sunk: total 46,440 GRT; 5 ships damaged: total 37,965 GRT; 1 ship taken as prize: total 2136 GRT	Scuttled 17 Mar 1941 southeast of Iceland after being depth-charged by the British destroyer HMS *Walker*. 3 dead and 40 survivors
U-100	VIIB	30-May-40	30 May 1940 – 17 Mar 1941	6 patrols. 25 ships sunk: total 135,614 GRT; 1 ship damaged beyond repair: total 2205 GRT; 4 ships damaged: total 17,229 GRT	Sunk 17 Mar 1941 southeast of Iceland after being rammed and depth-charged by the destroyers HMS *Walker* and HMS *Vanoc*. U-100 was the first U-boat sunk after being located on the surface in poor visibility by radar. 38 dead and 6 survivors
U-101	VIIB	11-Mar-40	11 Mar 1940 – 28 Feb 1942	10 patrols. 22 ships sunk: total 112,618 GRT; 1 warship sunk: total 1209t/1190 tons; 2 ships damaged: total 9113 GRT	to 26. Flottille

BOATS THAT SERVED WITH 7TH FLOTILLA (110 BOATS)

U-Boat	Type	Commissioned	Flotilla(s)	Patrols	Fate
U-102	VIIB	27-Apr-40	27 Apr 1940 – 1 Jul 1940	1 patrol. 1 ship sunk: total 5219 GRT	Sunk with all hands 1 Jul 1940 southwest of Ireland by depth charges from the destroyer HMS *Vansittart*. 43 dead. Originally thought to have been lost to unknown causes in the Bay of Biscay on or after 30 Jun 1940
U-133	VIIC	5-Jul-41	5 Jul 1941 – 31 Dec 1941	3 patrols. 1 warship sunk: total 1951t/1920 tons	to 23. Flottille
U-135	VIIC	16-Aug-41	1 Dec 1941 – 15 Jul 1943 from 5. Flotille	7 patrols. 3 ships sunk: total 21,302 GRT; 1 ship damaged: total 4762 GRT	Sunk 15 Jul 1943 in the Atlantic by the sloop HMS *Rochester*, the corvettes HMS *Mignonette* and HMS *Balsam* and a US Navy PBY Catalina of Patrol Squadron VP-92. 5 dead and 41 survivors
U-207	VIIC	7-Jun-41	7 Jun 1941 – 11 Sep 1941	1 patrol. 2 ships sunk: total 9727 GRT	Sunk with all hands 11 Sep 1941 in the Straits of Denmark by depth charges from the destroyers HMS *Leamington* and HMS Veteran. 41 dead
U-221	VIIC	9-May-42	1 Sep 1942 – 27 Sep 1943 from 5. Flottille (training)	5 patrols. 11 ships sunk: total 69,589 GRT; 1 ship damaged: total 7197 GRT	Sunk with all hands 27 Sep 1943 southwest of Ireland by depth charges from a Handley-Page Halifax of No. 58 Sqn RAF. 50 dead
U-224	VIIC	20-Jun-42	1 Nov 1942 – 13 Jan 1943 from 5. Flottille (training)	2 patrols. 2 ships sunk: total 9535 GRT	Sunk 13 Jan 1943 in the Mediterranean west of Algiers by ramming and depth charges from the corvette HMCS *Ville de Quebec*. 45 dead and 1 survivor
U-227	VIIC	22-Aug-42	1 Apr 1943 – 30 Apr 1943 from 5. Flottille (training)	1 patrol	Sunk with all hands 30 Apr 1943 north of the Faroes by depth charges from an Australian Hampden aircraft of No. 455 Sqn. 49 dead
U-255	VIIC	29-Nov-41	1 Dec 1943 – 1 Sep 1944 from 13. Flottille	15 patrols. 10 ships sunk: total 47,529 GRT; 1 warship sunk: total 1219t/1200 tons; 1 ship damaged b/r: total 7191 GRT	to 13. Flottille
U-265	VIIC	6-Jun-42	1 Feb 1943 – 3 Feb 1943	1 patrol	Sunk with all hands 3 Feb 1943 south of Iceland by depth charges from a Boeing B-17 Flying Fortress of No. 220 Sqn RAF. 46 dead
U-266	VIIC	24-Jun-42	1 Jan 1943 – 15 May 1943 from 8. Flottille	2 patrols. 4 ships sunk: total 16,089 GRT	Sunk with all hands 15 May 1943 in the North Atlantic by depth charges from a Halifax of No. 58 Sqn RAF. 47 dead. Previously credited to a No. 86 Sqn Liberator, but that attack was against U-403 and did no damage
U-267	VIIC	11-Jul-42	1 Feb 1943 – 1 Oct 1944 from 8. Flottille	7 patrols. Last boat to leave the U-boat base at St Nazaire on 23 Sep 1944	to 33. Flottille
U-274	VIIC	7-Nov-42	1 Aug 1943 – 23 Oct 1943 from 8. Flottille	2 patrols	Sunk with all hands 23 Oct 1943 southwest of Iceland by depth charges from destroyers HMS *Duncan* and HMS *Vidette*, and a Liberator of No. 224 Sqn RAF.48 dead
U-278	VIIC	16-Jan-43	1 Oct 1943 – 31 Dec 1943 from 8. Flottille	7 patrols. 1 ship sunk: total 7177 GRT; 1 warship sunk: total 1839t/1810 tons	to 11. Flottille
U-281	VIIC	8-May-43	1 Aug 1943 – 9 Nov 1944 from 8. Flottille	4 patrols	to 33. Flottille
U-285	VIIC	15-May-43	1 Aug 1944 – 30 Sep 1944 from 8. Flottille	3 patrols	to 11. Flottille
U-300	VIIC/41	29-Dec-43	1 Aug 1944 – 30 Sep 1944 from 8. Flottille	4 patrols. 2 ships sunk: total 7559 GRT; 1 ship damaged beyond repair: total 9551 GRT; 1 ship damaged: total 7176 GRT	to 11. Flottille
U-303	VIIC	7-Jul-42	1 Jan 1943 – 31 Mar 1943 from 8. Flottille	2 patrols. 1 ship sunk: total 4959 GRT	to 29. Flottille
U-310	VIIC	24-Feb-43	1 Aug 1944 – 4 Sep 1944 from 8. Flottille	6 patrols. 2 ships sunk: total 14,395 GRT	to 13. Flottille
U-338	VIIC	25-Jun-42	1 Mar 1943 – 21 Sep 1943 from 8. Flottille	3 patrols. 4 ships sunk: total 21,927 GRT; 1 ship damaged: total 7134 GRT	Missing with all hands in the North Atlantic on or after 20 Sep 1943. 51 dead. Previously recorded as having been sunk 20 Sep 1943 southwest of Iceland by a homing torpedo from a Liberator of No. 120 Sqn RAF. That attack was probably against U-386, and caused no damage
U-342	VIIC	12-Jan-43	1 Mar 1944 – 17 Apr 1944	2 patrols	Sunk with all hands 17 Apr 1944 southwest of Iceland by depth charges from a Catalina of No. 162 Sqn RCAF. 51 dead
U-358	VIIC	15-Aug-42	1 Feb 1943 – 1 Mar 1944 from 8. Flottille	6 patrols. 4 ships sunk: total 17,753 GRT; 1 warship sunk: total 1211t/1,192 tons	Sunk 1 Mar 1944 north of the Azores by depth charges and gunfire from the frigates HMS *Gould*, HMS *Affleck*, HMS *Gore* and HMS *Garlies*. 50 dead and 1 survivor
U-359	VIIC	5-Oct-42	1 Mar 1943 – 26 Jul 1943 from 8. Flottille	3 patrols	Sunk with all hands 26 Jul 1943 in the Caribbean south of Santo Domingo by depth charges from a US Navy Mariner of VP-32. 47 dead. Previously credited to another VP-32 Mariner on 28 Jul, but that attack actually destroyed U-159
U-364	VIIC	3-May-43	1 Nov 1943 – 31 Jan 1944 from 5. Flottille	2 patrols	Probably sunk with all hands 29 Jan 1944 in the Bay of Biscay by depth charges from a Halifax of No. 502 Sqn RAF. 49 dead. Originally loss was attributed to a Wellington of No. 172 Sqn RAF. That attack was probably against U-608, which shot down the aircraft before it could drop its charges
U-381	VIIC	25-Feb-42	1 Oct 1942 – 19 May 1943 from 5. Flottille	3 patrols	Missing with all hands south of Greenland on or after 9 May 1943, when the boat reported for the last time. 47 dead. Previously thought to have been sunk 19 May 1943 southeast of Cape Farewell, Greenland, by depth charges from the destroyer HMS *Duncan* and the corvette HMS *Snowflake*. That attack was actually against two boats, U-304 and U-636, and caused minor damage

BOATS THAT SERVED WITH 7TH FLOTILLA (110 BOATS)

U-Boat	Type	Commissioned	Flotilla(s)	Patrols	Fate
U-382	VIIC	25-Apr-42	1 Oct 1942 – 31 Oct 1944 from 5. Flottille	6 patrols. 1 ship damaged: total 9811 GRT	to 33. Flottille
U-387	VIIC	24-Nov-42	1 Jul 1943 – 31 Oct 1943 from 5. Flottille	15 patrols	to 13. Flottille
U-390	VIIC	13-Mar-43	1 Dec 1943 – 5 Jul 1944 from 5. Flottille	4 patrols. 1 auxiliary warship sunk: total 545 GRT; 1 ship damaged: total 7934 GRT	Sunk 5 Jul 1944 in the mouth of the Seine by depth charges from the destroyer HMS *Wanderer* and the frigate HMS *Tavy*. 48 dead and 1 survivor
U-397	VIIC	20-Nov-43	1 Jun 1944 – 30 Jun 1944 from 5. Flottille	No patrols	to 23. Flottille
U-403	VIIC	25-Jun-41	1 Sep 1941 – 30 Jun 1942 from 5. Flottille	7 patrols. 2 ships sunk: total 12,946 GRT	to 11. Flottille
U-406	VIIC	22-Oct-41	1 May 1942 – 18 Feb 1944 from 8. Flottille	11 patrols. 1 ship sunk: total 7452 GRT; 3 ships damaged: total 13,285 GRT	Sunk 18 Feb 1944 in the North Atlantic by depth charges from the frigate HMS *Spey*. 12 dead and 45 survivors
U-410	VIIC	23-Feb-42	1 Sep 1942 – 31 May 1943 from 5. Flottille	7 patrols. 7 ships sunk: total 47,244 GRT; 2 warships sunk: total 7006t/6895 tons; 1 ship damaged beyond repair: total 3722 GRT; 1 ship damaged: total 7134 GRT	to 29. Flottille
U-427	VIIC	2-Jun-43	1 Jun 1944 – 31 Jul 1944 from 8. Flottille	5 patrols	to 11. Flottille
U-434	VIIC	21-Jun-41	21 Jun 1941 – 18 Dec 1941	1 patrol	Sunk 18 Dec 1941 north of Madeira by depth charges from the escort destroyer HMS *Blankney* and the destroyer HMS *Stanley*. 2 dead and 42 survivors
U-436	VIIC	27-Sep-41	1 Feb 1942 – 30 Jun 1942 from 5. Flottille	8 patrols. 6 ships sunk: total 36,208 GRT; 2 ships damaged: total 15,575 GRT	to 11. Flottille
U-442	VIIC	21-Mar-42	1 Oct 1942 – 12 Feb 1943 from 5. Flottille	2 patrols. 4 ships sunk: total 25,417 GRT	Sunk with all hands 12 Feb 1943 west of Cape St Vincent by depth charges from a Hudson of No. 48 Sqn RAF. 48 dead
U-448	VIIC	1-Aug-42	1 Feb 1943 – 14 Apr 1944 from 8. Flottille	5 patrols	Sunk 14 Apr 1944 northeast of the Azores by depth charges from the frigate HMCS *Swansea* and the sloop HMS *Pelican*. 9 dead and 42 survivors
U-449	VIIC	22-Aug-42	1 May 1943 – 24 Jun 1943 from 8. Flottille	1 patrol	Sunk with all hands on 24 Jun 1943 northwest of Cape Ortegal, Spain, by depth charges from the sloops HMS *Wren*, HMS *Woodpecker*, HMS *Kite* and HMS *Wild Goose*. 49 dead
U-453	VIIC	26-Jun-41	26 Jun 1941 – 31 Dec 1941	17 patrols. 9 ships sunk: total 23,289 GRT; 1 warship sunk: total 848t/835 tons; 1 warship damaged beyond repair: total 1732t/1705 tons; 2 ships damaged: total 16,610 GRT	to 29. Flottille
U-454	VIIC	24-Jul-41	1 Nov 1941 – 1 Aug 1943 from 5. Flottille	10 patrols. 1 ship sunk: total 557 GRT; 1 warship sunk: total 1900t/1870 tons; 1 ship damaged: total 5395 GRT	Sunk at 14:00 1 Aug 1943 in the Bay of Biscay northwest of Cape Ortegal by depth charges from an Australian Sunderland of No. 10 Sqn. 32 dead and 14 survivors
U-455	VIIC	21-Aug-41	1 Jan 1942 – 29 Feb 1944 from 5. Flottille	10 patrols. 3 ships sunk: total 17,685 GRT	to 29. Flottille
U-551	VIIC	7-Nov-40	7 Nov 1940 – 23 Mar 1941	1 patrol	Sunk with all hands 23 Mar 1941 southeast of Iceland by depth charges from the ASW trawler HMS *Visenda*. 45 dead
U-552	VIIC	4-Dec-40	4 Dec 1940 – 30 Apr 1944	15 patrols. 29 ships sunk: total 163,529 GRT; 2 auxiliary warships sunk: total 747 GRT; 1 warship sunk (USS *Reuben James*, the first US warship sunk in WWII – 6 weeks before declaration of war): total 1209t/1190 tons; 3 ships damaged: total 26,910 GRT	to 22. Flottille
U-553	VIIC	23-Dec-40	23 Dec 1940 – 30 Nov 1942	10 patrols. 13 ships sunk: total 64,612 GRT; 2 ships damaged: total 15,273 GRT	to 3. Flottille
U-567	VIIC	24-Apr-41	1 Nov 1941 – 21 Dec 1941 from 3. Flottille	3 patrols. 2 ships sunk: total 6809 GRT	Sunk with all hands 21 Dec 1941 northeast of the Azores by depth charges from the sloop HMS *Deptford* and the corvette HMS *Samphire*. 47 dead
U-575	VIIC	19-Jun-41	19 Jun 1941 – 13 Mar 1944	10 patrols. 8 ships sunk: total 36,106 GRT; 1 warship sunk: total 1031t/1015 tons; 1 ship damaged: total 12,910 GRT	Sunk 13 Mar 1944 north of the Azores by depth charges from the frigate HMCS *Prince Rupert*, the destroyer USS *Hobson*, the destroyer escort USS *Haverfield*, a Wellington of No. 172 Sqn RAF, 2 Flying Fortresses of Nos. 206 and 220 Sqns RAF and a Grumman Avenger of VC-95 of the escort carrier USS *Bogue*. 18 dead and 37 survivors
U-576	VIIC	26-Jun-41	26 Jun 1941 – 15 Jul 1942	5 patrols. 4 ships sunk: total 15,450 GRT; 2 ships damaged: total 19,457 GRT	Sunk with all hands 15 Jul 1942 off Cape Hatteras by depth charges from 2 US Navy Kingfisher seaplanes of VS-9. Boat may also have been rammed by MV *Unicoi* which had previously hit the boat with its deck gun. 45 dead
U-577	VIIC	3-Jul-41	3 Jul 1941 – 31 Dec 1941	3 patrols	to 29. Flottille
U-578	VIIC	10-Jul-41	1 Sep 1941 – 6 Aug 1942 from 5. Flottille	5 patrols. 4 ships sunk: total 23,635 GRT; 1 warship sunk: total 1107t/1090 tons	Missing with all hands in the Bay of Biscay on or after 6 Aug 1942. 49 dead. Previously credited to depth charges from a Czech-crewed Wellington of No. 311 Sqn RAF, which caused minor damage to U-135
U-581	VIIC	31-Jul-41	1 Dec 1941 – 2 Feb 1942 from 5. Flottille	2 patrols. 1 auxiliary warship sunk: total 364 GRT	Sunk 2 Feb 1942 southwest of the Azores by the destroyer HMS *Westcott*. 4 dead and 41 survivors
U-593	VIIC	23-Oct-41	1 Mar 1942 – 31 Oct 1942 from 8. Flottille	16 patrols. 9 ships sunk: total 38,290 GRT; 3 warships sunk: total 2949t/2902 tons; 1 ship damaged b/r: total 8426 GRT; 1 warship damaged b/r: total 1651t/1625 tons; 1 ship damaged: total 4853 GRT; 1 warship damaged: total 1651t/1625 tons	to 29. Flottille
U-594	VIIC	30-Oct-41	1 Mar 1942 – 4 Jun 1943 from 8. Flottille	5 patrols. 2 ships sunk: total 14,390 GRT	Sunk with all hands 4 Jun 1943 west of Gibraltar by rockets from a Hudson of No. 48 Sqn RAF. 50 dead

BOATS THAT SERVED WITH 7TH FLOTILLA (110 BOATS)

U-Boat	Type	Commissioned	Flotilla(s)	Patrols	Fate
U-602	VIIC	29-Dec-41	1 Oct 1942 – 31 Dec 1942 from 5. Flottille	4 patrols. 1 warship damaged beyond repair: total 1565t/1540 tons	to 29. Flottille
U-607	VIIC	29-Jan-42	1 Aug 1942 – 13 Jul 1943 from 5. Flottille	5 patrols. 4 ships sunk: total 28,937 GRT; 2 ships damaged: total 15,201 GRT	Sunk 13 Jul 1943 in the Bay of Biscay northwest of Cape Ortegal by depth charges from a Sunderland of No. 228 Sqn RAF. 45 dead and 7 survivors
U-617	VIIC	9-Apr-42	1 Sep 1942 – 30 Nov 1942 from 5. Flottille	7 patrols. 8 ships sunk: total 25,879 GRT; 1 auxiliary warship sunk: total 810 GRT; 2 warships sunk: total 3759t/3700 tons	to 29. Flottille
U-618	VIIC	16-Apr-42	1 Sep 1942 – 14 Aug 1944 from 5. Flottille	10 patrols. 3 ships sunk: total 15,788 GRT	Sunk with all hands 14 Aug 1944 west of St Nazaire by depth charges from frigates HMS *Duckworth* and HMS *Essington* and a Liberator of No. 53 Sqn RAF. 61 dead
U-624	VIIC	28-May-42	1 Oct 1942 – 7 Feb 1943 from 8. Flottille	2 patrols. 5 ships sunk: total 39,855 GRT; 1 ship damaged: total 5432 GRT	Sunk with all hands 7 Feb 1943 in the North Atlantic by depth charges from a B-17 Flying Fortress of No. 220 Sqn RAF. 45 dead
U-641	VIIC	24-Sep-42	1 Mar 1943 – 19 Jan 1944	4 patrols	Sunk with all hands 19 Jan 1944 southwest of Ireland by depth charges from corvette HMS *Violet*. 50 dead
U-647	VIIC	5-Nov-42	1 Jun 1943 – 28 Jul 1943 from 5. Flottille	1 patrol	Missing with all hands on or after 28 Jul 1943 north of the Shetland Islands, position unknown, possibly mined. 48 dead
U-650	VIIC	26-Nov-42	1 May 1943 – 30 Sep 1944 from 5. Flottille	7 patrols	to 11. Flottille
U-662	VIIC	9-Apr-42	1 Oct 1942 – 21 Jul 1943 from 5. Flottille	4 patrols. 3 ships sunk: total 18,609 GRT; 1 ship damaged: total 7174 GRT	Sunk 21 Jul 1943 in the mouth of the Amazon by depth charges from a US Navy PBY Catalina of VP-94. 44 dead and 3 survivors
U-667	VIIC	21-Oct-42	1 Jun 1943 – 25 Aug 1944 from 5. Flottille	5 patrols. 1 ship sunk: total 7176 GRT; 2 warships sunk: total 1190t/1171 tons; 1 warship damaged b/r: total 1680t/1653 tons	Sunk 25 Aug 1944 in the Bay of Biscay near La Rochelle by a mine. 45 dead
U-678	VIIC	25-Oct-43	1 Jun 1944 – 7 Jul 1944 from 5. Flottille	1 patrol	Sunk with all hands 7 Jul 1944 southwest of Brighton by depth charges from the destroyers HMCS Ottawa and HMCS *Kootenay* and corvette HMS *Statice*. 52 dead
U-702	VIIC	3-Sep-41	1 Mar 1942 – 3 Apr 1942 from 5. Flottille	1 patrol	Missing with all hands after 3 Apr 1942 in the North Sea. In 1987 a wreck that had struck a mine was found during oil exploration off Norway, and may be U-702
U-704	VIIC	18-Nov-41	1 Jul 1942 – 1 Apr 1943 from 8. Flottille	5 patrols. 1 ship sunk: total 6942 GRT	to 21. Flottille
U-707	VIIC	1-Jul-42	9 Dec 1942 – 9 Nov 1943 from 8. Flottille	3 patrols. 2 ships sunk: total 11,811 GRT	Sunk with all hands 9 Nov 1943 east of Azores by depth charges from a Fortress of No. 220 Sqn RAF. 51 dead
U-708	VIIC	24-Jul-42	1 Oct 1943 – 1 Feb 1944 from 8. Flottille	No patrols	to 5. Flottille
U-710	VIIC	2-Sep-42	1 Apr 1943 – 24 Apr 1943 from 5. Flottille	1 patrol	Sunk with all hands 24 Apr 1943 south of Iceland by depth charges from a Flying Fortress of No. 206 Sqn RAF. 49 dead
U-714	VIIC	10-Feb-43	1 Aug 1943 – 10 Nov 1944 from 5. Flottille	6 patrols. 1 ship sunk: total 1226 GRT; 1 auxiliary warship sunk: total 425 GRT	to 33. Flottille
U-751	VIIC	31-Jan-41	31 Jan 1941 – 17 Jul 1942	7 patrols. 5 ships sunk: total 21,412 GRT; 1 warship sunk: total 11,177t/11,000 tons; 1 ship damaged: total 8096 GRT	Sunk with all hands 17 Jul 1942 northwest of Cape Ortegal, Spain, by depth charges from an Armstrong Whitworth Whitley and an Avro Lancaster of Nos. 61 and 502 Sqns RAF. 48 dead
U-765	VIIC	19-Jun-43	1 Apr 1944 – 6 May 1944 from 8. Flottille	1 patrol	Sunk 6 May 1944 in the North Atlantic by depth charges from 2 Swordfish flying from escort carrier HMS *Vindex*, and from frigates HMS *Bickerton*, HMS *Bligh* and HMS *Aylmer*. 37 dead and 11 survivors
U-962	VIIC	11-Feb-43	1 Aug 1943 – 8 Apr 1944 from 5. Flottille	2 patrols	Sunk with all hands 8 Apr 1944 NW of Finisterre by depth charges from sloops HMS *Crane* and HMS *Cygnet*. 50 dead
U-969	VIIC	24-Mar-43	1 Oct 1943 – 29 Feb 1944 from 5. Flottille	3 patrols. 2 ships damaged beyond repair: total 14,352 GRT	to 29. Flottille
U-974	VIIC	22-Apr-43	1 Nov 1943 – 19 Apr 1944 from 5. Flottille	1 patrol	Sunk 19 Apr 1944 off Stavanger, Norway, torpedoed by Norwegian submarine HNoMS *Ula*. 42 dead and 8 survivors
U-976	VIIC	5-May-43	1 Nov 1943 – 25 Mar 1944 from 5. Flottille	2 patrols	Sunk 25 Mar 1944 near St Nazaire by gunfire from two Mosquitoes of No. 248 Sqn RAF. 4 dead and 49 survivors
U-980	VIIC	27-May-43	1 Jun 1944 – 11 Jun 1944 from 5. Flottille	1 patrol	Sunk with all hands 11 Jun 1944 northwest of Bergen by depth charges from a Catalina of No. 162 Sqn RCAF. 52 dead
U-985	VIIC	24-Jun-43	1 Jan 1944 – 15 Nov 1944 from 5. Flottille	3 patrols. 1 ship sunk: total 1735 GRT	Damaged by a German mine in Norwegian waters. Stricken 15 Nov 1944. Captured at Kristiansand May 1945. Broken up
U-988	VIIC	15-Jul-43	1 Jun 1944 – 29 Jun 1944 from 5. Flottille	1 patrol. 1 ship sunk: total 2385 GRT; 1 ship damaged beyond repair: total 7058 GRT; 1 warship damaged beyond repair: total 940t/925 tons	Thought to have been sunk 29 Jun 1944 west of Guernsey by depth charges from frigates HMS *Domett*, HMS *Cooke*, HMS *Essington*, HMS *Duckworth*, and a Liberator of No. 244 Sqn. 50 dead. However, boat may have been sunk 11 days earlier by a Polish Wellington of No. 304 Sqn.
U-994	VIIC	2-Sep-43	1 Jun 1944 – 5 Jul 1944 from 5. Flottille	1 patrol	to 5. Flottille
U-1004	VIIC/41	16-Dec-43	1 Aug 1944 – 31 Oct 1944 from 31. Flottille	2 patrols. 1 ship sunk: total 1313 GRT; 1 warship sunk: total 996 GRT	to 11. Flottille
U-1191	VIIC	9-Sep-43	1 May 1944 – 12 Jun 1944 from 8. Flottille	1 patrol	Missing with all hands on or after 12 Jun 1944 in the English Channel. 50 dead
U-1192	VIIC	23-Sep-43	1 May 1944 – 31 Jul 1944 from 8. Flottille	1 patrol	to 24. Flottille
U-A	Turkish	20-Sep-39	Sep 1939 – Mar 1941 and Dec 1941 – Aug 1942	9 patrols. 7 ships sunk: total 40,706 GRT	Former Turkish *Badiray*. Second of 4 boats ordered from Germaniawerft. When war broke out she was commissioned into the German Navy. Given the U-A designation on 21 Sep 1939. To 2. Flottille Apr–Dec 1941

9 Unterseebootsflottille

The first combat flotilla to be founded after the outbreak of war, the 9th Flotilla was established in the autumn of 1941. After the organization of the unit had been settled, it was transferred to Brest at the beginning of 1942, where it would play its part in the Battle of the Atlantic.

BREST WAS ONE OF the first French bases to be used by U-boats, and was home to the 1st U-boat Flotilla as well as the 9th. The base was captured by the 5th Panzer Division in June 1940, and it quickly became clear that any plans to operate U-boats from it would have to be delayed: the retreating British had destroyed most of the port's facilities.

Urgent repair work began immediately, and within two months the first U-boat, U-85, had arrived for repairs. By the autumn of 1940, the port was fully operational. However, it became evident that any U-boats using the port would be vulnerable to air attack, and in January 1941 construction work began on the massive concrete U-boat pens that would become characteristic of such bases.

The bunkers were built on a huge scale. Five 'wet' pens could each accommodate up to three boats. Ten 'dry' pens were also built, in which single boats could be dry-docked for major repairs. Boats began using the pens from the autumn of 1941, although the facility was not completed until the summer of 1942.

Massive protection

The bunkers were subject to Allied air attack from the moment construction began. They were a massive target, more than 333m (1093ft) by 192m (630ft), but more than 80 large-scale raids during the war caused very little damage. Even when nine 'Tallboy' six-tonne (5.9-ton) bombs scored direct hits in

Commanders	
Kptlt. Jürgen Oesten *(Oct 1941 – Feb 1942)*	Korvkpt. Heinrich Lehmann-Willenbrock *(May 1942 – Sep 1944)*

9TH FLOTILLA INSIGNIA

The 9th Flotilla's 'Laughing Swordfish' was famous. Originally the emblem of Heinrich Lehmann-Willenbrock's U-96, it became the flotilla's insignia when the ace commander took over the unit from Jürgen Oesten.

August 1944, only five penetrated the 6m (20ft) of concrete on the roof, and caused no damage either to the interior or to the U-boats berthed there.

The 9th Flotilla was commanded by two of the U-boat arm's most respected aces. Jürgen Oesten commanded U-61, U-106 and U-861 in a career that would take him from the Arctic to the Far East. He was the first commander of the 9th Flotilla, leaving to become *U-Boot-Admiralstabsoffizier* with the *Admiral Nordmeer*, where he had a major part to play in directing the U-boat war in Arctic waters. When Oesten arrived at Brest he discovered that there were

▼ **The sinking of U-744**

This photograph shows two of the seven Canadian escorts that combined to destroy U-744 in the North Atlantic on 6 March 1944. Twelve U-boat crewmen were killed and another 40 captured.

9TH FLOTILLA	
Type	Boats assigned
Type VIIC	73
Type VIIC/41	5
Type VIID	6

ATLANTIC OCEAN

● Brest

no facilities available for his crew, all of the pre-war French barracks having been taken by the 1st Flotilla. Eventually he found a partially built hospital and helped by the *Organisation Todt* he completed this to house his crews.

He was succeeded as 9th Flotilla commander by Heinrich Lehmann-Willenbrock. The successful commander of U-96, Lehmann-Willenbrock was the model for *Der Alte*, the commander in Lothar-Günther Buchheim's best-selling *Das Boot*. As a *Sonderführer-Leutnant*, or War Correspondent, Buchheim accompanied U-96 on her seventh patrol, which provided the background for the book and the film and television series that followed.

Limited success

Brest was the third busiest of the U-boat bases in France, after Lorient and St Nazaire. Between them, the 1st and 9th Flotillas mounted 329 U-boat patrols between 28 August 1940 and 4 September 1944. However, having been formed after the end of the first 'Happy Time' the unit's boats did not run up the massive scores earlier commanders had achieved. Few boats sank more than three ships, and many

did not survive their first patrol. The flotilla paid a considerable price for its participation in the Battle of the Atlantic: 54 out of the 84 boats that saw service were sunk by enemy action, the majority going down with all hands.

The last U-boat to leave Brest was U-256, commanded by the flotilla commander, Korvkpt. Lehmann-Willenbrock. It left the port on 4 September 1944, reaching Bergen in Norway on 17 October. Both the 1st and 9th Flotillas were disbanded as U-boat activity ceased. Brest was captured by the US Army on 21 September 1944 after a fierce month-long battle.

▲ U-595

Type VIIC

Destroyed on 14 November 1942 northeast of Oran by depth charges from Hudsons of No. 608 Sqn RAF, assisted by five more aircraft from the same squadron. The crew beached the boat on the Algerian shore: all 45 survived.

Specifications

Crew: 44

Powerplant: Diesel/electric

Max Speed: 31.5/14.1km/hr (17/7.6kt) surf/sub

Surface Range: 12,040km (6500nm)

Displacement: 773/879t (761/865 tons) surf/sub

Dimensions (length/beam/draught): 67.1 x 6.2 x 4.8m (220.1 x 20.34 x 15.75ft)

Commissioned: 6 Nov 1941

Armament: 14 torpedoes (4 bow/1 stern tubes); 1 x 8.8cm (3.5in) and 2 x 2cm (0.8in) guns (1942)

Star commanders
1941–44

Although the flotilla was led by two highly successful aces, wartime conditions by the time it was founded meant that it had fewer 'star' captains than earlier U-boat formations.

▲ **Concrete protection**
The massive concrete U-boat pens built by the Organisation Todt on the French Atlantic coast proved impervious to Allied air attack.

Fregattenkapitän Heinrich Lehmann-Willenbrock

Born on 11 December 1911 in Bremen, Heinrich Lehmann-Willenbrock joined the *Reichsmarine* as part of Crew 31. In April 1939, he transferred to the U-boat force. After one patrol in U-5, he commissioned U-96, in which he made eight patrols, sinking 24 ships totalling over 170,000 GRT. Lehmann-Willenbrock was the sixth highest scoring U-boat ace of the war. Commander of the 9th Flotilla from 1942, he took the last U-boat out of Brest in September 1944. After the war he worked as a salvage contractor and as master of several merchant ships. He died on 18 April 1986 at Bremen.

Oberleutnant zur See Heinz Sieder

Born 28 June 1920 in Munich, Sieder joined the *Kriegsmarine* as part of Crew 38. After active service aboard the battlecruiser *Scharnhorst,* he transferred to the U-boat arm in April 1941. He commissioned the Type VIIC U-boat U-984 in June 1943.

In January 1944, he was attached to the 9th Flotilla in Brest. He was awarded the Knight's Cross for a patrol at the end of June 1944, in which he torpedoed a British destroyer and four merchant vessels, damaging three beyond repair.

Sieder died on 20 August 1944, when U-984 was sunk with all hands west of Brest by depth charges from the Canadian destroyers HMCS *Ottawa, Kootenay* and *Chaudiere.*

Oberleutnant zur See Hermann Stuckmann

Born on 2 January 1921 in Wuppertal-Barmen, Stuckmann joined the *Kriegsmarine* soon after the beginning of the war in Class X/39. In July 1941, he was attached to the U-boat force and served as watch officer for more than a year on U-571 under the command of Kptlt. Helmut Möhlmann. In July 1943, he commissioned the Type VIIC boat U-316, which he commanded until May 1944 as a school boat in the Baltic. In May 1944, he took command of the combat boat U-621, which operated against the Allied landing ships in the English Channel in 1944.

During these patrols he sank two landing ships. Stuckmann died when U-621 was sunk with all hands on 18 August 1944 in the Bay of Biscay near La Rochelle by depth charges from Canadian destroyers.

STAR COMMANDERS		
Commander	Patrols	Ships Sunk
Fregkpt. Heinrich Lehmann-Willenbrock	10	24
Oblt. zur See Heinz Sieder	4	3
Oblt. zur See Hermann Stuckmann	3	1

U-210

TYPE VIIC

Built by Germania Werft at Kiel, U-210 was laid down in March 1941 and was launched in December. The boat was commissioned in February 1942.

AFTER A PERIOD OF WORKING UP with the 5th Flotilla in the Baltic, U-210 was transferred to the 9th Flotilla at Brest. The boat's first patrol started at Kiel and was intended to finish at its new base, but as happened to so many boats in the later stages of the war, things did not go according to plan. The boat set off from Kiel on 18 July 1942, heading for the Norwegian Sea, from where it would prepare for its foray out into the Atlantic.

On 29 July, U-210 was ordered to intercept Convoy ON 115, which had been located in the central Atlantic and was being shadowed by U-164. U-210 reached the convoy the next day, but an alert and efficient escort force ensured that no U-boat was able to press home an attack.

The boat was then ordered to join the *Pirat* wolfpack, which was then establishing a patrol line well ahead of ON 115 in the hope of re-establishing contact. On 2 August, U-552 spotted the convoy to

U-210 Commander

Kptlt. Rudolf Lemcke *(Feb 1942 – Aug 1942)*

the east of Cape Race, and the wolfpack moved in to attack before the merchant ships could reach the Newfoundland Bank, where they would be within range of air cover from Canada. However, a thick fog which fell the next day – an ever-present hazard in these waters – meant that the attack had to be abandoned after two ships had been sunk.

U-210 was then ordered to join the *Steinbrinck* wolfpack patrolling about 645km (400 miles) to the northeast of Newfoundland in the path of Convoy SC 94. U-593 spotted the merchant ships on 5 August and U-210 closed on their position south of Cape Farewell. On 6 August, as U-210 approached the convoy submerged, it was located by the Canadian destroyer HMCS *Assiniboine*. An accurate depth-charge attack forced the boat to the surface, and the combatants engaged in a close-range gun battle, during which the U-boat commander, *Kapitänleutnant* Lemcke, was killed. The destroyer then rammed the U-boat, which sank leaving six dead. The 37 survivors were taken prisoner.

U-210 TIMETABLE		
Patrol Dates	**Operational Area**	**Ships Sunk**
18 Jul 1942 – 6 Aug 1942	North Atlantic	0

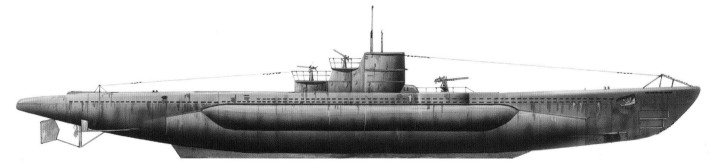

▲ **U-210**

Type VIIC

A typical boat of the Type VIIC, which made up the largest single class of submarine ever built, U-210 nevertheless had no chance to use its weapons against enemy convoys in its short, one-patrol career.

Specifications

Crew: 44

Powerplant: Diesel/electric

Max Speed: 31.5/14.1km/hr (17/7.6kt) surf/sub

Surface Range: 12,040km (6500 nm)

Displacement: 773/879t (761/865 tons) surf/sub

Dimensions (length/beam/draught): 67.1 x 6.2 x 4.8m (220.1 x 20.34 x 15.75ft)

Commissioned: 21 Feb 1942

Armament: 14 torpedoes (4 bow/1 stern tubes); 1 x 8.8cm (3.5in) and 2 x 2cm (0.8in) guns

U-256

TYPE VIIC

Commissioned as a standard Type VIIC at the end of November 1941, U-256 was one of a handful of boats converted as Flak platforms for use against Allied aircraft in the Bay of Biscay.

THE BOAT WAS BUILT at Bremer Vulkan and made its first combat patrol on its transfer from Kiel to 9th Flotilla at Brest. After pursuing Convoy SC 94 with the *Steinbrinck* wolfpack, U-256 joined the *Lohs* group west of Ireland. In the early hours of 25 August, the boat was damaged by depth charges while attacking Convoy ONS 122. Limping towards France and safety, U-256 was further damaged by an RAF Whitley bomber on 2 September. The damage was so bad that the boat was taken out of service in November 1942.

The submarine was converted to a Flak boat from May 1943, recommissioning as U-Flak 2 on 16 August 1943. In company with U-271, the boat left Lorient on 4 October 1943. Her mission was to rendezvous with and provide anti-aircraft protection for the 'milch cow' U-488 to the west of the Azores.

On 31 October, U-256 was on the surface when she was detected by the destroyer USS *Borie*. Diving, the Flak boat was subjected to three depth-charge attacks which caused some damage. Evading her attacker, U-256 returned to Brest in November.

The Flak conversions had not been a great success, and U-256 was rebuilt as a conventional Type VIIC boat in December and January. Seriously damaged

U-256 TIMETABLE		
Patrol Dates	**Operational Area**	**Ships Sunk**
28 Jul 1942 – 3 Sep 1942	Transit from Kiel to Lorient	0
4 Oct 1943 – 17 Nov 1943	Protecting tanker U-488 W of the Azores	0
25 Jan 1944 – 22 Mar 1944	W of Ireland/SW of Ireland	1
6 June 1944 – 8 June 1944	Channel invasion front	0
3 Sep 1944 – 17 Oct 1944	Transit from France to Bergen, Norway	0

U-256 Commanders

Kptlt. Odo Loewe *(Dec 1941 – Nov 1942)*   Korvkpt. Heinrich Lehmann-Willenbrock

Wilhelm Brauel *(Aug 1943 – June 1944)*   *(Sep 1944 – Oct 1944)*

on a patrol in June 1944, U-256 was the last boat left in Brest as Allied armies approached from Norway. Repaired and equipped with a *Schnorchel* on her last patrol, she was captained by Korvkpt. Heinrich Lehmann-Willenbrock, the commander of the 9th Flotilla, on her last voyage from France to Norway. The boat was decommissioned for the final time on 23 October 1944 at Bergen.

▼ Type VIIC Flak boat conning tower

The increased Allied air threat prompted Admiral Dönitz to authorize the development of 'Flak boats'. These were Type VII boats with extensively modified conning towers, which carried heavy anti-aircraft armament. Two quad 2cm (0.8in) Flakvierlings were mounted, together with a 3.7cm (1.5in) Flak gun. Although the Flak boats achieved some success, they could still be swamped by Allied fighter-bombers like the Mosquito, and the enlarged tower adversely affected both dive times and underwater handling.

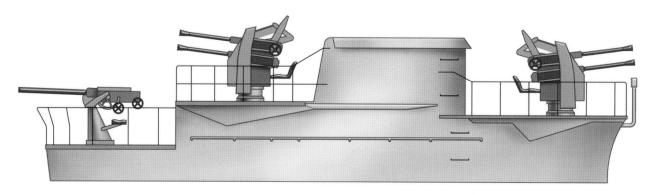

U-377

Type VIIC

Built at Howaldtswerke Kiel and commissioned in October 1941, U-377 had an active career in the Arctic and the Atlantic, but sank nothing in 12 patrols.

THE BOAT OPERATED with the 11th Flotilla against the PQ and QP convoys in the Arctic before transferring to the 9th Flotilla early in 1943. During the journey south, U-377 made the first penetration of British coastal waters for two years.

U-377 went missing with all 52 hands on or after 15 January 1944. The boat was originally thought to have been sunk on 17 January, southwest of Ireland, by depth charges from the destroyer HMS *Wanderer* and the frigate HMS *Glenarm*. However, there is a good chance that U-377 may have been sunk by one of its own acoustic (T5) homing torpedoes on 15 January. British codebreakers picked up at least two emergency messages from U-boats reporting damage from torpedo hits around that time, though there is no record that the

signals were ever received by the *Kriegsmarine* or by FdU *West*. No Allied units made any report of attacking a U-boat on that day. One of the signals was probably from U-305 and the other is likely to have been from U-377.

U-377 Commanders

Kptlt. Otto Köhler *(Oct 1941 – Aug 1943)*

Oblt. Gerhard Kluth *(Aug 1943 – Jan 1944)*

Oblt. Ernst-August Gerke *(Sep 1943 – Oct 1943)*

U-377 TIMETABLE

Patrol Dates	Operational Area	Ships Sunk
14 Feb 1942 – 28 Feb 1942	Transit from Kiel to Norway	0
6 Mar 1942 – 19 Mar 1942	Arctic, S of Jan Mayen Is	0
22 Mar 1942 – 25 Mar 1942	Patrol from Narvik aborted	0
5 Apr 1942 – 19 Apr 1942	Off Kola Peninsula, USSR	0
25 May 1942 – 29 May 1942	Arctic against convoy PQ 16	0
31 May 1942 – 2 June 1942	Moved to Trondheim for repair	0
20 Nov 1942 – 25 Nov 1942	Transferred to Bergen	0
30 Jan 1943 – 18 Mar 1943	Transit to France via Orkney and N Atlantic	0
15 Apr 1943 – 7 June 1943	Central and western N Atlantic	0
26 Aug 1943 – 30 Aug 1943	Atlantic patrol aborted	0
6 Sep 1943 – 10 Oct 1943	S of Iceland/off Newfoundland	0
15 Dec 1943 – 15 Jan 1944	NE of the Azores/West of Portugal	0

▲ **U-377**

Type VIIC

U-377 landed at least two weather detachments on Spitzbergen on her Arctic patrols, and was assigned to several wolfpacks in the North Atlantic after transferring to the 9th Flotilla, but had no successes in attacking convoys.

Specifications

Crew: 44

Powerplant: Diesel/electric

Max Speed: 31.5/14.1km/hr (17/7.6kt) surf/sub

Surface Range: 12,040km (6500nm)

Displacement: 773/879t (761/865 tons) surf/sub

Dimensions (length/beam/draught): 67.1 x 6.2 x 4.8m (220.1 x 20.34 x 15.75ft)

Commissioned: 2 Oct 1941

Armament: 14 torpedoes (4 bow/1 stern tubes); 1 x 8.8cm (3.5in) and 2 x 2cm (0.8in) guns

Attack on convoy SC 94
AUGUST 1942

During the summer of 1942 U-boats returned to the Atlantic convoy routes after wreaking havoc amid the unprotected shipping on the American coast and in the Caribbean.

THE CONVOY CONSISTED of 36 ships, escorted by Canadian Escort Group C1 (destroyer HMCS *Assiniboine* and corvettes HMCS *Chilliwack* and HMCS *Orillia*) and three Royal Navy corvettes, HMS *Nasturtium*, HMS *Dianthus* and HMS *Primrose*. Originating at Halifax, the slow eastbound convoy had left Sydney, Cape Breton Island, on 31 July 1942.

Ranged against the convoy were the eight boats of Group *Steinbrinck* – U-71, U-210, U-379, U-454, U-593, U-597, U-607 and U-704. These were reinforced by a number of newly arrived boats, including U-174, U-176, U-254, U-256, U-438, U-595, U-605, U-660 and U-705.

U-boat attacks

On 6 August, the *Assiniboine* sighted a submarine on the surface and attacked her using gunfire. The submarine, which was U210, returned fire, setting the destroyer's bridge on fire. The submarine was unable to dive and, eventually, the destroyer decided to ram her, sinking the U-boat. However, *Assiniboine* was so severely damaged she had to put back to St Johns for repairs, denying the convoy escort its largest and most mobile asset.

A massive underwater explosion on 8 August caused several merchant crews to abandon their vessels. Most, however, realizing that their ships had not been torpedoed, reboarded their vessels. The explosion may have been from a munitions ship, one of five sunk in a very short period of time by U-176 and U-379.

The repeated attacks by the *Steinbrinck* boats signalled that the *U-Bootwaffe* was back in the Atlantic with a vengeance: SC 94 lost 11 out of its 36 ships before it could reach Britain and safety.

CONVOY SC 94 BATTLE TIMETABLE	
Date	**Event**
5 Aug 1942	A group of 6 merchantmen and two escorts, separated from the convoy due to fog, are spotted by U-593. U-593 sinks one ship, and is then driven off by the escort, along with U-595 which had responded to U-593's sighting report
6 Aug	U-454 and U-595 try to penetrate the escort screen, but are severely damaged and have to return to port. U-210 attacks but is sunk by the *Assiniboine*
7 Aug	The *Steinbrinck* wolfpack is reinforced by six of the newly arrived outbound boats. Eleven boats attack the convoy overnight and into 8 August, but all fail to hit a target
8 Aug	After midday, U-176 sinks three ships. An almost simultaneous attack by U-379 accounts for two more. This is the first serious attack on an Atlantic convoy since the previous year, most U-boat strength having been diverted to operations off the US coast and the Caribbean. The crews of some of the merchantmen panic, and three are abandoned simply through fear of being attacked. One of the drifting vessels is sunk by U-176
8/9 Aug	The Polish destroyer *Blyskawica* and the British destroyer HMS *Broke* reinforce the convoy escort. U-379 is sunk by HMS *Dianthus*. Aggressive patrolling by the escorts keeps the U-boats away from the convoy, only U-595 and U-607 being able to mount attacks, which are unsuccessful
9 Aug	Most of the escort has been drawn away from the convoy, pursuing a contact, but long-range aircraft are now able to reach the area and provide cover. U-174, U-254, U-256 and U-704 all launch attacks, but are unable to get close enough to achieve any success
10 Aug	U-597 launches an unsuccessful attack. However, bad planning leaves the convoy temporarily uncovered by aircraft, and while the escorts are still pursuing contacts far astern, U-438 sinks three ships and U-660 destroys another

Wolfpack group *Leuthen*
SEPTEMBER–OCTOBER 1943

In contrast to the situation the previous summer, the U-boats attacking convoys in the summer and autumn of 1943 did so at their peril.

NEVERTHELESS, ALTHOUGH the battle had swung in favour of the escorts, Dönitz could still mount some effective attacks on the convoy routes. On 20 September 1943, 14 boats on patrol in the North Atlantic were ordered to establish patrol line *Leuthen*, stretching south-southwest of Iceland. Their aim was to locate and attack any ONS convoys that might have been passing through the area. They were to be reinforced by a number of other boats, which had been refuelling north of the Azores.

However, as that group moved north, one of the *Leuthen* boats, U-341, was spotted on the surface and sunk by a Canadian Liberator just east of the planned patrol line, alerting Allied anti-submarine forces to the presence of U-boats.

Convoy attack

On 20 September, U-270 spotted westbound convoy ON 202 near Cape Farewell. The *Leuthen* boats

were not yet in position, so they made best speed to attack the convoy, which had merged with convoy ONS 18 during the night. Five boats attacked the merchant ships, but most of the rest of the group targeted the escorts. The theory was that if the escort was sufficiently weakened, the U-boats would be free to attack the real target – the merchantmen. The U-boats claimed 10 destroyers sunk or damaged over the night of 20/21 September. In fact, three escorts were sunk and one was damaged.

Fog meant that the U-boats lost contact during 21 September. As it cleared in the afternoon of the 22nd, five boats regained contact and tried to attack, but were driven off. The operation was called off on 23 September as visibility again got worse and the convoy came under the protective umbrella of Newfoundland-based aircraft. In addition to the escort losses, six merchant ships had been lost and another damaged. U-229 and U-338 were sunk.

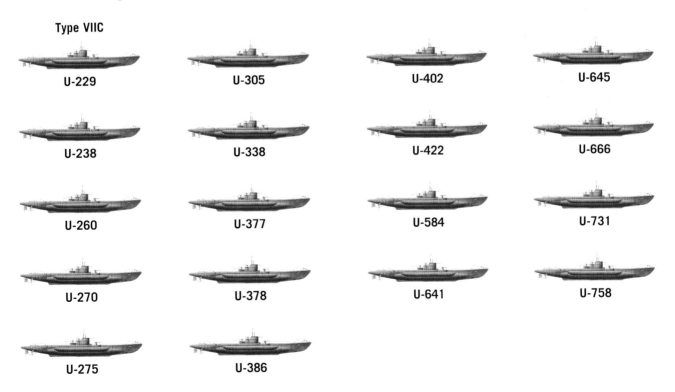

Type VIIC

U-229	U-305	U-402	U-645
U-238	U-338	U-422	U-666
U-260	U-377	U-584	U-731
U-270	U-378	U-641	U-758
U-275	U-386		

BOATS THAT SERVED WITH 9TH FLOTILLA (84 BOATS)

U-Boat	Type	Commissioned	Flotilla(s)	Patrols	Fate
U-89	VIIC	19-Nov-41	1 May 1942 – 12 May, 1943 from 8. Flottille	4 patrols. 4 ships sunk: total 13,815 GRT	Sunk with all hands 12 May 1943 in the North Atlantic by the destroyer HMS *Broadway*, the frigate HMS *Laganan* and an 811 Sqn Swordfish aircraft from the escort carrier HMS *Biter*. 48 dead
U-90	VIIC	20-Dec-41	1 Jul 1942 – 24 Jul 1942 from 8. Flottille	1 patrol	Sunk with all hands 24 Jul 1942 in the North Atlantic by the Canadian destroyer HMCS *St. Croix*. 44 dead
U-91	VIIC	28-Jan-42	1 Sep 1942 – 25 Feb 1944 from 5. Flottille	6 patrols. 4 ships sunk: total 26,194 GRT; 1 warship sunk: total 1307t/1375 tons	Sunk 26 Feb 1944 in the North Atlantic by the frigates HMS *Affleck*, HMS *Gore* and HMS *Gould*. 36 dead and 16 survivors
U-92	VIIC	3-Mar-42	1 Sep 1942 – 12 Oct 1944 from 5. Flottille	9 patrols. 2 ships sunk: total 17,612 GRT; 1 warship damaged b/r: total 1651t/1625 tons; 1 ship damaged: total 9348 GRT	Badly damaged 4 Oct 1944 in Bergen, Norway, by RAF bombs; decommissioned and scrapped
U-210	VIIC	21-Feb-42	1 Aug 1942 – 6 Aug 1942 from 5. Flottille (training)	1 patrol	Sunk 6 Aug 1942 in the North Atlantic south of Cape Farewell, Greenland, by ramming, depth charges and gunfire from the destroyer HMCS *Assiniboine*. 6 dead and 37 survivors
U-211	VIIC	7-Mar-42	1 Sep 1942 – 19 Nov 1943 from 5. Flottille (training)	5 patrols. 1 ship sunk: total 11,237 GRT; 1 warship sunk: total 1372t/1350 tons; 2 ships damaged: total 20,646 GRT	Sunk with all hands 19 Nov 1943 east of the Azores by depth charges from a Wellington aircraft of No. 179 Sqn RAF. 54 dead
U-213	VIID	30-Aug-41	1 May 1942 – 31 Jul 1942 from 1. Flottille	3 patrols. 1 special operation, landing an Abwehr agent on New Brunswick, Canada 14 May 1942	Sunk with all hands 31 Jul 1942 in the Atlantic east of the Azores by depth charges from the sloops HMS *Erne*, HMS *Rochester* and HMS *Sandwich*. 50 dead
U-214	VIID	1-Nov-41	1 May 1942 – 26 Jul 1944 from 5. Flottille (training)	11 patrols. 3 ships sunk: total 18,266 GRT; 1 warship sunk: total 1549t/1525 tons; 1 ship damaged: total 6507 GRT; 1 auxiliary warship damaged: total 10,552 GRT	Sunk with all hands 26 Jul 1944 in the English Channel southeast of Eddystone by depth charges from the frigate HMS *Cooke*. 48 dead
U-215	VIID	22-Nov-41	1 Jul 1942 – 3 Jul 1942 from 5. Flottille (training)	1 patrol. 1 ship sunk: total 7191 GRT	Sunk with all hands 3 Jul 1942 in the Atlantic east of Boston by depth charges from the anti-submarine trawler HMS *Le Tiger*. 48 dead
U-216	VIID	15-Dec-41	1 Sep 1942 – 20 Oct 1942	1 patrol. 1 ship sunk: total 4989 GRT	Sunk with all hands 20 Oct 1942 southwest of Ireland by 6 depth charges from a Liberator of No. 224 Sqn. 45 dead
U-217	VIID	31-Jan-42	1 Aug 1942 – 5 June 1943 from 5. Flottille (training)	3 patrols. 3 ships sunk: total 10,651 GRT	Sunk with all hands 5 Jun 1943 in mid-Atlantic by depth charges from Grumman TBF Avengers of the escort carrier USS *Bogue*. 50 dead
U-218	VIID	24-Jan-42	1 Sep 1942 – 30 Sep 1944 from 5. Flottille (training)	10 patrols. 3 ships sunk: total 698 GRT; 1 ship damaged: total 7361 GRT; 1 auxiliary warship damaged: total 7177 GRT	to 8. Flottille
U-230	VIIC	24-Oct-42	1 Feb 1943 – 30 Nov 1943 from 5. Flottille (training)	8 patrols. 1 ship sunk: total 2868 GRT; 3 warships sunk: total 3643t/3585 tons	to 29. Flottille
U-232	VIIC	28-Nov-42	1 May 1943 – 8 Jul 1943 from 5. Flottille (training)	1 patrol. On 24 Feb 1943, U-232 collided with and sank U-649 during training in the Bay of Danzig	Sunk with all hands 8 Jul 1943 west of Oporto by depth charges from a USAAF B-24. 46 dead
U-240	VIIC	3-Apr-43	1 Feb 1944 – 17 May 1944 from 5. Flottille (training)	1 patrol	Missing with all hands west of Norway after 17 May 1944. 50 dead. It was credited to depth charges from a Norwegian Sunderland of No. 330 Sqn RAF, but that target was probably U-668, which took no damage
U-244	VIIC	9-Oct-43	1 Aug 1944 – 31 Oct 1944	4 patrols	to 11. Flottille
U-248	VIIC	6-Nov-43	1 Aug 1944 – 31 Oct 1944 from 5. Flottille (training)	2 patrols	to 11. Flottille
U-254	VIIC	8-Nov-41	1 Aug 1942 – 8 Dec 1942 from 8. Flottille	3 patrols. 3 ships sunk: total 18,967 GRT	Sank 8 Dec 1942 southeast of Cape Farewell, Greenland, after a collision with U-221. 41 dead and 4 survivors
U-256	VIIC	18-Dec-41	1 Aug 1942 – 5 Oct 1944 from 8. Flottille (training)	5 patrols. 1 warship sunk: total 1321t/1300 tons	Heavily damaged 25 Aug 1942 and stricken in November 1942. Converted to U-Flak 2 in May 1943; commissioned for second time 16 Aug 1943. Converted back December 1943. Stricken 23 Oct 1944 in Bergen, Norway. Captured there and cannibalized
U-273	VIIC	21-Oct-42	1 May 1943 – 19 May 1943 from 8. Flottille	1 patrol	Sunk with all hands 19 May 1943 southwest of Iceland by depth charges from a Lockheed Hudson of No. 269 Sqn RAF. 46 dead
U-279	VIIC	3-Feb-43	1 Aug 1943 – 4 Oct 1943 from 8. Flottille	1 patrol. On its single patrol U-279 landed an agent on Iceland	Sunk with all hands southwest of Iceland 4 Oct 1943 by depth charges from a US Navy Ventura of VB-128. 48 dead. Originally credited to a British Liberator, which actually sank U-389
U-282	VIIC	13-Mar-43	1 Oct 1943 – 29 Oct 1943	1 patrol	Sunk with all hands 29 Oct 1943 southeast of Greenland by depth charges from the destroyers HMS *Vidette*, HMS *Duncan* and the corvette HMS *Sunflower*. 48 dead
U-283	VIIC	31-Mar-43	1 Feb 1944 – 11 Feb 1944 from 8. Flottille	1 patrol	Sunk with all hands 11 Feb 1944 southwest of the Faroes by depth charges from a Vickers Wellington of No. 407 Sqn RCAF. 49 dead
U-284	VIIC	14-Apr-43	1 Nov 1943 – 21 Dec 1943	1 patrol	Scuttled 21 Dec 1943 southeast of Greenland after severe sea damage. No casualties – 49 survivors. Entire crew rescued by U-629 and returned to Brest 5 Jan 1944
U-293	VIIC/41	8-Sep-43	1 Apr 1944 – 31 Jul 1944 from 8. Flottille	6 patrols. 1 warship damaged: total 1685t/1658 tons	to 11. Flottille
U-296	VIIC/41	3-Nov-43	1 Aug 1944 – 30 Sep 1944 from 8. Flottille	3 patrols	to 11. Flottille
U-302	VIIC	16-Jun-42	1 Nov 1943 – 6 Apr 1944 from 9. Flottille	10 patrols. 3 ships sunk: total 12,697 GRT	Sunk with all hands 6 Apr 1944 in the Atlantic northwest of the Azores by depth charges from the frigate HMS *Swale*. 51 dead
U-309	VIIC	27-Jan-43	1 Nov 1943 – 1 Oct 1944 from 11. Flottille	11 patrols. 1 ship damaged beyond repair: total 7219 GRT	to 33. Flottille
U-317	VIIC/41	23-Oct-43	1 June 1944 – 26 June 1944 from 4. Flottille	2 patrols	Sunk with all hands 26 June 1944 northeast of the Shetlands by depth charges from a Liberator of No. 86 Sqn RAF. 50 dead

BOATS THAT SERVED WITH 9TH FLOTILLA (84 BOATS)

U-Boat	Type	Commissioned	Flotilla(s)	Patrols	Fate
U-347	VIIC	7-Jul-43	1 Mar 1944 – 31 May 1944 from 8. Flottille	4 patrols	to 11. Flottille
U-348	VIIC	10-Aug-43	1 Apr 1944 – 11 Jul 1944 from 8. Flottille	9 (possibly as many as 15) patrols	to 8. Flottille
U-365	VIIC	8-Jun-43	1 Mar 1944 – 8 Jun 1944 from 5. Flottille	11 patrols. 1 ship sunk: total 7540 GRT, 3 warships sunk: total 1377t/1355 tons, 1 warship damaged: total 1737t/1710 tons	to 13. Flottille
U-377	VIIC	2-Oct-41	1 Mar 1943 – 15 Jan 1944 from 11. Flottille	12 patrols	Missing with all hands southwest of Ireland Sep 1944. 52 dead. May have been sunk by its own acoustic (T5) homing torpedo on 15 Jan
U-383	VIIC	6-June-42	1 Oct 1942 – 1 Aug 1943 from 8. Flottille	4 patrols. 1 ship sunk: total 423 GRT	Lost with all hands 1 Aug 1943 west of Brittany, probably as a result of severe damage by depth charges from a Sunderland of No. 228 Sqn RAF. 52 dead
U-388	VIIC	31-Dec-42	1 Jun 1943 – 20 Jun 1943 from 5. Flottille	1 patrol	Sunk with all hands 20 Jun 1943 southeast of Cape Farewell, Greenland, by depth charges from a US Navy PBY Catalina from Patrol Squadron VP-84. 47 dead
U-389	VIIC	6-Feb-43	1 Aug 1943 – 4 Oct 1943 from 5. Flottille	2 patrols	Sunk with all hands 4 Oct 1943 southwest of Iceland by depth charges from a Liberator of No. 120 Sqn RAF. 50 dead. Previously credited to a Hudson of No. 269 Sqn in Denmark Strait, but that attack on 5 Oct actually sank U-336
U-403	VIIC	25-Jun-41	1 Mar 1943 – 18 Aug 1943 from 11. Flottille	7 patrols. 2 ships sunk: total 12,946 GRT	Sunk with all hands 18 Aug 1943 off the West African coast near Dakar by depth charges from a French-crewed Wellington of No. 344 Sqn RAF. 49 dead. Previously credited to a Lockheed Hudson of No. 200 Sqn, which attacked with depth charges earlier the same day but inflicted only minor damage
U-407	VIIC	18-Dec-41	1 Sep 1942 – 30 Nov 1942 from 5. Flottille	12 patrols. 3 ships sunk: total 26,892 GRT; 1 ship damaged beyond repair: total 7176 GRT; 1 ship damaged: total 6207 GRT; 2 warships damaged: total 18,187t/17,900 tons	to 29. Flottille
U-408	VIIC	19-Nov-41	1 May 1942 – 30 Jun 1942 from 5. Flottille	3 patrols. 3 ships sunk: total 19,689 GRT	to 11. Flottille
U-409	VIIC	21-Jan-42	1 Sep 1942 – 30 Jun 1943 from 5. Flottille	6 patrols. 3 ships sunk: total 16,199 GRT; 1 ship damaged: total 7519 GRT	to 29. Flottille
U-412	VIIC	29-Apr-42	1 Oct 1942 – 22 Oct 1942 from 8. Flottille	1 patrol	Sunk with all hands 22 Oct 1942 northeast of the Faroes by depth charges from a Vickers Wellington of No. 179 Sqn RAF. 47 dead
U-421	VIIC	13-Jan-43	1 Nov 1943 – 31 Mar 1944 from 8. Flottille	2 patrols	to 29. Flottille
U-425	VIIC	21-Apr-43	1 Nov 1943 – 31 Dec 1943 from 8. Flottille	8 patrols	to 11. Flottille
U-438	VIIC	22-Nov-41	1 Aug 1942 – 6 May 1943 from 8. Flottille	4 patrols. 4 ships sunk: total 19,502 GRT; 1 ship damaged: total 5496 GRT	Sunk with all hands 6 May 1943 northeast of Newfoundland by depth charges from the sloop HMS *Pelican*. 48 dead
U-443	VIIC	18-Apr-42	1 Oct 1942 – 31 Dec 1942 from 8. Flottille	3 patrols. 3 ships sunk: total 19,435 GRT; 1 warship sunk: total 1104t/1087 tons	to 29. Flottille
U-447	VIIC	11-Jul-42	1 Mar 1943 – 7 May 1943 from 8. Flottille	2 patrols	Sunk with all hands 7 May 1943 west of Gibraltar by depth charges from 2 Lockheed Hudsons of No. 233 Sqn RAF. 48 dead
U-450	VIIC	12-Sep-42	1 Jun 1943 – 30 Nov 1943 from 8. Flottille	4 patrols	to 29. Flottille
U-473	VIIC	16-Jun-43	1 Jan 1944 – 6 May 1944 from 5. Flottille	2 patrols. 1 warship damaged beyond repair: total 1422t/1400 tons	Sunk 6 May 1944 southwest of Ireland by depth charges from the sloops HMS *Starling*, HMS *Wren* and HMS *Wild Goose*. 23 dead and 30 survivors
U-480	VIIC	6-Oct-43	1 Jun 1944 – 14 Oct 1944 from 5. Flottille	3 patrols. 2 ships sunk: total 12,846 GRT; 2 warships sunk: total 1803t/1775 tons	to 11. Flottille
U-482	VIIC	1-Dec-43	1 Aug 1944 – 30 Sep 1944 from 5. Flottille	2 patrols. 4 ships sunk: total 31,611 GRT; 1 warship sunk: total 1026t/1010 tons	to 11. Flottille
U-591	VIIC	9-Oct-41	1 Jun 1943 – 30 Jul 1943 from 11. Flottille	8 patrols. 4 ships sunk: total 19,932 GRT; 1 ship damaged: total 5701 GRT	Sunk 30 Jul 1943 in the South Atlantic near Pernambuco by depth charges from a US Navy Ventura of VB-127. 19 dead and 28 survivors
U-595	VIIC	6-Nov-41	1 Aug 1942 – 14 Nov 1942 from 8. Flottille	3 patrols	Destroyed 14 Nov 1942 northeast of Oran by depth charges from 2 Hudsons of No. 608 Sqn RAF, assisted by five more aircraft from the same squadron. The crew beached the badly damaged boat on the Algerian shore: all 45 survived
U-604	VIIC	8-Jan-42	1 Aug 1942 – 11 Aug 1943 from 5. Flottille	6 patrols. 6 ships sunk: total 39,891 GRT	Scuttled 11 Aug 1943 in the Atlantic just south of the equator after being damaged by depth charges from a US Navy Ventura of VB-129 and a PB4Y Liberator of VB-107. 14 dead. 31 survivors were picked up by U-185 and U-172, but 14 U-604 crewmen died when U-185 was subsequently sunk
U-605	VIIC	15-Jan-42	1 Aug 1942 – 31 Oct 1942 from 5. Flottille	3 patrols. 3 ships sunk: total 8409 GRT	to 29. Flottille
U-606	VIIC	22-Jan-42	1 Nov 1942 – 22 Feb 1943 from 11. Flottille	3 patrols. 3 ships sunk: total 20,527 GRT; 2 ships damaged: total 21,925 GRT	Sunk 22 Feb 1943 in the North Atlantic by depth charges from the Polish destroyer *Burza* and the US coastguard cutter *Campbell*. 36 dead and 11 survivors
U-621	VIIC	7-May-42	1 Oct 1942 – 18 Aug 1944 (as U-Flak 3 19 Aug 1943 – 1 Oct 1943) from 8. Flottille	10 patrols. 4 ships sunk: total 20,159 GRT; 1 auxiliary warship sunk: total 2938 GRT; 1 ship damaged: total 10,048 GRT; 1 warship damaged: total 1651t/1625 tons. Refitted as U-Flak 3 7 Jul 1943. Converted back later in the year	Sunk with all hands 18 Aug 1944 in the Bay of Biscay near La Rochelle by depth charges from the destroyers HMCS *Ottawa*, HMCS *Kootenay* and HMCS *Chaudiere*. 56 dead
U-631	VIIC	16-Jul-42	1 Jan 1943 – 17 Oct 1943 from 5. Flottille	3 patrols. 2 ships sunk: total 9136 GRT	Sunk 17 Oct 1943 southeast of Greenland by depth charges from the corvette HMS *Sunflower*

BOATS THAT SERVED WITH 9TH FLOTILLA (111 BOATS)

U-Boat	Type	Commissioned	Flotilla(s)	Patrols	Fate
U-633	VIIC	30-Jul-42	1 Mar 1943 – 10 Mar 1943 from 5. Flottille	1 patrol. 1 ship sunk: total 3921 GRT	Sunk with all hands 10 Mar 1943 in the North Atlantic, rammed by the British merchantman SS *Scorton*. 43 dead. Previously credited to a Flying Fortress of No. 220 Sqn on 7 Mar 1943, which actually unsuccessfullly attacked U-641
U-634	VIIC	6-Aug-42	1 Feb 1943 – 30 Aug 1943 from 5. Flottille	3 patrols. 1 ship sunk: total 7176 GRT	Sunk with all hands 30 Aug 1943 east of the Azores by depth charges from the sloop HMS *Stork* and the corvette HMS *Stonecrop*. 47 dead
U-638	VIIC	3-Sep-42	1 Feb 1943 – 5 May 1943 from 5. Flottille	2 patrols. 1 ship sunk: total 5507 GRT; 1 ship damaged: total 6537 GRT	Sunk with all hands 5 May 1943 northeast of Newfoundland by depth charges from HMS *Sunflower*. 44 dead. Previously credited to HMS *Loosestrife* the same day, an attack which actually sank U-192
U-659	VIIC	9-Dec-41	1 Sep 1942 – 4 May 1943 from 5. Flottille	5 patrols. 1 ship sunk: total 7519 GRT; 3 ships damaged: total 21,565 GRT	Sunk 4 May 1943 west of Cape Finisterre, after colliding with U-439. 44 dead and 3 survivors
U-660	VIIC	8-Jan-42	1 Aug 1942 – 31 Oct 1942 from 5. Flottille	3 patrols. 2 ships sunk: total 10,066 GRT; 2 ships damaged: total 10,447 GRT	to 29. Flottille
U-663	VIIC	14-May-42	1 Nov 1942 – 8 May 1943 from 11. Flottille	3 patrols. 2 ships sunk: total 10,924 GRT	Probably foundered with all hands 8 May 1943 west of Brest after being seriously damaged on 7 May by depth charges from an Australian Sunderland of No. 10 Sqn. 49 dead. Previously credited to a 58 Sqn Halifax, which most likely caused minor damage to U-124
U-664	VIIC	17-Jun-42	1 Nov 1942 – 9 Aug 1943 from 8. Flottille	5 patrols. 3 ships sunk: total 19,325 GRT	Sunk 9 Aug 1943 in the North Atlantic by depth charges from Avengers flying from the escort carrier USS *Card*. 7 dead and 44 survivors
U-709	VIIC	12-Aug-42	1 Mar 1943 – 1 Mar 1944 from 5. Flottille	5 patrols	Sunk with all hands 1 Mar 1944 north of the Azores by depth charges from the destroyer escorts USS *Thomas*, USS *Bostwick* and USS *Bronstein*. 52 dead
U-715	VIIC	17-Mar-43	1 Jun 1944 – 13 Jun 1944 from 5. Flottille	1 patrol	Sunk 13 Jun 1944 northeast of the Faroes by depth charges from a Canso (Canadian-built Catalina) of No. 162 Sqn RCAF. 36 dead and 16 survivors
U-739	VIIC	6-Mar-43	1 Nov 1943 – 31 Dec 1943 from 8. Flottille	8 patrols. 1 warship sunk: total 635t/625 tons	to 13. Flottille
U-744	VIIC	5-Jun-43	1 Dec 1943 – 6 Mar 1944 from 8. Flottille	2 patrols. 1 ship sunk: total 7359 GRT; 1 warship sunk: total 1651t/1625 tons; 1 warship damaged: total 1651t/1625 tons	Sunk 6 Mar 1944 in the North Atlantic. Damaged by torpedoes from destroyer HMS *Icarus*, then sunk by depth charges from HMS *Icarus*, destroyers HMCS *Chaudiere* and HMCS *Gatineau*, frigate HMCS *St. Catherines*, corvettes HMS *Kenilworth Castle*, HMCS *Fennel* and HMCS *Chilliwack*. 12 dead and 40 survivors
U-755	VIIC	3-Nov-41	1 Aug 1942 – 30 Nov 1942 from 5. Flottille	5 patrols. 1 ship sunk: total 928 GRT; 2 auxiliary warships sunk: total 2974 GRT	to 29. Flottille
U-759	VIIC	15-Aug-42	1 Feb 1943 – 15 Jul 1943 from 5. Flottille	2 patrols. 2 ships sunk: total 12,764 GRT	Sunk with all hands 15 Jul 1943 east of Jamaica by depth charges from a US Navy Mariner of VP-32. 47 dead. Previously credited to another VP-32 aircraft on 26 Jul 1943, which sank U-359
U-761	VIIC	3-Dec-42	1 Aug 1943 – 24 Feb 1944 from 8. Flottille	3 patrols	Damaged by British and American aircraft while trying to pass through the Straits of Gibraltar. Scuttled 24 Feb 1944 off Tangier to avoid being sunk by destroyers HMS *Anthony* and HMS *Wishart*. 9 dead and 48 survivors
U-762	VIIC	30-Jan-43	1 Aug 1943 – 8 Feb 1944	2 patrols	Sunk with all hands 8 Feb 1944 in the North Atlantic by depth charges from the sloops HMS *Woodpecker* and HMS *Wild Goose*. 51 dead
U-764	VIIC	6-May-43	1 Nov 1943 – 30 Sep 1944 from 8. Flottille	8 patrols. 1 ship sunk: total 638 GRT; 2 warships sunk: total 1723t/1696 tons	to 11. Flottille
U-771	VIIC	18-Nov-43	1 Jun 1944 – 31 Jul 1944 from 31. Flottille	2 patrols	to 11. Flottille
U-772	VIIC	23-Dec-43	1 Aug 1944 – 14 Oct 1944 from 31. Flottille	2 patrols	to 11. Flottille
U-951	VIIC	3-Dec-42	1 Jun 1943 – 7 Jul 1943 from 5. Flottille	1 patrol	Sunk with all hands 7 Jul 1943 northwest of Cape St Vincent by depth charges from a USAAF B-24 of the 1st A/S Sqn. 46 dead
U-954	VIIC	23-Dec-42	1 May 1943 – 19 May 1943 from 5. Flottille	1 patrol	Sunk with all hands 19 May 1943 southeast of Cape Farewell, Greenland, by depth charges from the frigate HMS *Jed* and the sloop HMS *Sennen*. 47 dead
U-955	VIIC	31-Dec-42	1 Apr 1944 – 7 Jun 1944	1 patrol. Landed 3 spies on Iceland 20 Apr 1944	Sunk with all hands 7 Jun 1944 N of Cape Ortegal by depth charges from a Sunderland of No. 201 Sqn RAF. 50 dead
U-966	VIIC	4-Mar-43	1 Aug 1943 – 10 Nov 1943 from 5. Flottille	1 patrol	Sunk 10 Nov 1943 near Cape Ortegal by depth charges from British, American and Czech aircraft. 8 dead and 42 survivors
U-979	VIIC	20-May-43	1 Aug 1944 – 14 Oct 1944 from 5. Flottille	3 patrols. 1 auxiliary warship sunk: total 348 GRT; 2 ships damaged: total 12,133 GRT	to 11. Flottille
U-984	VIIC	17-Jun-43	Jan 1944 – 20 Aug 1944 from 5. Flottille	4 patrols. 1 ship damaged: total 7240 GRT; 3 ships damaged beyond repair: total 21,550 GRT; 1 warship damaged beyond repair: total 1321t/1300 tons	Sunk with all hands 20 Aug 1944 west of Brest by depth charges from destroyers HMCS *Ottawa*, HMCS *Kootenay* and HMCS *Chaudiere*. 45 dead
U-989	VIIC	22-Jul-43	1 Feb 1944 – 30 Sep 1944 from 5. Flottille	5 patrols. 1 ship sunk: total 1791 GRT; 1 ship damaged: total 7176 GRT	to 33. Flottille
U-997	VIIC/41	23-Sep-43	1 May 1944 – 31 May 1944 from 5. Flottille	7 patrols. 1 ship sunk: total 1603 GRT; 1 warship sunk: total 107t/105 tons; 1 ship damaged: total 4287 GRT	to 13. Flottille
U-1165	VIIC/41	17-Nov-43	1 Jun 1944 – 1 Aug 1944 from 8. Flottille	4 patrols. 1 warship sunk: total 40t/39 tons	to 11. Flottille

10 Unterseebootsflottille

The 10th U-boat Flotilla was founded at Lorient on 15 January 1942 under the command of *Kapitänleutnant* Günther Kuhnke. From the start, the new flotilla was home to the long-range boats of the U-boat arm, supplementing and replacing those serving with the 2nd Flotilla.

THE FLOTILLA CAME INTO BEING just when the need for long-range boats became more pressing, after Japan attacked the US Pacific Fleet at Pearl Harbor and Hitler declared war on the United States in support of Germany's Tripartite Pact ally. Germany and Japan had already had some naval dealings.

As early as March 1941, Hitler had issued a directive in which the High Command was to freely offer military intelligence and technical information to the Japanese authorities. German merchant ships had been trapped in Japanese ports at the outbreak of war, and they were used as blockade runners over the next two years in an attempt to bring strategic materials home to Germany.

By 1942, merchant ships had little chance of getting supplies through the Allied blockade, and thoughts turned to using submarines to carry vital strategic materials. Admiral Dönitz was not in favour of diverting his U-boat force from where he saw the real battle was taking place – in the North Atlantic. However, Hitler was keen on using the U-boats in Asian waters, both to acquire strategic materials and to prey on British and Commonwealth trade in those distant waters. Part of his reasoning was that such attacks would force the Allies to dilute their escort strength to deal with the new threat.

Commander

Korvkpt. Günther Kuhnke *(Jan 1942 – Oct 1944)*

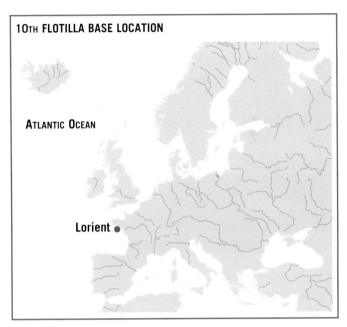

10TH FLOTILLA BASE LOCATION

ATLANTIC OCEAN

Lorient

Much of the burden of those operations fell on the newly formed 10th Flotilla. Finding crews able to deal with the difficulties of operating in such strange and dangerous waters was not easy, but there were enough former merchant seamen with Far Eastern experience scattered through the U-boat arm to provide a core of experience, and a number of officers had served in those waters with blockade runners and armed merchant raiders in the first years of the war.

Atlantic operations

Missions to exotic locations in Southeast Asia were only part of the 10th Flotilla's remit – the bulk of unit's boats operated in the Atlantic, mounting patrols from Greenland through the central Atlantic and the Caribbean to the coasts of South America and Southern Africa. The 10th Flotilla also numbered many of the specialist Type XIV supply submarines, the so-called milchcows, in its inventory. These were used to extend the

▼ U-464

U-464 was sunk by a Catalina from the US Navy's VP-73 patrol squadron in August 1942. Two crew were killed and the remaining 53 rescued.

10TH FLOTILLA	
Type	**Boats assigned**
Type IXC	26
Type IXC/40	41
Type IXD1	2
Type IXD2	4
Type XB	1
Type XIV	6

10TH FLOTILLA INSIGNIA

Overtly nationalistic or Nazi symbols were rare on U-boat insignia during World War II. The 9th Flotilla was the only unit that carried the *Balkenkreuz* more usually seen on aircraft or military vehicles.

endurance of all kinds of U-boats by providing refuelling, resupply and rearmament facilities in remote and unfrequented parts of the ocean.

The 10th Flotilla, like all French-based formations, had to leave its base in August 1944 as Allied armies smashed their way out of Normandy, advancing to

threaten many of the bases along the Atlantic coast of France. Most surviving boats of the 10th Flotilla were transferred to Norway, although a number were assigned to the 33rd Flotilla and were based in the Far East.

Korvettenkapitän Kuhnke left Lorient with the last flotilla boat, U-853, on 27 August 1944 and reached Flensburg, Germany, on 14 October. The flotilla was officially disbanded that month.

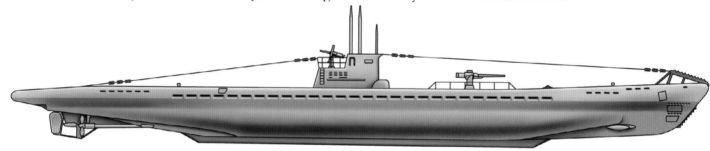

Specifications

Crew: 48–50

Powerplant: Diesel/electric

Max Speed: 33.9/13.5km/hr (18.3/7.3kt) surf/sub

Surface Range: 20,370km (11,000nm)

Displacement: 1138/1252t (1120/1232 tons) surf/sub

Dimensions (length/beam/draught): 76.8 x 6.8 x 4.7m (252 x 22.31 x 15.42ft)

Commissioned: 16 Oct 1941

Armament: 22 torpedoes (4 bow/2 stern tubes); 1 x 10.5cm (4.1in), 1 x 3.7cm (1.5in) and 1 x 2cm (0.8in) guns

▲ **U-160**

Type IXC

Commanded for three out of its four patrols by Knight's Cross holder Kptlt. Georg Lassen, U-160 served with the 10th Flotilla from March 1942 to July 1943. It sank 26 ships totalling more than 150,000 GRT before being tracked down and destroyed by aircraft from the escort carrier USS Santee.

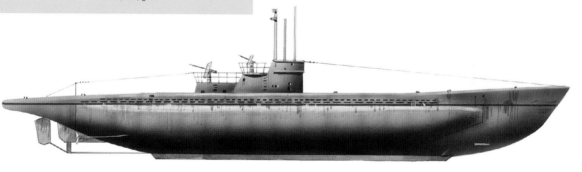

Specifications

Crew: 53

Powerplant: Diesel/electric

Max Speed: 26.7/11.7km/hr (14.4/6.3kt) surf/sub

Surface Range: 17,220km (9300nm)

Displacement: 1688/1932t (1661/1901 tons) surf/sub

Dimensions (length/beam/draught): 67.1 x 9.4 x 6.5m (220.16 x 30.83 x 21.33ft)

Commissioned: 5 Mar 1942

Armament: 2 x 3.7cm (1.5in) and 1 x 2cm (0.8in) guns

Fuel load: 439t (432 tons)

▲ **U-462**

Type XIV

This submarine tanker refuelled at least 50 boats on her first four patrols, but was damaged by aircraft on patrols five and six. Spotted off Cape Ortegal on her way into the Atlantic on patrol seven, she was sunk by aircraft and warships.

Star commanders
1941–44

The long-range boats of the 10th U-boat Flotilla achieved a considerable amount of success in 1941 and 1942, and the unit boasted several high-scoring commanders.

Korvettenkapitän Adolf Cornelius Piening

Born on 16 September 1910 in Süderende, Tondern, Piening joined the *Reichsmarine* with Crew 30. After service on the pocket battleship *Deutschland* and in torpedo boats and minesweepers, he transferred to U-boats in October 1940. In August 1941 he took command of U-155. In four patrols he sank 25 ships totalling 126,664 GRT as well as the escort carrier HMS *Avenger* (14,733 tonnes/14,500 tons).

He took command of the 7th Flotilla in March 1944. He made his final patrol in April 1945, laying mines off St Nazaire in U-255. In 1956, Adolf Piening joined the *Bundesmarine*, serving for 13 years and retiring as a *Kapitän zur See*. He died on 15 May 1984 in Kiel.

Piening was famous for introducing the so-called 'Piening Route' (hugging the coast of France and Spain), which he invented as a means of evading marauding Allied aircraft in the open waters of the Bay of Biscay.

Korvettenkapitän Helmut Witte

Helmut Witte was born on 6 April 1915 in Bojendorf, Holstein. He joined the Navy with Crew 34. In July 1940, Witte transferred to the U-boat force from surface craft. After the usual training, he became an officer on the newly commissioned U-107 under Kptlt. Hessler. Before he left the boat in July 1941, he had taken part in the most successful patrol of the war, during which U-107 sank 14 ships totalling nearly 87,000 GRT.

Witte commissioned U-159 in October 1941 and operated in the waters off Panama on his second patrol. On his third patrol, U-159 was a part of the *Eisbär* group, which operated in the waters off Cape Town in September 1942. In four patrols, he sank 23 ships for a total of 119,684 GRT.

Witte left U-159 in June 1943, serving from then until the end of the war in several staff positions. He was promoted to *Korvettenkapitän* on 20 April 1945. Helmut Witte died on 3 October 2005 at Duisburg.

STAR COMMANDERS		
Commander	Patrols	Ships Sunk
Korvettenkapitän Adolf Piening	8	25
Korvettenkapitän Helmut Witte	4	23
Korvettenkapitän Georg Lassen	4	26

Korvettenkapitän Georg Lassen

Born on 12 May 1915 in Berlin-Steglitz, Georg Lassen joined the Navy with Crew 35. For more than a year, he was I WO (*Erste Wacht Offizier*, or First Officer) aboard the successful U-29 commanded by *Kapitänleutnant* Otto Schuhart. They sank 11 ships for a total of 80,688 GRT as well as the 22,860-tonne (22,500-ton) aircraft carrier HMS *Courageous*. From January to September 1941, Kptlt. Georg Lassen was the commander of U-29, which at this time was a training boat in the 24th U-boat Flotilla.

On 16 October 1941, Lassen commissioned the Type IXC U-boat U-160, and on four patrols he sank 26 ships for a total of 156,082 GRT, damaging a further five ships totalling 34,419 GRT. On his first patrol as commander in March/April 1942, he sank or damaged six ships for a total of 43,560 GRT. On his last patrol, in South African waters, he sank or damaged six ships in less than five hours over the night of 3/4 March 1943 for a total of 41,076 GRT. Three days later he was awarded the Oak Leaves to the Knight's Cross.

Lassen left U-160 in May 1943, two months before the submarine was lost with all hands in the Atlantic, to become a tactics instructor at the 1st ULD (*U-Boot-Lehrdivision*).

CREW 37A EMBLEM

Kptlt. Hans-Jürgen Lauterbach-Emden, commander of the Type IXC/40 boat U-539, joined the *Kriegsmarine* with Crew 37A, and used his class insignia as a personal emblem on his first command.

U-459

TYPE XIV

In an attempt to extend the endurance of U-boats operating far out into the Atlantic, the *Kriegsmarine* developed a submarine tanker to support operational boats at sea.

U-459 WAS THE FIRST purpose-built 'milch cow', which were large boats designed to refuel combat boats at sea. They had no torpedo tubes but carried one 2cm (0.8in) and two 3.7cm (1.5in) AA guns for self-defence. The first of 10 such vessels commissioned between November 1941 and March 1943, U-459 set off on her first refuelling mission from Kiel in January 1942, returning to her new base at St Nazaire.

'Milch cow'

On her third and fourth patrols, U-459 was used to support the *Eisbär* and *Seehund* wolfpack groups, made up from long-range Type IX boats on their way to operational areas off the coast of South Africa.

U-459 Commander

Korvkpt. Georg von Wilamowitz-Möllendorf *(Nov 1941 – Jul 1943)*

After suporting the *Eisbär* boats in October 1942, U-459 had to be refuelled herself by fellow milchcow U-462 in order to make it back to her next new base at Bordeaux, where the boat was transferred to the operational control of the 12th Flotilla.

Air attack

The submarine was scuttled while heading out on her sixth patrol on 24 July 1943 near Cape Ortegal, Spain, after being badly damaged by two RAF Wellingtons from Nos. 172 and 547 Sqns. The first aircraft was shot down but crashed onto the boat's hull with only the rear gunner of the Wellington's crew surviving. A depth charge that landed

U-459 TIMETABLE		
Patrol Dates	**Operational Area**	**Boats Refuelled**
29 Mar 1942 –15 May 1942	NE of Bermuda	15
6 June 1942 – 19 Jul 1942	W of the Azores	16
18 Aug 1942 – 4 Nov 1942	S of St Helena	11
20 Dec 1942 – 7 Mar 1943	S of St Helena	4
20 Apr 1943 – 3 June 1943	Central N Atlantic	17
22 Jul 1943 – 24 Jul 1943	Bay of Biscay	0

Specifications

Crew: 53

Powerplant: Diesel/electric

Max Speed: 26.7/11.7km/hr (14.4/6.3kt) surf/sub

Surface Range: 17,220km (9300nm)

Displacement: 1688/1932t (1661/1901 tons) surf/sub

Dimensions (length/beam/draught): 67.1 x 9.4 x 6.5m (220.16 x 30.83 x 21.33ft)

Commissioned: 15 Nov 1941

Armament: 2 x 3.7cm (1.5in) and 1 x 2cm (0.8in) guns

Fuel load: 439t (432 tons)

▲ **U-459**

Type XIV

'Milch cows' like U-459 had no offensive role, and carried no torpedoes or torpedo tubes. The only armament fitted was defensive, since refuelling operations had to be carried out on the surface where the boats were vulnerable to air attack.

on the deck was pushed overboard: however, it exploded, damaging the submarine's steering gear.

While going around in circles in an attempt to evade the aircraft, U-459 was attacked by the second Wellington. Nineteen crewmen were killed and 41 (including the rear gunner of the downed Wellington bomber) survived, to be picked up by the Polish destroyer *Orkan*.

U-506
TYPE IXC

In five patrols with the 10th Flotilla, U-506 sank 14 ships totalling more than 70,000 GRT. In July 1943, it was assigned to the *Monsun* group in Asia, but it was never to arrive.

U-506 TOOK PART in the operations to rescue survivors after the sinking of SS *Laconia* in September 1942 off West Africa. About 1500 men were saved by three U-boats, an Italian submarine and by Vichy French vessels from Dakar.

U-506 TIMETABLE		
Patrol Dates	Operational Area	Ships Sunk
2 Mar 1942 – 25 Mar 1942	Transit from Kiel to Lorient via Heligoland	0
6 Apr 1942 – 15 June 1942	Florida/Gulf of Mexico	8
28 Jul 1942 – 7 Nov 1942	W African coast off Freetown	4
14 Dec 1942 – 8 May 1943	Central Atlantic/S Atlantic	2
6 Jul 1943 – 12 Jul 1943	Biscay, en route to the Far East	0

U-506 Commander

Kptlt. Erich Würdemann *(Sep 1941 – Jul 1943)*

Fate

U-506 was sunk on 12 July 1943 west of Vigo, Spain, by seven depth charges from a USAAF B-24 Liberator of A/S Sqn 1. Forty-eight crew were killed and six survived. This was one of the first boats detected using SC137 10cm (4in) radar, which the Germans could not detect.

About 15 men were seen in the water after the boat broke in two. The attacking pilot dropped a liferaft and a smoke flare to assist the surviving crew. Six men were picked up from the sea by a British destroyer on 15 July, three days after the sinking.

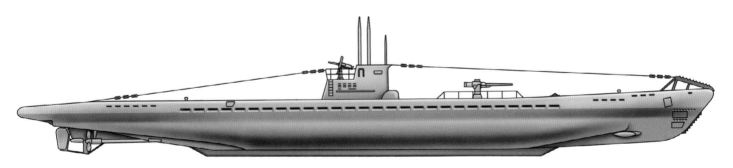

▲ **U-506**

Type IXC

U-506 underwent working-up training with the 4th Flotilla in the Baltic before transferring to the 10th Flotilla at Lorient for operations. The boat spent her combat career in the central Atlantic and in American waters.

Specifications

Crew: 48–50

Powerplant: Diesel/electric

Max Speed: 33.9/13.5km/hr (18.3/7.3kt) surf/sub

Surface Range: 20,370km (11,000nm)

Displacement: 1138/1252t (1120/1232 tons) surf/sub

Dimensions (length/beam/draught): 76.8 x 6.8 x 4.7m (252 x 22.31 x 15.42ft)

Commissioned: 15 Sep 1941

Armament: 22 torpedoes (4 bow/2 stern tubes); 1 x 10.5cm (4.1in), 1 x 3.7cm (1.5in) and 1 x 2cm (0.8in) guns

U-511
Type IXC

Laid down at Deutsche Werft, Hamburg, in February 1941, U-511 was launched in September and commissioned on 8 December of that year.

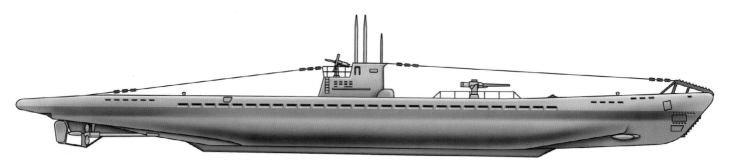

Specifications

Crew: 48–50

Powerplant: Diesel/electric

Max Speed: 33.9/13.5km/hr (18.3/7.3kt) surf/sub

Surface Range: 20,370km (11,000nm)

Displacement: 1138/1252t (1120/1232 tons) surf/sub

Dimensions (length/beam/draught): 76.8 x 6.8 x 4.7m (252 x 22.31 x 15.42ft)

Commissioned: 8 Dec 1941

Armament: 22 torpedoes (4 bow/2 stern tubes); 1 x 10.5cm (4.1in), 1 x 3.7cm (1.5in) and 1 x 2cm (0.8in) guns

▲ U-511

Type IXC

U-511 was one of a number of German Type IX boats that found their way into the service of the Imperial Japanese Navy in the last two years of the war. It was surrendered to the Americans in August 1945.

IN THE SUMMER OF 1942, while still working up in the Baltic the boat was detached to Peenemünde for use as a test platform in rocket experiments, possibly because Kptlt. Steinhoff's brother Dr Erich Steinhoff was a rocket scientist at Peenemünde at the time. A rack for six 30cm (11.8in) Wurfkörper 42 Spreng artillery rockets was fitted to the boat, missiles being launched successfully from the surface and submerged from as deep as 12m (39ft).

Although the experiments were technically successful, the U-boat staff did not proceed further with them. The rockets were not accurate enough to strike point targets such as ships. However, they might have functioned in a shore bombardment role had not the extra equipment on deck affected the boat's performance and handling underwater. The boat was assigned to the 10th Flotilla at Lorient

from August 1942, and mounted four patrols, three in the central Atlantic and the Caribbean and one to the U-boat base at Penang in Malaya. The boat carried passengers on this trip, including the German Ambassador to Tokyo, the Japanese Naval Attaché in Berlin, and some German scientists and engineers.

Fate

The boat was handed over to a Japanese crew, who took it on to Kure. It was sold to Japan on 16 September 1943 and became the submarine RO-500. Surrendered in August 1945, it was scuttled off Maizuru by the US Navy on 30 April 1946.

U-511 Commanders

Kptlt. Friedrich Steinhoff
(Dec 1941 – Dec 1942)

Kptlt. Fritz Schneewind
(Dec 1942 – Nov 1943)

U-511 TIMETABLE		
Patrol Dates	Operational Area	Ships Sunk
16 Jul 1942 – 29 Sep 1942	Transit from Kiel to Lorient via Caribbean	2
24 Oct 1942 – 28 Nov 1942	Off Moroccan Atlantic coast	0
31 Dec 1942 – 8 Mar 1943	Canaries/Azores/off Portuguese coast	1
10 May 1943 – 7 Aug 1943	Transit from Lorient to Penang	2

U-530
TYPE IXC/40

The Type IXC/40 was a marginally enlarged variant of the original Type IXC, with longer range and a more efficiently organized interior.

O N 23 JUNE 1944, on its way to the Caribbean, U-530 made a rendezvous west of the Cape Verde Islands with the Japanese submarine I-52. The huge Japanese boat (twice the tonnage of a Type IX) was heading for Europe with a cargo that included two tonnes (two tons) of gold plus other strategic materials. The German boat's mission was to supply the larger boat with a Naxos radar detector, two Naxos operators and a German navigator to help accomplish the last stage of its journey.

Unknown to the two Axis boats, Ultra intelligence had alerted the Allies to the rendezvous, and U-530 was being hunted by a US Navy task group led by the escort carrier USS *Bogue*. Immediately after making the transfer, U-530 headed for Trinidad,

U-530 Commanders

Kptlt. Kurt Lange *(Oct 1942 – Jan 1945)*

Oblt. Otto Wermuth *(Jan 1945 – Jul 1945)*

thus missing the attack made by Avengers from the *Bogue*. This was to be the last U-boat mission into the Caribbean. After the rendezvous, I-52 submerged, but was located by newly developed sonobuoys. The Avengers dropped two depth bombs, followed by Fido homing torpedoes. Two underwater explosions marked the end of I-52.

On being told of the end of the war, the crew of U-530, then off the American coast, refused to follow Admiral Dönitz's instructions. Heading south, they surrendered in the Mar del Plata, Argentina, on 10 July 1945. The crew was interned and the boat transferred to the United States and used for trials. It was sunk as a target on 28 November 1947 by a torpedo from USS *Toro*.

U-530 TIMETABLE

Patrol Dates	Operational Area	Ships Sunk
20 Feb 1943 – 22 Apr 1943	N Atlantic W of Ireland	2
29 May 1943 – 3 Jul 1943	SW of Canaries as a fuel tanker	0
27 Sep 1943 – 29 Sep 1943	Patrol aborted	0
3 Oct 1943 – 5 Oct 1943	Patrol aborted	0
17 Oct 1943 – 22 Feb 1944	Caribbean	1 damaged
22 May 1944 – 4 Oct 1944	Caribbean (last U-boat patrol in area)	0
3 Mar 1945 – 10 Jul 1945	US east coast	0

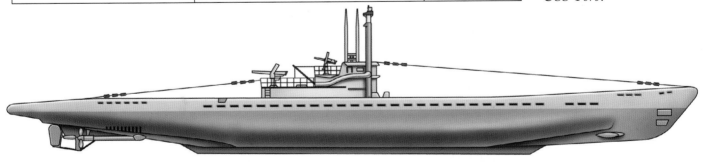

Specifications

Crew: 48–50

Powerplant: Diesel/electric

Max Speed: 33.9/13.5km/hr (18.3/7.3kt)

surf/sub

Surface Range: 20,370km (11,000nm)

Displacement: 1138/1252t (1120/1232 tons)

surf/sub

Dimensions (length/beam/draught): 76.8 x 6.9 x 4.7m (252 x 22.6 x 15.42ft)

Commissioned: 14 Oct 1942

Armament: 22 torpedoes; 1 x 10.5cm (4.1in), 1 x 3.7cm (1.5in) and 1 x 2cm (0.8in) guns

▲ **U-530**

Type IXC/40

U-530 made seven patrols under the control of the 10th Flotilla and the 33rd Flotilla, sinking just two merchant vessels totalling just over 12,000 GRT and damaging one more of 10,195 GRT.

Long-range operations
1941–45

Pre-war German planning had always envisaged the use of long-range submarines operating in concert with auxiliary cruisers or disguised merchant raiders in distant waters.

ADMIRAL KARL DÖNITZ WAS NOT in favour of the scheme, believing that the primary function of the U-boat was to sink enemy shipping. The best way to do that, he believed, was to operate where targets were most plentiful – on the convoy routes of the North Atlantic.

However, the *Oberkommando der Marine* (OKM, the Supreme Naval Command) had a wider view. By sending submarines farther afield, they could force the Royal Navy to stretch its anti-submarine assets over a much larger area. It would also force the introduction of the convoy system in the South Atlantic and the Indian Ocean, slowing the passage of war cargoes.

Initially, the long-range boats achieved considerable success. Author Bodo Herzog has listed the 16 most successful U-boats of November 1942, a particularly bad month for Allied shipping. Of the 16, only two were operating in the North Atlantic. Four were in the Caribbean, one was off the coast of West Africa, and no less than nine boats were successful in the South Atlantic and around the Cape of Good Hope.

Distant waters

Later, submarines were to operate even farther afield, making operational patrols in the Indian Ocean and in Southeast Asian waters. However, U-boats were still vulnerable in the early stages of a patrol. Many were lost to Allied aircraft as they traversed the lethal waters of the Bay of Biscay, while still more were destroyed by Allied hunter-killer groups deployed in the central Atlantic to block their passage as the boats moved south.

Replenishment of boats at sea
1941–44

Despite the development of the Type IX boats, long-range replenishment remained an issue for the *Kriegsmarine*.

EVEN THE LONG-RANGE Type IX boats lacked the endurance for extended operations in the South Atlantic and the Caribbean. Initially, they were to have been supported by supply ships, often disguised as neutral merchantmen. However, British success in cracking German naval codes meant that the locations of many supply rendezvous were known, especially after the capture of U-110 on 9 May 1941. In June 1941, nine out of ten supply ships were hunted down and sunk.

As a stop-gap, front-line boats were used as resupply platforms, but these could refuel or resupply only a handful of operational U-boats. The large Type XB minelayers were pressed into service as 'milch cows', or supply boats, and in 1941 these were joined by the purpose-designed Type XIV supply boat. Unarmed except for anti-aircraft defences, the Type XIVs could provide between 15 and 20 front-line boats with ammunition, fuel, water and food on a single patrol.

The first boat was U-459, which entered service with the 10th Flotilla on 1 April 1942. After some initial successes, the milch cows suffered the same fate as the surface supply vessels. Those that were not sunk in transit to their operational areas, far from the normal shipping lanes, were ruthlessly hunted down by Allied ships and aircraft, often operating on information provided by Ultra codebreakers.

BOATS THAT SERVED WITH 10TH FLOTILLA (82 BOATS)

U-Boat	Type	Commissioned	Flotilla(s)	Patrols	Fate
U-118	XB	6-Dec-41	1 Oct 1942 – 31 Oct 1942 from 4 Flottille	4 patrols. 3 ships sunk by mines: total 14,064 GRT; 1 warship sunk by mine: total 940t/925 tons; 2 ships damaged by mines: total 11,945 GRT	to 12. Flottille
U-155	IXC	23-Aug-41	1 Feb 1942 – 14 Aug 1944 from 4. Flottille	10 patrols. 25 ships sunk: total 126,664 GRT; 1 escort carrier (HMS *Avenger*) sunk: total 14,733t/14,500 tons; 1 auxiliary warship damaged: total 6736 GRT	to 33. Flottille
U-158	IXC	25-Sep-41	1 Feb 1942 – 30 Jun 1942 from 4. Flottille	2 patrols. 17 ships sunk: total 101,321 GRT 2 ships damaged: total 15,264 GRT	Sunk with all hands 30 Jun 1942 west of the Bermudas by depth charges from a US Navy Mariner of VP-74. 54 dead
U-159	IXC	4-Oct-41	1 May 1942 – 28 Jul 1943 from 4. Flottille	5 patrols. 23 ships sunk: total 119,684 GRT 1 ship damaged: total 265 GRT	Sunk with all hands 28 Jul 1943 south of Haiti by depth charges from a US Navy Mariner of VP-32. 53 dead. Previously credited to a Mariner from VP-32 on 15 Jul 1943 east of Jamaica.
U-160	IXC	16-Oct-41	1 Mar 1942 – 14 Jul 1943 from 4. Flottille	5 patrols. 26 ships sunk: total 156,082 GRT; 5 ships damaged: total 34,419 GRT	Sunk with all hands 14 Jul 1943 south of the Azores by a US Navy Avenger and Wildcats of the escort carrier *USS Santee*. 57 dead
U-163	IXC	21-Oct-41	1 Aug 1942 – 13 Mar 1943 from 4. Flottille	3 patrols. 3 ships sunk: total 15,011 GRT 1 warship damaged beyond repair: total 2032t/2000 tons	Sunk with all hands 13 Mar 1943 northwest of Cape Finisterre by depth charges from the Canadian corvette HMCS *Prescott*. 57 dead
U-164	IXC	28-Nov-41	1 Aug 1942 – 6 Jan 1943 from 4. Flottille	2 patrols. 3 ships sunk: total 8133 GRT	Sunk 6 Jan 1943 northwest of Pernambuco by depth charges from a US Navy Catalina of VP-83. 54 dead and 2 survivors
U-165	IXC	3-Feb-42	1 Sep 1942 – 27 Sep 1942 from 4. Flottille	1 patrol. 2 ships sunk: total 8396 GRT; 1 auxiliary warship sunk: total 358 GRT; 3 ships damaged: total 14,499 GRT; 1 auxiliary warship damaged: total 7252 GRT	Probably sunk with all hands 27 Sept 1942 in the Bay of Biscay west of Lorient by depth charges from a Czech-crewed Wellington of No. 311 Sqn RAF. 51 dead
U-166	IXC	23-Mar-42	1 Jun 1942 – 30 Jul 1942 from 4. Flottille	2 patrols. 4 ships sunk: total 7593 GRT	Sunk with all hands 30 Jul 1942 in the Gulf of Mexico by depth charges from the US Navy escort vessel PC-566. 52 dead. Originally thought to have been sunk by a single depth charge from a US Coast Guard J4F-1 aircraft, but that may have been an unsuccessful attack on U-171
U-167	IXC/40	4-Jul-42	1 Dec 1942 – 6 Apr 1943 from 4. Flottille	2 patrols. 1 ship sunk: total 4621 GRT; 1 ship damaged: total 7200 GRT	Scuttled 6 Apr 1943 near the Canary Islands after a depth charge attack by a Hudson aircraft of No. 233 Sqn the day before. All 50 crew members survived. It was raised in 1951 and transferred to Spain, where it was used commercially as an exhibit and as a film set
U-169	IXC/40	16-Nov-42	1 Mar 1943 – 27 Mar 1943 from 4. Flottille	1 patrol	Sunk with all hands 27 Mar 1943 south of Iceland by depth charges from a British B-17 Fortress. 54 dead
U-170	IXC/40	19-Jan-43	1 Jun 1943 – 31 Oct 1944 from 4. Flottille	4 patrols. 1 ship sunk: total 4663 GRT	to 33. Flottille
U-171	IXC	25-Oct-41	1 Jul 1942 – 9 Oct 1942 from 4. Flottille	1 patrol. 3 ships sunk: total 17,641 GRT	Sunk 9 Oct 1942 in the Bay of Biscay near Lorient by a mine. 22 dead and 30 survivors
U-172	IXC	5-Nov-41	1 May 1942 – 13 Dec 1943 from 4. Flottille	6 patrols. 26 ships sunk: total 152,778 GRT	Sunk 13 Dec 1943 in mid-Atlantic west of the Canary Islands after a 27-hour fight with Avenger and Wildcat aircraft of the escort carrier USS *Bogue* and by as many as 200 depth charges from the destroyers USS *George E. Badger*, USS *Clemson*, USS *Osmond Ingram* and USS *Du Pont*. 13 dead and 46 survivors
U-174	IXC	26-Nov-41	1 Aug 1942 – 27 Apr 1943	3 patrols. 5 ships sunk: total 30,813 GRT	Sunk with all hands 27 Apr 1943 south of Newfoundland by depth charges from a US Navy Ventura of VP-125. 53 dead
U-175	IXC	5-Dec-1941	1 Sep 1942 – 17 Apr 1943 from 4. Flottille	3 patrols. 10 ships sunk: total 40,619 GRT	Sunk 17 Apr 1943 southwest of Ireland by depth charges and gunfire from the US Coast Guard cutter USS *Spencer*. 13 dead and 41 survivors
U-176	IXC	15-Dec-41	1 Aug 1942 – 15 May 1943 from 4. Flottille	3 patrols. 10 ships sunk: total 45,850 GRT; 1 ship damaged: total 7457 GRT	Sunk with all hands 15 May 1943 northeast of Havana, by depth charges from the Cuban patrol boat CS 13 after being located by a US Navy OS2U-3 Kingfisher of VP-62. 53 dead
U-177	IXD2	14-Mar-42	1 Oct 1942 – 30 Nov 1942 from 4. Flottille	3 patrols. 14 ships sunk: total 87,388 GRT; 1 ship damaged: total 2588 GRT	to 12. Flottille
U-178	IXD2	14-Feb-42	1 Sep 1942 – 31 Oct 1942 from 4. Flottille	3 patrols. 13 ships sunk: total 87,030 GRT; 1 ship damaged: total 6348 GRT	to 12. Flottille
U-179	IXD2	7-Mar-42	1 Sep 1942 – 30 Sep 1942 from 4. Flottille	1 patrol. 1 ship sunk: total 6558 GRT	to 12. Flottille
U-180	IXD1	16-May-42	1 Feb 1943 – 1 Nov 1943 from 4. Flottille	2 patrols. 2 ships sunk: total 13,298 GRT	to 12. Flottille
U-181	IXD2	9-May-42	1 Oct 1942 – 31 Oct 1942	4 patrols. 27 ships sunk: total 138,779 GRT	to 12. Flottille
U-185	IXC/40	13-Jun-42	1 Nov 1942 – 24 Aug 1943 from 4. Flottille	3 patrols. 9 ships sunk: total 62,761 GRT; 1 ship damaged: total 6840 GRT	Sunk 24 Aug 1943 in mid-Atlantic by depth charges from 3 Avengers and Wildcats of the escort carrier USS *Core*. 29 dead and 22 survivors. 14 men who had been rescued from U-604 also died
U-186	IXC/40	10-Jul-42	1 Jan 1943 – 12 May 1943	2 patrols. 3 ships sunk: total 18,782 GRT	Sunk with all hands 12 May 1943 north of the Azores by depth charges from the destroyer HMS *Hesperus*. 53 dead
U-187	IXC/40	23-Jul-1942	1 Jan 1943 – 4 Feb 1943 from 4. Flottille	1 patrol	Sunk 4 Feb 1943 in the North Atlantic by depth charges from the destroyers HMS *Beverley* and HMS *Vimy*. 9 dead and 45 survivors
U-188	IXC/40	5-Aug-42	1 Feb 1943 – 20 Aug 1944 from 4. Flottille	3 patrols. 8 ships sunk: total 49,725 GRT; 1 warship sunk: total 1209t/1190 tons; 1 ship damaged: total 9977 GRT	Scuttled 20 Aug 1944 at the U-boat base in Bordeaux, unable to escape the Allied advance

BOATS THAT SERVED WITH 10TH FLOTILLA (82 BOATS)

U-Boat	Type	Commissioned	Flotilla(s)	Patrols	Fate
U-192	IXC/40	16-Nov-42	1 May 1943 – 6 May 1943 from 4. Flottille	1 patrol	Sunk with all hands 6 May 1943 in the North Atlantic southeast of Cape Farewell by depth charges from the corvette HMS *Loosestrife*. 55 dead. Previously thought to have been sunk 5 May by depth charges from the corvette HMS *Pink*.
U-193	IXC/40	10-Dec-42	1 Apr 1944 – 23 Apr 1944 from 2. Flottille	3 patrols. 1 ship sunk: total 10,172 GRT	Missing with all hands on or after 23 Apr 1944 in the Bay of Biscay. 59 dead. Previously listed as sunk 28 Apr 1944 in the Bay of Biscay west of Nantes by depth charges from an RAF Wellington aircraft.
U-194	IXC/40	8-Jan-43	1 Jun 1943 – 24 Jun 1943 from 4. Flottille	1 patrol	Sunk with all hands 24 Jun 1943 in the North Atlantic southwest of Iceland by a homing torpedo from a US Navy PBY Catalina of VP-84. 54 dead.
U-195	IXD1	5-Sep-42	1 Apr 1943 – 1 Sep 1943 from 4. Flottille	3 patrols. 2 ships sunk: total 14,391 GRT 1 ship damaged: total 6797 GRT	to 12. Flottille
U-459	XIV	15-Nov-41	1 Apr 1942 – 31 Oct 1942 from 4. Flottille	6 resupply patrols	to 12. Flottille
U-460	XIV	24-Dec-41	1 Jul 1942 – 31 Oct 1942 from 4. Flottille	6 resupply patrols	to 12. Flottille
U-461	XIV	30-Jan-42	1 Jul 1942 – 31 Oct 1942 from 4. Flottille	6 resupply patrols	to 12. Flottille
U-462	XIV	5-Mar-42	1 Aug 1942 – 31 Oct 1942 from 4. Flottille	7 resupply patrols	to 12. Flottille
U-463	XIV	2-Apr-42	1 Aug 1942 – 31 Oct 1942 from 4. Flottille	5 resupply patrols	to 12. Flottille
U-464	XIV	30-Apr-42	1 Aug 1942 – 20 Aug 1942 from 4. Flottille	1 resupply patrol	Sunk 20 Aug 1942 southeast of Iceland by a US Navy PBY Catalina. 2 dead and 53 survivors
U-506	IXC	15-Sep-41	1 Feb 1942 – 12 Jul 1943 from 4. Flottille	5 patrols. 14 ships sunk: total 69,893 GRT; 1 ship damaged beyond repair: total 6821 GRT; 3 ships damaged: total 23,354 GRT. U-506 took part in the *Laconia* rescue operations in September 1942	Sunk 12 Jul 1943 west of Vigo, Spain, by 7 depth charges from a USAAF B-24 Liberator of A/S Sqn 1. 48 dead and 6 survivors. This was one of the first boats detected by centimetric airborne radar
U-508	IXC	20-Oct-41	1 Jul 1942 – 12 Nov 1943	6 patrols. 14 ships sunk: total 74,087 GRT	Sunk with all hands 12 Nov 1943 in the Bay of Biscay north of Cape Ortegal by depth charges from a US Navy Liberator of VB-103. 57 dead
U-509	IXC	4-Nov-41	1 Jul 1942 – 15 Jul 1943	4 patrols. 5 ships sunk: total 29,091 GRT; 1 ship damaged beyond repair: total 7129 GRT; 3 ships damaged: total 20,014 GRT	Sunk with all hands 15 Jul 1943 northwest of Madeira by aerial torpedoes from Grumman TBF/TBM Avengers of the escort carrier USS *Santee*. 54 dead
U-510	IXC	25-Nov-41	1 Aug 1942 – 30 Sep 1944 from 4. Flottille	7 patrols. 11 ships sunk: total 71,100 GRT; 1 auxiliary warship sunk: total 249 GRT; 3 ships damaged beyond repair: total 24,338 GRT; 8 ships damaged: total 53,289 GRT	to 33. Flottille
U-511	IXC	8-Dec-41	1 Aug 1942 – 1 Sep 1943	4 patrols. 5 ships sunk: total 41,373 GRT; 1 ship damaged: total 8773 GRT	Sold to Japan 16 Sep 1943 and became the Japanese submarine RO-500. Surrendered at Maizuru Aug 1945. Scuttled in Gulf of Maizuru by US Navy 30 Apr 1946
U-512	IXC	20-Dec-41	1 Sep 1942 – 2 Oct 1942 from 4. Flottille	1 patrol. 3 ships sunk: total 20,619 GRT	Sunk 2 Oct 1942 north of Cayenne by depth charges from an B-18A aircraft of US Army Bomb Sqn 99. 51 dead and 1 survivor (who spent 10 days adrift on a liferaft)
U-513	IXC	10-Jan-42	1 Sep 1942 – 19 Jul 1943 from 4. Flottille	4 patrols. 6 ships sunk: total 29,940 GRT; 2 ships damaged: total 13,177 GRT	Sunk 19 Jul 1943 in the South Atlantic southeast of Sao Francisco do Sul by depth charges from a US Navy Mariner of VP-74. 46 dead and 7 survivors
U-514	IXC	24-Jan-42	1 Sep 1942 – 8 Jul 1943 from 4. Flottille	4 patrols. 4 ships sunk: total 16,329 GRT; 2 ships damaged: total 13,551 GRT; 2 ships damaged beyond repair: total 8202 GRT	Sunk with all hands 8 Jul 1943 northeast of Cape Finisterre by rockets from a Liberator of No. 224 Sqn RAF. 54 dead
U-515	IXC	21-Feb-42	1 Sep 1942 – 9 Apr 1944 from 4. Flottille	7 patrols. 21 ships sunk: total 131,769 GRT; 2 auxiliary warships sunk: total 19,277 GRT; 1 ship damaged beyond repair: total 4668 GRT; 1 warship damaged beyond repair: total 1372t/1350 tons; 1 ship damaged: total 6034 GRT; 1 warship damaged: total 1951t/1920 tons	Sunk 9 Apr 1944 north of Madeira by rockets from Avenger and Wildcat aircraft of the escort carrier USS *Guadalcanal*, and by depth charges from the destroyer escorts USS *Pope*, USS *Pillsbury*, USS *Chatelain* and USS *Flaherty*. 16 dead and 44 survivors
U-516	IXC	21-Feb-42	1 Sep 1942 – 30 Sep 1944 from 4. Flottille	6 patrols. 16 ships sunk: total 89,385 GRT; 1 ship damaged: total 9687 GRT	to 33. Flottille
U-517	IXC	21-Mar-42	1 Sep 1942 – 21 Nov 1942 from 4. Flottille	2 patrols. 8 ships sunk: total 26,383 GRT; 1 warship sunk: total 914t/900 tons	Sunk 21 Nov 1942 southwest of Ireland by depth charges from Albacores of the fleet carrier HMS *Victorious*. 1 dead and 52 survivors
U-523	IXC	25-Jun-42	1 Feb 1943 – 25 Aug 1943 from 4. Flottille	4 patrols. 1 ship sunk: total 5848 GRT	Sunk 25 Aug 1943 west of Vigo, Spain, by depth charges from the destroyer HMS *Wanderer* and the corvette HMS *Wallflower*. 17 dead and 37 survivors
U-524	IXC	8-Jul-42	1 Dec 1942 – 22 Mar 1943 from 4. Flottille	2 patrols. 2 ships sunk: total 16,256 GRT	Sunk with all hands 22 Mar 1943 south of Madeira by depth charges from a B-24 Liberator of USAAF A/S Sqn 1. 52 dead
U-525	IXC/40	30-Jul-42	1 Jan 1943 – 11 Aug 1943 from 4. Flottille	3 patrols. 1 ship sunk: total 3454 GRT	Sunk with all hands 11 Aug 1943 northwest of the Azores by depth charges and torpedoes from aircraft of the escort carrier USS *Card*. 54 dead
U-526	IXC/40	12-Aug-42	1 Feb 1943 – 14 Apr 1943 from 4. Flottille	1 patrol	Sunk 14 Apr 1943 in the Bay of Biscay near Lorient by mines. 42 dead and 12 survivors
U-527	IXC/40	2-Sep-42	1 Feb 1943 – 23 Jul 1943 from 4. Flottille	2 patrols. 1 ship sunk: total 5242 GRT; 1 ship damaged: total 5848 GRT	Sunk 23 Jul 1943 south of the Azores by depth charges from Grumman Avengers of the escort carrier USS *Bogue*. 40 dead and 13 survivors
U-528	IXC/40	16-Sep-42	1 Apr 1943 – 11 May 1943 from 4. Flottille	1 patrol	Sunk 11 May 1943 southwest of Ireland by depth charges from a Handley Page Halifax of No. 58 Sqn RAF and from the sloop HMS *Fleetwood*. 11 dead and 45 survivors
U-529	IXC/40	30-Sep-42	1 Feb 1943 – 12 Feb 1943 from 4. Flottille	1 patrol	Missing with all hands on or after 12 Feb 1943 in the North Atlantic. 48 dead. Previously credited to a Liberator of No. 120 Sqn RAF, but that attack on 15 Feb 1943 most likely accounted for U-225

BOATS THAT SERVED WITH 10TH FLOTILLA (82 BOATS)

U-Boat	Type	Commissioned	Flotilla(s)	Patrols	Fate
U-530	IXC/40	14-Oct-42	1 Mar 1943 – 30 Sep 1944 from 4. Flottille	7 patrols. 2 ships sunk: total 12,063 GRT; 1 ship damaged: total 10,195 GRT	to 33. Flottille
U-533	IXC/40	25-Nov-42	1 May 1943 – 16 Oct 1943 from 4. Flottille	2 patrols	Sunk 16 Oct 1943 in the Gulf of Oman by depth charges from a Bisley (late-model Blenheim) of No. 244 Sqn RAF. 52 dead and 1 survivor
U-535	IXC/40	23-Dec-42	1 Jun 1943 – 5 Jul 1943 from 4. Flottille	1 patrol	Sunk with all hands 5 Jul 1943 northeast of Cape Finisterre by depth charges from a Liberator of No. 53 Sqn RAF. 55 dead
U-537	IXC/40	27-Jan-43	1 Aug 1943 – 30 Sep 1944 from 4. Flottille	3 patrols	to 33. Flottille
U-539	IXC/40	24-Feb-43	1 Jul 1943 – 30 Sep 1944 from 4. Flottille	3 patrols. 1 ship sunk: total 1517 GRT; 2 ships damaged: total 12,896 GRT. U-539 was the first *Schnorchel*-equipped U-boat to go on a combat patrol, 2 Jan 1944	to 33. Flottille
U-540	IXC/40	10-Mar-43	1 Oct 1943 – 17 Oct 1943 from 4. Flottille	1 patrol	Sunk with all hands 17 Oct 1943 east of Cape Farewell, Greenland, by depth charges from Liberators of Nos. 59 and 120 Sqns RAF. 55 dead
U-541	IXC/40	24-Mar-43	1 Nov 1943 – 31 Oct 1944 from 4. Flottille	4 patrols. 1 ship sunk: total 2140 GRT	to 33. Flottille
U-542	IXC/40	7-Apr-43	1 Oct 1943 – 28 Nov 1943 from 4. Flottille	1 patrol	Sunk with all hands 28 Nov 1943 north of Madeira by depth charges from a Leigh Light-equipped Wellington of No. 179 Sqn RAF. 56 dead. Often confused with an attack by another 179 Sqn Wellington on the same night, which actually caused minor damage to U-391
U-543	IXC/40	21-Apr-43	1 Nov 1943 – 2 Jul 1944 from 4. Flottille	2 patrols	Sunk with all hands 2 Jul 1944 southwest of Tenerife by depth charges and a Fido homing torpedo from Grumman Avengers flying from the escort carrier *USS Wake Island*. 58 dead
U-544	IXC/40	5-May-43	1 Nov 1943 – 16 Jan 1944 from 4. Flottille	1 patrol	Sunk with all hands 16 Jan 1944 northwest of the Azores by depth charges and rockets from Grumman Avenger aircraft of the escort carrier USS *Guadalcanal*. 57 dead
U-546	IXC/40	2-Jun-43	1 Jan 1944 – 9 Nov 1944 from 4. Flottille	3 patrols. 1 warship sunk: total 1200 tons	to 33. Flottille
U-549	IXC/40	14-Jul-43	1 Jan 1944 – 29 May 1944 from 4. Flottille	2 patrols. 1 warship sunk: total 9393 tons; 1 warship damaged: total 1321t/1300 tons	Sunk with all hands 29 May 1944 after sinking the escort carrier USS *Block Island* southwest of Madeira, by depth charges from the US destroyer escorts USS *Eugene E. Elmore* and USS *Ahrens*. 57 dead
U-550	IXC/40	28-Jul-43	1 Feb 1944 – 16 Apr 1944 from 4. Flottille	1 patrol. 1 ship sunk: total 11,017 GRT	Sunk 16 Apr 1944 in the North Atlantic east of New York by depth charges and gunfire from the destroyer escorts USS *Gandy*, USS *Joyce* and USS *Peterson*. 44 dead and 12 survivors
U-804	IXC/40	4-Dec-43	1 Jul 1944 – 30 Sep 1944 from 4. Flottille	2 patrols. 1 warship sunk: total 1321t/1300 tons	to 33. Flottille
U-844	IXC/40	7-Apr-43	1 Oct 1943 – 16 Oct 1943 from 4. Flottille	1 patrol	Sunk with all hands 16 Oct 1943 southwest of Iceland by depth charges from Liberators of Nos. 59 and 86 Sqns RAF. 53 dead
U-845	IXC/40	1-May-43	1 Jan 1944 – 10 Mar 1944 from 4. Flottille	1 patrol. 1 ship damaged: total 7039 GRT	Sunk 10 Mar 1944 in North Atlantic by depth charges from destroyers HMS *Forester* and HMCS *St. Laurent*, corvette HMCS *Owen Sound* and frigate HMCS *Swansea*. 10 dead and 45 survivors
U-846	IXC/40	29-May-43	1 Dec 1943 – 4 May 1944 from 4. Flottille	2 patrols	Sunk with all hands 4 May 1944 in the Bay of Biscay north of Cape Ortegal, Spain, by depth charges from a Vickers Wellington of No. 407 Sqn RCAF. 57 dead
U-853	IXC/40	25-Jun-43	1 Apr 1944 – 1 Oct 1944 from 4. Flottille	3 patrols. 1 ship sunk: total 5353 GRT; 1 warship sunk: total 437t/430 tons	to 33. Flottille
U-855	IXC/40	2-Aug-43	1 Apr 1944 – 11 Sep 1944 from 4. Flottille	1 patrol	Missing with all hands on or after 11 Sep 1944 west of Bergen while returning from a weather patrol. 56 dead. Possibly mined in the Iceland–Faroes barrage. Previously credited to a Liberator of No. 224 Sqn RAF on 24 Sep 1944, but that attack actually sank U-763
U-857	IXC/40	16-Sep-43	1 Jun 1944 – 30 Sep 1944 from 4. Flottille	3 patrols. 2 ships sunk: total 15,259 GRT; 1 ship damaged: total 6825 GRT	to 33. Flottille
U-865	IXC/40	25-Oct-43	1 Jul 1944 – 19 Sep 1944 from 4. Flottille	1 patrol	Missing with all hands after leaving Trondheim, Norway, 9 Sep 1944. 59 dead. Known to have had a faulty *Schnorchel* – may have contributed to loss.
U-866	IXC/40	17-Nov-43	1 Aug 1944 – 30 Sep 1944 from 4. Flottille	1 patrol	to 33. Flottille
U-1221	IXC/40	11-Aug-43	1 Jul 1944 – 30 Nov 1944 from 4. Flottille	1 patrol	to 33. Flottille
U-1222	IXC/40	1-Sep-43	10. Flottille 1 Mar 1944 – 11 Jul 1944 from 4. Flottille	1 patrol; no ships sunk or damaged	Sunk with all hands 11 Jul 1944 west of La Rochelle by depth charges from a Short Sunderland of No.201 Sqn RAF. 56 dead.
U-1229	IXC/40	13-Jan-44	10. Flottille 1 Aug 1944 – 20 Aug 1944 from 10. Flottille	1 patrol; no ships sunk or damaged.	Sunk 20 Aug 1944 off Newfoundland while en route to Maine to land an agent, by depth charges of the escort carrier USS *Bogue*. 18 dead and 41 survivors. To 33. Flott.
U-1230	IXC/40	26-Jan-44	10. Flottille 1 Aug 1944 – 30 Sep 1944 from 31. Flottille	No patrols	to U-Abwehrschule
UD-3	Dutch O 21 class	8-June-41	10. Flottille Oct 42 – Feb 43 from 2. Flottille	3 patrols; 1 ship sunk (Norwegian ship *Indra*): total 5,041 GRT	Scuttled at Kiel on 3 May 1945

11 Unterseebootsflottille

The 11th Flotilla was founded on 15 May 1942 under the command of *Korvettenkapitän* Hans Cohausz. Based at Bergen in Norway, with boats operating from other ports stretching up beyond the Arctic Circle, the flotilla's primary mission was to interdict Allied supply lines to the USSR.

THE WESTERN ALLIES mounted a major effort to provide the USSR with war materials following the German invasion of Russia in June 1941. Seventy-eight convoys sailed between August 1941 and May 1945 with temporary pauses in the flow between July and September 1942, and March and November 1943. Early convoys sailed from Iceland, but after September 1942 they assembled at and sailed from Loch Ewe in Scotland. The route was around occupied Norway to the Soviet ports and was particularly dangerous due to the proximity of German air, submarine and surface forces and also because of the severe weather.

Outbound convoys carried the PQ designation while those returning to the Atlantic were known as QP or RA convoys. Hitler first began moving naval forces to Norway to forestall a potential invasion by the British, aimed at cutting German supplies of iron ore. However, having U-boats, destroyers, cruisers and capital ships in Norway meant that the *Kriegsmarine* had the chance to cut the flow of

11TH FLOTILLA BASE LOCATION

ATLANTIC OCEAN

● Bergen

▼ **Debris**

In the Barents Sea, a U-boat crew observe a patch of wreckage left behind by a recently destroyed US steamer.

Commanders

Fregkpt. Hans Cohausz *(May 1942 – Dec 1944)* — Fregkpt. Heinrich Lehmann-Willenbrock *(Dec 1944 – May 1945)*

9 FLOTILLA (1942–45)	
Type	Boats assigned
Type VIIC	121
Type VIIC/41	49
Type IXC/40	2
Type XB	1
Type XXI	6
Type XXIII	10

11TH FLOTILLA INSIGNIA

Given that the 11th Flotilla's main operational area was in the Arctic, it is not surprising that the unit's insignia should depict a polar bear riding on the back of a surfaced U-boat.

supplies from the United Kingdom and the United States to the Eastern Front.

In terms of numbers of ships sunk, the 11th Flotilla in Norway contributed little to the overall levels of U-boat successes, although there were occasional triumphs such as the massacre of Convoy PQ 17. Nevertheless, in combination with the *Luftwaffe,* its attacks forced the Allies to expend valuable resources in protecting the convoys. U-boats were also used to check on ice conditions and to set up weather stations on remote Arctic island groups. Submarines were even sent into the Siberian passage to try to intercept convoys coming from the Far East in the few months in summer when the passage was free of ice.

Following the Allied invasion of Normandy in 1944, Germany quickly lost the use of its ports in France, and the only area from which U-boats could set out on patrols into the Atlantic with relative safety was Norway. Most

of the surviving boats from France were sent north. The original French-based U-boat flotillas were disbanded, and the boats were taken onto the strength of the Norwegian flotillas. From there they continued to mount patrols against both Arctic and Atlantic convoys.

The final act of the 11th Flotilla's existence came with the introduction into service of the new high-speed 'Electro boats', the Type XXI and Type XXIII. Several Type XXIIIs became operational, and the first operational Type XXI boat, U-2511, was under 11th Flotilla orders. The flotilla was disbanded in May 1945 when Germany surrendered.

Kapitänleutnant Reinhart Reche

Born on 13 December 1915, Reche joined the German Navy as part of Crew 34. He made two patrols on U-751 before being promoted to command his own boat. One of the few captains to achieve success in the north, he commanded U-255 on nine patrols in the Arctic and played a major part in the destruction of convoy PQ 17. Reche left U-255 for a staff appointment in June 1943.

After the war, Reche joined the *Bundesmarine* and from 1959 to 1961 commanded the submarine training unit. He retired in 1974 as a *Kapitän zur See,* and died on 3 March 1993.

▲ **U-2326**

Type XXIII

The small Type XXIII boat had a short range and was lightly armed, but its high underwater speed made it a potentially deadly opponent in coastal waters. U-2326 survived the war, surrendering at Dundee on 14 May 1945.

Specifications

Crew: 14

Powerplant: Diesel/electric

Max Speed: 18.5/23.2km/hr (10/12.5kt) surf/sub

Surface Range: 2500km (1350nm)

Displacement: 236/260t (232/256 tons) surf/sub

Dimensions (length/beam/draught): 34.1 x 3 x 3.75m (112 x 10 x 12ft)

Commissioned: 10 Aug 1944

Armament: 2 torpedoes (2 bow tubes)

U-218

TYPE VIID

U-218 was a Type VIID U-boat, a slightly lengthened version of the standard design with a section added aft of the conning tower intended to hold and dispense mines.

LAID DOWN AT Germania Werft, Kiel, in March 1941, U-218 was commissioned on 24 January 1942. On her fifth patrol at the beginning of August 1943, six of the boat's crewmen were wounded by machine-gun fire in an attack by an RAF Wellington. The boat having sustained damage, its mission to the Caribbean was aborted. On 4 November 1943, U-218 claimed to have sunk a sailing vessel off Trinidad, but the sinking has never been confirmed.

In June 1944, U-218 went on her first *Schnorchel*-equipped patrol. The *Schnorchel* was faulty and several crewmembers were taken ill with carbon-

monoxide poisoning caused by diesel fumes. U-218 was to be transferred to Norway at the end of August 1944, but had to return to Kiel for a battery refit in October of that year. She returned to Norway for operations in March 1945.

U-218 was responsible for destroying the last British ship sunk as a result of the war. The steam fishing vessel *Kurd* went down on 10 July 1945, having struck a mine laid by the boat the previous August off Lizard Head.

Fate

U-218 surrendered in Bergen, Norway, on 8 May 1945 and sank while under tow to the Operation *Deadlight* scuttling grounds on 4 December 1945.

U-218 Commanders

Kptlt. Richard Becker *(Jan 1942 – Aug 1944)*   Kptlt. Rupprecht Stock *(Aug 1944 – May 1945)*

U-218 TIMETABLE

Patrol Dates	Operational Area	Ships Sunk
25 Aug 1942 – 29 Sep 1942	Transit from Kiel to Brest	0
25 Oct 1942 – 21 Nov 1942	W of Ireland/Gibraltar	0
7 Jan 1943 – 10 Mar 1943	Canaries/Azores	0
18 Apr 1943 – 2 June 1944	N Atlantic	0
29 Jul 1943 – 6 Aug 1943	Minelaying off Trinidad	0
19 Sep 1943 – 8 Dec 1943	Minelaying in the Caribbean	0
12 Feb 1944 – 7 May 1944	Minelaying in the Caribbean	0
13 June 1944 – 9 Jul 1944	Minelaying in the Channel	0
10 Aug 1944 – 23 Sep 1944	Minelaying in the Channel	1
22 Mar 1945 – 8 May 1945	Minelaying in Clyde estuary	1

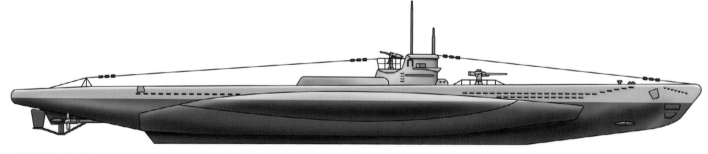

▲ **U-218**

Type VIID

Able to lay as many as 15 large ground mines, U-218 mounted 10 patrols between 1942 and the end of the war. Only two ships were sunk by its weapons, one in the Clyde estuary and one in the Channel after the end of the war.

Specifications

Crew: 44

Powerplant: Diesel/electric

Max Speed: 29.6/13.5km/hr (16/7.3kt) surf/sub

Surface Range: 8100km (4374nm)

Displacement: 980/1097t (965/1080 tons) surf/sub

Dimensions (length/beam/draught): 76.9 x 6.4 x 5m (252.3 x 21 x 16.4ft)

Commissioned: 24 Jan 1942

Armament: 14 torpedoes (4 bow/1 stern tubes); 15 mines; 1 x 8.8cm (3.5in) and 1 x 2cm (0.8in) guns

U-300
TYPE VIIC/41

Laid down at Bremer Vulkan, Vegesack, in April 1943, U-300 was commissioned in December of that year. It joined the 11th Flotilla in 1944.

AFTER WORKING UP with the 8th Flotilla in the Baltic for more than six months, U-300 was assigned to the 7th Flotilla at St Nazaire. However, by the time the boat went on its first operational patrol in the Atlantic, the U-boat force was abandoning its French bases, and at the end of the patrol U-300 was ordered to make for Bergen, where it would join the 11th Flotilla. The boat mounted two patrols in British coastal waters, sinking four ships totalling 17,370 GRT.

Fate
Having been sent to patrol off Gibraltar, U-300 was sunk on 22 February 1945 west of Cadiz by depth charges from the minesweepers HMS *Recruit* and HMS *Pincher* and the armed yacht/minesweeper USS *Evadne*. Eleven crewmen died and 42 became POWs.

U-300 TIMETABLE		
Patrol Dates	Operational Area	Ships Sunk
13 Jul 1944 – 17 Aug 1944	Hebrides/Iceland	0
4 Oct 1944 – 2 Dec 1944	S of Iceland	2
21 Jan 1945 – 22 Feb 1945	Off Gibraltar	0

U-300 Commanders

Oblt. Fritz Hein *(Dec 1943 – Feb 1945)*

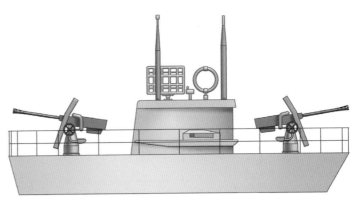

▲ **Type VII bridge conversion**

Designed to maximize anti-aircraft power, the Turm VII conversion carried two pairs of powerful 3.7cm (1.5in) Flak guns. Like the preceding Turm VII conversion, which was optimized for arctic operations, this alteration carried both forward-firing and aft-firing weaponry for better all-round protection. Had the war lasted longer, boats like U-300, a deep-diving Type VIIC/41, might well have been fitted with such armament. In any event, the boat was lost before conversion could take place.

▲ **U-300**

Type VIIC/41

Type VIIC/41 boats were virtually identical to other Type VIICs, but were constructed from thicker, stronger steel. This meant that they could dive more deeply than standard boats, and had more chance of avoiding depth charges.

Specifications
Crew: 44

Powerplant: Diesel/electric

Max Speed: 31.5/14.1km/hr (17/7.6kt) surf/sub

Surface Range: 12,040km (6500nm)

Displacement: 773/879t (761/865 tons) surf/sub

Dimensions (length/beam/draught): 67.2 x 6.2 x 4.8m (220.5 x 20.34 x 15.75ft)

Commissioned: 29 Dec 1943

Armament: 14 torpedoes (4 bow/1 stern tubes); 1 x 3.7cm (1.5in) and 2 x twin 2cm (0.8in) guns

U-486

TYPE VIIC

On her first patrol, U-486 sailed from Norway to the English Channel. She sent down three vessels in a notably successful combat debut at a time when few untried U-boats sank anything.

ON 18 DECEMBER 1944, U-486 sank the 6000 GRT *Silver Laurel*, sailing with Convoy BTC 10. Six days later, on the night of Christmas Eve, U-486 torpedoed the troopship SS *Leopoldville* in the English Channel just 8km (5 miles) from the port of Cherbourg, France. The *Leopoldville* was transporting 2235 soldiers of the US Army's 66th Infantry Division. The ship sank some two hours later.

So close to a major port, most of the passengers would normally have survived. However, everything that could go wrong with the rescue did go wrong. The escort commander, believing that the troopship could make port, ordered the escorts to hunt for the U-boat; calls for help were mishandled, rescue craft were slow to the scene and the weather was unfavourable.

When a secondary explosion hastened the vessel's sinking, 1000 troops were left in the freezing water. As many as 802 American soldiers died or were reported missing that night, together with 17 of the *Leopoldville*'s crew.

U-486 Commanders

Oblt. Gerhard Meyer *(Mar 1944 – Apr 1945)*

U-486 avoided the searching destroyers and frigates, and two days later she sank the frigate HMS *Capel*. Just 15 minutes later the boat damaged the frigate HMS *Affleck* beyond repair.

Fate

Despite being coated with Alberich anti-sonar material and equipped with a *Schnorchel*, U-486 was sunk with all 48 crew on 12 April 1945 northwest of Bergen, torpedoed by the Royal Navy submarine HMS *Tapir*. The U-boat had developed a *Schnorchel* problem, and was spotted by the British submarine, which was on patrol off the Norwegian ports, as U-486 surfaced on her way back into Bergen.

U-486 TIMETABLE

Patrol Dates	Operational Area	Ships Sunk
6 Nov 1944 – 20 Nov 1944	Transit from Kiel to Egersund	0
26 Nov 1944 – 15 Jan 1945	English Channel	3
9 Apr 1945 – 12 Apr 1945	British waters	0

▲ **U-486**

Type VIIC

Schnorchel-equipped U-boats entered service in large numbers in 1944. With the breathing device fitted, boats like U-486 could penetrate heavily defended waters with a reduced chance of being detected and destroyed.

Specifications

Crew: 44

Powerplant: Diesel/electric

Max Speed: 31.5/14.1km/hr (17/7.6kt) surf/sub

Surface Range: 12,040km (6500nm)

Displacement: 773/879t (761/865 tons) surf/sub

Dimensions (length/beam/draught): 67.1 x 6.2 x 4.8m (220.1 x 20.34 x 15.75ft)

Commissioned: 22 Mar 1944

Armament: 14 torpedoes (4 bow/1 stern tubes); 1 x 3.7cm (1.5in) and 2 x twin 2cm (0.8in) guns

U-2511

Type XXI

The best of the surviving U-boat commanders were assigned to the new, high-performance Type XXI submarines, but only a few of the many boats completed were ever declared operational.

On the evening of 3 May 1945, U-2511 set out from Bergen for her first and last patrol – the first operational mission by the revolutionary Type XXI *Elektroboot.*

Faster than any previous U-boat, with an integral *Schnorchel* allowing it to operate submerged as long as fuel and food held out, the Type XXI might have caused Allied escort forces some concern had it been available in any numbers. Fortunately very few were ready for action in the last days of the war, and none fired their weapons in anger. However, U-2511 came closest. Commanded by U-boat ace Adalbert Schnee, the boat was intended to patrol in the Caribbean, but on 4 May the captain received the cease-fire order that was to signal Germany's ultimate defeat.

A few hours later, north of the Faroes, U-2511 encountered a British task group. Schnee mounted

U-2511 Commanders

Korvkpt. Adalbert Schnee *(Sep 1944 – May 1945)*

a dummy attack on the heavy cruiser HMS *Norfolk*, approaching undetected to within 500m (547 yards).

Having proved a point to himself and his crew, Schnee turned U-2511 away, increasing the boat's submerged speed to a fast 29.6km/hr (16kt) to make his escape. U-2511 returned to Bergen on 5 May 1945.

Fate

U-2511 was surrendered at Bergen in May 1945. It was transferred to Lisahally, Northern Ireland, on 14 June that year for Operation *Deadlight,* and was sunk as a naval gunfire target on 7 January 1946.

U-2511 TIMETABLE		
Patrol Dates	**Operational Area**	**Ships Sunk**
16 Mar 1945 – 21 April 1945	Transit from Kiel to Bergen	0
3 May 1945 – 5 May 1945	Intended for the Caribbean	0

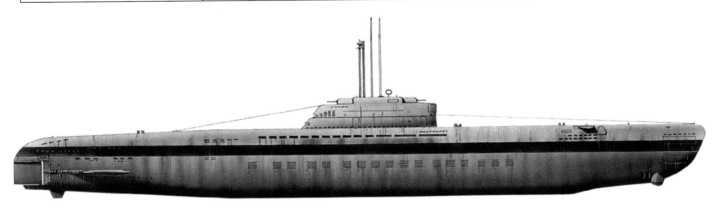

Specifications

Crew: 57

Powerplant: Diesel/electric

Max Speed: 28.9/32.6km/hr (15.6/17.6kt surf/sub)

Surface Range: 11,150km (6021nm)

Displacement: 1647/1848t (1621/1819 tons)

Dimensions (length/beam/draught): 76.7 x 6.6 x 6.3m (251.6 x 21.65 x 20.67ft)

Commissioned: 29 Sep 1944

Armament: 23 torpedoes (6 bow tubes); 2 x twin 2cm (0.8in) guns

▲ **U-2511**

Type XXI

Korvkpt. Schnee spoke with some of the officers of HMS Norfolk after the surrender, who were shocked to learn that the U-boat ace had got his fully armed Type XXI boat to within 500m (547 yards) of their cruiser without being detected.

Slaughter of PQ 17
27 June – 13 July 1942

The biggest convoy disaster of the war came when the British Admiralty overruled its commanders on the spot out of fear of a non-existent threat from German heavy units.

THIRTY-FIVE MERCHANTMEN LOADED with supplies set off into perilous Arctic waters on 27 June 1942. Convoy PQ 17 was carrying war matériel from Britain and the United States to the USSR. Through the course of 1942 on the northern route to Russia, Allied losses to German aircraft and U-boats had been increasing. In May, PQ 16 had lost seven ships, but PQ 17 was the largest and most valuable convoy to date. The boost to Soviet supplies which had been provided by PQ 16 was noticeable in spite of the losses, which prompted the Germans to redouble their efforts to break the convoy route to Archangelsk and Murmansk. Operation *Rösselsprung* was set up, involving the assembly of powerful air, surface and submarine forces in northern Norway.

PQ 17 was provided with a large escort for the time. Close escort was provided by six destroyers, four corvettes and two anti-aircraft vessels. Nearby was the close-support force of four cruisers, three destroyers, two submarines and two tankers. Distant cover in case the convoy was attacked by heavy German units was provided by the Royal Navy Home Fleet, centred

CONVOY PQ 17 BATTLE TIMETABLE	
Date	Event
27 June 1942	At 16:00 the ships of convoy PQ 17 leave their anchorage in Hvalfjordur, Iceland, and head northwards. The convoy consists of 35 ships and is heavily loaded with 297 aircraft, 594 tanks, 4246 lorries and gun carriers and 158,503 tonnes (156,000 tons) of cargo. (This was enough to equip an army of 50,000 men and was valued at $700 million at the time.) Shortly after leaving, one ship runs aground and returns to port
29 June	The convoy encounters heavy drift ice. Four merchantmen are damaged, with one having to return to port. This leaves 33 ships en route to Russia
1 July	The convoy is spotted by U-255 and U-408. U-456 joins the other boats and begins tracking the convoy. Further reconnaissance information is provided by BV 138 flying boats of the *Luftwaffe*
2 July	A number of U-boats attempt attacks on the convoy, but to little effect. They are joined in the evening by the first in a series of *Luftwaffe* torpedo attacks
3 July	U-boats and *Luftwaffe* torpedo planes continue to attack without success. However, British intelligence receives reports that a powerful German surface force is leaving Norwegian waters and heading northwards. The Admiralty calculates that *Tirpitz*, *Hipper*, *Scheer* and *Lützow* would intercept the convoy on the evening of 4 July
4 July	Two ships are sunk by U-457 and U-334. At around 22:00, the British Admiralty, fearing that *Tirpitz* and her consorts are about to strike, and knowing that the battleships of the Home Fleet are too far away to intervene, orders the escorts to run westwards and for the convoy to scatter and proceed independently towards Russia
5 July	Even though the German surface forces have not left port, the scattered merchantmen are vulnerable to U-boats and air attack. The slaughter begins almost immediately. *Luftwaffe* aircraft sink six ships, while the U-boats account for a similar number (U-88 and U-703 sinking two each, while U-334 and U-456 sink the others)
6 July	Two more vessels are lost, one to the *Luftwaffe* and one to U-255
7 July	The *Luftwaffe* sinks another ship, while U-255, U-457 and U-355 account for three more
8 July	U-255 sinks her third ship
10 July	U-251 and U-376 each sink one merchantman
13 July	U-255 sinks a derelict merchant ship that has been adrift since being struck by *Luftwaffe* bombs on 5 July

▲ KMS *Tirpitz*

The fear that the powerful battleship *Tirpitz* might attack the convoy caused the Admiralty to order PQ 17 to scatter. This left the merchantmen helpless against *Luftwaffe* torpedo planes and the *Kriegsmarine*'s U-boats.

on the battleship HMS *Duke of York*, flying the flag of Admiral Tovey, and the powerful new 406mm (16in) fast battleship USS *Washington*.

Against this force Germany fielded U-88, U-251, U-255, U-334, U-355, U-376, U-456, U-457, U-657 and U-703, together with a substantial *Luftwaffe* force equipped with Heinkel He 111H (torp), Ju 88A-4, Heinkel He 115C, Blohm und Voss Bv 138 and Focke-Wulf Fw 200 Kondor aircraft. Lurking nearby in Norwegian fiords were the battleship *Tirpitz*, the pocket battleships *Scheer* and *Lützow*, and the heavy cruiser *Hipper*.

In all, 24 of the 35 merchant ships from PQ 17 were sunk. In addition to the loss of life, material losses were extremely heavy. The 144,805 tonnes (142,518 tons) of shipping that went down took with it 3350 motor vehicles, 430 tanks, 210 bombers and 100,910 tonnes (99,316 tons) of general cargo, which included radar sets and ammunition.

The *Luftwaffe* had flown 202 sorties against the convoy, losing only five planes for the eight ships they sank. Three of the 11 surviving ships from PQ 17 were sunk on the return voyage from Russia in the next westbound convoy. One fell to U-255, becoming the boat's fifth victim.

The next convoy to do the northern route, PQ 18, sailed for Russia at the beginning of September, losing 13 ships (though three U-boats were sunk by the escorts). Convoy operations to Russia were suspended after the PQ 17 disaster and the losses to PQ 18 and were not resumed until JW 51 sailed in December 1942.

Specifications	
Crew: 44	Dimensions (length/beam/draught): 67.1 x 6.2
Powerplant: Diesel/electric	x 4.8m (220.1 x 20.34 x 15.75ft)
Max Speed: 31.5/14.1km/hr (17/7.6kt) surf/sub	Commissioned: 29 Nov 1941
Surface Range: 12,040km (6500nm)	Armament: 14 torpedoes (4 bow/1 stern tubes); 1
Displacement: 773/879t (761/865 tons) surf/sub	x 3.7cm (1.5in) and 2 x twin 2cm (0.8in) guns

▲ U-255

Type VIIC

U-255 was a very successful U-boat, carrying out 15 patrols and sinking 10 ships for a total 47,529 GRT. The U-boat was eventually sunk with all hands on 15 May 1943 in the North Atlantic by depth charges from a Halifax of No. 58 Sqn RAF.

U-Boat	Type	Commissioned	Flotilla(s)	Patrols	Fate
BOATS THAT SERVED WITH 11TH FLOTILLA (189 BOATS)					
U-88	VIIC	15-Oct-41	1 Jul 1942 – 12 Sep, 1942 from 7. Flottilla	3 patrols. 2 ships sunk: total 12,304 GRT	Sunk with all hands 12 Sep 1942 in the Arctic Ocean south of Spitzbergen by the destroyer HMS *Faulknor*. 46 dead
U-117	XB	25-Oct-41	15 Oct 1942 – 30 Nov 1942 from 1. Flottilla	5 patrols. 2 ships damaged by mines: total 14,269 GRT	to 12. Flottille
U-209	VIIC	11-Oct-41	1 Jul 1942 – 28 Feb 1943 from 6. Flottilla	7 patrols. 4 ships sunk: total 1356 GRT	to 1. Flottille
U-212	VIIC	25-Apr-42	1 Oct 1942 – 31 May 1943 from 8. Flottille (training)	15 patrols. 1 ship sunk: total 80 GRT	to 13. Flottille
U-218	VIID	24-Jan-42	1 Mar 1945 – 8 May 1945 from 8. Flottille	10 patrols. 2 ships sunk: total 552 GRT; 2 ships damaged: total 14,538 GRT; 1 auxiliary warship damaged: total 7177 GRT. Sank last British ship destroyed as result of the war: steam fishing vessel *Kurd* sunk 10 Jul 1945 by a minefield laid by U-218 the previous year off Lizard Head	Surrendered in Bergen, Norway, 8 May 1945. Sunk in Operation *Deadlight* 4 Dec 1945
U-244	VIIC	9-Oct-43	1 Nov 1944 – 8 May 1945	4 patrols	Surrendered at Lisahally, Northern Ireland, 14 May 1945. Sunk by naval gunfire after breaking cable while being towed out to the scuttling ground for Operation *Deadlight*
U-246	VIIC	11-Jan-44	1 Oct 1944 – 5 Apr 1945 from 3. Flottille	2 patrols	Missing with all hands Mar/Apr 1945 in the Irish Sea south of the Isle of Man. 48 dead. Sinking was credited to depth charges from the frigate HMS *Duckworth* off Land's End, but that attack probably sank U-1169
U-248	VIIC	6-Nov-43	1 Nov 1944 – 16 Jan 1945 from 9. Flottille	2 patrols	Sunk with all hands 16 Jan 1945 in the North Atlantic by depth charges from the destroyer escorts USS *Hayter*, USS *Otter*, USS *Varian* and USS *Hubbard*. 47 dead
U-251	VIIC	20-Sep-41	1 Jul 1942 – 31 May 1943 from 6. Flottilla	9 patrols. 2 ships sunk: total 11,408 GRT	to 13. Flottille
U-255	VIIC	29-Nov-41	1 Jul 1942 – 31 May 1943 from 8. Flottilla	15 patrols. 10 ships sunk: total 47,529 GRT; 1 warship sunk: total 1219t/1200 tons; 1 ship damaged b/r: total 7191 GRT	to 13. Flottille
U-269	VIIC	19-Aug-42	1 Apr 1943 – 31 Oct 1943 from 8. Flottille (training)	5 patrols	to 6. Flottille
U-275	VIIC	25-Nov-42	1 Oct 1944 – 10 Mar 1945 from 3. Flottille	9 patrols. 1 ship sunk: total 4934 GRT; 1 warship sunk: total 1107t/1090 tons	Sunk with all hands 10 Mar 1945 by a mine in the English Channel south of Newhaven. 48 dead
U-278	VIIC	16-Jan-43	1 Jan 1944 – 31 Aug 1944 from 7. Flottille	7 patrols. 1 ship sunk: total 7177 GRT; 1 warship sunk: total 1839t/1810 tons	to 13. Flottille
U-285	VIIC	15-May-43	1 Oct 1944 – 15 Apr 1945 from 7. Flottille	3 patrols	Sunk with all hands 15 Apr 1945 southwest of Ireland by depth charges from the frigates HMS *Grindall* and HMS *Keats*. 44 dead
U-286	VIIC	5-Jun-43	1 Aug 1944 – 4 Nov 1944 from 8. Flottille	4 patrols. 1 warship sunk: total 1168t/1150 tons	to 13. Flottille
U-286	VIIC	5-Jun-43	1 Mar 1945 – 29 Apr 1945 from 13. Flottille	4 patrols. 1 warship sunk: total 1168t/1150 tons	Sunk with all hands 29 Apr 1945 in the Arctic north of Murmansk by depth charges from the frigates HMS *Loch Insh*, HMS *Anguilla* and HMS *Cotton*. 51 dead
U-290	VIIC	24-Jul-43	1 Aug 1944 – 27 Aug 1944 from 6. Flottille	3 patrols	to 8. Flottille
U-293	VIIC/41	8-Sep-43	1 Aug 1944 – 4 Sep 1944 from 9. Flottille	6 patrols. 1 warship damaged: total 1685t/1658 tons	to 13. Flottille
U-294	VIIC/41	4-Oct-43	1 Aug 1944 – 5 Nov 1944 from 8. Flottille	5 patrols	to 13. Flottille
U-295	VIIC/41	20-Oct-43	1 Aug 1944 – 30 Sep 1944 from 8. Flottille	6 patrols. 1 warship damaged: total of 1168t/1150 tons	to 13. Flottille
U-296	VIIC/41	3-Nov-43	1 Oct 1944 – 12 Mar 1945 from 9. Flottille	3 patrols	Missing with all hands in the approaches to the North Channel on or after 12 Mar 1945. May have hit minefields T1 or T21 protecting the northern entrance to the Irish Sea. 42 dead
U-297	VIIC/41	17-Nov-43	1 Nov 1944 – 6 Dec 1944 from 8. Flottille	1 patrol	Sunk with all hands 6 Dec 1944 20km (12.4 miles) west of the Orkneys by depth charges from a Sunderland of No. 201 Sqn RAF. 50 dead. Previously listed missing in the Pentland Firth, but wreck found and identified May 2000
U-299	VIIC/41	15-Dec-43	1 Aug 1944 – 4 Nov 1944 from 8. Flottille	6 patrols	to 13. Flottille
U-300	VIIC/41	29-Dec-43	1 Oct 1944 – 22 Feb 1945 from 7. Flottille	3 patrols. 2 ships sunk: total 7559 GRT; 1 ship damaged beyond repair: total 9551 GRT; 1 ship damaged: total 7176 GRT	Sunk 22 Feb 1945 west of Cadiz by depth charges from minesweepers HMS *Recruit* and HMS *Pincher* and the armed yacht/minesweeper USS *Evadne*. 11 dead and 42 survivors
U-302	VIIC	16-Jun-42	1 Dec 1942 – 31 May 1943 from 8. Flottille	10 patrols. 3 ships sunk: total 12,697 GRT	to 13. Flottille
U-307	VIIC	18-Nov-42	1 May 1943 – 31 Oct 1943 from 8. Flottille	19 patrols. 1 ship sunk: total 411 GRT	to 13. Flottille
U-309	VIIC	27-Jan-43	1 Aug 1943 – 31 Oct 1943 from 8. Flottille	11 patrols. 1 ship damaged beyond repair: total 7219 GRT	to 9. Flottille
U-312	VIIC	21-Apr-43	1 Jan 1944 – 31 Aug 1944 from 6. Flottille	12 patrols	to 13. Flottille
U-313	VIIC	20-May-43	1 Jan 1944 – 14 Sep 1944 from 8. Flottille	14 patrols	to 13. Flottille
U-314	VIIC	10-Jun-43	1 Jan 1944 – 30 Jan 1944	2 patrols	Sunk with all hands 30 Jan 1944 in the Barents Sea southeast of Bear Island by depth charges from the destroyers HMS *Whitehall* and HMS *Meteor*. 49 dead
U-315	VIIC	10-Jul-43	1 Mar 1944 – 14 Sep 1944 from 8. Flottille	1 ship sunk: total 6996 GRT; 1 warship damaged beyond repair: total 1392t/1370 tons	to 13. Flottille

BOATS THAT SERVED WITH 11TH FLOTILLA (189 BOATS)

U-Boat	Type	Commissioned	Flotilla(s)	Patrols	Fate
U-318	VIIC/41	13-Nov-43	1 Aug 1944 – 4 Nov 1944 from 4. Flottille	8 patrols	to 13. Flottille
U-321	VIIC/41	20-Jan-44	1 Mar 1945 – 2 Apr 1945	2 patrols	Sunk with all hands 2 Apr 1945 southwest of Ireland by depth charges from a Polish Wellington of No. 304 Sqn. 41 dead
U-322	VIIC/41	5-Feb-44	1 Nov 1944 – 29 Dec 1944 from 4. Flottille	2 patrols. 1 ship sunk: total 5149 GRT; 2 ships damaged beyond repair: total 14,367 GRT	Sunk with all hands 29 Dec 1944 south of Weymouth by depth charges from the corvette HMCS *Calgary*. 52 dead. Previously thought to have been sunk 25 Nov 1944 west of the Shetlands by depth charges from the frigate HMS *Ascension*
U-324	VIIC/41	5-Apr-44	15 Mar 1945 – 8 May 1945 from 4. Flottille	No patrols	Surrendered at Bergen 8 May 1945. Broken up in Mar 1947
U-325	VIIC/41	6-May-44	1 Dec 1944 – 7 Apr 1945 from 4. Flottille	3 patrols	Missing with all hands on or after 7 Apr 1945 in the North Atlantic or on the southwest coast of Britain. 52 dead
U-326	VIIC/41	6-Jun-44	1 Mar 1945 – 25 Apr 1945 from 4. Flottille	1 patrol	Sunk with all hands 25 Apr 1945 west of Brittany in the Bay of Biscay by a homing torpedo from a US Navy PB4Y Liberator aircraft of VPB-103. 43 dead
U-327	VIIC/41	18-Jul-44	1 Feb 1945 – 27 Feb 1945 from 4. Flottille	3 patrols	Sunk with all hands 27 Feb 1945 in the western Channel by depth charges from the frigates HMS *Labuan*, HMS *Loch Fada* and the sloop HMS *Wild Goose*. But may have been sunk 3 Feb 1945 near Bergen by depth charges from the frigates HMS *Bayntun*, HMS *Braithwaite* and HMS *Loch Eck*. 46 dead
U-328	VIIC/41	19-Sep-44	2 May 1945 – 8 May 1945 from 4. Flottille	No patrols	Surrendered May 1945. Transferred to Scotland 30 May 1945 for Operation *Deadlight*. Sunk 30 Nov 1945
U-334	VIIC	9-Oct-41	1 Jul 1942 – 14 June 1943 from 3. Flottille	8 patrols. 2 ships sunk: total 14,372 GRT	Sunk with all hands 14 Jun 1943 southwest of Iceland by depth charges from the frigate HMS *Jed* and the sloop HMS *Pelican*. 47 dead
U-339	VIIC	25-Aug-42	1 Mar 1943 – 1 Apr 1943 from 8. Flottille	No patrols	to 22. Flottille
U-343	VIIC	26-Mar-43	1 Jun 1944 – 22 Aug 1944 from 3. Flottille	5 patrols. 1 warship sunk: total 1372t/1350 tons	Sunk with all hands 22 Aug 1944 in the Barents Sea northwest of Bear Island by depth charges from a Swordfish aircraft of the escort carrier HMS *Vindex*. 50 dead. Previously credited to the sloops HMS *Mermaid* and HMS *Peacock*, the frigate HMS *Loch Dunvegan* and the destroyer HMS *Keppel* on 24 Aug 1944. That attack actually sank U-354
U-347	VIIC	7-Jul-43	1 Jun 1944 – 17 Jul 1944 from 9. Flottille	4 patrols	Sunk with all hands 17 Jul 1944 west of Narvik by depth charges from a Liberator of No. 86 Sqn RAF. 49 dead. Originally credited to a Catalina that actually sank U-361
U-354	VIIC	22-Apr-42	15 Oct 1942 – 31 May 1943 from 1. Flottille	20 patrols. 1 ship sunk: total 7179 GRT; 1 warship sunk: total 1321t/1300 tons; 1 warship damaged beyond repair: total 11,603t/11,420 tons; 1 ship damaged: total 3771 GRT	to 13. Flottille
U-355	VIIC	29-Oct-41	1 Jul 1942 – 1 Apr 1944 from 5. Flottille	16 patrols. 1 ship sunk: total 5082 GRT	Missing with all hands in the Arctic while shadowing convoy JW 58 on or after 4 Apr 1944. 52 killed. Previously credited to the destroyer HMS *Beagle* and an Avenger from the escort carrier HMS *Tracker*. That attack damaged U-673
U-361	VIIC	18-Dec-42	1 Mar 1944 – 17 Jul 1944 from 8. Flottille	3 patrols	Sunk with all hands 17 Jul 1944 west of Narvik by depth charges from a Catalina of No. 210 Sqn RAF. 52 dead. Originally thought to have been sunk by a Liberator the same day, but that attack actually destroyed U-347
U-363	VIIC	18-Mar-43	1 Jun 1944 – 14 Sep 1944 from 8. Flottille	10 patrols	to 13. Flottille
U-376	VIIC	21-Aug-41	1 Jul 1942 – 28 Feb 1943 from 6. Flottille	8 patrols. 2 ships sunk: total 10,146 GRT	to 3. Flottille
U-377	VIIC	2-Oct-41	1 Jul 1942 – 28 Feb 1943 from 6. Flottille	12 patrols	to 9. Flottille
U-378	VIIC	30-Oct-41	1 Jul 1942 – 30 Apr 1943 from 3. Flottille	11 patrols. 1 warship sunk: total 1951t/1920 tons	to 3. Flottille
U-394	VIIC	7-Aug-43	1 Jun 1944 – 2 Sep 1944 from 1. Flottille	2 patrols	Sunk with all hands 2 Sep 1944 southeast of Jan Mayen island by rockets and depth charges from a Swordfish from the escort carrier HMS *Vindex* and from destroyers HMS *Keppel* and HMS *Whitehall* and sloops HMS *Mermaid* and HMS *Peacock*. 50 dead
U-396	VIIC	16-Oct-43	1 Oct 1944 – 23 Apr 1945 from 1. Flottille	5 patrols	Missing with all hands after the middle of Apr 1945 while returning from a weather-reporting patrol. 45 dead. Previously credited to an RAF Liberator on 23 Apr 1945 southwest of the Shetlands. This was probably against a false target
U-399	VIIC	22-Jan-44	1 Feb 1945 – 26 Mar 1945 from 5. Flottille	1 patrol. 1 ship sunk: total 362 GRT; 1 ship damaged beyond repair: total 7176 GRT	Sunk 26 Mar 1945 near Land's End by depth charges from the frigate HMS *Duckworth*. 46 dead and 1 survivor
U-400	VIIC	18-Mar-44	1 Nov 1944 – 15 Dec 1944 from 5. Flottille	1 patrol	Sunk with all hands on or after 15 Dec 1944, probably by a mine off Cornwall. 50 dead. Previously credited to the frigate HMS *Nyasaland* 17 Dec 1944, but that attack actually sank U-772
U-403	VIIC	25-Jun-41	1 Jul 1942 – 28 Feb 1943 from 7. Flottille	7 patrols. 2 ships sunk: total 12,946 GRT	to 9. Flottille
U-405	VIIC	17-Sep-41	1 Jul 1942 – 28 Feb 1943 from 1. Flottille	11 patrols. 2 ships sunk: total 11,841 GRT	to 6. Flottille

BOATS THAT SERVED WITH 11TH FLOTILLA (189 BOATS)

U-Boat	Type	Commissioned	Flotilla(s)	Patrols	Fate
U-408	VIIC	19-Nov-41	1 Jul 1942 – 5 Nov 1942 from 9. Flottille	3 patrols. 3 ships sunk: total 19,689 GRT	Sunk with all hands 5 Nov 1942 north of Iceland by depth charges from a US Navy PBY Catalina of VP-84. 45 dead
U-419	VIIC	18-Nov-42	1 Aug 1943 – 8 Oct 1943 from 8. Flottille	1 patrol	Sunk 8 Oct 1943 in the North Atlantic by depth charges from a Liberator of No. 86 Sqn RAF. 48 dead and 1 survivor
U-420	VIIC	16-Dec-42	1 Jul 1943 – 20 Oct 1943 from 8. Flottille	2 patrols	Missing with all hands after 20 Oct 1943 in the North Atlantic. 49 dead. Originally credited to a Liberator of No. 10 Sqn RCAF, which depth-charged a U-boat in the Atlantic on 26 Oct 1943, probably U-91, which was undamaged
U-425	VIIC	21-Apr-43	1 Jan 1944 – 14 Sep 1944 from 9. Flottille	8 patrols	to 13. Flottille
U-426	VIIC	12-May-43	1 Oct 1943 – 31 Oct 1943 from 8. Flottille	2 patrols. 1 ship sunk: total 6625 GRT	to 1. Flottille
U-427	VIIC	2-Jun-43	1 Aug 1944 – 4 Nov 1944 from 7. Flottille	5 patrols	to 13. Flottille
U-435	VIIC	30-Aug-41	1 Jul 1942 – 31 Jan 1943 from 1. Flottille	8 patrols. 9 ships sunk: total 53,712 GRT; 1 auxiliary warship sunk: total 2456 GRT; 3 warships sunk: total 869t/855 tons	to 1. Flottille
U-436	VIIC	27-Sep-41	1 Jul 1942 – 31 Aug 1942 from 7. Flottille	8 patrols. 6 ships sunk: total 36,208 GRT; 2 ships damaged: total 15,575 GRT	to 6. Flottille
U-456	VIIC	18-Sep-41	1 Jul 1942 – 30 Nov 1942 from 6. Flottille	11 patrols. 6 ships sunk: total 31,528 GRT; 1 auxiliary warship sunk: total 251 GRT; 1 warship (HMS *Edinburgh*) damaged: total 11,685t/11,500 tons	to 1. Flottille
U-457	VIIC	5-Nov-41	1 Jul 1942 – 16 Sep 1942 from 6. Flottille	3 patrols. 2 ships sunk: total 15,593 GRT; 1 ship damaged: total 8939 GRT	Sunk with all hands 16 Sep 1942 in the Barents Sea northeast of Murmansk by depth charges from the British destroyer HMS *Impulsive*. 45 dead
U-467	VIIC	15-Jul-42	1 Apr 1943 – 25 May 1943 from 5. Flottille	2 patrols	Sunk with all hands 25 May 1943 southeast of Iceland by a Fido homing torpedo from a US Navy PBY Catalina of Patrol Squadron VP 84. 46 dead
U-470	VIIC	7-Jan-43	1 Jul 1943 – 16 Oct 1943 from 5. Flottille	1 patrol	Sunk 16 Oct 1943 southwest of Iceland by depth charges from Liberators of Nos. 59 and 120 Sqns RAF. 46 dead and 2 survivors
U-472	VIIC	26-May-43	1 Jan 1944 – 4 Mar 1944 from 5. Flottille	1 patrol	Sunk 4 Mar 1944 in the Barents Sea southeast of Bear Island by naval gunfire and aerial rockets from the destroyer HMS *Onslaught* and Swordfish aircraft of the escort carrier HMS *Chaser*. 23 dead and 30 survivors
U-480	VIIC	6-Oct-43	15 Oct 1944 – 24 Feb 1945 from 9. Flottille	3 patrols. 2 ships sunk: total 12,846 GRT; 2 warships sunk: total 1803t/1775 tons	Sunk with all hands in the Channel some time in Feb 1945, probably in minefield Brazier D2. 48 dead. Previously credited to frigates HMS *Duckworth* and HMS *Rowley* 24 Feb 1945 southeast of Isles of Scilly. In fact they sank U-1208
U-482	VIIC	1-Dec-43	1 Oct 1944 – 16 Jan 1945 from 11. Flottille	2 patrols. 4 ships sunk: total 31,611 GRT; 1 warship sunk: total 1026t/1010 tons	Probably sunk with all hands 25 Nov 1944 west of the Shetlands by depth charges from frigate HMS *Ascension*. 48 dead. Previously recorded fates include loss to mines northwest of Malin Head around 7 Dec 1944 or to depth charges from sloops HMS *Peacock*, HMS *Starling*, HMS *Hart* and HMS *Amethyst* and frigate HMS *Loch Craggie* in the North Channel 16 Jan 1945
U-483	VIIC	22-Dec-43	5 Sep 1944 – 8 May 1945 from 3. Flottille	2 patrols. 1 warship damaged beyond repair: total 1321t/1300 tons	Surrendered at Trondheim. Transferred to Scotland 29 May 1945 for Operation *Deadlight*. Sunk 16 Dec 1945
U-485	VIIC	23-Feb-44	1 Nov 1944 – 8 May 1945 from 5. Flottille	2 patrols	Surrendered at Gibraltar 8 May 1945. Transferred to Scotland for Operation *Deadlight*. Sunk 8 Dec 1945
U-486	VIIC	22-Mar-44	1 Nov 1944 – 12 Apr 1945 from 5. Flottille	2 patrols. 2 ships sunk: total 17,651 GRT; 1 warship sunk: total 1102t/1085 tons; 1 warship damaged b/r: total 1102t/1085 tons	Sunk with all hands 12 Apr 1945 northwest of Bergen, torpedoed by the submarine HMS *Tapir*. 48 dead
U-586	VIIC	4-Sep-41	1 Jul 1942 – 31 May 1943 from 6. Flottille	12 patrols. 2 ships sunk: total 12,716 GRT; 1 ship damaged: total 9057 GRT	to 13. Flottille
U-589	VIIC	25-Sep-41	1 Jul 1942 – 14 Sep 1942 from 6. Flottille	8 patrols. 1 ship sunk: total 2847 GRT; 1 auxiliary warship sunk: total 417 GRT	Sunk with all hands 14 Sep 1942 in the Arctic Ocean southwest of Spitzbergen by depth charges from destroyer HMS *Onslow*, and from a Swordfish flying from the escort carrier HMS *Avenger*. 48 dead, including 4 *Luftwaffe* airmen the boat had rescued the previous day
U-591	VIIC	9-Oct-41	1 Jul 1942 – 31 May 1943 from 6. Flottille	8 patrols. 4 ships sunk: total 19,932 GRT; 1 ship damaged: total 5701 GRT	to 9. Flottille
U-592	VIIC	16-Oct-41	1 Jul 1942 – 28 Feb 1943 from 6. Flottille	10 patrols. 1 ship sunk: total 3770 GRT	to 6. Flottille
U-601	VIIC	18-Dec-41	1 Jul 1942 – 31 May 1943 from 5. Flottille	10 patrols. 3 ships sunk: total 8819 GRT	to 13. Flottille
U-606	VIIC	22-Jan-42	1 Sep 1942 – 31 Oct 1942 from 5. Flottille	3 patrols. 3 ships sunk: total 20,527 GRT; 2 ships damaged: total 21,925 GRT	to 9. Flottille
U-622	VIIC	14-May-42	2 Oct 1942 – 31 May 1943 from 8. Flottille	4 patrols	to 13. Flottille
U-625	VIIC	4-Jun-42	1 Nov 1942 – 31 May 1943 from 3. Flottille	9 patrols. 3 ships sunk: total 18,751 GRT; 2 auxiliary warships sunk: total 939 GRT	to 13. Flottille
U-629	VIIC	2-Jul-42	1 Dec 1942 – 31 Oct 1943 from 5. Flottille	11 patrols	to 1. Flottille
U-636	VIIC	20-Aug-42	1 Apr 1943 – 31 Oct 1943 from 5. Flottille	14 patrols. 1 ship sunk: total 7169 GRT	to 13. Flottille

U-Boat	Type	Commissioned	Flotilla(s)	Patrols	Fate
BOATS THAT SERVED WITH 11TH FLOTILLA (189 BOATS)

BOATS THAT SERVED WITH 11TH FLOTILLA (189 BOATS)

U-Boat	Type	Commissioned	Flotilla(s)	Patrols	Fate
U-639	VIIC	10-Sep-42	1 Apr 1943 – 31 May 1943 from 5. Flottille	4 patrols	to 13. Flottille
U-644	VIIC	15-Oct-42	1 Apr 1943 – 7 Apr 1943 from 5. Flottille	1 patrol	Sunk with all hands 7 Apr 1943 northwest of Narvik, Norway, torpedoed by HM Submarine *Tuna*. 45 dead
U-646	VIIC	29-Oct-42	1 Apr 1943 – 17 May 1943 from 5. Flottille	2 patrols	Sunk with all hands 17 May 1943 southeast of Iceland by depth charges from a Hudson of No. 269 Sqn RAF. 46 dead
U-650	VIIC	26-Nov-42	1 Oct 1944 – 9 Dec 1944 from 7. Flottille	7 patrols	Missing with all hands in the North Atlantic or the Arctic Ocean on or after 9 Dec 1944. 47 dead
U-657	VIIC	8-Oct-41	1 Jul 1942 – 17 May 1943 from 3. Flottille	7 patrols. 1 ship sunk: total 5196 GRT	Sunk with all hands 17 May 1943 east of Cape Farewell by depth charges from the frigate HMS *Swale*. 47 dead. Previously credited to a torpedo from US Navy PBY Catalina of VP-82 on 14 May, which probably did attack U-657 but is unlikely to have damaged the boat
U-663	VIIC	14-May-42	1 Oct 1942 – 31 Oct 1942 from 5. Flottille	3 patrols; 2 ships sunk: total 10,924 GRT	to 9. Flottille
U-674	VIIC	15-Jun-43	1 Feb 1944 – 2 May 1944 from 5. Flottille	3 patrols	Sunk with all hands 2 May 1944 northwest of Narvik by rockets from a Swordfish of the escort carrier HMS *Fencer*. 49 dead
U-680	VIIC	23-Dec-43	1 Oct 1944 – 8 May 1945 from 6. Flottille	4 patrols	Surrendered at Wilhelmshaven 8 May 1945. Transferred to Scotland for Operation *Deadlight*. Sunk as a gunfire target 28 Dec 1945
U-681	VIIC	3-Feb-44	1 Nov 1944 – 10 Mar 1945 from 31. Flottille	1 patrol	Struck a rock 10 Mar 1945 while submerged near the Isles of Scilly; forced to surface near the Bishop Rock and spotted by a US Navy PB4Y Liberator of VPB-103. Sunk by depth charges. 11 dead and 38 survivors
U-682	VIIC	17-Apr-44	1 Dec 1944 – 1 Feb 1945 from 31. Flottille	No patrols	to 31. Flottille
U-683	VIIC	30-May-44	1 Jan 1945 – 20 Feb 1945 from 31. Flottille	1 patrol	Missing with all hands on or after 20 Feb 1945 southwest of Ireland or in the English Channel. 49 dead. Previously thought to have been sunk 12 Mar 1945 near Land's End by depth charges from the frigate HMS *Loch Ruthven* and the sloop HMS *Wild Goose*; those attacks probably targeted the wreck of U-247
U-703	VIIC	16-Oct-41	1 Jul 1942 – 31 May 1943 from 6. Flottille	13 patrols. 5 ships sunk: total 29,523 GRT; 1 auxiliary warship sunk: total 559 GRT; 1 warship sunk: total 1900t/1870 tons	to 13. Flottille
U-711	VIIC	26-Sep-42	1 Apr 1943 – 31 May 1943 from 5. Flottille	12 patrols. 1 ship sunk: total 7176 GRT; 1 warship sunk: total 940t/925 tons; 1 ship damaged: total 20 GRT	to 13. Flottille
U-713	VIIC	29-Dec-42	1 Jul 1943 – 31 Oct 1943 from 8. Flottille	5 patrols	to 13. Flottille
U-716	VIIC	15-Apr-43	1 Jan 1944 – 30 Sep 1944 from 5. Flottille	10 patrols. 1 ship sunk: total 7200 GRT	to 13. Flottille
U-722	VIIC	15-Dec-43	1 Oct 1944 – 27 Mar 1945 from 1. Flottille	3 patrols. 1 ship sunk: total 2190 GRT	Sunk with all hands 27 Mar 1945 in the North Atlantic off the Hebrides by depth charges from the frigates HMS *Fitzroy*, HMS *Redmill* and HMS *Byron*. 44 dead
U-735	VIIC	28-Dec-42	1 Aug 1944 – 28 Dec 1944 from 8. Flottille	No patrols	Sunk on 28 Dec 1944 in Oslo Fjord near Horten by British bombs. 39 dead and 1 survivor
U-764	VIIC	6-May-43	1 Oct 1944 – 8 May 1945 from 9. Flottille	8 patrols. 1 ship sunk: total 638 GRT; 2 warships sunk: total 1723t/1696 tons	Surrendered 14 May 1945 at Lisahally, Northern Ireland. Sunk 2 Feb 1946 in Operation *Deadlight*
U-771	VIIC	18-Nov-43	1 Aug 1944 – 30 Sep 1944 from 9. Flottille	2 patrols	to 13. Flottille
U-772	VIIC	23-Dec-43	15 Oct 1944 – 30 Dec 1944 from 9. Flottille	2 patrols	Sunk with all hands 17 Dec 1944 south of Cork by depth charges from frigate HMS *Nyasaland*. 48 dead. Previously credited to a Canadian Wellington south of Weymouth 30 Dec 1944, which was probably an ineffective attack against U-486
U-773	VIIC	20-Jan-44	1 Oct 1944 – 8 May 1945 from 1. Flottille	3 patrols	Surrendered at Trondheim 8 May 1945. Transferred to Scotland for Operation *Deadlight*. Sunk 8 Dec 1945.
U-774	VIIC	17-Feb-44	1 Feb 1945 – 8 Apr 1945 from 31. Flottille	1 patrol	Sunk with all hands 8 Apr 1945 southwest of Ireland by depth charges from the frigates HMS *Calder* and HMS *Bentinck*. 44 dead
U-775	VIIC	23-Mar-44	1 Nov 1944 – 8 May 1945 from 31. Flottille	2 patrols. 1 ship sunk: total 1926 GRT; 1 warship sunk: total 1321t/1300 tons; 1 ship damaged: total 6991 GRT	Surrendered at Trondheim, Norway, on 8 May 1945. Transferred to Scotland for Operation *Deadlight*. Sunk by gunfire 8 Dec 1945
U-778	VIIC	7-Jul-44	1 Mar 1945 – 8 May 1945 from 31. Flottille	1 patrol	Surrendered at Bergen 8 May 1945. Transferred to Scotland for Operation *Deadlight*. Foundered while on tow 4 Dec 1945 northeast of Inishtrahull
U-825	VIIC	4-May-44	1 Dec 1944 – 8 May 1945 from 8. Flottille	2 patrols. 1 ship damaged beyond repair: total 8262 GRT; 1 ship damaged: total 7198 GRT	Surrendered at Portland 10 May 1945. Transferred to Northern Ireland for Operation *Deadlight*. Sunk 3 Jan 1946
U-826	VIIC	11-May-44	1 Jan 1945 – 8 May 1945 from 8. Flottille	1 patrol	Surrendered at Loch Eriboll, Scotland, 11 May 1945. Sunk 1 Dec 1945 in Operation *Deadlight*
U-827	VIIC/41	25-May-44	1 Mar 1945 – 5 May 1945 from 8. Flottille	No patrols	Scuttled 5 May 1945 in Flensburg Fjord
U-867	IXC/40	12-Dec-43	1 Sep 1944 – 19 Sep 1944	1 patrol	Sunk with all hands 19 Sep 1944 northwest of Bergen by depth charges from a Liberator of No. 224 Sqn RAF. 60 dead
U-901	VIIC	29-Apr-44	15 Mar 1945 – 8 May 1945	1 patrol	Surrendered at Stavanger. Transferred to Northern Ireland 29 May 1945 for Operation *Deadlight*. Sunk 5 Jan 1946

U-Boat	Type	Commissioned	Flotilla(s)	Patrols	Fate
BOATS THAT SERVED WITH 11TH FLOTILLA (189 BOATS)					
U-905	VIIC	8-Mar-44	1 Dec 1944 – 27 Mar 1945 from 31. Flottille	2 patrols	Sunk with all hands 27 Mar 1945 between the Hebrides and the Scottish mainland by depth charges from the frigate HMS *Conn*. 45 dead. Previously credited to a 120 Sqn Liberator 20 Mar 1945 southeast of Faroes, but this was probably a false target
U-907	VIIC	18-May-44	1 Dec 1944 – 8 May 1945 from 31. Flottille	2 patrols	Surrendered at Bergen. Transferred Scotland 29 May 1945 for Operation *Deadlight*. Sunk 7 Dec 1945
U-926	VIIC	29-Feb-44	15 Mar 1945 – 8 May 1945 from 4. Flottille	No patrols	Surrendered at Bergen, Norway, 8 May 1945. Taken into Norwegian service as HNMS *Kya*. Stricken 1962. One of only 3 U-boats left at Bergen after more than 30 boats were transferred to Scotland in late May and early Jun 1945
U-927	VIIC	27-Jun-44	1 Feb 1945 – 24 Feb 1945 from 4. Flottille	1 patrol	Sunk with all hands 24 Feb 1945 in the Channel southeast of Falmouth by depth charges from a Vickers Warwick of No. 179 Sqn RAF. 47 dead
U-956	VIIC	6-Jan-43	1 Jan 1944 – 30 Sep 1944 from 1. Flottille	13 patrols. 1 warship sunk: total 1209t/1190 tons; 1 ship damaged beyond repair: total 7176 GRT	to 13. Flottille
U-957	VIIC	7-Jan-43	1 Jan 1944 – 30 Sep 1944 from 3. Flottille	6 patrols. 2 ships sunk: total 7353 GRT; 2 warships sunk: total 614t/604 tons	to 13. Flottille
U-963	VIIC	17-Feb-43	1 Nov 1944 – 8 May 1945 from 1. Flottille	10 patrols	Scuttled 20 May 1945 on the Portuguese west coast. The crew was interned. 48 survivors
U-965	VIIC	25-Feb-43	1 Jan 1944 – 30 Sep 1944 from 5. Flottille	7 patrols	to 13. Flottille
U-978	VIIC	12-May-43	5 Sep 1944 – 8 May 1945 from 3. Flottille	2 patrols. 1 ship damaged beyond repair: total 7176 GRT. U-978 carried out the longest *Schnorchel* patrol of the war, 68 days submerged from Bergen, Norway, beginning 9 Oct 1944, returning 16 Dec	Transferred from Trondheim to Scotland 29 May 1945 for Operation *Deadlight*. Sunk 11 Dec 1945
U-979	VIIC	20-May-43	Oct 1944 – 24 May 1945 from 9. Flottille	3 patrols. 1 auxiliary warship sunk: total 348 GRT; 2 ships damaged: total 12,133 GRT	Scuttled 24 May 1945 at Amrum, Germany, after running aground
U-987	VIIC	8-Jul-43	1 Jun 1944 – 15 Jun 1944 from 1. Flottille	1 patrol	Sunk with all hands 15 Jun 1944 west of Narvik, torpedoed by the British submarine HMS *Satyr*. 53 dead
U-990	VIIC	28-Jul-43	1 Jan 1944 – 25 May 1944 from 5. Flottille	4 patrols. 1 warship sunk: total 1951t/1920 tons	Sunk 25 May 1944 west of Bodö by depth charges from a Liberator of No. 59 Sqn. 22 dead (including 2 rescued from U-476) and 51 survivors (including 18 from U-476)
U-991	VIIC	29-Jul-43	1 Sep 1944 – 8 May 1945 from 5. Flottille	1 patrol	Transferred from Bergen to Scotland 29 May 1945 for Operation *Deadlight*. Sunk 11 Dec 1945
U-992	VIIC	2-Aug-43	1 Jun 1944 – 30 Sep 1944 from 3. Flottille	8 patrols; 1 warship damaged beyond repair: total 1077t/1060 tons	to 13. Flottille
U-994	VIIC	2-Sep-43	1 Aug 1944 – 4 Nov 1944 from 5. Flottille	1 patrol	to 13. Flottille
U-1002	VIIC/41	30-Nov-43	1 Mar 1945 – 8 May 1945 from 31. Flottille	1 patrol	Transferred from Bergen to Scotland 30 May 1945 for Operation *Deadlight*. Sunk 13 Dec 1945
U-1003	VIIC/41	9-Dec-43	1 Sep 1944 – 23 Mar 1945 from 31. Flottille	2 patrols	Scuttled 23 Mar 1945 in the North Channel about 16km (10 miles) north of Malin Head after being rammed by the Canadian frigate HMCS *New Glasgow* 20 Mar 1945. 17 dead and 31 survivors
U-1004	VIIC/41	16-Dec-43	1 Nov 1944 – 8 May 1945 from 7. Flottille	2 patrols. 1 ship sunk: total 1313 GRT; 1 warship sunk: total 996t/980 tons	Transferred from Bergen to Scotland 30 May 1945 for Operation *Deadlight*. Sunk by gunfire 1 Dec 1945
U-1005	VIIC/41	30-Dec-43	1 Feb 1945 – 8 May 1945 from 31. Flottille	2 patrols	Transferred from Bergen to Scotland 30 May 1945 for Operation *Deadlight*. Foundered while under tow to the scuttling grounds 5 Dec 1945
U-1006	VIIC/41	11-Jan-44	1 Sep 1944 – 16 Oct 1944 from 11. Flottilla	1 patrol	Sunk 16 Oct 1944 southeast of Faroes by depth charges from the frigate HMCS *Annan*. 6 dead and 44 survivors
U-1009	VIIC/41	10-Feb-44	1 Nov 1944 – 8 May 1945 from 31. Flottille	2 patrols	Surrendered 10 May 1945 at Loch Eriboll, Scotland. Sunk by naval gunfire in Operation *Deadlight* 16 Dec 1945
U-1010	VIIC/41	22-Feb-44	1 Apr 1945 – 8 May 1945	1 patrol	Surrendered 14 May 1945 at Loch Eriboll, Scotland. Sunk by gunfire in Operation *Deadlight* 7 Jan 1946
U-1014	VIIC/41	14-Mar-44	1 Jan 1945 – 4 Feb 1945 from 31. Flottille	1 patrol	Sunk with all hands 4 Feb 1945 in the Hebrides by depth charges from frigates HMS *Loch Scavaig*, HMS *Nyasaland*, HMS *Papua* and HMS *Loch Shin*. 48 dead
U-1017	VIIC/41	13-Apr-44	1 Nov 1944 – 29 Apr 1945 from 31. Flottille	2 patrols. 2 ships sunk: total 10,604 GRT	Possibly sunk 29 Apr 1945 northwest of Ireland by depth charges from a Liberator of No. 120 Sqn RAF. 34 dead. It might have been U-398: both boats disappeared at about the same time
U-1018	VIIC/41	24-Apr-44	1 Dec 1944 – 27 Feb 1945 from 31. Flottille	1 patrol. 1 ship sunk: total 1317 GRT	Sunk 27 Feb 1945 south of Penzance by depth charges from the frigate HMS *Loch Fada*. 51 dead and 2 survivors
U-1019	VIIC/41	4-May-44	1 Dec 1944 – 8 May 1945 from 31. Flottille	1 patrol	Transferred from Trondheim to Scotland 29 May 1945 for Operation *Deadlight*. Sunk by gunfire 7 Dec 1945
U-1020	VIIC/41	17-May-44	1 Dec 1944 – Jan 1945? from 31. Flottille	1 patrol	Missing with all hands in the North Sea after leaving Horten 22 Nov 1944. 52 dead
U-1021	VIIC/41	25-May-44	1 Dec 1944 – 30 Mar 1945 from 31. Flottille	1 patrol	Missing with all hands south of the Bristol Channel on or after 14 Mar 1945. 43 dead. Probably sunk in British-laid minefield A1 or ZME 25
U-1022	VIIC/41	7-Jun-44	1 Feb 1945 – 8 May 1945 from 31. Flottille	1 patrol. 1 ship sunk: total 1392 GRT; 1 auxiliary warship sunk: total 328 GRT	Transferred from Bergen to Scotland 30 May 1945 for Operation *Deadlight*. Sunk 29 Dec 1945
U-1023	VIIC/41	15-Jun-44	1 Mar 1945 – 8 May 1945 from 31. Flottille	1 patrol. 1 warship sunk: total 340t/335 tons; 1 ship damaged: total 7345 GRT	Surrendered 10 May 1945 at Weymouth. Sunk in Operation *Deadlight* 7 Jan 1946

BOATS THAT SERVED WITH 11TH FLOTILLA (189 BOATS)

U-Boat	Type	Commissioned	Flotilla(s)	Patrols	Fate
U-1024	VIIC/41	28-Jun-44	1 Feb 1945 – 12 Apr 1945 from 31. Flottille	1 patrol. 1 ship damaged beyond repair: total 7176 GRT; 1 ship damaged: total 7200 GRT	Captured 12 Apr 1945 in the Irish Sea south of Isle of Man by the frigates HMS *Loch Glendhu* and HMS *Loch More*. Foundered while on tow 13 Apr 1945. 9 dead and 37 survivors
U-1051	VIIC	4-Mar-44	1 Jan 1945 – 26 Jan 1945 from 5. Flottille	1 patrol. 1 ship sunk: total 1152 GRT; 1 warship a total loss: total 1321t/1300 tons	Sunk with all hands 26 Jan 1945 south of Isle of Man, by ramming and depth charges from frigates HMS *Aylmer*, HMS *Calder*, HMS *Bentinck* and HMS *Manners*. 47 dead. Previously credited to the frigates HMS *Tyler*, HMS *Keats* and HMS *Bligh* in St George's Channel 27 Jan 1945 but they actually sank U-1172
U-1053	VIIC	12-Feb-44	1 Nov 1944 – 15 Feb 1945 from 5. Flottille	2 patrols	Sank with all hands plus some dockyard personnel in a diving accident 15 Feb 1945 near Bergen. 45 dead
U-1055	VIIC	8-Apr-44	1 Dec 1944 – 23 Apr 1945 from 5. Flottille	2 patrols. 4 ships sunk: total 19,413 GRT	Missing with all hands on or after 23 Apr 1945 in Atlantic or Channel. 49 dead. Originally credited to a US Navy PBY off Brest, but the boat destroyed was probably U-1107
U-1058	VIIC	10-Jun-44	1 Jan 1945 – 8 May 1945 from 5. Flottille	2 patrols	Surrendered at Lough Eribol, Northern Ireland 10 May 1945. Awarded to the USSR and became Soviet submarine S-82 in Nov 1945
U-1063	VIIC/41	8-Jul-44	1 Mar 1945 – 15 Apr 1945 from 5. Flottille	1 patrol	Sunk 15 Apr 1945 west of Land's End by depth charges from the frigate HMS *Loch Killin*. 29 dead and 17 survivors
U-1064	VIIC/41	29-Jul-44	1 Feb 1945 – 8 May 1945 from 5. Flottille	1 patrol. 1 ship sunk: total 1564 GRT	Transferred from Trondheim to Loch Ryan 29 May 1945. Awarded to the USSR and became Soviet submarine S-83 in Nov 1945
U-1104	VIIC/41	15-Mar-44	1 Feb 1945 – 8 May 1945 from 8. Flottille	1 patrol	Transferred from Bergen to Scotland 30 May 1945 for Operation *Deadlight*. Sunk by gunfire 1 Dec 1945
U-1107	VIIC/41	8-Aug-44	16 Feb 1945 – 30 Apr 1945 from 8. Flottille	1 patrol. 2 ships sunk: total 15,209 GRT	Sunk 30 Apr 1945 west of Brest by retro bombs from a US Navy PBY of VP-63. 37 dead and 10+ survivors. Previously credited to a US Navy Liberator, which actually sank U-326
U-1109	VIIC/41	31-Aug-44	16 Feb 1945 – 8 May 1945 from 8. Flottille	2 patrols	Transferred from Norway to Northern Ireland 31 May 1945 for Operation *Deadlight*. Sunk 6 Jan 1946 by submarine torpedoes
U-1163	VIIC/41	6-Oct-43	1 Aug 1944 – 30 Sep 1944 from 8. Flottille	4 patrols. 1 ship sunk: total 433 GRT	to 13. Flottille
U-1165	VIIC/41	17-Nov-43	1 Aug 1944 – 8 May 1945 from 9. Flottille	4 patrols; 1 warship sunk: total 40t/39 tons	Transferred from Narvik to Scotland 19 May 1945 for Operation *Deadlight*. Sunk 30 Dec 1945
U-1169	VIIC/41	9-Feb-44	1 Feb 1945 – 29 Mar 1945 from 8. Flottille	1 patrol	Sunk with all hands 29 Mar 1945 in the English Channel south of Lizard Point, by depth charges from the frigate HMS *Duckworth*. 49 dead. Previously thought to have hit a mine 5 Apr, but the boat sunk was U-242
U-1171	VIIC/41	22-Mar-44	1 Mar 1945 – 8 May 1945 from 8. Flottille	No patrols	Transferred from Stavanger to Scotland 29 May 1945. Used by the Royal Navy as submarine N 19. Broken up in 1949
U-1172	VIIC/41	20-Apr-44	1 Dec 1944 – 27 Jan 1945 from 8. Flottille	1 patrol. 1 ship sunk: total 1599 GRT; 1 ship damaged: total 7429 GRT; 1 warship (escort carrier *HMS Thane*) damaged: total 11,583t/11,400 tons	Sunk with all hands 27 Jan 1945 in St George's Channel by depth charges from frigates HMS *Tyler*, HMS *Keats* and HMS *Bligh*. 52 dead. Previously credited to frigates HMS *Aylmer*, HMS *Calder*, HMS *Bentinck* and HMS *Manners*, which actually sank U-1051
U-1195	VIIC	4-Nov-43	1 Jan 1945 – 7 Apr 1945 from 5. Flottille	1 patrol. 2 ships sunk: total 18,614 GRT	Sunk 7 Apr 1945 in the English Channel by depth charges from the destroyer HMS *Watchman*. 32 dead and 18 survivors
U-1199	VIIC	23-Dec-43	10 Nov 1944 – 21 Jan 1945 from 1. Flottille	2 patrols. 1 ship damaged beyond repair: total 7176 GRT	Sunk 21 Jan 1945 near the Scilly Isles by depth charges from the destroyer HMS *Icarus* and the corvette HMS *Mignonette*. 48 dead and 1 survivor
U-1200	VIIC	5-Jan-44	1 Sep 1944 – 11 Nov 1944 from 8. Flottille	1 patrol	Sunk with all hands 11 Nov 1944 south of Ireland by depth charges from corvettes HMS *Pevensey Castle*, HMS *Lancaster Castle*, HMS *Porchester Castle* and HMS *Kenilworth Castle*. 53 dead
U-1202	VIIC	27-Jan-44	1 Sep 1944 – 8 May 1945 from 8. Flottille	2 patrols. 1 ship sunk: total 7176 GRT	Stricken at Bergen 10 May 1945. Surrendered to Britain. Transferred to Norway in Oct 1948. Became the Norwegian submarine *KNM Kinn* 1 Jul 1951. Stricken 1 June 1961. Broken up at Hamburg in 1963
U-1203	VIIC	10-Feb-44	1 Dec 1944 – 8 May 1945 from 8. Flottille	1 patrol. 1 auxiliary warship sunk: total 580 GRT	Transferred from Trondheim to Scotland 29 May 1945 for Operation *Deadlight*. Sunk 8 Dec 1945
U-1206	VIIC	16-Mar-44	1 Feb 1945 – 14 Apr 1945 from 8. Flottille	1 patrol	Sank in a diving accident 14 Apr 1945 off Peterhead, Scotland. 4 dead and 46 survivors
U-1208	VIIC	6-Apr-44	1 Jan 1945 – 27 Feb 1945 from 8. Flottille	1 patrol. 1 ship sunk: total 1644 GRT	Sunk with all hands 27 Feb 1945 southeast of Isles of Scilly by depth charges from frigates *HMS Duckworth* and HMS *Rowley*. 49 dead. Sinking previously credited to sloop HMS *Amethyst* south of Ireland, but that attack destroyed U-1276
U-1209	VIIC	13-Apr-44	1 Nov 1944 – 18 Dec 1944 from 8. Flottille	1 patrol	Ran into Wolf Rock near the Scilly Isles and was scuttled 18 Dec 1944. 9 dead and 44 survivors
U-1231	IXC/40	9-Feb-44	1 Sep 1944 – 30 Sep 1944 from 31. Flottille	2 patrols	to 33. Flottille
U-1272	VIIC/41	28-Jan-44	1 Mar 1945 – 8 May 1945 from 8. Flottille	1 patrol	Transferred from Bergen to Scotland 30 May 1945 for Operation *Deadlight*. Sunk 8 Dec 1945

BOATS THAT SERVED WITH 11TH FLOTILLA (189 BOATS)

U-Boat	Type	Commissioned	Flotilla(s)	Patrols	Fate
U-1273	VIIC/41	16-Feb-44	1 Feb 1945 – 17 Feb 1945 from 8. Flottille	Training	Sunk 17 Feb 1945 by a mine in Oslofjord near Horten. 43 dead and 8 survivors
U-1276	VIIC/41	6-Apr-44	1 Nov 1944 – 20 Feb 1945 from 8. Flottille	1 patrol. 1 warship sunk: total 940t/925 tons	Sunk with all hands 20 Feb 1945 south of Waterford, Ireland, by depth charges from the sloop HMS *Amethyst*. 49 dead
U-1277	VIIC/41	3-May-44	1 Feb 1945 – 8 May 1945 from 8. Flottille	1 patrol	Scuttled 3 Jun 1945 off Capo de Mundo near Oporto, Portugal. No casualties – 47 survivors. Crew paddled ashore in rubber dinghies and were interned before being handed over to the British. Eventually released from POW camp in 1948
U-1278	VIIC/41	31-May-44	1 Dec 1944 – 17 Feb 1945 from 8. Flottille	1 patrol	Sunk with all hands 17 Feb 1945 northwest of Bergen by depth charges from the frigates HMS *Bayntun* and HMS *Loch Eck*. 48 dead
U-1279	VIIC/41	5-Jul-44	1 Feb 1945 – 3 Feb 1945 from 8. Flottille	1 patrol	Sunk with all hands 3 Feb 1945 northwest of Bergen by depth charges from the frigates HMS *Bayntun*, HMS *Braithwaite* and HMS *Loch Eck*. 48 dead
U-1302	VIIC/41	25-May-44	1 Jan 1945 – 7 Mar 1945 from 4. Flottille	1 patrol. 3 ships sunk: total 8386 GRT	Sunk with all hands 7 Mar 1945 in St George's Channel by depth charges from the frigates *HMCS La Hulloise*, HMCS *Strathadam* and HMCS *Thetford Mines*. 48 dead
U-2321	XXIII	12-Jun-44	1 Feb 1945 – 8 May 1945 from 32. Flottille	1 patrol. 1 ship sunk: total 1406 GRT	Surrendered at Kristiansand Süd, Norway. Taken to Loch Ryan 29 May 1945 for Operation *Deadlight*. Sunk 27 Nov 1945 by naval gunfire
U-2322	XXIII	1-Jul-44	1 Feb 1945 – 8 May 1945 from 32. Flottille	2 patrols. 1 ship sunk: total 1317 GRT	Surrendered at Stavanger, Norway. Taken to Loch Ryan 31 May 1945 for Operation *Deadlight*. Sunk 27 Nov 1945 by naval gunfire
U-2324	XXIII	25-Jul-44	1 Feb 1945 – 8 May 1945 from 32. Flottille	2 patrols	Surrendered at Stavanger, Norway. Taken to Loch Ryan 29 May 1945 for Operation *Deadlight*. Sunk 27 Nov 1945 by naval gunfire
U-2325	XXIII	3-Aug-44	1 Feb 1945 – 8 May 1945 from 32. Flottille	No patrols	Surrendered at Kristiansand Süd, Norway. Taken to Loch Ryan 29 May 1945 for Operation *Deadlight*. Sunk 28 Nov by naval gunfire
U-2326	XXIII	10-Aug-44	1 Feb 1945 – 8 May 1945 from 32. Flottille	2 patrols	Surrendered at Dundee, Scotland, 14 May 1945. Became the British submarine N 35. Transferred to France in 1946. Sank 6 Dec 1946 at Toulon in an accident. Raised and broken up
U-2328	XXIII	25-Aug-44	1 Apr 1945 – 8 May 1945 from 32. Flottille	No patrols	Surrendered at Bergen, Norway. Taken to Loch Ryan 30 May 1945 for Operation *Deadlight*. Took on water and sank while on tow to scuttling grounds 27 Nov 1945
U-2329	XXIII	1-Sep-44	15 Mar 1945 – 8 May 1945 from 32. Flottille	1 patrol	Surrendered at Stavanger, Norway. Taken to Loch Ryan in Jun 1945 for Operation *Deadlight*. Sunk 28 Nov 1945 by naval gunfire
U-2330	XXIII	7-Sep-44	16 Mar 1945 – 3 May 1945 from 32. Flottille	No patrols	Scuttled 3 May 1945 at Kiel
U-2334	XXIII	21-Sep-44	1 Apr 1945 – 8 May 1945 from 32. Flottille	No patrols	Surrendered at Kristiansand Süd, Norway. Taken to Loch Ryan 29 May 1945 for Operation *Deadlight*. Sunk 28 Nov 1945 by naval gunfire
U-2335	XXIII	27-Sep-44	1 Apr 1945 – 8 May 1945 from 32. Flottille	No patrols	Surrendered at Kristiansand Süd, Norway. Taken to Loch Ryan 29 May 1945 for Operation *Deadlight*. Sunk 28 Nov 1945 by naval gunfire
U-2502	XXI	19-Jul-44	1 Mar 1945 – 8 May 1945 from 31. Flottille	No patrols	Surrendered with 11th Flotilla. Taken from Oslo 3 Jun to N Ireland for Operation *Deadlight*. Sunk 2 Jan 1946
U-2503	XXI	1-Aug-44	1 Apr 1945 – 4 May 1945 from 31. Flottille	No patrols	Damaged en route from Kiel to Norway by rockets from Mosquitoes of Nos. 236 and 254 Sqns RAF. Beached on Danish coast and scuttled 4 May 1945. 13 dead
U-2506	XXI	31-Aug-44	1 Apr 1945 – 8 May 1945 from 31. Flottille	No patrols	Transferred from Bergen to Lisahally, Northern Ireland for Operation *Deadlight*. Sunk 5 Jan 1946
U-2511	XXI	29-Sep-44	15 Mar 1945 – 8 May 1945 from 31. Flottille	1 patrol. First operational mission by a Type XXI boat	Surrendered at Bergen May 1945. Transferred to Northern Ireland 14 Jun 1945 for Operation *Deadlight*. Sunk 7 Jan 1946 by naval gunfire.
U-2513	XXI	12-Oct-44	1 Apr 1945 – 8 May 1945 from 31. Flottille	No patrols	Surrendered at Horten 8 May 1945 and moved to Northern Ireland. Transferred to United States in Aug 1945 and used for trials. Sunk 7 Oct 1951 west of Key West, Florida, in rocket tests
U-3008	XXI	19-Oct-44	1 Apr 1945 – 8 May 1945 from 4. Flottille	Preparing for first patrol in last days of war	Transferred from Wilhelmshaven to Loch Ryan 21 Jun 1945. Transferred to United States for trials Aug 1945. Sunk after demolition tests in May 1954. Broken up at Puerto Rico

12 Unterseebootsflottille

Long-range U-boats had originally been assigned to the 2nd Flotilla, but as that unit became more involved in the main battle in the Atlantic, new Type IXs and supply boats were assigned to the 10th Flotilla before many transferred to the 12th Flotilla.

THE 12TH FLOTILLA WAS FOUNDED on 15 October 1942 under the command of *Korvettenkapitän* Klaus Scholtz. It was assigned to the U-boat base at Bordeaux, originally home to the Italian flotilla that had been participating (not very successfully) in the Battle of the Atlantic.

The first German U-boat to arrive at its new base in Bordeaux was U-178, which made port on 9 January 1943. Most of the long-range boats from the 10th Flotilla, which had been operating in the South Atlantic and the Indian Ocean, were transferred and the 12th Flotilla also took over the remaining large Italian submarines in the base after the Italian armistice in 1943. The base also saw a number of large Japanese boats arrive from the Far East, bringing diplomatic and military personnel.

During August 1944, most of the boats still in European waters left the base for Flensburg. The last two boats to leave Bordeaux were U-534 and U-857, which sailed on 25 August 1944.

The flotilla was disbanded in August 1944. Those members of the unit unable to hitch a ride on the boats attempted to make their way back to Germany overland under Fregkpt. Scholtz, but on 11 September 1944 were captured by US troops.

12TH FLOTILLA (1942–44)	
Type	Boats assigned
Type VIIF	3
Type IXD	24
Type XB	6
Type XIV	9
Type UIT	5

▲ **'Milch cow' under attack**
A Type XB boat on a resupply operation off the Cape Verde Islands in the summer of 1943 is attacked by Avengers and Wildcats of a US Navy escort carrier.

Commander
Fregkpt. Klaus Scholtz *(Oct 1942 – Aug 1944)*

12TH FLOTILLA INSIGNIA

The insignia of a wolf's head over a U-boat silhouette was mounted over a globe showing Eurasia, all within a black 'U' for U-boat. Few 12th Flotilla boats actually carried the unit insignia.

12TH FLOTILLA BASE LOCATION

ATLANTIC OCEAN

Bordeaux

Star commanders
1942–44

By the time the 12th Flotilla was established, the time for running up massive scores in distant waters had gone, as Allied intelligence and countermeasures made the U-boat task harder.

Kapitän zur See Werner Hartmann

Werner Hartmann was born on 11 December 1902 in the Harz Mountains. He joined the *Reichsmarine* not long after World War I with Crew 21. After command experience aboard light destroyers, he transferred to the U-boat arm in 1935. In U-26, he operated in Spanish waters during the Civil War.

On the outbreak of war, Hartmann was commander of U-37 of the 2nd U-boat Flotilla. In October 1939 he led the first attempt to direct a wolfpack from U-37, but Admiral Dönitz found that control from a land base was more effective. Hartmann then served in staff positions and training commands before going back to sea.

In November 1942, he took over U-198, one of the large Type IXD2 boats, and completed the third longest patrol of the war. Leaving Kiel in March 1943, U-198 operated off the eastern coast of South Africa, returning to Bordeaux on 24 September after 201 days at sea. In 1944, he became U-boat commander in the Mediterranean.

In his operational career of four patrols, Hartmann sank 26 ships for a total of 115,338 GRT. He joined the *Bundesmarine* when it was formed in the 1950s. He died on 26 April 1963.

Korvettenkapitän Eitel-Friedrich Kentrat

Born on 11 September 1906 in Stahlheim, Kentrat joined the *Reichsmarine* with Crew 28. Although not one of the highest-scoring commanders – only seven ships sunk for a total of 42,433 GRT in nine patrols – he became famous while commanding U-196 for carrying out the longest submarine combat patrol of the war.

U-196 left Kiel on 13 March 1943 and reached Bordeaux on 23 October 1943, after 225 days at sea, during which Kentrat took the boat into the Indian Ocean. The next patrol was also long, lasting more than five months.

Kentrat left U-196 in Penang in August 1944 to take command of the German naval detachment at Kobe in Japan, and also spent time with the Naval Attache in Tokyo. He returned to Germany, after more than two years in Allied captivity, in October 1947. He died on 9 January 1974, at Bad Schwartau.

STAR COMMANDERS		
Commander	Patrols	Ships Sunk
Kapitän zur See Werner Hartmann	4	26
Korvkptn Eitel-Friedrich Kentrat	9	7

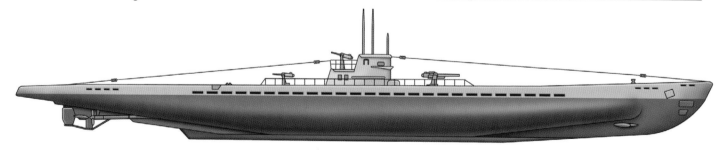

▲ **U-196**

Type IXD2

The original Type IXD was a very long-range submarine transport, but production quickly changed to the armed Type IXD2. U-196 was one of these boats, and completed the longest submarine patrol of World War II.

Specifications

Crew: 57

Powerplant: Diesel/electric

Max Speed: 35.6/12.8km/hr (19.2/6.9kt) surf/sub

Surface Range: 43,900km (23,700nm)

Displacement: 1616/1803t (1590/1775 tons) surf/sub

Dimensions (length/beam/draught): 87.6 x 7.5 x 5.4m (287.42 x 24.58 x 17.75ft)

Commissioned: 11 Sep 1942

Armament: 22 torpedoes (4 bow/2 stern tubes); 1 x 10.5cm (4.1in), 1 x 3.7cm (1.5in) and 1 x 2cm (0.8in) guns

U-118

TYPE XB

Laid down in March 1940 at Germania Werft in Kiel, U-118 was commissioned on 6 December 1941. This large Type XB boat was commanded by Werner Czygan for its entire career.

ALTHOUGH BUILT AS A MINELAYER, U-118 made only one patrol in that role. It was used as a supply boat on its other missions. On 12 June 1943, west of the Canary Islands, she was strafed by a Wildcat fighter

and then sunk by depth charges from eight Avenger aircraft flying from the escort carrier USS *Bogue*. Forty-three of her crew were killed; 16 survived.

U-118 Commander

Korvkpt. Werner Czygan

(Dec 1941 – Jun 1943)

U-118 TIMETABLE		
Patrol Dates	**Operational Area**	**Boats resupplied**
19 Sept 1942 – 16 Oct 1942	NW of the Azores	4
12 Nov 1942 – 13 Dec 1942	SE of the Azores	7
25 Jan 1943 – 26 Feb 1943	Minelaying W of Gibraltar (4 ships sunk)	11
25 May 1943 – 12 Jun 1943	WSW of the Canaries (sunk)	3 or 4

▲ U-118

Type XB

The largest submarines in service with the *Kriegsmarine* during World War II, the Type XB boats could carry 66 mines. However, the class handled poorly and its slow diving time meant that it was vulnerable to air attack.

Specifications

Crew: 52

Powerplant: Diesel/electric

Max Speed: 30.4/13km/hr (16.4/7kt) surf/sub

Surface Range: 26,760km (14,450nm)

Displacement: 1763/2143t (1735/2143 tons) surf/sub

Dimensions (length/beam/draught): 89.8 x 9.2 x 4.7m (294.58 x 30.16 x 15.42ft)

Commissioned: 6 Dec 1941

Armament: 66 mines; 11 torpedoes (2 stern tubes); 1 x 10.5cm (4.1in), 1 x 3.7cm (1.5in) and 1 x 2cm (0.8in) guns

U-461

TYPE XIV

The Third of the Type XIV submarine tankers to be built, U-461 was laid down at Deutsche Werke in Kiel early in December 1940 and was commissioned on 30 January 1942.

ON 9 DECEMBER 1942, on her third patrol, U-461 encountered two lifeboats from the merchant ship *Teesbank*, sunk four days previously by U-128. The U-boat gave the survivors some food and water, but took the captain aboard as a prisoner. On 30 July 1943, while in transit to her operational area in

U-461 Commander

Korvkpt. Wolf-Harro Stiebler *(Apr 1942 – Jul 1943)*

the Azores, U-462 was spotted in the Bay of Biscay northwest of Cape Ortegal by an RAF Liberator, which vectored an RAF Sunderland, a Catalina, an American Liberator and a Halifax on to the target. U-461 was in company with U-462 and U-504, and the three boats fought off their attackers, causing considerable damage, but being damaged themselves in the process. U-461 was sunk by a newly arrived Australian Sunderland of No. 461 Sqn. Fifty-three of the boat's crew

died and 15 survived. The other two boats were hunted down and destroyed soon afterwards by surface ships and aircraft.

U-461 TIMETABLE		
Patrol Dates	Operational Area	Boats resupplied
21 Jun 1942 – 16 Aug 1942	W of the Azores	11
7 Sep 1942 – 17 Oct 1942	NW of the Azores	15
19 Nov 1942 – 3 Jan 1943	N of St Paul Rocks/S of the Azores	12
13 Feb 1943 – 22 Mar 1943	S/SW of Azores	10
20 Apr 1943 – 30 May 1943	Central N Atlantic	13
22 Jul 1943 – 23 Jul 1943	Patrol aborted due to leaking tank	0
27 Jul 1943 – 30 Jul 1943	En route to Cape Verde Islands	0

Specifications

Crew: 53

Powerplant: Diesel/electric

Max Speed: 26.7/11.7km/hr (14.4/6.3kt) surf/sub

Surface Range: 17,220km (9300nm)

Displacement: 1688/1932t (1661/1901 tons) surf/sub

Dimensions (length/beam/draught): 67.1 x 9.4 x 6.5m (220.16 x 30.83 x 21.33ft)

Commissioned: 30 Jan 1942

Armament: 2 x 3.7cm (1.5in) and 1 x 2cm (0.8in) guns

Fuel load: 439t (432 tons)

▲ **U-461**

Type XIV

In its tanker role the Type XIV could carry 439 tonnes (432 tons) of fuel oil for supply to operational boats. This was enough to provide 12 Type VIIs with an extra four weeks of endurance, or five Type IXs with an extra eight weeks.

U-852

TYPE IXD2

A very long-range Type IXD2 boat, U-852 was to become notorious as the command of the only U-boat commander to be guilty of a major war crime.

U-852 WAS HEADING FOR the Indian Ocean to join the *Monsun* (Monsoon) wolfpack operating there. On its way south, the boat torpedoed and sank the Greek steamer *Peleus* off West Africa on the night of 13/14 March 1944. Since several *Monsoon* boats had been detected and sunk on their way to the Indian Ocean, Eck decided to erase all evidence of his actions so as not to alert Allied search forces.

After leaving the scene briefly, the boat returned after midnight and called on the survivors in boats, on rafts and in the water to approach the U-boat. As they did so, the German crew opened fire with machine guns, and threw hand grenades to destroy the rafts. The boat cruised around the wreckage,

U-852 Commander

Kptlt. Heinz-Wilhelm Eck

(Jun 1943 – May 1944)

firing occasional bursts before leaving the scene before dawn. However, three men survived and after a month adrift were rescued by a Portuguese steamer.

U-852 TIMETABLE		
Patrol Dates	Operational Area	Ships Sunk
18 Jan 1944 – 3 May 1944	Indian Ocean	2

After penetrating the Arabian Sea, U-852 was located by Wellingtons of Nos. 8 and 621 Sqns RAF flying out of Aden, which damaged the boat so badly it was forced to run aground. The submarine was scuttled on 3 May 1944 in the Arabian Sea off the Somali coast. Seven crew were killed and 59 survived, who were captured ashore by the Somaliland Camel Corps and a naval landing party.

Initially, Allied investigators were most excited by the Fa330 'Bachstelze' aircraft carried by the U-boat, a rotary-winged kite that could be quickly folded and unfolded. However, the crew of U-852 had neglected to destroy the submarine's log, which proved that the U-boat had sunk a ship off Freetown on 13 March.

War Crimes

Eventually it was established that the boat had been responsible for the massacre of the crew of the *Peleus* – which, contrary to the impression established by Hollywood, was the only such incident during the war. Eck, his 2nd Watch Officer, the Medical Officer, the Chief Engineer and one of the boat's petty officers were tried for war crimes in October 1945. The first three were found guilty, and were executed by firing squad on the Lüneberger Heide at the end of November 1945.

Milchkühe ('milk cows')
1942–44

The Type XIV U-boat was a modification of the Type IXD, designed to resupply other U-boats. Because of their ability to provide sustenance, the Type XIVs became known as *Milchkühe*.

The Type XIV had no offensive weaponry, but had a relatively heavy anti-aircraft gun fit. During the Battle of the Atlantic, the 'milk cows' and the large Type XB minelayers pressed into service in the resupply role successfully allowed medium-range Type VIIC boats to operate along the American coast during the second 'Happy Time' in the first half of 1942. They were also essential to the successful patrols of long-range Type IX boats operating in the South Atlantic, off the Cape of Good Hope and in the Indian Ocean.

The 'milk cows' acted as force multipliers, allowing operational U-boats much greater time on station. As such, they were priority targets for Allied anti-submarine forces, and the early German successes did not last long. Ultra intelligence from Allied codebreakers, High Frequency Direction Finding (HF/DF) systems that zeroed in and triangulated on U-boat radio communications, improved radar, expanded air coverage and increasingly aggressive ASW tactics meant that the

▶ **Resupplying**

Here, a 'milch cow' submarine replenishes two combat U-boats in the South Atlantic. The 'milk cow' supply boats proved vital in attacking distant sea lanes, where Allied escort levels were lighter and there was less air cover.

big boats were eventually hunted down and all but eliminated during the course of 1943.

Many were surprised on the surface as they were refuelling combat boats, neither submarine being able to submerge quickly. 'Milk cow' duty was especially hazardous – 289 sailors were killed out of an estimated total 'milk cow' complement of around 550 men.

New Types Cancelled

Ten boats of this type were commissioned, but their increasing vulnerability meant that 14 planned Type XIVs were cancelled in May 1944. Also cancelled was further work on the Type XX design. This would have been an even larger transport boat, but the first would not have been ready until the summer of 1945 at the earliest.

Monsoon boats
1943–44

The idea of stationing U-boats in Malaya for operations in the Indian Ocean was first proposed by the Japanese in December 1942. However, as supplies and basing support were not available the idea was initially turned down. By 1943, however, German attitudes had changed.

Admiral Dönitz was not in favour of diverting strength from the main operational areas in the Atlantic. However, on 5 April 1943 it was decided to send U-178 to Penang to establish a naval base there. U-511 would eventually be given to the Japanese in return for rubber.

When the war in the Atlantic turned decisively in favour of the Allies in May 1943, it was decided to carry the underwater battle farther afield into less heavily protected sea lanes. The Indian Ocean was still almost on a peacetime footing, with few escorted convoys and many ships sailing individually.

Long-range boats already operating around South Africa were ordered to be replenished and sent into the Arabian Sea. More boats were also to be deployed, and were expected to arrive at the end of the monsoon season in September 1943. As a result, the group was given the name *Monsun* – German for monsoon.

Disappointing results

The *Monsun* group was expected to wreak the same kind of havoc in the Indian Ocean as the U-boats had done off the American coast in the early months of 1942. However, the boats had great difficulty in simply reaching their distant operational area – losses were incurred along the way, and the deployment was further complicated by the fact that many of the 'milk cow' resupply boats had been sunk. Of the initial 11 *Monsun* U-boats, four were destroyed in

transit and two – one of which sank – were diverted on emergency refuelling duties, so effectively only five boats managed to break through.

Once in the Indian Ocean, results were less than satisfactory, due in large part to the fact that Allied signals intelligence was able to locate the German operational areas, which enabled the authorities to route shipping away from the prowling U-boats.

Most of the boats were from the 12th Flotilla, but from September 1944, with the loss of the French U-boat bases, control was passed to the 33rd Flotilla, which was set up at Penang.

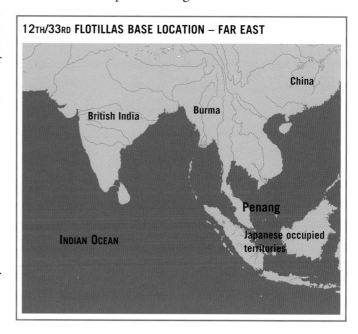

12TH/33RD FLOTILLAS BASE LOCATION – FAR EAST

China

British India Burma

Penang

INDIAN OCEAN Japanese occupied territories

BOATS THAT SERVED WITH 12TH FLOTILLA (47 BOATS)

U-Boat	Type	Commissioned	Flotilla(s)	Patrols	Fate
U-117	XB	25-Oct-41	1 Dec 1942 – 7 Aug 1943 from 11 Flotille	5 patrols. 2 ships damaged by mines: total 14,269 GRT	Sunk with all hands in the North Atlantic while supplying U-66 on 7 Aug 1943 by depth charges and a Fido homing torpedo from five Avenger aircraft of the escort carrier USS *Card*. 62 dead
U-118	XB	6-Dec-41	1 Nov 1942 – 12 June 1943 from 10 Flotille	4 patrols. 3 ships sunk by mines: total 14,064 GRT; 1 warship sunk by mine: total 940t/925 tons; 2 ships damaged by mines: total 11,945 GRT	Sunk 12 Jun 1943 west of the Canary Islands by depth charges from eight Avenger aircraft from the escort carrier USS *Bogue*. 43 dead and 16 survivors
U-119	XB	2-Apr-42	1 Feb 1943 – 24 June 1943 from 4 Flotille	2 patrols. 1 ship sunk by mine: total 2937 GRT; 1 ship damaged by mine: total 7176 GRT	Sunk with all hands 24 Jun 1943 in the Bay of Biscay northwest of Cape Ortegal by ramming and depth charges from the sloop HMS *Starling*. 57 dead
U-177	IXD2	14-Mar-42	1 Dec 1942 – 6 Feb 1944 from 10. Flottille	3 patrols. 14 ships sunk: total 87,388 GRT; 1 ship damaged: total 2588 GRT	Sunk 6 Feb 1944 in the South Atlantic west of Ascension Island by depth charges from a US Navy Liberator of VB-107. 50 dead and 15 survivors
U-178	IXD2	14-Feb-42	1 Nov 1942 – 1 Aug 1944 from 10. Flottille	3 patrols. 13 ships sunk: total 87,030 GRT; 1 ship damaged: total 6348 GRT	Scuttled 25 Aug 1944 at Bordeaux, France, as she was not seaworthy in time to escape the advancing US Army
U-179	IXD2	7-Mar-42	1 Oct 1942 – 8 Oct 1942 from 10. Flottille	1 patrol. 1 ship sunk: total 6558 GRT	Sunk with all hands 8 Oct 1942 in the South Atlantic near Cape Town by depth charges from the destroyer HMS *Active*. 61 dead
U-180	IXD1	16-May-42	1 Apr 1944 – 23 Aug 1944 from 10. Flottille	2 patrols. 2 ships sunk: total 13,298 GRT	Missing with all hands on or after 23 Aug 1944 in the Bay of Biscay west of Bordeaux. Some sources ascribe the loss to mines. 56 dead
U-181	IXD2	9-May-42	1 Nov 1942 – 30 Sep 1944	4 patrols. 27 ships sunk: total 138,779 GRT	to 33. Flottille
U-182	IXD2	30-Jun-42	1 Dec 1942 – 16 May 1943	1 patrol. 5 ships sunk: total 30,071 GRT	Sunk with all hands 16 May 1943 northwest of Madeira, by depth charges from the destroyer USS *MacKenzie*. 61 dead
U-195	IXD1	5-Sep-42	1 May 1944 – 30 Sept 1944 from 10. Flottille	3 patrols. 2 ships sunk: total 14,391 GRT; 1 ship damaged: total 6797 GRT	to 33. Flottille
U-196	IXD2	11-Sep-42	1 Apr 1943 – 30 Sept 1944	3 patrols. 3 ships sunk: total 17,739 GRT. U-196 completed a 225-day patrol from 13 Mar to 23 Oct 1943, the longest submarine patrol of WWII	to 33. Flottille
U-197	IXD2	10-Oct-42	1 Apr 1943 – 20 Aug 1943 from 4. Flottille	1 patrol. 3 ships sunk: total 21,267 GRT; 1 ship damaged: total 7181 GRT	Sunk with all hands 20 Aug 1943 south of Madagascar by depth charges from Catalinas of Nos. 259 Sqn and 265 Sqn RAF. 67 dead
U-198	IXD2	3-Nov-42	1 Apr 1943 – 12 Aug 1944 from 4. Flottille	2 patrols. 11 ships sunk: total 59,690 GRT	Sunk with all hands 12 Aug 1944 near the Seychelles by depth charges from the frigate HMS *Findhorn* and the Indian sloop HMIS *Godavari*. 66 dead
U-199	IXD2	28-Nov-42	1 May 1943 – 31 July 1943 from 4. Flottille	1 patrol. 2 ships sunk: total 4181 GRT	Sunk 31 Jul 1943 in the South Atlantic east of Rio de Janeiro by depth charges from a US Navy Mariner and a Brazilian Catalina and Hudson. 49 dead and 12 survivors
U-200	IXD2	22-Dec-42	1 Jun 1943 – 24 Jun 1943 from 4. Flottille	1 patrol	Sunk with all hands 24 Jun 1943 southwest of Iceland by 2 depth charges from a Liberator of No. 120 Sqn RAF. 68 dead (including 7 Brandenburg commandos aboard for a special mission)
U-219	XB	12-Dec-42	1 Jul 1943 – 30 Sep 1944	2 patrols	to 33. Flottille
U-220	XB	27-Mar-43	1 Sep 1943 – 28 Oct 1943	1 patrol. 2 ships sunk: total 7199 GRT (in a field of 66 magnetic SMA mines laid off of St Johns, Canada	Sunk with all hands after supplying U-603 on 28 Oct 1943 in the North Atlantic by depth charges from Avenger and Wildcat aircraft of the escort carrier USS *Block Island*. 56 dead
U-233	XB	22-Sep-43	1 Jun 1944 – 5 Jul 1944 from 4. Flottille (training)	1 patrol	Sunk 5 Jul 1944 while on a minelaying patrol southeast of Halifax by ramming, depth charges and gunfire from the destroyer escorts USS *Baker* and USS *Thomas*. 32 dead and 29 survivors
U-459	XIV	15-Nov-41	1 Nov 1942 – 24 Jul 1943 from 10. Flottille	6 resupply patrols	Scuttled 24 Jul 1943 near Cape Ortegal, Spain, after being badly damaged by two Wellingtons from Nos. 172 and 547 Sqns. 19 dead and 41 survivors
U-460	XIV	24-Dec-41	1 Nov 1942 – 4 Oct 1943 from 10. Flottille	6 resupply patrols	Sunk 4 Oct 1943 north of the Azores by Avengers and Wildcats of the escort carrier USS *Card*. 62 dead and 2 survivors. Fate often confused with U-422, which was sunk nearby on the same day by USS *Card* aircraft.
U-461	XIV	30-Jan-42	1 Nov 1942 – 30 Jul 1943 from 10. Flottille	6 resupply patrols	Sunk 30 Jul 1943 in the Bay of Biscay northwest of Cape Ortegal by an Australian Sunderland of No. 461 Sqn. 53 dead and 15 survivors
U-462	XIV	5-Mar-42	1 Nov 1942 – 30 Jul 1943 from 10. Flottille	8 resupply patrols	Sunk 30 Jul 1943 in the Bay of Biscay by gunfire from the sloops HMS *Wren*, HMS *Kite*, HMS *Woodpecker*, HMS *Wild Goose* and HMS *Woodcock* after being forced to the surface by a Handley Page Halifax of No. 502 Sqn. 1 dead and 64 survivors
U-463	XIV	2-Apr-42	1 Nov 1942 – 16 May 1943 from 10. Flottille	5 resupply patrols	Sunk with all hands 16 May 1943 in the Bay of Biscay by depth charges from a Halifax of No. 58 Sqn RAF. 57 dead. Originally credited to another 58 Sqn Halifax the previous day, but that attack actually destroyed U-266
U-487	XIV	21-Dec-42	1 Apr 1943 – 13 Jul 1943 from 4. Flottille	2 resupply patrols	Sunk 13 Jul 1943 in the central Atlantic by Grumman Avenger and Wildcat aircraft from the escort carrier USS *Core*. 31 dead and 33 survivors
U-488	XIV	1-Feb-43	1 May 1943 – 26 Apr 1944 from 4. Flottille	3 resupply patrols	Sunk with all hands 26 Apr 1944 west of Cape Verde by depth charges from the destroyer escorts USS *Frost*, USS *Huse*, USS *Barber* and USS *Snowden*. 64 dead

BOATS THAT SERVED WITH 12TH FLOTILLA (47 BOATS)

U-Boat	Type	Commissioned	Flotilla(s)	Patrols	Fate
U-489	XIV	8-Mar-43	1 Aug 1943 – 4 Aug 1943 from 4. Flottille	1 resupply patrol	Sunk 4 Aug 1943 southeast of Iceland by a Sunderland of No. 423 Sqn RCAF. 1 dead and 53 survivors
U-490	XIV	27-Mar-43	1 Apr 1944 – 12 Jun 1944 from 4. Flottille	1 resupply patrol	Sunk 12 Jun 1944 northwest of the Azores by depth charges from aircraft of the escort carrier USS *Croatan*, and from the destroyer escorts USS *Frost*, USS *Huse* and USS *Inch*. No casualties – 60 survivors.
U-847	IXD2	23-Jan-43	1 Jul 1943 – 27 Aug 1943 from 4. Flottille	1 patrol	Sunk with all hands 27 Aug 1943 in the Sargasso Sea by Fido homing torpedoes from Avenger and Wildcat aircraft flying from the escort carrier USS *Card*. 62 dead
U-848	IXD2	20-Feb-43	1 Aug 1943 – 5 Nov 1943 from 4. Flottille	1 patrol. 1 ship sunk: total 4573 GRT	Sunk with all hands 5 Nov 1943 in the South Atlantic southwest of Ascension Island by depth charges from 3 US Navy PB4Y Liberators of VB-107 and 2 B-25 Mitchells of the USAAF 1st Composite Sqn. 63 dead
U-849	IXD2	11-Mar-43	1 Oct 1943 – 25 Nov 1943 from 4. Flottille	1 patrol	Sunk with all hands 25 Nov 1943 in the South Atlantic west of the mouth of the Congo by depth charges from a US Navy Liberator of VP-107. 63 dead
U-850	IXD2	17-Apr-43	1 Nov 1943 – 20 Dec 1943 from 4. Flottille	1 patrol	Sunk with all hands 20 Dec 1943 west of Madeira by depth charges and Fido homing torpedoes from 5 Avengers and Wildcats of the escort carrier USS *Bogue*. 66 dead
U-851	IXD2	21-May-43	1 Feb 1944 – 27 Mar 1944 from 4. Flottille	1 patrol	Missing, presumed sunk with all hands, in the North Atlantic on or after 27 Mar 1944. 70 dead
U-852	IXD2	15-Jun-43	1 Feb 1944 – 3 May 1944 from 4. Flottille	1 patrol. 2 ships sunk: total 9972 GRT	Scuttled 3 May 1944 in the Arabian Sea off the Somali coast after running aground during an attack by 6 Wellingtons of Nos. 8 and 621 Sqns RAF. 7 dead and 59 survivors
U-859	IXD2	8-Jul-43	1 Apr 1944 – 23 Sep 1944 from 4. Flottille	1 patrol. 3 ships sunk: total 20,853 GRT	Sunk 23 Sep 1944 near Penang in the Strait of Malacca, torpedoed by HM Submarine *Trenchant*. 47 dead and 20 survivors
U-860	IXD2	12-Aug-43	1 Apr 1944 – 15 Jun 1944	1 patrol	Sunk 15 Jun 1944 south of St Helena by depth charges and rockets from Avenger and Wildcat aircraft of the escort carrier USS *Solomons*. 42 dead and 20 survivors
U-861	IXD2	2-Sep-43	1 Apr 1944 – 30 Sep 1944 from 4. Flottille	2 patrols. 4 ships sunk: total 22,048 GRT; 1 ship damaged: total 8139 GRT	to 33. Flottille
U-862	IXD2	7-Oct-43	1 May 1944 – 30 Sep 1944 from 4. Flottille	2 patrols. 7 ships sunk: total 42,374 GRT	to 33. Flottille
U-863	IXD2	3-Nov-43	1 Jul 1944 – 29 Sep 1944 from 4. Flottille	1 patrol	Sunk with all hands 29 Sep 1944 in the South Atlantic southeast of Recife, Brazil, by depth charges from 2 US Navy PB4Y Liberators of VB-107. 69 dead
U-871	IXD2	15-Jan-44	1 Aug 1944 – 26 Sep 1944 from 4. Flottille	1 patrol	Sunk with all hands 26 Sep 1944 northwest of the Azores by depth charges from a B-17 Flying Fortress of No. 22 Sqn RAF. 69 dead
U-1059	VIIF	1-May-43	1 Jan 1944 – 19 Mar 1944 from 5. Flottille	1 torpedo transport patrol	Left Bordeaux with replacement torpedoes for the Monsoon boats operating in the Far East. Sunk 19 Mar 1944 southwest of the Cape Verde Islands by Avengers and Wildcats from the escort carrier USS *Block Island*. 47 dead and 8 survivors
U-1061	VIIF	25-Aug-43	1 Jan 1944 – 1 Mar 1944	5 torpedo transport patrols	Surrendered in Bergen, Norway, May 1945. Transferred to Scotland for Operation *Deadlight*. Sunk by naval gunfire 1 Dec 1945
U-1062	VIIF	19-Jun-43	1 Jan 1944 – 30 Sep 1944	3 torpedo transport patrols	Sunk with all hands 30 Sep 1944 in central Atlantic by depth charges from the destroyer escort USS *Fessenden*. 55 dead. Boat was returning from Asia: it had left Norway 3 Jan 1944 with 39 torpedoes for Monsoon boats, reaching Penang 19 Apr 1944
UIT-21	Italian Calvi class	10-Sep-43	Oct 1943 – 15 Apr 1944	No patrols	Commissioned as the *Giuseppe Finzi* in 1936. Taken over as a long-range transport boat at Bordeaux following the Italian capitulation on 9 Sep 1943. In too poor repair for operations, and decommissioned 15 Apr 1944. Scuttled 25 Aug 1944
UIT-22	Italian Liuzzi class	10-Sep-43	Oct 1943 – Mar 1944	1 patrol	Launched as the *Alpino Bagnolini* 28 Oct 1939. Taken over as a long-range transport boat at Bordeaux following the Italian capitulation on 9 Sep 1943. Sunk with all hands 11 Mar 1944 south of the Cape of Good Hope by South African Catalinas of No. 262 Sqn. 43 dead
UIT-23	Italian Liuzzi class	10-Sep-43	Dec 1943 – Feb 1944	1 patrol	Commissioned as the Italian submarine *Reginaldo Giuliani* in March 1940. Seized by Japan at Penang following the Italian capitulation. Handed over to the Germans at Singapore Sep 1943. Torpedoed 14 Feb 1944 in the Strait of Malacca by British submarine HMS *Tallyho*. 26 dead and 14 survivors
UIT-24	Italian Marcello class	10-Sep-43	Dec 1943 – Sep 1944	6 patrols	Commissioned 23 Sep 1939 as the *Comandante Capellini*. Already in use as a transport boat when taken over by the Germans, following the Italian capitulation, at Sabang in the Far East on 10 Sep 1943. Transferred to 33. Flottille in 1944
UIT-25	Italian Marconi class	12-Dec-43	Dec 1943 – Sep 1944	3 patrols	Originally commissioned as the Italian submarine *Luigi Torelli* May 1940. Seized by Japan at Singapore following the Italian Armistice in 1943. Handed over to Germany and commissioned as a long-range transport in Dec 1943. Transferred to 33. Flottille

13 Unterseebootsflottille

The first U-boats to operate in Norwegian waters were supporting the German invasion of the country in 1940. By 1942, it became clear that boats operating from Norway would be able to strike both into the Atlantic and against the increasing numbers of Arctic convoys.

THE 13TH FLOTILLA was established at the port of Trondheim, well to the north of the main U-boat base at Bergen, from which the boats of the 11th Flotilla sailed. The new flotilla was set up in June 1943 under the command of *Korvettenkapitän* Rolf Rüggeberg. Boats were often forward deployed even farther north at Narvik or Hammerfest. This had the advantage of taking them out of the range of easy air attack from Britain, while at the same time bringing the boats closer to the main convoy route from Iceland or the UK, around the North Cape and into the USSR.

Commander

Korvkpt. Rolf Rüggeberg
(Jun 1943 – May 1945)

Arctic missions

Although the primary task of the U-boats was to find and attack the convoys bringing much-needed supplies from the Western Allies to the Soviets, who were bearing the brunt of the ground war, they were also used for a variety of other missions. Boats regularly mounted weather patrols, gathering information on ice and weather conditions, and monitoring the extent of the summer and winter pack ice, which determined how far north the convoys could go. U-boats also supported *Luftwaffe* reconnaissance flights, providing fuel for Blohm und Voss Bv 138 flying boats.

13TH FLOTILLA BASE LOCATION

Trondheim

ATLANTIC OCEAN

Possibly the most important mission was the setting-up and retrieval of temporary weather stations. Meteorological conditions in the polar regions have a great effect on the weather in continental Europe, and data from the region allowed for more accurate forecasting.

In September 1944, the flotilla was reorganized thanks to the influx of surviving boats forced to flee the French bases. It was finally disbanded in May 1945, when Germany surrendered.

13TH FLOTILLA INSIGNIA

The Viking ship on a white cross was an appropriate symbol for a unit based in Norway. About 10 of the flotilla's boats have been recorded as carrying the flotilla insignia.

13TH FLOTILLA (1943–45)	
Type	**Boats assigned**
Type VIIC	47
Type VIIC/41	8

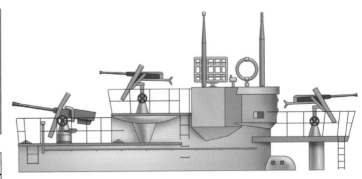

▲ **Type VIIC conversion VI with twin 2cm (0.8in) guns**
The conversion VI tower was developed to give Arctic-service boats increased forward-facing firepower in the shape of an extra twin 2cm (0.8in) mount.

U-255

TYPE VIIC

Laid down at Bremer Vulkan in Vegesack, U-255 was launched in October 1941, and went on its first operational patrol in June 1942. It was one of the most successful of all Arctic boats.

U-255 WAS ONE OF THE first German units to locate the ill-fated Convoy PQ 17, which it did on 1 July 1942, halfway through the boat's first operational patrol. U-255 sank four ships in the attack on PQ 17, and accounted for one damaged derelict a few days later. On its second patrol U-255 shelled two Soviet wireless stations, and on its third, the U-boat was damaged by an RAF Catalina south of Jan Meyen Island.

U-255 Commanders

Kptlt. Reinhart Reche *(Nov 1941 – Jun 1943)*
Oblt. Erich Harms *(Jun 1943 – Aug 1944)*

Oblt. Helmuth Heinrich
(Mar 1945 – May 1945)

Between July and September 1943, U-255 was deployed on its first patrol with the 13th Flotilla. Moving eastwards along the northern coast of the USSR, the boat established a secret seaplane base on Novaya Zemlya and searched for convoys on the summer route to Siberia, without success.

In February 1944, U-255 began operating in the Atlantic, and was transferred to the 7th Flotilla at St Nazaire. The boat was damaged by air attack and in August 1944, it was decommissioned. Although cut

Specifications

Crew: 44

Powerplant: Diesel/electric

Max Speed: 31.4/14.1km/hr (17/7.6kt) surf/sub

Surface Range: 12,040km (6500nm)

Displacement: 773/879t (761/865 tons) surf/sub

Dimensions (length/beam/draught): 67.1 x 6.2 x 4.8m (220.1 x 20.34 x 15.75ft)

Commissioned: 29 Nov 1941

Armament: 14 torpedoes (4 bow/1 stern tubes); 1 x 8.8cm (3.5in) and 1 x 2cm (0.8in) guns

U-255 TIMETABLE		
Patrol Dates	**Operational Area**	**Ships Sunk**
15 Jun 1942 – 15 Jul 1942	Northern waters	4
4 Aug 1942 – 9 Sep 1942	Spitzbergen/Soviet Arctic	0
13 Sep 1942 – 25 Sep 1942	Greenland Sea	1
29 Sep 1942 – 3 Oct 1942	Transit to Kiel for refit	0
7 Jan 1943 – 18 Jan 1943	Transit from Kiel to Hammerfest	0
23 Jan 1943 – 9 Feb 1943	Barents Sea	3
22 Feb 1943 – 15 Mar 1943	Norwegian Sea	2
29 Mar 1943 – 29 Apr 1943	Northern waters	0
19 Jul 1943 – 19 Sep 1943	Soviet waters/Novaya Zemlya	1
26 Feb 1944 – 11 Apr 1944	North Atlantic	1
6 Jun 1944 – 15 Jun 1944	Bay of Biscay	0
17 Apr 1945 – 21 Apr 1945	Minelaying off the French Coast	0
22 Apr 1945 – 8 May 1945	Moved between La Pallice and St Nazaire several times	0
8 May 1945 – 15 May 1945	Transit to Loch Alsh and surrender	0

▲ **U-255**

Type VIIC

U-255's combat debut came in the Allied disaster of Convoy PQ 17. The boat was one of the first to locate the convoy, and it benefited when the Admiralty in London ordered the convoy to scatter, picking off four out of the eight vessels sunk by the U-boats in the massacre that followed.

off, St Nazaire remained in German hands to the end of the war. U-255 was repaired and manned by personnel at the base at the end of 1944, and carried out minelaying in April 1945.

U-255 sank 10 vessels in northern waters, totalling 53,873 GRT. It also accounted for an American destroyer escort on one of its two Atlantic patrols.

Fate

The boat left St Nazaire on 8 May 1945, and was surrendered to the Royal Navy at Loch Alsh, Scotland, on the 19th. It was then moved to Loch Ryan, where it became one of 116 boats disposed of in Operation *Deadlight*. It was sunk as a target by aircraft on 13 December 1945.

U-354
TYPE VIIC

Launched at Flensburger Schiffsbau in January 1942, U-354 was commissioned in April 1942. Although initially on the strength of the 1st Flotilla, the boat spent its entire career in Norway.

U-354 REACHED BERGEN in October 1942, and over the next 18 months mounted at least 11 patrols in northern waters. However, like most boats in the region, she contributed little to the tonnage of Allied merchant shipping sunk by the U-boat arm, accounting for only two vessels sunk – although the crew claimed several Soviet vessels damaged, none of which were ever confirmed.

The boat was more successful in her final hours. On 22 August 1944, on her last patrol, U-354 unexpectedly came across a Royal Navy carrier task force off Vannoy Island. The British had just attacked the battleship *Tirpitz* at Kaafiord. The U-boat attacked the British ships, torpedoing the escort carrier HMS *Nabob* and the frigate HMS *Bickerton*. U-354 was then driven off by Fleet Air Arm aircraft. *Bickerton* was so badly damaged she had to be scuttled by a torpedo from a destroyer. The *Nabob* was towed to Scapa Flow, and saw no more wartime service.

Fate

U-354 was sunk with all hands on 24 August 1944 northeast of North Cape by depth charges from the sloops HMS *Mermaid* and HMS *Peacock*, the frigate HMS *Loch Dunvegan* and the destroyer HMS *Keppel*. Fifty-one crewmembers were killed.

U-354 Commanders

Kptlt. Karl-Heinz Herbschleb	Oblt. Hans-Jürgen Sthamer
(Apr 1942 – Feb 1944)	*(Feb 1944 – Aug 1944)*

U-354 TIMETABLE

Patrol Dates	Operational Area	Ships Sunk
10 Oct 1942 – 17 Oct 1942	Transit from Kiel to Skjomenfiord	0
29 Oct 1942 – 30 Nov 1942	Arctic Ocean	1
19 Dec 1942 – 15 Jan 1943	Arctic Ocean	1
18 Jan 1943 – 20 Jan 1943	Transit from Narvik to Trondheim	0
11 Mar 1943 – 4 Apr 1943	Northern waters	0
28 Apr 1943 – 30 Apr 1943	Transit to Hammerfest	0
9 May 1943 – 15 Jun 1943	Northern waters	0
25 Jul 1943 – 27 Jul 1943	Transit to Skjomenfiord	0
4 Aug 1943 – 22 Sep 1943	Soviet waters	0
22 Oct 1943 – 23 Oct 1943	Transit to Tromso	0
25 Oct 1943 – 6 Dec 1943	Spitzbergen/Bear Island	0
7 Dec 1943 – 5 Jan 1944	Bear Island	0
3 Jan 1944 – 4 Jan 1944	Transit to Trondheim	0
2 Mar 1944 – 5 Mar 1944	Transit to Narvik	0
8 Mar 1944 – 12 Apr 1944	Northern waters	0
18 Apr 1944 – 4 May 1944	S of Bear Island	0
6 May 1944 – 10 May 1944	Transit to Bergen	0
24 Jun 1944 – 28 Jun 1944	Transit to Bogenbucht	0
30 Jun 1944 – 28 Jul 1944	Northern waters	0
21 Aug 1944 – 24 Aug 1944	Northern waters	1

U-636

Type VIIC

Launched in June 1942 at the Blohm und Voss yard in Hamburg, U-636 spent most of its career on patrol in the Arctic, operating successively with 11th Flotilla and 13th Flotilla.

IN SPITE OF THE FACT that she was a very busy combat boat, carrying out no less than 15 patrols in the last two years of the war, U-636 achieved little success.

First patrol

By the time she went on her first patrol in May 1943, Allied escort techniques had been honed to an extremely fine level, and Ultra intelligence enabled the convoy planners to route ships away from known U-boat concentrations. As a result, although U-636 was assigned to at least eight wolfpacks, the boat rarely sighted Allied merchant ships or was driven off by alert escorts when she did.

U-636 TIMETABLE		
Patrol Dates	**Operational Area**	**Ships Sunk**
17 Apr 1943 – 28 Apr 1943	Transit from Kiel to Trondheim	0
2 May 1943 – 8 Jun 1943	SW of Iceland/SE of Greenland	0
24 Jul 1943 – 7 Aug 1943	Minelaying in Pechora Sea	0
14 Aug 1943 – 30 Aug 1943	Minelaying in Kara Sea	1 (2?)
5 Sep 1943 – 9 Sep 1943	Transit from Narvik to Bergen	0
24 Oct 1943 – 26 Oct 1943	Transit from Bergen to Trondheim	0
27 Oct 1943 – 17 Nov 1943	Minelaying in Soviet waters	0
18 Nov 1943 – 27 Dec 1943	S of Spitzbergen	0
30 Dec 1943 – 8 Jan 1944	Northern waters	0
26 Jan 1944 – 2 Feb 1944	Northern waters	0
8 Apr 1944 – 3 May 1944	Northern waters	0
27 Jun 1944 – 24 Jul 1944	Norwegian Sea	0
25 Aug 1944 – 12 Sep 1944	Minelaying in Pechora Sea	0
25 Sep 1944 – 3 Oct 1944	SW of Bear Island	0
6 Oct 1944 – 12 Nov 1944	E of Bear Island	0
4 Dec 1944 – 30 Jan 1945	N of Kola Inlet	0
1 Apr 1945 – 21 Apr 1945	Northwest of Ireland	0

U-636 Commanders

Kptlt. Hans Hildebrandt

(Aug 1942 – Feb 1944)

Oblt. Eberhard Schendel

(Feb 1944 – Apr 1945)

▲ **U-636**

Type VIIC

U-636 was one of a number of U-boats that penetrated deep into Soviet waters, carrying out minelaying patrols as far as the Kara Sea and into the estuary of the Yenisey River.

Specifications

Crew: 44

Powerplant: Diesel/electric

Max Speed: 31.5/14.1km/hr (17/7.6kt) surf/sub

Surface Range: 12,040km (6500nm)

Displacement: 773/879t (761/865 tons) surf/sub

Dimensions (length/beam/draught): 67.1 x 6.2 x 4.8m (220.1 x 20.34 x 15.75ft)

Commissioned: 20 Aug 1942

Armament: 14 torpedoes (4 bow/1 stern tubes); 1 x 3.7cm (1.5in) and 2 x twin 2cm (0.8in) guns (1944)

The boat's only success came from a minelaying operation in the Kara Sea which probably sank a Soviet freighter and may have destroyed a minesweeper. In June 1944, U-636 was attacked by an RAF Liberator, but severely damaged the aircraft before it could complete its attack. In October 1944, U-636 set up a clandestine weather station on Hopen Island in the Barents Sea.

U-636 was sunk with all hands on 21 April 1945 west of Ireland by depth charges from frigates HMS *Bazely*, HMS *Drury* and HMS *Bentinck*. Forty-two crewmembers were killed.

Arctic convoys
1941–45

When Hitler invaded the Soviet Union in June 1941, Stalin's USSR and the United Kingdom became allies in the war against Germany.

THE BRITISH AGREED to supply the Soviet Union with matériel and goods via convoys through the Arctic seas, the quantity of such assistance increasing dramatically when the United States entered the war in December 1941. The destinations were the northern ports of Murmansk and Arkhangelsk. To reach them, the convoys had to travel dangerously near the German-occupied Norwegian coastline. Convoys headed for Northern Russia were known as PQ convoys and those heading back were designated as QP convoys. Early convoys suffered few losses, but by the spring of 1942 the *Kriegsmarine* had concentrated significant U-boat and *Luftwaffe* strength in Norway, and sinkings began to increase.

Dreadful losses
The PQ/QP convoys were routed from Iceland to North Russia and back to Scotland. Eleven out of 18 convoys (eastbound PQ 7A, PQ 8, PQ 13, PQ 14, PQ 16, PQ 17 and PQ 18 and westbound QP 10, QP 11, QP 14 and QP 15) were intercepted by the Germans. In all, 29 ships of nearly 160,000 GRT were sunk by U-boats, with many more destroyed by *Luftwaffe* bombs and torpedoes.

After the losses suffered by PQ 16, PQ 17 and PQ 18, the Allies suspended Arctic convoy operations until the end of 1942, when increased numbers of escorts enabled more effective protection to be provided for the vulnerable merchant ships. The new convoys were redesignated as JW (eastbound) and RA (westbound). Thus from December 1942 the JW/RA system replaced the PQ/QP convoys. There were 21 JW convoys, comprising 552 merchant ships,

▲ **Depth charges**
Improvements in escort protection and the widespread use of depth charges drastically reduced the losses suffered by the Allies' Arctic convoys.

and 20 RA convoys composed of 492 ships overall. The increase in escort efficiency can be measured by the fact that only nine RA ships were were sunk by U-boats and two by the *Luftwaffe*, while only five JW ships were sunk by U-boats.

The U-boat arm felt the difference, too. Four U-boats were lost while attacking PQ convoys (three in the battle for PQ 18 alone), while a further seven were destroyed in attacks on JW convoys. No U-boats were lost in attacks on QP-routed vessels, but nine were sunk in attacks on RA convoys.

Wolfpack groups *Keil* and *Donner*
APRIL–MAY 1944

The *Keil* and *Donner* groups were two wolfpacks established at the end of March 1944, intended to attack eastbound Arctic convoys headed for the Soviet Union.

THE TWO GROUPS WERE given patrol areas near the edge of the ice pack to the south of Bear Island. No eastbound convoy was sighted, but late on the evening of 28 April a *Luftwaffe* reconnaissance aircraft spotted the westbound convoy RA 59.

Groups *Donner* and *Keil* were ordered to combine to mount an attack, and made contact on the afternoon of 30 April. However, by this stage in the war Allied escort tactics were very efficient, and convoys were generally protected by one or more escort carrier groups. Only U-711 managed to break through to the merchant ships, sinking the 7176-GRT American freighter SS *William S. Thayer*. Over the next two days and nights, the combined wolfpacks made repeated attacks against the escorts, but without success. Several explosions were heard, but all came from torpedoes blowing up at the ends of their runs without having hit a target.

The convoy escort was more successful: U-277 was sunk by depth charges on 1 May, as was U-959 a day

▲ **Trondheim pens**

The Type VII boat U-861 and the larger Type IX boat U-995 lie moored outside the 'Dora' bunker at Trondheim following their surrender in May 1945. Many of the Donner and Keil boats would have spent time here.

later, while U-674 was also lost on 2 May, destroyed on the surface by rockets. In each case, the attack was delivered by Royal Navy Swordfish aircraft flying from the escort carrier HMS *Fencer*.

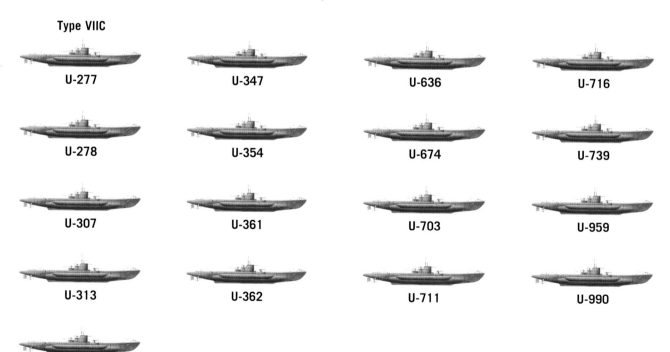

Type VIIC

U-277	U-347	U-636	U-716
U-278	U-354	U-674	U-739
U-307	U-361	U-703	U-959
U-313	U-362	U-711	U-990
U-315			

BOATS THAT SERVED WITH 13TH FLOTILLA (55 BOATS)

U-Boat	Type	Commissioned	Flotilla(s)	Patrols	Fate
U-212	VIIC	25-Apr-42	1 Jun 1943 – 31 Oct 1943 from 11. Flottille	15 patrols. 1 ship sunk: total 80 GRT	to 3. Flottille
U-251	VIIC	20-Sep-41	1 Jun 1943 – 30 Jun 1943 from 11. Flottille	9 patrols. 2 ships sunk: total 11,408 GRT	to 24. Flottille (training)
U-255	VIIC	29-Nov-41	1 Jun 1943 – 30 Nov 1943 from 11. Flottille	15 patrols. 10 ships sunk: total 47,529 GRT; 1 warship sunk: total 1219t/1200 tons; 1 ship damaged b/r: total 7191 GRT	to 7. Flottille
U-255	VIIC	29-Nov-41	1 Mar 1945 – 8 May 1945 from 7. Flottille	15 patrols. 10 ships sunk: total 47,529 GRT; 1 warship sunk: total 1219t/1200 tons; 1 ship damaged b/r: total 7191 GRT	Transferred to Scotland 14 May 1945 for Operation *Deadlight*. Sunk 13 Dec 1945
U-277	VIIC	21-Dec-42	1 Nov 1943 – 1 May 1944 from 6. Flottille	5 patrols	Sunk with all hands 1 May 1944 in the Arctic southwest of Bear Island by depth charges from a Swordfish of the escort carrier HMS *Fencer*. 50 dead
U-278	VIIC	16-Jan-43	1 Sep 1944 – 8 May 1945 from 11. Flottille	7 patrols. 1 ship sunk: total 7177 GRT; 1 warship sunk: total 1839t/1810 tons	Transferred to Scotland 19 May 1945 for Operation *Deadlight*. Sunk 31 Dec 1945
U-286	VIIC	5-Jun-43	5 Nov 1944 – 28 Feb 1945 from 11. Flottille	4 patrols. 1 warship sunk: total 1168t/1150 tons	to 11. Flottille
U-288	VIIC	26-Jun-43	1 Feb 1944 – 3 Apr 1944	2 patrols	Sunk with all hands 3 Apr 1944 in the Barents Sea southeast of Bear Island by depth charges and rockets from Swordfish, Avengers and Wildcats of the escort carriers HMS *Activity* and HMS *Tracker*. 49 dead
U-289	VIIC	10-Jul-43	1 May 1944 – 31 May 1944	2 patrols	Sunk with all hands 31 May 1944 in the Barents Sea southwest of Bear Island by depth charges from the destroyer HMS *Milne*. 51 dead
U-293	VIIC/41	8-Sep-43	5 Sep 1944 – 8 May 1945 from 13. Flottille	6 patrols. 1 warship damaged: total 1685t/1658 tons	Surrendered at Loch Alsh 11 May 1945. Sunk in Operation *Deadlight* 13 Dec 1945
U-294	VIIC/41	4-Oct-43	6 Nov 1944 – 28 Feb 1945 from 11. Flottille	5 patrols	to 14. Flottille
U-295	VIIC/41	20-Oct-43	1 Oct 1944 – 31 Mar 1945 from 11. Flottille	6 patrols. 1 warship damaged: total 1168t/1150 tons	to 14. Flottille
U-299	VIIC/41	15-Dec-43	5 Nov 1944 – 28 Feb 1945 from 11. Flottille	6 patrols	to 14. Flottille
U-302	VIIC	16-Jun-42	1 Jun 1943 – 31 Oct 1943 from 11. Flottille	10 patrols. 3 ships sunk: total 12,697 GRT	to 9. Flottille
U-307	VIIC	18-Nov-42	1 Nov 1943 – 29 Apr 1945 from 11. Flottille	19 patrols. 1 ship sunk: total 411 GRT	Sunk 29 Apr 1945 near Murmansk by depth charges from the frigate HMS *Loch Insh*. 37 dead and 14 survivors
U-310	VIIC	24-Feb-43	5 Sep 1944 – 8 May 1945 from 7. Flottille	6 patrols. 2 ships sunk: total 14,395 GRT	Surrendered 8 May 1945. Broken up at Trondheim, Norway, in Mar 1947
U-312	VIIC	21-Apr-43	1 Sep 1944 – 8 May 1945 from 11. Flottillle	12 patrols	Surrendered at Narvik, Norway, May 1945. Transferred to Scotland and sunk 29 Nov 1945 in Operation *Deadlight*
U-313	VIIC	20-May-43	15 Sep 1944 – 8 May 1945 from 11. Flottille	14 patrols	Surrendered at Narvik, Norway, 8 May 1945. Transferred to Scotland and sunk 27 Dec 1945 in Operation *Deadlight*
U-315	VIIC	10-Jul-43	15 Sep 1944 – 8 May 1945 from 11. Flottille	15 patrols. 1 ship sunk: total 6996 GRT; 1 warship damaged beyond repair: total 1392t/1370 tons	Stricken at Trondheim, Norway, 1 May 1945. Broken up in Mar 1947
U-318	VIIC/41	13-Nov-43	5 Nov 1944 – 28 Feb 1945 from 11. Flottille	8 patrols	to 14. Flottille
U-354	VIIC	22-Apr-42	1 Jun 1943 – 24 Aug 1944 from 11. Flottille	20 patrols. 2 ships sunk: total 9593 GRT; 1 warship sunk: total 1321t/1300 tons; 1 warship damaged beyond repair: total 11,603t/11,420 tons; 1 ship damaged: total 3771 GRT	Sunk with all hands 24 Aug 1944 northeast of North Cape by depth charges from the sloops HMS *Mermaid* and HMS *Peacock*, the frigate HMS *Loch Dunvegan* and the destroyer HMS *Keppel*. 51 dead. Originally credited to Swordfish of the escort carrier HMS *Vindex*, which actually destroyed U-344
U-360	VIIC	12-Nov-42	1 Jul 1943 – 2 Apr 1944 from 5. Flottille	7 patrols. 1 ship damaged: total 7153 GRT; 1 warship damaged: total 1565t/1540 tons	Sunk with all hands 2 Apr 1944 in the Norwegian Sea southwest of Bear Island by the destroyer HMS *Keppel*. 51 dead
U-362	VIIC	4-Feb-43	1 Mar 1944 – 5 Sep 1944 from 8. Flottille	7 patrols	Sunk with all hands 5 Sept 1944 in the Kara Sea near Krakovka by depth charges from the Soviet minesweeper T-116. 51 dead
U-363	VIIC	18-Mar-43	15 Sep 1944 – 8 May 1945 from 11. Flottille	10 patrols	Surrendered in Norway 8 May 1945. Transferred to Scotland for Operation *Deadlight* and was sunk 31 Dec 1945
U-365	VIIC	8-Jun-43	9 Jun 1944 – 13 Dec 1944 from 9. Flottille	11 patrols. 1 ship sunk: total 7540 GRT; 3 warships sunk: total 1377t/1355 tons, 1 warship damaged: total 1737t/1710 tons	Sunk with all hands 13 Dec 1944 in the Arctic east of Jan Mayen Island by depth charges from Royal Navy Swordfish flying from the escort carrier HMS *Campania*. 50 dead
U-366	VIIC	16-Jul-43	1 Mar 1944 – 5 Mar 1944 from 5. Flottille	2 patrols	Sunk with all hands 5 Mar 1944 in the Arctic Ocean northwest of Hammerfest by rockets from a Royal Navy Swordfish flying from the escort carrier HMS *Chaser*. 50 dead
U-387	VIIC	24-Nov-42	1 Nov 1943 – 9 Dec 1944 from 7. Flottille	15 patrols	Sunk with all hands 9 Dec 1944 in the Barents Sea near Murmansk by depth charges from the corvette HMS *Bamborough Castle*. 51 dead
U-425	VIIC	21-Apr-43	15 Sep 1944 – 17 Feb 1945 from 11. Flottille	8 patrols	Sunk 17 Feb 1945 in the Barents Sea near Murmansk by depth charges from the sloop HMS *Lark* and the corvette HMS *Alnwick Castle*. 52 dead and 1 survivor
U-427	VIIC	2-Jun-43	5 Nov 1944 – 28 Feb 1945 from 11. Flottille	5 patrols	to 14. Flottille
U-586	VIIC	4-Sep-41	1 Jun 1943 – 30 Sep 1943 from 11. Flottille	12 patrols. 2 ships sunk: total 12,716 GRT; 1 ship damaged: total 9057 GRT	to 6. Flottille
U-622	VIIC	14-May-42	1 Jun 1943 – 24 Jul 1943 from 11. Flottille	4 patrols	Sunk 24 Jul 1943 at Trondheim during a raid by heavy bombers of the 8th USAAF

BOATS THAT SERVED WITH 13TH FLOTILLA (55 BOATS)

U-Boat	Type	Commissioned	Flotilla(s)	Patrols	Fate
U-625	VIIC	4-Jun-42	1 Jun 1943 – 31 Oct 1943 from 11. Flottille	9 patrols. 3 ships sunk: total 18,751 GRT; 2 auxiliary warships sunk: total 939 GRT	to 1. Flottille
U-636	VIIC	20-Aug-42	1 Nov 1943 – 21 Apr 1945 from 11. Flottille	14 patrols. 1 ship sunk: total 7169 GRT	Sunk with all hands 21 Apr 1945 west of Ireland by depth charges from the frigates HMS *Bazely*, HMS *Drury* and HMS *Bentinck*. 42 dead
U-639	VIIC	10-Sep-42	1 Jun 1943 – 28 Aug 1943 from 11. Flottille	4 patrols	Sunk with all hands 28 Aug 1943 in the Kara Sea north of Mys Zhelaniya, torpedoed by the Soviet submarine S-101. 47 dead
U-668	VIIC	16-Nov-42	1 Jun 1944 – 8 May 1945 from 6. Flottille	6 patrols	Surrendered at Narvik, Norway, 8 May 1945. Transferred to Scotland for Operation *Deadlight*. Sunk 31 Dec 1945
U-673	VIIC	8-May-43	21 Jun 1944 – 31 Jul 1944 from 6. Flottille	5 patrols	to 6. Flottille
U-703	VIIC	16-Oct-41	1 Jun 1943 – 16 Sep 1944 from 11. Flottille	13 patrols. 5 ships sunk: total 29,523 GRT; 1 auxiliary warship sunk: total 559 GRT; 1 warship sunk: total 1900t/1870 tons	Missing with all hands on or after 16 Sep 1944 east of Iceland. 54 dead
U-711	VIIC	26-Sep-42	1 Jun 1943 – 4 May 1945 from 11. Flottille	12 patrols. 1 ship sunk: total 7176 GRT; 1 warship sunk: total 940t/925 tons; 1 ship damaged: total 20 GRT	Sunk 4 May 1945 near Harstad, Norway, by Avengers and Wildcats of the escort carriers HMS *Searcher*, HMS *Trumpeter* and HMS *Queen*. U-711 was damaged while alongside the depot ship *Black Watch*. The in-port watch of 12 men cut her loose from the sinking depot ship, but they had to abandon the boat and it sank nearby. 40 dead (killed aboard the *Black Watch* when it blew up) and 12 survivors. U-711 was the last U-boat sunk by the Royal Navy Fleet Air Arm
U-713	VIIC	29-Dec-42	1 Nov 1943 – 24 Feb 1944 from 11. Flottille	5 patrols	Sunk with all hands 24 Feb 1944 in the Arctic northwest of Narvik by depth charges from the destroyer HMS *Keppel*. 50 dead
U-716	VIIC	15-Apr-43	1 Oct 1944 – 31 Mar 1945 from 11. Flottille	10 patrols. 1 ship sunk: total 7200 GRT	to 14. Flottille
U-737	VIIC	30-Jan-43	1 Jul 1943 – 19 Dec 1944 from 8. Flottille	8 patrols	Sank 19 Dec 1944 in the Vestfjorden after a collision with minesweeper MRS 25. 31 dead and 20 survivors
U-739	VIIC	6-Mar-43	1 Jan 1944 – 8 May 1945 from 9. Flottille	8 patrols. 1 warship sunk: total 635t/625 tons	Surrendered at Wilhelmshaven 8 May 1945. Transferred to Scotland for Operation *Deadlight*. Sunk as a target by aircraft 16 Dec 1945
U-742	VIIC	1-May-43	1 Jun 1944 – 18 Jul 1944 from 6. Flottille	2 patrols	Sunk with all hands 18 Jul 1944 west of Narvik by depth charges from a Catalina of No. 210 Sqn RAF. 52 dead. The pilot, Flying Officer Cruickshank, was awarded the Victoria Cross for pressing home the attack even though his aircraft was badly damaged, one of his crew had been killed and he and another crewman were wounded
U-771	VIIC	18-Nov-43	1 Oct 1944 – 11 Nov 1944 from 11. Flottille	2 patrols	Sunk with all hands 11 Nov 1944 in the Andfjord near Harstad, Norway, by torpedoes from HM Submarine *Venturer*. 51 dead
U-921	VIIC	30-May-43	1 Jun 1944 – 2 Oct 1944	3 patrols	Missing with all hands northwest of Narvik after 2 Oct 1944. 51 dead. Previously credited to depth charges from aircraft of the escort carrier HMS *Campania* 30 Sep 1944 northwest of Hammerfest. That was against U-636 and U-968 and caused no damage
U-956	VIIC	6-Jan-43	1 Oct 1944 – 8 May 1945 from 11. Flottille	13 patrols. 1 warship sunk: total 1209t/1190 tons; 1 ship damaged beyond repair: total 7176 GRT	Surrendered 13 May 1945 at Loch Eriboll, Scotland. Sunk by naval gunfire in Operation *Deadlight* 17 Dec 1945
U-957	VIIC	7-Jan-43	1 Oct 1944 – 21 Oct 1944 from 11. Flottille	6 patrols. 2 ships sunk: total 7353 GRT; 2 warships sunk: total 614t/604 tons	Collided with a German supply vessel in the Lofoten Islands 19 Oct 1944. Decommissioned at Trondheim 21 Oct 1944. Transferred to England 29 May 1945. Broken up
U-959	VIIC	21-Jan-43	1 Mar 1944 – 2 May 1944 from 5. Flottille	2 patrols	Sunk with all hands in the Arctic southeast of Jan Mayen Island 2 May 1944 by depth charges from a Swordfish of the escort carrier HMS *Fencer*. 53 dead
U-965	VIIC	25-Feb-43	1 Oct 1944 – 30 Mar 1945 from 11. Flottille	7 patrols	Sunk with all hands 30 Mar 1945 north of Scotland by depth charges from frigates HMS *Rupert* and HMS *Conn*. 51 dead. Formerly credited to the Conn on 27 Mar, but that attack probably sank U-905
U-968	VIIC	18-Mar-43	1 Mar 1944 – 8 May 1945 from 5. Flottille	7 patrols. 2 ships sunk: total 14,386 GRT; 1 warship sunk: total 1372t/1350 tons; 1 ship damaged beyond repair: total 7200 GRT; 1 warship damaged beyond repair: total 1372t/1350 tons; 1 ship damaged: total 8129 GRT	Surrendered 16 May 1945 at Loch Eriboll, Scotland. Sunk 29 Nov 1945 in Operation *Deadlight*
U-992	VIIC	2-Aug-43	1 Oct 1944 – 8 May 1945 from 11. Flottille	8 patrols. 1 warship damaged beyond repair: total 1077t/1060 tons	Transferred from Narvik to Scotland 19 May 1945 for Operation *Deadlight*. Sunk by gunfire 16 Dec 1945
U-994	VIIC	2-Sep-43	5 Nov 1944 – 8 May 1945 from 11. Flottille	1 patrol	Transferred from Trondheim to Scotland 19 May 1945 for Operation *Deadlight*. Sank while on tow to the scuttling grounds 5 Dec 1945
U-995	VIIC/41	16-Sep-43	1 Jun 1944 – 28 Feb 1945 from 5. Flottille	9 patrols. 3 ships sunk: total 1560 GRT; 1 auxiliary warship sunk: total 633 GRT; 1 warship sunk: total 107t/105 tons; 1 ship damaged beyond repair: total 7176 GRT	to 14. Flottille
U-997	VIIC/41	23-Sep-43	1 Jun 1944 – 1 Mar 1945 from 9. Flottille	7 patrols. 1 ship sunk: total 1603 GRT; 1 warship sunk: total 107t/105 tons; 1 ship damaged: total 4287 GRT	to 14. Flottille
U-1163	VIIC/41	6-Oct-43	1 Oct 1944 – 8 May 1945 from 11. Flottille	4 patrols. 1 ship sunk: total 433 GRT	Transferred from Kristiansand to Scotland 29 May 1945 for Operation *Deadlight*. Sunk by aircraft 11 Dec 1945

14 Unterseebootsflottille

Formed late in the war after the U-boat force had been forced to flee its French bases, the 14th Flotilla was based at Narvik under the command of *Korvettenkapitän* Helmut Möhlmann. Operating against Arctic convoys, it never had a strength of more than eight boats.

OPERATING IN THE FAR NORTH, the 14th Flotilla made the last operational patrols of the war against the Arctic convoys. The boats achieved little against the by now highly efficient Allied escorts, but all eight survived the war to be surrendered to the British in May 1945. All bar U-995 were destroyed in Operation *Deadlight*: U-995 survives to this day as a war memorial at Laboe, near Kiel.

Oberleutnant zur See Hans-Georg Hess

Born on 6 May 1923 in Berlin, Hans-Georg Hess joined the *Kriegsmarine* as a 16-year-old volunteer in 1940. After service aboard minesweepers, he transferred to the U-boat arm in April of 1942. After officer training, he served aboard U-466 in the Atlantic and Mediterranean. Promoted to *Oberleutnant* in March 1944, he took command of U-995 in September 1944.

The boat made five patrols under his command, sinking five ships and damaging one. Hess was awarded the Knight's Cross in February 1945 as one

of the few late-war commanders to have had any success in the Arctic.

U-427

Laid down on 27 July 1942 at Danziger Werft, Danzig, the Type VIIC boat U-427 was commissioned on 2 June 1943 under the command of Oblt. Graf Karl-

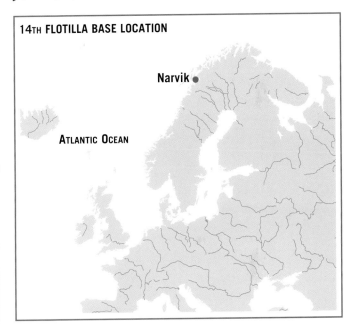

14TH FLOTILLA BASE LOCATION

Narvik

ATLANTIC OCEAN

Commander
Korvkpt. Helmut Möhlmann *(Dec 1944 – May 1945)*

▲ **U-427**

Type VIIC

In her short career in northern waters, U-427 led an active life. From protecting German coastal convoys against marauding British destroyers and cruisers, the boat went on to mount attacks on the last Arctic convoys of the war.

Specifications	
Crew: 44	Dimensions (length/beam/draught): 67.1 x 6.2
Powerplant: Diesel/electric	x 4.8m (220.1 x 20.34 x 15.75ft)
Max Speed: 31.5/14.1km/hr (17/7.6kt) surf/sub	Commissioned: 2 Jun 1943
Surface Range: 12,040km (6500nm)	Armament: 14 torpedoes (4 bow/1 stern tubes); 1
Displacement: 773/879t (761/865 tons) surf/sub	x 3.7cm (1.5in) and 2 x twin 2cm (0.8in) guns

14TH FLOTILLA	
Type	Boats assigned
Type VIIC	2
Type VIIC/41	6

U-427 Commander

Oblt. Graf Karl-Gabriel von Gudenus *(Jun 1943 – May 1945)*

Gabriel von Gudenus. From August 1944, U-427 was used to escort German coastal convoys, carrying out 18 missions before February 1945. The boat also mounted five combat patrols with the 13th and 14th Flotillas. On the night of 11/12 January, the boat attacked a British cruiser squadron that had damaged two merchantmen, but missed. On the night of 29 April 1945, U-427 attacked convoy RA 66, launching torpedoes against the destroyers HMCS *Haida* and *Iroquois*, but scoring no hits. The escorts fought back and dropped a total of 678 depth charges on U-427's estimated position during a hunt which lasted several hours. However, the boat managed to avoid damage, and worked its way clear. This was one of the last attacks made by the U-boat arm on an Arctic convoy.

Fate

U-427 was surrendered at Narvik, Norway, at the end of the war and was transferred to Loch Eriboll in Scotland for Operation *Deadlight*. The boat was sunk by naval gunfire on 21 December 1945.

U-995

U-995 was a Type VIIC/41 boat and was laid down on 25 November 1942 at Blohm und Voss in Hamburg. The submarine was commissioned on 16 September 1943 under the command of *Kapitänleutnant* Walter Köhntopp, who was succeeded on 10 October 1944 by *Oberleutnant* Hans-Georg Hess. The boat received its working up training with the 5th Flotilla before becoming operational with the 13th Flotilla in June 1944. It was transferred to the 14th Flotilla on 1 March 1945. The boat made nine patrols, sinking four ships for a total of nearly 2200 GRT. It also sank a Soviet minesweeping trawler and damaged a 7000-GRT American freighter beyond repair.

Fate

U-995 was surrendered to Britain at Trondheim in May 1945. The boat was given to Norway in October 1948, becoming the Norwegian submarine *Kaura* on 1 December 1952. Stricken in 1965, it was returned to Germany in 1970, restored to wartime standard and installed as a war memorial and museum ship at Laboe near Kiel in October 1971.

14TH FLOTILLA INSIGNIA

The flotilla's operational area in northern waters was appropriately represented by a U-boat on top of the world, backed by the midnight sun. However, there is no record that any of its boats carried the insignia.

BOATS THAT SERVED WITH 14TH FLOTILLA (8 BOATS)					
U-Boat	Type	Commissioned	Flotilla(s)	Patrols	Fate
U-294	VIIC/41	4-Oct-43	1 Mar 1945 – 8 May 1945 from 13. Flottille	5 patrols	Surrendered at Narvik. Transferred to Scotland for Operation *Deadlight*. Sunk 31 Dec 1945
U-295	VIIC/41	20-Oct-43	1 Apr 1945 – 8 May 1945 from 13. Flottille	6 patrols. 1 warship damaged: total: 1168t/1150 tons	Surrendered at Narvik May 1945. Transferred to Scotland at the end of May for Operation *Deadlight*. Sunk 17 Dec 1945
U-299	VIIC/41	15-Dec-43	1 Mar 1945 – 8 May 1945 from 13. Flottille	6 patrols	Transferred from Bergen to Scotland 29 May 1945 for Operation *Deadlight*. Sunk 4 Dec 1945
U-318	VIIC/41	13-Nov-43	1 Mar 1945 – 8 May 1945 from 13. Flottille	8 patrols	Surrendered at Narvik, Norway, 8 May 1945. Transferred to Scotland for Operation *Deadlight*. Sunk 21 Dec 1945
U-427	VIIC	2-Jun-43	1 Mar 1945 – 8 May 1945 from 13. Flottille	5 patrols	Surrendered at Narvik, Norway. Transferred to Scotland for Operation *Deadlight*. Sunk 21 Dec 1945
U-716	VIIC	15-Apr-43	1 Apr 1945 – 8 May 1945 from 13. Flottille	10 patrols. 1 ship sunk: total 7200 GRT	Surrendered at Narvik 8 May 1945. Transferred to Scotland for Operation *Deadlight*. Sunk by aircraft 11 Dec 1945
U-995	VIIC/41	16-Sep-43	1 Mar 1945 – 8 May 1945 from 13. Flottille	9 patrols. 3 ships sunk: total 1560 GRT; 1 auxiliary warship sunk: total 633 GRT; 1 warship sunk: total 107t/105 tons; 1 ship damaged beyond repair: total 7176 GRT	Surrendered to Britain at Trondheim May 1945. Transferred to Norway Oct 1948, becoming the Norwegian submarine *Kaura* 1 Dec 1952. Stricken in 1965. Returned to Germany; survives as a war memorial and museum at Laboe, near Kiel
U-997	VIIC/41	23-Sep-43	1 Mar 1945 – 8 May 1945 from 13. Flottille	7 patrols. 1 ship sunk: total 1603 GRT; 1 warship sunk: total 107t/105 tons; 1 ship damaged: total 4287 GRT	Transferred from Narvik to Northern Ireland 19 May 1945 for Operation *Deadlight*. Sunk by aircraft 13 Dec 1945

23 Unterseebootsflottille

German naval planners between the wars had always considered the Mediterranean to be a potential operational zone. However, when Germany had to commit forces to the region in 1941, it was in a very different war from that which had been envisaged.

ADOLF HITLER HAD NO intention of getting involved in southern Europe, but when his fellow fascist dictator Mussolini got into trouble in the Balkans, the Mediterranean and North Africa, Germany had to commit military forces to help its ally in the theatre.

Originally, the *Kriegsmarine* had anticipated that France would be the major enemy, but in the event it was British and Commonwealth forces in North Africa and the British Mediterranean Fleet that were encountered in battle.

Air power could provide much of the support needed by Germany's expeditionary force in Africa, the *Deutsches Afrika Korps*. However, true control would come only by denying the British command of the sea. The *Kriegsmarine* was too weak to make any

Commander

Kptlt. Fritz Frauenheim *(Sep 1941 – May 1942)*

difference on the surface, but the U-boat arm might be able to interfere with troop and resupply convoys that supported the British armies in North Africa, and it was decided to send a small force to the eastern Mediterranean.

A new flotilla, the 23rd, was established in Greece to control the boats. Founded on 11 September 1941 under the command of *Kapitänleutnant* Fritz Frauenheim, it was too small to be really effective and in May 1942 it was disbanded, its boats and missions being taken over by the larger 29th Flotilla. The 23rd Flotilla itself was reformed in 1943 as a training unit in the Baltic.

Kapitänleutnant Hans Heidtmann

Born on 8 August 1914 near Lübeck, Heidtmann joined the German Navy in Crew 34. He moved onto U-boats in January 1938, and made six non-combat patrols as acting commander of U-2 and U-14. From July 1940 he was commander of the school boat U-21 with the 21st Flotilla.

In February 1941, he commissioned the Type VIIC boat U-559. He carried out two patrols in the North Atlantic, sinking one ship before being deployed to the Mediterranean, passing safely through the Straits of Gibraltar on 26 September 1941.

Over the next 12 months U-559 carried out a further eight patrols, sinking at least three ships and an Australian sloop. U-559 was sunk in October 1942 by British destroyers, whose crews managed to capture vital codebooks before the boat went down. Heidtmann died on 5 April 1976 in Hamburg.

23RD FLOTILLA INSIGNIA

Most of the boats assigned to the 23rd Flotilla wore individual insignia. Indications are that the 'White Donkey', thought to be the flotilla's device, was carried only by Hans Heidtmann's U-559.

23RD FLOTILLA BASE LOCATION

ATLANTIC OCEAN

Salamis •

MEDITERRANEAN SEA

23RD FLOTILLA (1941–42)	
Type	**Boats assigned**
Type VIIB	3
Type VIIC	6

U-75

TYPE VIIB

Built by Bremer Vulkan, Vegesack, U-75 was laid down in December 1939 and launched on 18 October 1940. It served initially with the 7th Flotilla before transferring to the Mediterranean.

U-75'S FIRST THREE patrols were in the Atlantic, during which the boat sank four merchant ships totalling more than 25,000 GRT. On her third patrol, U-75 made a rendezvous with the disguised commerce raider *Orion* off the Azores, escorting the vessel into the estuary of the Gironde from where it entered Bordeaux.

In September 1941, U-75 left St Nazaire with orders to pass through the Straits of Gibraltar to operate in the Mediterranean. She was one of six boats of the *Goeben* group, the first Type VII boats to enter the Mediterranean. Their orders were to operate in the eastern Mediterranean to interdict supplies being sent by the British from Alexandria to Tobruk. U-75 encountered a British convoy on

U-75 Commander

Kptlt. Helmuth Ringelmann *(Dec 1940 – Dec 1941)*

12 October and sank two troop-carrying lighters, or barges, by torpedo and gunfire. After making an unsuccessful attack on a destroyer, U-75 entered her new base at Salamis on 2 November.

Fate

U-75 left on her last patrol off the Egyptian coast on 22 December 1941. On 28 December, the boat torpedoed a British freighter off Mersa Matruh. In a radio message, the captain reported another sinking, but this has never been confirmed. Soon afterwards, British forces tracked down the boat, and it was sunk by a depth-charge attack from the fleet destroyer HMS *Kipling*. Fourteen of the crew died; 30 were taken prisoner.

U-75 TIMETABLE		
Patrol Dates	Operational Area	Ships Sunk
10 Apr 1941 – 12 May 1941	S of Iceland	1
29 May 1941 – 3 Jul 1941	Central N Atlantic	1
29 Jul 1941 – 25 Aug 1941	Central N Atlantic	2
27 Sep 1941 – 2 Nov 1941	Transit from St Nazaire to Salamis	2
22 Dec 1941 – 28 Dec 1941	Off Egyptian coast	1

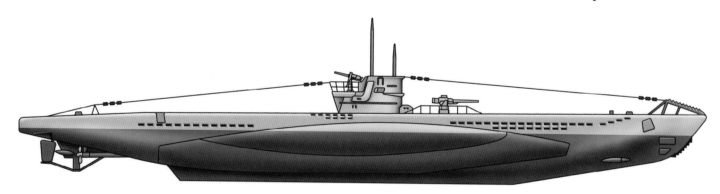

Specifications

Crew: 44

Powerplant: Diesel/electric

Max Speed: 31.9/14.8km/hr (17.2/8kt) surf/sub

Surface Range: 12,040km (6500nm)

Displacement: 765/871t (753/857 tons) surf/sub

Dimensions (length/beam/draught): 66.5 x 6.2 x 4.7m (218.1 x 20.34 x 15.4ft)

Commissioned: 19 Dec 1940

Armament: 14 torpedoes (4 bow/1 stern tubes); 1 x 8.8cm (3.5in) and 1 x 2cm (0.8in) guns

▲ **U-75**

Type VIIB

One of the first of the Kriegsmarine's front-line U-boats to operate in the Meditarranean, U-75 was tasked with providing support for the Afrika Korps by sinking British supply convoys in the eastern Mediterranean.

U-331
TYPE VIIC

Launched at Nordseewerke, Emden, in December 1940, U-331 was commissioned on 31 March 1941 under the command of *Kapitänleutnant* Freiherr Hans-Diedrich von Tiesenhausen.

ASSIGNED TO THE 1st U-boat Flotilla at St Nazaire, U-331 completed her combat training at Kiel. In July 1941, the boat left for her first patrol in the Atlantic, initially operating southeast of Greenland, but later moving to join a patrol line stretching between Gibraltar and the Azores. Although an attempt was made to attack Convoy HG 69, the boats were driven off by the British escorts.

In September 1941, U-331 left Lorient for the eastern Mediterranean as part of the six-boat *Goeben* group. On the way the boat exchanged gunfire

U-331 Commander

Kptlt. Freiherr Hans-Diedrich von Tiesenhausen *(Mar 1941 – Nov 1942)*

with a British convoy of troop-carrying barges. One crewman was killed in the firefight. One day later the boat put into her new base at Salamis.

On her third patrol in November 1941, U-331 landed commandos on the Egyptian coast near Ras Gibeisa. The soldiers' mission was to blow up the coastal railway, but they were captured.

A few days later, on 25 November 1941, U-331 encountered the British Mediterranean Fleet, which had left Alexandria the previous day. U-331 fired four torpedoes at the second battleship in line, the 31,599-tonne (31,100-ton) HMS *Barham*. The battleship blew up and sank, with the loss of 862 members of her crew; 449 survivors were picked up. After the patrol, von Tiesenhausen was flown to Berlin to be awarded the Knight's Cross.

◀ **Torpedo room**
Crewmembers of U-331 examine the torpedo tubes. On the back of one of the tubes is marked a kill, HMS Barham, which was sunk on 25 November 1941.

▲ **U-331**

Type VIIC

Although U-331 had little success against Allied merchant shipping, the boat was presented with one of the greatest prizes of the war when she encountered the British Mediterranean Fleet and sank the battleship HMS Barham.

Specifications

Crew: 44	Dimensions (length/beam/draught): 67.1 x 6.2 x 4.8m (220.1 x 20.34 x 15.75ft)
Powerplant: Diesel/electric	
Max Speed: 31.5/14.1km/hr (17/7.6kt) surf/sub	Commissioned: 31 Mar 1941
Surface Range: 12,040km (6500nm)	Armament: 14 torpedoes (4 bow/1 stern tubes);
Displacement: 773/879t (761/865 tons) surf/sub	1 x 8.8cm (3.5in) and 1 x 2cm (0.8in) guns

On her fifth patrol, off the Lebanese coast, U-331 engaged two small sailing vessels with gunfire. The U-boat had to leave the scene before the vessels were confirmed as sunk.

Fate

On 17 November 1942, after being badly damaged by a Lockheed Hudson of No. 500 Sqn RAF in the Mediterranean north of Algiers, U-331 signalled her surrender to the circling aircraft. However, the boat was attacked and destroyed by torpedo-equipped Albacores from the aircraft carrier HMS *Formidable*, which were unaware that the boat had capitulated. Thirty-two crewmembers were killed; 17 survived. The survivors were all picked up and taken into captivity.

U-331 TIMETABLE		
Patrol Dates	**Operational Area**	**Ships Sunk**
2 Jul 1941 – 19 Aug 1941	North Atlantic/Azores	0
24 Sep 1941 – 11 Oct 1941	Transit from Lorient to Mediterranean	0
12 Nov 1941 – 3 Dec 1942	Special operations off Libya	1
14 Jan 1942 – 28 Feb 1942	Off Tobruk	0
4 Apr 1942 – 19 Apr 1942	Minelaying off Beirut	2 (possibles)
9 May 1942 – 21 May 1942	Off Tobruk	0
25 May 1942 – 15 Jun 1942	Libyan coast	0
5 Aug 1942 – 10 Aug 1942	Balearic Islands	0
12 Aug 1942 – 19 Sep 1942	Balearic Islands	0
7 Nov 1942 – 17 Nov 1942	Algerian coast	1

▶ **Keeping watch**

The crew of a Type VIIC seek out targets in the Mediterranean in 1942. The U-boats were far less successful in the Mediterranean theatre, and Dönitz felt they would have been better deployed against convoys in the North Atlantic.

U-Boat	Type	Commissioned	Flotilla(s)	Patrols	Fate
BOATS THAT SERVED WITH 23RD FLOTILLA WHEN IT WAS A COMBAT UNIT (9 BOATS)					
U-75	VIIB	19-Dec-40	1 Oct 1941 – 28 Dec 1941 from 7. Flottille	5 patrols. 7 ships sunk: total 37,884 GRT; 2 warships sunk: total 756t/744 tons	Sunk 28 Dec 1941 in the Mediterranean near Mersa Matruh by depth charges from the destroyer HMS *Kipling*. 14 dead and 30 survivors
U-77	VIIC	18-Jan-41	1 Jan 1942 – 30 Apr 1942 from 7. Flottille	12 patrols. 14 ships sunk: total 31,186 GRT; 1 warship sunk: total 1067t/1050 tons; 1 ship damaged beyond repair: total 5222 GRT; 2 ships damaged: total 5384 GRT; 2 warships damaged: total 2926t/2880 tons	to 29. Flottille
U-79	VIIC	13-Mar-41	1 Oct 1941 – 23 Dec 1941 from 1. Flottille	6 patrols. 2 ships sunk: total 2983 GRT; 1 warship damaged beyond repair: total 635t/625 tons; 1 ship damaged: total 10,356 GRT	Sunk 23 Dec 1941 in the Mediterranean north of Sollum by depth charges from the destroyers HMS *Hasty* and HMS *Hotspur*. No fatalities – 44 survivors
U-83	VIIB	8-Feb-41	1 Jan 1942 – 30 Apr 1942 from 1. Flottille	12 patrols. 5 ships sunk: total 8425 GRT; 1 auxiliary warship sunk: total 91 GRT; 1 ship damaged: total 2590 GRT; 1 auxiliary warship damaged: total 6746 GRT	to 29. Flottille
U-97	VIIC	28-Sep-40	1 Nov 1941 – 30 Apr 1942 from 7. Flottille	13 patrols. 15 ships sunk: total 64,404 GRT; 1 auxiliary warship sunk: total 6833 GRT; 1 ship damaged: total 9718 GRT	to 29. Flottille
U-133	VIIB	5-Jul-41	1 Jan 1942 – 14 Mar 1942 from 7 Flottille	3 patrols. 1 warship sunk: total 1951t/1920 tons	Sunk with all hands 14 Mar 1942 near Salamis, Greece, by a German-laid mine. 45 dead
U-331	VIIC	31-Mar-41	1 Jan 1942 – 14 Mar 1942 from 7. Flottille	10 patrols. 1 auxiliary warship sunk: total 9135 GRT; 1 battleship (HMS *Barham*) sunk: total 31,599t/31,100 tons; 1 warship damaged: total 378t/372 tons	to 29. Flottille
U-371	VIIC	15-Mar-41	1 Nov 1941 – 14 Apr 1942 from 1. Flottille	19 patrols. 8 ships sunk: total 51,401 GRT; 1 auxiliary warship sunk: total 545 GRT; 2 warships sunk: total 2323t/2286 tons; 2 ships damaged b/r: total 13,341 GRT; 4 ships damaged: total 28,072 GRT; 2 warships damaged: total 2540t/2500 tons	to 29. Flottille
U-559	VIIC	27-Feb-41	1 Nov 1941 – 14 Apr 1942 from 1. Flottille	10 patrols. 4 ships sunk: total 11,811 GRT; 1 damaged: total 5917 GRT; 1 warship sunk: total 1077t/1060 tons	to 21. Flottille

29 Unterseebootsflottille

The 29th Flotilla was founded in December 1941 under the command of _Korvettenkapitän_ Franz Becker. Intended for Mediterranean operations, its boats came under the operational control of the _Kriegsmarine_'s Mediterranean Command rather than the U-boat Command.

WHILE THE 23RD FLOTILLA in Greece operated against Allied shipping in the east, the 29th Flotilla based at La Spezia concentrated on patrols in the central and western Mediterranean. When the 23rd Flotilla was disbanded, the 29th Flotilla assumed control of its boats and mission.

Boats also used the base facilities at Salamis, Pola, and in the south of France as forward-operating locations. The flotilla's headquarters was moved to Toulon in August 1943 as Allied troops gained a foothold in Italy.

End in the Mediterranean

The last U-boat attempting to enter the Mediterranean, U-731, was sunk on 15 May 1944 by the patrol vessel HMS _Kilmarnock_, the anti-submarine trawler HMS _Blackfly_ and two US Navy PBY Catalina aircraft from VP-63. On 21 May, U-boats gained their last success in the region when U-453 attacked Convoy HA 43, sinking one ship, but being sunk herself soon afterwards. In September 1944, the last of 68 U-boats to serve in

the Mediterranean were destroyed. U-407 was sunk south of the Greek island of Milos on the 19th. Five days later in raids on Salamis, USAAF aircraft damaged U-596 and U-565, which were scuttled. The 29th Flotilla was disbanded, as its other eight U-boats had all been destroyed or scuttled at Toulon.

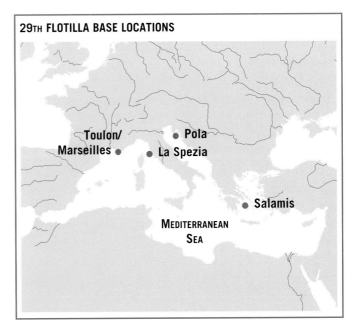

29TH FLOTILLA BASE LOCATIONS

Toulon/ Marseilles • Pola • La Spezia • Salamis

MEDITERRANEAN SEA

Commanders

Korvkpt. Franz Becker *(Dec 1941 – May 1942)*   Korvkpt. Gunther Jahn *(Aug 1943 – Sep 1944)*
Korvkpt. Fritz Frauenheim *(May 1942 – Jul 1943)*

29TH FLOTILLA INSIGNIA

The flotilla's insignia was originally worn by U-338. The boat rammed a dock crane on being launched, and became known as the 'Wild Donkey'. Three or four of the flotilla's boats are known to have used this emblem.

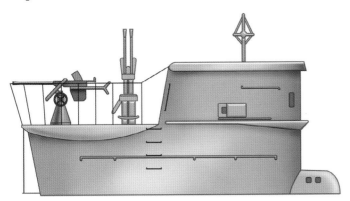

▲ **Type VIIC extended bridge**

The first attempt to improve the Type VIIC's defensive power came with an extension of the bridge platform to make room for two twin Breda 13.2mm (0.5in) heavy machine guns to supplement the standard single 2cm (0.8in) weapon. Even heavy machine guns were not enough, and the bridge structure was extended further to make room for extra single, and then twin, 2cm (0.8in) weapons. The diamond-shaped aerial is for the FuMB 2, the Biscay Cross, which gave warning of first-generation aircraft radars but was useless against centimetric equipment.

29TH FLOTILLA (1941–44)	
Type	**Boats assigned**
Type VIIB	3
Type VIIC	49

Star commanders
1941–44

The 29th Flotilla included in its number some of the busiest of all U-boat commanders, who made many patrols in the perilously shallow and clear waters of the Mediterranean.

Kapitänleutnant Freiherr Hans-Diedrich von Tiesenhausen

Born on 22 February 1913 in Latvia, von Tiesenhausen joined the Navy with Crew 34. He began his U-boat career on U-23 under *Kapitänleutnant* Otto Kretschmer. Together they completed three successful patrols and sank five ships for a total of 27,000 GRT, as well as one destroyer. He also served aboard U-93.

At the end of March 1941 von Tiesenhausen took command of U-331, in which he completed nine patrols with the 23rd and 29th Flotillas. On 25 November 1941, U-331 sank the battleship HMS *Barham*, for which achievement von Tiesenhausen received the Knight's Cross. U-331 was sunk in November 1942 off Algiers and von Tiesenhausen was taken prisoner. In 1947, he returned to Germany from a prison camp in Canada and worked as a joiner. In 1951, he emigrated to Canada. He died on 17 August 2000 at Vancouver in British Columbia.

Korvettenkapitän Helmut Rosenbaum

Born on 11 May 1913 near Leipzig, Rosenbaum joined the *Reichsmarine* with Crew 32. He

STAR COMMANDERS		
Commander	Patrols	Ships Sunk
Kptlt. Freiherr Hans-Diedrich von Tiesenhausen	10	2
Korvkpt. Helmut Rosenbaum	10	9
Oblt. Horst-Arno Fenski	6	8

commanded U-2 and U-73, sinking six ships and the aircraft carrier HMS *Eagle*. Rosenbaum died in an air crash on 10 May 1944 near Konstanza, Romania.

Oberleutnant zur See Horst-Arno Fenski

Born on 3 November 1918 in East Prussia, Fenski joined the *Kriegsmarine* with Crew 37b. He commanded U-34, U-410 and U-371, sinking six ships totalling 43,032 GRT as well as two warships totalling 7006 tonnes (6895 tons), including the cruiser HMS *Penelope* in February 1944. U-410 was destroyed by US bombs in March 1944. Oblt. Fenski then took over U-371, but on his first patrol with this boat he had to scuttle her after heavy depth-charge attacks. He spent two years as a prisoner of war. He died on 10 February 1965 at Hamburg.

▲ U-410

Type VIIC

Originally commanded by Korvettenkapitän Kurt Sturm, U-410 was taken over by *Oberleutnant* Horst-Arno Fenski in 1943. The boat was badly damaged by an American air raid on Toulon and was decommissioned in March 1944.

Specifications	
Crew: 44	Dimensions (length/beam/draught): 67.1 x 6.2 x 4.8m (220.1 x 20.34 x 15.75ft)
Powerplant: Diesel/electric	
Max Speed: 31.5/14.1km/hr (17/7.6kt) surf/sub	Commissioned: 23 Feb 1942
Surface Range: 12,040km (6500nm)	Armament: 14 torpedoes (4 bow/1 stern tubes); 1 x 2cm (0.8in) quad and 2 x twin 2cm (0.8in)
Displacement: 773/879t (761/865 tons) surf/sub	

U-73

Type VIIB

Commissioned on 31 October 1940, U-73 made five Atlantic patrols with the 7th Flotilla before moving to the Mediterranean, where she made 10 patrols with the 29th Flotilla.

DURING THE ACTION against Convoy MW 10 in March 1942, U-73's stern was shattered by a bombing attack and the boat was forced to limp the 1930km (1200 miles) back to La Spezia on the surface. In August 1942, the U-boat was part of the force deployed against Operation *Pedestal*, the major British effort to support a vital supply convoy trying to reach the beleaguered island of Malta. Early in the afternoon of the 11th, U-73 closed with the convoy near Majorca and sank the 22,960-tonne (22,600-ton) aircraft carrier HMS *Eagle*. Of the warship's crew of 1160, 260 died. U-73 tried to attack the escort force on its return from Malta, but

was unsuccessful, failing to hit the damaged cruiser HMS *Nigeria,* which had earlier been torpedoed by the Italian submarine *Axum.*

In August 1943, U-73 claimed two hits against the cruiser USS *Philadelphia* off the north coast of Sicily,

U-73 TIMETABLE		
Patrol Dates	**Operational Area**	**Ships Sunk**
8 Feb 1941 – 2 Mar 1941	W of British Isles	1
25 Mar 1941 – 24 Apr 1941	SW of Ireland	4
20 May 1941 – 24 Jun 1941	*Bismarck* escort N Atlantic/S Iceland	0
29 Jul 1941 – 2 Aug 1941	Mission aborted due to engine trouble	0
7 Aug 1941 – 7 Sep 1941	SW of Iceland	0
11 Oct 1941 – 11 Nov 1941	SE of Greenland	0
4 Jan 1942 – 20 Jan 1942	Through Straits of Gibraltar to Messina	0
31 Jan 1942 – 26 Feb 1942	Off Cyrenaica	0
16 Mar 1942 – 26 Mar 1942	Against convoy MW 10 Alexandria/Malta	0
20 Oct 1942 – 19 Nov 1942	W Med against Operation *Torch*	0
4 Aug 1942 – 5 Sep 1942	Against Malta resupply convoy *Pedestal*	1
22 Dec 1942 – 13 Jan 1943	W Mediterranean off Algeria	1
12 Jun 1943 – 1 Jul 1943	Off Algerian coast	1
2 Aug 1943 – 29 Aug 1943	Off N coast of Sicily	0
5 Oct 1943 – 30 Oct 1943	Special operations	0
4 Dec 1943 – 16 Dec 1943	Off Algerian coast	0

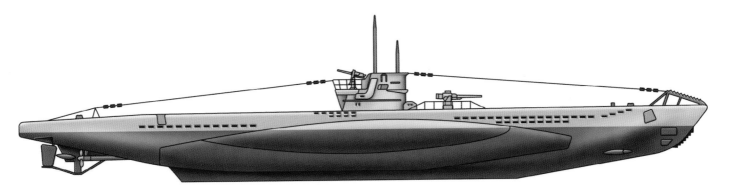

▲ **U-73**

Type VIIB

Type VIIB boats lacked the range of later variants, but in the relatively short-range war that was fought in the Mediterranean this was not a major handicap. U-73 was a particularly busy boat, making at least 16 combat patrols.

Specifications

Crew: 44

Powerplant: Diesel/electric

Max Speed: 31.9/14.8km/hr (17.2/8kt) surf/sub

Surface Range: 12,040km (6500nm)

Displacement: 765/871t (753/857 tons) surf/sub

Dimensions (length/beam/draught): 66.5 x 6.2 x 4.7m (218.1 x 20.34 x 15.4ft)

Commissioned: 31 Oct 1940

Armament: 14 torpedoes (4 bow/1 stern tubes); 1 x 8.8cm (3.5in) and 1 x 2cm (0.8in) guns

U-73 Commanders

Kptlt. Helmut Rosenbaum	Kptlt Horst Deckert
(Sep 1940 – Sep 1942)	*(Oct 1942 – Dec 1943)*

but they were never confirmed. In October 1943, U-73 landed an agent on the coast of Algeria. During the patrol she was attacked by the British submarine HMS *Ultimatum*, which claimed, wrongly, to have sunk the German boat.

U-73 was sunk on 16 December 1943 in the Mediterranean near Oran, Algeria, by depth charges and gunfire from the destroyers USS *Woolsey* and USS *Trippe*. Sixteen of the crew were killed and 34 survived.

U-371

Type VIIC

Laid down at Howaldtswerke Kiel in November 1939, U-371 commissioned in March 1941. She served with 1st Flotilla in the Atlantic and with 23rd and 29th Flotillas in the Mediterranean.

O N HER FIRST PATROL U-371 claimed to have torpedoed a large ship in the central Atlantic in addition to the Norwegian MV *Vigrid*, but no Allied loss has ever been confirmed.

In October 1943, U-371 claimed a ship to have 'probably been sunk' in addition to the American merchantman *James Russell Lowell,* the minesweeper HMS *Hythe* and the destroyer USS *Bristol,* but the attack has never been confirmed.

On her last patrol, U-371 fell victim to the first Allied 'Swamp' attack. During more than 24 hours of evasive manoeuvres, *Oberleutnant* Fenski took U-371 to a depth of over 200m (655ft) before eventually being forced to the surface. The crew abandoned the boat and it was destroyed.

Joseph E. Campbell, the French destroyer escort *Sénégalais* and the escort destroyer HMS *Blankney.* Three crewmen were killed and 49 survivors were taken prisoner.

U-371 Commanders

Oblt. Heinrich Driver *(Mar 1941 – Apr 1942)*	Kptlt. Waldemar Mehl *(May 1942 – Apr 1944)*
Kptlt. Karl-Otto Weber *(Mar 1942 – Apr 1942)*	Oblt. Horst-Arno Fenski *(Apr 1944 – May 1944)*
Kptlt. Heinz-Joachim Neumann *(Apr – May 1942)*	

Fate

U-371 was sunk at 04:09 on 4 May 1944 in the Mediterranean north of Constantine by depth charges from the destroyer escorts USS *Pride* and USS

U-371 TIMETABLE		
Patrol Dates	**Operational Area**	**Ships Sunk**
5 Jun 1941 – 1 July 1941	W of British Isles	1
23 Jul 1941 – 19 Aug 1941	SW of Ireland	2
16 Sep 1941 – 24 Oct 1941	Transit from Brest to Mediterranean	0
4 Dec 1941 – 10 Jan 1942	E Mediterranean off Egyptian coast	0
4 Mar 1942 – 25 Mar 1942	Off Tobruk	0
21 Apr 1942 – 9 May 1942	E Mediterranean	0
1 Jul 1942 – 7 Jul 1942	Central Mediterranean	0
5 Sep 1942 – 18 Sep 1942	E Mediterranean	0
12 Oct 1942 – 16 Oct 1942	Transit from Salamis to Pola	0
1 Dec 1942 – 4 Dec 1942	Transit from Pola to Messina	0
7 Dec 1942 – 10 Jan 1943	W Mediterranean	1
14 Feb 1943 – 3 Mar 1943	Algerian coast	1
7 Apr 1943 – 11 May 1943	Algerian coast	1
3 Jul 1943 – 12 Jul 1943	W Mediterranean	0
22 Jul 1943 – 11 Aug 1943	Algerian coast	1
21 Aug 1943 – 3 Sep 1943	W Mediterranean	0
7 Oct 1943 – 28 Oct 1943	Algerian coast	3
15 Nov 1943 – 23 Nov 1943	W Mediterranean	0
22 Jan 1944 – 13 Feb 1944	Off the Anzio beachhead	0
4 Mar 1944 – 25 Mar 1944	Algerian coast	2
23 Apr 1944 – 4 May 1944	Algerian coast	0

U-559

TYPE VIIC

Laid down at Blohm und Voss, Hamburg, on 1 February 1940, U-559 was commisioned on 27 February 1941 under the command of *Kapitänleutnant* Hans Heidtmann.

ON HER SECOND PATROL in the Atlantic, U-559 sank one ship. The boat also claimed another ship sunk and a third damaged, but neither were confirmed. After transiting the Straits of Gibraltar and covering the Mediterranean from west to east on her third patrol to join the 23rd Flotilla, U-559 claimed a hit on a British destroyer off Alexandria, but it has never been confirmed. In February 1941, U-559 observed two hits on an unidentified freighter already suffering from torpedo or bomb damage, but no confirmation of this has ever been made either. The boat transferred to the 29th Flotilla in April 1942, when the 23rd Flotilla was disbanded at Salamis.

Fate

U-559 was sunk on 30 October 1942 in the Mediterranean northeast of Port Said by depth charges from the destroyers HMS *Pakenham*, HMS *Petard* and HMS *Hero*, the escort destroyers HMS *Dulverton* and HMS *Hurworth*, and a Vickers Wellesley aircraft. Seven crewmembers died and 38 survived.

For more than 10 months, Allied codebreakers had been unable to crack the latest Enigma code used by U-boats. However, the sinking of U-559 enabled them to make a breakthrough. The wreck was boarded by three men from HMS *Petard*. They secured several secret documents and codebooks and were trying to recover the Enigma machine when the boat sank, taking two of the three men to their deaths. The items recovered greatly aided Allied codebreakers in their attempts to crack the Enigma code.

U-559 Commander

Kptlt. Hans Heidtmann

(Feb 1941 – Oct 1942)

U-559 TIMETABLE		
Patrol Dates	**Operational Area**	**Ships Sunk**
4 Jun 1941 – 5 Jul 1941	Denmark Strait/North Atlantic	0
26 Jul 1941 – 22 Aug 1941	Central N Atlantic	1
20 Sep 1941 – 20 Oct 1941	Transit from St Nazaire to Mediterranean	0
24 Nov 1941 – 4 Dec 1941	E Mediterranean	1
8 Dec 1941 – 31 Dec 1941	Off Tobruk	2
16 Feb 1942 – 26 Feb 1942	Off Bardia	0
4 Mar 1942 – 21 Mar 1942	E Mediterranean	0
24 Mar 1942 – 12 May 1942	Transit from Salamis to Pola and back	0
18 May 1942 – 22 Jun 1942	E Mediterranean	1
29 Aug 1942 – 21 Sep 1942	Central Mediterranean	0
29 Sep 1942 – 30 Oct 1942	E Mediterranean	0

Swamp tactics

1943–44

U-371, on its first patrol commanded by Oblt. Horst-Arno Fenski, was unlucky enough to be the first victim of a new and highly effective Allied sub-hunting tactic in the Mediterranean.

Known as the Swamp, this tactic took advantage of the fact that by 1943 the Allies had a large number of air and sea bases in the Mediterranean, from Gibraltar along the North African coast to Egypt and the Levant and on Malta. Overwhelming Allied strength meant that the area in which a U-boat was known or suspected to be operating could be packed with surface escorts and patrol aircraft in a very short time. The searchers knew where the U-boat had been if it had made an attack. They could make a fair estimate of its course after an attack – basically away from Allied bases and shipping routes. They knew how fast a U-boat could travel underwater, which meant that they could make an estimate of its position and where it would probably be over the next few hours. They would then systematically and continually search the area, forcing the submarine to remain beneath the waves until its batteries ran out of charge and it had try to escape on the surface.

U-371 was spotted recharging her batteries on the surface off Djidjelli on the Algerian coast on the night of 2/3 May 1944. The area was immediately swamped with six escorts and three aircraft squadrons. They hunted the boat until the early morning of 4 May, when Oblt. Fenski had to surface to save his crew. He managed to fight back, and torpedoed and damaged the US destroyer escort USS *Menges* and the French destroyer escort *Sénégalais* before finally being forced to abandon his boat.

Redoubled efforts

The longest Swamp operation occurred in May 1944. On 14 May, U-616 commanded by Oblt.

Siegfried Koitschka attacked the convoy GUS 39 and damaged two Allied merchantmen. Immediately the Allies began to swamp the area. Two convoy escorts gained a contact, and three US Navy destroyers left Oran to join the hunt. U-616 torpedoed two more merchantmen, and four more American destroyers joined the hunt along with British and US aircraft.

The U-boat temporarily eluded the searching Allied forces, but over the next two days continuous relays of Hudsons from No. 500 Sqn RAF made sporadic contact and damaged the boat in repeated depth-charge attacks. Late on 16 May, the boat was spotted by an RAF Wellington out of Gibraltar, and the destroyers closed in at high speed. Forced to the surface early on 17 May, U-616 was dispatched by gunfire in less than five minutes.

Only five hours later, U-960, commanded by Oblt. Günther Heinrich, unsuccessfully attacked the destroyer USS *Ellyson*, which was carrying survivors from U-616, off Oran. Another Swamp operation was called. U-960 was sunk two days later on 19 May, northwest of Algiers, by depth charges from the destroyers USS *Niblack* and USS *Ludlow* and from Vickers Wellingtons and Lockheed Venturas of Nos. 36 and 500 Sqns RAF. Twenty of the boat's 51 crewmembers were picked up alive.

___BOATS THAT SERVED WITH 29TH FLOTILLA (52 BOATS)					
U-Boat	Type	Commissioned	Flotilla(s)	Patrols	Fate
U-29	VIIA	16-Nov-36	1 Sep 1943 – 30 Nov 1943 from 24 Flottille (training)	7 patrols. 11 ships sunk: total 62,765 GRT; 1 aircraft carrier (*HMS Courageous*) sunk: total 22,861t/22,500 tons	to 21. Flottille
U-73	VIIB	31-Oct-40	1 Jan 1942 – 16 Dec 1943 from 7. Flottille	16 patrols. 8 ships sunk: total 43,945 GRT; 4 warships (including aircraft carrier *HMS Eagle*) sunk: total 23,315t/22,947 tons; 3 ships damaged: total 22,928 GRT	Sunk 16 Dec 1943 in the Mediterranean near Oran by depth charges and gunfire from the destroyers USS *Woolsey* and USS *Trippe*. 16 dead and 34 survivors
U-74	VIIB	31-Oct-40	1 Dec 1941 – 2 May 1942 from 7. Flottille	8 patrols. 4 ships sunk: total 24,694 GRT; 1 warship sunk: total 940t/925 tons; 1 ship damaged: total 97 GRT; 1 auxiliary warship damaged: total 11,402 GRT	Sunk with all hands 2 May 1942 east of Cartagena, Spain, by depth charges from the destroyers HMS *Wishart*, HMS *Wrestler* and depth charges from an RAF Catalina of No. 202 Sqn. 47 dead
U-77	VIIC	18-Jan-41	1 May 1942 – 28 Mar 1943 from 23. Flottille	12 patrols. 14 ships sunk: total 31,186 GRT; 1 warship sunk: total 1067t/1050 tons; 1 ship damaged beyond repair: total 5222 GRT; 2 ships damaged: total 5384 GRT; 2 warships damaged: total 2926t/2880 tons	Sunk 28 Mar 1943 east of Cartagena, Spain, by 4 depth charges and 1 bomb from 2 Hudson aircraft of Nos. 48 and 233 Sqns. 38 dead and 9 survivors
U-81	VIIC	26-Apr-41	1 Dec 1941 – 9 Jan 1944 from 1. Flottille	17 patrols. 23 ships sunk: total 39,711 GRT; 1 auxiliary warship sunk: total 1150 GRT; 1 aircraft carrier (*HMS Ark Royal*, 13 Nov 1941) sunk: total 22,963t/22,600 tons; 1 ship damaged beyond repair: total 5917 GRT; 2 ships damaged: total 14,143 GRT	Sunk 9 Jan 1944 at Pola by US bombs. 2 dead. Raised 22 Apr 1944 and broken up
U-83	VIIB	8-Feb-41	1 May 1942 – 4 Mar 1943 from 23. Flottille	12 patrols. 5 ships sunk: total 8425 GRT; 1 auxiliary warship sunk: total 91 GRT; 1 ship damaged: total 2590 GRT; 1 auxiliary warship damaged: total 6746 GRT	Sunk with all hands 4 Mar 1943 southeast of Cartagena by 3 depth charges from an RAF Hudson. 50 dead
U-97	VIIC	28-Sep-40	1 May 1942 – 16 Jun 1943 from 23. Flottille	13 patrols. 15 ships sunk: total 64,404 GRT; 1 auxiliary warship sunk: total 6833 GRT; 1 ship damaged: total 9718 GRT	Sunk west of Haifa 16 Jun 1943 by depth charges from an Australian Hudson aircraft of No. 459 Sqn. 27 dead and 21 survivors
U-205	VIIC	3-May-41	1 Nov 1941 – 17 Feb 1943 from 3. Flottille	11 patrols. 1 ship sunk: total 2623 GRT; 1 warship sunk: total 5537t/5450 tons	Sunk 17 Feb 1943 north of Cyrene in the Mediterranean by depth charges from the destroyer HMS *Paladin* and a South African Bisley (Blenheim) aircraft. 8 dead and 42 survivors
U-223	VIIC	6-Jun-42	1 Nov 1943 – 30 Mar 1944 from 6. Flottille	6 patrols. 2 ships sunk: total 12,556 GRT; 1 warship sunk: total 1966t/1935 tons; 1 ship damaged beyond repair: total 4970 GRT; 1 warship damaged beyond repair: total 1321t/1300 tons	Sunk 30 Mar 1944 in the Mediterranean north of Palermo by depth charges from destroyers HMS *Laforey* and HMS *Tumult* and escort destroyers HMS *Hambledon* and HMS *Blencathra*. 23 dead and 27 survivors

BOATS THAT SERVED WITH 29TH FLOTILLA (52 BOATS)

U-Boat	Type	Commissioned	Flotilla(s)	Patrols	Fate
U-230	VIIC	24-Oct-42	1 Dec 1943 – 21 Aug 1944	8 patrols. 1 ship sunk: total 2868 GRT; 3 warships sunk: total 3643t/3585 tons	Ran aground 21 Aug 1944 in the Toulon roads during the Allied invasion of southern France. Scuttled. No casualties – 50 survivors
U-301	VIIC	9-May-42	1 Jan 1943 – 21 Jan 1943 from 1. Flottille	3 patrols	Sunk 21 Jan 1943 in the Mediterranean west of Bonifacio, torpedoed by the submarine HMS *Sahib*. 45 dead and 1 survivor
U-303	VIIC	7-Jul-42	1 Apr 1943 – 21 May 1943 from 7. Flottille	2 patrols. 1 ship sunk: total 4959 GRT	Sunk 21 May 1943 in the Mediterranean south of Toulon by torpedoes from the submarine HMS *Sickle*. 20 dead and 28 survivors
U-331	VIIC	31-Mar-41	15 Apr 1942 – 17 Nov 1942 from 23. Flottille	10 patrols. 1 auxiliary warship sunk: total 9135 GRT; 1 battleship (HMS *Barham*) sunk: total 31,599t/31,100 tons; 1 warship damaged: total 378t/372 tons	Badly damaged 17 Nov 1942 in the Mediterranean north of Algiers by an RAF Hudson. U-331 signalled surrender, but was sunk by a torpedo from an Albacore of HMS *Formidable*. 32 dead and 17 survivors
U-343	VIIC	18-Feb-43	1 Feb 1944 – 10 Mar 1944 from 3. Flottille	4 patrols	Sunk with all hands 10 Mar 1944 in the Mediterranean south of Sardinia by depth charges from the minesweeper/trawler HMS *Mull*. 51 dead
U-371	VIIC	15-Mar-41	15 Apr 1942 – 4 May 1944 from 23. Flottille	19 patrols. 9 ships sunk: total 57,235 GRT; 1 auxiliary warship sunk: total 545 GRT; 2 warships sunk: total 2322t/2286 tons; 2 ships damaged beyond repair: total 13,341 GRT; 4 ships damaged: total 28,072 GRT; 2 warships damaged: total 2540t/2500 tons	Scuttled on 4 May 1944 in the Mediterranean north of Constantine after attack by depth charges from destroyer escorts USS *Pride* and USS *Joseph E. Campbell*, French destroyer escort *Sénégalais* and escort destroyer HMS *Blankney*. 3 dead and 49 survivors
U-372	VIIC	19-Apr-41	14 Dec 1941 – 4 Aug 1942 from 1. Flottille	8 patrols. 3 ships sunk: total 11,751 GRT; 1 auxiliary warship sunk: total 14,650 GRT	Sunk 4 Aug 1942 southwest of Haifa by depth charges from destroyers HMS *Sikh* and HMS *Zulu*, escort destroyers HMS *Croome* and HMS *Tetcott*, and a Wellington of No. 221 Sqn RAF. All 48 crew survived
U-374	VIIC	21-Jun-41	14 Dec 1941 – 12 Jan 1942 from 1. Flottille	3 patrols. 1 ship sunk: total 3349 GRT; 2 auxiliary warships sunk: total 992 GRT	Sunk 12 Jan 1942 in the western Mediterranean east of Cape Spartivento, torpedoed by submarine HMS *Unbeaten*. 42 dead and 1 survivor
U-375	VIIC	19-Jul-41	1 Jan 1942 – 30 Jul 1943 from 3. Flottille	11 patrols. 9 ships sunk: total 16,847 GRT; 1 ship damaged beyond repair: total 6288 GRT; 1 warship damaged: total 2693t/2650 tons	Sunk with all hands 30 Jul 1943 northwest of Malta by depth charges from the submarine chaser USS *PC-624*. 46 dead
U-380	VIIC	22-Dec-41	1 Dec 1942 – 11 Mar 1944 from 6. Flottille	12 patrols. 2 ships sunk: total 14,063 GRT; 1 ship damaged beyond repair: total 7178 GRT; 1 ship damaged: total 7191 GRT	Sunk 11 Mar 1944 in the Mediterranean near Toulon by US bombs. 1 dead
U-407	VIIC	18-Dec-41	1 Dec 1942 – 19 Sep 1944 from 9. Flottille	12 patrols. 3 ships sunk: total 26,892 GRT; 1 ship damaged beyond repair: total 7176 GRT; 1 ship damaged: total 6207 GRT; 2 warships damaged: total 18,187t/17,900 tons	Sunk 19 Sep 1944 south of the Greek island of Milos by depth charges from the destroyers HMS *Troubridge*, HMS *Terpsichore* and the Polish destroyer *Garland*. 5 dead and 48 survivors
U-409	VIIC	21-Jan-42	1 Jul 1943 – 12 Jul 1943 from 9. Flottille	6 patrols. 3 ships sunk: total 16,199 GRT; 1 ship damaged: total 7519 GRT	Sunk 12 Jul 1943 northeast of Algiers by depth charges from the destroyer HMS *Inconstant*. 11 dead and 37 survivors
U-410	VIIC	23-Feb-42	1 Jun 1943 – 11 Mar 1944 from 7. Flottille	7 patrols. 7 ships sunk: total 47,244 GRT; 2 warships sunk: total 7006t/6895 tons; 1 ship damaged beyond repair: total 3722 GRT; 1 ship damaged: total 7134 GRT	Damaged beyond repair 11 Mar 1944 at Toulon in the south of France by USAAF bombs
U-414	VIIC	1-Jul-42	1 May 1943 – 25 May 1943 from 6. Flottille	3 patrols. 1 ship sunk: total 5979 GRT; 1 ship damaged: total 7134 GRT	Sunk with all hands 25 May 1943 in the western Mediterranean by depth charges from the corvette HMS *Vetch*. 47 dead
U-421	VIIC	13-Jan-43	1 Apr 1944 – 29 Apr 1944 from 9. Flottille	2 patrols	Sunk 29 Apr 1944 in Toulon by US bombs
U-431	VIIC	5-Apr-41	1 Jan 1942 – 21 Oct 1943 from 3. Flottille	16 patrols. 7 ships sunk: total 9752 GRT; 1 auxiliary warship sunk: total 313 GRT; 2 warships sunk: total 3605t/3548 tons; 1 ship damaged beyond repair: total 6415 GRT; 1 ship damaged: total 3560 GRT; 1 warship damaged: total 457t/450 tons	Sunk with all hands 21 Oct 1943 near Algiers by depth charges from a Vickers Wellington of No. 179 Sqn RAF. 52 dead
U-443	VIIC	18-Apr-42	1 Jan 1943 – 23 Feb 1943 from 9. Flottille	3 patrols. 3 ships sunk: total 19,435 GRT; 1 warship sunk: total 1104t/1087 tons	Sunk with all hands 23 Feb 1943 in the Mediterranean near Algiers by depth charges from escort destroyers HMS *Bicester*, HMS *Lamerton* and HMS *Wheatland*. 48 dead
U-450	VIIC	12-Sep-42	1 Dec 1943 – 10 Mar 1944 from 9. Flottille	4 patrols	Sunk 10 Mar 1944 off the Italian coast south of Ostia by depth charges from escort destroyers HMS *Blankney*, HMS *Blencathra*, HMS *Brecon* and HMS *Exmoor* and destroyer USS *Madison*. No casualties – 42 survivors
U-453	VIIC	26-Jun-41	1 Jan 1942 – 21 May 1944 from 7. Flottille	17 patrols. 9 ships sunk: total 23,289 GRT; 1 warship sunk: total 848t/835 tons; 1 warship damaged beyond repair: total 1732t/1705 tons; 2 ships damaged: total 16,610 GRT	Sunk 21 May 1944 in the Ionian Sea northeast of Cape Spartivento by depth charges from destroyers HMS *Termagant* and HMS *Tenacious* and escort destroyer HMS *Liddesdale*. 1 dead and 51 survivors
U-455	VIIC	21-Aug-41	1 Mar 1944 – 6 Apr 1944 from 7. Flottille	10 patrols. 3 ships sunk: total 17,685 GRT	Missing with all hands in the Mediterranean on or after 2 Apr 1944, while returning from a patrol off Algiers. 51 dead. May have been sunk 6 Apr 1944 near La Spezia by a German mine
U-458	VIIC	12-Dec-41	1 Nov 1942 – 22 Aug 1943 from 3. Flottille	7 patrols. 2 ships sunk: total 7584 GRT	Sunk 22 Aug 1943 in the Mediterranean southeast of Pantelleria by depth charges from escort destroyer HMS *Easton* and Greek escort destroyer *Pindos*. 8 dead and 39 survivors
U-466	VIIC	17-Jun-42	1 Apr 1944 – 19 Aug 1944 from 3. Flottille	5 patrols	Damaged at Toulon 5 Jul 1944 by bombs from USAAF B-24s. Scuttled 19 Aug 1944 during the Allied invasion of southern France
U-471	VIIC	5-May-43	1 May 1944 – 6 Aug 1944 from 1. Flottille	3 patrols	Bombed in dry dock 6 Aug 1944 in Toulon by USAAF B-24 Liberator. Raised in 1945 and entered French service as the *Millé*. Redesignated Q339, and stricken 9 Jul 1963

BOATS THAT SERVED WITH 29TH FLOTILLA (52 BOATS)

U-Boat	Type	Commissioned	Flotilla(s)	Patrols	Fate
U-557	VIIC	13-Feb-41	5 Dec 1941 – 16 Dec 1941 from 1. Flottille	4 patrols. 6 ships sunk: total 31,729 GRT; 1 warship (HMS *Galatea*) sunk: total 5304t/5220 tons	Sank with all hands 16 Dec 1941 in the Mediterranean west of Crete, after being rammed by the Italian torpedo boat *Orione*, which had mistaken the U-boat for a British submarine. 43 dead
U-559	VIIC	27-Feb-41	15 Apr 1942 – 30 Oct 1942 from 23. Flottille	11 patrols. 4 ships sunk: total 11,811 GRT; 1 warship sunk: total 1077t/1060 tons	Sunk 30 Oct 1942 northeast of Port Said by depth charges from destroyers HMS *Pakenham*, HMS *Petard* and HMS *Hero*, escort destroyers HMS *Dulverton* and HMS *Hurworth*, and an RAF Wellesley. 7 dead and 38 survivors. Boarded by three British sailors, who recovered vital Enigma material before the boat sank, taking two of the boarders to their deaths
U-562	VIIC	20-Mar-41	1 Jan 1942 – 19 Feb 1943 from 1. Flottille	9 patrols. 6 ships sunk: total 37,287 GRT; 1 ship damaged: total 3359 GRT	Sunk with all hands 19 Feb 1943 in the Mediterranean northeast of Benghazi by depth charges from destroyer HMS *Isis*, escort destroyer HMS *Hursley* and a Wellington of No. 38 Sqn RAF. 49 dead
U-565	VIIC	10-Apr-41	1 Jan 1942 – 24 Sep 1944 from 1. Flottille	21 patrols. 3 ships sunk: total 11,347 GRT; 3 warships sunk (including cruiser HMS *Naiad* and HM Submarine *Simoom*): total 7829t/7705 tons; 3 ships damaged: total 33,862 GRT	Badly damaged by US bombs 19 Sep 1944 at Piraeus (Athens). 5 crewmen killed. Scuttled five days later
U-568	VIIC	1-May-41	1 Jan 1942 – 29 May 1942 from 3. Flottille	5 patrols. 1 ship sunk: total 6023 GRT; 2 warships sunk: total 1880t/1850 tons; 1 warship damaged: total 1656t/1630 tons	Sunk 29 May 1942 northeast of Tobruk by depth charges from destroyer HMS *Hero* and escort destroyers HMS *Eridge* and HMS *Hurworth*. No casualties – 47 survivors
U-573	VIIC	5-Jun-41	1 Jan 1942 – 2 May 1942	4 patrols. 1 ship sunk: total 5289 GRT	Damaged northwest of Algiers by depth charges from a Hudson of No. 233 Sqn RAF. 1 dead and 43 survivors. Interned at Cartagena 2 May 1942. Sold to Spain 2 Aug 1942. Became the Spanish submarine G 7 (later S-01). In commission until 1971 – the last WWII U-boat in service
U-577	VIIC	3-Jul-41	1 Jan 1942 – 15 Jan 1942 from 7. Flottille	3 patrols	Sunk with all hands 15 Jan 1942 northwest of Mersa Matruh by depth charges from a Royal Navy Swordfish of No. 815 Sqn. 43 dead. Previously credited to an RAF Sunderland on 9 Jan, which actually attacked U-568, causing minor damage
U-586	VIIC	4-Sep-41	1 Mar 1944 – 5 Jul 1944 from 6. Flottille	12 patrols. 2 ships sunk: total 12,716 GRT; 1 ship damaged: total 9057 GRT	Sunk 5 Jul 1944 at Toulon by bombs from USAAF B-24s of the 233rd BS
U-593	VIIC	23-Oct-41	1 Nov 1942 – 13 Dec 1943 from 7. Flottille	16 patrols. 9 ships sunk: total 38,290 GRT; 3 warships sunk: total 2949t/2902 tons; 1 ship damaged b/r: total 8426 GRT; 1 warship damaged b/r: total 1651t/1625 tons; 1 ship damaged: total 4853 GRT; 1 warship damaged: total 1651t/1625 tons	Sunk 13 Dec 1943 after a 32-hour chase in the western Mediterranean, by depth charges from the destroyer USS *Wainwright* and the escort destroyer HMS *Calpe*. No casualties – 51 survivors
U-596	VIIC	13-Nov-41	19 Nov 1942 – 24 Sep 1944 from 3. Flottille	12 patrols. 12 ships sunk: total 41,411 GRT; 1 warship sunk: total 250t/246 tons; 2 ships damaged: total 14,180 GRT	Scuttled 24 Sep 1944 Skaramanga Bay, Greece, after damage by US bombs. 1 crewman killed
U-602	VIIC	29-Dec-41	1 Jan 1943 – 19 Apr 1943 from 7. Flottille	4 patrols. 1 warship damaged beyond repair: total 1565t/1540 tons	Missing with all hands on or after 19 Apr 1943, when last message was sent from north of Oran. 48 dead. Wreck found in 2005 off the coast of Ibiza. Loss previously credited to an RAF Hudson, but that attack was against U-453 and caused no damage
U-605	VIIC	15-Jan-42	1 Nov 1942 – 14 Nov 1942 from 9. Flottille	3 patrols. 3 ships sunk: total 8409 GRT	Sunk with all hands 14 Nov 1942 near Algiers by depth charges from an RAF Hudson of No. 233 Sqn. 46 dead. Loss previously credited to corvettes HMS *Lotus* and HMS *Poppy* 13 Nov 1942, but in fact they attacked U-77, causing minor damage
U-616	VIIC	2-Apr-42	1 Jun 1943 – 17 May 1944 from 6. Flottille	9 patrols. 2 warships sunk: total 2216t/2181 tons; 2 ships damaged: total 17,754 GRT	Sunk 17 May 1944 east of Cartagena after a three-day battle with the destroyers USS *Nields*, USS *Gleaves*, USS *Ellyson*, USS *Macomb*, USS *Hambleton*, USS *Rodman* and USS *Emmons*, and an RAF Wellington. No casualties – 53 survivors
U-617	VIIC	9-Apr-42	1 Dec 1942 – 12 Sep 1943 from 7. Flottille	7 patrols. 8 ships sunk: total 25,879 GRT; 1 auxiliary warship sunk: total 810 GRT; 2 warships sunk: total 3759t/3700 tons	Ran aground in the Mediterranean near Melilla 12 Sep 1943, attacked by RAF Hudsons and Royal Navy Swordfish. Destroyed by gunfire from corvette HMS *Hyacinth* and minesweeper HMAS *Wollongong*. No casualties – 49 survivors
U-642	VIIC	1-Oct-42	1 Dec 1943 – 5 Jul 1944 from 6. Flottille	4 patrols. 1 ship sunk: total 2125 GRT	Sunk in port 5 July 1944 at Toulon by US bombs
U-652	VIIC	3-Apr-41	1 Jan 1942 – 2 Jun 1942 from 3. Flottille	8 patrols. 2 ships sunk: total 8152 GRT; 1 auxiliary warship sunk: total 558 GRT; 2 warships sunk: total 2784t/2740 tons; 2 ships damaged: total 9918 GRT; 1 auxiliary warship damaged: total 10,917 GRT	Badly damaged in the Mediterranean in the Gulf of Sollum by depth charges from a Royal Navy Swordfish. Scuttled 2 Jun 1942 by torpedoes from U-81. No casualties – 46 survivors
U-660	VIIC	8-Jan-42	1 Nov 1942 – 12 Nov 1942 from 9. Flottille	3 patrols. 2 ships sunk: total 10,066 GRT; 2 ships damaged: total 10,447 GRT	Scuttled 12 Nov 1942 in the Mediterranean off Oran, after depth-charge attack by corvettes HMS *Lotus* and HMS *Starwort*. 2 dead and 45 survivors
U-755	VIIC	3-Nov-41	1 Dec 1942 – 28 May 1943 from 9. Flottille	5 patrols. 1 ship sunk: total 928 GRT; 2 auxiliary warships sunk: total 2974 GRT	Sunk 28 May 1943 northwest of Majorca by rockets from a Hudson of No. 608 Sqn RAF. 40 dead and 9 survivors (picked up by the neutral Spanish destroyer *Velasco*)
U-952	VIIC	10-Dec-42	1 Feb 1944 – 6 Aug 1944 from 3. Flottille	5 patrols. 2 ships sunk: total 13,374 GRT; 1 warship sunk: total 940t/925 tons; 1 ship damaged: total 7176 GRT	Sunk 6 Aug 1944 in Toulon by US bombs
U-967	VIIC	11-Mar-43	1 Mar 1944 – 11 Aug 1944 from 29 Flottille	3 patrols. 1 warship sunk: total 1321t/1300 tons	Scuttled 11 Aug 1944 in Toulon. 2 crewmen killed
U-969	VIIC	24-Mar-43	1 Mar 1944 – 6 Aug 1944 from 7. Flottille	3 patrols. 2 ships damaged beyond repair: total 14,352 GRT	Destroyed 6 Aug 1944 in Toulon by USAAF bombs

30 Unterseebootsflottille

The 30th Flotilla was founded in October 1942 under the command of Kptlt. Helmut Rosenbaum. The operational area was the Black Sea, where a handful of Type II boats were sent to prevent Soviet reinforcements reaching areas being attacked by the *Wehrmacht* in the summer of 1942.

GETTING THE BOATS TO the Black Sea presented a major challenge. Type IIs lacked the range to reach the area, and in any case would not have been allowed to pass through the Bosphorous.

In order to get the boats to the operational area, they had to be broken down into manageable portions. Engines, keels, conning towers, deck sections, hydroplanes, batteries and propellers were removed. The hulls were barged up the Elbe towards Dresden, where each was moved onto two 70-tonne (69-ton) vehicles for transport at less than walking pace along the autobahn to Ingolstadt.

Again mounted on the pontoons that had been transported by rail from Dresden, the stripped boats were moved by water to Linz, where they were reassembled. From there, they went under their own power downriver to Konstanza.

30TH FLOTILLA BASE LOCATION

Konstanza (Romania)
BLACK SEA

MEDITERRANEAN SEA

Commanders

Kptlt. Helmut Rosenbaum
(Oct 1942 – May 1944)

Kptlt. Clemens Schöler *(May 1944 – Jul 1944)*
Kptlt. Klaus Petersen *(Jul 1944 – Oct 1944)*

▲ **Showing the strain**
The engine room was the hottest place to work in a U-boat, and was especially cramped on the smaller Type II submarines.

U-9

From 28 October 1942 to 11 August 1944, U-9 (formerly of 1st Flotilla) mounted 12 patrols in the Black Sea, operating out of Konstanza against Soviet coastal convoys off the Caucasus. In May 1943, she damaged a Soviet tanker beyond repair, and claimed another probably sunk in October. In March 1944 her crew claimed to have shot down two Soviet aircraft, and in March damaged a Soviet patrol vessel. U-9 claimed to have damaged another tanker in May 1944. U-9 was sunk in port on 20 August 1944 at Konstanza by bombs from Soviet aircraft.

U-19

From 21 January 1943 to 10 September 1944, U-19 mounted 11 patrols in the Black Sea, operating out of Konstanza against Soviet coastal convoys off the Caucasus. On 14 February 1943, she sank a Soviet freighter, and claimed damage to a passenger/troop ship on 23 March.

On 27 June 1944, U-19 sank a cargo barge, and on 29 August 1944 she sank a Soviet minesweeper after she had evacuated Konstanza following Romania's surrender. This was the last sinking by a U-boat in the Black Sea.

U-19 was scuttled on 10 September 1944 off the coast of Turkey in the Black Sea, in position 41.16N, 31.26E.

U-19 TIMETABLE (PRE-BLACK SEA DEPLOYMENT)		
Patrol Dates	Operational Area	Ships Sunk
25 Aug 1939 – 15 Sep 1939	Reconnaissance of North Sea	0
14 Oct 1939 – 18 Oct 1939	Minelaying off English E Coast	3
15 Nov 1939 – 20 Nov 1939	Minelaying off Orford Ness	1
4 Jan 1940 – 12 Jan 1940	NE Scotland	1
18 Jan 1940 – 28 Jan 1940	NE coast of England	4
12 Feb 1940 – 26 Feb 1940	E of the Shetlands	0
14 Mar 1940 – 23 Mar 1940	Pentland Firth/NE Scotland	4
3 Apr 1940 – 23 Apr 1940	Norwegian waters	0
May 1940 – Apr 1942	Training	0

Soviet advances

Two other flotilla boats – U-20 and U-23 – were also scuttled on 10 September 1944 near the Turkish coast, as Soviet troops advanced from the Ukraine towards the German base at Konstanza.

U-19 Commanders

Kptlt. Viktor Schütze (Jan 1936 – Sep 1937)

Kptlt. Hans Meckel (Sep 1937 – Nov 1939)

KrvKpt. Wilhelm Müller-Arnecke

(Nov 1939 – Jan 1940)

Kptlt. Joachim Schepke (Jan 1940 – Apr 1940)

Kptlt. Wilfried Prellberg (May 1940 – Jun 1940)

Kptlt. Peter Lohmeyer (Jun 1940 – Oct 1940)

Wolfgang Kaufmann (Oct 1940 – Nov 1940)

KrvKpt. Rudolf Schendel (Nov 1940 – May 1941)

Oblt. Gerhard Litterscheid (Jun 1941 – Feb 1942)

Kptlt. Hans-Ludwig Gaude

(Dec 1941 – Dec 1943)

Oblt. Willy Ohlenburg (Dec 1943 – Sep 1944)

Oblt. Hubert Verpoorten (Sep 1944 – Sep 1944)

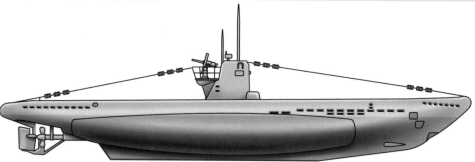

▲ U-19

Type IIB

Until the arrival of the six Type II boats operated by the 30th Flotilla, supported by torpedo boats, minesweepers and other small craft, the Soviet Navy had been the dominant force in the Black Sea.

Specifications

Crew: 25

Powerplant: Diesel/electric

Max Speed: 33/15.4km/hr (17.8/8.3kt) surf/sub

Surface Range: 3334km (1800nm)

Displacement: 283/334t (279/329 tons) surf/sub

Dimensions (length/beam/draught): 42.7 x 4.1 x 3.8m (140.1 x 13.5 x 12.5ft)

Commissioned: 16 Jan 1936

Armament: 6 torpedoes (3 bow tubes); 1 x 2cm (0.8in) gun

BOATS THAT SERVED WITH 30TH FLOTILLA (6 BOATS)					
U-Boat	Type	Commissioned	Flotilla(s)	Patrols	Fate
U-9	IIB	21-Aug-35	1 Oct 1942 – 20 Aug 1944 from 24. Flottille	19 patrols. 7 ships sunk: total 16,669 GRT; 1 warship sunk: total 561t/552 tons; 1 warship damaged: total 419t/412 tons	Sunk by Soviet aircraft 20 Aug 1944 at Konstanza, Black Sea
U-18	IIB	4-Jan-36	6 May 1943 – 25 Aug 1944 from 24. Flottille	14 patrols. 3 ships sunk: total 1985 GRT; 1 ship damaged: total 7745 GRT; 1 warship damaged: total 57t/56 tons	Scuttled 25 Aug 1944 at Konstanza, Black Sea
U-19	IIB	16-Jan-36	1 Oct 1942 – 10 Sep 1944 from 22. Flottille	20 patrols. 14 ships sunk: total 35,430 GRT; 1 warship sunk: total 448t/441 tons	Scuttled in the Black Sea 10 Sept 1944 off the coast of Turkey
U-20	IIB	1-Feb-36	1 Oct 1942 – 10 Sep 1944 from 21. Flottille	17 patrols. 14 ships sunk: total 37,669 GRT; 1 ship damaged beyond repair: total 844 GRT; 1 ship damaged: total 1846 GRT	Scuttled in the Black Sea 10 Sept 1944 off the coast of Turkey
U-23	IIB	24-Sep-36	1 Oct 1942 – 10 Sep 1944 from 21. Flottille	16 patrols. 7 ships sunk: total 11,094 GRT; 2 warships sunk: total 1433t/1410 tons; 3 ships damaged beyond repair: total 18,199 GRT; 1 ship damaged: total 1005 GRT; 1 warship damaged: total 57t/56 tons	Scuttled in the Black Sea 10 Sept 1944 off the coast of Turkey
U-24	IIB	10-Oct-36	1 Oct 1942 – 25 Aug 1944 from 21. Flottille	20 patrols. 1 ship sunk: total 961 GRT; 5 warships sunk: total 580t/571 tons; 1 ship a total loss: total 7886 GRT; 1 ship damaged: total 7661 GRT	Scuttled 25 Aug 1944 at Konstanza, Black Sea

33 Unterseebootsflottille

The 33rd Flotilla was founded in September 1944 under the command of *Korvettenkapitän* Georg Schewe. Nominally based at Flensburg, to the north of Kiel, the flotilla's boats were in fact scattered in operating bases from France to the Far East.

THE LOSS OR ISOLATION of the main U-boat operating bases in France in 1944 saw boats being transferred, where possible, to Germany or Norway. The long-range boats that had been controlled by 12th Flotilla at Bordeaux were now operating under the auspices of the 33rd Flotilla, though a number of its boats that had been undergoing repair were trapped in encircled bases like St Nazaire. However, a good proportion of the long-range boats had been at sea during the Allied invasion of Europe – operating in such diverse locations as off the South American coast, off South Africa, in the Indian Ocean and the Arabian Sea – or were alongside in the Japanese-held ports of Penang, Singapore and Batavia or at Kobe in the Home Islands.

33RD FLOTILLA BASE LOCATION – EUROPE

ATLANTIC OCEAN

● Flensburg

33RD FLOTILLA (1944–45)	
Type	Boats assigned
Type VIIC (incl 4 x Type VIIC/41)	18
Type IXC	3
Type IXC/40	41
Type IXD2 (incl 1 x Type IXD1)	9
Type XB	2
Italian UIT	2

U-boats still mounted offensive patrols from these bases, but at least as important was their transport function. A submarine will never make a good freighter, but the large Type IXD and Type XB boats could bring 200 tonnes (197 tons) or so of strategic materials, which would otherwise be unobtainable. Most of the boats still in the Far East when Germany surrendered in May 1945 were given to the Imperial Japanese Navy.

Commanders

Korvkpt. Georg Schewe
(Sep 1944 – Oct 1944)
Korvkpt. Günther Kuhnke
(Oct 1944 – May 1945)

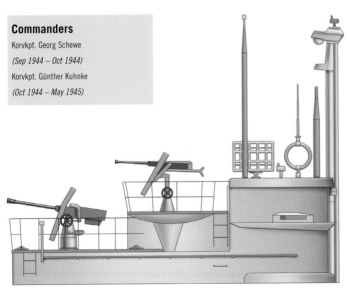

U-857 INSIGNIA

There is no photographic evidence that the 33rd Flotilla had a unit insignia. However, many of the boats used their own symbols, like the sword and oak leaves carried by the Type IXC/40 boat U-857.

◀ **Type VIIC 1945 conversion bridge**

The standard weapons fit on late-war conning towers included a single or twin 3.7cm (1.5in) mount aft with two twin 2cm (0.8in) C38 mounts side by side immediately aft of the armoured bridge. The increasingly cluttered towers were also fitted with Schnorchels, direction-finding loops and radar-warning aerials, in addition to the two periscopes standard since the beginning of the war.

Star commanders
1944–45

Operating in the distant and challenging waters of the Indian Ocean and Southeast Asia called for great seamanship skills from the captains and crews of the 33rd Flotilla's boats.

Fregattenkapitän Ottoheinrich Junker

Born on 12 July 1905 at Freiburg, Junker joined the *Reichsmarine* with Crew 24. One of the earliest members of the U-boat arm, he commanded the early Type VII boat U-33 before the war, going on to serve with the TEK (Torpedo Testing Command) before he commissioned U-532 in November 1942. After one Atlantic mission, Junker took the submarine to the Far East as one of the *Monsun* boats. In four patrols he sank eight ships for a total of 46,895 GRT. The boat returned from Jakarta in January 1945, and surrendered in England in May of that year. Junker died on 28 July 2000, aged 95.

STAR COMMANDERS		
Commander	Patrols	Ships Sunk
Fregattenkapitän Ottoheinrich Junker	4	8
Kapitänleutnant Alfred Eick	3	8

Kapitänleutnant Alfred Eick

Born on 9 March 1916 in Essen, Eick joined the *Kriegsmarine* with Crew 37. He commanded U-510 on three patrols, sinking eight ships totalling 56,972 GRT and damaging two more, as well as sinking one small auxiliary warship. He surrendered his boat at St Nazaire in May 1945.

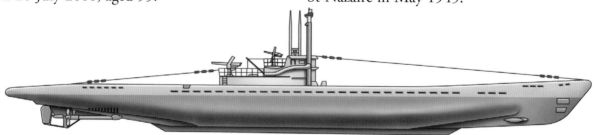

Specifications

Crew: 48–50

Powerplant: Diesel/electric

Max Speed: 33.9/13.5km/hr (18.3/7.3kt) surf/sub

Surface Range: 20,370km (11,000nm)

Displacement: 1138/1252t (1120/1232 tons) surf/sub

Dimensions (length/beam/draught): 76.8 x 6.9 x 4.7m (252 x 22.6 x 15.42ft)

Commissioned: 11 Nov 1942

Armament: 22 torpedoes (4 bow/2 stern tubes); 1 x 10.5cm (4.1in), 1 x 3.7cm (1.5in) and 1 x 2cm (0.8in) guns

▲ **U-532**

Type IXC/40

Commanded by torpedo expert Ottoheinrich Junker, U-532 surrendered at Liverpool on 10 May 1945. She was carrying a cargo of tin, rubber, wolfram and molybdenum.

U-195
TYPE IXD1

One of only two Type IXD1 boats, U-195 was commissioned in September 1942. The boat was fitted with experimental high-speed diesels, which proved unsatisfactory in service.

O N HER FIRST PATROL in South African waters, U-195 sank two ships. However, her six S-boat diesels, fitted to provide a higher surface speed, caused continual problems, and they also belched clouds of black smoke when in operation on the surface. They were replaced by standard Type

IX engines, and both U-195 and her sister, U-180, were converted to transport boats. They lost their torpedo armament, and carried up to 256 tonnes (252 tons) of cargo. In May 1945, U-195 passed to Japan, becoming the I-506 on 15 July. The boat was surrendered to the Allies at Jakarta in August 1945.

U-195 Commanders

Korvkpt. Heinz Buchholz	Oblt. Friedrich Steinfeldt
(Sep 1942 – Oct 1943)	*(Apr 1944 – May 1945)*

U-195 TIMETABLE

Patrol Dates	Operational Area	Ships Sunk
20 Mar 1943 – 23 Jul 1943	South Atlantic off South Africa	3
24 Aug 1944 – 28 Dec 1944	Transit from Bordeaux to Asia	0
19 Jan 1945 – 4 March 1945	Transit to France but returned to Batavia	0

Specifications

Crew: 55

Powerplant: Diesel/electric

Max Speed: 38.5/12.8km/hr (20.8/6.9kt) surf/sub

Surface Range: 18,335km (9900nm)

Displacement: 1636/1828t (1610/1799 tons)

Dimensions (length/beam/draught): 87.6 x 7.5 x 5.4m (287.42 x 24.58 x 17.75ft)

Commissioned: 11 Sep 1942

Armament: 24 torpedoes; 1 x 10.5cm (4.1in), 1 x 3.7cm (1.5in) and 1 x 2cm (0.8in) guns

▲ **U-195**

Type IXD1

U-195's last patrol was to be a cargo run back to France from the Dutch East Indies, but after about three weeks the boat developed a mechanical fault and was forced to return to Batavia, where she was given to the Japanese.

U-196

TYPE IXD2

Built by AG Weser at Bremen, U-196 was commissioned in September 1942 under the command of the experienced *Korvettenkapitän* Eitel-Friedrich Kentrat.

On its first patrol to the Indian Ocean, U-196 was at sea for 225 days before returning to Bordeaux, the longest submarine patrol of the war. In all that time she destroyed just two ships and damaged another.

The boat's second patrol, which ended at Penang, lasted some five months, and accounted for only one victim.

On its third patrol, under a new commander, U-196 put into Batavia before setting off into the Indian Ocean. The boat was declared missing with

U-196 TIMETABLE

Patrol Dates	Operational Area	Ships Sunk
13 Mar 1943 – 23 Oct 1943	Indian Ocean	2
16 Mar 1944 – 10 Aug 1944	Indian Ocean	1
30 Nov 1944 – 1 Dec 1944	East Indies	0

U-196 Commanders

Korvkpt. Eitel-Friedrich Kentrat	Korvkpt. Werner Striegler
(Sep 1942 – Sep 1944)	*(Oct 1944 – Dec 1944)*

all hands on 1 December 1944 south of Java, just one day after setting off, and may have been lost on the day of her departure as she traversed the Sunda Strait. All 65 crew were killed.

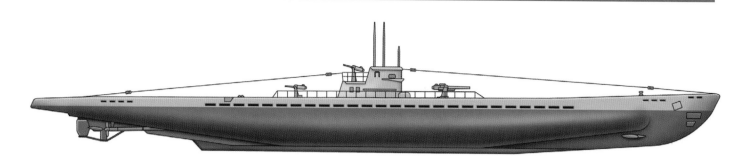

Specifications

Crew: 57

Powerplant: Diesel/electric

Max Speed: 35.6/12.8km/hr (19.2/6.9kt) surf/sub

Surface Range: 43,900km (23,700nm)

Displacement: 1616/1803t (1590/1775 tons)

Dimensions (length/beam/draught): 87.6 x 7.5
x 5.4m (287.42 x 24.58 x 17.75ft)

Commissioned: 11 Sep 1942

Armament: 22 torpedoes; 1 x 10.5cm (4.1in), 1
x 3.7cm (1.5in) and 1 x 2cm (0.8in) guns

▲ U-196

Type IXD2

Although not particularly successful in terms of sinking enemy ships, U-196, under the command of Eitel-Friedrich Kentrat, mounted two of the longest U-boat patrols undertaken during World War II.

U-510

TYPE IXC

Laid down at Deutsche Werft, Hamburg, at the beginning of November 1940, U-510 was commissioned there just over a year later, on 25 November 1941.

AFTER ITS INITIAL training with the 4th Flotilla, U-510 was assigned to the 10th Flotilla at Lorient. After four patrols in the central and western Atlantic, the boat was sent to the Indian

U-510 TIMETABLE		
Patrol Dates	Operational Area	Ships Sunk
7 Jul 1942 – 13 Sep 1942	Western Atlantic	2
14 Oct 1942 – 12 Dec 1942	Central Atlantic	0
16 Jan 1943 – 16 Apr 1943	Central Atlantic	2
3 Jun 1943 – 29 Aug 1943	Central Atlantic	3
3 Nov 1943 – 5 Apr 1944	Indian Ocean	6
12 Apr 1944 – 3 Dec 1944	Various ports in SE Asia and Japan	0
11 Jan 1945 – 23 Apr 1945	Transit from Batavia to St Nazaire	1

U-510 Commanders

Fregkpt. Karl Neitzel *(Nov 1941 – May 1943)*

Kptlt. Alfred Eick *(May 1943 – May 1945)*

Specifications

Crew: 48–50

Powerplant: Diesel/electric

Max Speed: 33.9/13.5km/hr (18.3/7.3kt) surf/sub

Surface Range: 20,370km (11,000nm)

Displacement: 1138/1252t (1120/1232 tons)

Dimensions (length/beam/draught): 76.8 x 6.8
x 4.7m (252 x 22.31 x 15.42ft)

Commissioned: 25 Nov 1941

Armament: 22 torpedoes; 1 x 10.5cm (4.1in), 1
x 3.7cm (1.5in) and 1 x 2cm (0.8in) guns

▲ U-510

Type IXC

On its third patrol, U-510 attacked the Trinidad-bound convoy BT 6 to the north of Cayenne. In addition to sinking two ships totalling over 10,000 GRT, the boat torpedoed and damaged a further six vessels totalling nearly 45,000 GRT.

Ocean. Late in 1944 as part of the 33rd Flotilla the boat shuttled between Penang, Singapore, Kobe in Japan and Batavia before returning to Europe. Surrendered to French forces at St Nazaire on 12 May 1945, she was taken into French Navy use and renamed the *Bouan* in French service. U-510 was decommissioned on 1 May 1959 as the Q176, and was broken up a year later.

The surrender of U-234

TYPE XB

After the loss of U-233 in July 1944, it was decided not to use U-234 as a minelaying boat. She was rebuilt as a long-range transport intended to ship vital cargoes to Japanese ports.

On 25 March 1945, U-234 left Kiel and a few days later reached Kristiansand, Norway. On board was a high-value cargo, which included technical drawings of advanced weapons, an Me-262 jet fighter in crates, several high-ranking German experts on various technologies, including rocketry and jets, two Japanese naval officers – Hideo Tomonaga and Genzo Shoji – and 560kg (1230lb) of uranium oxide intended for Japanese nuclear research laboratories in Osaka and Tokyo.

On 16 April 1945, U-234 left Norway en route to Japan. With such an important cargo the submarine's commander, *Kapitänleutnant* Fehler, had to avoid any possible contact with the enemy. U-234 ran deep and submerged for two weeks after leaving Kristiansand. Only after making it into the Atlantic did Kptlt. Fehler feel sufficiently confident to surface for two hours each night.

On 10 May, U-234 picked up a shortwave transmission carrying Karl Dönitz's announcement of Germany's surrender: 'My U-boat men … you have fought like lions … lay down your arms.' Instructions were given to proceed to the nearest Allied port, but U-234 was so positioned that several possible destinations existed. Fehler decided to head to the United States. Unwilling to be captured, Hideo Tomonaga and Genzo Shoji committed suicide by taking sleeping pills.

Nuclear surprise

On 14 May, an American boarding party took over and directed U-234 to Portsmouth, New Hampshire. Despite tight security, the arrival of U-234 at the docks became a major news event. Much of U-234's top secret cargo, 245 tonnes (240 tons) of documents and war materials, was shipped to Washington and opened out of sight of the press's cameras. The presence of so much uranium oxide was perhaps the biggest shock, indicating that both Germany and Japan had ongoing nuclear programmes.

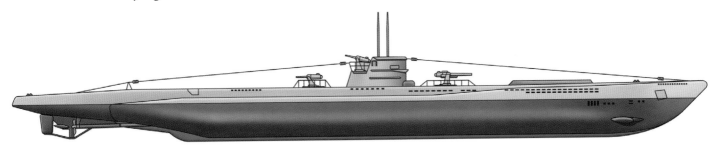

▲ **U-234**

Type XB

Built as minelayers, the large Type XB boats were used more often as milch cow supply boats or as submarine transports, bringing scarce strategic materials through the tight Allied blockade of the coast of occupied Europe.

Specifications	
Crew: 52	Dimensions (length/beam/draught): 89.8 x 9.2 x 4.7m (294.58 x 30.16 x 15.42ft)
Powerplant: Diesel/electric	
Max Speed: 30.4/13km/hr (16.4/7kt) surf/sub	Commissioned: 2 Mar 1944
Surface Range: 26,760km (14,450nm)	Armament: 66 mines; 11 torpedoes; 1 x 10.5cm (4.1in), 1 x 3.7cm (1.5in) and 1 x 2cm (0.8in) guns
Displacement: 1763/2177t (1735/2143 tons)	

Schnorchel patrols
1944–45

The submarine *Schnorchel* was invented by the Dutch just before World War II and perfected by the Germans during the war for use by U-boats.

UNTIL THE ADVENT of nuclear power, submarines were more properly described as submersibles: their limited underwater endurance meant that they were designed to operate on the surface most of the time. In the early years of the war, U-boats were safer on the surface than submerged because ASDIC and Sonar could detect boats underwater but were useless against a surface vessel. However, as the war progressed, the introduction of maritime patrol aircraft carrying ever more capable radar systems meant that a surfaced submarine became vulnerable on even the darkest of nights. As a result, U-boats were forced to spend more and more time submerged, and every time they surfaced to recharge their batteries they became targets.

Dutch invention

In 1940 the German conquest of the Netherlands gave the *Kriegsmarine* access to Dutch snorkel technology. The snorkel (*Schnorchel* in German) was a simple air tube that enabled submarines to travel at periscope depth while using diesels. In 1943, as more U-boats were lost, it was retrofitted to the VIIC and IXC classes and designed into the new XXI and XXIII types. The first boats to be fitted were U-57 and U-58, which ran trials in the Baltic in the summer of 1943. Boats began to use them operationally in early 1944, and by June 1944 about half of the boats stationed in France had them fitted. The Type VIICs U-211 and U-264 were the first operational boats to carry the equipment, but the first *Schnorchel* U-boat to leave for combat patrol was the U-539, which left France on 2 January 1944.

On Type VII boats the *Schnorchel* folded forward and was stored in a recess on the port side of the hull while on the Type IXs the recess was on the starboard side. The XXI and XXIII types both had telescopic masts that rose vertically through the conning tower close to the periscope.

Schnorchels were not perfect, however. A U-boat travelling at more than 11km/hr (6kt) risked damaging the tube, and hydrophones were made ineffective by the roaring of air being sucked down it. *Schnorchels* were fitted with automatic valves to prevent seawater from being sucked into the diesels, but when these valves slammed shut the engines would draw air from the boat before shutting down, causing a partial vacuum which was very painful and in extreme cases caused ruptured eardrums.

One further problem arose out of extended submerged operations: a boat which remained underwater for long periods could not easily dispose of garbage and human waste, adding further to the already foul conditions aboard.

▲ **U-3008 *Schnorchel***

This photograph shows the Schnorchel of U-3008, a Type XXI U-boat. Unlike earlier submarines, the Type XXI had a telescopic Schnorchel, which was raised from a special housing by electric motors.

BOATS THAT SERVED WITH 33RD FLOTILLA (76 BOATS)

U-Boat	Type	Commissioned	Flotilla(s)	Patrols	Fate
U-155	IXC/40	10-Sep-42	1 Oct 1944 – 6 Oct 1944 from 2. Flottille	10 patrols. 25 ships sunk: total 126,664 GRT; 1 warship sunk: total 14,006t/13,785 tons; 1 aux warship damaged: total 6736 GRT	Transferred from Wilhelmshaven to Scotland 30 Jun 1945 for Operation *Deadlight*. Sunk 21 Dec 1945
U-168	IXC/40	19-Jan-43	1 Nov 1944 – 8 May 1945 from 10. Flottille	4 patrols. 2 ships sunk: total 6568 GRT; 1 auxiliary warship sunk: total 1440 GRT; 1 ship damaged: total 9804 GRT	Sunk 6 Oct 1944 in the Java Sea by a torpedo from the Dutch submarine HrMs *Zwaardvisch*. 23 dead and 27 survivors
U-170	IXD2	9-May-42	1 Oct 1944 – 8 May 1945	4 patrols. 1 ship sunk: total 4663 GRT	Surrendered May 1945. Transferred from Norway to Scotland 29 May for Operation *Deadlight*. Sunk 30 Nov 1945
U-181	IXC/40	1-Apr-42	1 Oct 1944 – 23 Apr 1945 from 2. Flottille	6 patrols. 4 ships sunk: total 19,260 GRT; 1 ship damaged beyond repair: total 6993 GRT	In the Far East at the end of the war. Taken over by Japan in May 1945 and became the Japanese submarine I-501 on 15 Jul 1945. Surrendered in Singapore Aug 1945
U-183	IXC/40	24-Sep-42	1 Oct 1944 – 1 May 1945 from 2. Flottille	6 patrols. 1 ship sunk: total 7015 GRT; 1 warship sunk: total 599t/590 tons	Sunk 23 Apr 1945 in the Java Sea by a torpedo from the submarine USS *Besugo*. 54 dead and 1 survivor
U-190	IXD1	5-Sep-42	1 Oct 1944 – 8 May 1945 from 12. Flottille	3 patrols. 2 ships sunk: total 14,391 GRT; 1 ship damaged: total 6797 GRT	Surrendered at Bulls Bay, Newfoundland, 12 May 1945. Used for tests, and was sunk 21 Oct 1947 southwest of Newfoundland by naval gunfire and aircraft bombs
U-195	IXD1	11-Sep-42	1 Oct 1944 – 1 Dec 1944	3 patrols. 3 ships sunk: total 17,739 GRT	Taken over by Japan in May 1945 and became the Japanese submarine I-506 15 Jul 1945. Surrendered at Jakarta Aug 1945
U-196	IXC	23-Aug-41	15 Aug 1944 – 8 May 1945 from 10. Flottille	3 patrols. 3 ships sunk: total 17,739 GRT. U-196 completed a 225-day patrol from 13 Mar to 23 Oct 1943, the longest submarine patrol of WWII	Declared missing with all hands 1 Dec 1944 south of Java. 65 dead
U-219	XB	12-Dec-42	1 Oct 1944 – 8 May 1945	2 patrols	Taken over by Japan 8 May 1945 in Batavia and became the Japanese submarine I-505 on 15 Jul 1945. Surrendered at Djakarta Aug 1945; broken up in 1948
U-234	XB	2-Mar-44	1 Mar 1945 – 8 May 1945 from 5. Flottille (training)	1 patrol	Surrendered at Portsmouth, New Hampshire, 16 May 1945. No casualties, though two Japanese passengers committed suicide. U-234 carried technical drawings, a crated Me-262 jet fighter, 560kg (1230lb) of uranium oxide, German experts on various technologies and 2 Japanese officers. Sunk as a target by a torpedo from USS *Greenfish* off Cape Cod 20 Nov 1947
U-245	VIIC	18-Dec-43	1 Oct 1944 – 8 May 1945 from 3. Flottille	3 patrols. 3 ships sunk: total 17,087 GRT	Surrendered and transferred from Norway to Scotland 30 May 1945 for Operation *Deadlight*. Sunk 7 Dec 1945
U-260	VIIC	14-Mar-42	1 Nov 1944 – 12 Mar 1945 from 6. Flottille	9 patrols. 1 ship sunk: total 4893 GRT	Scuttled 12 Mar 1945 south of Ireland after being mined at 80m (260ft) depth. No casualties – 48 survivors. Whole crew interned in Ireland
U-262	VIIC	15-Apr-42	10 Nov 1944 – 2 Apr 1945 from 3. Flottille	10 patrols. 3 ships sunk: total 13,010 GRT; 1 warship sunk: total 940t/925 tons	Bombed at Gotenhafen in Dec 1944. Stricken at Kiel 2 Apr 1945. Broken up in 1947
U-267	VIIC	11-Jul-42	1 Oct 1944 – 4 May 1945 from 7. Flottille	7 patrols	Scuttled 4 May 1945 in Gelting Bay
U-281	VIIC	27-Feb-1943	10 Nov 1944 – 8 May 1945 from 7. Flottille	4 patrols	Surrendered at Kristiansand 8 May 1945. Transferred to Scotland for Operation *Deadlight*. Sunk 30 Nov 1945
U-309	VIIC	27-Jan-43	1 Oct 1944 – 16 Feb 1945	11 patrols. 1 ship damaged beyond repair: total 7219 GRT	Sunk with all hands 16 Feb 1945 in the North Sea off the northeast coast of Scotland by depth charges from the frigate HMCS *St. John*. 47 dead
U-382	VIIC	25-Apr-42	1 Nov 1944 – 23 Jan 1945 from 7. Flottille	6 patrols. 1 ship damaged: total 9811 GRT	Sunk in Jan 1945 at Wilhelmshaven by British bombs. Raised 20 Mar 1945 and scuttled 8 May 1945
U-398	VIIC	18-Dec-43	1 Nov 1944 – 17 Apr 1945 from 3. Flottille	2 patrols	Missing with all hands after 17 Apr 1945 in the North Sea or in the Arctic. 43 dead. May have been sunk by a Liberator of No. 120 Sqn RAF 29 Apr 1945. That attack is usually considered to have been against U-1017, but both boats disappeared at about the same time and in the same waters
U-510	IXC	25-Nov-41	1 Oct 1944 – 8 May 1945 from 10. Flottille	7 patrols. 14 ships sunk: total 78,526 GRT; 1 auxiliary warship sunk: total 249 GRT; 3 ships damaged beyond repair: total 24,338 GRT; 8 ships damaged: total 53,289 GRT	Surrendered at St Nazaire and ceded to France 12 May 1945. Renamed the *Bouan* in French service. Stricken 1 May 1959 as Q176. Broken up in 1960
U-516	IXC	21-Feb-42	1 Oct 1944 – 8 May 1945 from 10. Flottille	6 patrols. 16 ships sunk: total 89,385 GRT; 1 ship damaged: total 9687 GRT	Surrendered at Lough Foyle, Northern Ireland. Sunk 2 Jan 1946 in Operation *Deadlight*
U-518	IXC	25-Apr-42	1 Nov 1944 – 22 Apr 1945 from 10. Flottille	7 patrols. 9 ships sunk: total 55,747 GRT; 3 ships damaged: total 22,616 GRT	Sunk with all hands 22 Apr 1945 northwest of the Azores by depth charges from the destroyer escorts USS *Carter* and USS *Neal A. Scott*. 56 dead
U-530	IXC/40	14-Oct-42	1 Oct 1944 – 8 May 1945 from 10. Flottille	7 patrols. 2 ships sunk: total 12,063 GRT; 1 ship damaged: total 10,195 GRT	Surrendered in the Mar del Plata, Argentina, 10 Jul 1945. Transferred to the US and used for trials. Sunk as a target 28 Nov 1947 by a torpedo
U-532	IXC/40	11-Nov-42	1 Oct 1944 – 8 May 1945 from 2. Flottille	4 patrols. 8 ships sunk: total 46,895 GRT; 2 ships damaged: total 13,128 GRT	Surrendered at Liverpool 10 May 1945. Sunk by sub-launched torpedo as part of Operation *Deadlight* 9 Dec 1945
U-534	IXC/40	23-Dec-42	1 Nov 1944 – 5 May 1945 from 2. Flottille	3 patrols	Sunk 5 May 1945 in the Kattegat by depth charges from a British Liberator of No. 86 Sqn RAF after shooting down another Liberator. 3 dead and 49 survivors. Raised in 1993, the wreck has been on display at Birkenhead, near Liverpool, in England
U-537	IXC/40	27-Jan-43	1 Oct 1944 – 9 Nov 1944 from 10. Flottille	3 patrols	Sunk with all hands 9 Nov 1944 in the Java Sea east of Surabaya, torpedoed by the US submarine *Flounder*. 58 dead
U-539	IXC/40	24-Feb-43	1 Oct 1944 – 8 May 1945 from 10. Flottille	3 patrols. 1 ship sunk: total 1517 GRT; 2 ships damaged: total 12,896 GRT. U-539 was the first *Schnorchel*-equipped U-boat to go on a combat patrol on 2 Jan 1944	Surrendered at Bergen, Norway. Transferred to Scotland for Operation *Deadlight*. Foundered while on tow to the scuttling grounds 4 Dec 1945

BOATS THAT SERVED WITH 33RD FLOTILLA (76 BOATS)

U-Boat	Type	Commissioned	Flotilla(s)	Patrols	Fate
U-541	IXC/40	24-Mar-43	1 Nov 1944 – 8 May 1945 from 10. Flottille	4 patrols. 1 ship sunk: total 2140 GRT	Surrendered at Gibraltar 14 May 1945. Transferred to Northern Ireland for Operation *Deadlight*. Sunk 5 Jan 1946
U-546	IXC/40	2-Jun-43	10 Nov 1944 – 24 Apr 1945 from 10. Flottille	3 patrols. 1 warship sunk: total 1219t/1200 tons	Sunk 24 Apr 1945 northwest of the Azores by depth charges from 8 destroyer escorts (USS *Flaherty*, USS *Neunzer*, USS *Chatelain*, USS *Varian*, USS *Hubbard*, USS *Janssen*, USS *Pillsbury* and USS *Keith*). 26 dead and 33 survivors
U-547	IXC/40	16-Jun-43	1 Oct 1944 – 1 Nov 1944 from 2. Flottille	3 patrols. 2 ships sunk: total 8371 GRT; 1 auxiliary warship sunk: total 750 GRT	Damaged by mines in the Gironde near Pauillac 13 Aug 1944. Decommissioned at Stettin 31 Dec 1944
U-548	IXC/40	30-Jun-43	1 Oct 1944 – 19 Apr 1945 from 2. Flottille	4 patrols. 1 warship sunk: total 1468t/1445 tons	Sunk with all hands 19 Apr 1945 southeast of Nova Scotia by depth charges from destroyer escorts *USS Reuben James* and USS *Buckley*. 58 dead. Previously credited 30 Apr 1945 to the patrol frigate USS *Natchez* and the destroyer escorts USS *Coffman*, USS *Bostwick* and USS *Thomas*. That attack is more likely to have sunk U-879
U-714	VIIC	10-Feb-43	11 Nov 1944 – 14 Mar 1945 from 7. Flottille	6 patrols. 1 ship sunk: total 1226 GRT; 1 auxiliary warship sunk: total 425 GRT	Sunk with all hands 14 Mar 1945 in the North Sea off the Firth of Forth by depth charges from the South African frigate *Natal*. 50 dead
U-758	VIIC	5-May-42	15 Oct 1944 – 1 Mar 1945 from 6. Flottille	7 patrols. 2 ships sunk: total 13,989 GRT	Damaged at Kiel by British bombs and stricken 16 Mar 1945. Broken up postwar
U-763	VIIC	13-Mar-43	1 Oct 1944 – 31 Oct 1944 from 3. Flottille	4 patrols. 1 ship sunk: total 1499 GRT	to 24. Flottille
U-802	IXC/40	12-Jun-43	1 Dec 1944 – 8 May 1945 from 2. Flottille	4 patrols. 1 ship sunk: total 1621 GRT	Surrendered at Loch Eriboll, Scotland, 11 May 1945. Sunk 31 Dec 1945 as part of Operation *Deadlight*
U-804	IXC/40	4-Dec-43	1 Oct 1944 – 9 Apr 1945 from 10. Flottille	2 patrols. 1 warship sunk: total 1321t/1300 tons	Blown up with all hands 9 Apr 1945 in the Kattegat after massed rocket attack by 13 de Havilland Mosquitoes of the Banff Strike Wing (Nos. 143, 235 and 248 Sqns RAF). 55 dead. U-1065 was destroyed in the same action
U-805	IXC/40	12-Feb-44	1 Mar 1945 – 8 May 1945 from 4. Flottille	1 patrol	Surrendered to the US Navy 14 May 1945 near Portsmouth, New Hampshire.
U-806	IXC/40	29-Apr-44	1 Nov 1944 – 8 May 1945 from 4. Flottille	1 patrol. 1 warship sunk: total 683t/672 tons; 1 ship damaged: total 7219 GRT	Surrendered May 1945. Transferred from Wilhelmshaven to Scotland 22 Jun 1945 for Operation *Deadlight*. Sunk 21 Dec 1945
U-843	IXC/40	24-Mar-43	1 Oct 1944 – 9 Apr 1945 from 2. Flottille	4 patrols. 1 ship sunk: total 8261 GRT	Sunk 9 Apr 1945 in the Kattegat, west of Gothenburg, by rockets from Mosquitoes of the Banff Strike Wing (Nos. 143, 235 and 248 Sqns RAF). 44 dead and 12 survivors
U-853	IXC/40	25-Jun-43	1 Oct 1944 – 6 May 1945 from 10. Flottille	3 patrols. 1 ship sunk: total 5353 GRT; 1 warship sunk: total 437t/430 tons	Sunk with all hands 6 May 1945 off the American coast southeast of New London by depth charges from the destroyer USS *John D. Ericsson*, the destroyer escort USS *Atherton* and the patrol frigate USS *Moberly*. 55 dead
U-857	IXC/40	16-Sep-43	1 Oct 1944 – 7 Apr 1945 from 10. Flottille	3 patrols. 2 ships sunk: total 15,259 GRT; 1 ship damaged: total 6825 GRT	Missing with all hands Apr 1945 off the US east coast. 59 dead. May have been sunk by US escort vessels at the same time as U-879, or by a US Navy blimp (airship) which dropped a homing torpedo on a possible submarine 18 Apr 1945
U-858	IXC/40	30-Sep-43	1 Oct 1944 – 8 May 1945 from 2. Flottille	2 patrols	Surrendered at Delaware, US, 14 May 1945 – the first German warship to surrender to US forces. Scuttled at the end of 1947 after being used for torpedo trials by the US Navy
U-861	IXD2	2-Sep-43	1 Oct 1944 – 6 May 1945 from 12. Flottille	2 patrols. 4 ships sunk: total 22,048 GRT; 1 ship damaged: total 8139 GRT	Surrendered at Trondheim, Norway, 6 May 1945. Transferred to Northern Ireland 29 May 1945 for Operation *Deadlight*. Sunk 31 Dec 1945
U-862	IXD2	7-Oct-43	1 Oct 1944 – 6 May 1945 from 12. Flottille	2 patrols. 7 ships sunk: total 42,374 GRT	Taken over by Japan at Singapore 6 May 1945, and became the Japanese submarine I-502. Surrendered at Singapore in Aug 1945 and was scuttled 13 Feb 1946
U-864	IXD2	9-Dec-43	1 Nov 1944 – 9 Feb 1945 from 4. Flottille	1 patrol	Sunk with all hands 9 Feb 1945 west of Bergen by torpedoes from HM Submarine *Venturer*. 73 dead. Both boats were submerged – the only such event in naval history
U-866	IXC/40	17-Nov-43	1 Oct 1944 – 18 Mar 1945 from 10. Flottille	1 patrol	Sunk with all hands 18 Mar 1945 northeast of Boston by depth charges from destroyer escorts USS *Lowe*, USS *Menges*, USS *Pride* and USS *Mosley*. 55 dead
U-868	IXC/40	23-Dec-43	1 Oct 1944 – 5 May 1945 from 2. Flottille	2 patrols. 1 warship sunk: total 683t/672 tons	Surrendered at Bergen May 1945. Transferred to Scotland 30 May 1945 for Operation *Deadlight*. Sunk 30 Nov 1945
U-869	IXC/40	26-Jan-44	1 Dec 1944 – 11 Feb 1945 from 4. Flottille	1 patrol	Sunk with all hands 11 Feb 1945 off New Jersey by Hedgehogs and depth charges from the destroyer escorts USS *Howard D. Crow* and USS *Koiner*. 56 dead. Previously credited to destroyer escort USS *Fowler* and French submarine chaser *L'Indiscret* 28 Feb off the Moroccan coast near Rabat
U-870	IXC/40	3-Feb-44	1 Oct 1944 – 30 Mar 1945 from 4. Flottille	1 patrol. 2 warships sunk: total 1991t/1960 tons; 2 ships damaged beyond repair: total 11,844 GRT; 1 warship damaged: total 1422t/1400 tons	Sunk in port 30 Mar 1945 at Bremen by US bombs
U-873	IXD2	1-Mar-44	1 Feb 1945 – 8 May 1945 from 4. Flottille	1 patrol	Surrendered at Portsmouth, New Hampshire, 16 May 1945. Used for trials. Broken up 1948
U-874	IXD2	8-Apr-44	1 Mar 1945 – 8 May 1945 from 4. Flottille	No patrols	Transferred from Horten, Norway, to Northern Ireland 29 May 1945 for Operation *Deadlight*. Sunk 31 Dec 1945
U-875	IXD2	21-Apr-44	1 Mar 1945 – 8 May 1945 from 4. Flottille	No patrols	Transferred from Bergen, Norway, to Northern Ireland 30 May 1945 for Operation *Deadlight*. Sunk 31 Dec 1945

BOATS THAT SERVED WITH 33RD FLOTILLA (76 BOATS)

U-Boat	Type	Commissioned	Flotilla(s)	Patrols	Fate
U-877	IXC/40	24-Mar-44	1 Dec 1944 – 27 Dec 1944 from 4. Flottille	1 patrol	Sunk 27 Dec 1944 northwest of the Azores by Squid anti-submarine launcher of the corvette HMCS *St. Thomas*. No casualties – 56 survivors
U-878	IXC/40	14-Apr-44	1 Feb 1945 – 10 Apr 1945 from 4. Flottille	2 patrols	Sunk with all hands 10 Apr 1945 west of St Nazaire by depth charges from the destroyer HMS *Vanquisher* and the corvette HMS *Tintagel Castle*. 51 dead
U-879	IXC/40	19-Apr-44	1 Feb 1945 – 30 Apr 1945 from 4. Flottille	1 patrol. 1 ship damaged: total 8537 GRT	Sunk with all hands 30 Apr 1945 east of Cape Hatteras by depth charges from frigate USS *Natchez* and destroyer escorts USS *Coffmann*, USS *Bostwick* and USS *Thomas*. 52 dead. Previously credited to USS *Buckley* and USS *Reuben James* east of Boston 19 Apr 1945. They probably destroyed U-548
U-880	IXC/40	11-May-44	1 Dec 1944 – 16 Apr 1945 from 4. Flottille	1 patrol	Sunk with all hands 16 Apr 1945 in the North Atlantic by depth charges from the destroyer escorts USS *Stanton* and USS *Frost*. 49 dead
U-881	IXC/40	27-May-44	1 Mar 1945 – 6 May 1945 from 4. Flottille	1 patrol	Sunk with all hands 6 May 1945 southeast of Newfoundland by depth charges from the destroyer escort USS *Farquhar*. 53 dead
U-889	IXC/40	4-Aug-44	15 Mar 1945 – 8 May 1945 from 4. Flottille	1 patrol	Surrendered 15 May 1945 at Shelburne, Nova Scotia. Transferred to the US Navy 10 Jan 1946. Used for torpedo trials before being scuttled at the end of 1947
U-953	VIIC	17-Dec-42	15 Oct 1944 – 8 May 1945 from 3. Flottille	10 patrols. 1 ship sunk: total 1927 GRT	Transferred 29 May 1945 from Norway to England. Used by the Royal Navy as a trials boat. Broken up in 1950
U-989	VIIC	22-Jul-43	1 Oct 1944 – 14 Feb 1945 from 9. Flottille	5 patrols. 1 ship sunk: total 1791 GRT; 1 ship damaged: total 7176 GRT	Sunk with all hands 14 Feb 1945 in the Faroe Islands by depth charges from frigates HMS *Bayntun*, HMS *Braithwaite*, HMS *Loch Eck* and HMS *Loch Dunvegan*. 47 dead
U-1106	VIIC/41	5-Jul-44	16 Feb 1945 – 29 Mar 1945 from 8. Flottille	1 patrol	Sunk with all hands 29 Mar 1945 northeast of the Faroes by depth charges from a Liberator of No. 224 Sqn RAF. 46 dead
U-1170	VIIC/41	1-Mar-44	1 Oct 1944 – 3 May 1945 from 8. Flottille (training)	Training	Scuttled 3 May 1945 at Travemünde
U-1205	VIIC	2-Mar-44	1 Oct 1944 – 3 May 1945 from 8. Flottille (training)	Training	Scuttled 3 May 1945 at Kiel
U-1221	IXC/40	11-Aug-43	1 Dec 1944 – 3 Apr 1945 from 10. Flottille	1 patrol	Sunk 3 Apr 1945 at Kiel by US bombs. 7 dead and 11 survivors
U-1223	IXC/40	6-Oct-43	30 Dec 1944 – 15 Apr 1945 from 2. Flottille	1 patrol. 1 ship damaged: total 7134 GRT; 1 warship damaged beyond repair: total 1392t/1370 tons	Stricken 14 Apr 1945 and scuttled 5 May 1945 west of Wesermünde
U-1226	IXC/40	24-Nov-43	1 Oct 1944 – 28 Oct 1944 from 2. Flottille	1 patrol	Missing with all hands on or after 23 Oct 1944 in the Atlantic. 56 dead. In its last message on that date, the boat reported a *Schnorchel* defect, which may have contributed to its loss
U-1227	IXC/40	8-Dec-43	1 Jan 1945 – 10 Apr 1945 from 2. Flottille	1 patrol. 1 warship damaged beyond repair: total 1392t/1370 tons	Damaged at Kiel by British night bombing 9 Apr 1945 and stricken the next day. Scuttled 3 May 1945
U-1228	IXC/40	22-Dec-43	1 Nov 1944 – 8 May 1945 from 31. Flottille	2 patrols. 1 warship sunk: total 914t/900 tons	Surrendered at Portsmouth, New Hampshire, 17 May 1945. Scuttled by the US Navy 5 Feb 1946
U-1230	IXC/40	26-Jan-44	1 Oct 1944 – 8 May 1945 from 10. Flottille	1 patrol. 1 ship sunk: total 5458 GRT. The patrol included the landing of 2 agents on the US coast at Hancock Point in Maine	Transferred from Wilhelmshaven to Scotland 24 Jun 1945 for Operation *Deadlight*. Sunk by naval gunfire 17 Dec 1945
U-1231	IXC/40	9-Feb-44	1 Oct 1944 – 8 May 1945 from 11. Flottille	2 patrols	Surrendered at Lough Foyle, Northern Ireland, 14 May 1945. Ceded to the USSR and became the Soviet submarine N-25. Broken up in 1960
U-1232	IXC/40	8-Mar-44	1 Nov 1944 – 8 May 1945 from 31. Flottille	1 patrol. 3 ships sunk: total 17,355 GRT; 1 ship damaged beyond repair: total 7176 GRT; 1 ship damaged: total 2373 GRT	Stricken at Wesermünde Apr 1945. Captured by the British. Foundered and sank 4 Mar 1946 while under tow to the Operation *Deadlight* scuttling grounds
U-1233	IXC/40	22-Mar-44	1 Nov 1944 – 8 May 1945 from 31. Flottille	1 patrol	Transferred from Wilhelmshaven to Scotland 24 Jun 1945 for Operation *Deadlight*. Sunk by naval gunfire 29 Dec 1945
U-1235	IXC/40	17-May-44	1 Dec 1944 – 15 Apr 1945 from 31. Flottille	1 patrol	Sunk with all hands 15 Apr 1945 in North Atlantic by depth charges from destroyer escorts USS *Stanton* and USS *Frost*. 57 dead
U-1271	VIIC/41	12-Jan-44	1 Oct 1944 – 8 May 1945 from 8. Flottille	Training	Transferred from Bergen to Scotland 30 May 1945 for Operation *Deadlight*. Sunk 8 Dec 1945
U-1305	VIIC/41	13-Sep-44	16 Mar 1945 – 8 May 1945 from 4. Flottille	1 patrol. 1 ship sunk: total 878 GRT	Surrendered at Loch Eriboll, Scotland, 10 May 1945. Ceded to the USSR and became Soviet submarine S-84 Nov 1945
UIT-24	Italian Marcello class	10-Sep-43	Oct 1944 – May 1945 from 12. Flottille	6 patrols	Taken over by Japan at Kobe following the German surrender; recommissioned as I-503 10 May 1945. Scuttled at Kii Suido 16 April 1946 by the US Navy
UIT-25	Italian Marconi class	12-Dec-43	Oct 1944 – May 1945	3 patrols	Taken over by Japan at Kobe 10 May 1945 and commissioned as I-504. After the Japanese surrender the boat was scuttled by the Americans

U-Boat Training Flotillas

At the outbreak of war, the *Kriegsmarine*'s U-boat arm was dedicated to turning out some of the best-trained submariners in the world. Basic training, or school, units gave new U-boat men their first experience of manning a U-boat at sea. Operational training was carried out under the aegis of the Front flotillas. However, the expansion of the U-boat arm through the war years saw an equally large expansion in the training establishment, with specialist flotillas being set up to provide weapons and tactical training. Final operational, or 'working up', training was now provided by the 4th, 5th and 8th Flotillas, through which all boats passed before being assigned to a combat flotilla based in Norway or France.

4 Unterseebootsflottille

Before the war and in the first two years of the conflict, U-boats were assigned to one of the front flotillas, undergoing working-up training at the flotilla's German base before being declared operational. However, in 1941 the system changed.

FRONT FLOTILLAS WERE NOW BASED in France or Norway, and responsibility for working up U-boats to operational standard was passed to three new training flotillas, the 4th, 5th and 8th, which were based at Stettin, Kiel and Königsberg. Boats were assigned to one of the flotillas on commissioning, and went through a process that could last from three to seven months before being declared ready for operations.

Officers and senior crew members were assigned to a boat in the last stages of construction, up to three months before commissioning, in a process known as *Baubelehrung*, or familiarization training. The idea was to make them totally familiar with every aspect of the boat. A week or two before commissioning, they would be joined by the rest of the crew.

Although the boat was assigned to a training flotilla after the commissioning ceremony, the next stage in its working up was to pass through the U-boat Acceptance Command – the *Unterseeboots-abnehmenkommando*, or UAK. This was a two-week process in which all of the boat's systems were tested, diving trials were carried out and any faults were identified. From there, the boat passed on to the much-feared *Agru Front* for final tactical training.

4TH FLOTILLA BASE LOCATION

ATLANTIC OCEAN

● Stettin

U-3030 INSIGNIA

The 4th Flotilla had no recorded flotilla insignia other than standard training markings. Some boats acquired individual insignia: that carried by U-3030 was designed by the I WO (first officer) Oblt. Dr Hansmann.

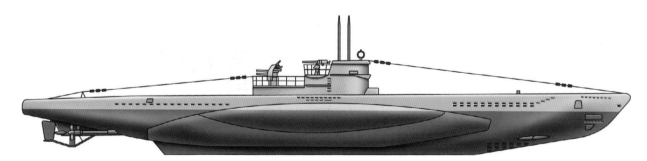

▲ **U-1025**

Type VIIC/41

One of the last Type VIIs to be commissioned, the Type VIIC/41 boat U-1025 was the same size as a standard Type VIIC, but was made from thicker steel and could dive more deeply. It was withdrawn from service after only two weeks due to defective batteries.

Specifications

Crew: 44	Dimensions (length/beam/draught): 67.2 x
Powerplant: Diesel/electric	6.2 x 4.8m (220.5 x 20.34 x 15.75ft)
Max Speed: 31.5/14.1km/hr (17/7.6kt) surf/sub	Commissioned: 12 Apr 1945
Surface Range: 12,040km (6500nm)	Armament: 14 torpedoes (4 bow/1 stern tubes);
Displacement: 771/874t (759/860 tons)	1 x 2cm (0.8in) quad and 2 x twin 2cm (0.8in)
surf/sub	guns (1944–45)

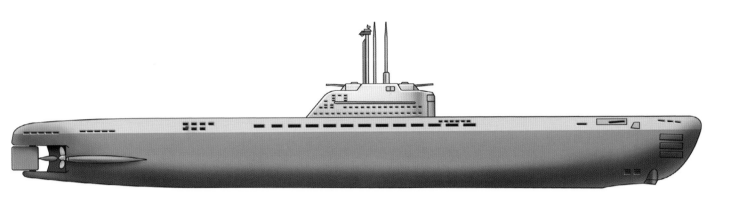

Specifications

Crew: 57

Powerplant: Diesel/electric

Max Speed: 28.9/31.9km/hr (15.6/17.2kt) surf/sub

Surface Range: 20,650km (11,150nm)

Displacement: 1647/1848t

(1621/1819 tons) surf/sub

Dimensions (length/beam/draught): 76.7 x 6.6 x 6.3m (251.7 x 21.7 x 20.7ft)

Commissioned: 20 Jul 1944

Armament: 23 torpedoes (6 bow tubes); 2 x twin 2cm (0.8in) gun turrets

▲ U-3001

Type XXI

U-3001 was one of the first Type XXI boats to be commissioned.

Commanders

Kptlt. Werner Jacobsen *(May 1941 – Aug 1941)*   Fregkpt. Heinz Fischer *(Aug 1941)*

Kptlt. Fritz Frauenheim *(Jul 1941)*

BOATS THAT TRAINED WITH THE 4TH FLOTILLA	
Type	**Boats ordered**
Type IX, IXC	U-37, U-38, U-129, U-130, U-153, U-154, U-155, U-156, U-157, U-158, U-159, U-160, U-161, U-162, U-163, U-164, U-165, U-166, U-171, U-172, U-173, U-174, U-175, U-176, U-504, U-505, U-506, U-507, U-508, U-509, U-510, U-511, U-512, U-513, U-514, U-515, U-516, U-517, U-518, U-519, U-520, U-521, U-522, U-523, U-524
Type IXC/40	U-167, U-168, U-169, U-170, U-183, U-184, U-185, U-186, U-187, U-188, U-189, U-190, U-191, U-192, U-193, U-194, U-525, U-526, U-527, U-528, U-529, U-530, U-531, U-532, U-533, U-534, U-535, U-536, U-537, U-538, U-539, U-540, U-541, U-542, U-543, U-544, U-545, U-546, U-547, U-548, U-549, U-550, U-801, U-802, U-803, U-804, U-805, U-806, U-841, U-842, U-843, U-844, U-845, U-846, U-853, U-854, U-855, U-856, U-857, U-858, U-865, U-866, U-867, U-868, U-869, U-870, U-877, U-878, U-879, U-880, U-881, U-883, U-889, U-1221, U-1222, U-1223, U-1234
Type IXD1, 2	U-177, U-178, U-179, U-180, U-181, U-182, U-195, U-196, U-197, U-198, U-199, U-200, U-847, U-848, U-849, U-850, U-851, U-852, U-859, U-860, U-861, U-862, U-863, U-864, U-871, U-872, U-873, U-874, U-875, U-876
Type VIIC	U-78, U-131, U-290, U-351, U-370, U-475, U-579, U-676, U-821, U-822, U-901, U-906, U-925, U-926, U-927, U-928
Type VIIC/41	U-317, U-318, U-319, U-320, U-321, U-322, U-323, U-324, U-325, U-326, U-327, U-328, U-929, U-930, U-1025, U-1301, U-1302, U-1303, U-1304, U-1305, U-1306, U-1307, U-1308
UA	UA (ex-Turkish)
Type XB	U-118, U-119, U-219, U-220, U-233
Type XIV	U-459, U-460, U-461, U-462, U-463, U-464, U-487, U-488, U-489, U-490
Type XXI	U-3001, U-3002, U-3003, U-3004, U-3005, U-3006, U-3007, U-3008, U-3009, U-3010, U-3011, U-3012, U-3013, U-3014, U-3015, U-3016, U-3017, U-3018, U-3019, U-3020, U-3021, U-3022, U-3023, U-3024, U-3025, U-3026, U-3027, U-3028, U-3029, U-3030, U-3031, U-3032, U-3033, U-3034, U-3035, U-3037, U-3038, U-3039, U-3040, U-3041, U-3044
Type XXIII	U-2321, U-2322, U-2323, U-2324, U-2325, U-2326, U-2336, U-2339, U-2343, U-2346, U-2347, U-2348, U-2349, U-2350, U-2351, U-2352, U-2353, U-2354, U-2355, U-2356, U-2357, U-2358, U-2359, U-2360, U-2361, U-2362, U-2363, U-2364, U-2365, U-2366, U-2367, U-2368, U-2369, U-2370, U-2371

4TH FLOTILLA BOATS LOST WHILE TRAINING/BOATS THAT MADE OPERATIONAL PATROLS WHILE TRAINING					
U-Boat	Type	Commissioned	Flotilla(s)	Patrols	Fate
U-78	VIIC	15-Feb-41	1 Mar 1945 – 16 Apr 1945 from 22. Flottille	No patrols – used as an electricity generator	Sunk 16 Apr 1945 at the electricity supply station at Pillau pier by Soviet artillery fire
U-319	VIIC/41	4-Dec-43	4 Dec 1943 – 15 Jul 1944 (operational from 1 Jun)	1 patrol	Sunk with all hands 15 Jul 1944 southwest of the Lindesnes, Norway, by depth charges from a Liberator of No. 206 Sqn RAF. 51 dead
U-579	VIIC	17-Jul-41	1 Mar 1945 – 5 May 1945 from 23. Flottille	Training	Sunk for a second time 5 May 1945 in the Kattegat by depth charges from a Liberator of No. 547 Sqn RAF. 24 dead
U-676	VIIC	4-Aug-43	16 Feb 1945 – 19 Feb 1945 from 8. Flottille	2 patrols	Sunk with all hands on or after 12 Feb 1945 in the Gulf of Finland, probably by a Soviet mine. 57 dead
U-803	IXC/40	7-Sep-43	7 Sep 1943 – 27 Apr 1944	Training	Sunk 27 Apr 1944 in the Baltic near Swinemünde by a mine. 9 dead and 35 survivors
U-854	IXC/40	19-Jul-43	19 Jul 1943 – 4 Feb 1944	Training	Sunk 4 Feb 1944 in the Baltic north of Swinemünde by mines. 51 dead and 7 survivors
U-872	IXD2	10-Feb-44	10 Feb 1944 – 29 Jul 1944	Training	Damaged 29 Jul 1944 at Bremen by US bombs. 1 crewman killed. Stricken 10 Aug 1944 and broken up
U-876	IXD2	24-May-44	24 May 1944 – 3 May 1945	Training	Damaged by British bombs 9 Apr 1945. Scuttled at Eckernförde 3 May 1945
U-906	VIIC	15-Jul-44	15 Jul 1944 – 31 Dec 1944	Training	Sunk in harbour at Hamburg 29 Dec 1944 by US bombs. Wreck further damaged in Apr 1945
U-2323	XXIII	18-Jul-44	18 Jul 1944 – 26 Jul 1944	Training	Sunk 26 July 1944 west of Möltenort by a mine. 2 dead and 12 survivors
U-2336	XXIII	30-Sep-44	16 Feb 1945 – 8 May 1945	1 patrol. 2 ships sunk: total 4669 GRT	Surrendered at Wilhelmshaven, Germany. Taken to Lisahally 21 Jun 1945 for Operation *Deadlight*. Sunk 3 Jan 1946 by naval gunfire
U-2351	XXIII	30-Dec-44	16 Feb 1945 – 1 Apr 1945 from 32. Flottille	Training	Taken out of service at Kiel in Apr 1945, after being bombed. Surrendered in May 1945. Transferred to Lisahally for Operation *Deadlight*. Sunk 3 Jan 1946 by naval gunfire
U-2359	XXIII	16-Jan-45	16 Feb 1945 – 2 May 1945 from 32. Flottille	Training	Sunk with all hands 2 May 1945 in the Kattegat by rockets from Mosquitoes of Nos. 143, 235 and 248 Sqns RAF, No. 333 Sqn RNoAF, and No. 404 Sqn RCAF. 12 dead
U-2365	XXIII	2-Mar-45	2 Mar 1945 – 8 May 1945	Training	Scuttled 8 May 1945 in the Kattegat. Raised in Jun 1956 and commissioned as *U-Hai* (S-170) in the German Federal Navy 15 Aug 1957. Sank 14 Sep 1966 in the North Sea after taking in water. Raised in 1966 and broken up
U-2367	XXIII	17-Mar-45	17 Mar 1945 – 5 May 1945	Training	Sank 5 May 1945 near Schleimünde after a collision with another U-boat. Raised in Aug 1956. Renamed *U-Hecht* (Pike) and commissioned in the Federal Navy 1 Oct 1957. Stricken 30 Sep 1968 and broken up at Kiel in 1969
U-3003	XXI	22-Aug-44	22 Aug 1944 – 4 Apr 1945	Trials boat	Sunk by bombs 4 Apr 1945 at Kiel
U-3004	XXI	30-Aug-44	30 Aug 1944 – 2 May 1945	Training	One of 3 type XXI boats buried in the wreckage of the Elbe II bunker in Hamburg
U-3007	XXI	22-Oct-44	22 Oct 1944 – 24 Feb 1945	Training	Sunk 24 Feb 1945 at Bremen, by bombs. 1 crewman killed
U-3032	XXI	12-Feb-45	12 Feb 1945 – 3 May 1945	Training	Sunk 3 May 1945 east of Fredericia by rockets from Typhoons of No. 184 Sqn RAF. 36 dead and 24 survivors

5 Unterseebootsflottille

**The 5th Flotilla was originally an operational unit, but was disbanded in January 1940.
It was re-established in June 1941 as a training flotilla, dedicated to working up new boats
to operational readiness.**

BOATS WHICH PASSED their acceptance trials at the UAK would then go through one of the technical training flotillas where crews would be put through a variety of simulated combat situations, learn how to fire live torpedoes, and undergo their first deep dives. These were carried out in a deep trench in the Baltic near the Danish island of Bornholm. Not all boats progressed, however. Those with serious faults often had to go back to the dockyard for repair, their crews being sent on an unexpected but not unwelcome leave until their boats were fixed.

Before the war, U-boat commanders were forbidden to take their vessels below 50m (165ft),

Commanders

Kptlt. Karl-Heinz Moehle

(June 1941 – Aug 1942)

Korvkpt. Hans Pauckstadt

(Sep 1942 – Nov 1942)

Korvkpt. Karl-Heinz Moehle

(Nov 1942 – May 1945)

U-3501 INSIGNIA

At least three different insignia designs have been claimed for the 5th Flotilla. The Type XXI boat U-3501 carried the insignia of Crew 37b, since that had been the intake with which the commander, Oblt. Helmut Münster, had joined the *Kriegsmarine*.

even though most U-boats had been designed for diving depths of 200m (655ft) or more.

Combat experience showed that boats and their crews had to be able to make deep dives to survive attacks by enemy escort vessels, but although training was changed to reflect the new reality, it was discovered that many boats had a faulty engine-room vent. Designed to close underwater, the vent often failed under pressure of a deep dive or from the blast of a nearby depth charge, and expensive modifications had to be made to all boats.

Torpedo Crisis

Live torpedo firing also highlighted some serious problems with the main weapons used by the U-boats. New torpedoes had been designed in the 1920s, but they had been tested only twice, and on both occasions they had failed. Even so, they were declared operational. As a result, in the first two years of the war the U-boat arm underwent a torpedo crisis, in which commanders could not be sure if the weapons they fired would detonate early or would even explode at all. By the time the 5th Flotilla had

BOATS THAT TRAINED WITH THE 5TH FLOTILLA	
Type	**Boats ordered**
Type IIB	U-11
Type VIIB	U-86
Type VIIC	U-91, U-92, U-134, U-135, U-208, U-210, U-211, U-221, U-224, U-225, U-226, U-227, U-228, U-229, U-230, U-231, U-232, U-235, U-236, U-237, U-238, U-239, U-240, U-241, U-242, U-243, U-244, U-245, U-246, U-247, U-248, U-249, U-250, U-257, U-258, U-259, U-262, U-301, U-333, U-336, U-337, U-348, U-353, U-354, U-355, U-360, U-364, U-365, U-366, U-374, U-375, U-380, U-381, U-382, U-384, U-385, U-386, U-387, U-388, U-389, U-390, U-391, U-392, U-393, U-394, U-396, U-397, U-398, U-399, U-400, U-403, U-407, U-408, U-409, U-410, U-435, U-436 , U-439, U-440, U-441, U-442, U-454, U-455, U-466, U-467, U-468, U-469, U-470, U-471, U-472, U-473, U-475, U-476, U-477, U-478, U-479, U-480, U-481, U-482, U-483, U-484, U-485, U-486, U-578, U-579, U-580, U-581, U-582, U-583, U-584, U-600, U-601, U-602, U-603, U-604, U-605, U-606, U-607, U-608, U-609, U-610, U-611, U-612, U-617, U-618, U-619, U-626, U-627, U-628, U-629, U-630, U-631, U-632, U-633, U-634, U-635, U-636, U-637, U-638, U-639, U-640, U-641, U-642, U-643, U-644, U-645, U-646, U-647, U-648, U-649, U-650, U-654, U-656, U-659, U-660, U-661, U-662, U-663, U-665, U-666, U-667, U-668, U-669, U-670, U-671, U-672, U-673, U-674, U-675, U-676, U-677, U-678, U-702, U-705, U-706, U-708, U-709, U-710, U-711, U-714, U-715, U-716, U-717, U-718, U-719, U-749, U-750, U-754, U-755, U-759, U-904, U-951, U-952, U-953, U-954, U-955, U-956, U-957, U-958, U-959, U-960, U-961, U-962, U-963, U-964, U-965, U-966, U-967, U-968, U-969, U-970, U-971, U-972, U-973, U-974, U-975, U-976, U-977, U-978, U-979, U-980, U-981, U-982, U-983, U-984, U-985, U-986, U-987, U-988, U-989, U-990, U-991, U-992, U-993, U-994, U-1051, U-1052, U-1053, U-1054, U-1055, U-1056, U-1057, U-1058, U-1131, U-1132, U-1161, U-1162, U-1195, U-1207, U-1210
Type VIIC/41	U-320, U-828, U-995, U-997, U-998, U-999, U-1001, U-1008, U-1063, U-1064, U-1065, U-1105, U-1108, U-1110, U-1168, U-1274, U-1275
Type VIID	U-213, U-214, U-215, U-216, U-217, U-218
Type VIIF	U-1059, U-1060, U-1061, U-1062
Type IXA	U-38
Type XB	U-234
Type XVIIA, B	U-792, U-793, U-794, U-795, U-1405, U-1406, U-1407
Type XXI	U-3501, U-3502, U-3503, U-3504, U-3505, U-3506, U-3507, U-3508, U-3509, U-3510, U-3511, U-3512, U-3513, U-3514, U-3515, U-3516, U-3517, U-3518, U-3519, U-3521, U-3522, U-3523, U-3524, U-3525, U-3526, U-3527, U-3528, U-3529, U-3530
Type XXIII	U-2332, U-2333, U-4701, U-4702, U-4703, U-4704, U-4705, U-4706, U-4707, U-4709, U-4710, U-4711, U-4712
British H class	UD-1 (ex-Dutch)
O 21 class	UD-3, UD-4 (ex-Dutch)
Aurore class	UF-2 (ex-French)

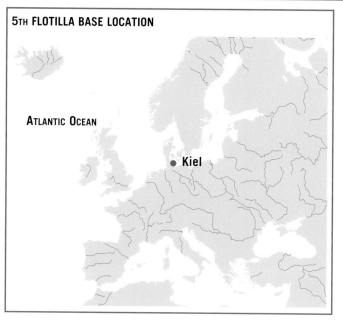

5TH FLOTILLA BASE LOCATION

ATLANTIC OCEAN

• **Kiel**

been set up as a training unit, things had improved, but they were still far from satisfactory.

The next stage in the training process was the much-feared *Agru Front*, the series of anti-convoy exercises in the Baltic which served as a boat's graduation from training.

The 5th Flotilla was founded as a training establishment in June of 1941. More than 330 boats passed through the flotilla while working up for operations, with at least eight boats being sunk in training accidents. Many more were destroyed by Allied air attack, and a number of boats that made operational patrols at the end of the war were destroyed by Allied warships. The flotilla was disbanded in May 1945.

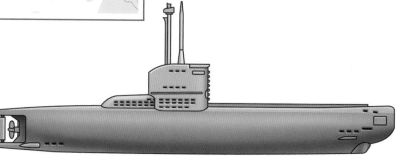

▲ **U-2332**

Type XXIII

U-2332 was one of a small number of Type XXIII boats that served with the 5th Flotilla. Most boats of this type trained with the 32nd Flotilla. The boat was scuttled on 5 May 1945.

Specifications

Crew: 14

Powerplant: Diesel/electric

Max Speed: 18/23.2km/hr (9.7/12.5kt) surf/sub

Surface Range: 4815km (2600nm)

Displacement: 238/262t (234/258 tons) surf/sub

Dimensions (length/beam/draught): 34.7 x 3 x 3.7m (113.9 x 9.9 x 12.1ft)

Commissioned: 18 Dec 1944

Armament: 2 torpedoes (2 bow tubes)

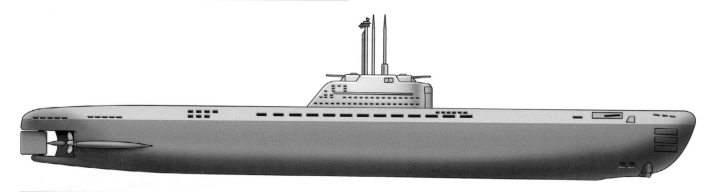

▲ **U-3523**

Type XXI

U-3523 was outward bound from Kiel in the last days of the war. She was sunk with all 58 hands on 6 May 1945 in the Skagerrak east of Arhus, Denmark, by depth charges from a Liberator of No. 86 Sqn RAF.

Specifications

Crew: 57

Powerplant: Diesel/electric

Max Speed: 28.9/31.9km/hr (15.6/17.2kt) surf/sub

Surface Range: 20,650km (11,150nm)

Displacement: 1647/1848t (1621/1819 tons)

surf/sub

Dimensions (length/beam/draught): 76.7 x 6.6 x 6.3m (251.7 x 21.7 x 20.7ft)

Commissioned: 23 Jan 1945

Armament: 23 torpedoes (6 bow tubes); 2 x twin 2cm (0.8in) gun turrets

5TH FLOTILLA BOATS LOST WHILE TRAINING/BOATS THAT MADE OPERATIONAL PATROLS WHILE TRAINING

U-Boat	Type	Commissioned	Flotilla(s)	Patrols	Fate
U-235	VIIC	19-Dec-42	19 Dec 1942 – 20 May 1943	Training	Sunk 14 May 1943 at the Germaniawerft dockyard, Kiel, by US bombs. Raised, repaired, and returned to service in Oct 1943. To 22. Flottille
U-237	VIIC	30-Jan-43	30 Jan 1943 – 20 May 1943	Training	Sunk 14 May 1943 at Kiel, by US bombs. Raised, repaired, and returned to service in Oct 1943. To 23. Flottille
U-239	VIIC	13-Mar-43	25 Jul 1944 – 5 Aug 1944	Training	Damaged 24 Jul 1944 at Kiel, by British bombs. 1 crewman killed. Stricken 5 Aug 1944 and broken up
U-242	VIIC	14-Aug-43	16 Feb 1945 – 5 Apr 1945 from 8. Flottille	7 patrols. 3 ships sunk: total 2595 GRT	Sunk with all hands 5 Apr 1945 by a mine in St Georges Channel. Originally thought to have been sunk 30 Apr 1945 in the Irish Sea west of Blackpool by depth charges from the destroyers HMS *Hesperus* and HMS *Havelock* but they were attacking the wreck of U-246
U-320	VIIC/41	30-Dec-43	1 Apr 1945 – 8 May 1945 from 4. Flottille	2 patrols	Damaged 8 May 1945 west of Bergen by depth charges from a Catalina of No. 210 Sqn RAF. Thought to have been sunk, but managed to get to Sotre near Bergen; beached and scuttled
U-348	VIIC	10-Aug-43	16 Feb 1945 – 30 Mar 1945 from 8. Flottille	Training	Sunk 30 Mar 1945 in Hamburg by US bombs during a daylight air raid. 2 crewmen killed
U-393	VIIC	3-Jul-43	1 Apr 1945 – 5 May 1945	Training	Attacked 4 May 1945 in Gelting Bay by USAAF tactical aircraft. 2 crewmen killed. Scuttled the next day in Flensburger Fjord. Previously credited to 6 Beaufighters, but that attack was against U-2351 and only caused minor damage
U-579	VIIC	17-Jul-41	17 Jul 1941 – 22 Oct 1941	Training	Sank in an Oct 1941 collision in the Baltic. Raised, returned to service Apr/May 1942 with 24. Flottille
U-580	VIIC	24-Jul-41	24 Jul 1941 – 11 Nov 1941	Training	Sank 11 Nov 1941 in the Baltic near Memel after a collision with the target ship *Angelburg*. 12 dead and 32 survivors
U-583	VIIC	14-Aug-41	14 Aug 1941 – 15 Nov 1941	Training	Sank with all hands 15 Nov 1941 near Danzig after colliding with U-153. 45 dead
U-649	VIIC	19-Nov-42	19 Nov 1942 – 24 Feb 1943	Training	Collided with U-232 24 Feb 1943 in the Baltic and sank. 35 dead and 11 survivors
U-670	VIIC	26-Jan-43	26 Jan 1943 – 20 Aug 1943	Training	Sank off Danzig after a collision with the target ship *Bolkoburg* 20 Aug 1943. 21 dead and 22 survivors
U-717	VIIC	19-May-43	16 Feb 1945 – 2 May 1945 from 8. Flottille	Training	Scuttled 2 May 1945 in the Wasserlebenbucht after being damaged by British bombs
U-718	VIIC	25-Jun-43	25 Jun 1943 – 18 Nov 1943	Training	Collided with U-476 18 Nov 1943 in the Baltic northeast of Bornholm and sank. 43 dead and 7 survivors
U-749	VIIC	14-Aug-43	1 Apr 1945 – 4 Apr 1945 from 24. Flottille	Training	Sunk 4 Apr 1945 at Germaniawerft in Kiel by US bombs. 2 crewmen killed
U-958	VIIC	14-Jan-43	16 Feb 1945 – 3 May 1945 from 8. Flottille	3 patrols. 1 ship sunk: total 40 GRT; 1 ship damaged: total 40 GRT	Decommissioned at Kiel Aug 1944. Scuttled 3 May 1945. Broken up in 1947
U-961	VIIC	4-Feb-43	4 Feb 1943 – 29 Mar 1944	1 patrol	Sunk with all hands 29 Mar 1944 east of Iceland by depth charges from the sloop HMS *Starling*. 49 dead
U-973	VIIC	15-Apr-43	15 Apr 1943 – 6 Mar 1944	2 patrols	Sunk 6 Mar 1944 northwest of Narvik by rockets from a Swordfish from the escort carrier HMS *Chaser*. 51 dead and 2 survivors
U-983	VIIC	16-Jun-43	16 Jun 1943 – 8 Sep 1943	Training	Sank 8 Sep 1943 after collision with U-988 in the Baltic. 5 dead and 38 survivors
U-998	VIIC/41	7-Oct-43	7 Oct 1943 – 27 Jun 1944	1 patrol	Damaged 16 Jun 1944 in Bergen by depth charges from a Norwegian Mosquito. Stricken 27 June 1944. Scrapped
U-1001	VIIC/41	18-Nov-43	16 Feb 1945 – 8 Apr 1945 from 8. Flottille	6 patrols	Sunk with all hands 8 Apr 1945 southwest of Land's End by depth charges from frigates HMS *Fitzroy* and HMS *Byron*. 45 dead
U-1008	VIIC/41	1-Feb-44	1 Mar 1945 – 6 May 1945 from 18. Flottille	No patrols	Sunk 6 May 1945 in the Kattegat north of Hjelm by depth charges from a Liberator of No. 86 Sqn RAF. All 44 crew survived
U-1054	VIIC	25-Mar-44	25 Mar 1944 – 16 Sep 1944	Training	Collided with ferry *Peter Wessel* at Kiel. Stricken 16 Sep 1944. Surrendered to Britain in 1945 and broken up
U-1060	VIIF	15-May-43	15 May 1943 – 27 Oct 1944	6 torpedo transport patrols	Ran aground and wrecked 27 Oct 1944 south of Bronnoysund after being damaged by rockets and depth charges from Fireflies and Barracudas of the fleet carrier HMS *Implacable*, and depth charges from Handley Page Halifaxes of No. 502 Sqn RAF and Czech Liberators of No. 311 Sqn. 12 dead and 43 survivors
U-1065	VIIC/41	23-Sep-44	23 Sep 1944 – 9 Apr 1945	1 patrol / Training	Sunk with all hands 9 Apr 1945 northwest of Göteborg by 10 rocket-firing Mosquitoes of Nos. 143 and 235 Sqns RAF. 45 dead
U-1131	VIIC	20-May-44	20 May 1944 – 30 Mar 1945	Training	Scuttled 29 Mar 1945 at Hamburg-Finkenwärder; further damaged afterwards by British bombs
U-1210	VIIC	22-Apr-44	16 Feb 1945 – 3 May 1945 from 8. Flottille		Sunk 3 May 1945 near Eckernförde by US bombs. 1 crewman killed
U-1274	VIIC/41	1-Mar-44	1 Mar 1945 – 16 Apr 1945 from 8. Flottille	1 patrol. 1 ship sunk: total 8966 GRT School boat	Sunk with all hands 16 Apr 1945 off the Northumberland coast by depth charges from the destroyer HMS *Viceroy*. 44 dead
U-3503	XXI	9-Sep-44	16 Feb 1945 – 8 May 1945 from 8. Flottille	Training	Scuttled 8 May 1945 in the Kattegat west of Göteborg, Sweden. Raised in 1946 and broken up. Previously credited to a Liberator of No. 86 Sqn RAF in the Kattegat 5 May 1945. The attack actually destroyed U-534
U-3505	XXI	7-Oct-44	16 Feb 1945 – 3 May 1945 from 8. Flottille	Training	Sunk by bombs 3 May 1945 in port at Kiel. 1 crewman killed
U-3506	XXI	16-Oct-44	16 Feb 1945 – 2 May 1945 from 8. Flottille	Training	One of 3 type XXI boats remaining buried in the wreckage of the Elbe II bunker in Hamburg
U-3508	XXI	2-Nov-44	16 Feb 1945 – 4 May 1945 from 8. Flottille	Training	Sunk 4 Mar 1945 at Wilhelmshaven by bombs
U-3509	XXI	29-Jan-45	29 Jan 1945 – 3 May 1945 from 8. Flottille	Training	Damaged by bombs in September 1944 in an air raid on the building slips. Repaired and completed. Scuttled 3 May 1945 in the Weser estuary
U-3512	XXI	27-Nov-44	16 Feb 1945 – 8 Apr 1945 from 8. Flottille	Training	Sunk 8 Apr 1945 at Kiel, by bombs
U-3519	XXI	6-Jan-45	16 Feb 1945 – 2 Mar 1945 from 8. Flottille	Training	Sunk 2 Mar 1945 north of Warnemünde by mines. 75 dead and 3 survivors
U-3523	XXI	23-Jan-45	23 Jan 1945 – 6 May 1945	Training	Sunk with all hands 6 May 1945 in the Skagerrak east of Arhus, Denmark, by depth charges from a Liberator of No. 86 Sqn RAF. 58 dead. Previously credited to a 224 Sqn Liberator the day before, but that attack caused only slight damage to U-1008
U-3525	XXI	31-Jan-45	31 Jan 1945 – 30 Apr 1945		Damaged by bombs 30 Apr 1945 in the western Baltic. Scuttled at Kiel 3 May 1945

8 Unterseebootsflottille

Like the 4th Flotilla, the 8th Flotilla was a training unit dedicated to working up newly commissioned U-boats to combat readiness before they departed to join a front flotilla. It was established at Königsberg in 1941, moving to Danzig in 1942.

THE BOATS ASSIGNED TO the 8th Flotilla typically went through a similar training process to those passing through the 4th or 5th Flotillas. After acceptance trials with the UAK and passing through the various technical flotillas, boats were assigned to the final graduating exercise at the *Technische Ausbildungsgruppe für Frontunterseeboote* – the Technical Training Group for Combat U-boats, otherwise known as the *Agru Front*. This final graduating exercise was a dreaded ordeal for

new crews. Boats which had a fair proportion of experienced men aboard had fewer problems, but late in the war experienced men were in short supply. The aim was to put the boat through a series of exercises intended to simulate as closely as possible true combat conditions.

Boats went out to sea with an experienced combat commander as training officer and assessor. During the exercises, he would arbitrarily decide that a piece of equipment was inoperative through combat damage or mechanical failure. He would then see how the captain dealt with the loss of a diesel while being chased by an escort, or how the crew would cope with a failure of the main lighting circuit in the middle of an attack, or what a command team might do if the main attack periscope failed during a night

Commanders

Kptlt. Wilhelm Schulz *(Oct 1941 – Jan 1942)*

Korvkpt. Hans Eckermann

(Jan 1942 – Jan 1943)

Kpt. z. S. Bruno Mahn *(Jan 1943 – May 1943)*

Korvkpt. Werner von Schmidt

(June 1943 – Apr 1944)

Fregkpt. Hans Pauckstadt

(May 1944 – Jan 1945)

BOATS THAT TRAINED WITH THE 8TH FLOTILLA	
Type	**Boats ordered**
Type VIIC	U-88, U-89, U-90, U-212, U-222, U-223, U-242, U-250, U-253, U-254, U-255, U-256, U-260, U-261, U-263, U-264, U-265, U-266, U-267, U-268, U-269, U-270, U-271, U-272, U-273, U-274, U-275, U-276, U-277, U-278, U-279, U-280, U-281, U-282, U-283, U-284, U-285, U-286, U-288, U-289, U-290, U-291, U-302, U-303, U-304, U-305, U-306, U-307, U-308, U-309, U-310, U-311, U-312, U-313, U-314, U-315, U-334, U-335, U-338, U-339, U-340, U-341, U-342, U-343, U-345, U-346, U-347, U-348, U-349, U-357, U-358, U-359, U-361, U-362, U-363, U-370, U-378, U-379, U-383, U-405, U-406, U-411, U-412, U-413, U-414, U-415, U-416, U-417, U-418, U-419, U-420, U-421, U-422, U-423, U-424, U-425, U-426, U-427, U-428, U-429, U-430, U-438, U-443, U-444, U-445, U-446, U-447, U-448, U-449, U-450, U-458, U-465, U-475, U-479, U-481, U-593, U-594, U-595, U-596, U-597, U-598, U-599, U-613, U-614, U-615, U-616, U-620, U-621, U-622, U-623, U-624, U-625, U-637, U-657, U-658, U-664, U-676, U-679, U-704, U-707, U-708, U-712, U-713, U-717, U-731, U-732, U-733, U-734, U-735, U-736, U-737, U-738, U-739, U-740, U-741, U-742, U-743, U-744, U-745, U-760, U-761, U-762, U-763, U-764, U-765, U-766, U-767, U-825, U-826, U-921, U-958, U-1102, U-1191, U-1192, U-1193, U-1199, U-1200, U-1201, U-1202, U-1203, U-1204, U-1205, U-1206, U-1207, U-1208, U-1209, U-1210
Type VIIC/41	U-292, U-293, U-294, U-295, U-296, U-297, U-298, U-299, U-300, U-827, U-828, U-1000, U-1001, U-1103, U-1104, U-1105, U-1106, U-1107, U-1108, U-1109, U-1110, U-1163, U-1164, U-1165, U-1166, U-1167, U-1168, U-1169, U-1170, U-1171, U-1172, U-1271, U-1272, U-1273, U-1274, U-1275, U-1276, U-1277, U-1278, U-1279
Type VIID	U-218
Type IXB	U-108
Type XVIIA, B	U-792, U-793, U-794, U-795, U-1405, U-1406
Type XXI	U-2501, U-2504, U-3501, U-3502, U-3503, U-3504, U-3505, U-3506, U-3507, U-3508, U-3510, U-3511, U-3512, U-3513, U-3514, U-3515, U-3516, U-3517, U-3518, U-3519, U-3520, U-3521, U-3522
Type XXIII	U-2339

8TH FLOTILLA INSIGNIA

U-boat insignia derived from a number of different sources. The 8th Flotilla was founded at Königsberg, but moved to Danzig in 1942, and the flotilla symbol incorporated the latter city's coat of arms.

8TH FLOTILLA BASE LOCATIONS

ATLANTIC OCEAN

Danzig ● Königsberg

attack. The stresses were real: more than 30 boats were lost in training accidents that killed over 850 U-boat men. Later in the war, these losses would be outstripped by the number of boats destroyed in port by Allied bombers or lost at sea when surprised on the surface by fighter-bombers.

Once a boat had passed the final exercise – no sure thing, as crews whose performance was unsatisfactory could be ordered to go through the whole process

Specifications

Crew: 19
Powerplant: Diesel/Walter turbine/electric
Max Speed: 16.7/44.4km/hr (9/24kt) surf/sub
Surface Range: 3408km (1840nm)
Displacement: 240/263t (236/259 tons) surf/sub

Dimensions (length/beam/draught): 41.5 x 3.3 x 4.3m (136.2 x 10.8 x 14.1ft)
Commissioned: 21 Dec 1944
Armament: 4 shortened 533mm (21in) torpedoes (2 bow tubes)

▲ U-1405

Type XVIIB

An experimental high-speed coastal boat powered by a Walter air-independent turbine, U-1405 was used as a training and trials vessel with the 8th Flotilla between December 1944 and January 1945.

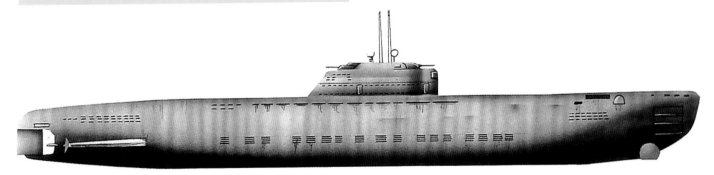

Specifications

Crew: 57
Powerplant: Diesel/electric
Max Speed: 28.9/31.9km/hr (15.6/17.2kt) surf/sub
Surface Range: 20,650km (11,150nm)
Displacement: 1647/1848t (1621/1819 tons)

surf/sub
Dimensions (length/beam/draught): 76.7 x 6.6 x 6.3m (251.7 x 21.7 x 20.7ft)
Commissioned: 28 Jun 1944
Armament: 23 torpedoes (6 bow tubes); 2 x twin 2cm (0.8in) gun turrets

▲ U-2501

Type XXI

This U-boat served with the 8th Flotilla from 21 November 1944 until the end of the war. It was commanded by Oblt. Otto Hübschen, but did not take part in any combat actions. U-2501 was scuttled on 3 May 1945 at Hamburg and eventually broken up.

again – it was returned to the dockyard for an overhaul while the crew went on their final leave.

After a boat had been declared *frontreif*, or combat ready, it was moved to the training flotilla's home base for final fitting-out, during which it would take on a full load of torpedoes, ammunition and supplies.

It was then transferred to a front flotilla, and its first operational patrol was made while in transit to its new home base.

In the last months of the war some 8th Flotilla boats were in combat against the Soviet Navy in the Baltic. The flotilla was disbanded in January 1945.

8TH FLOTILLA BOATS LOST WHILE TRAINING/BOATS THAT MADE OPERATIONAL PATROLS WHILE TRAINING					
U-Boat	Type	Commissioned	Flotilla(s)	Patrols	Fate
U-108	IXB	22-Oct-40	1 Sep 1943 – 11 Apr 1944 from 2. Flottille	Training	Sunk 11 Apr 1944 at Stettin, by bombs; raised and decommissioned 17 Jul 1944. Scuttled 24 Apr 1945
U-222	VIIC	23-May-42	23 May 1942 – 2 Sep 1942	Training	Sank 2 Sep 1942 in the Baltic west of Pillau after colliding with U-626. 42 dead and 3 survivors
U-250	VIIC	12-Dec-43	1 Jul 1944 – 30 Jul 1944 from 5. Flottille (training)	1 patrol. 1 warship sunk: total 57t/56 tons	Sunk 30 Jul 1944 in the Gulf of Finland by depth charges from the Russian submarine chaser MO-103. 46 dead and 6 survivors. Raised in Sept 1944 and commissioned into Soviet Navy from 12 Apr 1945
U-272	VIIC	7-Oct-42	7 Oct 1942 – 12 Nov 1942	Training	Collided with U-634 and sank 12 Nov 1942 near Hela. 29 dead and 19 survivors
U-290	VIIC	24-Jul-43	28 Aug 1944 – 15 Feb 1945 from 11. Flottille	3 patrols	to 4. Flottille
U-346	VIIC	7-Jun-43	7 Jun 1943 – 20 Sep 1943	Training	Sunk in a diving accident 20 Sep 1943 in the Baltic near Hela. 37 dead and 6 survivors
U-348	VIIC	10-Aug-43	12 Jul 1944 – 15 Feb 1945 from 9. Flottille	9 (possibly as many as 15) patrols	to 5. Flottille
U-370	VIIC	19-Nov-43	1 Aug 1944 – 15 Feb 1945 from 4. Flottille	12 patrols. 2 warships sunk: total 845t/832 tons	to 4. Flottille
U-423	VIIC	3-Mar-43	3 Mar 1943 – 17 June 1944	1 patrol	Sunk with all hands 17 Jun 1944 northeast of the Faroes on its way to join 3. Flottille by depth charges from a Norwegian-crewed Catalina of No. 333 Sqn RAF. 53 dead
U-446	VIIC	20-Jun-42	20 Jun 1942 – 21 Sep 1942	Training	Sunk 21 Sep 1942 near Kahlberg in the Gulf of Danzig by a British air-laid mine. 23 dead and 18 survivors. Raised 8 Nov 1942 and decommissioned. Scuttled 3 May 1945 near Kiel
U-475	VIIC	7-Jul-43	1 Aug 1944 – 15 Feb 1945 from 5. Flottille	4 patrols. 1 warship sunk: total 732t/720 tons; 1 warship damaged: total 57t/56 tons	to 4. Flottille
U-479	VIIC	27-Oct-43	1 Aug 1944 – 15 Nov 1944 from 5. Flottille	6 patrols. 1 warship damaged: total 57t/56 tons	Missing with all hands in the Gulf of Finland on or after 15 Nov 1944. 51 dead. Loss was attributed to ramming by Soviet submarine *Lembit*, but research indicates that most of *Lembit*'s official history was fabricated
U-481	VIIC	10-Nov-43	1 Aug 1944 – 8 May 1945 from 5. Flottille	3 patrols. 6 ships sunk: total 1217 GRT; 1 warship sunk: total 110t/108 tons; 1 ship damaged: total 26 GRT	Surrendered at Narvik, Norway. Transferred to Scotland for Operation *Deadlight*. Sunk 30 Nov 1945
U-637	VIIC	27-Aug-42	6 Jul 1944 – 1 Jan 1945 from 1. Flottille	3 patrols. 1 warship sunk: total 57t/56 tons	to 5. Flottille
U-676	VIIC	4-Aug-43	1 Sep 1944 – 15 Feb 1945 from 5. Flottille	2 patrols	to 4. Flottille
U-679	VIIC	29-Nov-43	1 Aug 1944 – 9 Jan 1945 from 31. Flottille	3 patrols. 1 warship sunk: total 40t/39 tons; 1 ship damaged: total 36 GRT	Sunk with all hands 9 Jan 1945 in the Baltic by depth charges from the Soviet patrol boat MO-124. 51 dead
U-717	VIIC	19-May-43	1 Aug 1944 – 15 Feb 1945 (operational 1 Aug 1944 – 1 Oct 1944) from 22. Flottille	5 patrols	to 5. Flottille
U-738	VIIC	25-Feb-42	20 Feb 1943 – 14 Feb 1944	Training	Sank 14 Feb 1944 in the Baltic near Gotenhafen after being hit in a collision by the steamship *Erna*. 22 dead and 24 survivors. Raised 3 Mar 1944 and broken up
U-745	VIIC	19-Jun-43	19 Jun 1943 – 4 Feb 1945 (operational from 1 May 1944)	4 patrols. 1 auxiliary warship sunk: total 140 GRT; 1 warship sunk: total 610t/600 tons	Built for Italy as submarine S-11; taken over after the armistice in 1943. Missing with all hands 30 Jan 1945 in the Gulf of Finland; probably hit a mine. 48 dead
U-958	VIIC	14-Jan-43	1 Aug 1944 – 15 Feb 1945 from 5. Flottille	3 patrols. 1 ship sunk: total 40 GRT; 1 ship damaged: total 40 GRT	to 5. Flottille
U-1000	VIIC/41	4-Nov-43	1 Aug 1944 – 29 Sep 1944	Training	Badly damaged by a mine 15 Aug 1944 in the Baltic. Stricken 29 September and scrapped
U-1164	VIIC/41	27-Oct-43	27 Oct 1943 – 24 Jul 1944 (operational from 1 Jul 1944)	Training	Stricken at Kiel 24 Jul 1944 after being damaged by British bombs
U-1166	VIIC/41	8-Dec-43	8 Dec 1943 – 22 Jul 1944	Training	Damaged by a torpedo accident 28 Jul 1944 at Eckernförde. Stricken at Kiel 28 Aug 1944. Scuttled in May 1945 at Kiel
U-1193	VIIC	7-Oct-43	1 Jun 1944 – 1 Aug 1944 from 24. Flottille	1 patrol	to 24. Flottille
U-2504	XXI	12-Aug-44	20 Nov 1944 – 3 May 1945 from 31. Flottille	Numerous construction faults limited the boat to training and experimental tasks only	Scuttled 3 May 1945 near Hamburg
U-3520	XXI	12-Jan-45	12 Jan 1945 – 31 Jan 1945	Training	Sunk with all hands by mines 31 Jan 1945 in the Baltic northeast of Bülk. 85 dead
U-3521	XXI	14-Jan-45	14 Jan 1945 – 15 Feb 1945	Training	to 5. Flottille
U-3522	XXI	21-Jan-45	21 Jan 1945 – 15 Feb 1945	Training	to 5. Flottille

18 Unterseebootsflottille

The 18th Flotilla, officially a training flotilla, existed for only two months early in 1945 and spent that time as a nominal combat formation in the Baltic Sea. However, none of its boats made any recorded operational patrols.

THE FLOTILLA WAS BASED AT HELA (now the Polish port of Hel) in the Baltic. Late in February 1945, as the the Red Army approached the town, the unit was evacuated. By using every inch of available space on board, some of the boats managed to cram in up to 100 civilian refugees and wounded soldiers. The flotilla was disbanded and surviving boats were transferred to the 5th Flotilla.

Commander

Korvkpt. Rudolf Franzius *(Jan 1945 – Mar 1945)*

18TH FLOTILLA BASE LOCATION

ATLANTIC OCEAN

● Hela

18TH FLOTILLA (5 BOATS)	
Type	**Boats ordered**
Type VIIC	U-1008, U-1161, U-1162
Type UA	UA
Type UD-4	UD-4

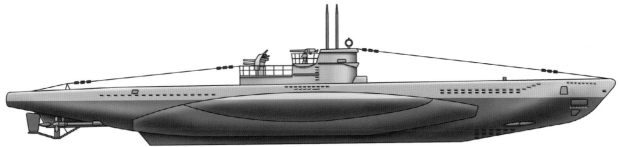

▲ U-1008

Type VIIC/41

Serving briefly with the 18th Flotilla as a trials boat before being transferred to the 5th Flotilla, U-1008 was sunk on 6 May 1945 in the Kattegat by depth charges from a Liberator of No. 86 Sqn RAF. All 44 crewmembers survived.

Specifications

Crew: 44

Powerplant: Diesel/electric

Max Speed: 31.5/14.1km/hr (17/7.6kt) surf/sub

Surface Range: 12,040km (6500nm)

Displacement: 771/874t (759/860 tons) surf/sub

Dimensions (length/beam/draught): 67.2 x 6.2 x 4.8m (220.5 x 20.34 x 15.75ft)

Commissioned: 1 Feb 1945

Armament: 14 torpedoes (4 bow/1 stern tubes); 1 x 2cm (0.8in) quad and 2 x twin 2cm (0.8in) guns

BOATS THAT SERVED WITH 18TH FLOTILLA					
U-Boat	**Type**	**Commissioned**	**Flotilla(s)**	**Patrols**	**Fate**
U-1008	VIIC/41	1-Feb-45	1 Feb 1945 – 28 Feb 1945 from 24. Flotille	Trials boat; nominally operational	to 5. Flottile
U-1161	VIIC	25-Aug-43	1 Feb 1945 – 28 Feb 1945 from 24. Flotille	Combat training/operational	Originally commissioned as Italian submarine S-8. Taken over by *Kriegsmarine* after the Italian Armistice. Transferred to 5. Flottile 1 Mar 1945
U-1162	VIIC	15-Sep-43	1 Feb 1945 – 28 Feb 1945 from 24. Flotille	Combat training/operational	Originally built as Italian submarine S-10. Taken over and completed by Germany after the Italian Armistice. Transferred to 5. Flottile 1 Mar 1945
UA	Turkish	20-Sep-39	Jan 1945 – Mar 1945 from 24. Flotille	School boat	Back to 24. Flottille. Scuttled 3 May 1945 at the Kiel Arsenal
UD-4	Dutch O 21 class	28-Jan-41	Jan 1945 – Mar 1945 from 24. Flotille	School boat	Taken out of service 19 Mar 1945. Scuttled 3 May 1945 at the Kiel Arsenal

19 Unterseebootsflottille

The 19th Flotilla was founded in October 1943 for training future U-boat commanders. After completing basic naval officer training, the prospective commander was sent on a 12-week training course, which included theory work and exercises at sea.

THE 19TH FLOTILLA specialized in teaching future officers the techniques of boat handling, before they were sent on to tactical and weapons courses with other flotillas. The submarines used were Type IIC coastal boats, all of which had been used for combat operations with the 1st Flotilla in the early months of the war. The commander training school was disbanded in May 1945, when Germany surrendered.

19TH FLOTILLA (4 BOATS)	
Type	Boats ordered
Type IIC	U-56, U-57, U-58, U-59

19TH FLOTILLA INSIGNIA

Although the 19th Flotilla had its own insignia of a stag's head, the four Type IIC boats assigned to the unit carried their own symbols, originally applied while they had been front boats with the 1st Flotilla.

19TH FLOTILLA BASE LOCATIONS

ATLANTIC OCEAN

● Kiel ● Pillau

Commander

Korvkpt. Jost Metzler *(Oct 1943 – May 1945)*

BOATS THAT SERVED WITH 19TH FLOTILLA (4 BOATS)					
U-Boat	Type	Commissioned	Flotilla(s)	Patrols	Fate
U-56	IIC	26-Nov-38	1 Jul 1944 – 28 Apr 1945 from 22. Flottille	Initial commander training	Sunk 28 Apr 1945 at Kiel by British aircraft bombs. 6 dead and 19 survivors
U-57	IIC	29-Dec-38	1 Jul 1944 – 3 May 1945 from 22. Flottille	Initial commander training	Sank 3 Sep 1940 at Brunsbüttel after an accidental collision with the Norwegian steamship *Rona*. 6 dead and 19 survivors. Raised in the same month, repaired and returned to service 11 Jan 1941. Scuttled 3 May 1945 at Kiel
U-58	IIC	4-Feb-39	1 Jul 1944 – 3 May 1945 from 22 Flottille	Initial commander training	Scuttled 3 May 1945 at Kiel
U-59	IIC	4-Mar-39	1 Jul 1944 – 1 Apr 1945 from 22. Flottille	Initial commander training	Scuttled in the Kiel Arsenal in May 1945

20 Unterseebootsflottille

During their initial officer training, prospective U-boat officers underwent the standard training experienced by all naval officers. They would have taken courses on weapons and weapons handling as well as ship handling and navigation.

ON COMPLETION THE CADET was promoted to the rank of *Fähnrich zur See*, or midshipman, before being attached to a surface warship, where he was expected to develop practical experience of ship handling. On finally passing out of the academy, a successful cadet was promoted to the rank of

Oberfähnrich sur See, or senior midshipman. Line officers destined for the *U-Bootwaffe* then went on to the U-boat training schools. In the second half of the war, these were located at Pillau, on the Baltic in the Bay of Danzig, and were supported by the 19th and 20th Flotillas. The Baltic was firmly under German control until near the end of the war, and the waters around Pillau offered reasonably safe training grounds for inexperienced crews.

U-boat training schools

The 20th Flotilla was founded in June 1943 as a training flotilla. Here, prospective submarine officers were given introductory courses in tactical training – *Vortaktische Ausbildung*. Classroom exercises were carried out in fully equipped U-boat simulators, during which trainees learned the trade of submarine warfare.

Eventually, the trainees would carry out numerous simulated attack runs on scale models of convoys. The passing grade was to make a total of 15 successful simulated attacks. Candidates also underwent practical submarine boat-handling training with the 19th Flotilla.

On completion of their training, the more promising candidates were posted directly to operational boats, where they served as 'apprentices' to experienced U-boat commanders. If they survived – which was no certainty after 1943 – they would be assigned to a new U-boat under construction, in the rank of *Leutnant*

20TH FLOTILLA BASE LOCATION

Pillau

ATLANTIC OCEAN

Commander

Korvkpt. Ernst Mengersen *(Jun 1943 – Feb 1945)*

zur See, or junior lieutenant. Other candidates were sent on to operational training flotillas, where they went through courses on underwater tactics and torpedo shooting.

The 20th Flotilla was in existence for less than two years, being formed at the height of the massive expansion of the U-boat arm in 1943, and being disbanded in February 1945.

21 Unterseebootsflottille

In the first years of the Third Reich, U-boat training was necessarily theoretical: until the shackles of the Treaty of Versailles had been thrown off, Germany was forbidden to build or operate submarines of any sort.

Prospective U-boat officers attended the *Unterseebootsabwehrschule* at Kiel, which as its name suggests had been given the cover identity of an anti-submarine warfare school. In fact, it was purely intended to train U-boat crews.

The announcement of German rearmament in 1935 saw the establishment of the 1st U-boat Flotilla and the setting up of a new training establishment at Neustadt, which was commonly known as the *Unterseebootsschule*.

Commanders

Kpt. z. S. Kurt Slevogt *(1935 – Oct 1937)*	Korvkpt. Otto Schuhart *(June 1943 – Sep 1944)*
Kptlt. Heinz Beduhn *(Nov 1937 – Mar 1940)*	Kptlt. Herwig Collmann
Korvkpt. Paul Büchel *(Mar 1940 – June 1943)*	*(Sep 1944 – Mar 1945)*

U-1 to U-6 were from the beginning designated as training boats, and formed the *Schulverband der U-Bootschule*. The *U-Bootwaffe* grew rapidly, and by the late 1930s the *Schulverband* had doubled in size. It was now known as the *Unterseebootsschulflottille*. In April of 1940, the school was renamed the

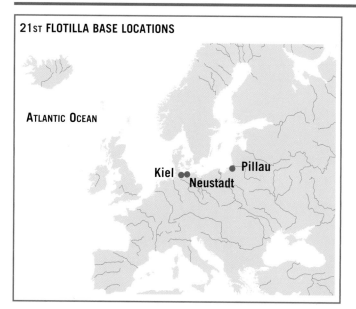

21ST FLOTILLA BASE LOCATIONS

ATLANTIC OCEAN

Kiel
Neustadt
Pillau

1. *Unterseebootslehrdivision*, or 1.ULD, and was moved to Pillau on the Bay of Danzig in the Baltic, where it was less vulnerable to British bomber attacks. A second *Lehrdivision*, 2.ULD, was set up at Gotenhafen later in 1940. Each of the ULDs was training up to 4000 U-boat men at any one time. Practical instruction was carried out aboard the flotillas attached to each *Lehrdivision* – the 21st Flotilla at Pillau and the 22nd Flotilla at Gotenhafen.

Specialists joined the U-boat arm already having learned a trade, which included diesel or electrical mechanic, wireless operator, torpedo mechanic, and cook. Members of the seaman branch performed the other functions, which included steering, working the hydroplanes, lookout, and gunners.

▲ **Ready for inspection**

A flotilla commander inspects the crew of a newly commissioned U-boat with the boat's commander. Ahead lay up to six months of tactical training before the boat could join a combat flotilla for operations.

21ST FLOTILLA INSIGNIA

Although the 21st Flotilla had its own insignia, there is no record of any of the boats assigned to the unit ever having carried it. Most former front boats in the flotilla had their own individual symbols.

21ST FLOTILLA (54 BOATS)	
Type	**Boats ordered**
Type IA	U-25
Type IIA	U-2, U-3, U-4, U-5, U-6
Type IIB	U-7, U-9, U-10, U-11, U-20, U-21, U-23, U-24, U-120, U-121
Type IIC	U-60, U-61, U-62
Type IID	U-139, U-141, U-148, U-151, U-152
Type VIIA	U-29, U-34
Type VIIB	U-48, U-101
Type VIIC	U-72, U-80, U-236, U-251, U-291, U-368, U-416, U-430, U-555, U-704, U-708, U-712, U-720, U-733, U-746, U-922, U-977, U-1101, U-1194, U-1195, U-1196, U-1197, U-1198, U-1201, U-1204
Type IX	U-38

Non-commissioned officers (NCOs) were promoted after a period of service in the ranks. During the war, they attended a purpose-built NCO training school at Plon. War pressures saw courses reduced to as little as two months, and by the end of the war some seamen were being drafted into U-boats without any training at all.

The 21st Flotilla's history ended in March 1945, when the unit was disbanded.

21ST FLOTILLA BOATS LOST WHILE TRAINING/BOATS THAT MADE OPERATIONAL PATROLS WHILE TRAINING					
U-Boat	**Type**	**Commissioned**	**Flotilla(s)**	**Patrols**	**Fate**
U-2	IIA	25-Jul-35	1 Jul 1940 – 8 Apr 1944 from *U-Bootschulflottille*	School boat. 2 patrols	Sank 8 Apr 1944 west of Pillau, in position 54.48N, 19.55E, after a collision with the German steam trawler *Helmi Söhle*. 17 dead and 18 survivors
U-5	IIA	31-Aug-35	1 Jul 1940 – 19 March 1943 from *U-Bootschulflottille*	School boat. 2 patrols	Sank 19 Mar 1943 west of Pillau in a diving accident. 21 dead and 16 survivors
U-7	IIB	18-Jul-35	1 Jul 1940 – 31 Jul 1944 from *U-Bootschulflottille*	School boat. 6 patrols. 2 ships sunk: total 4524 GRT	Sank with all hands 18 Feb 1944 west of Pillau in a diving accident. 29 dead
U-21	IIB	3-Aug-36	1 Jul 1940 – 5 Aug 1944 from 1. Flottille	School boat	Stranded 27 Mar 1940 after running aground off Oldknuppen Island following a navigational error. Interned in Norway at Kristiansand-Süd. Released to Germany 9 Apr 1940. Stricken 5 Aug 1944 at Pillau. Scrapped in Feb 1945.
U-72	VIIC	4-Jan-41	2 Jul 1941 – 30 Mar 1945 from 24. Flottille	School boat	Damaged 30 Mar 1945 in Bremen by American daylight bombers. Scuttled 2 May 1945
U-80	VIIC	8-Apr-41	1 Dec 1943 – 28 Nov 1944 from 23. Flottille	School boat	Sunk with all hands 28 Nov 1944 west of Pillau in a diving accident. 50 dead
U-139	IID	24-Jul-40	4 Oct 1940 – 30 Apr 1941	School boat; 2 patrols	to 22. Flottille
U-416	VIIC	4-Nov-42	1 Jul 1944 – 12 Dec 1944 from 23. Flottille	School boat	Sunk 30 Mar 1943 in the Baltic near Bornholm by a mine laid by the Soviet submarine L-3. Number of fatalities unknown. Raised in Apr 1943, and refurbished. Used for training from Oct 1943. Sank again 12 Dec 1944 northwest of Pillau after a collision with the German minesweeper M-203. 36 dead and 5 survivors

22 Unterseebootsflottille

As with the 21st Flotilla, the 22nd Flotilla was created to support one of the main U-boat training schools, where personnel assigned to the *U-Bootwaffe* were sent to gain their basic submarine training.

THE FLOTILLA WAS FOUNDED at Gotenhafen in January 1941, where it provided the training boats for 2. *Unterseebootslehrdivision*, or 2.ULD.

Before arriving at the ULD, a recruit had to go through basic naval training. In the pre-war years, applicants registered at the local *Wehrkreis*, or military district registration office, where they were given a medical. Initially, high educational standards were demanded of recruits destined for U-boats, but these were being relaxed by the time the 22nd Flotilla came into existence, and unskilled manual workers were now allowed to serve in the *U-Bootwaffe*.

Recruiting grounds

Curiously, the majority of lower-ranking volunteers for the *U-Bootwaffe* came from central Germany, far from the sea. Most were Protestant, and came from skilled blue-collar backgrounds. The standard period of enlistment both for seamen and for those who indicated that they would like to become NCOs was 12 years. Recruits were assessed and assigned to a specific trade by the *Kriegsmarine*.

One of the most important parts of a U-boat crewman's training at the U-boat school was in underwater escape techniques. Little did the recruits know, as they practised using breathing apparatus in the deep tanks at the U-boat schools, that the chances of escape from a submerged boat were almost nil.

Commanders

Korvkpt. Wilhelm Ambrosius	Korvkpt. Heinrich Bleichrodt
(Jan 1941 – Jan 1944)	*(Jul 1944 – May 1945)*
Korvkpt. Wolfgang Lüth *(Jan 1944 – Jul 1944)*	

Only if a boat was destroyed on the surface did any of the crew have a real chance of escaping.

The six Type II boats from the flotilla which were briefly operational during Operation *Barbarossa* achieved some success, sinking three Soviet submarines. However, in August 1941, U-144 suffered the same fate, when it was sunk by the Soviet submarine SC-307. The flotilla moved in early 1945 to Wilhelmshaven, where it was finally disbanded in May 1945 with Nazi Germany's surrender.

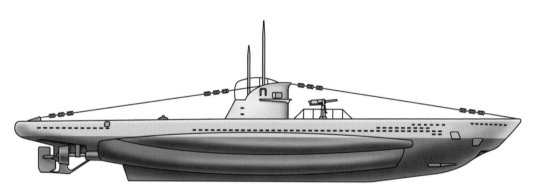

Specifications

Crew: 25	Dimensions (length/beam/draught): 44 x 4.9
Powerplant: Diesel/electric	x 3.9m (144.4 x 16.8 x 12.8ft)
Max Speed: 23.5/13.7km/hr (12.7/7.4kt) surf/sub	Commissioned: 15 Jun 1940
Surface Range: 6389km (3450nm)	Armament: 6 torpedoes (3 bow tubes);
Displacement: 319/370t (314/364 tons) surf/sub	1 x 2cm (0.8in) gun

▲ **U137**

Type IID

This was the last of the Type IIs to enter service. Many Type IID boats made operational patrols with the 1st and 3rd Flotillas before becoming training boats.

22ND FLOTILLA (47 BOATS)	
Type	**Boats assigned**
Type IIB	U-8, U-11, U-14, U-17, U-18, U-19
Type IIC	U-56, U-57, U-58, U-59
Type IID	U-137, U-138, U-139, U-140, U-142, U-143, U-144, U-145, U-146, U-147, U-149, U-150
Type VIIA	U-28, U-30
Type VIIC	U-71, U-78, U-96, U-235, U-239, U-316, U-339, U-349, U-350, U-351, U-369, U-552, U-554, U-555, U-560, U-717, U-721, U-924, U-1197, U-1198
Type VIIC/41	U-1103, U-1167
Type IX	U-37

22ND FLOTILLA BASE LOCATIONS

ATLANTIC OCEAN

● Gotenhafen

Wilhelmshaven ●

U-Boat	Type	Commissioned	Flotilla(s)	Patrols	Fate
22ND FLOTILLA BOATS LOST WHILE TRAINING/BOATS THAT MADE OPERATIONAL PATROLS WHILE TRAINING					
U-28	VIIA	12-Sep-36	1 Dec 1943 – 17 Mar 1944	School boat	Sunk by accident in port at Neustadt 17 Mar 1944. Raised in Mar 1944 and stricken 4 Aug 1944
U-30	VIIA	8-Oct-36	1 Dec 1943 – 12 Jan 1945 from 24. Flotille	School boat	Used in the last months of the war as a range boat. Scuttled 4 May 1945 in Kupfermühlen Bay
U-56	IIC	26-Nov-38	19 Dec 1940 – 30 Jun 1944 (operational Jun/Aug 1941) from 24. Flotille	School boat. 12 patrols. 3 ships sunk: total 8860 GRT; 1 auxiliary warship sunk: total 16,923 GRT; 1 ship damaged: total 3829 GRT	to 19. Flotille
U-96	VIIC	14-Sep-40	1 Jul 1944 – 15 Feb 1945 from 24. Flotille	School boat	Sunk 30 Mar 1945 by US bombs at Wilhelmshaven
U-139	IID	24-Jul-40	1 May 1941 – 2 May 1945 (operational 22 Jun 1941 – 31 Jul 1941)	School boat. 2 patrols	Scuttled 2 May 1945 at Wilhelmshaven
U-140	IID	7-Aug-40	1 Jan 1941 – 31 Mar 1945 (operational 22 Jun 1941 – 31 Aug 1941) from 1. Flotille	School boat. 3 patrols. 3 ships sunk: total 12,410 GRT; 1 warship sunk: total 209t/206 tons	to 31. Flotille
U-142	IID	4-Sep-40	19 Dec 1940 – 1 May 1945 (operational 22 Jun 1941 – 31 Aug 1941) from 24. Flotille	School boat. 4 patrols	Scuttled 2 May 1945 at Wilhelmshaven
U-144	IID	2-Oct-40	20 Dec 1940 – 10 Aug 1941 (operational from 22 Jun 1941)	School boat. 3 patrols. 1 warship sunk: total 209t/206 tons	Sunk with all hands 10 Aug 1941 in Gulf of Finland, torpedoed by the Russian submarine SC-307. 28 dead
U-149	IID	13-Nov-40	1 Jan 1941 – 8 May 1945 (operational 22 Jun 1941 – 31 Aug 1941) from 1. Flotille	School boat. 1 patrol. 1 warship sunk: total 209t/206 tons	Transferred from Wilhelmshaven to Scotland 30 Jun 1945 for Operation *Deadlight*. Sunk 21 Dec 1945 in position 55.40N, 08.00W

23 Unterseebootsflottille

The original 23rd Flotilla was a combat unit operating in the eastern Mediterranean in 1941 and 1942. Based at Salamis in Greece, it was disbanded and its surviving boats absorbed into the 29th Flotilla. However, the flotilla was revived a year later in the Baltic.

THE 23RD FLOTILLA WAS re-established in September 1943 as a training flotilla, under the command of *Korvettenkapitän* Otto von Bülow. Like the 19th and 24th Flotillas, its main purpose was to train future U-boat commanders.

Bülow was an experienced U-boat ace, and his task, along with the other experienced officers who served as instructors, was to present the trainee commanders with the kind of problems they could expect to face in combat.

Based at Danzig, the 23rd Flotilla was disbanded and evacuated in March 1945 as advancing Soviet forces approached the city.

23RD FLOTILLA (11 BOATS)	
Type	**Boats assigned**
Type VIIA	U-29
Type VIIB	U-52
Type VIIC	U-80, U-97, U-133, U-704, U-903, U-904, U-922, U-923, U-975

Commanders

Korvkpt. Otto von Bülow *(Aug 1943 – Mar 1945)*

23RD FLOTILLA BASE LOCATION

ATLANTIC OCEAN

Danzig

24 Unterseebootsflottille

The 24th Flotilla was founded in November 1939. Until March 1940 it was known as the *Unterseebootsausbildungsflottille* **(U-boat training school flotilla), and then until June 1940 it was redesignated as the 1.** *Unterseebootsausbildungsflottille.*

LIKE THE 23RD FLOTILLA, which though earlier numerically was actually founded later, the 24th Flotilla trained future U-boat commanders in a course known as the *Kommandantenschiesslehrgang*, or KSL. Each KSL course lasted four weeks, during which up to 12 U-boat officers received their final training in operations and tactics before being assigned to a boat in a front flotilla.

Before arriving at the 24th Flotilla, the prospective submarine commander would have served for at least six months aboard a surface warship, during which time he would have completed a naval armament course that would have introduced the basics of gunnery, torpedo operations and anti-aircraft defence.

Originally, the flotilla had been set up to provide officers with underwater attack training, which included the firing of training torpedoes at real targets, but in the middle of war the emphasis was changed to include training in underwater detection techniques, and in using the information so gained to escape an enemy attack.

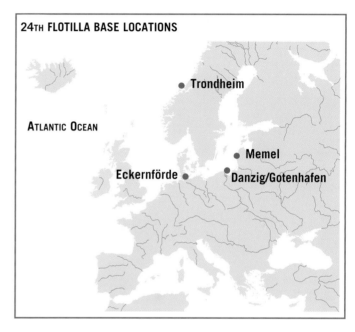

24TH FLOTILLA BASE LOCATIONS

ATLANTIC OCEAN

Trondheim

Memel

Eckernförde

Danzig/Gotenhafen

Baltic base

Initially based in the eastern Baltic, the flotilla was briefly moved to Norway during the early months of Operation *Barbarossa* to avoid conflicting with operational units, but was back at Memel by September 1941. The flotilla was disbanded in March 1945, as Allied troops advanced into Germany from east and west.

24TH FLOTILLA (53 BOATS)	
Type	**Boats assigned**
Type IIB	U-8, U-9, U-14, U-18, U-19, U-121
Type IID	U-56, U-142, U-143, U-148, U-151, U-152
Type VIIA	U-28, U-29, U-30, U-34
Type VIIB	U-46, U-52, U-101
Type VIIC	U-71, U-72, U-80, U-96, U-236, U-251, U-287, U-351, U-393, U-554, U-555, U-560, U-579, U-612, U-704, U-747, U-748, U-749, U-750, U-763, U-821, U-982, U-1161, U-1162, U-1192, U-1193, U-1195, U-1207
Type VIIC/41	U-999, U-1007, U-1008
Type IXA	U-38
Type IXB	U-103
UA	UA (ex-Turkish)
O 21 class	UD-4 (ex-Dutch)

Commanders

Korvkpt. Hannes Weingärtner	Fregkpt. Karl-Friedrich Merten
(Nov 1939 – Jun 1940)	*(Mar 1943 – May 1944)*
Kpt. z. S. R. Peters	Korvkpt. Karl Jasper *(May 1944 – Jul 1944)*
(Jul 1942 – Jan 1943)	Fregkpt. Karl-Friedrich Merten
	(Jul 1944 – Mar 1945)

24TH FLOTILLA INSIGNIA

There is scant evidence to suggest that any of the 24th Flotilla's boats used the official emblem, the stag's antler insignia. At least eight boats carried a white 'V' on the side of the conning tower.

25 Unterseebootsflottille

The 25th Flotilla was founded in April 1940. Its main purpose was to put newly commissioned boats still going through their working-up training through a course of live torpedo firing.

THE BOATS TOOK four weeks to complete their training before going on to a final tactical exercise with the 27th Flotilla. The 25th Flotilla operated until the end of the war, being disbanded on 13 May 1945.

Commanders

Korvkpt. Ernst Hashagen *(Apr 1940 – Dec 1941)*	Korvkpt. Robert Gysae *(Jan 1944 – Apr 1945)*
Korvkpt. Karl Jasper *(Dec 1941 – Aug 1943)*	Korvkpt. Wilhelm Schulz
Fregkpt. Karl Neitzel *(Aug 1943 – Jan 1944)*	*(Apr 1945 – May 1945)*

25TH FLOTILLA INSIGNIA

Although the 25th Flotilla had its own insignia of a U-boat silhouette on a white shield, none of the new boats that passed through wore it, since none of them were assigned permanently to the formation.

25TH FLOTILLA BASE LOCATIONS

ATLANTIC OCEAN

Trondheim

Libau

Travemünde

Danzig/Gotenhafen

26 Unterseebootsflottille

Like the 25th Flotilla, the 26th Flotilla was set up to put newly commissioned boats still going through their working-up training through a course of *Torpedoschiessausbildung*, or training in live torpedo firing.

THE 26TH FLOTILLA was founded in April 1941. The boats usually took three to four weeks to complete their training before going on to a final tactical exercise with the 27th Flotilla. The training torpedoes used were standard G7e weapons without warheads, and could be recognized by double white bands around the nose. Some weapons were fitted with lights to allow night shooting practice to be assessed.

The 26th Flotilla was disbanded in May 1945, when Germany surrendered.

Commanders

Korvkpt. Hans-Gerrit von Stockhausen *(Apr 1941 – Jan 1943)*	Fregkpt. Helmut Brümmer-Patzig *(Apr 1943 – Mar 1945)*
Korvkpt. Karl-Friedrich Merten *(Jan 1943 – Apr 1943)*	Korvkpt. Ernst Bauer *(Apr 1945 – May 1945)*

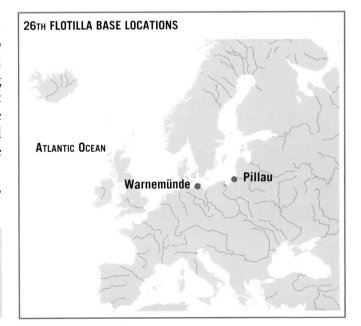

26TH FLOTILLA BASE LOCATIONS

ATLANTIC OCEAN

Warnemünde

Pillau

26TH FLOTILLA INSIGNIA

Unlike the 25th Flotilla, the 26th Flotilla did have boats permanently assigned, and there is no record that any of them carried the unit's official insignia. Most were former combat boats with their own symbols.

26TH FLOTILLA (7 BOATS)

Type	Boats assigned
Type VIIB	U-46, U-48, U-52, U-101
Type VIIC	U-80, U-351
Type IXA	U-37

27 Unterseebootsflottille

The 27th Flotilla was founded in January 1940 as a *TaktischeAusbildungUnterseeboote*, or tactical training flotilla. This was the final stage of training for new U-boat crews. After a boat was commissioned, it was sent to the U-boat Acceptance Command, where it was checked for mechanical or structural faults.

FROM THE ACCEPTANCE COMMAND the new boat was attached to a training flotilla, where instructors would put the new crews through a course designed to familiarize them with the kind of problems that occurred on operations. The crews would then would pass through one of the shooting flotillas, where they received practical instruction in firing torpedoes.

The graduation course was run by the *Technische Ausbildungsgruppe für Frontunterseeboote*, usually known as the *Agru Front*. The key element of the *Agru Front* course was the final war game, which came under the operational control of the 27th Flotilla. This was a simulated convoy battle in the Baltic. Boats usually arrived on the course in groups of 10 to 12, and a boat and its crew had to pass the course before being declared fit for operations.

By the later stages of the war, German training facilities were being put under severe strain, and the competent crews that had passed out early in the war were not matched by their successors. Before the war and in the early years of the conflict, all officers were seaman above all, and the relatively small numbers

of boats meant that the U-boat arm could pick and choose from officers who displayed real leadership ability. Unfortunately, by the later years of the war the massive increase in size of the U-boat arm meant that suitably capable officers were much harder to find.

Training strain

Recognizing the fall in quality, in 1943 the instructors added a 10-day pre-tactical course before the convoy exercise. However, this was not enough to make up for the deficiencies. A really bad performance meant that a boat could be held back for further training, taking part in the final war game twice or more. On some courses the instructors would have liked to fail

Commanders

Korvkpt. Ernst Sobe *(Jan 1940 – Dec 1941)*

Fregkpt. Werner Hartmann
(Dec 1941 – Oct 1942)

Korvkpt. Erich Topp *(Oct 1942 – Aug 1944)*

Kptlt. Ernst Bauer *(Oct 1944 – Mar 1945)*

27TH FLOTILLA (1 BOAT)

Type	Boats ordered
O 21 class	UD-4 (ex-Dutch)

27TH FLOTILLA BASE LOCATION

ATLANTIC OCEAN

Gotenhafen

every boat passing through. However, such was the pressure on the U-boat arm in the Atlantic that the staff at the *Agru Front* were forbidden to fail more than two boats per course.

Many years later, *Kapitänleutnant* Klaus Korth remembered how depressing it was to hear that crews he knew needed more training had been lost on their first or second operational patrols. However, there was little he or any other instructor could do. Any complaints went as far as Admiral Friedenburg, who agreed with the instructors, but were ignored by Admiral Dönitz and the naval high command, who needed boats at sea.

The 27th Flotilla was the last training station for new U-boats before they were overhauled, armed and filled with supplies for the long and dangerous voyage to their operational bases in France and Norway. The flotilla was finally disbanded in March 1945.

31 Unterseebootsflottille

The 31st Flotilla was founded in September 1943 as an initial training unit, tasked with taking inexperienced crews and giving them the basics of U-boat operations.

THE FLOTILLA BECAME the initial Type XXI training unit. Crews had to learn new techniques to handle the sheer speed of the revolutionary 'Electro Boat'. Some of the boats went on to the 4th and 11th Flotillas for operational training, but most were still undergoing basic training at the end of the war.

The flotilla was disbanded in May 1945 when Germany surrendered, but one boat did not come in quietly. The Type VIIC boat U-977 left Kristiansand, Norway, on 2 May 1945 for a combat patrol in the English Channel. When Germany surrendered a few days later, the boat was outbound in Norwegian waters. The commander, *Kapitänleutnant* Schäffer, did not wish to surrender and decided to head for

31st FLOTILLA BASE LOCATIONS

ATLANTIC OCEAN

Wilhelmshaven/
Wesermünde
Hamburg

Commanders

Kpt. z. S. Bruno Mahn	Korvkpt. Carl Emmermann
(Sep 1943 – Apr 1945)	*(Apr 1945 – May 1945)*

BOATS THAT TRAINED WITH THE 31ST FLOTILLA	
Type	**Boats ordered**
Type VIIC	U-708, U-712, U-720, U-721, U-722, U-733, U-746, U-747, U-748, U-768, U-771, U-772, U-773, U-774, U-775, U-776, U-777, U-778, U-779, U-903, U-905, U-907, U-922, U-924, U-975, U-977, U-982, U-1101, U-1132, U-1192, U-1193, U-1194, U-1196, U-1197, U-1198, U-1201, U-1204
Type VIIC/41	U-999, U-1000, U-1001, U-1002, U-1003, U-1004, U-1005, U-1006, U-1007, U-1008, U-1009, U-1010, U-1013, U-1014, U-1015, U-1016, U-1017, U-1018, U-1019, U-1020, U-1021, U-1022, U-1023, U-1024, U-1103, U-1167
Type IXC/40	U-1224, U-1225, U-1226, U-1227, U-1228, U-1229, U-1230, U-1231, U-1232, U-1233, U-1234, U-1235
Type XXI	U-2501, U-2502, U-2503, U-2504, U-2505, U-2506, U-2507, U-2508, U-2509, U-2510, U-2511, U-2512, U-2513, U-2514, U-2515, U-2516, U-2517, U-2519, U-2520, U-2521, U-2522, U-2523, U-2524, U-2525, U-2526, U-2527, U-2528, U-2529, U-2530, U-2531, U-2533, U-2534, U-2535, U-2536, U-2537, U-2538, U-2539, U-2540, U-2541, U-2542, U-2543, U-2544, U-2545, U-2546, U-2548, U-2551, U-2552

Argentina. Many of the crew were of the same mind, but those with families did not want to go. Schäffer gave the married men the chance to go to ashore, and 16 men, about a third of the crew, were landed on the Norwegian coast near Bergen on 10 May, where they were taken prisoner and transferred to England. On the same day, U-977 with its diminished crew submerged on a *Schnorchel* run to the Cape Verde Islands which was to last for 66 days – the second longest continuously submerged voyage of the war.

Crossing the equator on 23 July, U-977 arrived in Mar del Plata, Argentina, on 17 August after a voyage of 108 days. The boat and crew were interned and were later handed over to the Americans.

31ST FLOTILLA BOATS LOST WHILE TRAINING/BOATS THAT MADE OPERATIONAL PATROLS WHILE TRAINING					
U-Boat	Type	Commissioned	Flotilla(s)	Patrols	Fate
U-708	VIIC	24-Jul-42	16 Mar 1945 – 3 May 1945 from 21. Flottille	Initial training	Scuttled 3 May 1945 at Wilhelmshaven. Broken up in 1947
U-733	VIIC	14-Nov-42	1 Mar 1945 – 5 May 1945 from 21. Flottille	Initial training	Sank 9 Apr 1943 at Gotenhafen after a collision. Raised and repaired. Scuttled 5 May 1945 in Flensburg Fjord after being crippled by bombs and aircraft guns. Broken up in 1948
U-746	VIIC	4-Jul-43	1 Mar 1945 – 5 May 1945	Initial training	Scuttled 5 May 1945 in Gelting Bay, after being bombed. Broken up in 1948
U-747	VIIC	17-Jul-43	1 Apr 1945 – 1 Apr 1945 from 24. Flottille	Initial training	Destroyed 1 Apr 1945 in Hamburg, by US bombs
U-768	VIIC	14-Oct-43	14 Oct 1943 – 20 Nov 1943	Training	Sank after a collision with U-745 in the Gulf of Danzig 20 Nov 1943. No casualties – 44 survivors
U-776	VIIC	13-Apr-44	13 Apr 1944 – 8 May 1945	Training plus 1 patrol	Surrendered at Weymouth, England, 20 May 1945. On display in the Thames at Westminster from 24 May. Operated by the Royal Navy as trials boat N 65 before being sunk 3 Dec 1945 in Operation *Deadlight*
U-777	VIIC	9-May-44	9 May 1944 – 15 Oct 1944	Training	Sunk 15 Oct 1944 at Wilhelmshaven in a British air raid
U-977	VIIC	6-May-43	1 Mar 1945 – 8 May 1945 from 21. Flottille	Initial training	Crew refused to surrender at end of war. Interned at Mar del Plata, Argentina, 17 Aug 1945 after a trip from Norway that included 66 days submerged. Transferred to United States 13 Nov 1945. Torpedoed as submarine target off Boston 13 Nov 1946
U-982	VIIC	10-Jun-43	1 Mar 1945 – 9 Apr 1945 from 24. Flottille	Initial training	Destroyed 9 Apr 1945 at Hamburg in an RAF bombing raid
U-1007	VIIC/41	18-Jan-44	1 Mar 1945 – 2 May 1945 from 24. Flottille	Initial training	Scuttled 2 May 1945 at Lübeck after a rocket attack by 4 Typhoons of No. 245 Sqn RAF. 2 crewmen killed
U-1013	VIIC/41	2-Mar-44	2 Mar 1944 – 17 Mar 1944	Training	Collided with U-286 17 Mar 1944 in the Baltic east of Rügen and sank. 25 dead and 26 survivors
U-1015	VIIC/41	23-Mar-44	23 Mar 1944 – 19 May 1944	Training	Collided with U-1014 in the Baltic west of Pillau and sank. 36 dead and 14 survivors
U-1103	VIIC/41	8-Jan-44	1 Mar 1945 – 8 May 1945 from 22. Flottille	Initial Training	Transferred from Kiel to Scotland 23 Jun 1945 for Operation *Deadlight*. Sunk by naval gunfire 30 Dec 1945
U-1132	VIIC	24-Jun-44	1 Feb 1945 – 4 May 1945 from 5. Flottille	Training	Scuttled 4 May 1945 near Flensburg in Küpfermühlen Bay
U-1167	VIIC/41	29-Dec-43	1 Mar 1945 – 30 Mar 1945 from 22. Flottille	Initial Training	Sunk 30 Mar 1945 at Hamburg-Finkenwärder, after being damaged by British bombs. 1 crewman killed
U-1196	VIIC	18-Nov-43	1 Mar 1945 – 3 May 1945 from 21. Flottille	Initial Training	Stricken in Aug 1944 after a torpedo accident. Scuttled 3 May 1945 at Travemünde
U-1197	VIIC	2-Dec-43	1 Mar 1945 – 25 Apr 1945 from 21. Flottille	Initial Training	Damaged by bombs at Bremen and stricken at Wesermünde 25 Apr 1945. Sunk as a target by US Navy in the North Sea in Feb 1946
U-1201	VIIC	13-Jan-44	1 Mar 1945 – 8 May 1945	Training	Severely damaged by US bombs at Hamburg 11 Mar 1945. Scuttled 3 May 1945
U-1224	IXC/40	20-Oct-43	20 Oct 1943 – 15 Feb 1944	Training	Transferred to Japan as RO-501 15 Feb 1944. Sunk with all hands northwest of Cape Verde Islands 13 May 1944, en route to the Far East, by Hedgehog and depth charges from the destroyer escort USS *Francis M. Robinson*. 48 Japanese seamen killed
U-1234	IXC/40	19-Apr-44	19 Apr 1944 – 31 Jan 1945	Training	Collided with a steam tug in fog and sank at Gotenhafen 14 May 1944. 13 dead and 43 survivors. Raised, repaired and recommissioned 17 Oct 1944
U-2505	XXI	7-Nov-44	7 Nov 1944 – 3 May 1945	Training	One of 3 Type XXI boats buried in the wreckage of the Elbe II bunker in Hamburg
U-2509	XXI	21-Sep-44	21 Sep 1944 – 8 May 1945	Training	Sunk 8 Apr 1945 at Blohm und Voss, Hamburg, in a British bombing raid
U-2514	XXI	17-Oct-44	17 Oct 1944 – 8 Apr 1945	Training	Sunk 8 Apr 1945 at Hamburg by bombs
U-2515	XXI	19-Oct-44	19 Oct 1944 – 11 Mar 1945	Training	Damaged in Dec 1944 in the Baltic Sea by a mine. Sunk 17 Jan 1945 in dock at Hamburg, by bombs while damaged sections were being replaced
U-2516	XXI	24-Oct-44	24 Oct 1944 – 9 Apr 1945	Training	Sunk 9 Apr 1945 at Kiel, by bombs
U-2521	XXI	21-Nov-44	21 Nov 1944 – 3 May 1945	Training	Sunk 3 May 1945 in the Flensburg Fjord by rockets from Typhoons of No. 184 Sqn RAF. 44 dead. Previously credited to a British Liberator which actually sank U-579
U-2523	XXI	26-Dec-44	26 Dec 1944 – 17 Jan 1945	Training	Sunk 17 Jan 1945 in dock at Hamburg, by bombs
U-2524	XXI	16-Jan-45	16 Jan 1945 – 3 May 1945	Training	Scuttled 3 May 1945 southeast of the island of Fehmarn in the Kattegat after a rocket attack by Beaufighters of Nos. 236 and 254 Sqns RAF. 1 crewman killed
U-2530	XXI	30-Dec-44	30 Dec 1944 – 20 Feb 1945	Training	Sunk 31 Dec 1944 in a bombing raid on Hamburg. Raised in Jan 1945. Further damaged in raids 17 Jan 1945 and 20 Feb 1945
U-2537	XXI	21-Mar-45	21 Mar 1945 – 8 May 1945	Training	Sunk by US bombs 31 Dec 1944 while fitting out. Raised, damaged again 15 Jan 1945. Destroyed by British bombs 8 Apr 1945
U-2542	XXI	5-Mar-45	5 Mar 1945 – 3 Apr 1945	Training	Sunk 3 Apr 1945 on the Hindenburg Bank at Kiel, by bombs

32 Unterseebootsflottille

The 32nd Flotilla was founded in April 1944, primarily to train crews of the new high-performance Type XXI and XXIII 'electro boats'. However, only two of the larger boats were assigned, and after less than a month they were transferred to the 4th Flotilla.

THE TYPE XXIIIs WERE SMALL coastal boats, armed with only two torpedoes. Designed to mount short-duration patrols, they were equipped with *Schnorchels* and it was expected that they would spend most of their time submerged. As a result, they had no exterior decking, which caused considerable underwater drag on more conventional boats.

Type XXIIIs were equipped with a very large battery capacity, which meant that they were faster when submerged than on the surface. Very manoeuvrable, they could crash-dive in only nine seconds, which made them popular with crews, for whom Allied air attacks had become the major threat.

However, the sheer speed at which the boat could dive meant that crews had to be absolutely certain all hatches were secure: any water flowing into the boat could cause disaster, and U-2331 was lost in such a diving accident while training with 32nd Flotilla.

A further problem was the fact that the boat's safe operating depth had been vastly overestimated at some 250m (820ft), which was the kind of depth later Type VIIs could achieve safely. In fact, the true safe operating depth for the Type XXIII was only 80m (260ft), and crews had to be careful when crash-diving not to descend too rapidly.

The flotilla was originally located at Königsberg in East Prussia, but was transferred to Hamburg in January 1945 after Kurland was isolated by the advancing Red Army. The flotilla was disbanded in May 1945, when Germany surrendered.

Commanders

Fregkpt. Hermann Rigele	Korvkpt. Ulrich Heyse
(Apr 1944 – Mar 1945)	*(Mar 1945 – May 1945)*

32ND FLOTILLA (43 BOATS)

Type	Boats ordered
Type XXI	U-3001, U-3002
Type XXIII	U-2321, U-2322, U-2324, U-2325, U-2326, U-2327, U-2328, U-2329, U-2330, U-2331, U-2334, U-2335, U-2336, U-2337, U-2338, U-2339, U-2340, U-2341, U-2342, U-2343, U-2344, U-2345, U-2346, U-2347, U-2348, U-2349, U-2350, U-2351, U-2352, U-2353, U-2354, U-2355, U-2356, U-2357, U-2358, U-2359, U-2360, U-2361, U-2362, U-2363, U-2364

32ND FLOTILLA BASE LOCATIONS

ATLANTIC OCEAN

Hamburg

Königsberg

32ND FLOTILLA BOATS LOST WHILE TRAINING

U-Boat	Type	Commissioned	Flotilla(s)	Patrols	Fate
U-2331	XXIII	12-Sep-44	12 Sep 1944 – 10 Oct 1944	Training	Sank 10 Oct 1944 near Hela in an accident. 15 dead and 4 survivors
U-2338	XXIII	9-Oct-44	9 Oct 1944 – 4 May 1945	Training	Sunk 4 May 1945 east-northeast of Fredericia by Beaufighters of Nos. 236 and 254 Sqns RAF. 12 dead and 1 survivor
U-2340	XXIII	16-Oct-44	16 Oct 1944 – 30 Mar 1945	Training	Sunk 30 Mar 1945 at Hamburg by British bombs. Wreck broken up
U-2342	XXIII	1-Nov-44	1 Nov 1944 – 26 Dec 1944	Training	Sunk 26 Dec 1944 in the Baltic north of Swinemünde by a mine. 7 dead
U-2344	XXIII	10-Nov-44	10 Nov 1944 – 18 Feb 1945	Training	Collided with U-2336 and sank 18 Feb 1945 north of Heiligendamm. 11 dead and 3 survivors

Far East and the Pacific

DECEMBER 1941 – AUGUST 1945

In this vast war theatre, the prime conflict was between the rapidly expanding American submarine fleet, mostly attack boats, and the Japanese submarine fleet, built primarily with fleet operations in view.

WHEN THE JAPANESE ATTACKED Pearl Harbor on 7 December 1941, Japan had 63 operational submarines, the Dutch had 15 based at Surabaya, Java, and the Americans had 55. Great Britain had no submarines in the Pacific, and only two between February 1942 and July 1943.

British Submarines

HMS *Storm* was one of 15 S-class boats ordered in Britain's 1941 building programme. Commissioned on 23 July 1943, it made one patrol into the Arctic Ocean before being despatched to the Royal Navy base at Trincomalee, Ceylon, arriving on 20 February 1944. It operated in the Bay of Bengal and the Malacca Straits, on ocean patrol and covert missions. Two Japanese destroyers and a merchant vessel were sunk.

In September 1944, *Storm* was deployed to Fremantle, Western Australia, with one ballast tank modified to hold the extra fuel required to maintain patrols as far out as Java. The boat returned to Britain in April 1945, having travelled 114km (71,000 miles) and spent over 1400 hours submerged. It was scrapped in September 1949.

German Submarines

German U-boats also found their way into eastern waters. Eleven were to be transferred to a base in Japanese-held Penang, Malaya (12th, later 33rd, Flotilla) in mid-1943. But only five made it all the way, and their raiding activities in the Indian Ocean were of minor concern, largely through Allied decoding of their radio transmissions.

Japan

At the start of hostilities, Japan had 48 ocean-going I-class submarines and 15 were smaller RO-class; 29 were under construction; and 41 carried from one to three aircraft, a facility dropped by all other navies in the 1920s. Japanese submarines, though quite fast, were slow to dive and vulnerable to ASW techniques, while the Japanese Navy was surprisingly slow to develop its own radar and ASW capacity.

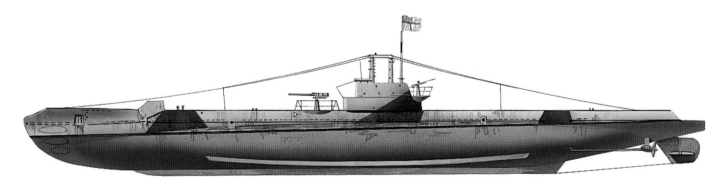

▲ HMS Storm

Royal Navy, S-class patrol submarine, Pacific, 1944

One of the third group of S-class boats, from the 1941 programme, Storm had a seventh external torpedo tube at the stern. Thirteen torpedoes were carried. D/F and radar aerials were added in 1944. It sank two Japanese warships, an army transport and 22 small craft. As with almost all submarines, its gunners had zero protection.

Specifications

Crew: 44	Submerged: 1006 tonnes (990 tons)
Powerplant: Twin screw diesel; electric motors	Dimensions (length/beam/draught): 61.8m x
Max Speed: Surfaced: 14.75 knots; Submerged:	7.25m x 3.2m (202ft 6in x 23ft 9in x 10ft 6in)
9 knots	Commissioned: May 1943
Surface Range: 15,750km (8500nm) at 10 knots	Armament: Six 533mm (21in) torpedo tubes; one
Displacement: Surfaced: 726 tonnes (715 tons);	76mm (3in) gun

The Japanese fleet had the most effective torpedoes available during World War II. The Type 95, a smaller submarine version of the Type 93 'long lance' (an American name, not used by the Japanese) developed from 1928, used pure oxygen to burn kerosene, instead of the compressed air and alcohol used in other nation's torpedoes. This gave them a range of up to 12km (7.5 miles) – about double that of their Allied counterparts – which also reduced their wake, making them harder to notice and avoid. The Type 95 also had by far the largest warhead of any submarine torpedo, initially 405kg (893lb), increased to 550kg (1210lb) late in the war.

Most importantly, the Type 95 used a simple contact exploder, and was far more reliable than its American counterpart, the Mark 14, until the latter was improved in late 1943. Japanese submarines also made extensive use of an electric torpedo, the Type 92. This weapon, with a 299kg (661lb) warhead, had modest performance compared to the Type 95, but emitted no exhaust and left no wake.

In one celebrated instance, I-19 of the 1st Submarine Flotilla fired six torpedoes at the carrier USS *Wasp* on 15 September 1942. Three hit the carrier, effectively destroying it. Of the three that missed, two travelled on into the path of another US task force, hitting and causing serious damage to the destroyer *O'Brien* and the battleship *North Carolina*.

RO-100 Series

The RO-100 series, also known as 'Kaisho' (small) or Type KS was an 18-strong class developed from 1940 and completed by 1944. Intended for coastal defence, with an operating depth of 75m (245ft), its size meant it carried a limited payload of eight 533mm (21in) torpedoes. During the war, the need to operate further out made life difficult for the class. RO-108 sank the US destroyer *Henley* off New Guinea in 1943 and RO-100s sank 33,021 tonnes (32,500 tons) of Allied merchant shipping, but the class was severely overextended. None survived the war, most of them sunk by American destroyers. The original RO-100 made eight patrols before being sunk by a mine off the Solomon Islands in November 1943.

The C1 Hei gata class of attack submarine was laid down in 1937–38, but not commissioned until March 1940 to October 1941. In all there were five: I-16, I-18, I-20, I-22 and I-24, intended specifically for attack on surface warships. Operational depth was

100m (330ft), and the class had a range of almost 26,000km (16,155 miles) and could remain at sea for up to 90 days. Twenty torpedoes were carried.

All participated in the surprise attack on Pearl Harbor by launching midget submarines, and I-24 also took part in the Battle of the Coral Sea and the attack on Sydney Harbour (May and June 1942). I-16 was converted to a transport in early 1943, carrying a landing craft. It was sunk off the Solomon

JAPANESE SUBMARINE CLASSES, 1939–45			
Class	Number	Launched	Note
C1	5	1940–41	Midget sub carrier
B1	20	1940–43	Patrol boat with seaplane or Kaiten
A/B	50	1940–43	Midget sub; 2-man crew
A1	3	1941–42	Seaplane carrier developed from J3
KD7	10	1942–43	Attack submarine
Kaisho type	18	1942–44	Coastal defence
Kaichu type	20	1943–44	Patrol submarine
B2	6	1943–44	Patrol submarine with seaplane or Kaiten
C3	3	1943–44	Long-range cruiser; cargo capacity
D1	12	1943–44	Landing craft; 110 troops
A2	1	1944	Long-range seaplane carrier
B3	3	1944	Patrol submarine with seaplane or Kaiten
C-type	15	1944	3-man crew; 47 completed by end of war
D-type	115	1944–45	5-man crew; 496 under construction mid-1945
AM	2	1944–45	Carried 2 seaplane bombers
Sen Toku I-400	3	1944–45	Long range; carried 3 float-planes
D2	1	1945	Cargo plus landing craft
Sen Taka	3	1945	Snorkel-fitted. Too late for combat duty
Sen Taka Sho	10	1945	Coastal patrol. 22 laid down
Sen Yu Sho	10	1945	Small supply boat
Sen Ho	1	1945	Submarine tanker and armament carrier

Islands by charges from a 'Hedgehog' ASW mortar from the US destroyer *England*, and none of the others survived the war.

In 1938, the Imperial Japanese Navy had built a small high-speed experimental submarine, designated 'Vesssel No. 71', capable of making over 21 knots (39km/h) submerged. From this, the much larger attack boat of class I-201 was developed, with 23 ordered from the Kure Navy Yard in 1943. But only eight were laid down, and three were completed before the Japanese surrender, but not put into operational service. These were

among the first submarines to travel faster when submerged than on the surface.

Faced with ever-more effective and aggressive ASW techniques, the Japanese desperately needed a boat that combined speed, fast diving, good underwater handling and quietness of operation along with its offensive capacity. Four electric motors developing 5000hp (3700kW) provided the underwater power.

The I-201 class, single-hulled, of streamlined design, with retractable deck guns, and snorkels, planned for large-scale production using prefabricated parts, was

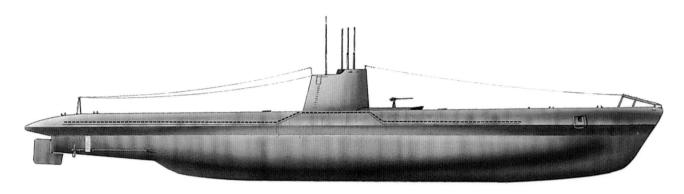

▲ RO-100

Imperial Japanese Navy, Type KS patrol submarine, Western Pacific, 1943

Completed in August 1942, this was the class leader. Assigned to SubRon 7, Submarine Division 13, of Japan's 8th Fleet, it was based at Rabaul, New Guinea, making combat patrols and supply runs in the region until sunk by a mine near Buin, Bougainville, on 25 November 1943.

Specifications

Crew: 75

Powerplant: Twin shaft diesel; electric motors

Max Speed: Surfaced: 14 knots; Submerged: 8 knots

Surface Range: 6485km (3500nm) at 12 knots

Displacement: Surfaced: 611 tonnes (601 tons); Submerged: 795 tonnes (782 tons)

Dimensions (length/beam/draught): 57.4m x 6.1m x 3.5m (188ft 3in x 20ft x 11ft 6in)

Commissioned: August 1942

Armament: Four 533mm (21in) torpedo tubes; one 76mm (3in) gun

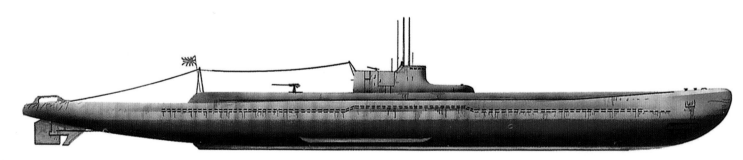

▲ C-1

Imperial Japanese Navy, midget submarine carrier

Based on the KD 6A type, though considerably larger, this was a fast boat on the surface. Unlike most big Japanese submarines, none of the class carried a float-plane. The midget submarine fittings were later replaced by attachments to hold small supply barges for landing supplies.

Specifications

Crew: 100

Powerplant: Twin shaft diesel; electric motors

Max Speed: Surfaced: 23.5 knots; Submerged: 8 knots

Surface Range: 25,928km (14,000nm)

Displacement: Surfaced: 2605 tonnes (2564 tons); Submerged: 3761 tonnes (3701 tons)

Dimensions (length/beam/draught): 108.6m x 9m x 5m (256ft 3in x 29ft 5in x 16ft 4in)

Commissioned: July 1938

Armament: Eight 533mm (21in) torpedo tubes; one 140mm (5.5in) gun

▲ **I-400 class**

I-400 and I-401, alongside USS *Proteus* after Japan's surrender in August 1945. The I-400 class was a serious attempt by the Imperial Japanese Navy to create a submarine aircraft carrier. The experiment proved to be an expensive flop and the class made no contribution to the war effort.

a potentially formidable submarine. But they had no influence on the war and were sunk or scuttled by the US Navy in the course of 1946.

I-351 (Sen-Ho or Sensuikan-Hokyu, 'submarine tanker') was planned in 1941 as a refuelling and supply craft for the Kawanishi H6K flying boats in remote places where onshore facilities could not be set up. Three were planned, but only I-351 was operational during the war, launched early in 1945 at Kure Navy Yard. With a capacity of 371 tonnes (365 tons) of gasoline fuel, twenty 250kg (550lb) bombs and 15 Type 91 aerial torpedoes, in addition to 11 tonnes (10.8 tons) of fresh water, it could substantially extend the striking range of the aircraft. It was well protected with four 533mm (21in) torpedo tubes, four 81mm (3in) mortars, and a battery of seven Type 96 25mm AA guns. It also carried 13-go radar equipment. I-351 survived in action for only six months before being sunk by the US Gato-class submarine *Bluefish* on 14 July 1945.

I-400 Class

The Sen-Toku I-400 class were the largest submarines built by any country before the appearance of nuclear-powered ballistic missile submarines. It was originally meant to number 18, and work started in January 1943. Within the partial double hull were two parallel cylindrical hulls. After the death of Admiral Yamamoto, sponsor of the class, the number was scaled back to five, of which only three were completed.

Unlike other Japanese aircraft-carrying submarines, they were attack rather than scouting vessels, with an operating range sufficient to make three round trips across the Pacific, or to circumnavigate the globe. To accommodate a hangar for three Aichi M6A Seiran bombers, the conning tower was offset to port.

A compressed-air 26m (85ft) catapult on the forward deck launched the aircraft, loaded with a 1800lb (800kg) bomb. An attack on the Panama Canal locks by Submarine Squadron 1, formed of the operational I-400 boats plus the aircraft-carrying I-13 and I-14, was devised in 1944–45, but abandoned in

Specifications

Crew: 100	Displacement: Surfaced: 1311 tonnes (1291
Powerplant: Twin screws diesel; electric motors	tons); Submerged: 1473 tonnes (1450 tons)
Max Speed: Surfaced: 15.7 knots; Submerged:	Dimensions (length/beam/draught): 79m x 5.8m
19 knots	x 5.4m (259ft 2in x 19ft x 17ft 9in)
Surface Range: 10,747km (5800nm) at 14 knots	Commissioned: July 1944
	Armament: Four 533mm (21in) torpedo tubes

▲ I-201

Imperial Japanese Navy, fast attack submarine, 1945

I-201 was completed on 2 February 1945 and assigned to various subdivisions of the 6th Fleet. An anechoic rubberized coating was applied to reduce noise. The bow planes were retractable. Ten Type 95 torpedoes were carried. The conning tower is notably small. It was sunk as a target on 23 May 1946.

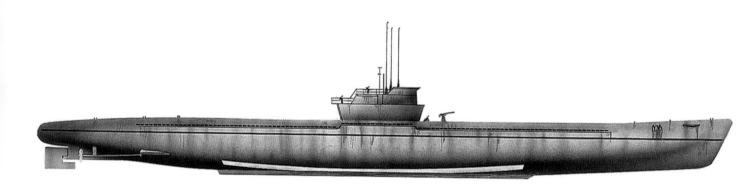

▲ I-351

Imperial Japanese Navy, flying-boat tender/transport submarine

Attached to Submarine Division 15 of the 6th Fleet, this boat made two return trips between its Sasebo base and Singapore in May to July 1945, picking up loads of rubber and other goods for the war effort. It never fulfilled its intended role as a flying-boat tender.

Specifications

Crew: 90	Displacement: Surfaced: 3568 tonnes (3512
Powerplant: Twin screws, diesel/electric motors	tons); Submerged: 4358 tonnes (4290 tons)
Max Speed: Surfaced: 15.8 knots; Submerged:	Dimensions (length/beam/draught): 110m x
6.3 knots	10.2m x 6m (361ft x 33ft 6in x 19ft 8in)
Surface Range: 24,076km (13,000nm) at	Commissioned: February 1944
14 knots	Armament: Four 533mm (12in) torpedo tubes

July 1945 in favour of attacking US carriers at the Ulithi Atoll base. Japan's surrender in August pre-empted this operation.

US Navy Submarines

Though originally planned as fleet boats, the US Navy's Gato class turned out to be well suited to the different kind of naval war that developed in the Pacific. Construction began on 11 September 1940 with USS *Drum*, at Portsmouth, New Hampshire, which was also the first to be commissioned, on 1 November 1941. Diving depth was 90m (300ft). Emulating the Germans' wolfpack system, Gato class

submarines operated as co-ordinated groups in the Yellow Sea and other areas.

The Gato class was the first to be fitted with air conditioning from the start. Many detail modifications were made in the course of the war, usually in order to accommodate radar, direction-finding and sonar equipment. While the array on masts and periscopes above the conning tower became ever more complex, the tower itself was progressively reduced in the interest both of lowering the profile and of reducing drag. USS *Barb*, refitted in 1945, was the first submarine to launch rocket shells against mainland targets; in 1954, it was passed to the Italian Navy

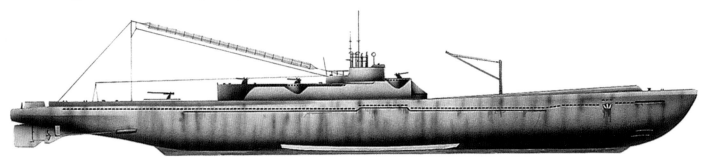

Specifications

Crew: 100	Displacement: Surfaced: 5316 tonnes (5233
Powerplant: Twin screw diesel; electric motors	tons); Submerged: 6665 tonnes (6560 tons)
Max Speed: Surfaced: 18.7 knots; Submerged:	Dimensions (length/beam/draught): 122m x 12m
6.5 knots	x 7m (400ft 1in x 39ft 4in x 24ft)
Surface Range: 68,561km (37,000nm) at	Commissioned: 1944
14 knots	Armament: Eight 533mm (21in) torpedo tubes;
	one 140mm (5.5in) gun

▲ I-400

Imperial Japanese Navy, aircraft-carrying strategic raider, 1945

Great ingenuity went into the folding and collapsible equipment, including a retrieval crane. The three I-400s were fitted with Mk3 Model 1 air search radar, Mk2 Model 2 surface search radar, and an E 27 radar detector. I-400 had a German snorkel system from May 1945. All were sunk as targets in 1946.

Specifications

Crew: 80	Displacement: Surfaced: 1845 tonnes (1816
Powerplant: Twin screw diesel; electric motors	tons); Submerged: 2463 tonnes (2425 tons)
Max Speed: Surfaced: 20 knots; Submerged:	Dimensions (length/beam/draught): 94m x 8.2m
10 knots	x 5m (311ft 3in x 27ft x 17ft)
Surface Range: 19,311km (10,409nm) at	Commissioned: April 1942
10 knots	Armament: 10 533mm (21in) torpedo tubes

▲ USS Barb

US Navy, Gato-class patrol/attack submarine, Pacific 1944

Barb made five patrols off Europe before deploying to Pearl Harbor in September 1943. On seven Pacific patrols it sank 17 ships of 96,628GRT, including the escort carrier Unyo on 17 September 1944, making it the US Navy's most successful combat submarine. Members of its crew mounted the only land incursion into Japan, in July 1945.

as *Enrico Tazzoli*; the profile shows its post-Guppy programme appearance.

Another Gato boat, USS *Grouper*, was refitted as a model of the post-war hunter-killer *SSK*. From 4 February 1943, when USS *Balao* was commissioned, the Gato class was supplemented by 122 boats of a similar – but in various ways – improved version, which was capable of operating down to 122m (400ft) with a range of 20,000km (12,400 miles), and able to remain submerged for 48 hours at a stretch. By August 1945, 56 Japanese submarines remained in service, many of them by now in bad or damaged condition; and, of these, only nine were large attack submarines. In the course of the war, 126

US SUBMARINE CLASSES, 1940–45			
Class	Number	Launched	Note
Tambor	6	1940–41	2 lost
Mackerel	2	1941	
Gar	6	1941	5 lost
Gato	73	1941–44	19 lost
Balao	113	1943–45	9 lost
Tench	28	1944–45	

were built (excluding midget submarines) and 127 were lost: 70 to surface ships, 19 to other submarines, 18 to aircraft, and the remainder to other causes.

▲ **USS Drum (Gato class)**

US Navy, Gato class patrol/attack submarine

The first Gato-boat to be commissioned and enter combat, it is seen here in World War II mode. After heavy depth-charging it was given a Balao-type conning tower at the end of 1943. The complex rig above the shears reflects the variety of sensory and communications equipment now carried.

Specifications

Crew: 80

Powerplant: Twin screw diesels; electric motors

Max Speed: Surfaced: 20 knots; Submerged: 10 knots

Surface Range: 22,236km (12,000nm) at 10 knots

Displacement: Surfaced: 1845 tonnes (1816 tons); Submerged: 2463 tonnes (2425 tons)

Dimensions (length/beam/draught): 95m x 8.3m x 4.6m (311ft 9in x 27ft 3in x 15ft 3in)

Commissioned: May 1941

Armament: 10 533mm (21in) torpedo tubes

Specifications

Crew: 80

Powerplant: Twin screw diesels; electric motors

Max Speed: Surfaced: 20 knots; Submerged: 10 knots

Surface Range: 19,300km (10,416nm) at 10 knots

Displacement: Surfaced: 1845 tonnes (1816 tons); Submerged: 2463 tonnes (2425 tons)

Dimensions (length/beam/draught): 94.8m x 8.2m x 4.5m (311ft 3in x 27ft x 15ft)

Commissioned: February 1942

Armament: 10 533mm (21in) torpedo tubes

▲ **USS Grouper (Gato class)**

US Navy, Gato class patrol/attack submarine, later test-boat

Commissioned on 12 February 1942, Grouper made nine war patrols, and in 1946 was the first submarine fitted with a combat information centre. From then on it was a test boat, becoming the first designated SSK on 2 January 1951. Later a floating laboratory, AGSS-214, it was finally scrapped in 1970.

Late war submarine development
1944–45

While Britain and the United States concentrated on enlarging their fleets of proven designs, Germany worked to develop new and more efficient submarine types, while also building huge numbers to established designs.

GERMANY PROVED TO BE ahead of the Allies in submarine design, although by this point in the war the Allies had developed effective air and sea submarine counter-measures.

Germany

Between 1943 and 1945, 118 U-boats of Type XXI were commissioned. Effectively this introduced a new generation of combat submarine. The streamlined outer hull covered a pressure-hull in figure-of-eight cross-section, the upper section of greater diameter than the lower.

The Type XXI had much improved crew facilities with a deep-freeze for food, a shower compartment and better accommodation. A hydraulic reload system enabled all six tubes to be reloaded in 10 minutes, less than the manual loading time of one tube on the Type VIIC. Greater electrical power, with three times the battery capacity of the Type VIIC, gave the Type XXI a much wider underwater range, enabling it to traverse the Bay of Biscay at a depth that minimized the risk of detection. It could reach 280m (919ft), a greater depth than any other submarine of the time. The four electric motors, two of them designed for silent running, gained it the name of 'Elektroboot'. Prefabrication and welding of eight separate sections were used to speed up building time to a hoped-for six months.

Seventeen completed or almost-completed Type XXIs were destroyed in yards between December 1944 and May 1945. As a result, only four were combat ready at the time of Germany's surrender, and only U-2511 and U-3008 undertook any offensive patrols. Neither sank anything, though on the day of surrender, 4 May, U-2511 made a demonstration run at the British cruiser *Norfolk*, which did not even notice the U-boat's presence.

U-3001 was one of the first Type XXI submarines to be commissioned, on 20 July 1944, and was assigned to the 32nd Training Flotilla at Konigsberg (now Kaliningrad), but quickly passed on to the 4th, at Stettin (Szczecin). From November 1944 to May 1945, it was based at KLA (Warship Training Section), Bremen. Always a training boat, it made

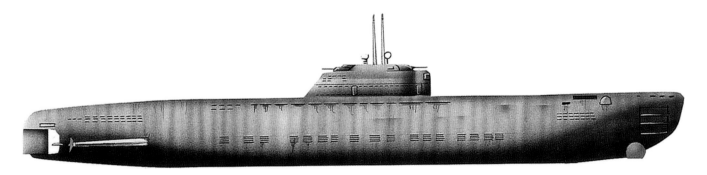

▲ **'Elektroboot' U-3001**

German Navy, Type XXI, 'Elektroboot,' coastal submarine, Stettin, 1944

Twenty-three torpedoes could be carried, or a split load of 14 torpedoes and 12 TMC mines. Passive/active sonar enabled blind firing from 49m (160ft), using LUT guidable torpedoes. It could travel submerged for three days before recharging. With no open deck top, its tower heralded the later fin or sail type.

Specifications

Crew: 57

Powerplant: Diesel; electric motors

Max Speed: 28.9/31.9km/hr (15.6/17.2kt) surf/sub

Surface Range: 20,650km (11,150nm)

Displacement: 1647/1848t (1621/1819 tons)

Dimensions (length/beam/draught): 76.7 x 6.6 x 6.3m (251.7 x 21.7 x 20.7ft)

Commissioned: 20 July 1944

Armament: 23 torpedoes (6 bow tubes); two twin 2cm (0.8in) gun turrets no wartime patrols, and was scuttled on 3 May 1945 northwest of Wesermünde.

By the end of 1941, the Type II submarine was in active service only in the Black Sea. A new smaller boat was needed to work in the North and Baltic Seas, to which Dönitz added the Mediterranean and Black Seas. This required the hull to be sectionable to sizes that could be carried by railway. The initial design was complete by 30 June 1943 and construction began not only in Germany but also at shipyards in occupied territories. The first was U-2321, launched on 17 April 1944 and commissioned 12 June. The Type XXIII was a single-hull boat, of all-welded construction. Like the Type XXI, being built in parallel, it was of streamlined construction and had a 'creep' electric motor. From April 1944 to May 1945, 61 entered service, out of 280 ordered, though only six are known to have carried out operational patrols, resulting in the sinking of five Allied ships.

Most Type XXIII boats were assigned to the 32nd Training Flotilla, though 13 joined the 5th Flotilla at Kiel, and 10 were active with the 11th Flotilla at Bergen, Norway. Despite having only two torpedo tubes, no gun and no spare torpedoes, the Type XXIIIs, because of their speed and stealth, could have been a powerful aid to Germany's war effort.

U-2326 was one of only three Type XXIII boats to survive the war. Surrendered at Dundee, Scotland, it became the British N25, then was passed to France

▲ **Type XXI**
The launch of a Type XXI U-boat at Kiel, sometime during 1943.

in 1946, but sank in an accident off Toulon in the same year.

Two Type IXD boats were commissioned in September 1942, U-195 as IXD1 and U-196 as IXD2, as large fast attack boats. U-196 made the longest patrol of any World War II submarine, from 13 March to 23 October 1943, to the Indian Ocean. U-195 sank three ships off South Africa in March to July 1943, but in the following year it was disarmed and converted at Bordeaux as a transport, carrying 256 tonnes (252 tons) of strategic war materials. Originally fitted with experimental high-speed diesel

engines, these proved unreliable and smoky, and were replaced by standard Type IX diesels. In May 1945, U-195 was taken over by the Japanese Navy at Batavia as I-506, for a brief period before being surrendered to the Americans in August.

Other Navies

HMS *Sanguine* was one of the last of the S-class to be completed before the end of the war brought the building programme to a halt. It was commissioned on 13 May 1945, too late for active service in European waters. In 1958, it was sold to the Israeli Navy, as was a sister boat, *Springer*, in 1959; they were renamed *Rahav* and *Tanin*. Numerous S-class boats were disposed of to other navies in the post-war years. Three, *Saga*, *Spearhead* and *Spur*, went to Portugal in 1948–49; and *Spiteful*, *Sportsman*, *Statesman* and *Styr* were passed to France in 1951–52. The last British S-class was scrapped in 1962.

In the course of the war the Italian Navy developed the Flutto class of medium submarines. Twelve of Type 1 were ordered and 10 completed by August 1943. Orders were placed for 24 of Type 2, but only three were launched and none commissioned during the war; all were captured at Monfalcone by German forces after Italy's surrender. Type 3 was to consist of 12 boats, but none was completed. The design was very much in line with Italian practice, but with a conning tower of reduced size.

Eight of the Flutto 2 boats were given UIT numbers to indicate U-boats of Italian provenance. One of the Flutto 1 class, *Nautilo*, scuttled in 1945, was raised and served in the Yugoslav post-war fleet as *Sava*. *Marea* was passed to Soviet Russia in 1949. The only surviving Flutto 1 boat in Italian hands was *Vortice*. After a major refit in 1951–53, it was recommissioned into the Italian Navy and served until August 1967.

Japan's Ha 201 Sensuikan Taka-Ko gata (small fast submarine) was comparable in type and purpose to Germany's Type XXIII, and constructed in a similar manner, in prefabricated sections using five different yards. Experience gained in the testing of 'Vessel No. 71' in 1938 was incorporated into the streamlined design. Home defence was the aim and 79 boats were planned for production in a crash programme beginning in January 1945.

Only 10 were completed and none undertook active patrols. Armed with only four torpedoes, they

GERMAN SUBMARINE CLASSES, 1935–45			
Class	Number	Launched	Note
Type IIA	6	1934–35	Double-hull design; coastal boats
Type IIB	24	1935–36	
Type IA	2	1936	
Type VIIA	10	1935–37	Two served in Spanish Civil War
Type IX hull	8	1936–39	Ocean-going; double
Type VIIB	24	1936–40	
Type IIC	8	1937–40	
Type IXB	14	1937–40	
Type VIIC	568	1938–44	Attack boat; single hull
Type IID	16	1939–40	
Type IXC	54	1939–42	
Type XB	8	1939–44	Minelayer
Type VIID	6	1940–42	Minelayer
Type XIV	10	1940–43	'Milch Cow' supply boats
Type IXC/40	87	1940–44	
Type IXD1	2	1940–42	
Type IXD2	28	1940–44	
Type VIIC/41	91	1941–45	
Type VIIF	4	1941–43	Supply boats
Type IXD42	2	1942–44	
Type XVIIA	6	1942–44	Experimental
Type XVIIB	3	1943–44	Experimental
Type XVIII	1	1943–44	Experimental; not completed
Type XXI	118	1943–45	'Elektroboot' developed from Type XVIII
Type XXIII	61	1943–45	Coastal; only 6 operational

were highly manoeuvrable and capable of short bursts of high speed while submerged, which would have made them dangerous to surface craft. They could dive to 100m (330ft). With only a 7.7mm (0.3in) AA machine gun, they were vulnerable to air attack, but a form of snorkel allowed them to stay submerged for lengthy periods. Limited storage space restricted their sea-time to 15 days.

Midget Submarines

Numerous countries, notably Italy and Japan on the Axis powers, and Great Britain among the Allies, invested in midget submarines: boats of under 150 tonnes (148 tons) with a crew in single numbers,

normally operated from a mother ship. The Japanese 'Kaiten' craft were really manned torpedoes and their construction in the later phase of the war was an act of desperation.

The British and Italian designs, though certainly high risk, were not suicide craft. Their aim was to engage in covert operations where a large vessel would not be able to penetrate. After 1939, the Royal Navy took an interest in the midget submarine, and two prototypes, X-3 and X-4, were built, leading to the X-5, with a four-man crew, and 20 were constructed. The most celebrated exploit of these X-boats was the attempt on the German battleship *Tirpitz* and other capital ships anchored in the

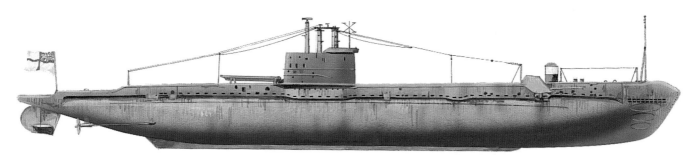

▲ HMS Sanguine

Royal Navy, S-class patrol submarine

S-boats had served in the Mediterranean during World War II, and Sanguine, without air conditioning, was often uncomfortable for its crew. Internal temperatures sometimes reached 40°C (104°F). But it remained active until 1966. Tanin participated in the Six-Day War of June 1967. Both were scrapped in 1968.

Specifications

Crew: 44	Submerged: 1006 tonnes (990 tons)
Powerplant: Twin screw diesel; electric motors	Dimensions (length/beam/draught): 61.8m x
Max Speed: Surfaced: 14.7 knots; Submerged:	7.25m x 3.2m (202ft 6in x 23ft 9in x 10ft 6in)
9 knots	Commissioned: February 1945
Surface Range: 15,750km (8500nm) at 10 knots	Armament: Six 533mm (21in) torpedo tubes; one
Displacement: Surfaced: 726 tonnes (715 tons);	76mm (3in) gun

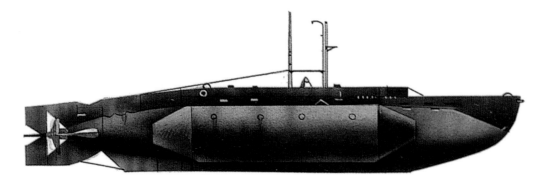

Specifications

Crew: 4	Submerged: 30 tons (29.5 tons)
Powerplant: Single screw diesel; electric motors	Dimensions (length/beam/draught): 15.7m x
Max Speed: Surfaced: 6.5 knots; Submerged:	1.8m x 2.6m (51ft 6in x 6ft x 8ft 6in)
5 knots	Commissioned: March 1942
Surface Range: 926km (500nm)	Armament: Two 1994kg (4400lb) detachable
Displacement: Surfaced: 27 tonnes/tons;	amatol charges

▲ HMS X-5

Royal Navy, midget submarine type, Norway, 1943

The X-boats had a passage-crew in transit and an operations crew for combat. An airlock allowed a diver to leave and re-enter. They could dive to 91m (300ft). Twenty were built, seven lost in action or accident, and one is preserved. Six XE-boats, as used at Singapore, were also constructed.

▲ **HMS** *Sanguine*

Commissioned on 13 May 1945, this was the last S-class to be completed. Note the sonar dome, the absence of a deck gun and the redesigned conning tower.

Altafjord, on the Norwegian coast. X-craft were used in other theatres too, including successful missions to sink Japanese ships at Singapore in July 1945.

The Germans developed a range of midget submarines, including the Seehund type of 1944, of which 285 were built (1000 were intended), but their introduction had a negligible effect on the closing stage of the war. Japan used Ko-hyoteki type midget submarines in the attacks at Pearl Harbor (1941) and Sydney Harbour (29 May 1942); 101 were built in

all. In 1945, Japan produced around 210 Kairyu 'sea dragon' two-man midget submarines and about 420 Kaiten 'human torpedoes'. Although Kaitens were sent on around 100 missions, only one significant strike was made, sinking the convoy escort USS *Underhill* on 24 July 1945.

Last US Wartime Classes

At the end of the war, the US Navy possessed a large and up-to-date submarine fleet, though many were

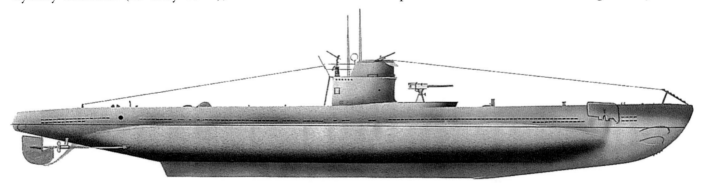

Specifications

Crew: 50

Powerplant: Twin screw diesel engines; electric
  motors

Max Speed: Surfaced: 16 knots; Submerged:
  8 knots

Surface Range: 6670km (3600nm) at 12 knots

Displacement: Surfaced: 1130 tonnes (1113

tons); Submerged: 1188 tonnes (1170 tons)

Dimensions (length/beam/draught): 64m x 6.9m
  x 4.9m (210ft 7in x 22ft 11in x 16ft 2in)

Commissioned: Not launched

Armament: Six 533mm (21in) torpedo tubes; one
  100mm (3.9in) gun

▲ **Ferro**

Italian Navy, Flutto II-class patrol submarine

Ferro was given the German number UIT-12, but no further work was carried out and it was blown up on the slipway on 1 May 1945. One of the Flutto II boats, Bario (numbered UIT 7 in 1943–45), was salvaged from the Monfalcone yards, rebuilt at Taranto in 1957–61, renamed Pietro Calvi, and served until 1972.

USS *TENCH*

The submarines of the Tench class were a developed version of the previous Gato and Balao classes, fitted with improved interior machinery and ballast tank arrangements. A total of 29 were completed for the United States during or immediately following World War II, and most never made a war patrol.

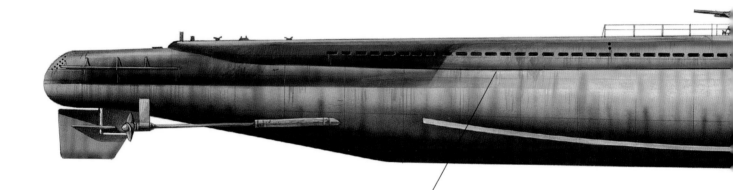

Sargo battery

Two 126-cell Sargo batteries were carried in forward and after compartments. Designed by the Bureau of Steam Engineering, they were named for USS *Sargo* whose commissioning C.O., Lieutenant E. E. Yeomans, suggested the design. Cells had two concentric hard rubber cases with a layer of soft rubber between them. This helped to prevent leakage of sulphuric acid in the event of depth charging or ramming. The Sargo battery was the standard design for US submarines to the end of the war.

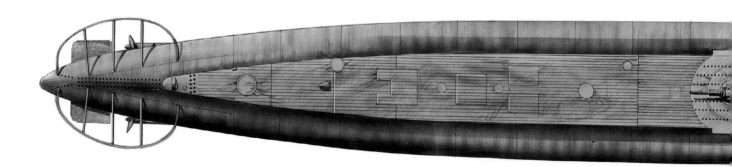

LF loop antenna

This was mounted between the periscopes, although later Tench-class boats had it mounted on a bracket aft of the SJ mast.

Guppy 1A refit programme (1951)

The profile shows *Tench* in wartime form. Under Guppy IA, the pointed fleet bow was retained and the motors, already slow-speed type, were not modernized, although the auxiliary diesel generator was replaced by air-conditioning equipment. With the Guppy project, the tower ceased to hold a control station and came to be known as the sail (USA) or fin (Great Britain).

Fairwater

The fairwater has been minimized: the extent of the lip on the after gun platform is so great as to require a support stanchion.

Ballast tanks

Re-planning of the ballast tanks also allowed space for an additional four torpedoes compared with the Balao and Gato boats.

Dive planes

Forward diving planes were stowed ready-tilted in dive position so that when extended they would immediately force the bow down. Diving to periscope depth could be achieved in 30–40 seconds.

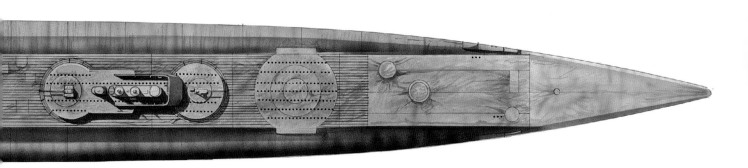

SOVIET SUBMARINE CLASSES, 1939–45			
Class	Number	Launched	Note
Series XIIIb L20	6	1940–41	Minelayer
Series Xb Shch 135	20	1940–47	Patrol
Series XIIb M30	45	1937–41	Coastal patrol
Series IXb S4	31	1939–41	Pre-war class; 4 to China, 1955
Series XIV K1	7	1939–41	Minelayer; continuation of pre-war type
Series XV M204	10	1941	Continuation of pre-war class
Ronis	2	1927	Seized from Latvia, 1940; coastal
Kalev	2	1936	Seized from Estonia 1940; minelayer
S3-4	2	1941	Seized from Romania 1944
TS4	1	1936	Seized from Romania 1944

battle-worn and in need of reconditioning. *Entemedor* of the Balao class (originally to be named 'Chickwick') was commissioned in April 1945 and made only one wartime patrol.

In 1945–48, it was based at West Coast ports and made several cruises in Far Eastern waters, based at Subic Bay. Placed on the reserve list in 1948, it was recommissioned in October 1950 during the Korean War. It saw service in the Atlantic in 1951–52, and was extensively modernized in 1952. In 1973, it was sold to Turkey and renamed *Preveze*, serving until 1987.

The Tench class was a refinement of the Balao type, which they resembled very closely. Originally 134 were to be constructed but, with the end of the war, 101 were cancelled or scrapped while under construction, and 33 remained as the United States' most up-to-date submarine prior to the post-war modernization programmes. While exceeding the Balao class in displacement by only some 40.6 tonnes (40 tons), they did have a better organized interior layout as well as greater hull strength. Only a few of the class, including *Tench* itself, participated in wartime operations. USS *Pickerel* was one of those not completed until after the war, in 1949. Fourteen were sold to other navies between 1964 and 1973: four to Brazil, two each to Turkey

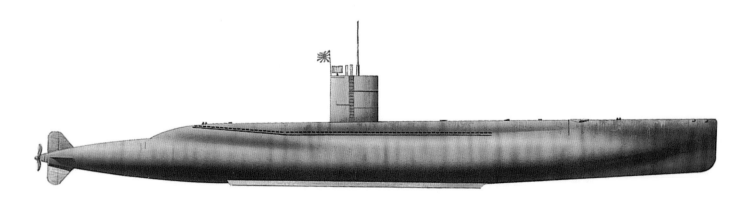

▲ Ha 201

Imperial Japanese Navy, coastal defence submarine

The class was intended to work in co-ordinated groups, but this never happened. Ha 201 was first of the class, completed on 31 May 1945, and assigned to Submarine Division 33, then Submarine Division 52. Surrendered at the Sasebo base on 2 September 1945, it was used for target practice, tied against the large I-402, in April 1946, and finally scuttled.

Specifications

Crew: 22

Powerplant: Single shaft diesel; electric motor

Max Speed: Surfaced: 10.5 knots; Submerged: 13 knots

Surface Range: 5559km (3000nm) at 10 knots

Displacement: Surfaced: 383 tonnes (377 tons);

Submerged: 447 tonnes (440 tons)

Dimensions (length/beam/draught): 50m x 3.9m x 3.4m (164ft x 13ft x 11ft 3in)

Commissioned: May 1945

Armament: Two 533mm (21in) torpedo tubes; one 7.7mm AA gun

and Italy, and one each to Canada, Greece, Pakistan, Peru, Taiwan, and Venezuela.

A combination of damage repair, major refits, different techniques at the various shipyards, and constant efforts to reduce the submarines' profile, both against visual and electronic reconnaissance, plus the requirement for ever-faster diving times, meant that although the Gato-Balao-Tench classes all had an overall resemblance, no two boats looked exactly the same and, in fact, were likely to show distinct differences, especially in the form of the conning tower and the arrangement of periscope shears, aerials and antennas.

SUBMARINE STRENGTHS, 1939 AND 1945 COMPARED				
Country	1939	1945	War Build	War Losses
Germany	57	448*	1171	780
Great Britain	60	162	178	76
Italy	107	57	38	88
Japan	63	46	111	128
Russia	218	163	54	109
United States	99	274	227	52

*Includes 222 U-boats scuttled in May 1945, 156 surrendered, and others never deployed in action

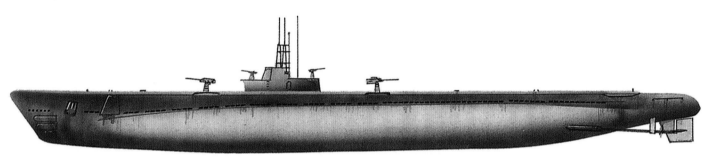

Specifications

Crew: 80

Powerplant: Twin screw diesel engines, electric motors

Max Speed: Surfaced: 20 knots; Submerged: 8.7 knots

Surface Range: 20,372km (11,000nm) at 10 knots

Displacement: Surfaced: 1854 tonnes (1825 tons); Submerged: 2458 tonnes (2420 tons)

Dimensions (length/beam/draught): 95m x 8.3m x 4.6m (311ft 9in x 27ft 3in x 15ft 3in)

Commissioned: December 1944

Armament: Ten 533mm (21in) torpedo tubes; one 127mm (5in) gun

▲ **USS Entemedor**

US Navy, Balao-class patrol submarine

Entemedor returned to base at Seattle on 22 September 1945, and served with the Pacific Fleet at Subic Bay in 1946-47. In reserve between 1948 and 1950, it was recommissioned in October 1950, joined the Atlantic Fleet, went through a GUPPY IIA refit in 1952, and did stints with the 6th Fleet in the Mediterranean up to 1962.

Specifications

Crew: 22

Powerplant: Four diesel engines; two electric motors

Max Speed: surfaced: 20.2 knots; Submerged: 8.7 knots

Surface Range: 20,372km (11,000nm) at 10 knots

Displacement: Surfaced: 1595 tonnes (1570 tons); Submerged: 2453 tonnes (2415 tons)

Dimensions (length/beam/draught): 95.2m x 8.31m x 4.65m (311ft 8in x 27ft 3in x 15ft 3in)

Commissioned: December 1944

Armament: One or two 127mm (5in) guns; 10 533mm (21in) torpedo tubes for 28 torpedoes

▲ **USS Pickerel**

US Navy, Tench-class patrol submarine, Pacific 1949

Pickerel was launched on 8 February 1944. In 1949, it deployed to Submarine Division 11 at Pearl Harbor, and thereafter remained in the Pacific. In 1962, it received a GUPPY III refit, then joined the 7th Fleet at Yokosuka, Japan. After Vietnam combat deployment on Yankee Station, it was transferred to Italy in 1972 as Primo Longobardo.

Chapter 4

The Cold War: 1946–89

Submarines had proved their worth so effectively
during the war years that it was beyond doubt they would
be key elements in future naval strategy. But there were
big challenges: how to arm them, how to extend undersea
cruising range and duration, and how to improve detection
and weapons-guidance systems. And not least, how to attack
and destroy a hostile and well-protected submarine.
Initially these challenges were met by seeking to develop
and improve on existing designs, but within 10 years this
gave way to a new approach, starting from first principles.
It became clear that application of new technologies,
from nuclear reactors to microchips, would expand the
role and power of the submarine in ways hardly
thought of in 1945.

◀ **USS _Dallas_**

USS _Dallas_ (SSN-700) was the first boat of the Los Angeles class to have the Mk 117 fire control system
installed. Commissioned in 1981, it is fitted to carry a Dry Deck Shelter, visible behind the sail.

A new era

Modernization is the key-word as submarine requirements are re-assessed in the light of the increasingly tense relationship between the Western powers and the Soviet bloc.

THE END OF THE WAR brought rationalization of the submarine fleets of the victorious Allied powers, with the older and more decrepit boats going for scrapping or target practice. Following their surrender in May and August 1945, all submarine design and construction in Germany and Japan came to a sudden end.

But these countries had been the most inventive and original wartime submarine builders, so surviving boats, and future plans, were closely scanned by the Allies. This was particularly true of the German boats, since the merits of the Type XXI and XXIII were already well known. The US, British and Soviet navies all possessed intact vessels of Type XXI and were startled to find just how much more advanced the German boats were.

These formed the basis of experiment and design in the later 1940s and into the 1950s. Attention focused particularly on three aspects: the snorkel, which enabled the submarine to stay underwater; the improvement of submarine speed; and their ability

to launch missiles against surface or land targets. A pattern was developed, of a smooth hull, uncluttered deck, no gun, streamlined fin or sail, and snorkel as a standard fitting.

The geopolitical background of the time was dominated by the hostile rivalry between the Soviet Union and the United States, each with its allies, forming the Warsaw Pact nations in the former case; and in the latter, the North Atlantic Treaty Organization (NATO), in 1949. The Soviet possession of nuclear technology and atomic weapons from 1949 raised the stakes enormously. A new arms race began, with the submarine an essential element. US production of a nuclear reactor compact enough to fit in a submarine's hull brought about the era of the 'true' submerged vessel that could travel underwater for weeks rather than days or hours. USS *Nautilus* and the hundreds of US and Soviet nuclear boats that followed, along with smaller British, French and, later, Chinese fleets revolutionized ideas about large-scale warfare. With such submarines,

▲ **HMS** *Explorer*

HMS *Explorer*, one of two experimental submarines, was nicknamed 'Exploder' as a consequence of her many accidents.

▲ **USS** *Philadelphia*
Launched in 1974, the USS *Philadelphia* was a Los Angeles-class nuclear attack submarine. It was decommissioned in 2010.

armed with long-range nuclear missiles, came the concept of the 'deterrent'. Any first strike against a superpower would be answered by a retaliatory strike from submarines at unknown locations. Mutual devastation was assured.

Missile Platforms

From the 1950s, the development of the submarine was linked to that of rocket-type weapons that could be fired from under the surface. As the missiles became larger and heavier, so the boats had to be more capacious in order to maximize their firepower. This led to some strange-looking designs until massive submarines, which could hold vertically mounted intercontinental ballistic missiles (ICBMs) within the hull, were built. The difficulties and hazards of launching a jet-propelled missile from a submarine included the problems of powering the actual launch, of maintaining stability, and of guiding the missile towards a target. From the early firings of Loon rockets, derived from the German V-1 and launched from a deck-mounted rack on US test-vessels, remarkable progress was made. The United States pressed on with solid-fuel rocket engines, while the Soviets for a long time continued with liquid-fuel missiles.

Nuclear submarines required advanced technology, under strict (if sometimes broken) secrecy. Most navies continued to employ, and to improve, submarines with diesel-electric drive. These were smaller, far less expensive, and fitted a well-tried range of tactical roles and missions. Only the US Navy gave up on developing new conventional designs, though it continued to use existing classes through most of the Cold War period.

On several occasions the Cold War threatened to become a 'hot' one. The Korean War in 1951 led to the rapid recommissioning of many US submarines from reserve, though they played little part in the land-based conflict. Four British submarines were part of the Suez invasion force in 1956. Both sides deployed submarines in the Cuban Missile Crisis of October 1962.

War between India and Pakistan in 1971 included the first submarine battles since 1945. British and Argentinian submarines were in action in the Falklands/Malvinas War in 1982. But by the 1980s, the long stalemate was beginning to end. The Strategic Arms Limitation (SALT I) agreement reduced the number of land-based missiles but had little effect on submarine numbers.

America and the Soviet Union
1946–54

The US and Soviet navies push ahead with new submarine types and modifications, mostly taken from German designs.

IN THE SOVIET UNION, Project 613 was put in hand from 1946, for a new class of submarine, later codenamed 'Whiskey' by NATO, a further improved version of the Type XXI. Originally designated as coastal patrol submarines, they were in fact fully sea-going boats. At least 215 were built between 1951 and 1958, in five configurations. The peak years of construction were 1953–56. *Whiskey I* had twin 25mm (0.98in) guns mounted in the sail. *Whiskey II* had two additional 57mm (2.2in) guns. *Whiskey III* had no guns. *Whiskey IV* had the 25mm guns restored and was also fitted with a snorkel. *Whiskey V* had the guns removed and a streamlined sail fitted, and most of the class were modified to this design.

Whiskey class submarines were supplied to Albania (4), Bulgaria (2), China (5), Egypt (7), Indonesia (14), North Korea (4) and Poland (4). In addition, China constructed 21 from Soviet-supplied parts, as Type 03. The class had a long life and 45 were still on the active list with the Soviet Navy in 1982. With the possible exception of some North Korean boats, all Whiskeys are now decommissioned.

Project 615, initiated in the late 1940s, was intended to provide the Soviet fleet with a coastal attack submarine of the most up-to-date type. Before the war, the Soviets had already been working on a closed-cycle engine that did not require to draw air from above the surface, and the experimental craft M-401 had been launched in 1941 and tested in the secluded waters of the Caspian Sea. Liquid oxygen mixed with purified exhaust gases powered the underwater motor.

Although streamlined, the class, codenamed Quebec by NATO, carried a twin 45mm (1.8in) AA gun in its earlier versions, faired into the forward end of the tower. The Quebecs remained an under-armed type, with no spare torpedo capacity for the four bow-mounted tubes. Thirty were built between 1952 and 1957, out of an original 100 planned. At this time they were the only submarines in the world using air-independent propulsion. Although some notable performances were achieved, the fuel caused frequent problems because of its tendency to catch fire. Two boats were lost. The Soviet Navy's development of nuclear submarines overtook the Quebecs, although they were modernized in the later 1950s under Project M615. By the time the last was retired, in the 1970s, the AIP motor had been replaced by a conventional

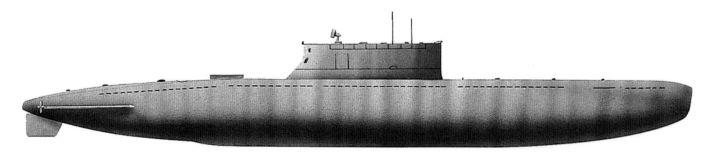

▲ **Whiskey class**

Soviet Navy patrol/missile submarine

Prefabrication and welded assembly were used to speed up production of the large numbers in this class. Between 1956 and 1963, 13 were converted to carry the Soviet Union's first guided missiles. Others were used as radar pickets and in intelligence-gathering missions.

Specifications

Crew: 50	Dimensions (length/beam/draught): 76 x 6.5 x
Powerplant: Twin shaft; diesel-electric	5m (294.3 x 21.3 x 16ft)
Max Speed: (33.3/26km/hr (18/14kt) surf/sub	Commissioned: 1949 (1st unit)
Surface Range: 15,890km (8580nm)	Armament: Four 533mm (21in) and two 406mm
Displacement: 1066/1,371t (1050/1350 tons)	(16in) torpedo tubes
surf/sub	

electric one. One of the Project 615 boats was used for research on developing an anechoic coating, with results that were to be applied to most Soviet combat submarines.

United States

USS *Cusk* (Balao class) and USS *Carbonero* (Gato class) were adapted in 1946–47 to fire air-breathing 'Loon' missiles, derived from the German V-1 pulse-jet rocket. A single missile was held in a tank-like hangar and fired from a rack mounted on the afterdeck. Both boats remained in service as guided-missile testing vehicles.

Parallel to the early missile operations, Project Guppy (Greater Underwater Propulsion Programme) was set up to enhance the capacities of the existing fleet. From June 1946, the programme passed through seven phases until 1963. It began with the intensive examination and testing of two Type XXI U-boats, U-2513 and U-3008, but further refinements and improvements were soon being added. USS *Odax* and *Pomodon*, Tench-class boats commissioned in 1945, were adapted in 1947. The deck guns were taken off, the bridge and shears structure adapted to reduce drag, capstans and deck cleats were made retractable, and the bow was redesigned from the sharp 'fleet bow' to a rounded 'Guppy bow'. Battery power was greatly increased and the boats were fitted with new sonar and radar equipment. The Guppy 1A programme was

THE LEGACY OF TYPE XX1	
Country	Derivative
France	E 48; Aréthuse
Great Britain	Explorer; Porpoise
Russia	Zulu; Whiskey; Romeo
United States	Guppy programme; Tench class

somewhat less comprehensive, fitted to nine Balao and one Tench boat in 1951. Guppy II included reconstruction of the sail to carry the array of masts required for snorkel induction, snorkel exhaust, periscopes and communication. A submarine sail might now support 12 or 13 separate antennas for range- and direction-finding, communications at different frequencies, and radar for both surface and air search. Guppy IIA also installed a new sail and a Guppy bow, as well as new motors. The 'Fleet Snorkel' conversion was a partial-Guppy, providing only snorkel equipment and an ESM mast. The pointed fleet bow was retained and the engines were not modernized, though the auxiliary motor was replaced by air-conditioning equipment. With the Guppy project, the conning tower ceased to hold a control station and came to be known as the sail (United States) or fin (Great Britain).

As a consequence of the development of rockets and with the increasing threat of the long-range bomber, radar detection was given a high priority

▲ Quebec class

Soviet Navy coastal submarine, Black Sea

This was the only AIP-engined submarine to be in series production before the 1990s, but technical problems limited its usefulness. It had two main diesel engines plus the closed cycle engine and an electric 'creep motor'. Theoretically capable of remaining 14 days submerged, they suffered numerous accidents and the design was abandoned after 1957.

Specifications

Crew: 30

Powerplant: Three shafts; two diesel engines; one 900hp (670kW) AIP diesel; creep motor

Max. speeds: 33/30km/hr (18/16kt) surf/sub

Surface Range: 5090km (2750nm) at 9kt

Displacement: 460.4/548.6t (460/540 tons)

Dimensions (length/beam/draught): 56 x 5.1 x 3.8m (183.75 x 16.4 x 12.5ft)

Commissioned: 1952

Armament: Four 533mm (21in) torpedo tubes; eight torpedoes

and a group of Gato, Balao and Tench class boats were fitted as 'radar-picket' boats in the Migraine Programme, which went through three phases between 1946 and 1952.

The Korean War

USS *Pickerel*, Tench class, was launched in December 1944 but not commissioned until 1949, benefitting from the Guppy II programme developments, including a snorkel and batteries with a total of 504 cells. *Pickerel* was then deployed in the Korean War zone, but submarines played relatively little part in the conflict. No US boat fired a a shot, but they were intensively used for reconnaissance and surveillance,

occasionally catching sight of Soviet submarines engaged in similar activities. *Pickerel* would be further modernized in 1962 under the Guppy III programme; and, during the Vietnam War in the later 1960s, it provided support for the carrier group based on 'Yankee Station' in the Gulf of Tonkin. On 18 August 1972, *Pickerel* was transferred to the Italian Navy, where it served as *Primo Longobardo* until 1980.

The first post-war design was closely related to the Guppy programme. USS *Tang* and its five sisters, commissioned between 1951 and 1952, were intended as fast attack boats, following on from the Tench class. Submerged speed was 18.3 knots compared to

▲ USS Volador

US Navy, Tench-class attack submarine, SS-490, Pacific 1949–70

Commissioned on 1 October 1948, *Volador* was with the Pacific Fleet until 1970, on reconnaissance patrols in the Korean War and earning three campaign stars in the Vietnam War. Note the three housings for PUFFS (BQG-4) passive underwater fire-control feasibility study. In 1980, it was transferred to Italy as *Gianfranco Gazzana Priaroggia*.

Specifications

Crew: 81	surf/sub
Powerplant: Twin shaft; four diesel engines; two electric motors	Dimensions (length/beam/draught): 95.2 x 8.32 x 4.65m (311.75 x 27.25 x 15.25ft)
Max Speed: 37.4/53km/hr (20.2/8.7kt) surf/sub	Commissioned: 1 October 1948
Surface Range: 20,372km (11,000nm) at 10kt	Armament: 28 x 533mm (21in) torpedoes; 10 tubes
Displacement: 1595/2,453t (1570/2415 tons)	

Specifications

Crew: 83	Displacement: 1585/2296t (1560/2260 tons) surf/sub
Powerplant: Twin shaft; diesel-electric	Dimensions (length/beam/draught): 82 x 8.3 x 5.2m (269.2 x 27.2 x 17ft)
Max. speeds: 28.7/34km/hr (15.5/18.3kt) surf/sub	Commissioned: 25 October 1951
Surface Range:18,530km (10,000nm) at 10kt	Armament: Eight 533mm (21in) torpedo tubes

▲ USS Tang

US Navy, patrol submarine, SS-306

The design was intended to keep the hull length as short as possible and to be adaptable to a future closed-cycle power plant. When *Tang* was transferred to Turkey in 1980, successive modifications meant the boat was 609.6 tonnes (600 tons) heavier and 22ft (6.5m) longer than on its launch in 1951.

15.5 knots on the surface. The six forward torpedo tubes were the prime armament, with the two aft tubes intended for ASW countermeasures weapons. The original four General Motors 'pancake' engines, with radial cylinders arranged round a vertical crankshaft, were not successful and were replaced in 1956 by three conventional Fairbanks-Morse 10-cylinder opposed-piston diesels. The Tang class carried 26 torpedoes. Diving capacity was 213m (700ft).

USS *Tang* was retired in 1980 as the oldest diesel-electric submarine in the US Navy and the last to serve in the Atlantic Fleet, to which it was transferred in 1978 after long service in the Pacific. Even then it still had more than 20 years of active life ahead, being transferred to the Turkish Navy as *Pirireis* and serving until 2004.

Operational requirements stiffened as the Cold War intensified. On the Atlantic side, boats patrolled the GIUK Gap, the area between Greenland, Iceland and the British Isles through which Soviet ships had to pass to reach the open Atlantic; also the exits from the Baltic and Black Seas, and from the Mediterranean. Despite the investment in the Guppy programme and the Tang class, and the undoubted improvements they brought, certain US Navy officers felt that a more radical approach was needed, starting from a blank sheet and using every device of modern design and technology to produce a true underwater warship. This resulted in the one-off experimental

THE GUPPY PROGRAMME			
Phase	Year	No. of boats	Note
1	1946–47	2	
II	1947–51	24	
IA	1951	10	
Fleet Snorkel		28	
IIA	1952–54	17	
IB	1953–55	4	Allied Navy boats
III	1959–63	9	

boat *Albacore*, built at the naval yard at Kittery, Maine, and commissioned on 5 December 1953. Ostensibly designed as a 'target boat' for hunter-killer practice, it immediately became clear that *Albacore* was virtually uncatchable. With a submerged speed of 33 knots and an unprecedented ability for steep dives and tight turns, it outperformed any existing submarine.

Aircraft technology was freely drawn on for control systems. Built as a testbed, *Albacore* went through a succession of modifications and conversions through the 1960s. These included sound-proofing contra-rotating propellers on the shaft, dive brakes, a redesigned bow and new battery systems, as well as underwater drag-chutes (not a success). The US Navy and its allies learned a great deal from *Albacore*, and vindication of the project came in 1956 when the combination of teardrop hull and nuclear propulsion

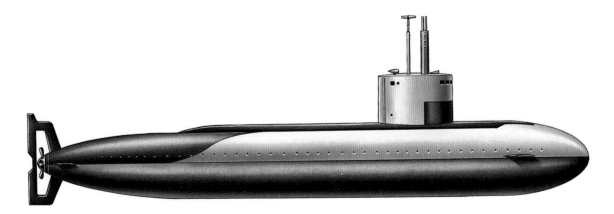

Specifications

Crew: 52–60

Powerplant: Single shaft; two diesel engines; one electric motor,

Max Speed: 46.3/61km/hr (25/33kt) surf/sub

Surface Range: Not released

Displacement: 1524/1880t (1500/1850 tons) surf/sub

Dimensions (length/beam/draught): 62.2 x 8.4 x 5.6m (204 x 27.6 x 15.6ft)

Commissioned: 5 December 1953

Armament: nil

▲ **USS Albacore**

US Navy, test submarine, 1953

After many experiments and wind-tunnel tests, the teardrop hull had an intriguing resemblance to some of the earliest submarines. The pressure hull was constructed from new HY-80 high-yield steel. The single screw was originally incorporated with the rudder and stern planes, but in 1955–56 was relocated behind them.

US POST-WAR DIESEL-ELECTRIC SUBMARINES				
Class	Type	Number	Year	Note
Barracuda	ASW	3	1944–51	Retired in 1950s
Tang	Attack	6	1949–52	Retired by 1975
Albacore	Experimental	1	1953	Retired 1972
Grayback	SSG	2	1954–58	Withdrawn as SSG 1964
Barbel	Attack	3	1956–59	Retired by 1990

was established with USS *Skipjack*, and has remained the basis of submarine design since. *Albacore* was decommissioned in 1972 and stricken in 1980; it remains as a memorial boat in Portsmouth, New Hampshire.

USS *Mackerel*, with sister boat *Marlin*, were the smallest American submarines to be built since the 'C' class of 1909, intended as training craft for personnel who would then transfer to the fleet boats. Originally nameless, known as T-1 and T-2, they were commissioned in 1953 and named in 1956. *Marlin* was assigned to the submarine base at Key West, Florida (SubRon 12) from January 1954 and served as a training boat and target ship. Both were decommissioned on 31 January 1973. *Marlin* is preserved far from the sea at Omaha, Bebraska.

Converging Lines of Development

In the early 1950s, the US Navy was following two lines of submarine development that would ultimately converge. One was typified by the design and building of USS *Albacore*, where a traditional form of propulsion was used with a revolutionary hull and controls. The other kept to the long-established torpedo-boat hull-form, but with a wholly new and equally revolutionary form of power plant: the nuclear reactor. Once the construction of the compact reactor became technically feasible, its application to submarines was only a matter of time, although it did not seem like that to the pioneers who had to persuade the naval supremos and the US Congress. In July 1951, the Congress authorized construction of a

▲ **USS *Skate***

USS *Skate* (SSN-578), commissioned in December 1957, was the first submarine to surface at the North Pole and first to cross the Atlantic Ocean without surfacing.

nuclear-powered submarine, the keel was laid at the Electric Boat yard in Groton Connecticut on 14 June 1952, it was launched as *Nautilus* on 21 January 1954, and commissioned on 30 September of that year. Apart from its nuclear drive, *Nautilus* was modelled on the Tang class. The naval reactors programme had been running since 1948, and by March 1953 a viable compact reactor had been constructed. The S2W naval reactor, a pressurized water reactor, was built by the Westinghouse Corporation. On 17 January 1955, *Nautilus* went to sea for the first time and in the next two years

covered distances unthinkable for a conventional submarine. On 3 August 1958, it became the first vessel to pass beneath the North Pole, using an inertial navigation system developed by North American Aviation. *Nautilus* served with US naval units in the Atlantic and Mediterranean. In 1960, it was assigned to the Sixth Fleet. By the mid-1960s, a range of more advanced nuclear submarines was in operation and *Nautilus* spent its final active years as a training boat. It was decommissioned on 3 March 1980, by which time it had travelled over half a million nautical miles.

Specifications

Crew: 18

Powerplant: Single shaft; diesel-electric

Max Speed: 14.8/17.6km/hr (8/9.5kt) surf/sub

Surface Range: 3706km (2000nm) at 8kt

Displacement: 308/353t (303/347 tons) surf/sub

Dimensions (length/beam/draught): 40 x 4.1 x 3.7m (131.2 x 13.5 x 12.2in)

Commissioned: 20 November 1953

Armament: One 533mm (21in) torpedo tube

▲ USS Marlin

US Navy, coastal submarine, SS-205

In 1966–67, *Mackerel* was adapted to test deep-sea rescue equipment, including keel-mounted wheels for moving on the ocean floor, thrusters, TV cameras and extensible arms, all of which were eventually used on the deep submergence vehicle NR-1. *Marlin* had a more conventional career participating in ASW training and exercises.

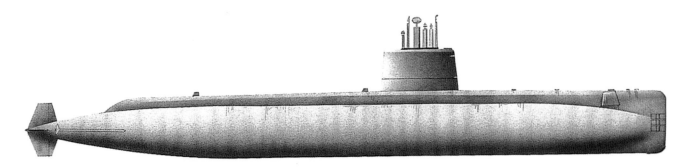

Specifications

Crew: 105

Powerplant: Twin shaft; one S2W pwr; turbines

Max Speed: 37/42.6km/hr (20/23kt) surf/sub

Surface Range: Unlimited

Displacement: 3589.7/4,167.8t (3533/ 4102 tons) surf/sub

Dimensions: 97 x 8.4 x 6.6m (323.55 x 27.8 x 21.75ft)

Commissioned: 30 September 1954

Armament: Six 533mm (21in) torpedo tubes

▲ USS Nautilus

US Navy, nuclear submarine, SSN-571, 1954

An extraordinary range of *technical* challenges were solved between 1951 and 1954 to make the US nuclear submarine a safe and effective vessel. Unlike any previous submarine, *Nautilus* had only one engine, and the absence of fuel tanks, batteries and double motors meant a welcome increase of crew space.

New roles for submarines
1955–64

For most navies, nuclear power was not an option. But all took an interest in the new capacity of submarines to fire tactical missiles.

APART FROM TWO BRITISH BOATS acquired in the immediate post-war period, China's first submarine classes originated in the Soviet Union. In 1956, China began construction of 21 boats identical to the Whiskey class. The Soviet Union then developed an advance on the Whiskey classes, Project 633, a diesel-electric attack boat given the name *Romeo* by NATO.

China

After 20 Soviet boats had been built, the designs were passed to China, under the Friendship and Mutual Assistance Treaty, and production began in 1962 at the Jiangnan yard in Shanghai. In China it was known as Type 033 and the first was launched in December 1965. Between 1962 and 1984 a total of 84 were built for the People's Liberation Army Navy, plus others for other countries. Over that period the Chinese made a range of modifications to the design. From the start, the Type 033 had eight torpedo tubes compared to the *Romeo*'s six. It could also carry 28 mines as an alternative to its 14 533mm (21in) torpedoes. A slightly greater displacement made it roomier and increased fuel capacity gave it

a range of almost double the original Romeos. Now obsolete, the Romeos survive perhaps only in the North Korean fleet, though other navies may have mothballed versions.

China went on to develop its Type 035 (Ming class) submarine from the Type 033. Of similar hull dimensions, it is a more advanced boat in all respects. Twenty were built from the early 1970s. The final six, commissioned between 1996 and 2001, were intended as a stopgap because of delays with the new generation Type 039, and are classed Type 035B. With an improved fire control system, and damping tiles to reduce noise, they carry 18 Yu-4 (SAET-60) passive homing surface-target torpedoes, capable of travelling 15km (9.3 miles) at 40 knots.

France

Requin was one of six boats of the Narval class completed between 1957 and 1960, intended as long-range patrol/attack submarines. They stand in line from the German Type XXI but were a more advanced design in many respects. The snorkel system was entirely new, and increased electrical power gave them a submerged range of 740km

▲ **Romeo class**

Soviet/Chinese patrol-attack submarine

Type 033 boats were built for Algeria, Bulgaria, Egypt and Syria. In addition, 22 were built in North Korea. They also provided the basis of the Chinese-designed Type 035 Ming class, of which 21 were built from 1971, most of them in the 1990s.

Specifications

Crew: 60

Powerplant: Twin shaft; diesel-electric

Max Speed: 29.6/24 km/hr (16/13kt) surf/sub

Surface Range: 29,632km (16,000nm) at 10kt

Displacement: 1351/1727t (1330/1700 tons) surf/sub

Dimensions (length/beam/draught): 77 x 6.7 x 4.9m (252.65 x 22 x 16.1ft)

Commissioned: 1958 (Russia), 1962 (China); first units

Armament: Eight 533mm (21in) torpedo tubes

(400 nautical miles) compared to the Type XXIs' 537km (290 nautical miles). They could operate at a depth of 400m (1300ft) and were significantly quieter. The least satisfactory aspect was the Schneider 2-stroke diesels, which were replaced in 1966–70 by diesel-electric motors based on the SEMT-Pielstick 12PA4-185 type. Major refits at the same time resulted in the removal of the two stern tubes, and the fitting of a new fin based on the Daphné class, as well as updating of sensory equipment. Later, *Requin* and *Dauphin* were used as testbeds for sonar and other electronic equipment to be installed on the nuclear-powered Triomphant class. *Requin,* the French Navy's last conventionally powered submarine, was finally disposed of as a target in 1992.

The India–Pakistan War

In 1958–60, France built four small boats of the Aréthuse class, modelled on the German Type XXIII, for use as hunter-killer boats in the Mediterranean. They were followed by a larger boat, the Daphné class of patrol/attack submarines, 11-strong, all completed between 1961 and 1970. Two were lost, in 1968 and 1970, the blame being attached to faults in the snorkel design.

Numerous boats of this type were sold to other countries. The Portuguese Navy acquired four in 1967–69 (one sold on to Pakistan in 1975), the South African Navy got three in 1970–71, and the Spanish got four in 1973–75. The best known are perhaps the trio sold to Pakistan in 1970, particularly PNS *Hangor*, which torpedoed the Indian ASW

▲ Daphné

French Navy, attack submarine, also Pakistan Navy, 1971

The four stern torpedo tubes were externally mounted and not reloadable while submerged. Based first at Lorient, then Toulon from 1972, *Daphné* underwent a major refit in 1967–68 and was last used in 1989 to test the new French Murène torpedo. It was sunk as a missile target in November 1994.

Specifications

Crew: 45	Displacement: 884/1062t (870/1045 tons) surf/sub
Powerplant: Two diesel engines: two electric motors	Dimensions: 58 x 7 x 4.6m (189.77 x 22.45 x 15ft)
Max Speed: 25/29.6km/hr (13.5/16kt) surf/sub	Commissioned: 20 Jun 1959
Surface Range: 8334km (400nm) at 5kt	Armament: 12 552mm (21.7in) torpedo tubes

▲ Requin

French Navy, Narval-class patrol submarine

The Narval class owes its origin to U-2518, renamed *Roland Morillot*. They were built in seven 10m (33ft) sections that were then welded together, the first French construction of this kind. After the 1966–70 refits, they joined the 2nd squadron at Lorient.

Specifications

Crew: 63	
Powerplant: Twin shaft; diesel-electric	Dimensions (length/beam/draught): 78.4 x 7.8 x 5.2m (257 x 26 x 17ft)
Max Speed: 29.6/33.3 km/hr (16/18kt) surf/sub	Commissioned: 3 December 1955
Surface Range: 27,795km (15,000nm) at 8kt	Armament: Eight 550mm (21.7in) torpedo tubes
Displacement:1661/1941t (1635/1910 tons) surf/sub	

FRENCH POST-WAR SUBMARINES (DIESEL-ELECTRIC)				
Class	Type	Number	Year	Note
Aurore	Patrol	5	1949–54	Pre-war class; modernized
E 48		2	1948	Experimental
Narval	Patrol	6	1957–86	
Aréthuse	Attack	4	1958–81	
Daphné	Attack	11	1964–70	Also for Pakistan (4), Portugal (4), South Africa (3), Spain (4)
Agosta	Attack	4	1977–2001	4 for Spain, 3 for Pakistan
Scorpène	Multi-role		2005	French/Spanish, then French only

frigate *Khukri* during the brief India–Pakistan war in November to December 1971.

This was the first submarine 'kill' since World War II. The engagement happened off India's west coast on 9 December 1971, when *Khukri* and a sister frigate *Kirpan* were sent to intercept *Hangor*. *Kirpan* was fired at, but the torpedo missed. *Khukri*, coming to attack, was struck and rapidly sank. Evading depth charges from *Kirpan* (and damaging its stern with a torpedo), *Hangor* eventually returned to base despite intense efforts by Indian air and surface craft to destroy it.

On 4 December, *Hangor*'s sister boat *Ghazi* had sunk in the Bay of Bengal, perhaps from an explosion of one of its own mines. *Hangor* was withdrawn in 2006 and is now a museum boat. France struck its remaining Daphné-class boats in the 1990s.

Great Britain

In the 1950s, it was assumed that the Royal Navy would continue to play a worldwide role, extending to Far Eastern waters. Two almost identical long-range patrol/attack submarines, the Porpoise and Oberon classes, were introduced in 1959. Endurance was built in, with glass-reinforced plastic used in construction of the casing. Their quietness compared to contemporary US and Soviet boats made them very useful in clandestine operations, when it might be necessary to lurk very close to a potentially hostile coastline or harbour in order to gather intelligence or to land special forces. Payload for the forward tubes was 20 Tigerfish torpedoes, the stern tubes were pre-loaded for anti-submarine defence. Electronics, sonar and radar were upgraded during the class's 30-year-plus career.

▲ **HMS Oberon**

Royal Navy, O-class patrol submarine

Thirteen of the class were commissioned into the Royal Navy. The prime difference to the Porpoise boats was better internal soundproofing and hulls constructed of high-strength QT28 steel, increasing diving capacity to 340m (1115ft). Two Admiralty V16 diesels of 3680hp (2744kW) powered two 3000hp (2237kW) electric motors.

Specifications

Crew: 69

Powerplant: Twin shaft; two diesel-electric motors

Max Speed: 22.2/31.5 km/hr (12/17.5kt) surf/sub

Surface Range: 11,118km (6000nm) at 10kt

Displacement: 2,063/2,449t (2,030/2,410 tons) surf/sub

Dimensions (length/beam/draught): 90 x 8.1 x 5.5m (295.25 x 26.5 x 18ft)

Commissioned: 18 July 1959

Armament: Eight 533mm (21in) torpedo tubes

Six Oberons were built for the Royal Australian Navy. These used American Mark 48 torpedoes, and the radar and sonar systems were Sperry Micropuffs passive ranging sonar and Krupp CSU3-41 attack sonar. Their stern tubes were sealed off and in the 1980s they were fitted with subsonic Harpoon missiles and designated as SSGs. Three were also built for Canada, three for Brazil and two for Chile. The Oberons were generally regarded as a very effective submarine. In effect, they were the last diesel-electric class to be in regular use by the Royal Navy.

Britain had experimented with hydrogen-peroxide drive, but by 1956 it was evident that any first-class naval power needed to have nuclear submarines on a par with those being built by the United States and the Soviets. HMS *Dreadnought* was the first, launched on 21 October 1960 and powered by a US S5W pressurized water reactor, designed for the US Skipjack class (the aft machinery area was known as 'the American sector'). The hull design also resembled *Skipjack*'s, though navigational and combat systems were largely based on British technology. Commissioned on 17 April 1963, *Dreadnought* was

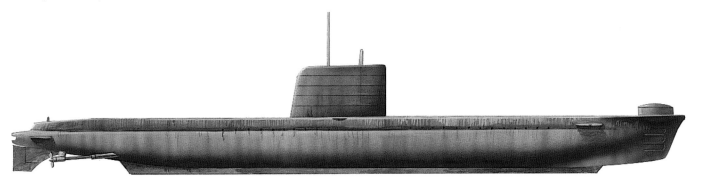

Specifications

Crew: 71	Displacement: 2062/2444t (2030/2405 tons) surf/sub
Powerplant: Twin shaft; two diesel-electric motors	Dimensions (length/beam/draught): 73.5 x 8.1 x 5.5m (241 x 26.5 x 18ft)
Max Speed: 22.2/31.5 km/hr (12/17kt) surf/sub	Commissioned: 22 September 1959
Surface Range: 16,677km (9000nm) at 10kt	Armament: Eight 533mm (21in) torpedo tubes

▲ HMS Walrus

Royal Navy, Porpoise-class patrol submarine

Eight of this class were built. The 'Snort' air-breathing system, shared with the Oberons, was a robust but efficient one intended to operate in rough sea conditions. Diving depth was 300m (984ft). Air and surface radar warning systems operated from periscope depth. All were decommissioned by 1988.

Specifications

Crew: 88	Displacement: 3556/4064t (3500/4000 tons) surf/sub
Powerplant: Single shaft; S5W pwr; steam turbines	Dimensions (length/beam/draught): 81 x 9.8 x 8m (265.75 x 32.25 x 26.25ft)
Max Speed: 37/55.5km/hr (20/30kt) surf/sub	Commissioned: 17 April 1963
Surface Range: Unlimited	Armament: Six 533mm (21in) torpedo tubes

▲ HMS Dreadnought

Royal Navy, nuclear patrol submarine (SSN)

To obtain a new US reactor design was a considerable achievement for the British, though future Royal Navy nuclear boats would have British reactors. A major refit and refuelling was carried out in 1970. *Dreadnought* surfaced at the North Pole on 3/4 March 1971.

BRITISH POST-WAR SUBMARINES (DIESEL-ELECTRIC)				
Class	Type	Number	Year	Note
Explorer	Test boat	2	1958	Experimental, HTP motor
Stickleback	Midget	4	1954–55	Improved XE-class
Porpoise	Patrol	8	1956–59	
Oberon	Multi-role	13	1960–67	14 built for export
Upholder	Patrol	4	199–93	Transferred to Canada 1998

DUTCH POST-WAR SUBMARINES				
Class	Type	Number	Year	Note
Dolfijn	Patrol	2	1954–60	Decommissioned
Zwaardvis	Patrol	2	1966–72	Decommissioned by 1995
Walrus	Patrol	4	1985–94	Conversion and refitting programme from 2013

inevitably used as a training and testing boat, though it was a fully effective SSN (fast attack), whose high underwater speed of 30 knots made it suitable for use as an escort to fast carrier groups. In 1980 it was withdrawn following damage to the machinery, which was not considered repairable, and the hulk remains at Rosyth naval dockyard. *Dreadnought,* built rapidly with US help, remained a one-off. Next to come was HMS *Valiant,* commissioned 18 July 1966, one of two hunter-killer boats (*Warspite* being the other, commissioned April 1967). Though based in many ways on *Dreadnought,* apart from being somewhat larger, there were two major differences: the pressurized-

water reactor was built by Rolls-Royce, and the two steam turbines by English Electric, and a 'rafting' system was used to install the machinery so that it did not bear directly on the hull, with a great improvement in quiet running. Rafting later became a common feature of nuclear submarines.

In Cold War operations, the two Valiant class served primarily in ASW roles, shadowing Soviet SSBNs (ballistic missile submarines) or task force groups and patrolling the lanes through which Soviet submarines passed into the open Atlantic. *Warspite* was decommissioned in 1991 and *Valiant* in 1994, because of cracks in the primary-to-secondary cooling system.

Specifications

Crew: 116

Powerplant: Single shaft; one pwr; steam turbines

Max Speed: 37/53.7km/hr (20/29kt) surf/sub

Surface Range: Unlimited

Displacement: 4470/4979t (4400/4900 tons)

Dimensions (length/beam/draught): 86.9 x 10.1 x 8.2m (285 x 33.25 x 27ft)

Commissioned: 18 July 1966

Armament: Six 533mm (21in) torpedo tubes

▲ **HMS Valiant**

Royal Navy, SSN, South Atlantic 1982

Unlike *Dreadnought,* *Valiant* had a Paxman diesel-electric auxiliary drive for silent running. In 1967, it made a 28-day submerged transit from Singapore to Britain, of 19,312km (12,000 miles). It spent 101 days patrolling the Argentinian coast in 1982, on surveillance and air-warning reconnaissance duty. Refits were undertaken in 1970, 1977 and 1989.

Netherlands

On 16 December 1960, *Dolfijn* was commissioned into the Royal Dutch Navy, after six years construction. The four boats of this ocean-going patrol-attack class were the first home-built submarines for the Dutch Navy since World War II. The design was a unique one incorporating three separate pressure hulls in a triangular arrangement, inside an external casing. The crew inhabited the top one; the other two contained the engines, batteries and storage space. The arrangement, complex and expensive to build, allowed a maximum diving depth of 300m (984ft), unusual for the late 1950s. The boats were commissioned between 1960 and 1966, the second pair having been held back while the possibility of nuclear propulsion was considered, and rejected.

Another unusual feature was an even division of the eight torpedo tubes between bow and stern. Minelaying via the tubes was also possible. *Dolfijn* was broken up in 1985; the others in the class survived into the 1990s, with *Zeehond* being used as a demonstrator for AIP propulsion by the RBM shipyard in Rotterdam between 1990 and 1994.

The Soviet Union

Project 641 was intended to provide a more up-to-date patrol/attack boat than the Whiskey class and the subsequent 1952 Zulu class, both World War II derivatives, and the resultant design, noted as Foxtrot by NATO, fulfilled the objective. The first of the class was laid down in 1957 and commissioned in

1958: construction continued until 1983. In all, 58 were built for the Soviet Navy, and a further 20 or so for other countries. The Foxtrots were powered by three Kolomna diesel engines and three electric motors, driving three propeller shafts. These made the boats relatively noisy, and their submerged speed of 15 knots did not allow for rapid chasing or shadowing. Nevertheless, the Foxtrot class played an important role in the Soviet Navy for more than 20 years, as a submarine that could be deployed almost anywhere. That included the North and West Atlantic Oceans.

The Cuban Missile Crisis

Foxtrot submarines were involved in the tense encounters that took place during the Cuban missile crisis of 16–28 October 1962. Four of the class were deployed to Cuban waters on 1 October. Although they did not have combat orders, all (unknown to the United States) were carrying a torpedo with a nuclear warhead. A Zulu-class boat, B-75, armed with two nuclear warheads, was also in the Atlantic under instruction to protect Soviet shipping between the Soviet Union and Cuba. Aware of the presence of Soviet submarines in the North Atlantic, the Pentagon ordered US Navy units on 23 October to track them and 'induce' them to surface and identify themselves. This involved the use of small-size practice depth charges.

Three Foxtrots, B-36, B-59, and B-130, were forced to the surface either by depth-charges or

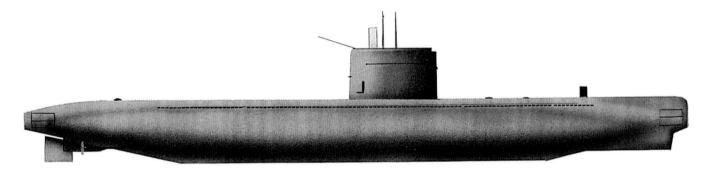

Specifications

Crew: 64	Displacement: 1518/1855t (1494/1826 tons)
Powerplant: Twin shaft; two diesel engines;	surf/sub
two electric motors	Dimensions (length/beam/draught): 80 x 8 x
Max Speed: 26.8/31.5km/hr (14.5/17kt) surf/sub	4.8m (260.8 x 25.75 x 15.75ft)
Surface Range: Details not available	Commissioned: 16 December 1960
	Armament: Eight 533mm (21in) torpedo tubes

▲ **Dolfijn**

Netherlands Navy, patrol submarine

The triple-hull formation was not continued by the Dutch Navy in future submarine classes, due to the later use of higher-grade steel and the improvement of welding techniques, which gave monohulled boats equivalent performance at less cost.

FOXTROT CLASS

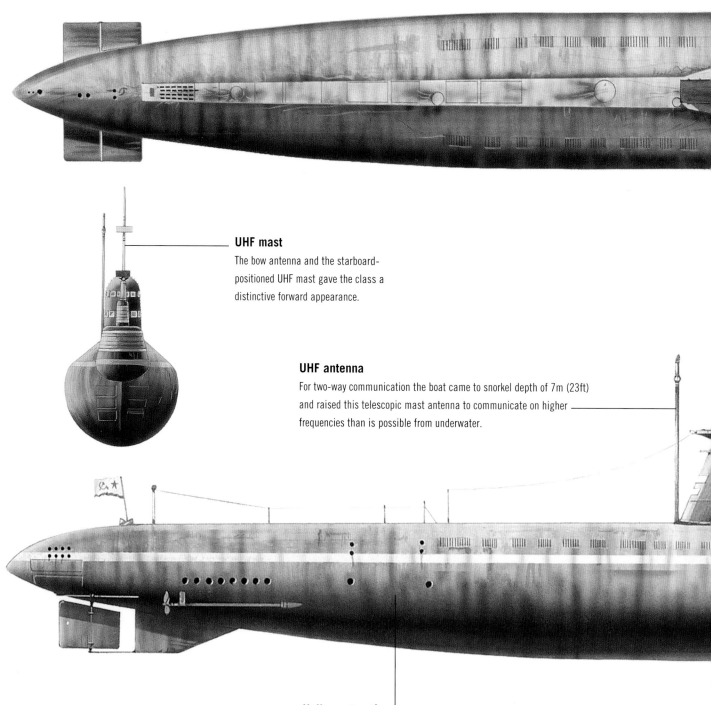

UHF mast
The bow antenna and the starboard-
positioned UHF mast gave the class a
distinctive forward appearance.

UHF antenna
For two-way communication the boat came to snorkel depth of 7m (23ft)
and raised this telescopic mast antenna to communicate on higher
frequencies than is possible from underwater.

Hull construction
The outer hull was formed from 9.5mm (0.37in) steel. The pressure
hull was formed from 22.2mm (0.87in) AK-25 high tensile steel with
a yield strength of 590MPa (5501 tons/sq ft).

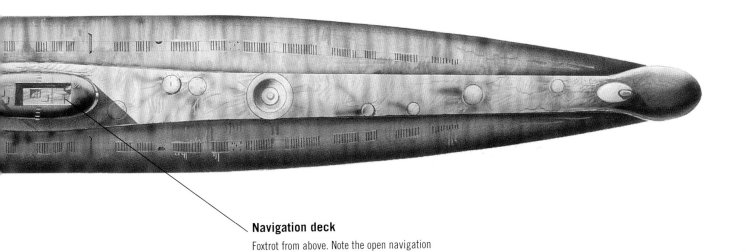

Navigation deck
Foxtrot from above. Note the open navigation
deck on top of the sail.

Bridge structure
Introduced on the Foxtrots, this construction was typical of later
Russian classes. Snorkel intake and exhaust were located at the rear.
Additional sonar arrays were incorporated in the sides of the sail.

Passive sonar
Feniks passive search/
attack sonar.

Antenna
Underwater telephone antenna
MG-18 and passive sonar antenna.

Torpedos
There was no spare torpedo storage for the 406mm (16in) aft
tubes and the four torpedoes had to be replaced in dock or from
a supply tender.

through battery exhaustion. A fourth, B-4, evaded US efforts to make it surface. The *Zulu* was recalled by Moscow when US President Kennedy announced the 'quarantine' zone around Cuba on 22 October. Meanwhile, in the Pacific, *Zulu B-88*, also with atomic warheads, was sent on patrol close to Pearl Harbor, with instructions to attack if war should break out. For a few days world security was on a knife-edge and submarines were on the brink of losing their deterrent role and unleashing a nuclear war. US submarines were put into a state of battle readiness at every East Coast base and submarines monitored the movements of Soviet shipping. On both sides, nuclear submarines, armed with ICBMs, were on full alert.

The Golf submarines had an unmistakable profile, with the sail extended into a long missile silo. Designated as Project 629, this was the first purpose-built Soviet ballistic missile submarine. Design began in the mid-1950s, after six Zulu boats had been modified to carry Scud missiles. Twenty-three were commissioned between 1958 and 1962. The first design allowed for carrying three R-11FM (SS-N-4) missiles with a range of around 150km (93 miles), and which had to be launched from the surface.

Sixteen of the class were modified in 1966–72 (Project 629A) to carry R-21 (SS-N-5) Sark missiles with a range of 1400km (870 miles), which could be launched while the submarine was submerged and

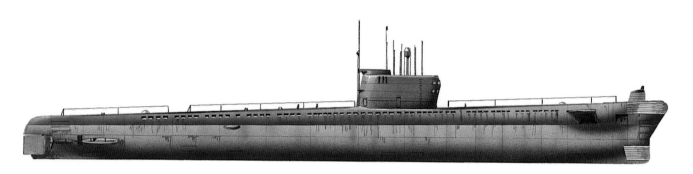

Specifications

Crew: 80

Powerplant: Triple shaft; three diesels engines; three electric motors

Max Speed: 33.3/29.6km/hr (18/16kt) surf/sub

Surface Range:10,190km (5500nm) at 8kt

Displacement: 1950/2500t (1191/2540 tons) surf/sub

Dimensions (length/beam/draught): 91.5 x 8 x 6.1m (300.18 x 26.25 x 20ft)

Commissioned: 1959 (first units)

Armament: 10 533mm (21in) torpedo tubes

▲ Foxtrot

Soviet Navy, patrol-attack submarine

Foxtrots carried the Soviet ensign in every ocean region. They were the last Soviet submarines to be constructed with old-style hulls, though the sail was of streamlined design. Their successors would be given the teardrop hull format.

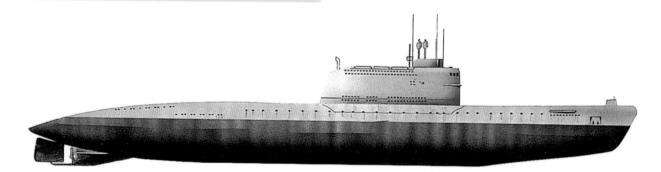

▲ Golf I

Soviet Navy, missile submarine

The keel was deepened in mid-section to accommodate the tubes of the missile silo. Like the Foxtrots, they had triple diesel-electric motors driving three propeller shafts and were not quiet in the water, except when using their slow-speed creep motor.

Specifications

Crew: 86

Powerplant: Triple shaft; three diesel-electric motors

Max Speed: 31.5/26km/hr (17/14kt) surf/sub

Surface Range: 36,510km (19,700nm) at 10kt

Displacement: 2336/2743t (2300/2700 tons)

Dimensions (length/beam/draught): 100 x 8.5 x 6.6m (328 x 27.9 x 21.6ft)

Commissioned: 1958

Armament: Three SS-N-4 SLBM; 10 533mm (21in) torpedo tubes

moving. These were known as Golf II. One of these, *K-129*, sank northwest of Oahu in the Pacific on 8 March 1968, with the loss of all its crew. Three R-21 nuclear missiles and two nuclear torpedoes were on board. SOSUS detector equipment registered the incident and the United States ran a semi-secret operation, Project Azorian, in 1974 to retrieve the wreck, using the SSNs *Halibut* and *Seawolf* as search vehicles. Part of the wreck was retrieved, but the details of the operation remain cloaked in secrecy.

By 1990, the Soviet Navy had withdrawn all its Golf-class boats. Ten were sold to North Korea in 1993, for scrapping. A Chinese version of the *Golf I* was built in 1966 and may still be in commission as a missile-testing platform.

On 16 September 1955, the Zulu class B-67 launched the first submarine-launched ballistic missile (SLBM), the R-11FM. From 1956, some Whiskey class submarines were adapted to carry guided missiles, initially the SS-N-3 Shaddock cruise missile. The first prototype, identified by NATO as Whiskey single-cylinder, carried only one missile, but six more were converted between 1958 and 1960 to carry two (Whiskey two-cylinder). The missile tubes were fitted aft of the sail. A further six were fitted with a lengthened sail to hold four vertically mounted Shaddocks (Whiskey long bin). B-67 was the first Soviet submarine to fire from a submerged position, on 10 September 1960, only two months after USS SSBN *George Washington* made a submerged launch of a Polaris A1. The first

launch of a nuclear-armed SLBM was on 20 October 1961 from a Project 629 submarine on the Novaya Zemlya Arctic test ground.

United States

In the United States, the Guppy programme was entering its final phase. Guppy III (1959–63) was a major operation that involved fitting a new 4.5m (15ft) central section to nine boats that had already been through Guppy II. This accommodated the increasing amount of electronic support measures (ESM), sonar and fire control equipment. The sail was heightened to raise the bridge and allow it to be manned in severe weather. Numerous Guppy boats were transferred to other navies between the 1950s and the mid-1970s, and two survived into the twenty-first century: *Thornback* (Turkish *Uluc Ali Reis*) decommissioned in 2000, and *Greenfish* (Brazilian *Amazonas*) scrapped in 2004.

Many early missile experiments were made with adapted fleet submarines. USS *Grayback* was commissioned at Mare Island, California, on 7 March 1958. Originally intended as attack submarines, it and USS *Growler* were converted on the slip to carry Regulus I sea-to-surface missiles. Four missiles were mounted in a hangar set in the bulbous bow. In September 1958, *Grayback* carried out the first successful launch of a Regulus missile from a submarine, establishing the role of the submarine as a vessel capable of striking land targets. *Grayback* subsequently went on Pacific operational patrols as

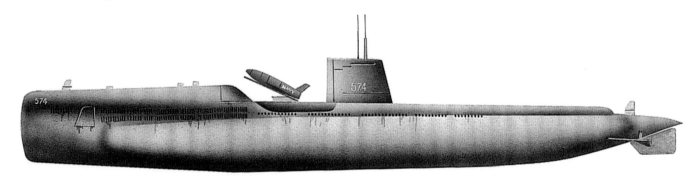

▲ USS Grayback

US Navy, missile submarine, SSG-574

The large missile hangar is the defining feature. For designers, its size and danger of flooding in a following sea was a major problem. The launcher was mounted on a turntable. The Regulus boats formed SubRon I at Pearl Harbor from 1958 to 1964.

Specifications

Crew: 84	Dimensions (length/beam/draught): 98.2 x 9.1 x
Powerplant: Twin shaft; two diesel-electric	5.8m (322.3 x 30 x 19ft)
motors	Commissioned: 7 March 1958
Max Speed: 37/31.5km/hr (20/17kt) surf/sub	Armament: Four Regulus I missiles; eight
Surface Range: 14,825km (8000nm) at 10kt	533mm (21in) torpedo tubes
Displacement: 2712/3708t (2670/3650 tons)	

an SSG, its rockets armed with nuclear warheads, inaugurating the concept of the 'strategic deterrent' that was to govern Cold War thinking and planning for 30 years. It was active until 25 May 1964, when it was decommissioned, with the abandonment of the Regulus programme. In 1967–68 it was converted to an amphibious transport submarine (LPSS) , with the former missile chambers used to hold troops and SEAL swimmer delivery craft. In this configuration it was used in Vietnam War operations, including Operation Thunderhead in June 1972, intended to rescue US prisoners of war from North Vietnam. *Grayback* was finally decommissioned on 15 January 1984, and sunk as a target on 13 April 1986. *Growler* is preserved as a museum boat in Brooklyn.

Nuclear Program

The progress of nuclear technology and the performance of the first nuclear submarines determined the US Navy to press on with nuclear propulsion. An order was placed in July 1955 for USS *Skate*, lead ship of a class of four, and it was commissioned on 23 December 1957. The design was based on the Tang class and they were among the smallest nuclear powered attack submarines. At the time, however, they were considered large boats, and were certainly effective in operation. *Skate* went on sub-Arctic patrols and was the first boat to surface at the North Pole (17 March 1959). Most of its almost 30-year career was spent with Atlantic Fleet, based at New London, Connecticut. Before the Skate class

had completed building, a new hunter-killer class, led by USS *Skipjack*, was built between 1956 and 1961. Constructed from HY-80 steel, these six boats had the teardrop hull design that had also been used in the Navy's final diesel-electric class, the three Barbel fast attack boats, built simultaneously (1956–59). In both classes, the command centre was located not in the tower but within the hull.

The S5W pressurized-water reactor, first installed in this class, became the standard for future classes until the 1970s. The Skipjack boats were very fast, with a submerged speed in excess of 29 knots, and were widely deployed, including Arctic patrols on the Soviet exit-route from Murmansk. Some were deployed in tactical forces during the Vietnam War. One of the class, USS *Scorpion*, was lost on 5 June 1968 off the Azores, returning from a patrol in the Mediterranean Sea. The cause of the disaster remains unidentified, but was most probably a mechanical failure. *Skipjack* was decommissioned and struck from the register on 19 April 1990.

Up to 1962, submarines played a key strategic role as radar picket boats, equipped with air search radar to give early warning of missile or aircraft attacks aimed at land bases or at fleet groups. Designated SSR or SSRN for nuclear boats, these had begun with the conversion of fleet submarines under the Migraine Programme, but the speed and endurance of the nuclear submarine made it much more suitable for the picket role, attached to fast carrier groups. USS *Triton*, commissioned on 10

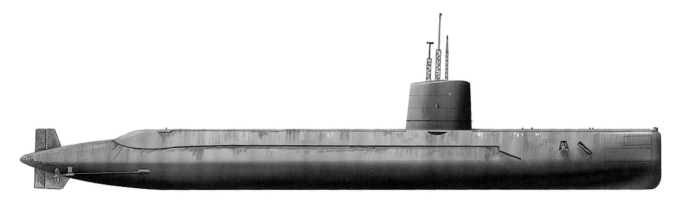

Specifications

Crew: 95	Dimensions (length/beam/draught): 81.5 x 7.6
Powerplant: Twin shaft; one pwr	x 6.4m (267.6 x 25 x 21ft)
Max Speed: 37/46.3km/hr (20/25kt) surf/sub	Commissioned: 23 December 1957
Surface Range: Unlimited	Armament: Six 533mm (21in) torpedo tubes
Displacement: 2611/2907t (2570/2681 tons)	

▲ USS Skate

US Navy, SSN-578

The world's first production-line nuclear submarine, *Skate* had dimensions similar to the Tang class; its greater weight was caused by the need for radiation shielding of its S3W reactor. Towed sonar was at first of the 'clip-on' kind, but two of the class later had integral reeled arrays installed.

▲ **Submarine launcher**
Halibut launching a Regulus missile from the deck. The streamlined hangar can clearly be seen.

November 1959, was built for radar picket duty, and assigned to SubRon 10, an all-nuclear unit based at New London, Connecticut. *Triton* fielded a range of detection equipment, not only AN/SPS-26 3-D long-range air search radar but also towed sonar gear. But only two years after commissioning, the $109 million craft was obsolete, its picket role taken over by carrier-based aircraft.

Triton was converted to SSN status as an attack submarine. It has been suggested that it was also considered as a NECPA (National Emergency Command Post Afloat) for use as a mobile command centre. But its career was short and it was decommissioned in 1969, the first US nuclear submarine to be taken out of service.

Polaris Deployed

Caught at a disadvantage by Soviet development of missile-carrying submarines, the United States mounted a powerful response in the late 1950s. The crucial weapon was a new missile, the Polaris A1, a relatively lightweight (13,063kg/28,800lb) two-stage solid-fuel rocket that had been developed with remarkable speed since December 1956, with a first

test launch in September 1958, the first submerged launch on 20 July 1960 and the first operational patrol in November 1960. Intended from the start as an SLBM, while Polaris was being tested, a Skipjack-class nuclear submarine then under construction, USS *Scorpion* (which was intended as an SSN), was extended with a new 40m (130ft) centre section to carry 16 missile launch tubes, and renamed *George Washington*, the first SSBN.

The Polaris A1's range of 2200km (1370 miles) and the quantity carried by the new SSBNs placed the United States firmly in the lead of missile development. In 1964–65, the Polaris missile was upgraded to A3. Later, *George Washington* was assigned to the Pacific Fleet's Pearl Harbor base. In 1983 it completed the last of 55 patrols as an SSBN, its missiles were removed, as were those of two others of the class, and it served for two years as an SSN before being decommissioned on 24 January 1985.

Commissioned a few days after *George Washington*, on 4 January 1960, USS *Halibut* was the first submarine specifically designed to launch guided missiles. Laid down as a conventionally powered boat, it was completed as a nuclear-powered one. It carried five Regulus I missiles, with a single launcher, and worked through 1961–64 with the Pacific Fleet. Overhauled at Pearl Harbor in 1965, with Regulus now obsolete, *Halibut* was redesignated an SSN, participating in ASW patrols and exercises until 1968. At Mare Island yard it was transformed into an undersea reconnaissance and retrieval vessel, and in this role participated in the attempted raising of the Soviet K-129 as well as engaging in seabed espionage. *Halibut* was decommissioned on 30 June 1976.

In January 1958, the construction order was given for the SSN USS *Thresher*, lead boat of a class of SSNs, an advance on the Skipjacks, with many new technological features, including deep-diving mechanisms, with a test depth of 400m (1300ft), advanced sonars, four midships-angled torpedo tubes also capable of launching the SUBROC ASW missile, and a high level of machinery-quieting, with the turbines supported on British-type 'rafts'.

Commissioned on 3 August 1961, *Thresher* was extensively tested and exercised through 1962. On 10 April 1963, it failed to surface from deep diving tests and was lost with all hands in the ocean east of Cape Cod. Intensive research followed the disaster, resulting in the SUBSAFE programme, providing the maximum reasonable assurance of quality in all systems exposed to sea pressure, or critical to recovery from flooding. A further 13 submarines of the class

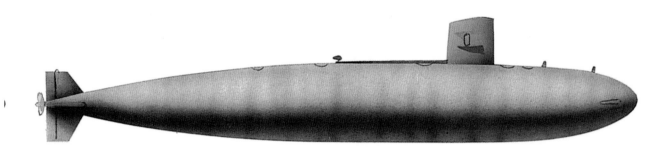

▲ **USS Skipjack**

US Navy, SSN-585, 1965

Skipjack had a single-hull design, with the sail set well forward, carrying the diving planes. This transference from bow-mounting reduced flow-noise past the bow sonar and made it much more effective. It was also the first single-shaft nuclear submarine, with the propeller set aft of the rudder and diving plane gear.

Specifications

Crew: 106

Powerplant: Single shaft; one S5W pwr; steam turbines

Max Speed: 33.3/55.5km/hr (18/30kt) surf/sub

Surface Range: Unlimited

Displacement: 3124/3556t (3075/3500 tons) surf/sub

Dimensions (length/beam/draught): 76.7 x 9.6 x 8.5m (251.75 x 31.5 x 27.8ft)

Commissioned: 15 April 1959

Armament: Five 533mm (21in) torpedo tubes

Specifications

Crew: 172

Powerplant: Twin shaft; one S4G pwr; steam turbines

Max Speed: 50/37km/hr (27/20kt) surf/sub

Surface Range: Unlimited

Displacement: 6035/7905t (5940/7780 tons) surf/sub

Dimensions (length/beam/draught): 136.3 x 11.3 x 7.3m (447.5 x 37 x 24ft)

Commissioned: 10 November 1959

Armament: Six 533mm (21in) torpedo tubes

▲ **USS Triton**

US Navy, radar/reconnaissance nuclear submarine, SSRN-586

The largest submarine yet built, it was the only US nuclear submarine with two reactors: it had two S4G pressurized-water reactors driving twin propellers. Each reactor could function independently of the other. In early 1960, it was the first vessel to circumnavigate the globe underwater.

were built between 1958 and 1967, and the class name was passed to the second boat, *Permit*. All shared the forward-set sail, though some were given an enlarged version, as well as heavier machinery, under the SUBSAFE programme, adding 3m (9ft 10in) to their length. The class was distributed between the Atlantic and Pacific Fleets, serving on a mixture of routine patrols and special intelligence-gathering and surveillance missions.

The 10 James Madison SSBNs, which were built from 1962 to 1964, marked a new step in missile, rather than submarine, development, being almost identical in dimensions to the 19 boats of the preceding Lafayette class. They were armed, however, with 16 Polaris A3 missiles, whose range

was 1900km (1180 miles) greater than that of the A2, and which had three re-entry vehicles for each warhead, the first multiple re-entry vehicle missile. Guidance, fire control and navigational systems were all improved from the Lafayettes.

Built at Mare Island, California, *Daniel Boone* served first with the Pacific Fleet at Guam, then later with Submarine Squadron 14 at the forward base of Holy Loch, Scotland. It was modified in 1976–78 to carry Poseidon C-3 missiles with the Mark 88 fire-control system, and in 1980 was the first of the Madison class to go on patrol with the new Trident C-4. After almost 30 years of service and 75 patrols, *Daniel Boone* was decommissioned on 18 February 1994.

▲ USS Halibut

US Navy, guided-missile submarine, SSGN-587

This was the first boat fitted with the SINS inertial navigation system designed for ballistic submarines. The bulging single-shell hangar was in effect a secondary pressure hull, later adapted as a hangar, with a sea-lock, for a towed underwater search vehicle.

Specifications

Crew: 99	Dimensions (length/beam/draught): 106.7 x 8.9 x
Powerplant: Single shaft; one S3W pwr; turbines	6.3m (350 x 29.5 x 20.75ft)
Max Speed: 27.8/26km/hr (15/14kt)	Commissioned: 4 January 1960
Surface Range: Unlimited	Armament: Five Regulus I or four Regulus II
Displacement: (2670/3650 tons) surf/sub	missiles; six 533mm (21in) torpedo tubes

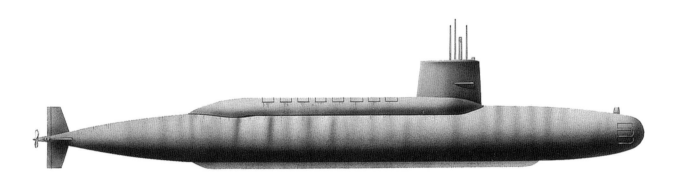

Specifications

Crew: 112	Dimensions (length/beam/draught): 116.3 x 10 x
Powerplant: Single shaft; one S5W pwr; turbines,	8.8m (381.7 x 33 x 28.8ft)
Max Speed: 37/56.5km/hr (20/30.5kt) surf/sub	Commissioned: 30 December 1959
Surface Range: Unlimited	Armament: 16 Polaris AI SBM; six 533mm (21in)
Displacement: 6115/6998t (6019/6888 tons) surf/sub	torpedo tubes

▲ USS George Washington

US Navy, ballistic missile submarine, SSBN-598

George Washington was commissioned on 30 December 1959, the first of a class of five SSBNs, each with two crews, to ensure full utilization of the boat's capacity. Between 28 October 1960 and 21 January 1961 it made its first patrol, and from April 1961 was based at the Holy Loch, Scotland.

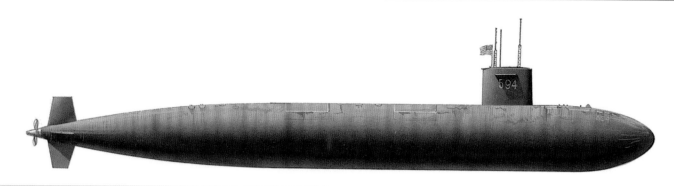

Specifications

Crew: 134

Powerplant: Single shaft; one S5W pwr; steam
turbines,

Max Speed: 33.3/50km/hr (18/27kt) surf/sub

Surface Range: Unlimited

Displacement: 3810/4380t (3750/4311 tons)
surf/sub

Dimensions (length/beam/draught): 84.9 x 9.6 x
8.8m (278.5 x 31.65 x 28.8ft)

Commissioned: 3 August 1961

Armament: Four 533mm (21in) torpedo tubes

▲ USS Thresher

US Navy, Thresher/Permit class, SSN-593

The loss of *Thresher* was a major shock, as this was considered the best nuclear submarine yet. The class was the first to carry the spherical sonar array that could track fast submarines in all three dimensions. These boats could detect the standard Mk 37 ASW torpedo, and outrun it.

Specifications

Crew: 140

Powerplant: Single shaft; one S5W pwr; steam
turbines,

Max Speed: 37/64.8km/hr (20/35kt) surf/sub

Surface Range: Unlimited

Displacement: 7366/8382t (7250/8250 tons)

surf/sub

Dimensions (length/beam/draught): 130 x 10 x
10m (425 x 33 x 33ft)

Commissioned: 23 April 1964

Armament: 16 Polaris A2/A3 SBM; four 533mm
(21in) torpedo tubes

▲ USS Daniel Boone

US Navy, James Madison class, SSBN-629

The James Madison-class submarines were in direct line from the Ethan Allen class of 1960, through the Lafayettes (1963), but had improved guidance, fire-control, navigational and missile-launching systems. Gas generators had already replaced compressed-air launchers with the Lafayette class.

The race for missile superiority
1965–74

The deep-sea lanes are now patrolled by ICBM-carrying SSBN 'Boomers'. But conventional submarines have not lost their attack role.

CHINA'S FIRST NUCLEAR submarine class, Type 091 or Han, had a hull design closely resembling the US 'teardrop' form, with diving planes fitted to the sail. Five were commissioned between 1974 and 1990. Propulsion was by a single pressurized-water reactor. Although little is known for certain about

Chinese nuclear submarine development, the long construction period indicates that the later boats may differ considerably in internal layout and weapons and other systems.

In successive refits all have been modernized to a degree, with the most essential feature being improved radiation shielding. Three are believed to remain in service, fitted with anechoic tiles to dampen their (considerable) noise and with Type H/SQ2-262B sonar replacing the original Type 603. The class can fire C-801 anti-ship missiles in addition to SET-65E and Type 53-51 torpedoes; or carry 36 mines.

Despite their limitations, the Chinese Han class brought China into the club of nuclear submarine operators and provided a solid base for further development.

Denmark

Though constructed by the Copenhagen Naval Dockyard, the Danish submarines *Narhvalen* and *Nordkaperen* were German designs, based on the Type 205, with certain differences and modifications. The hulls were formed of magnetic steel, as the non-magnetic steel used on the Type 205 had serious corrosion problems. *Narhvalen* was commissioned on 27 February 1970, and with its sister ship was used as a patrol/attack submarine to police the sensitive Kattegat and Skagerrak waters as well as participating

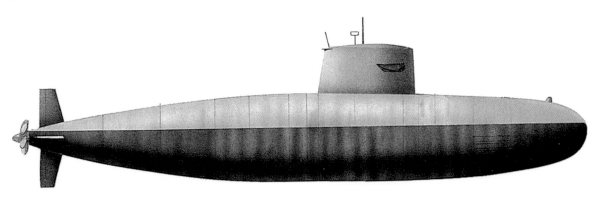

▲ Han

Chinese Navy, Type 091 SSN

Han-class deployments are believed to be infrequent, although in the past they have shadowed US Naval groups and one boat infringed territorial limits off a Japanese island in 2004. They are assigned to the PLA Navy's North Sea Fleet, at the the Qingdao naval base.

Specifications

Crew: 120

Powerplant: Single shaft; one pwr

Max Speed: 37/51.8km/hr (20/28kt) surf/sub

Surface Range: Unlimited

Displacement: 4572/5588.25t (4500/5500 tons) surf/sub

Dimensions (length/beam/draught): 90 x 8 x 8.2m (295.25 x 26.25 x 27ft)

Commissioned: 1972

Armament: Six 533mm (21in) torpedo tubes; 18 torpedoes; 36 mines

▲ Narhvalen

Danish Navy, patrol submarine, Skagerrak 1970

Failure to communicate with its command base, due to a radio failure, caused fears that *Narhvalen* had sunk in the *Skagerrak* in September 1970. In 1994, it and *Nordkaperen* went through a major refit, and it continued with coastal and NATO patrols until decommissioned in October 2003.

Specifications

Crew: 19

Powerplant: Twin shaft; two diesel engines; two electric motors

Max Speed: 18/31.5km/hr (10/17kt) surf/sub

Surface Range: Details not available

Displacement: 442/517t (453/509 tons) surf/sub

Dimensions (length/beam/draught): 44 x 4.55 x 3.98m (144.35 x 14.9 x 13ft)

Commissioned: 27 February 1970

Armament: Eight 533mm (21in) torpedo tubes

in wider-scale NATO exercises. Their longest known patrol was a 41-day cruise from the Baltic Sea to the Faeroe Islands, with only 5 per cent of the time spent on the surface. Since 2004 the Danish Navy no longer has submarines.

France

Laid down in 1964, commissioned in December 1971 after lengthy trials, *Redoutable* was France's first SSBN (known to the French as SNLE), and lead-boat of a class of six. Four were completed by 1976, and the final two in 1980 and 1985. The first two carried France's M1 SLBMs; the others had the

much superior M4, a three-stage missile with a range of 5300km (3290 miles). Each has six 150kT MIRV warheads. *Redoutable* and its sisters formed part of the Force Océanique Stratégique (FOST) set up to ensure at least one French SSBN was operational at any time. *Redoutable* made 51 operational patrols over 20 years before being decommissioned in 1991. All the class are now withdrawn.

France did not abandon the diesel-electric submarine and in 1977 introduced the Agosta class for patrol/attack duties. Four were built at Cherbourg for the French Navy in 1977–78 and four at Cartagena for the Spanish Navy in 1983–85. A

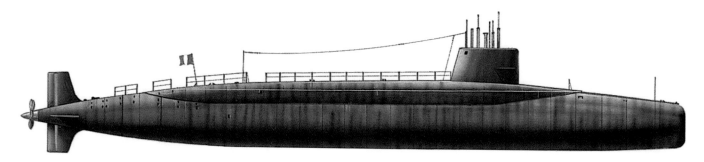

▲ Le Redoutable

French Navy, SSBN

Redoutable carried 18 L5 dual-purpose and F17 anti-ship torpedoes in addition to the missile armament. It was the only member of its class not to be retrofitted with Aerospatiale M4 ballistic missiles. Following its withdrawal, the five remaining boats were officially designated as the Inflexible class.

Specifications

Crew: 142

Powerplant: Single shaft; one pwr; turbines

Max Speed: 37/51.8km/hr (20/28kt) surf/sub

Surface Range: Unlimited

Displacement: 7620/9144t (7500/9000 tons) surf/sub

Dimensions (length/beam/draught): 128 x 10.6 x 10m (420 x 34.8 x 32.8ft)

Commissioned: 1 December 1971

Armament: 16 SLBM; SM-39 Exocet; four 533mm (21in) torpedo tubes

Specifications

Crew: 54

Powerplant: Single shaft; two diesel engines; one electric motor

Max Speed: 23.1/32.4km/hr (12.5/17.5kt) surf/sub

Surface Range: 15,750km (8500nm) at 9kt

Displacement: 1514/1768t (1490/1740 tons) surf/sub

Dimensions (length/beam/draught): 67.6 x 6.8 x 5.4m (221.75 x 22.45 x 17.75ft)

Commissioned: 11 February 1978

Armament: Four 550mm (21.7in) tubes; 40 mines

▲ Agosta

French Navy, patrol-attack submarine

The class was designed with Mediterranean deployment in mind. Use of HLES 80 steel enabled it to dive to 350m (1150ft). Its torpedo tubes were a new design, with rapid pneumatic-ram reload, which could fire at any speed and depth. It carried 23 torpedoes.

further two, originally ordered by South Africa, were sold to Pakistan in 1979–80.

Pakistan also has three Agosta 90B or Khalid class boats, built between 1999 and 2006, to a modernized design with upgraded weapons and sensor systems. Automated systems require a crew of only 36 compared to the Agosta's 54. The French Agosta boats have been decommissioned.

Germany

Eleven boats, numbered U1 to U12 (excluding U3) formed this class of attack submarines, which were intended for use in the Baltic Sea. This sea is shallow, which explains why they had a test depth of 100m (330ft), not very great for a modern submarine. The hulls were formed of a non-magnetic steel that turned out to have severe corrosion problems, though the problem was resolved by the time U9 to U12 were built, in 1967–69. U1 and U2, originally Type 201, were rebuilt as Type 205s with normal steel. In the Baltic, accurate sensory equipment is of vital importance and the first sea trials of the *Bundesmarine* CSU90 sonar array were conducted by a Type 205. U4 to U8 had brief careers, all

Specifications

Crew: 21

Powerplant: Single screw; diesel-electric

Max Speed: 18/.5/32.4km/hr (10/17.5kt) surf/sub

Surface Range: 7040km (3800nm) at 10kt

Displacement: 425.457t (419/450 tons) surf/sub

Dimensions (length/beam/draught): 43.9 x 4.6 x 4.3m (144 x 15 x 14ft)

Commissioned: 10 September 1968

Armament: Eight 533mm (21in) torpedo tubes

▲ **U-12**

Federal German Navy, Type 205 coastal submarine, Baltic Sea, 1968

A clear line of development can be traced from the Type 201 to the Type 205 and beyond. Working from the FGR submarine base at Eckernförde, *U-12* was reclassified as Type 205B while trialling new sonar systems. *U-1* was used as a test-boat for AIP propulsion in 1988.

Specifications

Crew: 21

Powerplant: Single shaft; diesel-electric

Max Speed: 18.5/31.5km/hr (10/17kt) surf/sub

Surface Range: 7.040km (3800nm) at 10kt

Displacement: 457/508t (450/500 tons) surf/sub

Dimensions (length/beam/draught): 48.6 x 4./6 x 4.5m (159.45 x 15.16 x 14.8ft)

Commissioned: 1974

Armament: Eight 533mm (21in) torpedo tubes

▲ **U-20**

Federal German Navy, Type 206 coastal submarine, 1974

Mines have always been a major element in Baltic naval operations, and the Type 206 was designed both to avoid them and to lay them. The compact hull design allows for eight bow tubes for wire-guided torpedoes: Type DM2A1 (Seeaal) on the Type 206 boats, and DM2A3 (Seehecht) on the 206As. Diving depth was 200m (656ft).

BRITISH NUCLEAR SUBMARINES				
Class	Type	Number	Year	Note
Dreadnought	Hunter-killer	1	1960	Stricken 1982
Valiant	Hunter-killer	2	1963–70	Stricken 1990–92
Resolution	SSBN	4	1966–68	Stricken 1990s
Churchill	Hunter-killer	3	1970–71	Stricken 1990–92
Swiftsure	Hunter-killer	6	1971–79	All stricken by 2010
Trafalgar	Hunter-killer	7	1981–91	4 in service, 2016
Vanguard	SSBN	4	1992–99	
Astute	SSN	3	2006–	3 under construction

being scrapped by 1974, while U12 was not decommissioned until 2005.

The follow-on class, Type 206, was built between 1968 and 1975, and like the 205s had hulls of high-strength non-magnetic steel. Twelve were modernized in the early 1990s as Type 206A. New features included the DBQS-21D sonar, new periscopes, a new LEWA weapons control system and GPS navigation. External containers enabling the boats to carry 24 ground mines were fitted. From 2010, all 206 and 206A boats were decommissioned.

Great Britain

With the introduction of the Resolution class of SSBN, the role of maintaining Britain's weapons of nuclear deterrence passed from the Air Force to the Navy. Four suitable submarines were ordered, and the first to be commissioned was HMS *Resolution* on

2 October 1967. Bow and stern sections were constructed separately, and the US-designed missile compartment inserted between them. Resemblances to the US Navy's Lafayette class were clear, though the British boats had bow-mounted hydroplanes, and other specifically British features included the 'rafting' of the main machinery, an automated hovering system and welded hull valves.

Like the Valiant class, it had a Rolls Royce pressurized-water reactor and English Electric turbines. Sixteen Polaris A3 were carried. Operational patrols did not begin until 15 June 1968, with the class based with the 10th Submarine Squadron at Faslane, Scotland. As with other SSBNs, each boat had two crews serving alternate missions. In the course of the 1980s they were converted to carry the Polaris AT-K missile, with the British Chevaline MRV warhead. All were decommissioned between 1992 and 1996.

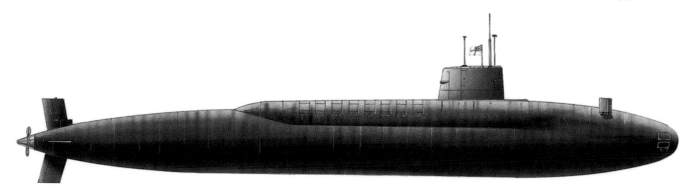

▲ **HMS Resolution**

Royal Navy, SSBN

HMS Resolution made its first Polaris launch on 15 February 1968, and remained in service for another 26 years, with a major upgrading of weapons and other systems in 1984. In 1991, it made the Royal Navy's longest Polaris patrol, of 108 days.

Specifications

Crew: 154

Powerplant: Single shaft; one pwr; steam turbines

Max Speed: 37/46.3km/hr (20/25kt) surf/sub

Surface Range: Unlimited

Displacement: 7620/8535t (7500/8400 tons)

surf/sub

Dimensions: 129.5 x 10.1 x 9.1m (425 x 33 x 30ft)

Commissioned: 2 October 1967

Armament: 16 Polaris A3TK SBM; six 533mm (21in) torpedo tubes

An updated version of the Valiant fleet submarine class, the Churchill class was formed of three SSNs commissioned in 1970–71. HMS *Churchill* was the first. As built, they were fitted with a Type 21 sonar array, replaced in the late 1970s by a Type 2020 hull-mounted array and a Type 2026 towed array. The six 533mm (21in) tubes could fire Mark 8 and Tigerfish torpedoes. From 1981, Harpoon anti-ship missiles were also carried. The Churchills were propelled by a shrouded pump-jet propulsor, quieter than any propeller and which produced the same speed for

fewer revolutions. This feature was maintained in the next class of fleet submarines, the six Swiftsure boats, except for *Swiftsure* itself.

This class, commissioned between 1973 and 1981, showed a change in hull design, more cylindrical than its predecessors and 4m (13ft) shorter than the Churchills. The fin was reduced and retractable diving planes were placed below the water-line. They had a maximum diving depth of 600m (1980ft) and an underwater speed in excess of 30 knots. Both anti-submarine and anti-surface attack was envisaged,

Specifications

Crew: 116	surf/sub
Powerplant: Single shaft; one pwr; steam turbines	Dimensions (length/beam/draught): 86.9 x 10.1 x 8.2m (285 x 33.25 x 27ft)
Max Speed: 37/53.7km/hr (20/29kt) surf/sub	Commissioned: 9 November 1971
Surface Range: Unlimited	Armament: Six 533mm torpedo tubes; Tigerfish torpedoes
Displacement: 4470/4979t (4400/4900 tons)	

▲ HMS Conqueror
Royal Navy, Churchill class SSN, Falklands, 1982

The Churchill class was essentially an improved version of the two Valiant boats. HMS *Conqueror* sank the Argentinian cruiser *General Belgrano* with Mk 8 torpedoes of World War II type on 2 May 1982 during the Falklands/Malvinas War. Later the class's torpedo armament was modernized.

Specifications

Crew: 116	surf/sub
Powerplant: Single shaft; one pwr; steam turbines	Dimensions (length/beam/draught): 82.9 x 9.8 x 8.5m (272 x 32.4 x 28ft)
Max Speed: 37/55.5km/hr (20/30kt) surf/sub	Commissioned: 17 April 1973
Surface Range: Unlimited	Armament: Five 533mm torpedo tubes; Tomahawk and Sub Harpoon SSMs
Displacement: 4471/4979t (4400/4900 tons)	

▲ HMS Swiftsure
Royal Navy, SSN

The class were deployed both for ASW screening duties with task-force groups and on independent patrol with anti-ship and anti-submarine capability. Like the Valiant and Churchill classes, they had an auxiliary diesel generator, 112-cell battery and electric motor. *Spartan* and *Splendid* were involved in the Falklands campaign of 1982. *Swiftsure* was decommissioned in 1992.

with the Mk 24 Tigerfish torpedo and the Sub Harpoon missile.

The comprehensive sonar suite featured the Type 2074 (active/passive search and attack), Type 2007 (passive), Type 2046 (towed array), 2019 (intercept and ranging) and Type 2077 (short range classification). HMS *Splendid* was the first British submarine to be fitted with Tomahawk cruise missiles, and fired them at land targets during the 1999 NATO strikes against Serbia. Last to be decommissioned was HMS *Sceptre* in 2010.

Italy

After training experience with ex-US submarines, Italy completed its first home-built submarines in 1968. These formed the four-strong Enrico Toti class, small vessels that were intended as interceptors and attack boats. The four torpedo tubes could fire the Whitehead Motofides A184 wire-guided torpedo, intended both for anti-ship and anti-submarine engagements, with a range of some 25km (15.5 miles) and an active/passive acoustic homing head with advanced counter-measures to spot enemy decoys.

Enrico Toti served in the Mediterranean Sea, achieving 220,480km (137,000 miles) on patrol duty round the coasts of Italy. All were decommissioned in 1991–93. *Enrico Toti* is preserved as a museum boat at Milan.

Japan

Japan's first fleet submarines since World War II were the Oshio class of 1967. In fact, *Oshio* itself differed significantly from the other four, with a larger bow structure and with a preliminary sonar fit. Also, the others were built of NS46 high-tensile steel and could operate at greater depths. *Harushio*, third to be commissioned, was more typical. They were multi-purpose boats, for patrol, surveillance, reconnaissance and crew training. The two stern torpedo tubes, intended for ASW defence, were later removed. All in the class were decommissioned by 1986.

The Soviet Union

The Echo class of SSGN falls into two groups: Project 659, the first five boats, was designated Echo I by NATO, and Project 675, the following 29, were Echo II. The Echo I boats, completed between 1960 and 1962, carried six launchers for the P-5 Pyatyorka (SS-N-3C Shaddock B) cruise missile. Their role was essentially a strategic one as they did not possess the fire-control and radar-detection equipment needed for attack boats.

Between 1969 and 1974, the cruise missiles were removed and the submarines converted to SSNs. All were deployed in the Pacific Fleet. Echo II were built at Severodvinsk and Komsomolsk between 1962 and 1967 for anti-ship warfare, with aircraft carriers particularly in mind. They carried eight P-6 (SS-N-

▲ **Enrico Toti**

Italian Navy, coastal patrol submarine, 1967

Two Fiat MB820 diesels generated 2220hp (1640kW). Only six torpedoes were carried, but they were of a highly efficient kind. Built by Fincantieri in Monfalcone, the Toti class can be compared to the French Aréthuse and the German Type 205 classes in size and functions.

Specifications

Crew: 26	sub
Powerplant: Single shaft; diesel engines; electric motor	Dimensions (length/beam/draught): 46.2 x 4.7 x 4m (151.66 x 15.46 x 13ft)
Max Speed: 25.8/27.8km/hr (14/15kt) surf/sub	Commissioned: 12 March 1967
Surface Range: 5556km (3000nm) at 5kt	Armament: Four 533mm (21in) torpedo tubes
Displacement: 532/591t (524/582 tons) surf/	

ITALIAN POST-WAR SUBMARINES				
Class	Type	Number	Year	Note
Da Vinci	Attack	3	1954–66	ex-US Gato class, 1942–43
Torricelli	Attack	2	1955–75	ex-US Balao class, 1944–45
Longobardo	Attack	2	1974–87	ex-US Tench class, 1948
Piomarta	Attack	2	1975–87	ex-US Tang class, 1952
Enrico Toti	Attack	4	1965–97	
Nazario Sauro	Attack	8	1970–93	4 in service (III and IV Sauro)
U-212A	Patrol	4	2006–09	Co-built with Germany

JAPANESE POST-WAR SUBMARINES				
Class	Type	Number	Year	Note
Kuroshio	Patrol	1	1955	ex USS *Mingo*; stricken 1966
Oyashio	Patrol	1	1960	Stricken 1976
Asashio	Attack	4	1964–69	In service to 1986
Uzushio	Attack	7	1968–78	Teardrop hull; in service 1971–96
Yushio	Attack	10	1980–89	In service to 2006
Harushio	Patrol	7	1987–97	4 used in training
Oyashio	Patrol	11	1994–2006	In service
Soryu	Patrol	9	2009	7 commissioned, 2 fitting out

3a Shaddock A) anti-ship cruise missiles, which could only be fired from a surfaced position. In order to effect guidance of a fired missile, the boat had to remain surfaced until mid-course correction and final target selection had been made: the element of vulnerability is clear.

Fourteen boats were modified to carry the P-500 Bazalt (SS-N-12 Sandbox) anti-ship cruise missile.

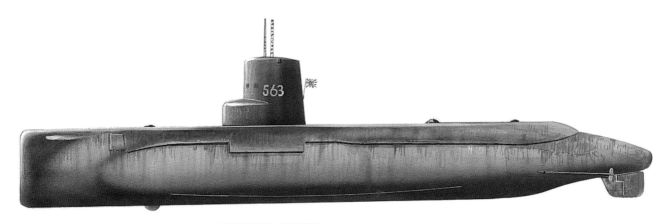

Specifications

Crew: 80

Powerplant: Twin shaft; two diesel engines; two electric motors

Max Speed: 25.8/33.3km/hr (14/18kt) surf/sub

Surface Range: 16,677km (9000nm) at 10kt

Displacement: 1650/2150t (1624/2116 tons)

Dimensions (length/beam/draught): 88 x 8.2 4.9m (288.65 x 27 x 16.18ft)

Commissioned: 25 February 1967

Armament: Eight 533mm (21in) torpedo tubes

▲ **Harushio**

Japanese Maritime Self-Defence Force, Oshio class patrol submarine, 1967

The Oshio class were built by Mitsubishi and Kawasaki at Kobe. Two Kawasaki diesels produced 2900hp each (2162kW) and the two electric motors developed 6300hp (4698kW). Innovations included aircraft-type controls and a five-bladed propeller.

This had a range of 550km (340 miles) and three were further upgraded with the P-1000 Vulkan (GRAU 3M70) with a 700km (430-mile) range. But by the early 1980s, the Echo I and II were becoming obsolete. All of Echo I were decommissioned by 1989; Echo II were decommissioned between 1989 and 1995.

Project 667A began in 1962 and the first submarine, K-137, was launched in 1964 and commissioned into the Northern Fleet at the end of 1967. Between 1967 and 1974, 33 more were added. The hull was cylinder-shaped and the front hydroplanes were re-sited on the sail. There was a touch of irony in their NATO designation of 'Yankee', as the Soviets were considered to have used stolen US plans in designing the class. As usual with Soviet practice, two reactors were installed, of the pressurized-water type. To reduce noise, new propellers were devised, the pressure hull was covered with sound-absorbing rubber and the external hull with antihydroacoustic coating. The footings under the propulsion systems were also isolated by rubber buffers.

The Yankee I SSBNs were equipped with the 'Cloud' battle management system, which could receive signals up to a depth of 50m (165ft) with the help of a Paravan towed antenna. The first four employed the Sigma navigation system, whereas the

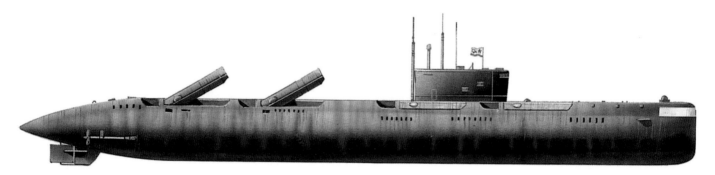

▲ Echo class
Soviet Navy, SSGN/SSN

The launch tubes, installed above the pressure hull, are shown in erected mode. Six missiles were carried. Echo II submarines carried eight and were 5 m (16.5ft) longer to accommodate the additional tubes. At least four Echo class boats are believed to have suffered serious accidents.

Specifications

Crew: 90	surf/sub
Powerplant: Twin shaft; one pwr; two steam turbines	Dimensions (length/beam/draught): 110 x 9 x 7.5m (360.9 x 29.5 x 24.58ft)
Max Speed: 37/51.8km/hr (20/28kt) surf/sub	Commissioned: 1960
Surface Range: Unlimited	Armament: As SSGN, six SS-N-3C cruise missiles; two 406mm (16in) torpedo tubes
Displacement: 4572/5588t (4500/5500 tons)	

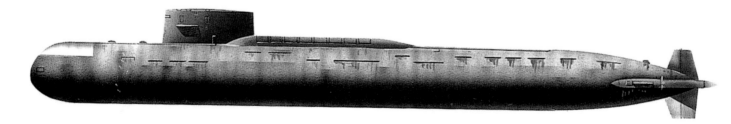

Specifications

Crew: 120	Dimensions (length/beam/draught): 129.5 x 11.6 x 7.8m (424.9 x 38 x 25.6ft)
Powerplant: Two shaft; two pwr; turbines	Commissioned: 1967
Max Speed: 37/55.5km/hr (20/30kt) surf/sub	Armament: 16 SS-N-6 SBM; six 533mm (21in) torpedo tubes
Surface Range: Unlimited	
Displacement: 7925/9450t (7800/9300 tons) surf/sub	

▲ Yankee class
Soviet Navy, SSBN

Through the 1970s, at least three Yankee submarines were stationed at strategic distances from the US mainland, with one or two on the way out or home, some of which must have passed close to US submarines on similar missions in the opposite direction.

SOVIET POST-WAR DIESEL-ELECTRIC SUBMARINES				
Project/(NATO name)	Type	Number	Year	Note
613, 664, 665 (Whiskey)	Coastal	236	1949–58	5 variants; retired by 1989
611 (Zulu)	Attack	26	1952–57	
615 (Quebec)	Coastal	30	1952–57	Retired in 1970s
633 (Romeo)	Attack	20	1957–61	560 planned; 113 exported
641 (Foxtrot)	Attack	74	1957–83	Retired by 2000
651 (Juliet)	Missile	16	1967–69	Retired by 1994
641B (Tango)	Attack	18	1972–82	None still in service
877 (Kilo)	Attack	24	1980–82	Some still active
636 (Improved Kilo)	Attack	49	1982–	Some still active; 30+ for export
677 Lada	Patrol	1	2004	Project reinstated 2014, under construction

▲ **Charlie I**

Soviet Navy, SSGN

This was the first Soviet SSGN capable of launching surface-to-surface missiles without having to surface first. With a high submerged speed and armed with SS-N-15 anti-submarine missiles, it also had hunter-killer capabilities.

Specifications

Crew: 100

Powerplant: Single shaft; one pwr; steam turbine

Max Speed: 37/50km/hr (20/27kt) surf/sub

Surface Range: Unlimited

Displacement: 4064/4877t (4000/4800 tons) surf/sub

Dimensions (length/beam/draught): 94 x 10 x 7.6m (308 x 32.75 x 25ft)

Commissioned: 1967

Armament: Eight SS-N-7 cruise missiles; six 533mm (21in) torpedo tubes

Specifications

Crew: 31

Powerplant: Single shaft; liquid-metal reactor; two steam turbines,

Max Speed: 37/77.8km/hr (20/42kt) surf/sub

Surface Range: Unlimited

Displacement: 2845/3739t (2800/3680 tons)

surf/sub

Dimensions (length/beam/draught): 81 x 9.5 x 8m (265.75 x 31.18 x 26.25ft)

Commissioned: 1970

Armament: Six 533mm (21in) torpedoes, nuclear warheads; 36 mines

▲ **Alfa class**

Soviet Navy, high-speed SSN

The appearance of this class caused hurried rethinking in the US submarine command, which assumed, incorrectly, that it was capable of operating at very deep levels. Faster submarines, and deep-running torpedoes, were made a high priority.

follow-on ships were equipped with the Tobol – the first Soviet satellite-linked navigational system.

The Yankee class were armed with 16 R-27 (SS-N-6 Serb) missiles, carried within the hull, unlike their predecessors. They had to come relatively close to the United States to target inland centres like Chicago or Kansas City. Nevertheless, they were a powerful threat, and the first Soviet SSBN to seriously challenge US boats. As a result of changing strategic requirements, and the arms limitation agreements, a number of variant Yankee types appeared, in most cases without ballistic missiles, and carrying cruise missiles or converted to SSN. Decommissioning of the class, in all configurations, began in the late 1980s and was complete by 1995.

Between 1968 and 1972, 11 Project 670A Charlie I submarines were commissioned. A compact SSGN, it was unique among Soviet boats at the time by having a single reactor and propeller. The Charlie I was originally designed to carry the SS-N-9 anti-shipping cruise missile. When this was not ready in time, the SS-N-7, a modified version of the SS-N-2 Styx, was substituted. Either 11 or 12 Charlie I submarines, carrying eight SS-N-7s of approximately 48km (30-mile) range, were built between 1967 and 1972 at a rate of about two a year.

Six Charlie II submarines, each with 8 SS-N-9s of 96km (60-mile) range, followed between 1972 and 1980. Charlie II carried the SS-N-9 missile originally planned for the Charlie I class, along with

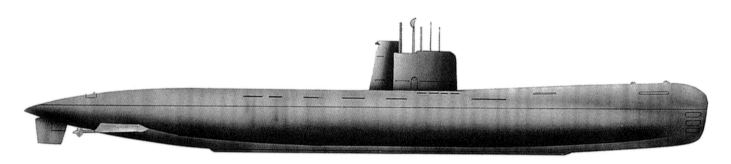

Specifications

Crew: 60	surf/sub
Powerplant: Twin shaft; diesel-electric	Dimensions (length/beam/draught): 92 x 9 x 7m
Max. speeds: 37/29.6km/hr (20/16kt) surf/sub	(301.85 x 29.5 x 24ft)
Surface Range: 22,236km (12,000nm) at 10kt	Commissioned: 1971
Displacement: 3251/3962t (3200/3900 tons)	Armament: Six 533mm (21in) torpedo tubes

▲ Tango class

Soviet Navy, patrol-attack submarine

Unprecedentedly high battery capacity enabled the Tango class to run submerged for a week before requiring to use their snorkels. A rubberized hull coating helped to make them hard to detect. They carried 24 torpedoes. The fin design is distinctive.

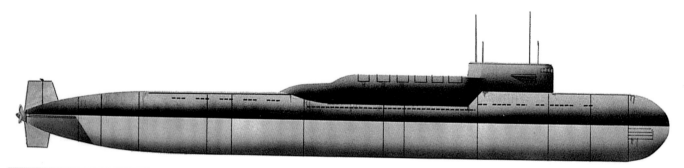

Specifications

Crew: 120	Dimensions (length/beam/draught): 150 x 12 x
Powerplant: Single shaft; two pwr; turbines	10.2m (492 x 39.33 x 33.5ft)
Max Speed: 35.2/46.3km/hr (19/25kt) surf/sub	Commissioned: 1971
Surface Range: Unlimited	Armament: 12 SS-N-8 SBM; six 457mm (18in)
Displacement: 7925/10,160t (7800/10,000 tons) surf/sub	torpedo tubes

▲ Delta class

Soviet Navy, SSBN

The Delta class reverted to the Soviet two-reactor arrangement (pressurized water-cooled system), with twin propellers. Capable of operating under the Arctic ice-cap, it was equipped with the Tobol-B navigation system and the Cyclone-B satellite navigation system.

an improved fire control system. In January 1988, the Soviets leased a Charlie I to India, where it served until January 1991 as the *Chakra*. Since the mid-1990s, all Charlie I and Charlie II have been on the reserve list.

In 1972, the Soviet Union completed the world's first titanium-hulled submarine, which was also the fastest, with a maximum underwater speed believed to be 44.7 knots. Numbered K-222, it remained a one-off, known as the Papa class by NATO, but was followed by the Lira class submarine (Project 705). Known as *Alfa*, no one could say this was lifted from US designs.

The profile, with the sail blending smoothly into the hull, was unique. Its hull was also made of titanium, stronger and lighter than steel. It could travel at 41 knots and, it was believed, could outdive the US Mk 48 torpedo. As a high-speed interceptor craft, the Alfa class was really ahead of its time, and only seven were built, between 1971 and 1981. Its level of automation made it complex to operate, and there were difficulties with the reduced crew levels, especially in problematic situations. Its reactor (a single one) was a new design with a lead-bismuth liquid-metal cooling system, which despite its power gave numerous operating difficulties. All were decommissioned by 1990.

The Soviets, however, had not given up on building conventionally powered boats, and so, between 1972 and 1982, 18 diesel-electric submarines of Project 641B Som (Catfish; Tango class to NATO) were built.

These were large attack submarines; their size being dictated by the need for ever-more complex electronic systems as well as more sophisticated weaponry. The diesel powerplant was identical to that of the later Foxtrots. Tango boats were deployed with the Black Sea and Northern fleets and were capable of long-range reconnaissance and intelligence-gathering missions.

After the shock of the Alfa class, the Soviet Navy unveiled what was perhaps a more serious threat to the security of the NATO powers, Project 667B Murena (Eel), or the Delta 1 class. This large SSBN was a major step forward from the Yankees, equipped with R-29 (SS-N-8 Sawfly) missiles with a range of 7800km (4846 miles).

The United States' new Poseidon missiles did have such a range. The first Delta I, K279, was completed in 1972, and a further 17 were built up to 1980. All the Delta I boats were decommissioned by the end of the twentieth century.

Spain

By the 1970s, the Spanish Navy was badly in need of modern submarines. It had five ex-US Balao class boats of World War II vintage, all ready for retirement. To replace them, it acquired four submarines of the French Daphné design, built under licence in Cartagena in 1973–75, and known as the Delfin class after the first to be commissioned.

The sonar suite comprised DUUA-2B, DSUV 22A, and DUUX-2A, and a DLT-D-3 fire control system was installed. In general, the electronics

▲ **Marsopa**

Spanish Navy, Delfin/Daphné class patrol submarine

Marsopa's last major outing was to take part in the Spontex 3 exercise in May 2003, a NATO combined-operations test with ships of many nations, to see whether the 'Blues' could effect a troop landing against the opposition of the 'Orange' vessels. It was decommissioned in 2006.

Specifications

Crew: 45	surf/sub
Powerplant: Twin shaft; two diesel engines; two electric motors	Dimensions (length/beam/draught): 58 x 7 x 4.6m (189.66 x 22.33 x 15ft)
Max Speed: 24.9/29.6km/hr (13.5/16kt) surf/sub	Commissioned: 1975
Surface Range: 8338km (4300nm) at 5kt	Armament: 12 552mm (21.7in) torpedo tubes
Displacement: 884/1062t (870/1045 tons)	

SWEDISH POST-WAR SUBMARINES				
Class	Type	Number	Year	Note
Hajen	Patrol	6	1954–58	Decommissioned
Draken	Patrol	6	1960–61	Decommissioned
Sjöörmen	Patrol	5	1967–68	Decommissioned
Näcken	Patrol	3	1978–79	Decommissioned
Västergötland	Patrol	2	1983–90	Active
Gotland	Patrol	3	1992–97	Active
Södermanland	Patrol	2	2003–04	Improved Västergötland
A26	Patrol	2	2015	For delivery by 2022

were an improvement on the French boats. Based at Cartagena, though deployed at different times both on Spain's Atlantic and Mediterranean coasts, the Delfin class participated in exercises with US Naval groups. All are now decommissioned.

Sweden

With the Sjöörmen class, Sweden once again claimed a place among the leaders of diesel-electric submarine design. Five boats formed the class, commissioned between July 1968 and September 1969. They incorporated numerous features developed by the Kockums shipbuilding form and the Swedish Navy, including a form of the x-rudder first seen on USS *Albacore*. Anechoic tiles damped the sound and the submerged speed of 20 knots was fast for a conventional submarine of the time.

In Swedish service until the early 1990s, they were modernized and refitted for tropical waters and became Singapore's Challenger class, four for service plus one for spare parts.

United States

The United States launched 41 SSBNs between 1960 and 1966. This massive force fielded 656 Polaris nuclear missiles, and comprised five classes, all generally similar in size, appearance and performance, but each one incorporating successive improvements in electronic systems.

Many were adapted for roles other than that of missile submarine. Benjamin Franklin class USS *George Washington Carver* was commissioned on 15 June 1966 and was deployed from the forward base at Rota, Spain. The prime difference between the

▲ Sjoormen

Swedish Navy, ASW patrol submarine

Anti-submarine action was the prime purpose of the class, and its short length and round Albacore-type hull make it highly manoeuvrable. It is also very quiet-running. In 1984–85, all were upgraded with new Ericsson IBS-A17 combat data and fire-control systems.

Specifications

Crew: 18

Powerplant: Single shaft; four diesel engines; one electric motor

Max Speed: 27.8/37km/hr (15/20kt) surf/sub

Surface Range: Not available

Displacement: 1143/1422t (1125/1400 tons)

surf/sub

Dimensions (length/beam/draught): 51 x 6.1 x 5.8m (167.25 x 20 x 19ft)

Commissioned: 31 July 1976

Armament: Four 533mm (21in) and two 400mm (15.75in) torpedo tubes

Franklins and the preceding James Madison class was quieter machinery, giving them a low acoustic signal for the time. All were powered by the well-tried S5W pressurized-water reactor. Following overhaul in 1977, its Polaris A3 missiles were replaced by Poseidon C-3, but it was not among those further converted to carry Trident-1 missiles. *George Washington Carver* was decommissioned on 18 March 1993.

On 12 July 1969, USS *Narwhal* was commissioned. This was a one-off SSN, built to hold the new S5G reactor, a pressurized-water reactor but with a different cooling system to the S5W. Based on 'natural circulation', with the reactor set low and steam generators set high, its advantage was greater quietness in operation.

Narwhal was indeed a very quiet boat and was used in many stealth operations off the Soviet coasts. Some of its innovatory systems were adopted for the subsequent Ohio class, but the US Navy did not adopt the 'natural cooling' system. It was deactivated on 16 January 1999.

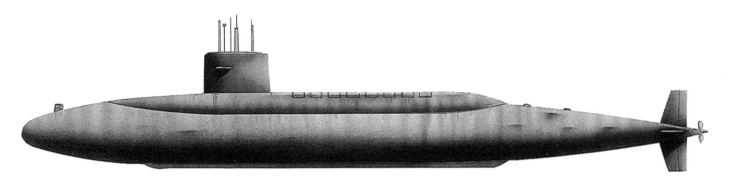

▲ USS George Washington Carver

US Navy, Lafayette class, SSBN-656

Built at Newport News, Virginia, *George Washington Carver* made 73 patrols as a 'Boomer' up to 1991. Conversion to SSN of a large submarine with only four torpedo tubes and a large sealed missile silo can hardly have been very effective, even though it could fire Mk45 nuclear-tipped torpedoes. Decommissioned 18 March 1993.

Specifications

Crew: 140

Powerplant: Single shaft; one S5W pwr; steam turbines

Max Speed: 37/55.5km/hr(20/30kt) surf/sub

Surface Range: Unlimited

Displacement: 7366/8382t (7250/8250 tons)

surf/sub

Dimensions (length/beam/draught): 129.5 x 10 x 9.6m (425.8 x 32.8 x 31.8ft)

Commissioned: 15 June 1966

Armament: 16 Trident C4 SLBM and four 533mm (21in) torpedo tubes

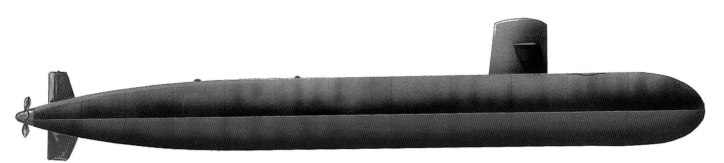

Specifications

Crew: 141

Powerplant: Single shaft; one SSG natural circulation pwr; turbines

Max Speed: 33.3/48.2km/hr (18/26kt) surf/sub

Surface Range: Unlimited

Displacement: 4251/5436t (4450/5350 tons)

surf/sub

Dimensions (length/beam/draught): 95.9 x 11.6 x 7.9m (314.66 x 38 x 25.9ft)

Commissioned: 12 July 1969

Armament: SUBROC and Sub Harpoon missiles; four 533mm (21in) torpedo tubes

▲ USS Narwhal

US Navy, SSN-671

The four torpedo tubes were mounted amidships to allow for a bow-mounted sonar system in addition to a towed sonar array. Many of *Narwhal's* features remain classified; it could probably hold remote-control underwater vehicles, and had sophisticated detection equipment for eavesdropping on Soviet communications. Decommissioned 1 July 1999.

Last years of the Cold War
1975–89

The long stand-off gradually begins to ease, but nuclear submarines remain the key elements in global strategy and gain new tactical roles.

ALTHOUGH PLANNED and ordered before the Falkland/Malvinas War of 1982, the Argentinian Navy did not take delivery of the TR-1700 Santa Cruz class submarine until 1984. Designed by Thyssen-Nordseewerke, they are the biggest submarines built in Germany since World War II.

Originally six boats were provided for: two to be built in Germany and four others under licence in Argentina – two more TR-1700s and two smaller TR-1400 types (later revised back to TR-1700). In the event, construction on the remaining four was suspended in the 1990s, though plans exist to restart the programme. The TR-1700 class is a long-range, high-speed SSK with a diving depth of 300m (990ft), and operating endurance of 30 days, extendable to 70 days. While intended as attack boats, they also have the capacity to carry and land small parties of special forces. *Santa Cruz* was modernized in 1999–2001 in a Brazilian yard, and its sister *San Juan* is also undergoing a refit. The Argentinian Navy still states an intention to develop nuclear submarines.

Brazil

Brazil's Tupi class patrol submarine was inaugurated in 1989. Designed and built by Howaldtswerke-Deutsche Werft (HDW) in Kiel, Germany, a variant on the German U-209 class, it was followed by three others built at the Arsenal de Marinha at Rio in 1994–99. Operating from the Almirante Castro e Silva base on Moncague Island, the Tupi boats are armed with British Tigerfish wire-guided torpedoes and Brazilian anti-submarine torpedoes developed by the Naval Research Institute. An 'improved Tupi' boat, *Tikuna*, was launched in March 2005. The hull design of this vessel was intended to be adaptable to hold a nuclear reactor and turbine drive.

China

The Type 092 (NATO codename *Xia*) was China's first ballistic missile submarine. Laid down in September 1970, it shared the hull form of the Type 091, but lengthened to hold the missile compartment, under a raised deck behind the sail. The pressurized-

▲ **Santa Cruz**

Argentinian Navy, TR-1700 type patrol-attack submarine

Based at Mar del Plata, this high-performance boat has four MTU diesels driving a single shaft, and a Varta-made battery of 8 x 120 cells. A diver's lockout is fitted. Sonar is an STW Atlas Elektronik CSU-83 suite with Thales DUUX-5 passive array, and an integrated battle and data system, with plotting table, is fitted.

Specifications

Crew: 29

Powerplant: Single shaft; diesel-electric

Max Speed: 27.8/46.3km/hr (15/25kt) surf/sub

Surface Range: 22,224km (12,000nm) at 8kt

Displacement: 2150/2,300t (2116/2264 tons) surf/sub

Dimensions (length/beam/draught): 66 x 7.3 x 6.5m (216.58 x 23.9 x 21.25ft)

Commissioned: October 1984

Armament: Six 533mm (21in) torpedo tubes

CHINESE NUCLEAR SUBMARINES				
Class	Type	Number	Year	Note
Type 091 Han	Patrol/attack	5	1974–91	1 decommissioned by 2014
Type 092 Xia	SSBN	1	1983	Status unclear
Type 093 Shang	fast attack	2	2006	4 (093G) in construction
Type 094 Jin	SSBN	4	2006	5th fitting out

water reactor and turbo-electric drive are also taken from the Type 091.

Launch did not take place until 1981 and it was officially commissioned in August 1983. The *Xia* initially carried 12 JuLang I (CSS-N-3) single-warhead ballistic missiles, first tested on 30 April 1982, though successful submerged firing from the *Xia* was not made until September 1987. During a major refit between 1995 and 2001, longer-range JuLang 1A SLBMs were installed. Since the mid-

1980s, the *Xia* has been based at Qingdao naval base, and remains technically on the active list.

France

Having established its nuclear striking force with the Redoutable class, the French Navy began to develop an SSN from 1974 and the class leader *Rubis* was laid down in December 1976. Eight boats were planned and six were eventually completed. *Rubis* was commissioned on 23 February 1983.

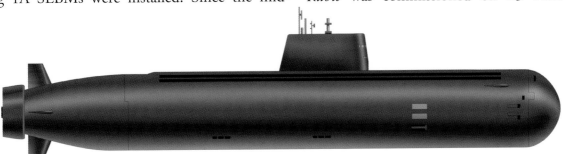

▲ **Tupi**

Brazilian Navy, Type 209/1400 patrol-attack submarine

Brazil shares with Argentina a stated desire to develop a nuclear reactor to power submarines. Meanwhile, the Tupi class is powered by four German 12V 493 A280 GAA 31L diesels from MTU, driving four Siemens alternators rated at 1.8mW, giving a total output of 9655hp.

Specifications

Crew: 30

Powerplant: Four diesel engines; four alternators; single electric motor

Max Speed: 18/44.4km/hr (10/24kt) surf/sub

Surface Range: 20,000km (11,000nm) at 10kt

Displacement: 1422.4/1586t (1400/1550 tons)

surf/sub

Dimensions (length/beam/draught): 61.2 x 6.25 x 5.5m (200.8 x 20.5 x 18ft)

Commissioned: 1989

Armament: Eight 533mm (21in) torpedo tubes; 16 torpedoes

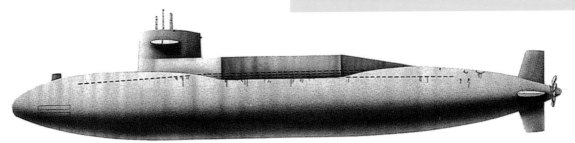

▲ **Xia**

Chinese Navy, SSBN

The prime value of the *Xia* to the PNLA has been in solving technical problems whose solutions can be applied to the following Type 094 class. To mount an effective nuclear deterrent requires at least three SSBNs, of which at least one has to be at sea at any given time.

Specifications

Crew: 140

Powerplant: Single shaft; one pwr; turbo-electric drive

Max Speed: 40.6km/hr (22kt) submerged

Surface Range: Unlimited

Displacement: Not released

Dimensions (length/beam/draught): 120 x 10 x 8m (393.58 x 33 x 26.16ft)

Commissioned: April 1961

Armament: 12 JL1 SBM; six 533mm (21in) torpedo tubes

Substantial redesign was made with the final two boats, incorporating a rounded bow rather than the original blunt front, and the first four boats were rebuilt between 1989 and 1995 to the same shape, which considerably reduced their noise level and also provided space for upgraded sonar equipment.

The relatively light weight of the French-designed K48 pressurized-water reactor helped to keep the boats to an exceptionally compact size for SSNs, though they were provided with diesel-electric auxiliary motors. The weapons control system is the DLA 2B and DLA 3, with the SAT ('système d'armes tactique') tactical data system. Based at Toulon, the class is set to be displaced over the next few years by the Barracuda class SSN.

Great Britain

From 1983, the Trafalgar class has formed the basis of the Royal Navy's hunter-killer submarine capacity. Ordered in April 1977, *Trafalgar* was completed in 1983 and all seven were in service by July 1986.

Developed from the Swiftsure class, the Trafalgars have a new reactor core, pump-jet propulsion and anechoic-tiled hulls. Technical problems have dogged the class and in August 2000 only one boat was operational, while others underwent refit or repair. HMS *Tireless* was stranded at Gibraltar for much of 2000 with a leak in the reactor primary cooling circuit. By 2005, it was officially stated that the problems had been resolved.

In 2001, HMS *Trafalgar* took part in Operation Veritas, launching Tomahawk missiles against targets in Afghanistan. HMS *Triumph* was part of the support fleet for the invasion of Iraq in 2003, again firing Tomahawks against land targets. During the Libyan campaign of 2011, *Triumph* fired six Tomahawks against Libyan air defence systems. HMS *Trafalgar* was decommissioned in 2009 and *Turbulent* in 2012; the others are scheduled to be gradually replaced as the Astute class enters service.

In the early 1980s, British naval planners considered that there was still a role for conventionally powered

FRENCH NUCLEAR SUBMARINES				
Class	Type	Number	Year	Note
Le Redoutable	SSBN	5	1972–80	Decommissioned
Rubis	SSN	4	1988	All active
Amethyste	SSN	2	1992–93	Improved Rubis
Le Triomphant	SSBN	4	1997–2010	All active
Barracuda	SSN	4	2017–27	In progress

▲ **Rubis**

French Navy, Rubis class SSGN

The class carry Exocet SM39 anti-ship missiles, fired from the torpedo tubes; ECAN L5 mod three torpedoes equipped with active and passive homing to a range of 9.5km (6 miles); and ECAN F17 mod-2 torpedoes, wire-guided, with active and passive homing to a range of 20km (12 miles). They can carry 14 missiles/torpedoes.

Specifications

Crew: 67

Powerplant: Single shaft; one auxiliary diesel-
 electric motor

Max Speed: 46.3km/hr25/25kt)

Surface Range: Unlimited

Displacement: 2423 /2713t (2385/2670 tons)

surf/sub

Dimensions (length/beam/draught): 72.1 x 7.6 x
 6.4m (236.5 x 24.9 x 21ft)

Commissioned: 23 February 1983

Armament: Exocet SSM; four 533mm (21in)
 torpedo tubes

submarines, and in 1983 orders were placed for four Type 2400 boats, beginning with HMS *Upholder*; plans for a further eight were cancelled. *Upholder* was finally commissioned in June 1990 and all four were in service by 1993. Despite initial problems with the torpedo firing systems, they were regarded as an effective class, though the hoped-for export sales did not happen. By the early 1990s, it was decided that diesel-electric submarines were not to form part of the British fleet and the Upholders were decommissioned. In 1998, they were sold to Canada and commissioned as the Victoria class in the Royal Canadian Navy between 2000 and 2004, two stationed at Esquimalt, British Columbia, and two at Halifax, Nova Scotia.

Israel

The first Israeli Navy submarines were former British S- and T-class boats of World War II, and the Gal class were its first modern boats. Based on the German Type 206A, they were built for the specific needs of Israel as a small, manoeuvrable boat intended for coastal and inshore operations. Although a German design, they were built in the British yard of Vickers at Barrow in Furness. *Gal* grounded on its way from England to Israel, but was repaired, and was commissioned in 1976, followed by two others. The full mission history of these boats has not been published, but they were undoubtedly involved in many clandestine landing operations, especially during periods of hostilities such as the 1982 Lebanon war. In 1983, they were

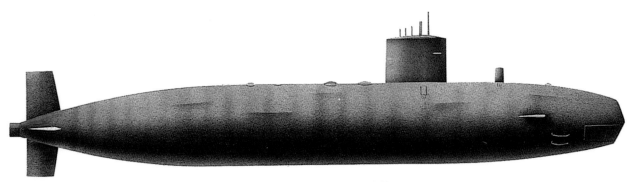

▲ HMS Torbay

Royal Navy, Trafalgar class SSN

The class was first fitted with Type 2020 sonar, but *Torbay* was re-equipped with Type 2076 passive search towed array, claimed to be the most advanced and effective in the world. Electronic warfare and decoy systems are: two SSE Mk8 launchers for Type 2066 and Type 2071 torpedo decoys; RESM Racaul UAP passive intercept; CESM Outfit CXA; and SAWCS decoys.

Specifications

Crew: 130

Powerplant: One pwr; turbines; pump-jet

Max Speed: 37/59.1km/hr (20/32kt) surf/sub

Surface Range: Unlimited

Displacement: 4877/5384t (4800/5300 tons) surf/sub

Dimensions (length/beam/draught): 85.4 x 10 x 8.2m (280.16 x 33.16 x 27ft)

Commissioned: 7 February 1987

Armament: Tomahawk and Sub Harpoon SSM, five 533mm (21in) torpedo tubes

Specifications

Crew: 47

Powerplant: Single shaft; diesel-electric

Max Speed: 22.2/37km/hr (12/20kt) surf/sub

Surface Range: 14,816km (8000nm) at 8kt

Displacement: 2203/2494t (2168/2455 tons) surf/sub

Dimensions (length/beam/draught): 70.3 x 7.6 x 5.5m (230.6 x 25 x 17.6ft)

Commissioned: June 1990

Armament: Sub harpoon SSM; six 533mm (21in) torpedo tubes

▲ HMS Upholder

Royal Navy, patrol submarine

The streamlined teardrop-form single hull is of NQ 1 high-tensile steel. Glass-fibre fins reduce both weight and noise and enable a 20-knot underwater speed. Much of the technology of the nuclear fleet was incorporated, with high levels of automation. A five-man lockout chamber is fitted in the fin.

upgraded to carry the UGM-84 Harpoon missile and its fire-control system. The original Mk37 torpedoes were replaced in 1987 by NT37E types. Further overhauls in 1994–95 provided improved sensors and fire-control systems. The class was decommissioned in 2003. *Gal* is kept as a museum boat in Haifa.

Italy

After the Enrico Toti boats of the 1960s, the next class was the four Sauro patrol submarines, completed between 1980 and 1982, Italy's last home design. The Sauros were much larger, with a wider range and greater versatility than their predecessors.

The tall sail had wide hydroplanes and an extended rear lip. Test diving depth for the class was 300m (984ft), though the hull strength can withstand pressures down to 600m (1970ft) for a brief period. In the 1980s and 1990s, two improved Sauro classes appeared, each of two boats.

Giuliano Prini was the second boat of the Salvatore Pelosi class of 1988–89. The Primo Longobardo class of 1993 had improved combat systems, and were significantly upgraded in 2004, being given new acoustic sensors, Harpoon anti-ship missiles, the ATLAS Elektronik ISUS 90-20 weapons control system, and new communications.

▲ Nazario Sauro

Italian Navy, patrol-attack submarine

Problems with the batteries caused delay in commissioning *Nazario Sauro*, and the second unit, *Carlo Fecia de Cossato*, was commissioned before it (1979 and 1980 respectively). Anti-ship and ASW operations were the designers' prime concern. The Sauros carried 12 torpedoes.

Specifications

Crew: 45

Powerplant: Single shaft; diesel-electric

Max Speed: 20.3/37km/hr (11/20kt) surf/sub

Surface Range: 12,970km (7000nm) at 10kt

Displacement: 1479/1657t (1456/1631 tons) surf/sub

Dimensions (length/beam/draught): 63.9 x 6.8 x 5.7m (209.6 x 22.33 x 18.66ft)

Commissioned: 1980

Armament: Six 533mm (21in) torpedo tubes

Specifications

Crew: 22

Powerplant: Single shaft; two diesel engines; one electric motor

Max Speed: 20.3/31.5km/hr (11/17kt) surf/sub

Surface Range: 7038km (3800nm) at 10kt

Displacement: 427/610t (420/600 tons) surf/sub

Dimensions (length/beam/draught): 45 x 4.7 x 3.7m (147.7 x 15.4 x 12.18ft)

Commissioned: December 1976

Armament: Eight 533mm (21in) torpedo tubes

▲ Gal

Israeli Navy, Type 206 patrol-attack submarine

It is likely that Israel's submarines have been used more often and intensively than any others in coastal and offshore operations, including much activity along the Lebanese coast in the late 1970s and 1980s. Short but intensive patrols and missions are the normal pattern.

The four improved Sauros are now expected to be replaced by Todaro-class boats between 2018 and 2022. A proposal to sell them to the United States for refurbishment and onward sale to Taiwan came to nothing.

Japan

Japan's 10-strong Yuushio class of attack submarine was a development of the preceding Uzushio class, larger and with enhanced diving capacity, the test diving depth being 275m (902ft). Commissioned between 1980 and 1989, they were of double-hull construction and follow the US practice of midship-mounted, outward-angled torpedo tubes in order not to impede the operation of the bow sonar array. From 1984, new boats were fitted to carry the Sub-Harpoon anti-ship missile, and all but *Yuushio* were retrofitted for this weapon. *Yuushio* was used as a training boat from 1996, and the last of the class to be in service was withdrawn in 2008.

The Harushio class, which progressively took over from the Yuushios, was slightly larger than the Yuushios and with improved noise reduction, anechoic material being applied to the hull and fin surfaces. The profiles were very similar, though the Harushio class sail was somewhat higher and shorter. Greater hull strength, using NS 110 high-strength steel, enabled a diving depth of at least 300m (984ft) and perhaps as great as 500m (1640ft). Seven boats were built between 1989 and 1997, with the last,

Asashio, built to a modified design and with greater systems automation, reducing its crew to 71. None of the class remains in active service.

Netherlands

The Dutch Navy began evaluation of its Walrus class of modern diesel-electric attack submarines in 1972, but it was 1990 before the first was commissioned, and four were in service by July 1994. They have an X-configuration of four combined rudders and stern diving planes, used also on the Swedish Sjöormen class, the Australian Collins class and the German Type 212A, which is a major aid to quiet operation. Diving depth, officially 300m (984ft), is probably nearer 400m (1310ft), due to a hull fabricated from French MAREI high-tensile steel. The Dutch submarines lead active lives, on regular patrols and also operating in the North Sea and Atlantic with other NATO vessels, but going as far afield as the Caribbean and the Somali coast in joint ventures against piracy and drug-running.

Peru

One of the most widely used submarine types is the German-designed Type 209. Development work began in the late 1960s and the first boats were launched in 1971. The Type 209 has never been used by the German Navy, but between 1971 and 2008, 61 were commissioned for 13 other navies. It is closely based on the IKL Type 206 design. Single-hulled,

▲ **Giuliano Prini**

Italian Navy, 'improved Sauro' class patrol submarine

Very little different to the Sauros in dimensions, outline and internal layout, the Pelosi class have the same armament but improved sonar, with IPD-703 active/passive, MD1005 passive flank and M5 intercept. Operational endurance is 45 days. They are based with the Second Submarine Group at Augusta, Sicily.

Specifications

Crew: 50

Powerplant: Single shaft; diesel-electric

Max Speed: 20.3/35.2km/hr (11/19kt) surf/sub

Surface Range: 17,692km (9548nm) at 11kt

Displacement: 1500/1689t (1476/1662 tonnes) surf/sub

Dimensions (length/beam/draught): 64.4 x 6.8 x 5.6m (211.16 x 22.25 x 18.4ft)

Commissioned: 1989

Armament: Six 533mm (21in) torpedo tubes

with a test depth of 500m (1640ft), it is a versatile craft that lends itself to many tasks and can carry a variety of different armaments. In 1975, the Peruvian Navy acquired two Type 209/1100 submarines, and between 1980 and 1983 a further four of Type 209/1200. The four Type 209/1200 boats are being upgraded at the Callao and Chimbote yards with new sonar, fire control and communications systems in a programme due to be completed by 2022.

The Soviet Union

From 1972, Soviet Russia developed the Project 667 BDR Kalmar class, codenamed Delta III by NATO. Fourteen were built between 1976 and 1982, double-hulled, with a large, broad turtle-back missile silo set behind the sail. The 16 missiles were R-29R (SS-N-18, Stingray), the first multiple-warhead rockets to be carried on Soviet submarines. Delta III boats were assigned both to the Northern Fleet (at Sayda and Olyenya, then Yagyelnaya from the early 1990s) and the Pacific Fleet based on the Kamchatka Peninsula. Rather than operate in the Atlantic, they were often stationed under thinner sections of the Arctic ice-cap. The sail-mounted hydroplanes could be rotated to vertical when breaking through ice. Withdrawal began in the mid-1990s, and in 2016 no more than three remained active.

Between 1985 and 1992, seven Delta IV boats were built, under Project 667BDRM. Very similar to the Delta IIIs, they are quieter in operation,

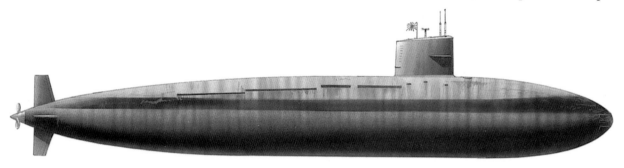

Specifications

Crew: 75	surf/sub
Powerplant: Single shaft; diesel-electric	Dimensions (length/beam/draught): 76 x 9.9 x
Max Speed: 22.2/37km/hr (12/20kt) surf/sub	7.5m (249.25 x 32.5 x 24.6ft)
Surface Range: 17,603km (9500nm) at 10kt	Commissioned: 1980
Displacement: 2235/2774t (2200/2730 tons)	Armament: Six 533mm (21in) torpedo tubes

▲ Yuushio

Japanese Maritime Self-Defence Force, patrol submarine

The Japanese Maritime Self-Defence Force is more reticent than some navies about its submarines. The torpedoes carried on the Yuushio class were Type 89 active-passive with a maximum range of 50km (31 miles). Electronic equipment included ZQQ-5 bow sonar (modification of the US BQS-4) and the ZQR towed array.

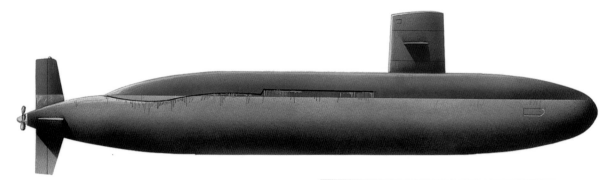

▲ Harushio

Japanese Maritime Self-Defence Force, long-range patrol submarine

This class had a 4630km (2877-mile) greater range than the *Yuushio*, giving it a longer sea endurance. Its greater displacement was accounted for by increased fuel capacity and more electronic equipment. Crew levels in both classes were the same.

Specifications

Crew: 75	Dimensions (length/beam/draught): 77 x 10 x
Powerplant: Single shaft; diesel-electric	7.75m (252.6 x 32.8 x 25.33ft)
Max Speed: 22.2/37km/hr (12/20kt) surf/sub	Commissioned: 1990
Surface Range: 22,236km (12,000nm) at 10kt	Armament: Sub Harpoon SSM; six 533mm (21in)
Displacement: surfaced 2489t (2450/2750 tons)	torpedo tubes
surf/sub	

with more effective hydroacoustic coating and new five-bladed propellers. Six were in service with the Northern Fleet in 2016, though due for replacement by new Borei-class SSBNs.

Simultaneous with the Delta III class was a new fast attack boat in the form of Project 671RTM, Shchuka (Pike), known to NATO as Victor III. Between 1978 and 1992, a total of 26 were added to the fleet. The Victor IIIs have a 6m (20ft) hull extension forward of the fin and a pod mounted above the upper rudder, from which a towed sonar array could be extended. This enlargement provided for the additional electronic equipment required to

process data from the towed array and two new flank arrays. Another prime requirement of the design was quiet running: the Victor I and Victor II classes had been shown to be too easily traceable. Clusterguard anechoic coatings decrease noise levels and bow hydroplanes retract into the hull at high underwater speeds or when surfaced. It is likely that the four Victor III boats commissioned in 1988–92 will remain in service until their reactor core lives expire around 2020.

In the late 1970s, the Rubin Design Bureau was working on Project 941, *Akula*, an SSBN that could carry 20 long-range missiles, each with up to 10

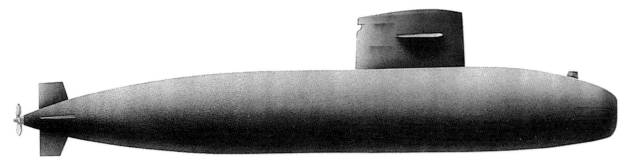

▲ Walrus

Netherlands Navy, patrol-attack submarine

In 2000, the entire class was temporarily withdrawn while problems with the closing valves on the diesel exhaust system were dealt with. From 2007, the four Walrus boats have been refitted and upgraded and can now fire the Mk 48 mod-7 torpedo.

Specifications

Crew: 49	Dimensions (length/beam/draught): 67.5 x 8.4 x
Powerplant: Single shaft; diesel-electric	6.6m (222 x 27.6 x 21.66ft)
Max Speed: 24/37km/hr (13/20kt) surf/sub	Commissioned: 1990
Surface Range: 18,520km (10,000nm) at 9kt	Armament: Four 533mm (21in) torpedo tubes
Displacement: 2490/2800t (2450/2775 tons)	

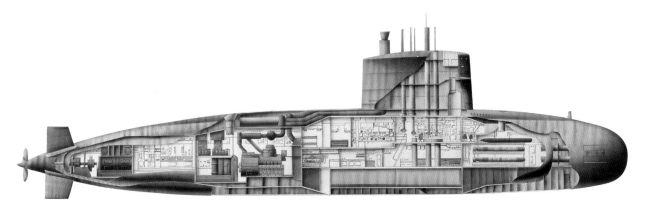

▲ Zeeleeuw

Netherlands Navy, Walrus class patrol-attack submarine

The hull form is based on the *Zwaardvis* (1972), but with ESM radar systems upgraded in 2000; Thomson Sintra TSM 2272 Eledone Octopus, GEC Avionics Type 2026 towed array, Thomson Sintra DUUX 5B passive ranging and intercept sonar; and DECCA 1229 surface search radar. Fire Control is HSA SEWACO VIII action data automation, GTHW integrated.

Specifications

Crew: 49	surf/sub
Powerplant: Single shaft; diesel-electric	Dimensions (length/beam/draught): 67.5 x 8.4 x
Max Speed: 24/37km/hr (13/20kt) surf/sub	6.6m (222 x 27.6 x 21.66ft)
Surface Range: 18,520km (10,000nm) at 9kt	Commissioned: 1988
Displacement: 2490/2800t (2450/2775 tons)	Armament: Four 533mm (21in) torpedo tubes

Specifications

Crew: 35

Powerplant: Single shaft; four diesel engines;
one electric motor

Max Speed: 18/40.6km/hr (10/22kt) surf/sub

Surface Range: 4447km (2400nm) at 8kt

Displacement: 1122/1249t (1105/12340 tons)
surf/sub

Dimensions: 56 x 6.2 x 5.5m (183.75 x 20.25
x 18ft)

Commissioned: 19 December 1980

Armament: Eight 533mm (21in) torpedo tubes

▲ Angamos

Peruvian Navy, Type 209/1200 patrol-attack submarine

Formerly named *Casma*, *Angamos* is one of the four submarines scheduled for upgrading by 2022, with a new combat direction system, new sonar and an upgraded Sepa Mk 3 fire-control system, improved hydrophones and signal processing capacity, replacement of SST-4 torpedoes with the AEG SUT 264 mod 3, and a major overhaul of the propulsion systems.

MIRV nuclear warheads – a total of 200 nuclear weapons. This was comparable with the US Ohio class, but Trident missiles were much lighter than the the Soviet RSM-52 (SS-N-20 Sturgeon), and the submarine had to be scaled accordingly. Given the reporting name Typhoon by NATO, it was the largest submarine yet to be constructed. The design includes features for travelling under ice and ice-breaking through ice cover up to 3m (9ft 10in) thick. The new-design stern fin has horizontal hydroplanes fitted behind the screws, and the nose horizontal hydroplanes are retractable into the hull. In the main body, two pressure hulls lie parallel with a third, smaller pressure hull above them, producing the bulge just below the sail; and two other pressure hulls for torpedoes and steering gear. Maximum diving depth is 400m (1312ft). *Typhoon* can spend at least 120 days submerged.

Between 2005 and 2010 the Typhoon-class *Dmitri Donskoy* was used to carry out flight tests of a new solid fuel SLBM, the SS-N-30 Bulava, reported to have a range of more than 8000km (5000 miles). Six Typhoons were commissioned, with a seventh launched but never completed. Three have been scrapped, with two on reserve. Current deployment is limited to the *Dmitriy Donskoy*.

The Oscar class nuclear-powered cruise missile attack submarine, displacing around 18,289 tonnes (18,000 tons) submerged, was designed, as with earlier SSGNs, primarily to attack US aircraft carrier battle groups. Though said to be slow to dive and cumbersome in manoeuvre, they are credited with a submerged speed of about 30 knots – sufficient to keep pace with their targets. *Oscar II* is about 10m (33ft) longer than *Oscar I*, with a substantially enlarged fin, and replaces *Oscar I*'s four-bladed propeller with a seven-bladed screw. It carries three times as many anti-ship cruise missiles as earlier Charlie and Echo II class submarines. The missiles are launched underwater from tubes fixed at an angle of approximately 400 and arranged in two rows of 12 each, on each side of the sail. The two Oscar I boats were stricken in 1996. Around five Oscar II remained active at the end of 2015, three with the Northern Fleet and two with the Pacific Fleet.

Rubin Bureau designed a new diesel-electric submarine in the late 1970s, Project 877 Paltus (*Halibut*), or *Kilo*. The first entered service with the Soviet Navy in 1980, and 23 others were added up to 1992. Exports were made to Algeria, China, India, Iran, Poland, Romania and Vietnam. It was superseded by Type 636, Improved Kilo, one of the quietest diesel submarines yet built, and equipped with a multi-purpose combat and command system. Most of the Type 636 boats are still active or in reserve. Orders from other countries include 10 for the People's Republic of China, delivered 1997–2005, and two for Algeria (2009). Vietnam took delivery of a 6th Improved Kilo in 2016. Sales to Egypt and Venezuela are also being explored.

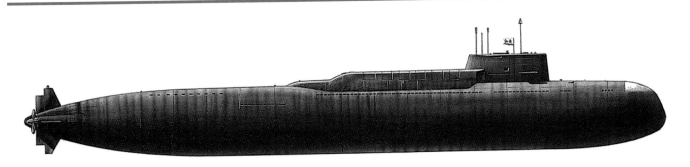

Specifications

Crew: 130

Powerplant: Twin shaft; two pwr; turbines

Max Speed: 26/44.4km/hr (14/24kt) surf/sub

Surface Range: Unlimited

Displacement: 10,791/13.463t (10,550/
13,250 tons) surf/sub

Dimensions (length/beam/draught): 160 x 12 x
8.7 (524.9 x 39.4 x 28.5ft)

Commissioned: 30 December 1976

Armament: 16 SS-N-8 SLBM; four 533mm (21in)
torpedo tubes

▲ Delta III

Soviet Navy, Kalmar class SSBN

The Delta III was fitted with the Almaz-BDR battle-management system for firing deep-water torpedoes. It had the Tobo-M-1 and then the Tobol-M-2 inertial navigation systems and a hydroacoustic navigational system codenamed by NATO as 'Bumblebee', using hydroacoustic buoys to determine position.

▲ Victor III

Soviet Navy, SSN

The class is powered by two OK-300 pressurized water reactors with two turbine generators, driving a single shaft. Two auxiliary diesel-electric motors are provided. The radiated noise level is very low, comparable with the US Los Angeles boats. Maximum diving depth is 400m (1312ft).

Specifications

Crew: 100

Powerplant: Single shaft; two VM-4T pwr; steam
turbine

Max Speed: 44.4/55.5km/hr (24/30kt) surf/sub

Surface Range: Unlimited

Displacement: 4775 x 7305t (4700/7190 tons)

Dimensions (length/beam/draught): 104 x 10 x
7m (347.75 x 32.8 x 23ft)

Commissioned: 1972

Armament: SS-N-15/16/21 SSM; six 533mm
(21in) torpedo tubes

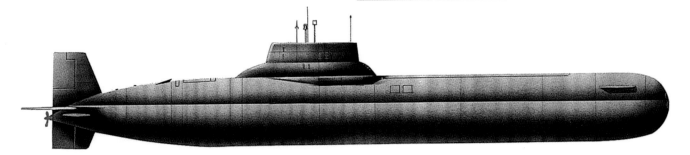

Specifications

Crew: 175

Powerplant: Twin shaft; two pwr; turbines

Max Speed: 44.4/46.3km/hr (12/25kt) surf/sub

Surface Range: Unlimited

Displacement: 18,797/26,925t (18,500/
26,500 tons) surf/sub

Dimensions (length/beam/draught): 171.5 x 24.6
x 13m (562.6 x 80.6 x 42.5ft)

Commissioned: 12 December 1981

Armament: 20 SS-N-20 SLBM; four 630mm
(25in) and two 533mm (21in) torpedo tubes

▲ Typhoon

Soviet Navy, SSBN

The two reactors drive two 50,000hp steam turbines and four 3200kW turbogenerators. Twin propellers are seven-blade, fixed-pitch shrouded. The two built-in thrusters on the bow and stern are telescopic turning screw rudders, powered by a 750kW motor. Despite their huge bulk, these are perhaps the quietest Soviet submarines yet built.

▲ Oscar I

Soviet Navy, SSGN

Like most Soviet submarines, the *Oscar* had a double hull – an inner pressure hull and an outer hydrodynamic hull, with 20cm (8in) of rubber between them to muffle sounds. The 3.5m (11.5ft) separation between the *Oscar*'s inner and outer hulls provided significant reserve buoyancy and improved survivability against conventional torpedoes.

Specifications

Crew: 130

Powerplant: Twin shaft; two pwr; turbines,

Max Speed: 40.7/55.5km/hr (22/30kt) surf/sub

Surface Range: Unlimited

Displacement: 11,685/13,615t (11,500/13,400 tons) surf/sub

Dimensions (length/beam/draught): 143 x 18.2 x 9m (469.18 x 59.66 x 29.5ft)

Commissioned: April 1980

Armament: SS-N-15/16/19 SSM; four 650mm (25.6in) and four 533mm (21in) torpedo tubes

▲ Kilo

Soviet Navy, patrol-attack submarine

Kilo is formed of six watertight compartments separated by transverse bulkheads in a pressurized double-hull. This design and the submarine's good reserve buoyancy lead to increased survivability if the boat is holed, even with one compartment and two adjacent ballast tanks flooded.

Specifications

Crew: 45

Powerplant: Single shaft; three diesels; three electric motors,

Max Speed: 27.8/44.4km/hr (15/24kt) surf/sub

Surface Range: 11,112km (6000nm) at 7kt

Displacement: 2494/393t (2455/3143 tons)

surf/sub

Dimensions (length/beam/draught): 69 x 9 x 7m (226.4 x 29.5 x 23ft)

Commissioned: 1980 (first units)

Armament: Six 533mm (21in) torpedo tubes

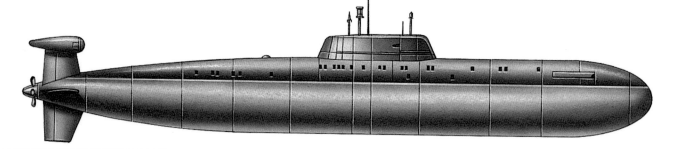

Specifications

Crew: 61

Powerplant: Single shaft; one pwr; single turbine

Max Speed: 18/59.2km/hr (10/32kt) surf/sub

Surface Range: Unlimited

Displacement: 7112/8230t (7000/8100 tons) surf/sub

Dimensions (length/beam/draught): 107 x 12.5 x 8.8m (351 x 41 x 28.9ft)

Commissioned: 1987

Armament: SS-N-15 and SS-N-21 SSMs; four 650mm (25.6in) and four 533mm (21in) torpedo tubes

▲ Sierra

Soviet Navy, SSN

The hull has six major compartments: torpedo room and battery; crew quarters, officers' mess and galley; command centre, computer complex and diesel generators; reactor; main switchboard, pumps and geared turbines; and electric motors, steering gear and pumps. A crew escape chamber is capable of bringing up the entire crew from a depth of 460m (1510ft).

▲ Kilo class

A Kilo-class submarine makes contact with warships from the Indian Navy. The Kilo class can be easily identified by their teardrop-shaped hull.

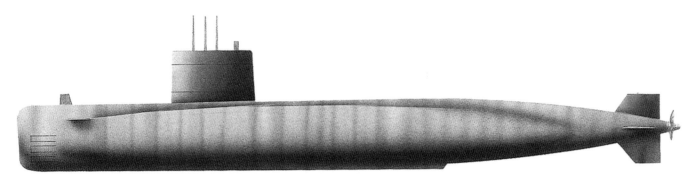

▲ Galerna

Spanish Navy, Agosta-type patrol-attack submarine

Two of *Galerna's* sister boats, *Tramontana* and *Mistral*, were engaged in Operation Protector off the coast of Libya during March to June 2011. *Mistral* is currently undergoing a major refit at Cartagena, intended to keep it viable until 2020, leaving two of the class in service; the fourth has been withdrawn.

Specifications

Crew: 54	surf/sub
Powerplant: Single shaft; diesel-electric	Dimensions (length/beam/draught): 67.6 x 6.8 x
Max Speed: 22.2/37km/hr (12/20kt) surf/sub	5.4m (221.75 x 22.33 x 17.75ft)
Surface Range: 13,672km (7378nm) at 9kt	Commissioned: 1983
Displacement: 1473/1753t (1450/1725 tons)	Armament: Four 551mm (21.7in) torpedo tubes

For 10 years, Project 945 had been working on an attack submarine that could outfight any other, resulting in a single SSN, commissioned in September 1984, with a second in 1987, both classified by NATO as Sierra I. With some different features, two more Project 945A Kondor (Sierra II) were completed in 1992 and 1993, after the fall of the Soviet Union.

Hull construction is of titanium alloy, providing very deep diving capability, to 700m (2300ft) with an outer maximum of 800m (2625ft) and the ability to avoid magnetic anomaly detection. Further

additions to the class were cancelled in favour of of the new Project 971 Akula class. The first Sierra I, named first *Karp*, then *Tula*, has been withdrawn. Its sister, *Krab*, is on the active list, as are the two Sierra II, *Nizhniy Novgorod* and *Pskov*.

Spain

Four submarines of the French Agosta class, built at Cartagena, were commissioned in 1983–86. Designated SSK, they are versatile and adaptable boats, forming the main element of the Spanish Navy's submarine arm into the twenty-first century.

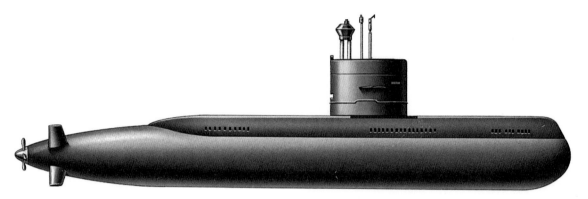

▲ **Näcken**

Swedish Navy, patrol-attack submarine

US Kollmorgen periscopes were fitted and all boats had the Data Saab NEDPS combined ship control and action information system. Wire-guided torpedoes of passive Type 613 for anti-ship strikes were fitted, as well as Type 431 active/passive anti-submarine torpedoes fired from the 400mm (15.7in) tubes.

Specifications

Crew: 19	Dimensions (length/beam/draught): 44 x 5.7 x
Powerplant: Single shaft; diesel-electric	5.5m (144.33 x 18.66 x 18ft)
Max Speed: 37/46.3km/hr (20/25kt) surf/sub	Commissioned: 25 April 1980
Surface Range: 3335km (1800nm) at 10kt	Armament: Six 533mm (21in) and two 400mm
Displacement: 996/1168t (980/1150 tons)	(15.7in) torpedo tubes
surf/sub	

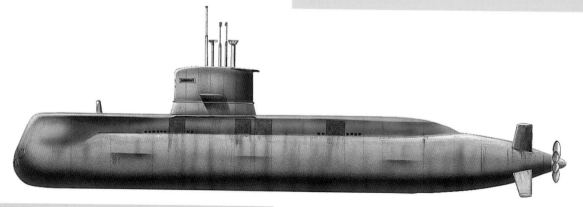

Specifications

Crew: 28	Dimensions (length/beam/draught): 48.5 x 6.1 x
Powerplant: Single shaft; diesel-electric	5.6m (159.18 x 20 x 18.4ft))
Max Speed: 19.8/37km/hr (11/20kt) surf/sub	Commissioned: 27 November 1987
Surface Range: Not released	Armament: Six 533mm (21in) and three 400mm
Displacement: 1087/1161t (1070/1143 tons)	(15.75in) torpedo tubes
surf/sub	

▲ **Västergotland**

Swedish Navy, patrol-attack submarine

A high-performance single-hulled patrol-attack submarine. Bow and stern parts were built at the Karlskrona yard, and the central section by Kockums at Malmö. They have x-format stern control planes and other features include a Pilkington Optronics search periscope with night vision.

Sea endurance range is 45 days and diving depth is 300m (984ft). Sensors and processing equipment include Thomson CSF DRUA 33 radar, Thomson Sintra DSUV 22, DUUA 2D, DUU 1D, DUUX 2 sonar plus DSUV 62A towed array. Updating and upgrading of equipment has taken place. In 2011, *Galerna* was fitted with a WECDIS NAV/C2S system, which integrates information from the navigation sensors with official ENC (electronic nautical cartography) data. Three of the four were still active in 2016.

Sweden

Sweden ordered three new submarines in 1972, from Kockums at Karlskrona. Commissioned in 1980–81, officially the A-14 type, they were usually known as the Näcken class, after the lead boat. Of compact design, with teardrop hull and two internal decks, their prime function was to intercept incursions into Swedish territorial waters. Deep diving was not required and maximum operational depth was 150m (490ft), but they were highly manoeuvrable. In 1987–88, *Näcken* was lengthened by 8m (26ft 3in) to accommodate two United Stirling Type V4 closed-cycle engines, with liquid-oxygen fuel. The AIP drive gave it a submerged endurance of 14 days. The electronics were updated in the early 1990s, but were all withdrawn later in the decade, except *Näcken*, transferred to Denmark as *Kronborg* on a

buy-or-lease arrangement between 2001 and 2005, and currently stored at Karlskrona.

Four SSK boats of the A-17 or Västergotland class were commissioned between 1987 and 1989. In 2003–04, the second two were refitted, extended by 12m (37ft), and provided with Stirling-type AIP engines as tested on *Näcken*. New weapons systems and stealth improvements were incorporated, and in this form they were redesignated as the Södermanland class, considered by many experts to be the quietest and most effective 'conventional' submarines in service anywhere. The first two boats were refitted for service in high-salinity tropical waters and sold to Singapore in 2008 as the Archer class. Sweden's two Södermanland-class boats remain in service.

Taiwan

At times during the Cold War, relations between Taiwan (Republic of China) and the People's Republic of China were extremely tense. For coastal defence, Taiwan ordered two SSK type boats from the Netherlands. As the Hai Lung (Sea-dragon) class, a modified version of the Dutch *Zwaardvis* attack submarine, they were commissioned in October 1987 and April 1988.

Beijing's diplomatic pressure prevented a further sale of four boats in 1992, and so far Taiwan has been unable to enlarge its submarine fleet. In 2008, the

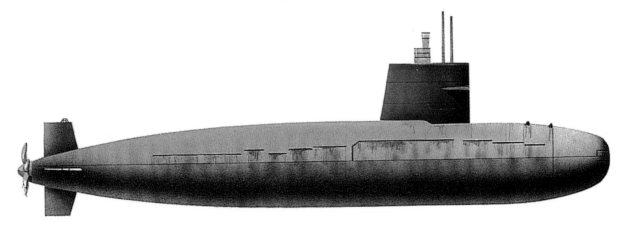

Specifications

Crew: 67

Powerplant: single shaft; three diesel engines; one electric motor

Max Speed: 19.8/37km/hr (11/20kt) surf/sub

Surface Range: 19,000km (10,241nm) at 9kt

Displacement: 2414/2702t (2376/2660 tons) surf/sub

Dimensions (length/beam/draught): 66 x 8.4 x 7.1m (216.5 x 27.6 x 23.33ft)

Commissioned: 1987

Armament: Six 533mm (21in) torpedo tubes

▲ Hai Lung

Taiwanese Navy, improved Zwaardvis-type patrol submarine

The Zwaardvis type teardrop hull design was in turn based on that of USS *Barbel*, the last US diesel-electric submarine. *Hai Lung's* dimensions were almost identical. Power came from three diesel engines rated at 42,000hp (3100kW) driving a Holec electric motor of 5100hp (3800kW) and a single shaft.

United States allowed the sale of UGM-84 Harpoon Block II missiles to Taiwan and it is believed that the two Hai Lung boats have the capacity to deploy these, in addition to their AEG SUT dual-purpose wire-guided, active/passive homing torpedoes. In 2014, Taiwan announced plans to acquire from four to eight new submarines, either home-built or bought from other builders.

United States

The Los Angeles or 688 class of fast attack submarine is numerically the largest in the world, with 62 commissioned between 1976 and 1996. They are equipped for anti-submarine warfare, intelligence gathering, show-of-force missions, insertion of special forces, strike missions, mining, and search and rescue. The last 23 boats, built since 1982, beginning with USS *San Juan*, known as Improved 688, incorporate upgraded weapons and electronic systems, are quieter in operation and are configured for under-ice operation, with the diving planes moved from the sail to the bow.

Other developments include an improved propulsion system and Navstar Global Positioning System (GPS) guidance capability. The Los Angeles class has participated in all US global operations. Nine were deployed in the Gulf War in 1991, during which Tomahawk missiles were launched from two of the submarines. Twelve were deployed in support of Operation Iraqi Freedom in March to April 2003. All launched Tomahawk TLAM missiles. Later operations have included strikes on targets in

▲ **USS *Los Angeles***

USS *Los Angeles* was the Navy's longest-serving vessel when it was decommissioned in February 2011.

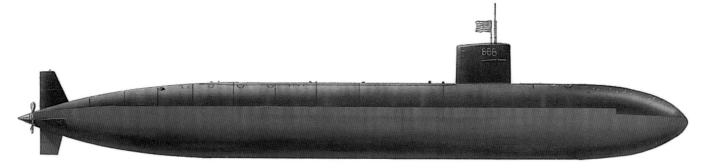

▲ **USS Los Angeles**

US Navy, SSN-688

The hull contains two separate watertight compartments, with crew, weapons and control space forward, and most machinery systems aft. The GE PWR S6G reactor needs refuelling only after 30 years' operation. Maximum diving depth is at least 450m (1475ft). Five have been adapted with Dry Dock shelters to allow entrance and exit of SEAL forces.

Specifications

Crew: 133

Powerplant: Single shaft; one S6G pwr; turbines

Max Speed: 37/59.2km/hr (20/32kt) surf/sub

Surface Range: Unlimited

Displacement: 6180/7038t (6082/6.927 tons) surf/sub

Dimensions (length/beam/draught): 110.3 x 10.1 x 9.9m (362 x 33 x 32.25ft)

Commissioned: 13 November 1976

Armament: Tomahawk Land Attack missiles; Harpoon SSM; four 533mm (21in) torpedo tubes

Yemen (2009) and Libya (2011). Forty-three remain on active duty.

USS *San Francisco*, commissioned on 24 April 1981, was stationed from 1981 to 1986 at Pearl Harbor. Following a modernization there in 1989–90, it was deployed in the Western Pacific and from 2002 was based at Apra Harbor, Guam. On 8 January 2005, travelling submerged at approximately 61m (200ft) and at full speed of 25 knots, it struck an uncharted undersea mountain. The forward ballast tanks ruptured and the sonar dome was wrecked, but the inner hull was not breached and the crew were able to bring the boat to the surface. A number of failures in procedures were later identified. *San Francisco*, with a normal life expectancy to 2017, was repaired, its bow section replaced by that of the about-to-be-retired USS *Honolulu*; and in 2009 it resumed service based at San Diego, California.

The basis of the United States' strategic nuclear deterrent remains the Ohio class of SSBN, the largest submarines built for the US Navy, with 18 commissioned between 1981 and 1997.

They carry up to 24 submarine-launched ballistic missiles with multiple independently targeted warheads. Originally, these were Trident I C4, but from the ninth boat, USS *Tennessee*, they carry the Trident II D5, and older boats have been retrofitted. Following the START II arms limitation treaty of June 1992, four were altered from SSBN to SSGN, carrying Tomahawk missiles and capable of tactical operations with special operations forces. Conversion was not completed until 2008. All in this class carry highly sophisticated counter-measures systems, including AN/WLY-1 from Northrop Grumman, providing automatic response against torpedo attack.

Fourteen Ohio-class SSBNs were on the active list in April 2016. The four SSGN boats are also still in service.

Specifications

Crew: 133	Dimensions (length/beam/draught): 110.3 x 10.1
Powerplant: Single shaft; one S6G pwr;, turbines	x 9.9m (362 x 33 x 32.25ft)
Max Speed: 37/59.2km/hr (20/32kt) surf/sub	Commissioned: 24 April 1981
Surface Range: Unlimited	Armament: Tomahawk Land Attack missiles;
Displacement: 6180/7038t (6082/6.927 tons)	Harpoon SSM; four 533mm (21in) torpedo tubes
surf/sub	

▲ **USS San Francisco**

US Navy, Los Angeles class SSN-711

As of 2011, 42 of the Los Angeles class were on the active list, assigned to home ports at: Groton, Connecticut; Norfolk, Virginia; Pearl Harbor, Hawaii; San Diego, California; Apra Harbor, Guam; and Bremerton, Washington. The class is evenly divided between the Atlantic and Pacific Fleets.

▲ **USS Ohio**

US Navy, SSGN-726

The Ohio class like all SSBNs is designed for long-term patrols and they can remain submerged for up to 70 days. The main machinery is the GE PWR S8G reactor with two turbines providing 60,000hp (44,740kW) and driving a single shaft. Major overhauls are required only at 15-year intervals.

Specifications

Crew: 155	18,750 tons) surf/sub
Powerplant: Single shaft; one S8G pwr;, two	Dimensions (length/beam/draught): 170.7 x 12.8
turbines	x 11m (560 x 42 x 36.4ft)
Max Speed: 44.4/51.8km/hr (24/28kt) surf/sub	Commissioned: 11 November 1981
Surface Range: Unlimited	Armament: 24 Trident C4 SLBMs; four 533mm
Displacement: 16,360/19,050t (16,764/	(21in) torpedo tubes

USS *LOS ANGELES*

This cutaway of USS *Los Angeles* shows just how much equipment has to be packed into a hull 110m (362ft) long and 10m (32ft) wide, along with 133 personnel.

Air and water processing

Atmosphere control equipment replenishes oxygen used by the crew, and removes carbon dioxide and other atmosphere contaminants. Two distilling plants convert salt water to fresh for drinking, washing and the propulsion plant.

Decoy canisters

Noise-making decoy canisters can be ejected as part of anti-detection measures.

Control and attack room

Nerve centre of the submarine.

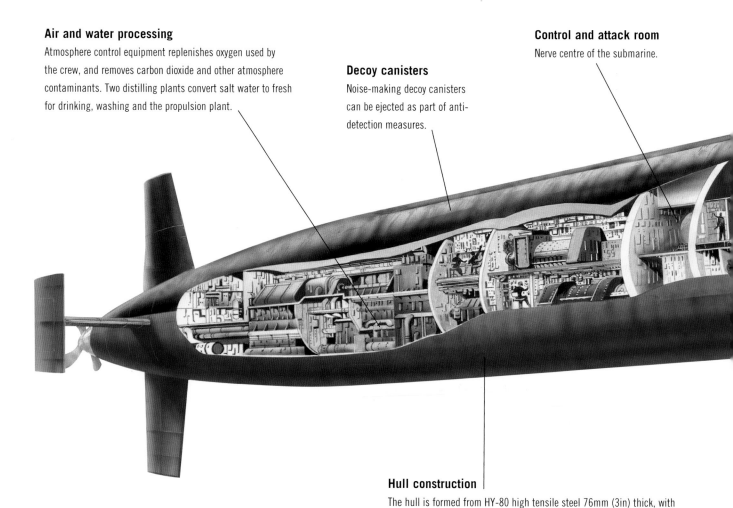

Hull construction

The hull is formed from HY-80 high tensile steel 76mm (3in) thick, with a test depth of 290m (950ft).

Bridge

In the forward top portion of the sail is the bridge. When the submarine is on the surface, the Officer of the Deck shifts his watch from the control room to here. Mess and berthing deck, plus galley. Hot meals are prepared four times a day, in line with the six-hour watches.

Data handling

Sonar processing and analysis room.

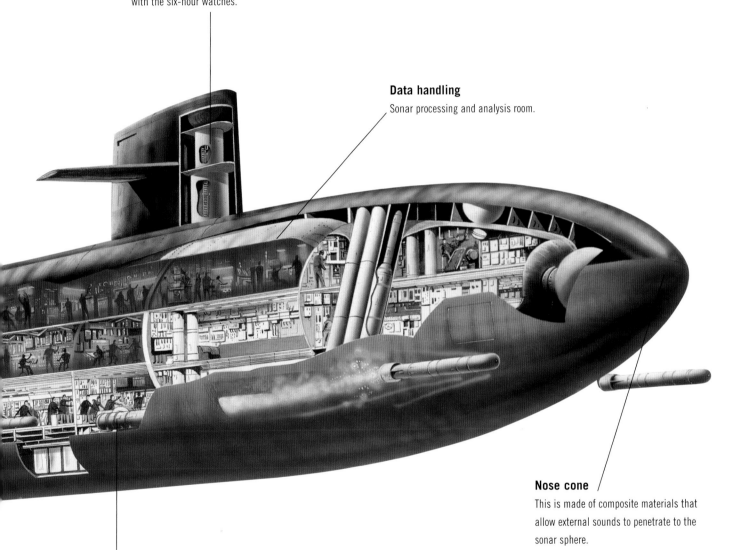

Nose cone

This is made of composite materials that allow external sounds to penetrate to the sonar sphere.

Armament

Torpedo and missile storage room holding 24 weapons, also housing controls for the vertical cruise missile launch tubes.

Chapter 5

Modern Era:
1990–Present

While the US and Russian submarine fleets
continued their patrols and exercises, the end of the Soviet
Union signalled a lower level of rivalry and tension, and the
numbers of nuclear submarines carrying long-range missiles
were greatly reduced. In submarine deployment, attention
switched from oceanic strategy to regional hot spots and
theatres of localized action. China, France, Great Britain,
Russia and the United States all developed new classes
of nuclear submarines, with the emphasis on hunter-killer
abilities, and other nations announced their intention to
join the nuclear club. Meanwhile, new self-contained
power systems and a high level of 'stealth' qualities
also brought about renewed interest in the potential
of the non-nuclear submarine.

◀ **USS *Seawolf* (SSN-21)**

Seen here on trials in 1997, *Seawolf* proved quieter and more manoeuvrable than the Los
Angeles class. But its high cost ruled out further development.

Regional security

With the ending of the Cold War, international naval issues switched from superpower confrontation to the problems raised by regional rivalries and instabilities. This brought a focus on the tactical deployment of submarines in combined and shoreline operations.

AT A STEADY 25 KNOTS, a typical SSN (fast-attack submarine) will cover 1110km (690 miles) in 24 hours, and 7773km (4830 miles) in seven days. Anywhere on the open seas is within a few days' reach, at most, of a nuclear submarine. By contrast, the diesel-engined British submarine *Onyx* took almost four weeks to reach the Falklands war zone in 1982.

From 1990, the world political scene has been typified by localized hot spots and problem areas.

Although all the nuclear-armed powers kept missile submarines at sea on secret patrol, the number of US and Russian active 'boomers' was greatly reduced. In 1989, over 400 nuclear submarines were operational or under construction. By 2011, three quarters had been decommissioned or dismantled. The majority of remaining boats, and of new builds, were designated SSN, or hunter-killers, though this plays down their versatility in intelligence-gathering, special operations

▲ **Collins class**

The Australian Navy Collins class consists of six diesel-electric submarines armed with torpedoes and Harpoon anti-shipping missiles. The blunt-ended bow and the hydroplanes set forward on the fin are trademarks of the class.

EVOLUTION OF THE GERMAN SUBMARINE FROM 1962							
Type	Year	Surface displacement tons/tonnes	Submerged displacement tons/tonnes	Speed knots	Range km/miles	Propulsion	Armament
201	1962–64	350/356	443/450	17.5	4800/2982	D/E	Torpedoes/mines
205	1967–70	450/456	500/508	17	7800/4847	D/E	Torpedoes/mines
206	1968–75	450/456	490/498	17	8300/5157	D/E	Torpedoes/mines
209	1971–	1427/1450	1781/1810	22.5	20,000/12,427	D/E	Torpedoes; UGM-84 missile
212	2002	1663/1690	1801/1830	20	14,800/9196	D/E +AIP	Torpedoes; short-range missiles
214	2007–	1690/1717	1830/1860	20	19,300/11,992	D/E +AIP	Torpedoes; UGM-84 missile

and in firing missiles at static land targets, in the course of regional operations. SSNs' roles in operations like the Libyan campaign in 2011 and the Iraq War of 2005 have been largely restricted to providing defence and support to task force groups. Bombardment of land targets from submarines was a minor aspect. Possibly secret operations along coastlines were also involved.

Nuclear Submarines

By 2016, the US Navy had 75 active nuclear submarines, of which 18 carried ballistic or guided missiles and the rest were SSNs (the US SSN force has been cut by almost 40 per cent since 1994; one consequence of reduction has been to extend crew deployment from six to seven months at a time, from March 2007). The Russian Navy had approximately 22 SSN-type nuclear boats and 26 missile carriers. Great Britain had seven SSN and four SSBN, while France had six SSN and four SSBN, and China was believed to have some 13 nuclear submarines, mostly of SSN type. India has joined the nuclear submarine club, and Argentina and Brazil have announced the same ambition or intention.

Important advances have also been made with non-nuclear submarines. On more than one occasion in the last two decades, a non-nuclear boat has shown itself capable of passing undetected through supposedly unerring detection systems. The US Navy got a shock in late 2007 when a Chinese Type 039 – completely undetected – surfaced in the middle of a carrier group, well within striking range of the nuclear carrier *Kitty Hawk*.

The ocean floor is nowadays mapped almost as extensively as the land surface. Highways and lurking areas are identified, followed and used. On one such route, the French missile boat *Le Triomphant* and the British SSN *Vanguard* were involved in a glancing collision in mid-Atlantic in February 2009 (both were repaired). Submarines can cut telephone cables and lay others, and plant 'road signs' either for their own use or to mis-route others.

Slowdown

In recent years, submarine construction has slowed, and not merely because of global economic downturn. Submarines and their attack, detection and defence systems have become hugely expensive. When a new one, even of conventional drive, costs in excess of $400 million, buyers hesitate. Yet world demand for reliable, effective and up-to-date submarines is greater than ever. The French Scorpène competes for orders against such rivals as the German Type 214 and the Russian Kilo.

Even the United States, in planning the Virginia-class SSN from around 2004, had to institute the Technology Barriers programme with the aim of halving the cost of new submarines without reducing their effectiveness. It included: propulsion concepts not constrained by a centreline shaft; externally stowed and launched weapons (especially torpedoes); conformal alternatives to the existing spherical sonar array; technologies that eliminate or substantially simplify current hull, mechanical and electrical systems; and automation to reduce crew workload (and numbers) for standard tasks.

Submarines today
1990–2016

The submarine has come a long way from the submersible torpedo boats of a century ago.

POSSESSING MORE DESTRUCTIVE power than all the capital ships of World War I, whether seen as a weapon of aggression or an instrument of peace-keeping, the submarine is unquestionably a marvel of technology and a key piece in international power-play.

Australia
The Royal Australian Navy (RAN) contracted for six diesel electric SSK boats with the Swedish builders, Kockums in June 1987. Construction work was done partially in Sweden and partially at Adelaide, and the boats were commissioned into the RAN between 1996 and 2003. Australia's strategic concerns required a long-range boat, and the Collins class, with a range of 18,496km (11,500 miles) at 10 knots, and a sea endurance of 70 days, are capable of extended patrols.

Sophisticated electronic systems are standard, including the ES-5600 electronic support sensor. Two Strachan and Henshaw submerged signal and decoy ejectors (SSDE) are carried; the forged unit containing the ejector barrel and water ram is welded into the hull. *Collins* deploys the Thales Underwater

Systems Scylla active and passive bow array sonar, and passive flank, intercept and ranging arrays.

The class has been subject to numerous problems and no more than two or three are operational at any one time. Their service life is expected to last until 2025, and further refitting with US assistance is in progress. In 2016 the Australian government is due to decide on a replacement type, with Japan, France and Sweden competing for the contract.

China
China maintains development of diesel-electric submarines. The Type 039 (codenamed Song by NATO) was first commissioned in June 1999: an ocean-going SSK with a teardrop-shaped hull. Revisions to the design came early, and only the first boat has a sail with a stepped-up rear section; all subsequent boats are classed as 039G. A multi-role combat and command system provides all the data needed for control of the boat and for the firing of torpedoes and missiles. This is likely to be an updated derivative of the combat/command system used in the Ming class submarines. The integrated sonar

▲ **Collins**

Royal Australian Navy, patrol submarine

The *Collins* has a single skew-back propeller, powered by three Hedemora/Garden Island Type V18B/14 four-stroke turbo charged diesels, each providing 1475kW. Jeumont Schneider of France supplied the three 1400kW 440V DC generators. The main motor is a water cooled DC shunt, double armature motor with rated power of 5250kW.

Specifications

Crew: 42

Powerplant: Single shaft; Diesel-electric

Max Speed: 18/37km/hr (10/20kt) surf/sub

Surface Range: 18,496km (9982nm) at 1kt

Displacement: 3100/3407t (3051/3353 tons) surf/sub

Dimensions (length/beam/draught): 77.8 x 7.8 x 7m (255.18 x 25.6 x 23ft)

Commissioned: 27 July 1996

Armament: Sub Harpoon SSM; six 533mm (21in) torpedo tubes

system comprises an active/passive medium-frequency spherical bow-mounted equipment and passive low-frequency reach arrays. The countermeasures suite comprises just the Type 921-A radar warning receiver and directional finder. The diesel-electric propulsion arrangement comprises four German MTU 16V396 SE diesel engines, four alternators and one electric motor, powering a single shaft.

Thirteen Song boats are in service, along with 15 of the considerably larger Type 039A Yuan class (introduced in 2006 and ultimately to number 20) that have AIP propulsion. Their prime use is likely to be in maintaining Chinese claims to islands like the Spratly group in the South China Sea, and monitoring the US observation-ships stationed just off China's territorial limits.

The next generation of Chinese attack submarines is the Type 093 (NATO codename Shang) replacement for the Han class. Two boats have been launched, and the first, after four years of trials, was commissioned into the PNLA Navy in 2006. The second may also be in service. Powered by a pressurized-water reactor and with a new bow sonar and three flank arrays (H/SQG-207) on each side of the hull, it can fire wire-guided torpedoes and launch YJ-82 AshMs anti-ship missiles. Further Type 093 submarines have been reported as under construction, but may be abandoned in favour of a new-design Type 095.

▲ **Type 039 Song class**

Chinese Navy, Type 039 multi-role submarine

The Song class is driven by one large seven-bladed propeller, and the primary machinery is located on shock-absorbent mountings for reduced vibration and minimized underwater noise radiation. The stealthiness of the design is further enhanced by the use of anechoic tiling similar to that used on the Russian Kilo-class boats.

Specifications

Crew: 60

Powerplant: Single dhsft; three diesel engines

Max Speed: 27.8/41km/hr (15/22kt)

Surface Range: Not available

Displacement: 1700/2250t (1673/2215 tons) surf/sub

Dimensions (length/beam/draught): 74.9 x 8.4 x 5.3m (245.7 x 27.5 x 17.4ft)

Commissioned: June 1999

Armament: Six 533mm (21in) torpedo tubes; 18 torpedoes/missiles or 36 mines

▲ **Shang class**

Chinese Navy, Type 093 SSN

Few details are known for certain, but the Shang class is double-hulled and has six torpedo tubes, for anti-surface and anti-submarine torpedoes and also for anti-ship missiles. It may also be fitted to launch land-attack cruise missiles. Closed-loop fire control enables discharge of all missiles in two minutes.

Specifications

Crew: about 100

Powerplant: Single shaft; one gas-cooled reactor

Max Speed: 64.8km/hr (35kt) submerged

Surface Range: Unlimited

Displacement: c6090–7110t (6000-7000 tons) surf/sub

Dimensions (length/beam/draught): 110 x 11 x 10m (361 x 36 x 32.8ft)

Commissioned: 2006

Armament: Six launch tubes for torpedoes/ YJ-82 anti-ship missiles

Specifications

Crew: 111

Powerplant: Single shaft; one pwr, pump-jet; diesel auxiliary

Max Speed: 37/46.3km/hr (20/25kt) surf/sub

Surface Range: Unlimited

Displacement: 12,842/14,335t (12,640/

14,565 tons) surf/sub

Dimensions (length/beam/draught): 138 x 17 x 12.5m (453 x 77.75 x 41ft)

Commissioned: 21 March 1997

Armament: 16 M45/TN75 SLBM; four 533mm (21in) torpedo tubes

▲ Le Triomphant

French Navy, SSBN

In line with French policy and planning, the electronic systems used are mostly of French manufacture. Sensors and processing systems are Thales DMUX 80, Sonar DUUX 5, Donar DSUV 61B VLF. Racal Decca navigation radar is installed. Thales also supply the DR3000U electronic support system.

Specifications

Crew: 31

Powerplant: Diesel-electric motors; battery/AIP

Max Speed: 22/37km/hr (12/20kt) surf/sub

Surface Range: 12,000km (6500nm) at 8kt

Displacement: 1870t (1840.4 tons) submerged

Dimensions (length/beam/draught): 70 x 6.2 x 5.8m (229.6 x 20.3 x 19ft)

Commissioned: From 2005

Armament: Six 533mm (21in) launch tubes for torpedoes/SM39 Exocet, or 30 mines

▲ Scorpène

French CM-2000 patrol submarine

The *Scorpène* hull can carry 18 heavyweight torpedoes or missiles, or 30 mines. It can fire the latest wire-guided torpedo types and can be adapted as an anti-ship, anti-submarine or dual-purpose attack boat.

Specifications

Crew: 60

Powerplant: One K15 reactor; turboreductors; pump jet

Max Speed: 26/46km/hr (14/25kt) surf/sub

Surface Range: Unlimited

Displacement: 4765/5300t (4689/5216.3 tons)

Dimensions (length/beam/draught): 99.4 x 8.8 x 7.3m (326 x 28.9 x 24ft)

Commissioned: Not yet in commission

Armament: Four 533mm (21in) launch tubes for torpedoes; MDCN SCALP and Exocet SM39 Block2 missiles

▲ Barracuda

French Navy, new generation SSN

The high level of automation integrated into the submarine's operational and mission systems will allow the submarine a complement of 60 (in two crews) compared to 78 in the Rubis and Amethyste Classes. The operational cost will be reduced by 30 per cent compared to that of the Rubis Class.

France

In 1997, *Le Triomphant* entered service as the first of the French Navy's new class of SSBN. Three more were commissioned between 2000 and 2010 and since then at least one has been permanently on patrol, armed with 16 M45 ballistic missiles. The final boat, *Le Terrible*, has been fitted with the enhanced M51 version as of 2010, with 12 multiple independently targetable re-entry vehicles (MIRVs) and a range of 8000km (5000 miles), and these will be fitted to the other members of the class by 2018. France's SSBNs are based at Ile Longue, Brest.

Through the DCNS (formerly DCN) company of Cherbourg, France is a contender in the export market for non-nuclear submarines. Originally in conjunction with the Spanish Navantia company, the *Scorpène* diesel-electric attack boat was developed. The joint programme collapsed with Spain opting for Navantia's S-80 design built in association with the US Lockheed-Martin Corporation (this much-delayed project is due to see its first launch in 2017).

Though the French Navy uses only nuclear submarines, DCNS continued to develop Scorpène as an export-only project. The basic form is the CM-2000 with diesel-electric propulsion, but also on offer are the lengthened AM-2000 with the French MESMA system of air-independent propulsion, and the CA-2000, a smaller version intended for coastal operations. Sales have been made to Chile, Brazil, Malaysia and India, with design variations made to suit these navies' requirements. In India it is known as the Kalvari class, with one undergoing sea trials and five more on order. Plans to acquire a further three have been announced.

In France, the Barracuda project has been under way since 1998 in order to ensure availability of a state-of-the-art nuclear attack submarine from 2017. Six boats are planned. The Barracuda class will have a displacement of about 4100 tonnes (4035 tons) surfaced, an increase of 70 per cent compared to the Amethyste-class submarines.

The class (first boat to be named *Suffren*) incorporates a range of diving, safety and damage control technologies and an integrated platform management system (IPMS). Many of the technologies developed by DCN for the Le Triomphant class and by Izar and DCN for the Agosta and Scorpène Classes are being incorporated.

A range of stealth technologies will minimize the acoustic, magnetic, radar and visual signatures, enabling silent running and manoeuvrability for the ASW role. DCN and Thales are creating a

CURRENT CONVENTIONAL SUBMARINES (I)							
Type	Year	Surface displacement tons/tonnes	Submerged displacement tons/tonnes	Speed knots	Range km/miles	Propulsion	Armament
Kilo Russia et al	1981	2300/2350	3000/3048	25	12,070/7,500	D/E	Torpedoes; missiles
Hai Lung Taiwan	1986	2338/2376	2618/2660	20	20,000/12,427	D/E	Torpedoes
Archer Singapore	1987/2011	1070/1050	1130/1150	20		D/E +AIP	Torpedoes; mines
Collins Australia	1996	3003/3051	3300/3353	25	12,070/7,500	D/E	Torpedoes; UGM-84 Harpoon; mines
Victoria Canada	1990	2220/2255	2455/2494	20	20,000/12,427	D/E	Torpedoes
Dolphin I Israel	1997–	1640/1666	1900/1930	20		D/E	Torpedoes; missiles (nuclear warheads)
Dolphin II Israel	2014–	2050/ 2083	2400/2438	25+		D/E	AIP torpedoes; missiles (nuclear warheads)

bespoke combat system, integrating active and passive sensors, electronic, optronic and optical sensors and data processing, signal processing of downloaded external tactical data, fire control, communications and navigation.

Germany

The HDW Type 214 is a strong contender among the diesel-electric submarines available for international sales. Diesel-electric propulsion, with a low-noise seven-blade skew-back propeller, is backed up by an AIP system using Siemens polymer electrolyte membrane (PEM) hydrogen fuel cells. Eight 533mm (21in) torpedo tubes can fire heavyweight torpedoes and four can also fire Sub-Harpoon missiles. Twenty-four torpedoes/missiles can be carried. The diesel generator plant is mounted on a swinging deck platform with double elastic mounts for noise and vibration isolation.

In most cases, only the lead ship has been built by ThyssenKrupp Howaldtwerke. Confirmed customers building the class under licence include South Korea (Son Won II class) with six vessels by 2015 and six more to be completed by 2020; Turkey with an order for six (Type 214TN) confirmed in July 2011, suffering delay and unlikely to be commissioned before 2018; Portugal with two delivered in 2010–11; and Greece, with one boat, *Papanikolis*, in service.

Another is undergoing upgrade and two have been awaiting launch since 2013, the delay due to Greece's financial crisis, a change in ownership of the Skaramagas shipyards, evidence of corruption in the purchasing process, and criticisms of Papanikolis's performance.

Specifications

Crew: 27

Powerplant: Single shaft; diesel-electric; battery; fuel-cell AIP

Max Speed: 22.2/37km/hr (12/20kt) surf/sub

Surface Range: 19,300km (10,420nm)

Displacement: 1690/1860t (1663.3/ 1830.6 tons) surf/sub

Dimensions (length/beam/draught): 65 x 6.3 x 6m (213.25 x 20.6 x 19.6ft)

Commissioned: 4 November 2010

Armament: Eight 533mm (21in) launch tubes for torpedoes/missiles

▲ **Papanikolis**

German-designed Type 214 multi-role submarine

Type 214 is a high-performance boat capable of diving to 400m (1312ft) or more, and with an endurance period of 84 days. As an export-sales boat, many features vary between those of different navies, but all share the pressure hull of HY-80/HY-100 high tensile steel, shaped to optimize hydrodynamic and stealth aspects.

Type	Year	Surface displacement tons/tonnes	Submerged displacement tons/tonnes	Speed knots	Range km/miles	Propulsion	Armament
Oyashio Japan	1996	2706/2750	3937/4000	20		D/E	Torpedoes; UGM-84 torpedoes; missiles
Song China	1999		2214/2250	22		D/E +AIP	Torpedoes; Yu-4 missiles; mines
Scorpène CM2000 France et al	2005–	1540/1565	1673/1700	20	12,000/7,546	D/E +AIP	Torpedoes; Exocet SM39; mines

CURRENT CONVENTIONAL SUBMARINES (II)

Great Britain

The Royal Navy deploys four SSBNs, all of the Vanguard class, built between 1986 and 1999. They are the largest submarines built by Britain, designed specifically as carriers for the Trident D5 SLBM. The two periscopes are a CK51 search model and a CH91 attack model, both with TV and thermal imaging cameras in addition to conventional optics. The Thales Underwater Systems Type 2054 composite sonar is fitted. This is a multi-mode, multi-frequency system, incorporating the 2046, 2043 and 2082 sonars. The Type 2043 is a hull-mounted active/passive search sonar, the Type 2082 a passive intercept

and ranging sonar, and the Type 2046 a towed array sonar operating at very low frequency, providing a passive search capability. Upgrading of the sonars includes open-architecture processing. Navigational search capability is provided by a Type 1007 I-band navigation radar installation.

The Vanguard submarines are based at Faslane on the Firth of Clyde. The oldest two have both undergone major refits, *Vanguard* in 2002–04 and *Victorious* in 2004–06. *Vigilant* completed a refit in 2012. From 2017, they will be progressively withdrawn. Development work on a successor class is in progress.

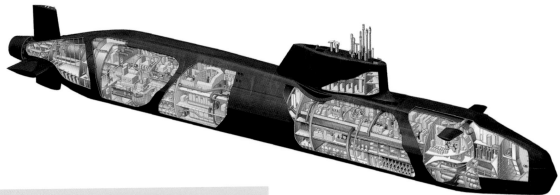

Specifications

Crew: 135	Dimensions (length/beam/draught): 97 x 11.3 x
Powerplant: Single shaft; one pwr; two turbines,	10m (323 x 37 x 33ft)
Max Speed: 56+km/hr/29+kt (submerged)	Commissioned: 27 August 2010
Surface Range: Unlimited	Armament: Six 533mm (21in) launch tubes for
Displacement: 7000/7400t (6889/7283 tons)	Spearfish torpedoes/Tomahawk Block IV TLAM;
surf/sub	38 weapons

▲ **HMS Astute**

Royal Navy, new generation SSN

Astute's six 533mm (21in) torpedo tubes discharge Spearfish torpedoes and mines. There is capacity for a total of 38 torpedoes and missiles. The BAE Systems Spearfish is wire-guided with an active/passive homing head. Range is 65km (40 miles) at 60kt. Spearfish is fitted with a directed-energy warhead.

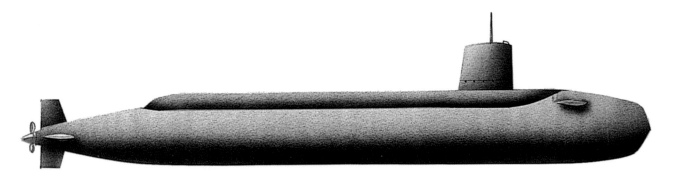

Specifications

Crew: 135	Dimensions (length/beam/draught): 149.9 x 12.8
Powerplant: Single shaft; one RR pwr; two	x 12m (491.8 x 42 x 39.4ft)
turbines; pump-jet propulsor	Commissioned: 14 August 1993
Max Speed: 46.3km/hr (25kt) submerged	Armament: 16 Trident D5 SLBM; four 533mm
Surface Range: Unlimited	(21in) torpedo tubes
Displacement: 15,900t (15,649 tons) surf/sub	

▲ **HMS Vanguard**

Royal Navy, SSBN

A new design of pressurized-water reactor was installed, the PWR2, with a 25-year life, driving two GEC turbines, with a single pump-jet propulsor giving a maximum submerged speed of 25 knots. Auxiliary power is supplied by two 6MW steam turbine generators and two Paxman MW diesel alternators.

CURRENT CONVENTIONAL SUBMARINES (III)							
Type	Year	Surface displacement tons/tonnes	Submerged displacement tons/tonnes	Speed knots	Range km/miles	Propulsion	Armament
Type 214 Germany	2007	1663/1690	1830/1860	20		D/E + AIP	Torpedoes; UGM-84 torpedoes; missiles
Soryu Japan	2009	2854/2900	4134/4200	20		D/E + AIP	Torpedoes; UGM-84 Harpoon missiles
Lada Russia	2010	1737/1765	2657/2700	21	12,000/7,546	D/E + AIP	Torpedoes; RPK-6 missiles

Britain's new SSN class is named after HMS *Astute*, and is intended to be formed of seven boats, over a construction period extending towards 2020. The nuclear reactor is the PWR2, shared with the Vanguard SSBNs. Comprehensive counter-measures include decoys and electronic support measures (ESM). The ESM system is the Thales Sensors Outfit UAP(4). Outfit UAP(4) has two multifunction antenna arrays mounted on the two non-hull penetrating optronics masts from Thales Optronics and McTaggart Scott. The CM010 mast includes thermal imaging, low light TV and colour CCD TV sensors. The RN's Eddystone Communications band Electronic Support Measures (CESM) system provides advanced communications, signal intercept, recognition, direction-finding and monitoring capability.

Astute is fitted with I-band navigation radars. The sonar is the Thales Underwater Systems 2076 integrated passive/active search and attack suite with bow, intercept, flank and towed arrays; also the latest version of the Thales S2076 integrated suite. Atlas Hydrographic provided the DESO 25 high-precision echosounder, capable of precise depth measurements down to 10,000m (32,800ft). Raytheon Systems provide the Successor IFF (identification friend or foe) naval transponder system for the class.

India

Arihant, India's first home-constructed nuclear submarine, was commissioned on 23 February 2016. Launched on 26 July 2009, its design owes a good deal to the Russian Akula class. The original intention was to make it a patrol-attack submarine, but this was changed to the SSBN format. Powered by an 80MW pressurized water reactor, *Arihant* has four missile launch tubes with capacity to make underwater and under-ice discharge. It is currently equipped with K-15 SLBMs, with a range of 700–750 km (434–465 miles), though the aim is to replace them with longer-range missiles. A second boat, *Aridhaman*, is under construction, and plans for a further two have been announced.

Israel

Israel's Type 800 or Dolphin class submarine, based on the German Type 209, is modified to such an extent that it is really a class in its own right. The first of six boats was commissioned in 1999 and three were in service by 2000. A further three were ordered in 2006 and 2011, with modifications including AIP propulsion. Two were delivered by late 2015, with the third due in 2018. Much of the sensory and control equipment is installed in Israel. Patrol, surveillance, interception, attack, special operations and minelaying are all regular roles. Underwater swimmers can be deployed from a wet-and-dry compartment in the hull.

The US Navy recorded a cruise missile launched from an Israeli submarine in the Indian Ocean as travelling 1500km (930 miles). It is generally assumed, though unconfirmed officially, that Israel possesses nuclear weapons and tactical warheads that can be fitted to submarine-fired missiles. The Dolphin class uses the ISUS 90-1 TCS weapon control system supplied by STN Atlas Elektronik, for automatic sensor management, fire control, navigation, and operations. Radar warning and active surface search are fitted. The sonar suite includes the Atlas Elektronik CSU 90 hull-mounted passive and active search and attack sonar.

The class is normally stationed at Haifa on the Mediterranean coast, but is deployed in accordance with perceived security requirements and have been known to operate in the Red Sea from Eilat.

Japan

Japan's Oyashio class is a larger version of the *Harushio*, primarily to allow more space for flank-mounted sonar. The first of 11 boats was laid down at the Kawasaki yard in Kobe in January 1994 and commissioned on 16 March 1998; the last was commissioned on 10 March 2008. All were built at Kobe by Kawasaki or Mitsubishi, and have capability both for anti-submarine and anti-surface operations. The propulsion system integrates two Kawasaki 12V25S diesel engines, two Kawasaki alternators and two Toshiba main motors, with a total power output of 7700hp (5742kW). From the late 1970s, an ever-increasing proportion of Japan Maritime Self-Defence Force (JMSDF) systems has been of Japanese origin, and the Oyashio class is equipped with Japanese-designed radar and electronics. Its sonar systems are based on US designs, but have been modified to suit Japanese requirements. The six HU-605 533mm tubes have 20 reloads for Type 89 wire-guided active/passive homing torpedoes or UGM-84D Harpoon anti-ship missiles.

▲ Arihant

Indian Navy, SSBN

Arihant is fitted with a combination of two sonar systems – Ushus and Panchendriya. Ushus is state-of-the-art sonar built for Kilo-class submarines. Panchendriya is a unified submarine sonar and tactical control system, which includes all types of sonar (passive, surveillance, ranging, intercept and active). It also features an underwater communications system.

Specifications

Crew: 96	Dimensions (length/beam/draught): 110 x 11 x
Powerplant: Single shaft; one pwr	9m (361 x 36 x 29.5ft)
Max Speed: 28/44km/hr (15/24kt) surf/sub	Commissioned: Due 2012
Surface Range: Unlimited	Armament: Six 533mm (21in) launch tubes; 12
Displacement: about 5800–7700/8200–13,000t	K-15 SLBM
(5708–7578/8070–12,795 tons)	

Specifications

Crew: 35	1900 tons) surf/sub
Powerplant: Single shaft; three diesel engines;	Dimensions (length/beam/draught): 57 x 6.8 x
diesel-electric	6.2m (187 x 22 x 20ft)
Max Speed: 37km/hr (20kt) submerged	Commissioned: 1999
Surface Range: Not released	Armament: Four 650mm (25.5in) and six 533mm
Displacement: 1666.3/1930.5t (1640/	(21in) launch tubes

▲ Dolphin

Israeli Navy, variant of German Type 209 patrol submarine

No less than 10 bow torpedo tubes are fitted, six of them 533mm (21in) for launching DM2A3 wire guided torpedoes. An unusual feature is the four 650mm (26in) torpedo tubes. These can be used to launch Israeli-built nuclear-armed Popeye Turbo cruise missiles (a variant of the Popeye standoff missile).

All of the Oyashio class were in service in 2016, with one converted as a training boat. None have AIP, but this feature is integral to the 16SS or Soryu class, introduced in 2009, the largest Japanese submarines since World War II. Their capacity for operating very close to the seabed, combined with virtual silence under AIP, give formidable performance. Seven were in service by March 2016, with two more at the fitting-out stage. These and any further boats will have Japanese lithium-ion AIP rather than the Kockum-Stirling liquid-oxygen fuelled engines of the earlier vessels. They are also

the first Japanese submarines to be offered for export sale.

Russia

The cruise missile submarines of Project 949A, built between 1985 and 1996, known to NATO as Oscar II, are updated, quietened and enlarged versions of Oscar I. As standard with Soviet nuclear submarines, they have double hulls, two nuclear reactors and twin propeller shafts. An elongated sail reinforced for ice-breaking with multiple retractable masts has an open bridge as well as an enclosed bridge station beneath

▲ Oyashio

Japanese Maritime Self-Defence Force, patrol submarine

The new boats share the double hulls and anechoic coating of the previous class, but the revised outer casing, in 'leaf coil' rather than 'teardrop' form, gives them a slightly different appearance and the fin is of a more efficient hydrodynamic shape.

Specifications

Crew: 69	Dimensions (length/beam/draught): 81.7 x 8.9
Powerplant: Single shaft; diesel-electric	x 7.4m (268.1 x 29.2 x 24.25ft)
Max Speed: 22.2/37km/hr (12/20kt) surf/sub	Commissioned: 16 March 1998
Surface Range: Not released	Armament: Sub Harpoon SSM; six 533mm (21in)
Displacement: 2743/3048t (2700/3000 tons)	torpedo tubes
surf/sub	

Specifications

Crew: 65	surf/sub
Powerplant: Two Kawasaki 12V diesels; four	Dimensions (length/beam/draught): 84 x 9.1 x
Kawasaki-Kockums V4-275R Stirling engines	8.5m (275.5 x 30 x 27.9ft)
Max Speed: 24/37km/hr (13/20kt) surf/sub	Commissioned: 2009
Surface Range: 11,297km (6100nm) at 6.5kt	Armament: Six 533mm (21in) launch tubes for
Displacement: 2900/4200t (2854/4134 tons)	torpedoes; Sub-Harpoon missiles; mines

▲ Soryu

Japanese Maritime Self-Defence Force, long-range patrol submarine

In addition to the twin Kawasaki 12/V 25/25 SB-type diesels, it has four Kawasaki-Kockums V4-275R Stirling AIP engines. *Soryu* carries 20 Type 89 wire-guided torpedoes or a combination of these and Harpoon missiles.

it. Missiles are launched from a submerged position, from tubes fixed at an angle of approximately 40°. The tubes, arranged in two rows of 12, are each covered by six hatches on each side of the sail, with each hatch covering a pair of tubes. The launchers are placed between the inner pressure hull and the outer hydrodynamic hull.

As attack submarines, these are the largest to be built (only the Typhoon and Ohio class missile boats are bigger) and it is notable that construction went on after the collapse of the Soviet Union – a tribute to their general reliability as well as their versatility in uses ranging from shadowing carrier battle groups to attack on coastal and inland targets. Some of the later Oscar II boats remain on the active list in both the Northern and Pacific fleets,

with three currently noted as in overhaul and three others in service.

K-141, *Kursk*, was commissioned on 30 December 1994 and deployed with the Northern Fleet. On 12 October 2000, it sank in the Barents Sea, with the loss of all 118 persons on board. It was raised in October 2001 in a salvage operation carried out by two Dutch companies, Mammoet Worldwide and Smit International, and towed to the naval shipyard in Murmansk. The forward weapons compartment was cut out prior to lifting and sections were later lifted in May 2002. Wreckage remaining on the seabed was blown up. The nuclear reactors and Granit cruise missiles were all recovered. The cause of the disaster was revealed as the explosion of a Type 65 high-test peroxide

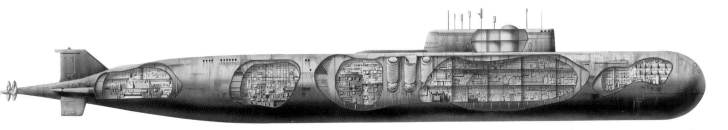

▲ Oscar II

Russian Navy, Oscar II class SSGN, Barents Sea, 2000

Oscar II is equipped with 24 SS-N-19 Granit cruise missiles with a range of 550km (342 miles). The missile weighs 6.9 tonnes (6.8 tons) with a warhead weighing 1000kg (2205lb). Its speed is Mach 1.5. Under the START arms limitation treaty, nuclear warheads for these missiles were replaced with high explosive warheads.

Specifications

Crew: 112

Powerplant: Twin shaft; two OK-650b reactors; steam turbines

Max Speed: 30/59km/hr (16/32kt) surf/sub

Surface Range: Unlimited

Displacement: 13,615–14,935/16,663–24,835t

(13,400–14,700/16,400–24,000 tons) surf/sub

Dimensions (length/beam/draught): 154 x 18.2 x 9m (505.2 x 60 x 29.5ft)

Commissioned: December 1994

Armament: 24 SS-N-19 Granit missiles; two 650mm and four 533mm (21in) launch tubes

Specifications

Crew: 107

Powerplant: One OK-650B reactor; turbine; pump-jet

Max Speed: 28/54km/hr (15/29kt) surf/sub

Surface Range: Unlimited

Displacement: 14,720/24,000t (14,488/ 23,621 tons) surf/sub

Dimensions (length/beam/draught): 170 x 13.5 x 10m (557.75 x 44.25 x 32.8ft)

Commissioned: Due 2012

Armament: 16 RSM-56 Bulava SLBM; six 533mm (21in) launch tubes for torpedoes/RPK-2 Viyuga cruise missiles

▲ Borei

Russian Navy, new-generation SSBN

A single OK-650B nuclear reactor, also used on the preceding classes, provides power and these are the first Russian submarines to have pump-jet propulsion. The Borei class has a more compact and also more hydrodynamically efficient hull design compared to its SSBN predecessors. Diving depth is believed to be 450m (1480ft).

▲ USS Seawolf

US Navy, SSN-21

Its hull, built of HY-100 steel, enables diving capability to 610m (2000ft); maximum submerged speed is 35 knots, and it is designed to operate below the ice cap. The bow diving planes are retractable. Full acoustic cladding is applied and at a 'silent' speed of 20 knots, it is virtually undetectable.

Specifications

Crew: 140

Powerplant: Single shaft; one S6W pwr; one secondary motor

Max Speed: 33/65km/hr (18/35kt) surf/sub

Surface Range: Unlimited

Displacement: 8738/9285t (8600/9138 tons)

Dimensions (length/beam/draught): 107 x 12 x 10.9m (353 x 40 x 35ft)

Commissioned: 1997

Armament: Eight 660mm (25.9in) launch tubes for Mk 48; torpedoes; Tomahawk or Sub-Harpoon missiles; 50 weapons

(HTP) torpedo, triggering another explosion in the weapons compartment, causing the vessel to sink. The blast was caused by a leakage of the highly volatile torpedo propellant, which then came in contact with kerosene and metal. Although it was believed that *Kursk*, in common with other Oscar II boats, had an emergency crew escape capsule, it appears, unfortunately, to have been impossible to activate this rescue device.

Project 955, the Borei class of SSBN, is intended to replace the Delta IV and Typhoon classes. As the fourth generation of Russian nuclear submarine, this class is well endowed with new features. Ten boats will form the class, with three in service as of December 2014 and four in construction to be commissioned between 2017 and 2020. A further three, designated Project 955A, will incorporate updated features. The class will be divided evenly between the Northern and Pacific fleets.

The class has been designed around the new RSM-56 Bulava missile (SS-NX-30), a three-stage missile using both solid (stages one and two) and liquid fuel (stage three). By far the most sophisticated missile design to emanate from Russia, it is understood to possess a range of defence-penetration systems including evasive manoeuvring, mid-course counter-measures and decoys, and warhead shielding against physical and electromagnetic pulse damage. It carries up to 10 hypersonic MIRV warheads with a range of 9000km (5592 miles) and a yield of 100–150kT. The first three Borei submarines will carry 16 Bulavas, but later boats will have 20. The missile

FOURTH GENERATION AMERICAN AND RUSSIAN NUCLEAR SUBMARINES COMPARED							
Class/Type	Year	Surface displacement tons/tonnes	Submerged displacement tons/tonnes	Speed knots	Test Depth m/feet	Propulsion	Armament
Borei SSBN	2010	14,488/14,720	23,621/24,000	29	450/1,476	1 OK-650B	16 RSM-56 Bulava
Yasen SSGN	2011	8600/8738	13,800/14021	35+	600/1,968	1 KPM PWR	24 Granat SLCM
Seawolf SSGN	2005	8600/8738	9138/9284	35+	610/2,000	1 S6W PWR	50 Tomahawk
Virginia SSGN	2004	N/A	7800/7925	32	240/787	1 SNG PWR	12 Tomahawk

was successfully fired from the first Borei, *Yuri Dolgorkiy*, in June 2011. The class is expected to be the mainstay of Russia's strategic missile capability into the 2040s.

Russia's fourth-generation SSN attack submarine is the subject of Project 885, also known as the Granei or Yasen class. Like its SSBN counterpart, it represents a large step forward. A new-type single KPM pressurized water reactor provides power to a single propeller shaft (it is not thought that the class has pump-jet propulsion). The first of the class, *Severodvinsk*, was launched on 15 June 2010 and was commissioned into the Russian Navy on 17 June 2014. A second was laid down on 24 July 2009 and is under construction, while a contract for a further four was signed on 9 November 2011. The class will carry cruise missiles, of a type not yet specified. Delivery dates and deployment have not been made public.

United States

The Seawolf class, originally envisaged as the follow-on to the Los Angeles attack submarines, was the first completely new US submarine design for 30 years. But only three were built before new strategic requirements ended the programme in favour of developing the Virginia class. *Seawolf* is nevertheless a very advanced boat with many features that make it a formidable element in the US ocean armoury. Powered by a GE PWR S6W reactor and two turbines, it has a pump-jet propulsor and a secondary propulsion submerged motor.

The eight 660mm (26in) tubes enable silent 'swimout' torpedo launches, but also launch a variety of other missiles and remotely operated vehicles. Combat data system, fire control, counter-measures and sonar equipment, all fully up to date when *Seawolf* was commissioned in 1997, have been upgraded. The third class member, USS *Jimmy Carter,* was adapted for seabed and special forces operations by the insertion of a 30m (99ft) 'multi-mission platform' section, allowing for deployment and recovery of remote-operating vehicle (ROV) units and SEAL forces. All three remain in service as of 2016, *Seawolf* and *Connecticut* based at SubBase Bangor and *Jimmy Carter* at Naval Base Kitsap, in Washington State.

Considerably smaller and less costly than the 'billion-dollar' *Seawolf*, the Virginia class was designed to assume the attack-submarine role in the post-Cold War context. Rather than deep-sea encounters, coastal and hot-spot operations were considered most likely. Signals from the masts' sensors are transmitted through fibre optic data lines through signal processors to the control centre. Visual feeds from the masts are displayed on LCD interfaces in the command centre.

It is the first US submarine to employ a built-in Navy SEAL staging area allowing a team of nine men to enter and leave the submarine. With a newly designed anechoic coating, isolated deck structures and new design of propulsor to achieve low acoustic signature, it is claimed that the noise level of the *Virginia* is as low as that of the *Seawolf* class. At least 30 boats are planned. As of early 2016, twelve were in service, five under construction or fitting out, and orders for a further 11 were in place.

Specifications

Crew: 135

Powerplant: One S9G pwr; pump-jet propulsors

Max Speed: 46km/hr (25kt) submerged

Surface Range: Unlimited

Displacement: 7900t (7800 tons) submerged

Dimensions (length/beam): 115 x 10m (377 x 34ft)

Commissioned: 23 October 2004

Armament: 12 vertical BGM-109 Tomahawk cruise missile tubes; four 533mm (21in) torpedo tubes; 38 weapons

▲ USS Virginia
US Navy, SSN-774

Instead of a traditional periscope, the class utilizes a pair of telescoping photonics masts located outside the pressure hull. Each mast contains high-resolution cameras, along with light-intensification and infrared sensors, an infrared laser rangefinder and an integrated Electronic Support Measures (ESM) array.

USS *VIRGINIA*

The Virginia class is intended to assume the US Navy's attack- and multi-mission submarine role in the post-Cold War context. Its use of modular construction and commercial, off-the-shelf technology is intended both to hold down costs and to provide flexibility in updating its electronic systems.

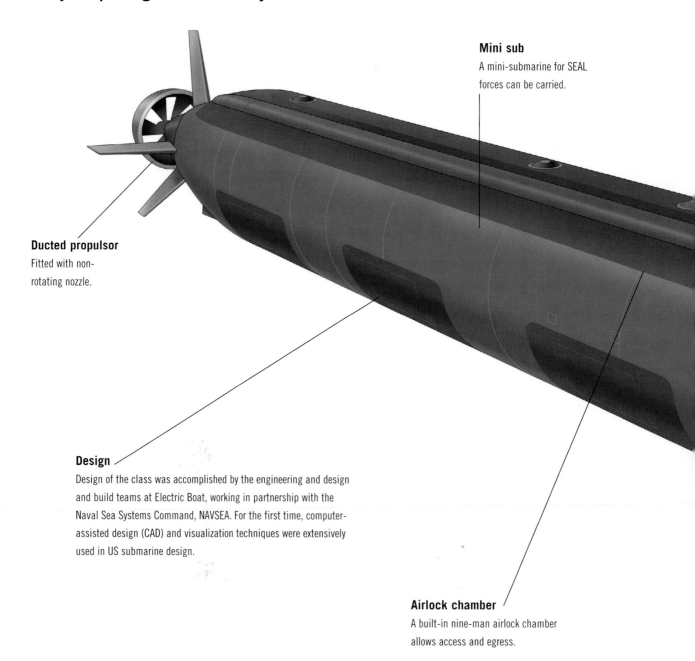

Mini sub
A mini-submarine for SEAL forces can be carried.

Ducted propulsor
Fitted with non-rotating nozzle.

Design
Design of the class was accomplished by the engineering and design and build teams at Electric Boat, working in partnership with the Naval Sea Systems Command, NAVSEA. For the first time, computer-assisted design (CAD) and visualization techniques were extensively used in US submarine design.

Airlock chamber
A built-in nine-man airlock chamber allows access and egress.

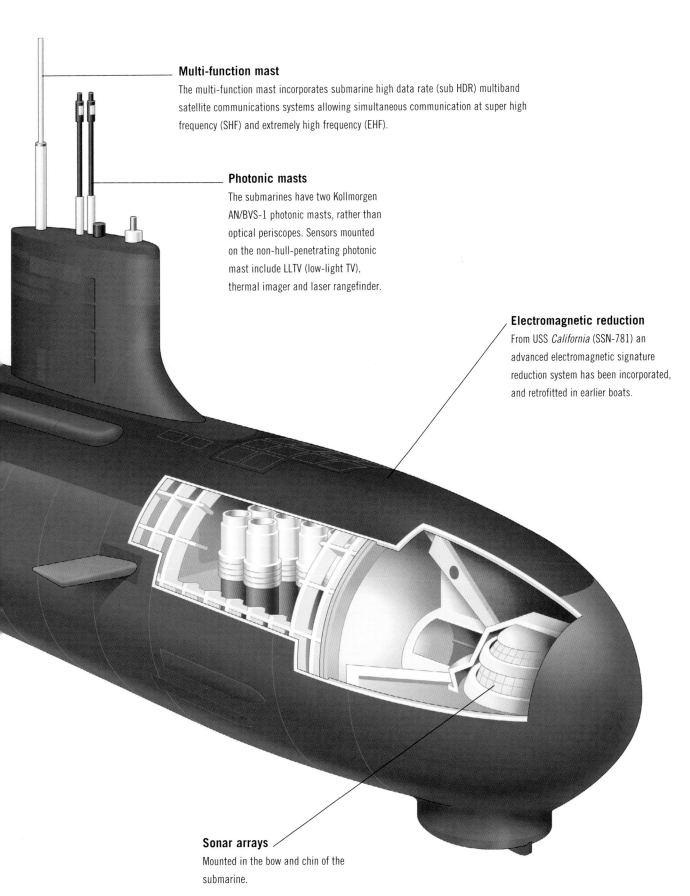

Multi-function mast

The multi-function mast incorporates submarine high data rate (sub HDR) multiband satellite communications systems allowing simultaneous communication at super high frequency (SHF) and extremely high frequency (EHF).

Photonic masts

The submarines have two Kollmorgen AN/BVS-1 photonic masts, rather than optical periscopes. Sensors mounted on the non-hull-penetrating photonic mast include LLTV (low-light TV), thermal imager and laser rangefinder.

Electromagnetic reduction

From USS *California* (SSN-781) an advanced electromagnetic signature reduction system has been incorporated, and retrofitted in earlier boats.

Sonar arrays

Mounted in the bow and chin of the submarine.

Submarine strengths
2016

The submarine remains a key element of modern military naval power.

TODAY, 40 COUNTRIES possess a total of 455 naval submarines, ranging from Portugal's two to the USA's 67. Sheer numbers are no clear indication of strength, however (see tables on pages 370–371).

Portugal's two Tridente-class boats are the German Type 214 – very up-to-date vessels equipped with air-independent propulsion, which play useful roles in NATO exercises both as hunters and as quarry. Canada has four submarines but though modernized, their design goes back to the 1970s. Australia lists six submarines, all of the Collins class, which have encountered numerous mechanical and technical problems since their commissioning between 1996 and 2003, with sometimes only one of the six available for service (after much work, the class has

become more reliable and a programme is in hand to extend their operational lives beyond 2030). North Korea's 20 or so Romeo-class submarines are obsolescent.

The Anatomy of Undersea Power

The United States's submarine force remains the world's largest and also the most powerful. An Ohio-class SSBN carrying 24 Trident II missiles has the capacity to fire 288 multiple independently targeted re-entry vehicles (MIRV). The Virginia class, armed with Tomahawk missiles (also nuclear-capable) was designed with both open-ocean and coastal operations in view. But the Virginia boats displace 7800 tons (7925 tonnes) and some analysts of

Specifications

Crew: 27–30

Powerplant: One MTU 16v 396 turbocharged diesel-generator set developing 2881hp (2150kW), one Siemens Permasyn Type FR6439 motor, 4023hp (3MW)

Max Speed: Surfaced: 12 knots (22.2km/h; 13.8 mph); Submerged: 20 knots (37km/h; 23 mph)

Surface Range: 8000nm (14,816km; 9206 miles)

at 8 knots (14.8km/h; 9.2 mph)

Displacement: Surfaced: 1450 tonnes (1430 tons); Submerged: 1830 tonnes (1800 tons)

Dimensions: Length: 56m (183ft 9in); Beam: 7m (23ft); Draught: 6m (19ft 8in)

Commissioned: October 2005

Armament: Six 533mm (21in) tubes for 24 Atlas Elektronik DM2A4 torpedoes

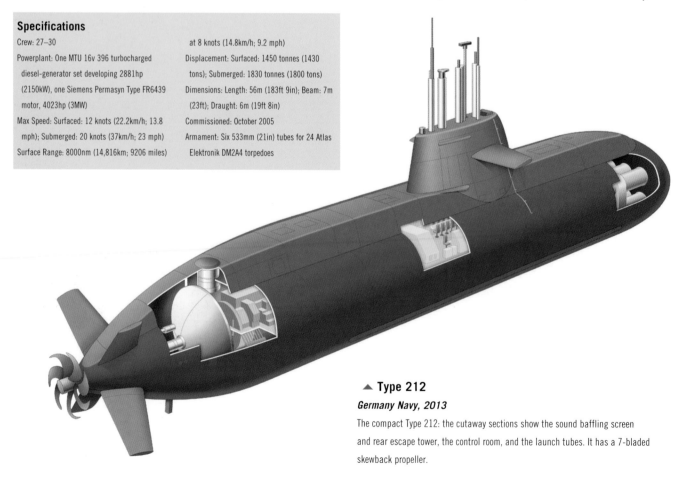

▲ **Type 212**

Germany Navy, 2013

The compact Type 212: the cutaway sections show the sound baffling screen and rear escape tower, the control room, and the launch tubes. It has a 7-bladed skewback propeller.

naval strategy have questioned their ability to reach action points that would be accessible to smaller vessels. Even the largest of modern 'conventional' submarines, Japan's Soryu class, displaces only 4124 tons (4200 tonnes).

After a 20-year gap between 1990 and 2010, Russia has resumed a vigorous submarine-building programme, which encompasses both nuclear and non-nuclear vessels. Its new designs of Borei SSBN and Yasen SSGN stand comparison with their American rivals, though the discrepancy in numbers is still substantial. With the 'Improved Kilo' and the Lada class – intended as an an even-more-improved Kilo, but subject to a major redesign after the launch of a pilot vessel in 2010 – Russia still has a strong interest in non-nuclear submarines.

The next-largest nuclear fleet is that of the People's Republic of China. With the introduction of the Jin class SSBN, China is able to join the USA, Russia, France and Britain in keeping a missile submarine on secret patrol at all times, as a deterrent to attack. While China's future plans are not known, it is most probable that developmental work is going ahead on improved versions of the

Jin class and of the Shang class SSN, to match the quality of Russian and US vessels. The other established nuclear submarine powers, Great Britain and France, maintain the minimum number of boats necessary to sustain a deterrent role and to preserve an up-to-date technological base.

Underwater drive using batteries or liquid oxygen makes the 'conventional' submarine, designed for stealth in other ways too, actually quieter than a nuclear submarine. Its silence and lengthy underwater endurance give it operational advantages in limited-range and littoral operations. Interest in acquiring or enlarging submarine strength is strongest where neighbouring nations have conflicting interests or difficult relationships, with Bangladesh and Myanmar (Burma), India and Pakistan, Israel and Iran, North and South Korea as examples. Bangladesh has three Improved Kilo boats on order for 2019. Pakistan concluded an eight-boat package with China in late 2015, with four Type 039A submarines to be built in each country (Type 039A is an export version of the Yuan submarine which does not incorporate AIP). North Korea has built over 60 small coastal submarines with a range of

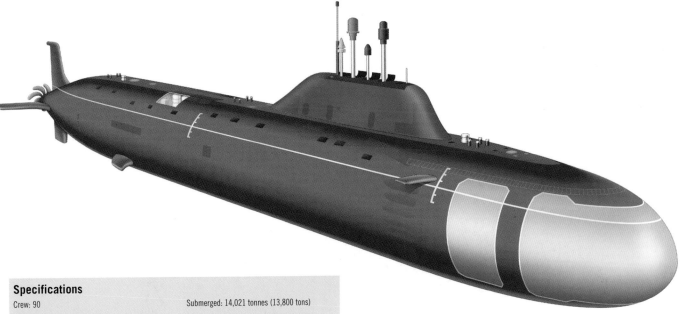

Specifications

Crew: 90

Powerplant: One KPM pressurized water reactor
43,000hp (200MW); single screw

Max Speed: Surfaced: 20 knots (37km/h);
Submerged: 35 knots (64.8km/h; 40.2 mph)

Surface Range: Unlimited

Displacement: Surfaced: 8737 tonnes (8600 tons);

Submerged: 14,021 tonnes (13,800 tons)

Dimensions: Length: 119m (390ft 5in); Beam:
13.5m (44ft 3in); Draught: 8.4m (27ft 6in)

Commissioned: 2014

Armament: Eight silos for SL weapons; eight
650mm (25.3in) and two 533mm (21in)
torpedo tubes

▲ **Yasen class**

Russian Navy, new generation class SSGN

It is known to be designed for a dive depth of up to 600m (1970ft) and for a maximum submerged speed in excess of 35 knots. This class is the first Russian submarine to be equipped with a spherical sonar, designated as Irytysh-Amfora. To accommodate this large-size array, the torpedo tubes are set at an angle.

NATIONAL SUBMARINE STRENGTHS 2016			
Country	Number	Type/class	Note
Algeria	2	Improved Kilo	Project 636M
	2	Kilo	From 1980s
Argentina	1	Type 209	
	2	TR 1700	
Australia	6	Collins	2000
Bangladesh	2	Ming Class	2016
Brazil	5	Type 209	
	4	Scorpène	Due 2017
Canada	4	Victoria class	1990–93
Chile	2	Scorpène	
	2	Type 209	Updated 2009
China	2	Han Type 091	SSN
	4	Shang Type 093	SSN
	4	Jin Type 094	SSBN
	1	Xia Type 092	SSGN
	17	Ming	
	12	Kilo	
	13	Song Type 039	
	15	Yuan Type 039A	
Colombia	2	Type 209/1200	
	2	Type SX-506	
Ecuador	2	Type 209	
Egypt	4	Type 209/1400	First delivered 2016
	4	Romeo	Modernized
France	6	SSN	
	4	SSBN	

NATIONAL SUBMARINE STRENGTHS 2016			
Country	Number	Type/class	Note
Germany	6	Type 212	
Great Britain	3	Astute SSN	4 on order
	4	Trafalgar SSN	
	4	Vanguard SSBN	
Greece	1	U-214 type	2 incomplete
	7	Type 209	Upgraded from 2010
India	9	Kilo Type 877EM	
	4	Type 209/1500	
	2	Foxtrot	Training
	1	Scorpène	Kalvari class
	1	Arihant SSBN	
	1	Chakra II SSN	Russian lease
Indonesia	2	Cakra class	Germany, 1980s
Iran	3	Kilo	
	2	Fateh	2011–2015
	1	Nahang	2006
	14	Ghadir	Small boats
	1	Besat class	2013
Israel	3	Dolphin I	
	2	Dolphin II	
Italy	2	Type 212	Todaro class
	2	Sauro IV	
	2	Sauro III	
Japan	7	Soryu	3 in progress
	10	Oyashio	
Malaysia	2	Scorpène	

around 50nm and appears to have constructed a larger vessel of similar dimensions to the Type 214s deployed by the South Korean Navy.

This was probably the vessel reported as making a successful missile launch from below the surface in May 2015. The South Koreans are also working to a plan known as KSS-III, for nine large boats of around 3000–3500 tonnes/tons to be commissioned from 2022, which with boats currently on order will bring their fleet up to 27 modern submarines. Iran, too, has set up its own design and construction facilities and claims to be developing an approximately 1200-tonne/ton class, Besat, which will be able to fire cruise missiles from below the surface.

Life-extension and Disposal

Many countries are taking measures to extend the lives of existing submarines, for example by replacing outdated sonar equipment and installing new communications systems, and by installing later-generation torpedoes and missiles. This is expensive, but much less costly than building a new submarine. While it is common nowadays for buyer-countries to insist on assembling new submarines in their own shipyards, the only countries still designing as well as building non-nuclear submarines are China, France, Germany, Japan, Iran, North Korea, South Korea, Russia, Spain and Sweden. Iran and North Korea build for their own fleets only, and

NATIONAL SUBMARINE STRENGTHS 2016			
Country	Number	Type/class	Note
Netherlands	4	Walrus	Undergoing upgrade
North Korea	1	New type, 2015	VL missile
	c22	Romeo	
	c40	Yono	Small boats
	c22	Sang O	Coastal infiltration
Norway	6	Ula class	1987–92
Pakistan	3	Agosta 90B	
	2	Agosta 70	
Peru	4	Type 209/1200	
	2	Type 209/1100	
Poland	1	Kilo	
	4	Kobben	From Norway, 2002–03
Portugal	2	Tridente	Type 214
Russia	3	Delta III SSBN	1979–82
	6	Delta IV SSBN	1984–90
	1	Typhoon SSBN	
	3	Borei SSBN	2013–14
	7	Oscar II SSGN	1989–96
	1	Sierra I SSN	1987
	2	Sierra II SSN	1990–93
	4	Victor III SSN	1990–92
	10	Akula SSN	1989–2000
	1	Yasen SSN	2014
	16	Kilo	1981–90
	4	Improved Kilo	2014–15
	1	Lada	2010
Singapore	2	Sjoormen type	Challenger class
	2	Västergötland	Archer class
South Africa	3	Type 209/1400	From 2006
South Korea	4	Son-Won-Il	Type 214
	9	Chang-Bogo	Type 209/1200
Spain	3	S-70 Galerna	
	4	S-80	Under construction

NATIONAL SUBMARINE STRENGTHS 2016			
Country	Number	Type/class	Note
Sweden	3	Gotland	AIP drive
	2	Sodermanland	AIP drive
Taiwan	2	Hai Lung	Zwaardvis class
	2	Hai Shih	Tench class
Turkey	6	U-214 type	On order 2016
	6	Ay class	Type 209/1200
	4	Preveze class	Type 209TI/1400
	4	Gür class	Type 209T2/1400
United States	18	Ohio SSBN	
	39	Los Angeles SSN	
	3	Seawolf SSN	
	12	Virginia SSN	5 building
Venezuela	2	Type 209	Believed inactive
Vietnam	5	Improved Kilo	Sixth due mid-2016

electronic equipment made to fit the spaces available. Modular design was introduced in the interest of keeping down costs, but also makes it possible to keep very high-specification technology secret even from the submarine's designers, as well as to replace outdated kit.

Any navy seeking to operate modern submarines must ensure that it can provide the funds not only for construction, but for maintenance over several decades, for periodic major refits, for provision of base facilities, and for ultimate disposal of decommissioned boats. While disposal costs are particularly high for nuclear submarines – it costs the US Navy between $25 and $50 million for each boat – they are also very considerable for the sophisticated new-generation conventional submarines. There are now many more decommissioned nuclear submarines than active ones, and though they are defuelled, their reactors will remain radioactive for very many years. No country has yet resolved the issue of effective disposal. The USA's Ship/Submarine Recycling Program for nuclear vessels, centred at Puget Sound Naval Shipyard, separates and seals reactor compartments. At least one reactor, the first one installed in USS *Seawolf*, was dumped in the Atlantic depths, but that is no longer considered an acceptable option.

Spain, compelled to drastically redesign its S-80 AIP submarine originally intended for service from 2012, is not seeking foreign orders at present. The modular design form adopted for modern submarines makes it easier for buyer-navies to instal their own choice of

TYPE 094 JIN CLASS

China's second-generation nuclear-powered SSBN has significantly extended the country's range of potential strategic engagement.

Launch tubes

Silos for 12 launch tubes for the JL-2 SLBM, each capped with up to six nuclear warheads.

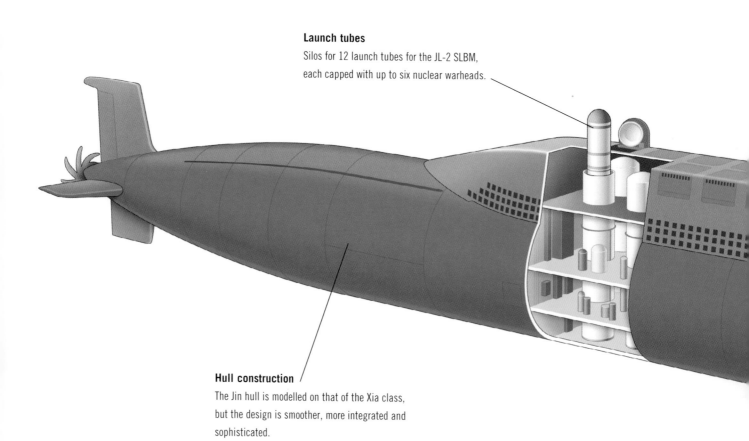

Hull construction

The Jin hull is modelled on that of the Xia class, but the design is smoother, more integrated and sophisticated.

Specifications

Crew: Undisclosed

Powerplant: Nuclear reactor, single screw

Max Speed: Surfaced: undisclosed; Submerged:
  20 knots+ (37km/h+; 23 mph+) (estimated)

Range: Unlimited

Surface Range: Unlimited

Displacement: Surfaced: 8128 tonnes (8000
  tons); Submerged: 11,176 tonnes (11,000 tons)

Dimensions: Length: 135m (442ft 11in); Beam:
  12.5m (41ft); Draught: 8m

Commissioned: 2007

Armament: 12 JL-2 SLBMs; six 533mm (21in)
  torpedo tubes

Range
Each Jin-class boat is able to conduct patrols lasting approximately 60 days, and with five submarines to deploy, near-continuous at-sea deterrence can be maintained, although refit time may present problems.

Torpedoes
Other armament includes six 533mm (21in) torpedo tubes. Chinese torpedoes are assumed to be based on Russian models and to include in their range a development of the Shkval 'rocket torpedo' that travels at high speeds enveloped in its own bubble of gas to avoid water resistance.

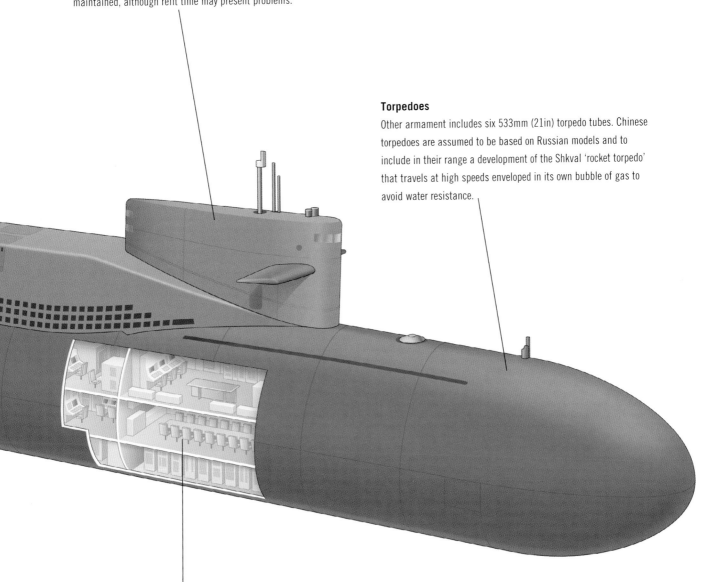

Control room
Navigation, fire control, counter-measures and sonar systems may be less technically advanced than on American and Russian submarines, although the successor Type 096 will certainly show significant upgrading of these aspects.

Rescue Systems

Modern submarines are often fitted with exit chambers allowing swimmers or pieces of equipment to be despatched or admitted. These are for use relatively near the surface. It is standard practice now to incorporate at least one and usually two escape systems that allow the crew to leave a damaged submarine at depths down to around 180m (600ft). The Russian Navy prefers to use detachable escape pods. In the case of the HABETaS system developed by ThyssenKrupp Marine Systems and the British AMITS company, potential rescue capacity from a depth of 250m (960ft) is claimed. This system is fitted in the Netherlands' Walrus class and to all new boats built by the Howaldtswerke yard in Kiel.

The ISMERLO organization exists to facilitate the rapid call-out and deployment of rescue equipment to any location in the world. Though operated under NATO control, with its base at Northwood in England, any country may register with it. If the crew of a disabled submarine is unable to vacate the boat,

standard procedure is to locate the craft using a robot vehicle (ROV), assess its situation, then use a manned submarine rescue vehicle (SRV) to attach itself to an escape hatch. The SRV can take out 12 crewmembers at a time and has battery power to make 10 trips before recharging.

Remote Control

The increasing use of remote-control technology in military operations extends to the submarine world. The concept of the UUV (unmanned underwater vehicle) is already a reality in civilian use, and both the US and Russian navies are working on prototype models. The US Navy is testing a vessel known as the LDUUV (large displacement unmanned underwater vehicle) that can be deployed from a Virginia-class submarine. Initially such craft are seen as engaging in reconnaissance work, including the launching of aerial drones, and mine detection. A Russian project, however, is believed to be centred on a UUV which would be capable of approaching any coastline

▲ **Type 094 Jin class**

Photographed on exercise, flying the Chinese flag and a naval ensign, a Jin-class submarine displays the typical hump of an SSBN.

▲ USS *Connecticut* (SSN-22)

The second of the three Seawolf-class boats, *Connecticut* was commissioned on 11 December 1998. It is based at Bremerton in Washington State with Submarine Development Squadron Five.

with a 1-megaton (equal to a million tons of TNT) weapon. Much developmental work remains to be done, not least in communications and directional control, before vehicles of this kind can be effectively deployed. But to naval planners the prospect is alluring. Such a vessel would be virtually undetectable and require none of the high-cost, space-consuming facilities essential to keep a human crew alive and in a good state of morale.

Planners are preoccupied by the longer-term future role of the naval submarine. Britain's four Vanguard-class SSBNs will reach the end of their working lives in the 2020s, and to ensure continuity of Britain's continuous at-sea deterrent, a successor class would have to be ready by then, capable of firing Trident II D5 SLBMs. The debate is not only concerned with the huge cost of a new SSBN class, but with whether the essential secrecy of a nuclear submarine's location at sea can be preserved in the face of new sensor technology designed to detect large objects moving even at great depths. SSBNs are at their most vulnerable at the approaches to their bases, and several

navies, including the Chinese, are working on new forms of propulsion and navigation for underwater gliders and 'robotic fish', which would co-operate in shoal or spread formations, capable of pursuing and attacking a target. The USA is also developing an autonomous surface craft, the ACTUV (ASW Continuous Trail Unmanned Vessel) intended for coastal work in tracing and pursuing diesel-electric/AIP submarines, with the aim of negating their 'stealth' advantage.

Though the stakes in terms of firepower grow ever-higher, and the technology involved becomes ever-more sophisticated, the underlying reality remains what it has always been since the inception of the submarine as a weapon of war – the contest between the stealth and destructive power of the submarine and the effectiveness of the measures used against it.

Index of Submarine names

General Index